Oracle8™ Administration and Management

Michael Ault

WILEY COMPUTER PUBLISHING

John Wiley & Sons, Inc.

New York • Chichester • Weinheim• Brisbane • Singapore • Toronto

Publisher: Robert Ipsen
Editor: Robert Elliott
Managing Editor: Brian Snapp
Electronic Products, Associate Editor: Mike Sosa
Text Design & Composition: Publisher's Design and Production Services, Inc.

Designations used by companies to distinguish their products are often claimed as trademarks. In all instances where John Wiley & Sons, Inc., is aware of a claim, the product names appear in initial capital or ALL CAPITAL LETTERS. Readers, however, should contact the appropriate companies for more complete information regarding trademarks and registration.

This text is printed on acid-free paper.

This publication is designed to provide accurate and authoritative information in regard to the subject matter covered. It is sold with the understanding that the publisher is not engaged in rendering legal, accounting, or other professional service. If legal advice or other expert assistance is required, the services of a competent professional person should be sought.

The content of this book is based on Release Candidate 8.0.2 and 8.0.3 of Oracle8™. There may have been changes made to the product since these releases. Therefore, screen shots and examples may not be identical to the final product.

For current information about Oracle8, you should visit www.oracle.com/

Library of Congress Cataloging-in-Publication Data

Ault, Michael R.
    Oracle8 administration and management / Michael Ault.
      p.   cm.
    "Wiley Computer Publishing."
    Includes index.
    ISBN 0-471-19234-1 (pbk. : alk. paper)
    1. Relational databases. 2. Oracle (Computer file). 3. Database
management. I. Title.
QA76.9.D3A938 1997
005.75′65—dc21   976-36223
                                        CIP

Printed in the United States of America
10 9 8 7 6 5 4 3 2 1

Dedication

As with the first edition, I would like to dedicate this book to my loving and patient wife and daughters, Susan, Marie, and Michelle, who have put up with my ill-humor, raging at the computer, and in-general unrefined behavior during its writing. I would also like to thank Oracle Corporation for their excellent classes and references. I would also like to thank all the contributors to Oracle Open World, and IOUG-A, and the participants on the CompuServe Forums for keeping my knowledge and abilities honed. I want to thank Savant Corporation for the use of their Q product, and last but certainly not least, RevealNet, Inc. for the Dictionary Lite product and assistance throughout the development process.

Contents

Acknowledgments

This book would not exist without the generous support and assistance of the people at John Wiley and Sons, especially Bob Elliott, Brian Calandra, and Brian Snapp. I would also like to thank Jerry Recht from Oracle Corporation for his help in obtaining the latest versions of Oracle software and documentation during the book's development. I would also like to thank my manager, John Dailey, of DMR-Trecom for his support during the entire development period.

Introduction

SO YOU'VE CHOSEN ORACLE . . . NOW WHAT?

Oracle® Corporation's Oracle8™ is one of the first relational database systems to take the plunge into the object-oriented paradigm. So what can it do for you?

Oracle's power comes from its ability to allow users quick and accurate data retrieval. This is the main strength of a relational system. With Oracle's new object-oriented extensions it now allows real-world modeling with the power of the relational engine behind the model. This merging of object and relational technology has led to one of the most powerful object-relational databases available. Object-relational databases provide a logical, generally straightforward presentation of data. The tabular relational format expanded to include the varray, nested table, and object views, as well as to allow storage of methods with data, presents data in a new way that is still familiar to those of us brought up in the relational paradigm. This allows users to query information and easily get the data they need and only the data they need. How is it done?

This is accomplished through the tabular format of a relational database with the object-oriented extensions added in a clear, straightforward method. The logical collection of *related* data and methods and the data objects' *relationships* to each other form the database. Through its SQL, SQL*Plus, ORA*Forms and other tools, Oracle allows developers, users, and administrators to get a look at their data like never before.

The purpose of this book is to provide the administrator responsible for maintaining and administrating the Oracle database with a set of tools to make their job easier. It is hoped that through example and real-world scenarios the database administrator or manager will gain valuable insight into the workings of the Oracle database management system. Numerous examples of reports and the SQL, SQL*Plus, and PL/SQL code used to generate them will be given. The interpretation of these reports will also be covered.

Oracle provides a great database administration toolset. Unfortunately, few beginning DBAs have the prerequisite knowledge to put these tools to good use. This book is intended to remedy that. In the chapters to follow, all phases of Oracle database administration and management will be covered: from initial installation, to day-to-day maintenance, to the all-important backup, recovery, and disaster recovery procedures that could mean the difference between being a successful DBA and being given the boot.

A Brief Overview of Oracle8

Oracle version 8 is an *object-relational database management system* (ORDBMS). As was discussed before, a traditional RDBMS stores data in tables called *relations*. These relations are two-dimensional representations of data where the rows, called *tuples* in relational jargon, represent records, and the columns, called *attributes,* are the pieces of information contained in the record. Oracle8 provides new object-oriented extensions to the Oracle RDBMS, forming a new entity, the object-relational database. In an object-relational database, columns can represent either a single value (as in standard relational databases), a varray (a fixed number of additional records), or a REF to a second table where a variable amount of data can be stored. This takes the two-dimensional relational view and adds a third dimension. In addition, in an object-relational database, procedures known as methods can be tied to the tables. Methods are above and beyond the old concept of triggers, as we shall see later.

Oracle provides a rich set of tools to allow design and maintenance of the database. The major Oracle tools are listed below.

RDBMS Kernel	This is the database engine, the workhorse of Oracle.
SQL	This is the relational language—Structured Query Language.
SQL*Plus	This is Oracle's addition to SQL.
PL/SQL	Stands for Procedural Language SQL, allows procedural processing of SQL statements.
SQL*DBA	Database administrator's toolset; includes a Monitor utility. This is obsolete with 7.3.
SQL*Loader	This allows data entry from ASCII flat files into Oracle tables.
EXPORT/IMPORT	These tools allow data and structure information to be removed and inserted from Oracle databases into or out of archives.
SQL*Report	This is Oracle's first report writer language.
ORA*Forms	If the RDBMS is the workhorse, this is the jockey. Forms allows ease of access to data, reports, and procedures.

ORA*Reports	This is Oracle's standard report writer. It is GUI based and includes menuing.
CONTEXT	This allows access to text-based data stored in Oracle.
Oracle*Graphics	This product allows graphic representation of Query results.
Developer2000	This provides for generation of forms reports and 3GL code based on the inputs to Designer2000.
Designer2000	This allows generation of ERD, FHD, Matrix, and Dataflow diagrams from CASE*Dictionary.
Oracle Webserver and developer tools	
Oracle Video Server and development tools	
SEDONA	Oracle's new object-oriented Broker tool
SVRMGR	Oracle's replacement tool for SQLDBA.
Oracle Enterprise Manager	Provides the capability to manage multiple instances across your entire enterprise.
Oracle Enterprise Backup	Provides automated backup and recovery options for Oracle.
Oracle Precompilers	Provides interface to most major 3GL languages.
Oracle Procedure Builder	Provides easy-to-use interface for the development of Oracle procedures.

and many, many, more!

In order to fully understand the structures that make up an Oracle database, the ability to use the above tools is critical. As a database administrator or manager you will become intimately familiar with at least the first eleven of the above tools, with the possible exception of SQL*Report.

Oracle is more than just a collection of programs that allow ease of data access. Oracle can be compared to an operating system that overlays the operating system of the computer on which it resides. Oracle has its own file structures, buffer structures, global areas, and tunability above and beyond those provided within the operating system. Oracle controls its own processes, controls its own records and consistencies, and cleans up after itself.

Oracle as it exists on your system (with the exception of DOS or OS/2) consists of executables, five to nine detached processes, a global memory area, data files, and maintenance files. It can be as small as a couple of Megabytes, or as large as a massive globe-spanning construction of gigabytes. A diagram showing a typical Oracle7 and Oracle8 environment is shown in Figures I.1 and I.2; you may want to refer to these diagrams as you read the next sections.

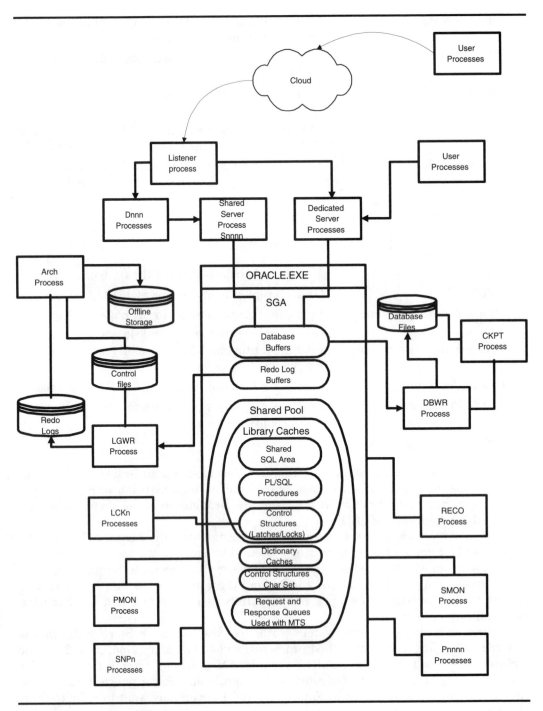

FIGURE I.1   Oracle7 structures.

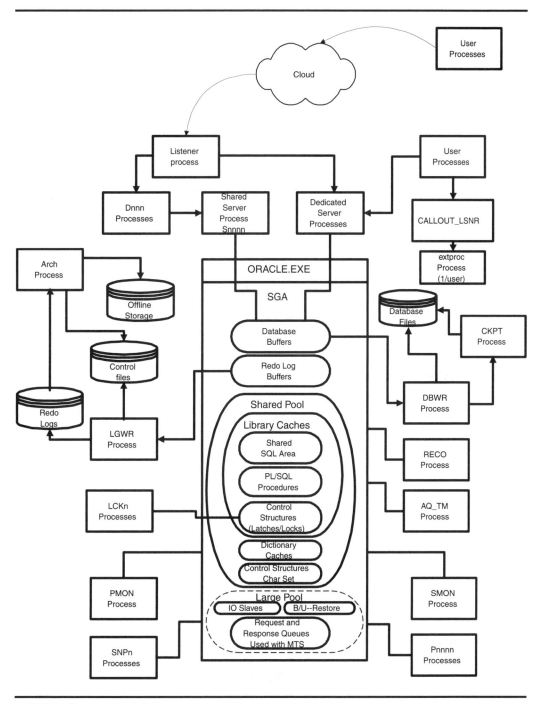

FIGURE I.2   Oracle8 structures.

Let's look at a typical Oracle system that operates in either VMS or UNIX environments.

On VMS, NT (threads), or UNIX there may be a minimum of eight detached processes for Oracle7; for Oracle8, this jumps to nearly a dozen. Four of these are the base Oracle processes and these processes are started every time Oracle is started up on a system; the additional processes may be started if the database is using archiving, uses TCPIP, or is being run in parallel and/or distributed mode. The Oracle job queues, snapshot processes, advanced queuing options, and callout processes all add to the process count. These processes are listed below.

DBWR—Database Writer	This process handles data transfer from the buffers in the SGA to the database files.
LGWR—Log Writer	This process transfers data from the redo log buffers to the redo log database files.
SMON—System Monitor	This process performs instance recovery on instance startup and is responsible for cleaning up temporary segments. In a parallel environment, this process recovers failed nodes.
PMON—Process Monitor	This process recovers user processes that have failed and cleans up the cache. This process recovers the resources from a failed process.
ARCH—Archiver Process	This process is active only if archive logging is in effect. It writes the redo log data files that are filled into the archive log data files.
RECO—Distributed Transaction Recoverer	This is an Oracle7 process that resolves failures involving distributed transactions.
LCK*n*—Lock Process	This process is used for interinstance locking in an Oracle7 parallel server environment.
D*nnn*—Dispatcher	This process allows multiple processes to share a finite number of Oracle7 servers. It queues and routes process requests to the next available server.
S*nnn*—Servers	This Oracle7 process makes all the required calls to the database to resolve a user's requests. It returns results to the D*nnn* process that calls it.
LISTENERTCPIP server	If you are running TCPIP, this process, known as the listener process, will be running as well (only one per node).

CKPxx	This is the checkpoint process that can be started to optimize the checkpoint operation for Oracle logging.
Snpxx	These are snapshot process queues.
Aq_tnxx	These are the advanced queuing processes. As of 8.0.2, there can be only one set, but later releases should allow for more.
EXTPROC	These are the callout queues; there will be one for each session performing callouts. It is hoped that Oracle will multithread these processes or it could result in the callout feature being unusable in a large multiuser environment. As of the 8.0.2 beta this also was not working with environments where multithreaded server was enabled. This functionality has been promised in 8.0.3.

On a UNIX system, this additional process may be present:

ARCHMON—Archive Monitor	This is a process on UNIX that monitors the archive process and writes the redo logs to the archives. It will require a dedicated window or terminal on BSD systems.

On multiuser-capable systems, each user process may spawn several subprocesses depending on the type of activities being done by that process. Depending on how Oracle is configured, a single parallel query may start dozens of query slave processes for a single user!

The global memory area, called the System Global Area (SGA) is an area of CPU memory that is reserved for Oracle use only. It contains buffers that are used to speed transaction throughput and help maintain the system integrity and consistency. No data is altered directly on the disk; it all passes through the SGA. The size and configuration of the SGA is defined by a file called the initialization file or INIT.ORA file, which can contain information on each type of buffer or shared pool area in the SGA.

There are also shared programs that make up a typical instance. These can be as few as one (e.g., the ORACLE kernel) or as complex as the entire toolset. Placing the toolset into shared memory (on VMS) reduces the memory requirements for each user.

As was said before, Oracle can be viewed as an operating system that overlays your existing operating system. It has structures and constructs that are unique to it alone. The major area of an Oracle installation is of course the database. In order to access an Oracle database you must first have at least one *instance* of Oracle that is assigned to that database. An instance consists of the subprocesses, global area, and related structures that are assigned to it. Multiple instances can attach to a single database. Many of an instance's and database's characteristics are determined when it is created. A single VMS, NT, or UNIX platform can have several instances in operation simultaneously; on VMS and some UNIX systems they can be attached to their own database or may share one.

The document set for Oracle weighs in at over 60 pounds and is not light reading by any means. It takes at least a single CD-ROM to contain it all.

A Brief Overview of Relational Jargon

Some of you are no doubt wondering what the heck this book is talking about. Relations, tuples, attributes—what are they? Ninety percent of any field is learning the jargon—the language specific to that field. With Oracle, the jargon is that of relational databases. Much of this jargon can be attributed to Dr. Codd who formulated the rules, called "Normal Forms," for data and formulated the relational algebra upon which relational databases are designed.

You may have already been exposed to such topics as "Normal Forms," "tuples," and "primary and foreign keys." It is not the intention of this book to give a full course in relational theory. We will, however, attempt to clarify the meaning of this "relational speak" so those without a formal grounding in relational terminology can find the book as valuable as those who know it all.

We've already mentioned tables, tuples, and attributes and touched on relationships. Let's look at relationships a bit more as they apply to relational databases. Stop for a moment and consider the company where you work or perhaps are consulting for. The company has employees, or, let's say, the company employs workers. The reverse is also true; a worker is employed by a company. This is a relationship. A relationship is a logical tie between information that is contained in entities. In this case, the information is from the entities: A: the company, and B: the workers.

Can a worker have more than one job? Of course. Can a company have more than one worker? Yes. So let's restate the relationship:

A Company may employ one or more Workers. A Worker may be employed by one or more Companies.

This is called a "many-to-many" relationship. Of course, other types of relationships exist. Within a company, a worker usually only works for one department at a time, while a department may have many workers. This is called a "one-to-many" relationship. Generally speaking, most many-to-many relationships can be broken down into one-to-many relationships; one-to-many relationships form a majority of the relationships in a relational database. A relationship is between two *entities*. In the above example, "Worker" and "Company" are entities. An entity is always singular in nature. In most cases, an entity will map into a table. A diagram showing the logical structure of a relational database is called an entity relationship diagram (ERD). Figure I.3 shows a simple entity relationship diagram.

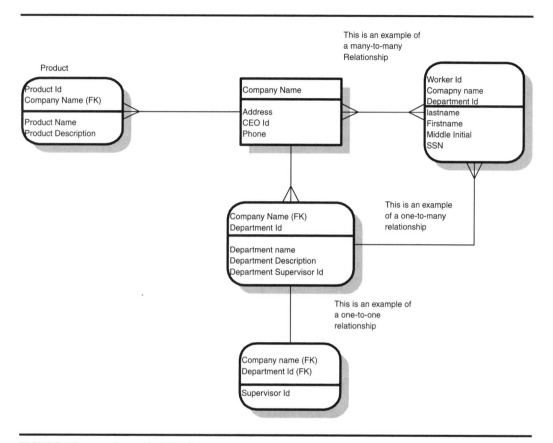

FIGURE I.3   Example ERD diagram.

Another aspect of a relational database is its functions. Without functions, a database would have no purpose. Functions start at a high level, such as "Provide a means of tracking and reporting the work history of employees." Functions can be broken down, or if you wish, decomposed, until they are atomic in nature. A fanatic would break down a function until it consisted of operations involving individual attributes, such as add, delete, update, and retrieve.

For example, say we wished to retrieve a record (or *tuple)* from a table, update one of its columns (or *attributes),* and then return the row to the table. In one case, it could be considered one function, *update of attribute x.* In a different light, it could be decomposed into the individual retrieves, modifies, and updates of the columns. In most cases it isn't required to go into great and gory detail. The functions a database perform are shown in a function hierarchy diagram. Entities (and hence, tables) and relations map into functions. Figure I.4 shows a simple function hierarchy diagram (FHD).

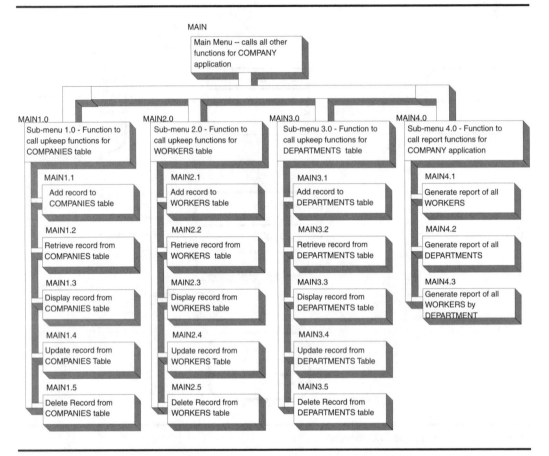

FIGURE I.4   Example of a simple function hierarchy diagram.

The final aspect of a relational database is its modules. A module may perform one or more *functions*. A module may map into a form, a report, a menu or a procedure. For example, a single module representing a form can handle numerous atomic functions, such as add, update, retrieve, and delete, of a table, or even a group of tables, and data records.

Let's summarize. A relational database is made up of entities consisting of attributes. These entities and attributes can be mapped into a table. Each occurrence of an entity adds a row to the table it maps to. These rows are called tuples. Each entity relates to one or more other entities by means of relationships. Relationships must be valid in both directions and must have degree such as *one to many* or *many to many*. Relationships must also show optionality, such as *may be* or *must be*.

Functions are used to tell what is done with the entities and relations. Entities and relations map into functions. Modules implement functions and map into forms, reports, menus, or procedures.

All of this depends on Dr. Codd's rules. The entire set of rules are complex and, to most of us, rather obtuse at times. Luckily, they have been used to produce the rules of Normalization. These, simply stated, are:

- **Precursor:** *Each occurrence of an entity is uniquely identifiable by a combination of attributes and/or relationships.*
- **1st Normal Form:** *Remove repeated attributes or groups of attributes to their own entity.*
- **2nd Normal Form:** *Remove attributes dependent on only part of the unique identifier.*
- **3rd Normal Form:** *Remove attributes dependent on attributes that are not a part of the unique identifier.*

In short, to be in third normal form all attributes in an entity must relate directly to the identifier and only to the identifier.

This unique identifier is called the *primary key*. It can be a unique number such as a social security number, or a combination of attributes, called a concatenated or combination key, such as last name and date of birth. Generally speaking, these primary keys are used to enforce relations by mapping the keys into related entities where they become *foreign keys*.

For those who want a more detailed discussion of entity relationship diagrams, normalization, and other related (no pun intended) topics, the books listed below are recommended:

Atre, S., *Data Base: Structured Techniques for Design, Performance and Management.* New York, NY: John Wiley & Sons, 1988.

Barker, Richard, *CASE*METHOD Entity Relationship Modeling.* Reading, MA: Addison-Wesley, 1990.

Barker, Richard, *CASE*METHOD Function and Process Modeling.* Reading, MA: Addison-Wesley, 1990.

Barker, Richard, *CASE*METHOD Tasks and Deliverables.* Reading, MA: Addison-Wesley, 1990.

Brathwaite, Ken S., *RELATIONAL DATABASES Concepts, Design and Administration.* New York: McGraw-Hill, 1988.

Date, C. J., *Introduction to Database Systems Volume 1, 4th Edition.* Reading, MA: Addison-Wesley, 1995.

A Brief Overview of Object-Oriented Jargon

No doubt many of you know a great deal more about object-oriented technology than I do or would ever want to know. However, it won't hurt to go over a few of the basic terms and buzzwords in this new paradigm.

The heart of the object-oriented world is of course the object. So what is an object? In *Visual Basic 5: Object Oriented Programming* (1997, Coriolis Press), Gene Swartzfager explains: "An object is a software package that contains a collection of related procedures and data."

A procedure is in turn called a method, and data elements are called attributes. So an object is a software package that contains methods and attributes. Objects, to fall completely into the object-oriented universe, must be independent of each other. This makes them ideal for use as reusable modules since each can be maintained independently of the other *as long as proper interface and messaging standards are implemented and enforced.* Unfortunately, most shops forget that last little caveat.

Objects communicate via messages. A message usually has three parts: the object name, one of the object's methods (or members), and an attribute list. Objects are contained in *classes* that define each member of an object's class. A single object is called an *instance* of that object. The only differences between particular instances of objects in a class are the attributes that the particular class objects operate against.

Other terms that bounce around in objectspeak are encapsulation, polymorphism, and inheritance. (I once knew a programmer who suffered from encapsulated polymorphism, but since he had inherited it there was nothing that could be done.) What are these three principles of object-oriented technology?

Encapsulation is simply the feature of an object-oriented program that means it is completely standalone; that is, it is not dependent on another object nor is another object dependent upon it for its function. Since an encapsulated object is passed attributes and returns attributes with no other external communication required (i.e., no global or public variables, no external calls to other objects or methods) it is said to implement data hiding or binding.

Polymorphism allows a single method to be used by multiple classes or objects. An example would be overloading of an Oracle PL/SQL function to handle multiple datatypes. An overloaded function (or procedure) in PL/SQL simply has several functions or procedures of the same name and argument structure except that one of the passed arguments is a different datatype. The user has no idea that multiple functions or procedures exist; he or she simply calls the function or procedure and gets the results back.

Inheritance is just what it appears. We have touched on the concept of classes. Classes can be subdivided into super-classes and subclasses. Inheritance allows subclasses to inherit behaviors from their super-class. Generally speaking, a super-class will be a general class of generic functions with subclasses that exhibit more and more specialized behavior. Oracle8 will not support inheritance until release 8.2 at the earliest.

In Oracle we have some Oracle8-specific definitions for the Oracle object-oriented extensions. These involve how Oracle uses object technology. Let's look at some of these Oracle-specific definitions to complete this discussion of object-oriented jargon.

- **Object Type:** An object type (called *abstract data types* in early release documentation) are datatypes that define Oracle objects. An Oracle object is one instance of an Oracle object type. Oracle objects can be persistent, such as tables or views, or may be transient, such as a memory construct in PL/SQL. The CREATE TYPE command is used to create an Oracle object type. Persistent object types will have an object identifier (OID) while nonpersistent object types will not.

- **Object Table:** An object table is a table of Oracle object types. If a pre-Oracle8 table is ported to Oracle8, it doesn't automatically become an object table. To get a relational table to behave as if it were an object table, it must be made part of an object view. Only objects represented by true object tables have OIDs. Object tables were referred to as extent tables or typed tables in early Oracle8 documents.

- **Object Identifier (OID):** As was said before, only objects stored in an object table have an OID. The OID is guaranteed to be globally unique and consists of a 128-byte hexadecimal value. By itself an OID cannot be used to locate an object instance, only a REF (discussed later) which contains location data can be used for locating an object instance.

- **Object:** A single instance of an object datatype which may or may not have an associated OID. If the object is from an object table it will have an OID; if it is from Oracle Call Interface variables or PL/SQL variables it will not.

- **Nested Object:** An object is said to be nested if its object type is used to specify a single column in an object table.

- **Nested Tables:** The CREATE TYPE command can be used to create a type that is actually a table. This table type can then be used to create a table of that type which can be used as a column in a second object table. This results in a nested table. Don't worry if this is confusing now; in the next few chapters you will see examples which should reduce the fog factor.

- **Datatypes:** There are three types of datatype in Oracle8: built-in, library, or user-defined. Built in are the standard NUMBER, DATE, VARCHAR2, LONG, LONG RAW, BLOB, etc. User-defined are specialized types built by users or VARs, and library types are types built by a third party and supplied to the user (generally a specialized form of the user-defined datatype).

- **LOBS:** New in Oracle8 is extended coverage for large objects (LOBS). There are several types of LOB: a character LOB (CLOB), binary LOB (BLOB), national character LOB (NCLOB), and a LOB stored externally to the database, a BFILE which is generally to be used for long binary files such as digitized movies or audio tracks.

- **External Procedures:** Another new Oracle8 feature is the ability to call procedures that don't reside in the database from PL/SQL. By procedures we mean a 3GL program. Currently (8.0.2) only C is supported but more languages will be available by the time general release of Oracle 8 is accomplished. These are also referred to as 3GL callouts. One problem with these is that for each process that makes a 3GL callout a new callout process is created, and since they don't yet work with MTS this will effectively double the number of operating system processes required in an environment that uses callouts.

- **Constructor:** This is an Oracle kernel-generated method to instantiate an Oracle object type instance. It is differentiated from a user-created method in that it is system created and automatically applied when a call is made to an object type or when an object type is needed and does not have an implicit or explicit SELF parameter (to use a bit of objectspeak).
- **Forward Type Definition:** I prefer to call this a type-in-type. Essentially, it means you can define an object type and then use that type in a second, third, or any number of subsequent type definitions. In this special case, both types refer to each other in their definition. For you C programmers, this is identical to forward declaration. An example of this type of type-in-type definition will be shown in a later section.
- **Object View:** An object view allows normal relational tables to be referenced like objects in an object relational database. The object view process supplies synthesized OIDs for relational rows. Later sections will demonstrate this technique.

What Exactly Is a Database Administrator?

A database administrator (DBA) should not be confused with a data administrator. While a data administrator is responsible for administering data via naming conventions and data dictionaries, a database administrator is responsible for administering the physical implementation of a database. This can include or overlap the database management function. In fact, this book will blur the two together since the functions of one are closely related to the other. The DBA provides support and technical expertise to the DA and users.

The DBA position is constantly changing and expanding. It may encompass physical design and implementation, performance monitoring and tuning, even testing and configuration of interface programs such as X-Window emulators for use with the database.

The database administrator must have the freedom required to move data files in coordination with the system manager to optimize database access. The DBA should work hand-in-hand with the system administrator to ensure proper use is made of available resources. There is no more sure formula for failure than that involving a company where the database administrator and the system administrator are at war.

Let's list the major jobs of a database administrator, according to the *Oracle8 Server Administrator's Guide*, Release 8.0, Beta-2, Part No. A50648-1, Copyright © 1989, 1997, Oracle Corporation:

- Installing and upgrading the Oracle server and application tools
- Allocating system storage and planning future storage requirements for the database system
- Creating primary database storage structures (tablespaces) after application developers have designed an application
- Creating primary objects (tables, views, indexes) once application developers have designed an application

- Modifying the database structure, as necessary, from information given by application developers
- Enrolling users and maintaining system security
- Ensuring compliance with your Oracle license agreement
- Controlling and monitoring user access to the database
- Monitoring and optimizing the performance of the database
- Planning for backup and recovery of database information
- Maintaining archived data on tape
- Backing up and restoring the database
- Contacting Oracle Corporation for technical support

In an ideal structure, there is a data administrator who is a direct report to a director or other senior manager. This DA is "off to the side," rather like the executive officer on a Navy ship. Also reporting to this level of management should be the database administrator. The DA and DBA need to work closely together to be sure that the physical and logical structure of the database, through the data dictionary, are closely tied. The database administrator may also hold the database management function, or this may be a separate position. Beneath this level are the application administrators, who control individual applications. Beneath the application administrators may be the development and maintenance staffs, or these may be in a separate directorate. This structure is shown in Figure I.5. If the database is sufficiently large, especially under Oracle8 due to its more complex security requirements, a security administrator may also be required.

All of the above positions must work closely together. The DA must talk to the DBA; the DBM and DBA must work closely together to optimize the database system. The application managers need to ensure their applications meet naming rules and conventions and coordinate their resource utilization with the DBM and DBA.

As can be seen, the DBA is central to the proper running of a database system. They coordinate activities related to the database, assist with design, development, and testing, and provide monitoring and tuning. Given the DBA's importance let's look at what it takes to find a good DBA.

Selecting a Proper DBA Over the last few years I have been interviewed for and have interviewed several dozen candidates for Oracle-related positions. The positions ranged from entry-level developer to senior-level DBA. Many of the interviews were for DBA-level positions. In this period I learned that it is very difficult to hire, or be hired, as a DBA unless you know exactly who or what you are looking for when you use the title DBA. This section will attempt to clear up the misconceptions about the Oracle DBA position, specify the levels within the DBA position, and give some idea of how to interview and be interviewed for Oracle DBA positions.

To be a full-charge DBA, a candidate must be knowledgeable in all of these areas:

- Installation
- Configuration management

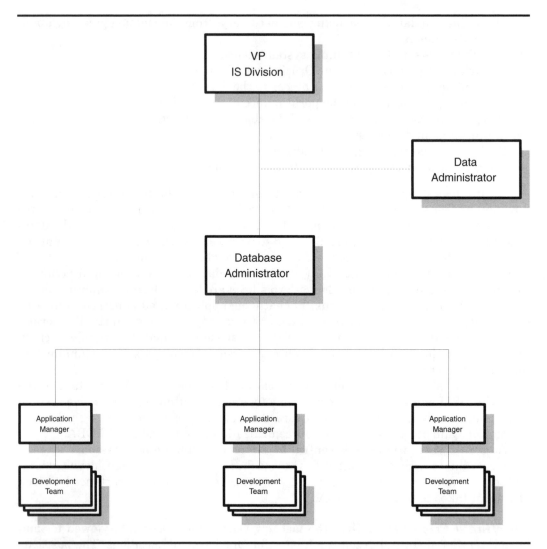

FIGURE I.5   Sample Information Systems Data Administration Org Chart.

- Security
- Monitoring and tuning
- Backup and recovery
- Troubleshooting
- Vendor interface

Desired Personality Traits of a DBA Many times, managers concentrate on technical qualities and overlook personality. Virtually every category shown above means a DBA will have to interface with other personnel, be they vendors, users, developers, or managers. This indicates the DBA should exhibit the following traits:

- Self-confidence
- Curiosity
- Tenacity
- Tactful
- Self-starter
- Detail oriented

Why Are These Traits Important? I have had several underlings that lacked self-confidence; they constantly asked my feelings on every decision major or minor and showed no initiative. As a beginning DBA under a full-charge DBA, this may be all right, but if the person *is* the full-charge DBA then who are they going to depend on for their decisions if they have no self-confidence? Interviews should include questions on problems and how they were solved. The answers should demonstrate self-confidence. One thing to remember is that to not know an answer is not bad, but to not know where to find an answer is bad.

The Oracle database system is constantly changing. Not all of these changes are documented. Curiosity is a requirement to be a good DBA. If a DBA isn't curious they are passive and wait for things to be told them. A curious DBA will install the latest version and immediately begin searching out the differences and improvements and how they can be applied to make his or her job better (read easier). A curious DBA will have multiple references they purchased with their own money and will have read them. One of my interview questions involves what references the candidate has and uses. Needless to say, if they respond with only the documentation set and haven't even read that, then their stock looses value rapidly. Curiosity will also drive them to understand the Oracle data dictionary and any utilities or packages provided by Oracle. Many of my interview questions deal with these Oracle internals. Lack of knowledge about the data dictionary tables and views and the Oracle-provided utilities and packages is unforgivable in a full-charge DBA.

Troubleshooting requires a bulldog-like tenacity, getting a hold and not letting go until the problem is solved. Many times a DBA will give up on a problem that would have been solved with the next solution they tried. As a SYSOP for the CompuServe ORAUSER forum I see questions daily that should have been solved by the person asking them, if they were tenacious and curious. I use troubleshooting questions from my own experience and from experiences I see many times on the ORAUSER and ORASUPP forums on CompuServe.

A self-starting employee is important for any position. Doubly so for a DBA. A DBA must be able to wade in and make things happen, not just wait for things to happen. A self-starting DBA obtains or develops their own scripts to monitor such items as table sizes, tablespace usage, SGA usage, in short, all of the items that can get them in trouble if ignored. Questions dealing with level of experience in PL/SQL, SQL, and SQL*Plus will show how many scripts the DBA candidate has developed. Some operations in PL/SQL and SQL*Plus are generally only used by DBAs so questions concerning specific techniques will expose those who have written their own scripts and those who haven't.

Dealing with developers and managers, not to mention users, requires tact. A tactless DBA will make nothing but enemies for your department. Tact has been called the ability to tell someone to go to Hades and have them anxious for the trip. Many times developers, managers, and users will make unreasonable requests; the DBA must have tact to field and deflect these requests without burning bridges. How a person acts during the interview process will show their level of tact.

The final trait, being detail oriented, is very important. Being detail oriented means that they don't have to be told to cross-check details. It also means they actively document quirks in the installation "just in case." The indications of a detail-oriented person are such things as bringing a daytimer or scheduler to the interview, showing up ahead of time, and asking questions that indicate they have researched the company they are interviewing with. This detail orientation will show up in their knowing the Oracle internals and understanding the relationships between the views, tables, and dynamic performance tables. Usually a detail-oriented person will take the time to research the database on their own.

Knowledge Required of a DBA A good DBA candidate will know all of the areas discussed above. A DBA must be familiar with both installation and update on the platform that your system is running against. Each platform has its own quirks and idiosyncrasies. A DBA experienced on Windows-NT will have difficulty performing an installation on UNIX or DEC-VMS. Updates can raise havoc with production machines if they are done incorrectly. DBA candidates should be able to answer specific questions concerning installation and upgrade of Oracle systems on your platform. They should exhibit the curiosity to ask about your platform and any modifications to the standard installation that exist upon it during the interview process.

Configuration management involves database sizing, file placement, and specification of storage media. A full-charge DBA will be familiar with system topics such as RAID levels, disk sharing, disk shadowing, solid state disks, optical storage and their application to the Oracle database environment. On UNIX they should also be familiar with the cost and benefits associated with use of raw devices and when raw device usage is mandatory.

Understanding Oracle security options is vital to the DBA job. A demonstrated knowledge of system and object level privileges, roles, and profiles is required for any DBA. Understanding how the operating system security options interface with the Oracle options is also important. Additional requirements such as use of Secure Oracle and implementation of SQLNET are also considerations.

One of the critical aspects of the DBA job is the monitoring and tuning of the database and any applications. Monitoring and tuning requires a detailed understanding of the Oracle data dictionary, the tkprof, and explain plan utilities and understanding how both the cost-based and rule-based optimizers function. Detailed understanding of what can and can't be done via indexing, use of hints, and SQL statement tuning is vital to a DBA. A DBA candidate should demonstrate knowledge of:

- DBA_ views, ALL_ views, and USER_ views
- SYS owned "$" tables
- V$ dynamic performance tables

All of these are a part of the Oracle data dictionary. In addition, the DBA candidate should have knowledge of the DBMS_* series of packages and how they can be used to facilitate tuning and script development and the UTL*.SQL series of utility scripts and their usage in tuning and monitoring.

A DBA candidate must understand all of the backup and recovery options. Use of the import and export utilities, and use of cold and hot backups are all vital topics that a DBA must understand. Interview questions concerning types of database backups used and how the utilities can be used are asked in order to show level of knowledge in this area. An additional topic that should be covered in this phase of the interview are recovery scenarios involving partial recovery at the table, tablespace, and database levels.

Troubleshooting is a binary ability. Usually people will either have the knack or they won't. Troubleshooting requires an analytical approach where the problem is laid out in discrete parts and each is attacked in a methodological fashion until the problem is solved. Troubleshooting also involves the ability to admit when you don't know something but having the tenacity to say "But I can look it up." Questions on troubleshooting must come from real life and should involve multiple steps and critical thinking to solve. Questions on the most difficult problem they have encountered and how they solved it are asked in order to test their troubleshooting ability.

A final bit of knowledge required of a DBA is the ability to communicate clearly either orally or via written materials. Since a major portion of a DBA job will involve interaction with others on multiple levels within a company environment, your DBA must speak, think, and write clearly and concisely. A review of their resume with particular attention to any publishing credits will help with determining their abilities in this regard. Presentations at user groups, local or national, magazine articles, or just articles in local user group publications all show the ability to communicate.

At a professional level, look for jobs where they wrote documentation or procedures. Most candidates with advanced degrees such as Masters or PhDs will have had to have written and communicate to get to that level of education. Ask them to bring their dissertation or examples of their writing to the interview. Candidates should be sure to bring examples of this type of ability to the interview. The ability to communicate clearly in spoken word and to take and give instructions and to understand complaints is vital. As qualified technically as a candidate may be, if they cannot communicate they will not succeed.

What Level of DBA Do I Need? DBAs range from DBBS level (database baby sitters) to full-charge DBAs. What level do you need? If you place a full-charge, fire-breathing DBA in a job where all that they have to do is monitor an older version of

Oracle and ensure backups are taken they will soon tire of the job and leave. On the other hand, if you hire a DBBS for a position where initiative, drive, tenacity, and troubleshooting skills are critical, you are asking for trouble. Be sure that you get the right candidate for the right job. I would rather hire a technically inexperienced DBA that showed all of the personality traits discussed above, than a DBBS that could rewrite Oracle, if someone told him to, that is.

A database baby sitter usually has a good-looking resume that is full of projects and jobs involving Oracle. However, most of these jobs will have involved third-party applications that were preinstalled and only required monitoring. If they can't answer in-depth questions concerning the DBA_ views or the V$ tables then chances are they are DBBS rather than DBA level candidates. Another key indicator is a lack of knowledge about the Oracle utilities such as import, export, and the tuning tools tkprof and explain plan. A final indicator is lack of knowledge concerning the DBA task-related DBMS_* packages.

If all you need is someone to monitor a third-party database application via a preconfigured monitoring tool and only take action when the tool tells them a problem has happened, then hire a DBBS. You will waste a DBA and no one will be happy if you get an overqualified person into a low-level job.

If you need a full-charge DBA, don't hire a DBBS unless they show the curiosity and tenacity to use deep-end learning to pull themselves up to the level of a full DBA. Deep-end learning is like when someone is thrown into a pool at the deep end to learn to swim. Usually there won't be time to send them to the multitude of classes required to give them full knowledge, so they will have to learn as they go. Get them involved with the Oracle forums and user groups and purchase whatever references they require. I suggest a full paper copy of the Oracle manuals which is theirs alone. An on-line reference such as the Oracle Administrator product from RevealNet is also a good idea since it will provide battle-tested solutions to many problems. As a last resort, the Oracle references on CD can also be used. I have found them difficult to use and their search engine is deplorable, but as a last resort they work. The newer versions using Java are much better, but at least to me, nothing replaces a paper manual for ease of use (besides, you can use it even during a power outage— by candlelight!).

Developing Questions for Interviews Interview questions should be diligently researched and the expected answers listed. Where open-ended questions are used the interviewer should have the level of knowledge required to judge the answers' correctness. The questions should be broken into categories and each should be assigned a point value based on either a scale such as from 0–5 or according to difficulty. At the conclusion of the interview technical ability evaluation should be based on the results from these points. Your interview questions should be reviewed by technically competent personnel for accuracy and applicability. Appendix A shows some example interview questions. These questions are included on the attached CD-ROM in Acrobat Reader format.

Prequalification of Candidates Candidates used to have two sources for Oracle knowledge; experience and/or Oracle Corporation training classes. Experience speaks for itself and can be judged as to depth and level. Training was only as good as what the candidate put into it. What I mean by this is that the candidate could either gain much from the experience of Oracle training if they took the will to learn and curiosity with them to class, or they could take nothing away from the class if they practiced passive learning. Since Oracle training is not graded, everyone receives certification regardless of participation. Now many vendors offer Oracle classes. Indeed with the plethora of classes available it is difficult if not impossible to judge the quality of training a candidate may have received. One item that will assist hiring managers is the recent introduction of the Oracle Certification Exam offered by Sylvan Learning Systems (The Cauncy Group). This exam tests candidates' knowledge in all areas of the DBA skill set. The test was created by battle-tested DBAs, and in order to pass, a candidate will in almost all cases have to have had actual experience as an Oracle DBA and will have to have knowledge from multiple Oracle references. The test was developed by over a dozen experienced DBAs and has been certified against hundreds of DBA candidates. While obtaining an Oracle certification from this exam is no absolute guarantee that a candidate is fully qualified, it can be used as an acid test to separate the wheat from the chaff.

Always check a candidate's references. Speak to previous employers if possible and find out about a candidate's past work history. Many people will interview wonderfully but won't function in the job.

Appearance A candidate who doesn't take the time put the right foot forward by maintaining a proper appearance probably doesn't have the wherewithal to perform adequately in the job. Clean, appropriate clothing and proper grooming show that the candidate is willing to make the effort to please the employer. Candidates who are sloppy in appearance and mannerisms will bring this to the job and their interactions with other parts of the company.

There is no magic formula for determining if a candidate can perform adequately or to always ensure an employer will properly evaluate a candidate's abilities. However, if proper preparation is done by both the employer and candidate then successful hiring or acquisition of a proper position can be made less a matter of chance.

CHAPTER 1

Installation of Oracle

Oracle installation is a complex topic. The method used to install the database system and toolset is very platform dependent. With the new CD-based installs, much of the platform dependencies have been reduced, but you as DBA need to be aware of the differences that apply to your platform. These differences will generally be explained in the release documents and platform-specific installation and user's guide provided with your software distribution. However, there are topics which are universal that involve structure and layout issues. This chapter will present these topics and give a general idea of the way to proceed with your installation.

1.1 THINGS TO CONSIDER BEFORE INSTALLATION

Regardless of what system you are installing Oracle on, there are several major considerations that you must address before you install. When thinking about these items, plan for your data space needs for at least a year in advance. These items are:

How many data files will the database require?

What size of global area will the database require?

What are the database's archive requirements?

How many disk drives are available for Oracle files?

How many instances and/or databases does your installation require?

Is there a need for shared instances?

Will the database be distributed?

Do you want single task or independent tools?

How many users will the database need to support, both total and concurrent?

The answers to the previous questions will determine the entire course of the installation.

Optimal Flexible Architecture (OFA)

In accordance with Cary V. Millsap of the Oracle National Technical Response Team, the OFA process involves following three rules:

1. Establish an orderly operating system directory structure in which any database file can be stored on any disk resource.
   a. Name all devices that might contain Oracle data in such a manner that a wild card or similar mechanism can be used to refer to the collection of devices as a unit.
   b. Make a directory explicitly for storage of Oracle data at the same level on each of these devices.
   c. Beneath the Oracle data directory on each device, make a directory for each different Oracle database on the system.
   d. Put a file X in the directory /u??/ORACLE/D (or on VMS DISK2:[ORACLE.D]) if and only if X is a control file, redo log file, or data file of the Oracle database whose DB_NAME is D. X is any database file.

TIP   You may wish to add an additional directory layer if you will have multiple Oracle versions running at the same time. This additional layer includes the version level.

---

2. Separate groups of segments (data objects) with different behavior into different tablespaces.
   a. Separate groups of objects with different fragmentation characteristics in different tablespaces (e.g., don't put data and rollback segments together).
   b. Separate groups of segments that will contend for disk resources in different tablespaces (e.g., don't put data and indexes together).
   c. Separate groups of segments representing objects with differing behavioral characteristics in different tablespaces (e.g., don't put tables that require daily backup in the same tablespace with ones that require yearly backup).

3. Maximize database reliability and performance by separating database components across different disk resources. A caveat for RAID environments: consider also spreading datafiles across multiple controller volume groups.
   a. Keep at least three active copies of a database control file on at least three different physical drives.

b. Use at least three groups of redo logs in Oracle7. Isolate them to the greatest extent possible on hardware serving few or no files that will be active while the RDBMS is in use. Shadow redo logs whenever possible.

c. Separate tablespaces whose data will participate in disk resource contention across different physical disk resources. (You should also consider disk controller usage.)

Minimum OFA Configuration

The minimum suggested configuration would consist of five data areas, either disks, striped sets, RAID sets, or whatever else comes down the pike in the next few years. These areas should be as separate as possible, ideally operating off of different device controllers to maximize throughput. The more heads you have moving at one time, the faster your database will be. The disk layout should minimize disk contention. For example:

DISK1: Oracle executables and user areas, a control file, the SYSTEM tablespace, redo logs

DISK2: Data-data files, a control file, tool-data files

DISK3: Index-data files, a control file

DISK4: Rollback segment-data files, export files

DISK5: Archive log files

1.2   ORACLE STRUCTURES AND HOW THEY AFFECT INSTALLATION

As can be seen from the previous section, an Oracle database is not a simple construct. Much thought must go into file placement, size of global areas, number of control files, and numerous other structural issues before installation. It is a testament to the resiliency of the Oracle RDBMS that even if most of the decisions are made incorrectly, the database that results will still function, albeit, inefficiently.

The structures are as follows:

Oracle executables

Data files—data, index, temporary, rollback

Redo logs

Control files

Export files

Archive logs

Placement of any LOB or BFILE storage structures

Let's examine each of these.

Executables

The Oracle executables are the heart of the system. Without the executables the system is of course worthless since the data files are only readable by Oracle processes. The Oracle executables should be on a disk reserved for executables and maybe some user files. Disk speed is not a big issue, but availability is of major concern. The executables will require 150 to over 200 megabytes or more of disk space. The installation process will create a directory structure starting at a user-specified root directory. There will usually be a subdirectory for each major product installed.

Data Files

Data files are the physical implementations of Oracle tablespaces. Tablespaces are the logical units of storage that would roughly compare to volume groups in an operating system. Each tablespace can have hundreds of tables, indexes, rollback segments, constraints, and other internal structures mapped into it. In return, these are then mapped into the data files that correspond to the tablespaces. Only a limited number of data files can be associated with a tablespace. The total number of data files for the entire database is set by the MAXDATAFILES parameter at creation (VMS defaults to 32, UNIX, 16).

Redo Logs

As their name implies, redo logs are used to restore transactions after a system crash or other system failure. The redo logs store data about transactions that alter database information. Each database should have at least two groups of two logs each on separate physical non-RAID5 drives; if no archive logging is taking place, three or more groups with archive logging in effect. These are relatively active files and if made unavailable, the database cannot function. They can be placed anywhere except in the same location as the archive logs. Archive logs are archive copies of filled redo logs and are used for point-in-time recovery from a major disk or system failure. Since they are backups of the redo logs it would not be logical to place the redo logs and archives in the same physical location. Size of the redo logs will determine how much data is lost for a disaster affecting the database.

Control Files

An Oracle database cannot be started without at least one control file. The control file contains data on system structures, log status, transaction numbers and other important information about the database. The control file is generally less than one megabyte in size. It is wise to have at least two copies of your control file on different disks, three for OFA compliance. Oracle will maintain them as mirror images of each other. This ensures that loss of a single control file will not knock your database out of the water. You cannot bring a control file back from a backup; it is a living file that corresponds to current database status. In both Oracle7 and Oracle8, there is a CREATE CONTROL FILE command that allows recovery from loss of a control file. However, you must have detailed knowledge of your database to use it properly. The section of the recovery chapter that deals with backup and recovery of control files explains in detail how to protect yourself from loss of a control file. It is easier to maintain extra control file copies.

Exports and Archives

Export and archive files affect the recoverability of your database should some disaster befall it. Export files, created by the export utility supplied by Oracle, are copies of a database's data and structure at a given point in time. There are several types of exports that will be covered in the section on backup and recovery. Export files should be stored in a separate location from archive files.

Archive files, as was stated before, are archived copies of the redo logs. They provide the capability to recover to a specific point-in-time for any tablespace in the database. For any application considered to be production or mission-critical, archive logging must be turned on. These files can be stored to disk, tape, or even optical storage such as WORM. Using operating system backups such as BACKUP on VMS or TAR on UNIX, and with the application of archive logs, a database can be quickly recovered after disaster.

After each successful backup of a shut-down Oracle database, the associated archive and export files may be removed and either placed in storage or deleted. In an active database these files may average tens of megabytes per day; storage for this amount of data needs to be planned for. Just for example, at one installation doing Oracle development with no active production databases, 244 megabytes of archives and over 170 megabytes of exports were generated in a one-week period. If archive logging is turned on, and you run out of archive disk space, the database stops after the last redo log is filled. Plan ahead and monitor disk usage for instances using archive logging.

1.3 SYSTEM CONSIDERATIONS

Within each Oracle installation there are several operating system considerations that must be taken into account. These affect how Oracle uses global memory and process memory areas. The DBAs will be responsible for tuning and maintaining these areas.

What Is a PAD?

The PAD is only used on VMS systems. The SGA PAD file size is specified when you create the database for the first time. This parameter determines how much process memory is reserved for the System Global Area (SGA). If your settings in the INIT.ORA file (to be covered later) cause the SGA to be larger than the SGA PAD, the instance will not start up. Make the PAD as large as you ever expect to need. The SGA will only use as much as it needs. To increase the PAD requires a complete relink of all products on Oracle7, which should be avoided if possible.

On UNIX systems, the shared memory parameters determine your maximum SGA. The critical parameters are: SHMMAX and SHMSEG under HP-UX, for example. Please refer to your system documentation and the current version of your installation guide for information on setting these parameters. On both systems, increasing SGA size will increase performance; however, too large of an SGA will result in swapping and severe performance degradation.

On NT the memory is dynamically configured although such factors as memory interleave and cache memory configuration can dramatically improve or degrade performance.

What Is an SGA and How Does It Apply to Me?

SGA refers to a Shared Global Area. As the term *global* implies, this area is accessible to all Oracle processes and users. Each instance will have its own SGA. Oracle processes and users must share large amounts of data. If all of the processes had to get the data from the disk, the IO load would soon render response times that would be totally unacceptable. To prevent this, Oracle uses global memory areas, that is, CPU memory. This memory is dedicated to use for Oracle alone. In Oracle7 the SGA contains data buffer areas, redo log buffers, and the shared pool (context areas). Each area is important to the database's overall performance. On Oracle8 an additional area, the LARGE POOL, is also configured.

The shared pool context areas and database buffers provide immediate access to data that has been preread from either the data dictionary tables or the data tables. The Oracle kernel process uses an LRU (least recently used) algorithm to write data back to the disks. Data is never altered on the disks directly, but is altered in memory first.

The redo buffers contain row change information, transaction commit history, and checkpoint history. This data is written into the redo logs and eventually to the archive logs. A commit will force a disk write as will the filling of a redo log buffer or the reaching of a predefined checkpoint.

For Oracle7 the queue and request areas store data that is being transferred between processes such as servers and other Oracle7 processes. The shared SQL area stores all SQL statements in a parsed form. When a user or process issues a SQL command, the shared SQL area is checked to see if the command already exists in parsed form; if it does, this shared version is used. If the multithreaded server option is utilized, some of the user process global area is also placed in the shared pool. Under Oracle8 the LARGE POOL area is an optional extension to the SGA. If configured via its initialization parameters the LARGE POOL takes over the session-level memory needs for MTS or XA sessions. The LARGE POOL is also used for IO slaves and during Oracle backup and restore operations.

What Is a PGA and How Does It Apply to Me?

The PGA is the Process Global Area. This is memory reserved for each process that uses Oracle. It contains the Context Area. Oracle sets this area's size based on the values of the initialization parameters:

OPEN_LINKS	the number of database links allowed open per user
DB_FILES	the number of database files allowed for the database (up to the value of MAX_DATAFILES)
LOG_FILES	the maximum number of redo log file groups (up to the value of MAX_LOGFILES)

The PGA will also contain session-related information if MTS is not used. In environments where MTS is used the session information is placed in the SHARED_POOL region of the SGA. This session information consists of the user's private SQL area and other session-specific data. The PGA will always hold the user's stack information.

Another contributor to each processes memory footprint is the size of the SORT_AREA_SIZE and SORT_AREA_RETAINED_SIZE parameters. When a process executes a sort memory the size of SORT_AREA_SIZE is allocated to the user. If SORT_AREA_RETAINED_SIZE is also set, then this amount of memory is reduced to that value and allowed to grow to SORT_AREA_SIZE. If the sort requires more space than is specified in SORT_AREA_SIZE, the sort is broken into SORT_AREA_SIZED chunks which are swapped out to disk as needed.

1.4 SOME SYSTEM-SPECIFIC NOTES

Under each operating system there are items a DBA needs to be aware of and take into account when installing Oracle on a specific operating system. This section is an attempt to consolidate these system-specific notes in one location.

VMS-Specific Notes

As was stated earlier, VMS defaults to a MAXDATAFILES setting of 32. If you don't correct this, the system control files must be rebuilt in order to increase it. I suggest setting it to the maximum allowed.

Memory Requirements To run Oracle on VMS you must have at least 16 Mb of system memory. To load the complete product set requires 325,000 blocks of disk space for version 7, at least twice as much for Oracle8. If you comply with OFA rules you will need additional disk space to accommodate the tablespaces required. The maximum datafile size is based on 16-bit addressing and thus is limited to two gigabytes. Even though Oracle runs on 32-bit platforms and 64-bit platforms this limit is still in effect.

VMS SYSGEN Parameters SYSGEN parameters of interest are listed below.

Parameter	*V7 Value*
GBLPAGES	8000 + 2 for every 1 K of PAD for V7
VIRTUALPAGECNT	> than Max. user PGFLQUO
GBLSECTIONS	17

There are other requirements that may change with time and versions of the software; please be sure to check your installation and administration guide for all values before altering them.

Data Files The limit for maximum open files for Oracle7 is 1022. The minimum data file size for Oracle7 is 5 Mb for the *first* (SYSTEM) file; there is no limit after that. The maximum number of redo logs allowed is 255. For VMS, the maximum number of extents, that is, the number of times a table, rollback segment, or index can be extended, is based on database block size. For the VMS system, the minimum block size is 2 K bytes; this yields a maximum number of extents of 121. For a 4 K byte block size the maximum is 249 and for an 8 K byte block size it will be 505.

UNIX-Specific Notes

Data Files As was stated before, UNIX defaults to a value of 30 for MAXDATAFILES on UNIX systems. On older versions of UNIX there may be a kernel-based limit of 60 open files per process. This can be overcome by altering the OPEN_MAX value in the limits.h file. Under some versions of UNIX this may be different; look under configurable Kernel parameters. Another UNIX-specific limit is on the total number of file extents. The Oracle7 documentation gives the following information on maximum extents for various block sizes: .5 K block size—25 extents, 1 K block—57, 2 K block—121, 4 K block—249, 8 K—505. This implies that a close watch on database table extents must be maintained for UNIX and that proper design and table sizing is critical.

System Global Area (SGA) In some cases, the SGA may exceed the available shared memory; the UNIX administrator must relink the kernel to allow larger programs if this occurs. There are system-specific shared memory parameters that control the maximum size of the SGA. These should be reviewed under configurable kernel parameters for your version of UNIX. The installation guide for your Oracle system will delineate which parameters to look at for your UNIX system. Under the UP-UX implementation the size of the SGA is limited to the size of swap space on the available disk drives. The parameters which control how the SGA grows on a HP-UX system are SHMMAX, the size of a shared memory area, and SHMSEG, the number of shared memory areas a process can access.

Rollback Segments Most systems are not using the parallel instance option of Oracle. Because of this, private rather than public rollback segments should be used. This will allow a single rollback segment to be taken off-line for consolidation. If you will have large transactions such as batch updates with numerous updates and adds between commits, a second INIT.ORA file should be created which brings on-line a single large rollback segment to be used during batch operations.

Raw Devices If you have tuned your application, compressed datafiles and tables, tuned IO and all applicable SGA parameters, and still cannot get the performance you want on UNIX, then consider using RAW devices. Oracle is capable of reading and writing directly to raw devices. This can increase Oracle performance for disk IO by over 50% and ensures data integrity is maintained. One limitation is that Oracle data file names are restricted to a specified syntax when raw devices are used. Another is that the entire raw partition has to be used for only one file, which can lead to wasted disk space unless the areas are carefully planned. This will require the DBA to keep an accurate map of what devices belong to which tablespaces, log files, and so on. Another method is to turn off UNIX buffering. Whether the option of removing UNIX buffering is open to you depends on the version of UNIX you are using.

There are also limitations on types of backup that can be used. Many third-party software packages that are designed for use with Oracle support backup of RAW devices. If you don't have one of these packages I suggest ensuring you have enough formatted (cooked) file systems to support a "dd" to a cooked file system followed by a normal backup.

There is some debate as to whether the reported up to 50% increase in speed of access is due to the RAW device usage, or whether a good deal of it is an artifact of the conversion process from a cooked system to a RAW. Generally a system with bad performance has other problems, such as chained rows and excessive table extents as well as improper placement of indexes, tables, redo, and rollback. The DBA converts to RAW by exporting, dropping the database, doing the RAW partitions, recreating the database, and then importing. Usually files will be placed better due to lessons learned. The chained rows and multiple table extents are eliminated by the export/import, and another major performance problem, brown indexes, is fixed by the import rebuild of the indexes. Voila! The system is 50% faster and RAW gets the credit when doing all of the above to the database on a cooked file system would have given the same improvements.

If you want to use a shared instance (Oracle's Parallel Server option) you must use RAW devices on UNIX since there are no UNIX file systems that support the proper sharing of disks in other than a RAW state.

Archives To implement Archive logging on BSD-type systems, the archmon process must be started as a separate process that communicates via SQL*NET over TCP/IP to the arch process. This will require that the SQL*NET TCP/IP process orasrv be running. The archmon process must be run from a dedicated window or terminal.

1.5   ORACLE AND DISK USAGE

One of the major arguments against relational database systems has been speed. It is said that relational systems are slow. It has been found, however, that with proper tuning of Oracle applications and operating system as well as proper file placement, Oracle performance is excellent. Conversely, if you try to place Oracle on an insufficient number of disks, performance will suffer.

How Many Is Enough?

Some applications will do fine with two disks. It's not great, mind you, but the system will function. Other applications, such as large complex systems involving numerous indexes, data tables, and tablespaces, may require dozens. To reduce disk contention and maximize database reliability, it is suggested that the DBA utilize OFA procedures to place database files. The next sections cover file placement for some basic disk layouts.

One Disk (Surely You Jest) For other than DOS, OS/2, WINDOWS-NT, or MAC-based, single-user databases, it is foolish and very dangerous to even consider using a single disk to hold all Oracle files. A single disk failure or crash could completely destroy your system. Since there are no file placement options with one disk, let's go on to the next configuration.

Two Disks (Just Barely Adequate) At least with two disks you can achieve separation of data and indexes and can separate redo logs from archive log files. This gives you some redundancies in recovery options. The file placement is shown below.

DISK1: Oracle executables, index data files, redo logs, export files, a copy of the control file

DISK2: Data data files, rollback segment data file, temporary user data files, archive log files, a copy of the control file

As you can see, an attempt is made to spread IO between the two disks. Indexes and data are on separate platters, as are redo logs and rollback segments. Additional recoverability in case of disk crash is given by having exports on one drive and archive log files on the other. While infinitely better than only one disk, having only two disks is still an extremely vulnerable condition and is not recommended.

Three Disks (Nearly There) With three drives available we improve the chances that the database can be recovered from disk crashes. We can also reduce the disk contention caused by sharing disks between highly active files in flagrant disregard for OFA rules. Let's look at the three-disk layout:

DISK1: Executables, redo logs, rollback segments, export files, copy of the control file

DISK2: Data data files, temporary user data files, a copy of the control file

DISK3: Archive log files, indexes, a copy of the control file

Again, an attempt is made to spread IO evenly across the platters. While this is better than one or two disks, there is still contention between redo logs and rollback segments, indexes, and archives.

Four Disks (Just About Right) Four disks are much better. Now we can spread the disk intensive rollbacks and redo logs. In addition, we can isolate the archives away from the indexes. Let's look at the structure:

DISK1: Executables, redo log files, export files, a copy of the control file

DISK2: Data data files, temporary user data files, a copy of the control file

DISK3: Indexes, a copy of the control file

DISK4: Archive logs, rollback segments

Now we have succeeded in spreading IO even further. Redo logs and rollback segments have been separated and because archive logs will not be as active as redo logs, there will be less contention in this configuration. Since in most installations exports will be done during off hours, there should be little contention between the redos and exports.

Five Disks (Oracle Nirvana) Well, this may not be Nirvana, but it is an excellent minimum configuration. Five disks allow OFA compliance and permit maximum spread of IO load. Let's look at a five-disk spread:

DISK1: Executables, a copy of the control file, redo logs, the SYSTEM tablespace data files

DISK2: Data data files, temporary user data files, a copy of the control file

DISK3: Index data files, a copy of the control file

DISK4: Rollback segment data files, export files

DISK5: Archive log files

Now we have minimum contention. By moving export files to tape, we can eliminate one additional source of database lockup. By monitoring DISK5 and periodically removing archive log files to tape we can eliminate another. If we really wanted to push OFA, we could add a disk for redo logs.

Other authors recommend larger configurations and in some cases it is warranted. If you have several large tables consideration should be given to placing these, and their indexes, on separate platters. Most of this type of consideration is application dependent. With some of the giant databases we are now seeing (hundreds of gigabytes aren't uncommon anymore) and with pedabyte sizes now available through Oracle8 it seems silly to talk about a mere 5, 7, or 100 disks. If you can use RAID0-1 and stripe data across multiple platters, do it. Of course don't do what one inexperienced system administrator did and try to do RAID5 sets with two disks each.

As was previously stated, the more we can spread our tablespaces across multiple disks the better Oracle likes it. If you have the disk resources, spread Oracle as thin as you can. While a five-disk configuration performs well and is easy to maintain, the more the merrier.

Disk Striping, Shadowing, RAID, and Other Topics

Unless you've been living in seclusion from the computer mainstream, you will have heard of the above topics. Let's take a brief look at them and how they will affect Oracle.

Disk Striping Disk striping is the process by which multiple smaller disks are made to look like one large disk. This allows extremely large databases, or even extremely large single-table tablespaces, to occupy one logical device. This makes managing the resource easier since backups only have to address one logical volume instead of several. This also provides the advantage of spreading IO across several disks. If you will need several gigabytes of disk storage for your application, striping may be the way to go. One disadvantage to striping: If one of the disks in the set crashes, you lose them all.

Disk Shadowing or Mirroring If you will have mission-critical applications that you absolutely cannot allow to go down, consider disk shadowing or mirroring. As its name implies, disk shadowing or mirroring is the process whereby each disk has a shadow or mirror disk that data is written to simultaneously. This redundant storage allows the shadow disk or set of disks to pick up the load in case of a disk crash on the primary disk or disks; thus the users never see a crashed disk. Once the disk is brought back on-line, the shadow or mirror process brings it back in sync by a process appropriately called "resilvering." This also allows for backup, since the shadow or mirror set can be broken (e.g., the shadow separated from the primary), a backup taken, and then the set resynchronized.

The main disadvantage to disk shadowing is the cost: For a two-gigabyte disk farm, you need to purchase four gigabytes of disk storage.

RAID—Redundant Arrays of Inexpensive Disks The main strength of RAID technology is its dependability. In a RAID 5 array, the data is stored as are check sums and other information about the contents of each disk in the array. If one disk is lost, the others can use this stored information to recreate the lost data. This makes RAID very attractive. RAID has the same advantages as shadowing and striping at a lower cost. It has been suggested that if the manufacturers would use slightly more expensive disks (RASMED—redundant array of slightly more expensive disks) performance gains could be realized. A RAID system appears as one very large, reliable disk to the CPU. There are several levels of RAID to date:

RAID-0—Known as disk striping

RAID-1—Known as disk shadowing

RAID-0/1—Combination of RAID-0 and RAID-1

RAID-2—Data is distributed in extremely small increments across all disks and adds one or more disks that contain a Hamming code for redundancy. RAID-2 is not considered commercially viable due to the added disk requirements (10–20% must be added to allow for the Hamming disks).

RAID-3—This also distributes data in small increments but adds only one parity disk. This results in good performance for large transfers, but small transfers show poor performance.

RAID-4—In order to overcome the small transfer performance penalties in RAID-3, RAID-4 uses large data chunks distributed over several disks and a single parity disk. This results in a bottleneck at the parity disk. Due to this performance problem RAID-4 is not considered commercially viable.

RAID-5—This solves the bottleneck by distributing the parity data across the disk array. The major problem is it requires several write operations to update parity data. The performance hit is only moderate and the other benefits outweigh this minor problem.

RAID-6—This adds a second redundancy disk that contains error-correction codes. Read performance is good due to load balancing, but write performance suffers due to RAID-6 requiring more writes than RAID-5 for data update.

For the money, I would suggest RAID0/1, that is, striped and mirrored. It provides nearly all of the dependability of RAID5 and gives much better write performance. You will usually take at least a 20% write performance hit using RAID5. For read-only applications RAID5 is a good choice, but in high transaction/high performance environments the write penalties may be too high.

New Technologies

Oracle is a broad topic; topics related to Oracle and Oracle data storage are even broader. This section will touch on several new technologies such as Optical Disk, RAM disk, and tape systems that should be utilized with Oracle systems whenever possible. Proper use of Optical technology can result in significant savings when large volumes of static data are in use in the database (read only). RAM drives can speed access to index and small table data by several fold. High speed tapes can make backup and recovery go quickly and easily. Let's examine these areas in more detail.

Optical Disk Systems WORM (write once, read many) or MWMR (multiple write, multiple read) optical disks can be used to great advantage in an Oracle system. Their main use will be in storage of export and archive log files. Their relative immunity to crashes and long shelf life provide an ideal solution to the storage of the immense amount of data that proper use of archive logging and exports produce. As access speeds improve, these devices will be worth considering for these applications in respect to Oracle. Another area where they have shown great benefits is in read-only tablespaces.

Tape Systems Nine track, 4 mm, 8 mm, and the infamous TK series from DEC can be used to provide a medium for archive logs and exports. One problem with this is the need at most installations for operator monitoring of the tape devices to switch cartridges and reels. With the event of stacker-loader drives for the cartridge tapes, this limitation has all but been eliminated in all but the smallest shops.

RAM Drives (Random Access Memory) While RAM drives have been around for several years, they have not seen the popularity their speed and reliability should be able to claim. One of the problems has been their small capacity in comparison to other storage mediums. Several manufacturers offer solid state drives of steadily increasing capacities. For index storage these devices are excellent. Their major strength is their innate speed. They also have onboard battery backup sufficient to back up their contents to their built-in hard drives. This backup is an automatic procedure invisible to the user, as is the reload of data upon power restoration. The major drawback to RAM drives is their high cost. The rapid reductions in memory chip costs with the equally rapid increase in amount of storage per chip may soon render this drawback nonexistent.

1.6   INSTALLATION GUIDELINES

Installation of Oracle is a complex topic. On the one hand, Oracle has automated the process to a large extent; on the other hand, if you don't have your ducks in a row before you start, your success is doubtful. This section will cover installation on VMS, NT, and UNIX and attempt to point out the pitfalls that may be on the path to a proper installation. Since the product is growing and changing with each release, this section cannot, nor is it intended to, replace the installation guides provided by Oracle. Instead, this section should provide general guidelines for the DBA who is facing installation or upgrade of the Oracle products.

Generic Installation Issues

In any installation, whether it be on UNIX or VMS, there are certain items which must be addressed. These include:

Disk space availability

DBA account setup

Training

File layout

Tablespace layout

Database-specific topics

We will cover these topics and hopefully provide the DBA the information to arrive at logical answers to installation questions that may arise.

Disk Space Availability Disk space availability probably messes up more installations than any other. On VMS, NT, and UNIX, Oracle requires contiguous space for its tablespace data files. When you are talking about files that at a minimum are megabytes in size, this can become quite an issue. Disk fragmentation doesn't seem to be a problem under UNIX.

With most modern systems, disk space is allocated dynamically. This means that as a file needs space, it is granted space wherever it is available on a disk. On active systems, where files are created, updated, and deleted or moved to different disks, this results in fragmentation. This results in problems for the DBA.

Under VMS, the fragmentation of disk assets is a performance issue for the system administrator; for a DBA attempting to install Oracle, it can be a show stopper. A disk may show that it has several megabytes available, but if those megabytes are spread out in 512 K chunks across the platter, they are useless to Oracle. It is very frustrating to get a message telling you the system cannot allocate enough contiguous space when multiple megabytes are available. How can this be prevented?

The best way to prevent disk fragmentation from stopping an Oracle install is to install to freshly formatted, or virgin disks. Unfortunately, most DBAs will be installing on existing systems and this won't be an option. The next best way is to coordinate with the system administrator to have the disks defragmented before the installation. On VMS this means either using an on-line defragmentation utility (be sure it is Oracle compatible), or using VMS BACKUP to back up and restore the disks involved in the installation. Since this can take several hours if the disks are large and the only backup media is TK70, you don't spring this on the system administrator an hour or two before the install; it will need to be coordinated days in advance.

The Oracle DBA Account Other than the SYSTEM account on VMS and the ROOT or SUPERUSER account on UNIX, the Oracle DBA account, usually called ORACLE, will be one of the most powerful accounts on the system. This is required due to the Oracle system being more like an operating system rather than just a set of executables. In order to start up and shut down, create the required files, and allow global sharing of the kernel and perhaps the tools, the Oracle DBA account needs much broader privileges than a normal user account. The account must have the privilege to create directories, files, and other system objects; it will also require the ability to place objects in shared memory.

The second largest contributor to a bad install experience is an underprivileged Oracle DBA account. The account *must* be set up as stated in the installation documentation for the install to be successful. After the installation, some adjustment of account privileges can be done if the system administrator just can't stand for an account out of his realm of control having such broad privileges, but not until *after* the install is complete.

In most cases, the privileges removed by an overzealous system administrator will have to be periodically reinstated for code relinks, special file work, and of course, upgrades. This will soon convince most system administrators to set them and leave them. After all, if you can't be trusted with the required privileges to do your job, should you be trusted with the job? It is advised that the Oracle DBA be sent to at least an introductory course in system administration so as to know what not to do with the privileges. A course in system tuning is also advised.

Training It has been said that success in a new venture usually depends on three things: training, training, and training. This is especially true in the realm of the Oracle DBA. Oracle Corporation, and many third-party vendors, offer numerous classes at locations across the United States and Europe. There are also many sources for computer-based training (CBT) as well as on line references such as the RevealNet, Inc. Oracle Administrator (which I helped to author and a part of which is included on the accompanying CD). These classes are Oracle specific and address issues that DBAs, developers, and managers need to be aware of and take into account. With most Oracle purchases you can negotiate training units, or TUs. Use them; they are worth their weight in gold. While there have been a few successful seat-of-the-pants Oracle installations, most end up in trouble. The Oracle Masters programs are especially useful in that they take the guesswork out of what classes you should take. Consult with Oracle training about schedules and classes. For large Oracle installations with large numbers of developers and administrators, Oracle will provide on-site classes that may significantly reduce your training costs. Another good program is the Chauncey Group DBA certification program. For a small fee you can go to any Sylvan Learning Center and take an examination that will determine if you have the prerequisite knowledge to be a DBA on Oracle. However, if you don't have at least two years of experience in Oracle and some training, don't waste your money, I helped develop this exam; it isn't a piece of cake by any means.

If you have training on-site, don't allow outside interruptions to intrude upon the class. These can be disruptive and are rude to the instructor. Besides, it wastes your training money.

Would you allow a first-time driver to just jump into the car and drive off? It is amazing how many sites turn new and complex systems over to personnel with perhaps a good background in databases, but no experience whatsoever in Oracle. Yes, there are generic issues, but there are enough details specific to Oracle alone that training is highly recommended. If it costs $12,000 to fully train a DBA, isn't it worth it? How much money would it cost if the system were down for several days while an inexperienced DBA pored through the manuals and tried to communicate intelligently with the Oracle help line? What if a critical application was destroyed because of something the DBA did or didn't do? At one site, an experienced DBA, new to the Oracle database system, didn't follow the normal database data file-naming convention recommended by Oracle. Even though backups were taken, they didn't get the one SYSTEM data file that was named incorrectly. As a result, when an application required recovery due to data corruption, the system couldn't be restored. This resulted in the users abandoning the application and investing hundreds of hours reinventing it on MAC systems.

In my incarnation as a SYSOP on the CompuServe ORAUSER forum, I answer newbie questions on a daily basis that can usually be answered by looking at the manuals. Don't waste support analysts' (and my) time by asking us questions that you can answer yourself. Besides, I have found I learn better if I look it up rather than have someone tell me; I'm sure you have too.

Disk Layout

If you've read up to this point, you should realize that disk layout is critical to efficient operation of Oracle systems. There are several topics you need to consider when designing your disk layout.

1. What are the sizes and available space on the disks to be used with Oracle?
2. Is this disk used for other non-Oracle applications?
3. Has the disk been defragmented (if VMS)?
4. Is this a RAW device (if UNIX)?
5. What is the speed of the disk?
6. Is this a RAM or optical disk?

Let's look at each of these questions and how the answers affect Oracle.

What are the sizes and available space on the disks to be used with Oracle? Obviously if there isn't enough space on the disk, you can't use it. If the size is too small to handle projected growth, then you might want to look at another disk. Oracle files can be moved, but not with that section of the database active. If you enjoy coming in after or before hours or on weekends, then by all means put your database files on an inappropriately sized disk.

Is this disk used for other non-Oracle applications? This is a many-sided question. From the Oracle point of view, if you have a very active non-Oracle application it will be in contention for the disk with Oracle at every turn. If the non-Oracle application, such as word processing or a calculation program that uses intermediate result files, results in disk fragmentation (on VMS) this is bad if the data file co-located with it has to grow and can't allocate more contiguous space.

From the viewpoint of the other application, if we are talking about export files, archive log files, or growing data files, an asset we need to operate may be consumed, thus preventing our operation. Look carefully at the applications you will be sharing the disk assets with; talk with their administrators and make logical usage projections.

Has the disk been defragmented? (for VMS). This was covered before but bears repeating. A fragmented disk is of little use to Oracle on VMS. Oracle needs contiguous disk space for its data files. If the disk hasn't been defragmented, have it checked by the system administrator for fragmentation and defragment it if required.

Is the disk a RAW device? (for UNIX). If the disk is a RAW device, this restricts your capability for file naming. Be sure you maintain an accurate log of tablespace mapping to raw devices. Map tablespace and other assets locations ahead of time. Remember, an entire RAW partition must be used per Oracle datafile, they can not be sub partitioned with re-doing the entire RAW setup, If you must use RAW plan it!

What is the speed of the disk? By speed of disk we are referring to the access and seek times. The disk speed will drive disk throughput. Another item to consider when looking at disk speed is whether or not the disk is on a single or shared controller. Is the DSSI chained? All of these questions affect device throughput. Generally, data files and indexes should go on the fastest drives; if you must choose one or the other, put indexes on the fastest. Rollback segments and redo logs can go on the slowest drives as can archive logs and exports.

Is the disk a RAM or optical disk? Ultimately the RAM and optical usage ties back to disk speed. A RAM drive should be used for indexes due to its high speed. It is probably not a good candidate for data files due to the RAM drive's current size limitations; this may change in the future.

An optical drive, due to its relative slowness, is excellent for archives and exports, but probably shouldn't be used for other Oracle files. A possible exception might be large image files (BLOBS) or large document files. Usually, unless you have a rewritable CD system, the tablespaces placed on a CDROM will be read only.

With the storage capacities of most optical drives, they make excellent resources for archive logs and exports. They can conceivably provide a single point-of-access for all required recovery files, even backups. This solves the biggest recovery bottleneck; restoration of required files from tape.

Database-Specific Topics

There are numerous items to consider before installation:

Number and size of database tablespaces, file placement, number of potential applications

SGA and PAD issues (just SGA for UNIX)

Number of users, both developer and application

Number and placement of control files

Number and placement of redo logs

Number and placement of rollback segments

Will this database be shared between multiple instances?

Will this database be distributed?

Should the tools be linked single task or independent (two task)?

Let's examine each of these as they relate to installation of Oracle:

Number and Size of Database Tablespaces, File Placement, Number of Potential Applications This is a disk space and create script related issue. The number of potential applications will drive the number and size of database tablespaces above and beyond the five base tablespaces. You will recall that these are:

SYSTEM—Contains files owned by the SYS and SYSTEM user.

TOOLS—Contains files usually owned by SYSTEM but that apply to the Oracle developer's toolset; these files contain base information and details of forms, reports, and menus.

ROLLBACK—Contains the private rollback segments; its size will depend on number of rollback segments and expected transaction size.

DEFAULT USER—Tablespace in which users can create and destroy temporary, nonapplication-related tables such as those used in SQL*REPORT for intermediate queries.

TEMPORARY USER—Tablespace for sorts, joins, and other operations that require temporary disk space for intermediate operations. If this tablespace is not available and default tablespace is not set for each user, these tables will be created and dropped in the SYSTEM tablespace, resulting in fragmentation. Additionally, a poorly designed join or overly ambitious select statement could result in filling the SYSTEM area and halting the database.

Each application should have its own tablespace. If there are several small applications, you might want to put them in a single large tablespace, but if you can avoid this it makes application management easier. Each application should also have its own index tablespace. This results in a simple formula for determining the number of tablespaces:

5 + 2 times the number of applications expected

Some applications may require multiple tablespaces such as in the case where for performance you want to separate out large tables from the rest of the application. In one case, a single application generated 13 tablespaces. Most applications aren't as complicated as this and will only require two tablespaces. Of course the purists will claim each table should be in its own tablespace, but this is overkill in many cases.

Sizing of tablespaces is a difficult question. Each tablespace will have unique requirements. Here are some general guidelines:

The SYSTEM tablespace, if you split out the tool tables, should only require 40 to 90 megabytes of disk space.

The TOOLS tablespace will depend entirely on the amount of development you expect. At one site with 16 applications being developed, nearly 90 megabytes were required for the TOOLS tables.

The ROLLBACK tablespace will again be driven by the number and size of rollback segments you require. The number and size of rollback segments is driven by the number of transactions per rollback segment, the number of users, and the maximum size of nonbatch transactions. With Oracle7 and Oracle8 you can create a large rollback segment and leave it off-line until it is needed for a large transaction and then use the SET TRANSACTION USE ROLLBACK SEGMENT command to utilize it after bringing it on-line. The number of rollback segments is driven by the number of expected transactions and can be estimated by the equation:

NUMBER OF TRANSACTIONS / TRANSACTIONS PER ROLLBACK SEGMENT

The number of transactions will be driven by the number of users and types of database operations they will be doing. In fact, if the Oracle kernel sees a violation of the above formula, it will bring on-line any available public rollback segments.

The DEFAULT USER tablespace size will depend upon the number of users you want to assign to it and the estimated size of tables they will be using. In most cases 10 to 20 megabytes is sufficient. If you expect heavy usage, assign quotas to each user.

The TEMPORARY USER tablespace should be up to twice the size of your largest table if you use RULE-based optimization and up to four times the size of your largest table for COST-based, and is also dependent on the number of users and the size of sorts or joins they perform. An improperly designed join between large tables can fill a temporary area fast. For example, an unrestricted outside join of two thousand row tables will result in a one-million-row temporary sort table. If those rows are each several hundred bytes long, there goes your temporary space. Unfortunately, there isn't much that can be done other than training developers or ad-hoc query generators not to do unrestricted joins of large tables. If a temporary tablespace gets filled, the users who are assigned to it cannot perform operations requiring temporary space, or, worse, the temporary space may be taken from the SYSTEM area. There is a valid argument for having several temporary areas if you have a large number of users. In one instance, a 10-megabyte temporary tablespace was completely filled by a single multitable outside join using DECODE statements.

If you have the disk space, placing the TEMPORARY USER tablespaces on a disk of its own will improve query and report performance due to reduction of disk contention, especially for large reports or queries.

If you will be using the Oracle DESIGNER*2000 products, you will require two additional tablespaces for the DESIGNER tables and indexes. These tablespaces must be created before you attempt to install the DESIGNER tables. The same rules as for the TOOLS tablespace apply for these tablespaces. Follow the sizing guidelines provided by the Oracle documentation for these tablespaces.

SGA and PAD Issues As was discussed previously, in VMS, PAD size governs the maximum size to which the SGA can grow. In UNIX, the parameters controlling shared memory usage are the limiting factor. In either case, before you create the database, serious thought has to be given to how much you expect the SGA to grow over the next year. Sizing the PAD larger than what you need right now will not harm the VMS system, nor will overspecifying the shared memory parameters on a UNIX platform.

The size of the SGA is controlled by buffer sizes, and the buffer sizes are controlled by the database block size, which is specified at database creation and cannot be changed without rebuilding the database. This usually defaults to 2 K. I usually suggest at least 4 K, and in most cases 8 K works best.

The three major components of the SGA are the database buffers, large buffers, and the shared pool. The SGA also contains the redo log buffers. The ideal situation would be to size the SGA to hold the entire database in memory. For small systems, this may be a real situation; for most, it is not feasible. Therefore, you must decide how much to allocate. Many times, especially for development databases, this will be a rough SWAG (scientific wild-assed guess). For systems already designed with detailed data storage estimates, it may be better defined. A general rule of thumb for a pure Oracle system (no other applications) is 50 to 60% of available RAM for your SGA. Note that for small databases this may be overkill.

Oracle provides tools to analyze buffer performance. Unfortunately, they can only be used once a system is operating and running under a normal load; so for our discussion of installation, they are useless. The estimate, therefore, will depend on average query or report size expected multiplied times the number of expected concurrent users plus a 50% fudge factor for recursive gets (when an unindexed row is queried and the database has to rifle through its records recursively). This yields the formula:

(# users [×] size of average query or report in bytes) [×] 1.5

The average report size can be estimated by taking the average line length times the number of lines.

If you have no idea whatsoever, make the buffer area at least 10 to 20 meg or so (you will usually outgrow the 4-meg default rather quickly). Make the shared pool at least 9 to 12 meg (not the 3 meg it will default to).

We will discuss the actual parameters in the INIT.ORA file that control SGA size when we get to the section on tuning. What you need to know right now is that the default initialization file provided by Oracle has three default ranges: small, medium, and large. Choose the set of parameters that corresponds to what you anticipate needing and comment out the rest. The PAD size is specified during the installation and the shared memory parameters should be set before installation as well.

One thing to remember: If you overspecify the shared memory or PAD size you may get into a situation known as swapping. This is where all or part of your application is swapped out to disk because physical memory just isn't large enough to hold it all. Needless to say, this has a very negative impact on performance.

Number of Users—Administrative, Developer, and Application We've already looked at the responsibilities of the DBA or administrative user; what are the normal responsibilities of the other user types? According to the Oracle7 Server Administrator's Guide, they are:

Developmental responsibilities:

1. Design and develop database applications.
2. Design the database structure for an application.
3. Estimate storage requirements for an application.
4. Specify modifications of the database structures for an application.
5. Keep the database administrator informed of required changes.
6. Tune the *application* (not the database!) during development.
7. Establish an application's security requirements during development.

Application user's responsibilities:

1. Entering, modifying, and deleting data, where permitted
2. Generating reports of data

All Oracle databases have these three types of users: administrative, developmental, and application. As their names imply, administrative users administer and maintain the database itself; developmental users develop applications and systems; and application users use the developed applications and systems.

These three types of users have different needs. The space and disk needs of a developer are usually greater than those of an application user. For example, a developer using Oracle CASE tools and Ora*Reports on a VMS system may require 150,000 blocks of paged memory, while an application user may do fine with only 20,000. A developer system may get by with a smaller SGA because, generally speaking, developers will work with a subset of all the data expected, while a production database user will need a larger SGA because the data set is much larger. Administrative users usually have the same quotas as a developmental user, but their privileges are greater.

On VMS the Process Global Area as governed by the working set variables in the user's UAF file will determine the number of database cursors the user can have open. On UNIX the user environment control variables in the kernel will perform the same function. These may have to be tailored for each type of user.

Generally speaking, you will need five or more subprocesses available to each Oracle user. This will allow a menu to call a form to call a report, etc. Expect the process requirements to double if you use parallel query/update/delete options. This may mean that parameters affecting total system process counts and individual user process counts may have to be modified. It is suggested that you and the system administrator sit down and hammer out the requirements for your Oracle system before you install it. This will prevent unpleasant surprises for both of you. It may also require upgrading your system's memory. It is best to be forewarned as to the limits for your operating platform before you run head on into them.

The number of each of these types of users will tell you about required SGA sizing, disk resource requirements, and required system memory. Sixteen megabytes is required just to run Oracle . . . how much will your users require on top of this?

Number and Placement of Control Files Control files are probably the smallest and most important files in the Oracle system. They contain the following data:

Names of the database and redo log files

Timestamp of database creation

Begin/end of rollback segments

Checkpoint information

Current redo log file sequence number

This data is critical for database operation and at least one control file is required for database startup. There are methods for rebuilding a control file, but it is much easier to maintain, or rather have Oracle maintain, multiple copies of the control file.

Oracle recommends two copies on separate disk resources. For OFA compliance, three are required. Obviously, if they are on the same platter, the same disaster can waste all of them; therefore, they should be placed on different physical disks. More than three copies is a bit paranoid, but if it makes you feel safer, have as many as you wish; only one usable, current file is required for startup.

Number and Placement of Redo Logs Oracle requires at least two groups of one redo log. If you are archiving, three are suggested. In a number of installations up to six have been defined. If you do a lot of update activity with numerous users, more than six may be required. When a log fills, the next one in the queue is opened and the previously active log is marked for archive (if you have archiving enabled). The logs are archived on a first-in, first-out basis so, depending on the speed that the log groups can be written to disk or tape, more than one log group may be waiting to be archived. One redo log group is used at a time with multiple users writing into it at the same time. The size of the redo logs in a group depends on one critical piece of data: How much data can you afford to lose on a system crash?

You see, the smaller the log group size, the more often it is written to disk and the less data (timewise) is lost. The larger the log group size, the less often it is written to disk and the more data (timewise) is lost. For instance, if your log groups are filling every ten minutes, then you may lose ten minutes' worth of data should the disk(s) crash that holds that redo log group's files. It has been demonstrated on an active system that a one-megabyte redo log group may only last a few minutes. In an inactive or read-only type situation, a one-megabyte system may last for hours. It is all dependent on how the database is being used and the size of the redo log group. Remember, a group of three one-meg redo logs is actually only treated as a single one-megabyte redo log (the other two files are mirrors). If you mirror redo logs by placing the group members on separate disks (not just separate file systems, be sure it is separate physical disks) then your ability to recover from a disk crash increases manifold.

You have to balance the needs for restoration and minimal data loss against time to recover data. Obviously if you have archiving happening every minute and your normal work day is eight hours, you will have 480 logs written to disk daily. Over a five-day work week, this turns into 2400 files. If you have to restore from a crash or other disaster, you may have to apply all of these to your last backup to bring the database current to the time of the crash. In one case, a DBA had to apply 9000+ files to recover his system because he hadn't looked at how often his redo logs were archiving; needless to say, he pays more attention now. The minimum size for redo log groups is 50 K.

In the section on database tuning we will discuss how to determine if you have a sufficient number of redo log groups and how to optimize your archive process.

Number and Placement of Rollback Segments Another item controlled by the number of users and the transaction load on the system is the number of rollback segments. The formula, as stated before, is:

NUMBER OF TRANSACTIONS / NUMBER OF TRANSACTIONS PER ROLLBACK SEGMENT

This will yield number of rollback segments needed. They should be sized to handle the maximum expected live transaction.

The placement of rollback segments is decided based upon resource contention prevention. Put them where they won't cause contention with other Oracle files. Transactions are spread across all active rollback segments. Usually it is a good idea to locate the rollback segments in a tablespace or tablespaces dedicated to just rollback segments. This allows the DBA to easily manage these resources.

The size of rollback segments is based upon three items:

- Average number of simultaneous active transactions
- Average number of bytes modified per transaction
- Average duration of each transaction

The longer a transaction, the larger the rollback segment it will require. One is automatically created when the database is created. This initial rollback segment is for SYSTEM tablespace use. If you have plans for more than one tablespace, you will need a second rollback segment. Of course, this second segment will have to be created in the SYSTEM tablespace. Once the ROLLBACK tablespace is defined, and additional rollback segments created, the second rollback segment in the SYSTEM tablespace should be placed off line or dropped.

Each rollback segment must be created with a minextents value of at least 2 and a maxextents based on the number of rollback segments in the tablespace, the size specified for each extent, and the size of the ROLLBACK tablespace. Each of the extents should be the same size; that is, initial should equal next and pctincrease has to be set to zero percent (look at the STORAGE statement specification in Appendix B on the CD-ROM for an explanation of these parameters). If you intend to do large batch transactions it may be advisable to create a large rollback segment used only for batch operations. This single large segment can be left off-line until needed and then activated and used for a specific transaction using the SET TRANSACTION USE ROLLBACK SEGMENT command.

Will the Tools Be Linked Single Task or Independent (Two-Task)? This question deals with the way the Oracle tools, such as ORA*Forms, ORA*ReportWriter, or DESIGNER, address the Oracle kernel. See Figure 1.1 for a graphical demonstration of this concept.

If the tools are linked single task, they address a specific node's Oracle kernel by default. To access another node or another system a connect string must be used (connect strings will be covered in a later section). This mode is useful for a single-node database situation and saves on memory and task usage. This is generally used where a client/server architecture is not used. It has been demonstrated that relinking some tools single task, such as the import and export utilities, will increase their performance by up to 30%

If the tools are linked independent, or two-task, a connect string must always be used. It is called two-task because the tools must run as one task while the Oracle executable runs as another. Two-task is generally used in a client/server situation. This allows the following benefits:

1. This allows client machines to perform CPU-intensive tasks, offloading these tasks from the server.

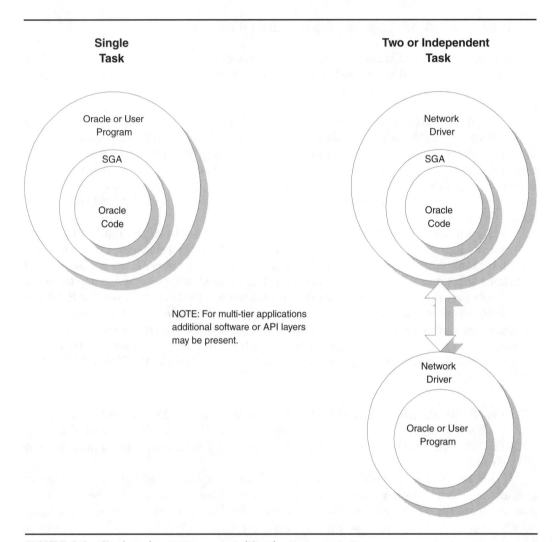

FIGURE 1.1 Single-task verses two or multi-task structure.

2. This allows movement of tools from one environment to another (such as from a development area to a production one) without relinking.

3. It allows the Oracle7 server to be relinked without relinking all of the tools.

However, two-task tools can reduce throughput depending on the machine they are installed upon. The DBA needs to consider the costs versus the benefits when deciding whether to use single or two-task linked tools.

Will This Database Be Shared Between Multiple Instances? A shared database allows a number of instances to access the same database. This allows the DBA to spread the SGA usage for a large database system across the CPUs of several machines. The CPUs must be part of the same CLUSTER. This is also known as a *parallel* or shared database. In order to use this option on UNIX the disks that are shared must be configured as RAW devices.

This requires what is known as a *loosely coupled system;* a set of clustered VAX Sequent or SGI (Silicon Grahpics) machines is an excellent example. This parallel server mode has the following characteristics, according to the Oracle *Parallel Server Administrator's Guide,* version 7:

1. An Oracle instance can be started on each node in the loosely coupled system.
2. Each instance has its own SGA and set of detached processes.
3. All instances share the same database files and control files.
4. Each instance has its own set of redo log groups.
5. The database files, redo log files, and control files reside on one or more disks of the loosely coupled system.
6. All instances can execute transactions concurrently against the same database and each instance can have multiple users executing transactions concurrently.
7. Row locking is preserved.

Since the instances must share locks, a lock process is started, LCKn. In addition, the GC_ parameters must be configured in the INIT.ORA files.

If the answer to the question at the beginning of this subsection is yes, the DBA needs to know how many instances will be sharing this database; this parameter will be used to determine INIT.ORA parameters. This answer is also important when determining the number and type of rollback segment. Rollback segments can either be private and only used by a single instance, or public, and shared between all instances that access the database.

The DBA will need to know the names for all instances sharing a database. They should also know the number of users per instance. Figure 1.2 illustrates this concept.

Another aspect of this concept of a parallel instance is the multithreaded database. Essentially this uses queue logic and shared processes (the Dnnn processes) to allow multiple users to share the same executable image. Under the other implementations a single process was allotted to each user. Each thread is associated with its own set of redo logs.

Will This Database Be Distributed? A distributed database, as its name implies, has its data files spread across several databases in different locations. This requires that there be DBAs in these distributed locations. The major consideration will be network reliability. This is especially true when two-phase commit is used. Under two-phase commit, if one of your distributed database nodes goes down, you can't update tables that undergo two-phase commit with that node's data.

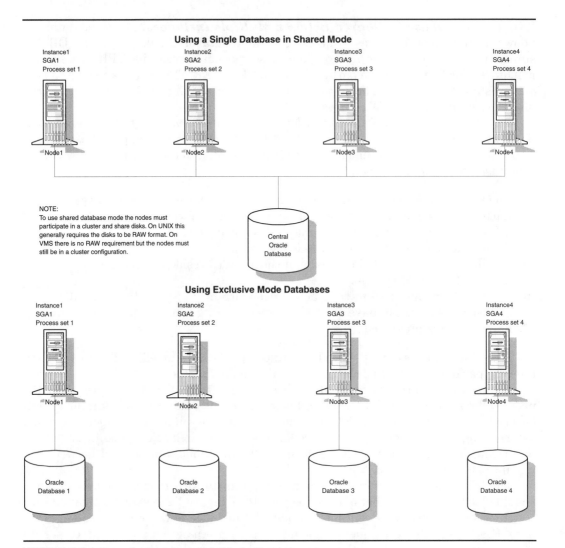

FIGURE 1.2   Shared versus Exclusive Mode Databases.

According to the Oracle7 *Server Administrators Guide*, the DBA needs to consider the following items in a distributed environment:

1. The number of transactions posted from each location
2. The amount of data (portion of table) used by each node
3. The performance characteristics and reliability of the network
4. The speed of various nodes and the capacities of its disks
5. The criticality of success if a node or link is down
6. The need for referential integrity between tables

A distributed database appears to be one database to the user but is in fact a collection of database tables in separate databases spread across several locations. These databases are of course on different computer systems that are connected by a network.

The computers, or *nodes* in a distributed database environment, will act as both clients and servers depending upon whether they are requesting data from another database on a different node, or providing data to a different node as it is requested.

Each site is autonomous, that is, managed independently. The databases are distinct, separate entities that are sharing their data. The benefits of site autonomy are:

1. The various databases cooperating in the distributed environment can mirror the local organization's needs and desires. This is especially useful at sites where there may be two organizations that need to share some, but not all, data. An example would be two Aerospace companies cooperating on the Space Platform. They may need to share data about design, but not want to share financial information.
2. Local data is controlled by the local database administrator. This limits the responsibility to a manageable level.
3. Failure at one node is less likely to affect other nodes. The global system is at least partially available as long as a single node of the database is active. No single failure will halt all processing or be a performance bottleneck. For example, if the Pittsburgh node goes down, it won't affect the Omaha node, as long as Omaha doesn't require any of Pittsburgh's data.
4. Failure recovery is on a per-node basis.
5. A data dictionary exists for each local database.
6. Nodes can upgrade software independently, within reason.

As DBA you will need to understand the structures and limits of the distributed environment if you are required to maintain a distributed environment. The features of a two-phase commit as well as naming resolution and the other distributed topics will be covered later in the book. Figure 1.3 shows a distributed database structure.

1.7 INSTALLATION GUIDELINES FOR VMS

Before beginning installation, the DBA needs to consider a very important topic. This topic deals with the question: Why am I installing Oracle? The answer drives the way Oracle is installed and how you configure your disk system for its installation. If you are installing Oracle to support a third-party provided system, such as DLB's Monitor or Recorder products, PE-Nelson's LIMS, or even Oracle's Financials, each of these has specific requirements and should be reviewed before you start installation. Another case in its entirety is when you are installing Oracle in support of in-house development. In the case of in-house development, you have to consider the entire development environment and how to structure it to take full advantage of the Oracle product. Let's examine this.

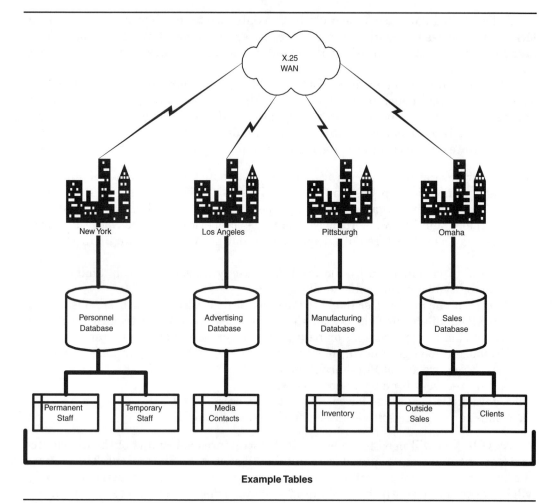

Example Tables

FIGURE 1.3   Example of a distributed database.

The Development Environment

The location and access methods for the Oracle and Oracle CASE toolsets is fixed and not alterable by the developer. How the developer uses these tools and locates the modules thus created is, however, under his or her control. The developer has the choice of co-locating all modules in one directory, leading to confusion and difficulty in isolating one module or subtype of modules from the rest, or, logically organizing a directory structure that facilitates access to each type of module. Obviously, the latter form of organization is more efficient and should be used.

The Development Directories It is suggested that the development environment directory structure be set up as follows:

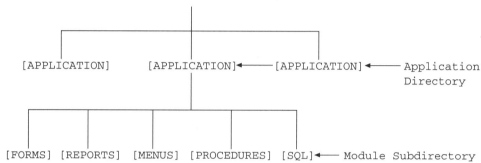

As can be seen, this provides a directory for each application, and under each application, all of its modules.

Environmental Logicals or Symbols To prevent the developer from having to use excessively long path names, a logical symbol definition for each of the subdirectories is created. For an application called CDMS, for example, the logical definitions for VMS would be:

```
$! CDMS_LOGICALS.COM - Example DCL routine for VMS to set Logicals
$!
$ DEFINE CDMS$FORMS  DIA1:[M_ORACLE.DEVELOPMENT.CDMS]
$ DEFINE CDMS$REPORT DIA1:[M_ORACLE.DEVELOPMENT.CDMS]
$ DEFINE CDMS$MENU    DIA1:[M_ORACLE.DEVELOPMENT.CDMS]
$ DEFINE CDMS$PROC DIA1:[M_ORACLE.DEVELOPMENT.CDMS]
$ DEFINE CDMS$SQL         DIA1:[M_ORACLE.DEVELOPMENT.CDMS]
$ EXIT
```

Once these definitions are set for a particular developer, via a command file executed upon entry to the development environment, the developer can use them in place of the full path specification in reports, menus, and procedures.

This also facilitates transfer to a production environment. The entire directory structure is transferred to production from the application level down. The logical definitions are altered to reflect this move and the rest of the code can remain as is.

VMS Symbol Definitions To facilitate movement to and from the different subdirectories, symbols or keys can be defined to provide the SET DEFAULT commands as needed. For example:

```
$! CDMS_SYMBOLS.COM -  Example command procedure for VMS symbols
$!
$ CDMSF :== "SET DEFAULT CDMS$FORMS"
$ CDMSR :== "SET DEFAULT CDMS$REPORTS"
$ CDMSM :== "SET DEFAULT CDMS$MENUS"
$ CDMSP :== "SET DEFAULT CDMS$PROC"
$ CDMSS :== "SET DEFAULT CDMS$SQL"
$!
$ EXIT
```

VMS Key Definitions For developers desiring to use keystrokes to facilitate movement between directories, the numeric PF1-PF4 and 0-9 keys can be defined as direct key strokes to execute these commands. For example:

```
$! CDMS_KEYS.COM - Example key definintion file for DCL
$!
$ DEFINE/KEY PF1 "SET DEFAULT CDMS$FORMS"/TERMINATE
$ DEFINE/KEY PF2 "SET DEFAULT CDMS$REPORTS"/TERMINATE
$ DEFINE/KEY PF3 "SET DEFAULT CDMS$MENUS"/TERMINATE
$ DEFINE/KEY PF4 "SET DEFAULT CDMS$PROC"/TERMINATE
$ DEFINE/KEY KP0 "SET DEFAULT CMDS$SQL"/TERMINATE
$!
$ EXIT
```

Use of the Development Environment Once the development environment is established, the developer uses the symbols or key strokes to move between the subdirectories as needed. Each type of module is generated in its own subdirectory. The logicals are used in forms, menus, procedures, and SQL scripts to identify module locations.

When the developer switches between projects, he or she simply executes a single command procedure that alters all logical, symbol, and key definitions to reflect the new application's locations. For example, to enter the CDMS application development environment, a developer could run the following DCL script:

```
$! CDMS_SETUP.COM - DCL Command procedure for CDMS Environment
$!
$ @DIA1:[M_ORACLE.DEVELOPMENT.CDMS.PROCEDURES]CDMS_LOGICAL.COM
$ @CDMS$PROC:CDMS_SYMBOLS.COM
$ @CDMS$PROC:CDMS_KEYS.COM
$ SET DEFAULT DIA1:[M_ORACLE.DEVELOPMENT.CDMS]
$!
$ EXIT
```

A similar script would be developed for each new application. A similar method uses a predefined list of applications and a DCL menu to automatically assign a developer to his or her environment. The DBA can even utilize SQL*Menu to provide ease of access to all tools, including CASE, and the developer only needs to enter his or her user name and password for Oracle once for the entire work session.

A Generic VMS Installation Procedure

The following guidelines assume you will be installing Oracle in compliance with OFA guidelines and with an eye toward the information provided in all of the previous sections. If you follow this general procedure, along with the installation guide provided by Oracle, you should have a successful Oracle installation.

General Procedure for Installation of Oracle on VAX/VMS-based Platforms:

1. Review all installation documents sent with the software.
2. Using the guides provided in the documentation, establish the proper operating system environment. This will entail coordinating changes to the SYSGEN parameters with the system manager and possibly require alterations to the basic system user account quotas.

Example SYSGEN parameters for Oracle version 7 (exclusive):

GBLPAGES	At least 16500 free contiguous global pages in exclusive mode; if SGA is larger than the one created by the distributed INIT.ORA, add 2 pages for each 1 K of additional SGA.
VIRTUALPAGECNT	Larger than the largest PGFLQUO granted to an Oracle user.
GBLSECTIONS	At least 17 Global Sections.

Example SYSGEN parameters for Oracle version 7 (parallel):

MIN_GBLSECTIONS should be increased by: (8 * #images) + #instances + #global sections for each product installed shared in memory.

MIN_GBLPAGES should be equal to or greater than: (15,100 * #instances) + #global pages for each product installed shared in memory.

Formulas for ORACLE7 increases to node-based parameters in parallel mode:

SRPCOUNT	(ORACLE7 locks) X (# of instances in the cluster)
SRPCOUNTV	(ORACLE7 locks) X (# of instances in the cluster)
IRPCOUNT	ORACLE7 locks
IRPCOUNTV	ORACLE7 locks
LOCKIDTBL	(ORACLE7 locks) X (# of instances in the cluster)
LOCKIDTBL_MAX	(ORACLE7 locks) X (# of instances in the cluster)
RESHASHTBL	(1/4) X (LOCKIDTBL) with a maximum of 8192
LOCKDIRWT	Use the Digital Equipment Corporation documentation for the proper setting of this parameter for your system.

Example user quotas for Oracle Version 7:

ASTLM	Parallel mode: 24 or greater
BYTLM	20480 or greater
ENQLM	Exclusive mode: 5 or greater, Parallel mode: 100 or greater
FILLM	3 + (#LOGFILES) * (#MEMBERS/LOGFILE GROUP) + (#CONTROL FILES) + (#DATABASE FILES) or greater; 100 is recommended
MAXDETACH	#DATABASES * [8 + #THREADS *[[(# LOCK PROCESSES/ THREAD)
	+ (#DISPATCHERS/THREAD) + (#MULTI-THREADED SERVERS/THREAD)]]
MAXJOBS	0 or greater then MAXDETACH
PGFLOQUO	20,480 + (2 * SGA pad size in kilobytes) or greater
WSQUOTA	4096 or greater
WSDEFAULT	1024 or greater
WSQUOTA	2048 or greater

3. Provide a detailed description of the Oracle DBA account requirements with explanations of the reasons behind the quota and privilege requirements to the system manager and have him or her create the required account.

   Set quotas in the high range of those listed above. In addition, the DBA account will require the following privileges:

   SYSNAM
   GRPNAM
   CHMKNL
   PRMMBX (If TCP/IP is to be used)
   GROUP
   WORLD
   ORA_DB rights identifier

TIP   ORA_DBA is the generic rights identifier that can access, start up, and shut down all instances. If you wish finer control of who has access to what databases, use the SID in the identifier. For example, if the SID is PROD, then the rights identifier would be ORA_PROD_DBA. This would restrict the user to only being able to start up and shut down the PROD database. The Oracle7 administrator may also require the OSOPER and OSDBA identifiers.

---

4. Have the system administrator review the available disks for space availability, speed of access, and fragmentation status. If needed, have the system administrator defragment the disks.

5. Obtain from the system manager the disks, their speeds, and their available capacities. Prepare an installation map showing file placement.

   Disk space requirements for Oracle7 code:

   > 100,000 blocks for basic product set
   > 15,000 blocks for link space
   > 115,000 blocks for Oracle7 code and executables
   > 25,000 blocks for a minimal instance.

6. Define a list of required system logicals to point to disk locations. These should be descriptive and allow use of wild cards to address the entire setup. For example:

   ```
   ORA_MAIN, ORA_DATA, ORA_INDEXES, ORA_RBK, ORA_ARCHIVE.
   ```

7. Define the required directory structure on each disk. The structure should start with a generic top-level directory, such as Oracle7 or Oracle8 and then have subdirectories for each application. If desired, use the Oracle convention of DB_ followed by the SID name of the database to name these directories. Under these secondary directories it might be advisable to further subdivide the directory into file types if multiple file types will be stored there. Remember, if you have fewer than five disks available, you can still assign five logicals in preparation for the time when you may have more room to spread the files. This will allow you to redefine logicals instead of entire file names.

8. Write down how many users you are planning on.

9. Write down how many redo logs you will need.

10. Write down how many rollback segments you will need.

11. Write down which disks you want to place the CONTROL files on.

12. Write down what you want to call your instance (SID). This can be up to six characters long.

13. Write down what you want to call your database. This can be up to eight characters long.

14. Write down the size for your PAD file (in K, default is 2048 K or 2 meg).

15. Write down the number of data files you will need (remember, you will need at least five, with two additional for each application). What size should they be, in megabytes? Write it all down. Map out locations if you have more than one data disk. Do you have any large tables that might require their own tablespace area? It has been reported that Oracle prefers 500-meg data files. If your application is that large, use 500-meg data files to make up your large tablespaces. This is also an easier size to back up to tape and move from disk to disk if required.

16. Write down where you want your archive logs written to.

17. Write down where exports should go.

18. Make a list of your initial users, their default applications, and any that require the ability to create files.

19. If you have space available, have the system manager copy the installation save sets from tape onto a disk. Your access time will be dramatically increased. Place each tape in its own subdirectory. This is required because each set of files will have its own BOOT.BCK file. If you put the save sets in one large directory, these files will become confused and cause installation problems. If you are installing from compact disk, this step is not required.

20. Set your default directory to the top-level directory on the executable drive. The VMS command is "SET DEFAULT disk:[directory]." It is suggested that the actual executables not be installed into a directory used as a login directory. Set up a subdirectory under the top-level directory such as [ORACLE7.DBA] and have the DBA account log in at that directory.

21. Once you are in the top-level directory, unbundle the RDBMS save set using the commands in the following Tip:

TIP   If you didn't have the disk space to unload the save sets from tape, do the following first (otherwise, proceed to step b):

a. Mount the RDBMS tape into or onto the tape drive; issue the command:

```
$ MOUNT/FOREIGN devicename
```

b. Unbundle the BOOT.BCK save set using the following command:

```
$ BACKUP/LOG devicename:BOOT.BCK/SAVE []*.*/NEW/OWN=PARENT
```

---

22. Use the Oracle install procedure, ORACLEINS.COM, to load the required products from the RDBMS save sets.

a. This procedure is invoked by the following command:

```
$ @ORACLEINS
```

b. When ORACLEINS displays the "ORACLE Installation Startup Menu" choose the first selection, "Create a new ORACLE system.."

c. When prompted for the Oracle root directory, press enter to accept the default value and continue. If it is not, enter the proper directory and press enter.

d. When prompted for the location of the save sets you want to load, enter the directory for the next save set if you used the preloaded save sets or enter the tape drive from which you are loading the save sets.

e. When the "Main Menu" appears, choose the "Software Installation and Upgrade Menu."

f. When the "Software Installation and Upgrade Menu" appears, choose the "Select Products to Load" option.

g. When the list of applicable products from the save set is displayed, choose those you are licensed for from the menu by entering their number from the list. If you want to load all of the products, enter an "A." To exit the menu with your selections enter an "E." If you make a mistake, exit the menu with a "Q" entry and start over.

h. When the "Software Installation and Upgrade Menu" is displayed, choose the "Load and Build Selected Products" menu item.

TIP   The products will be loaded first, then the procedure will prompt you "Do you want to reconfigure the products or exit before building? (N):." Enter a "Y" unless this is the last product save set you wish to unbundle.

---

i. If this is not the last save set, return to step 21 and load the next BOOT.BCK.

j. If this is the last save set, go on by selecting the "Select Build Configuration Options." Configure all products per your system requirements and then exit the item with an "E" to return to the "Software Installation and Upgrade Menu." Be sure that in the RDBMS Configuration Options you specify the maximum PAD size you will require from step 14.

k. Select the "Build Selected Products" item. It is suggested that the OPTION item be built first if you are using the TPO option, and then build SQL*NET followed by any tools not built by the previous procedures. If you select all tools to be built from the first, it may result in products being linked multiple times.

TIP   The OPTION product must be loaded and built if you ever intend to use TPO. If it is not selected, it will not be built by the other build procedures.

---

23. Use steps 21 and 22 to unbundle the other product save sets. (You will have to load the BOOT.BCK save sets for each product from their own save set directory or tape.) The first BOOT.BCK is unloaded into the top-level or ROOT directory; all others are loaded into the INSTALL directory created when the first BOOT.BCK was unbundled.

24. Load all desired products before building any of them. Many of the products are dependent upon each other and will relink several times if you build the products as you load them. Use the load and build option from the ORACLEINS menu, once the product is linked, answer "Y" when the procedure asks if you wish to reconfigure, then exit from the reconfigure menu.

25. Once all products are loaded, you can begin building them. Build the products in the following order:

OPTION (TPO)

SQL*NET (SQL*NET is used by virtually all of the products; it will link just about all of them for you)

Any tools not linked by the SQL*NET build.

26. Once all of the products have been successfully built, use ORACLEINS to create an instance by selecting the "Instance Creation, Startup, and Shutdown Menu" item.

27. From the "Instance Creation, Startup, and Shutdown Menu," select the "Create a New Instance and Database" option.

28. Enter a unique SID (the one you wrote down in step 12).

29. Enter a unique database name (the one from step 13).

30. Check the defaults for the various system files displayed.

   a. Ensure redo logs are placed as you desire.

   b. Verify that the size of the redo logs is what you need.

   c. Be sure the database (actually the SYSTEM tablespace) is sized for future expansion.

   d. Verify control files are placed properly.

   e. Enter your needed MAXDATAFILES from step 15. Enter your MAXLOGFILES from step 9. (This will correspond to the maximum number of log file groups.)

   f. Enter MAXINSTANCES, the maximum number of instances that may access a single database.

   g. Enter MAXLOGMEMBERS, the maximum number of copies against a single log file.

   h. Enter MAXLOGHISTORY, the maximum number of redo logs that can be recorded in the archive history of the control file.

Once you are completely satisfied with the defaults, exit with an "E" to begin instance setup.

31. The procedure will build the instance directory structure, create database build and maintenance scripts, and create database startup and shutdown scripts. When asked if you want to continue, you have two options:

   a. If you don't want more than two control files and two redo log groups created at this point, and don't want archive logging, answer "Y" or press return.

   b. If you need to add more control files or redo logs, or want archive logging, you must add this additional data to the creation script, answer "N," and exit the ORACLEINS procedure.

If you answered "Y," the procedure will build and start your initial instance.

32. If you chose "Y" in step 31, go on to step 34. If you chose "N" and exited the ORA-CLEINS procedure, return to the Oracle root directory (use a SET DEFAULT [-]) and execute a directory command (DIR).

33. If you have returned to the root directory, set your default directory to DB_<value of your SID> and then use the EDT or EVE editor to modify the CREATE_<SID>.SQL file so it includes the additional redo logs, control files, and archive log parameters. (Refer to Appendix B on the CD-ROM for the proper syntax to use.) Once you have finished the modifications, there is a .COM procedure named the same as the .SQL procedure to create your instance.

34. Once the instance is created and operational, add a second rollback segment using the procedure in the *Administration Manual*. Once this second rollback segment is created, shut down the instance and add the ROLLBACK_SEGMENTS statement to your INIT.ORA file with the name of the new rollback segment as its parameter. Restart the instance.

TIP   Every Oracle database is created with two default users. These users are SYS, which owns all the base tables, and SYSTEM, which is intended to be the DBA account for high-level DBA work. These accounts are created with the default passwords "CHANGE_ON_INSTALL" and "MANAGER." These passwords should be changed immediately after all products have had their tables loaded. If you don't you have left a significant security hole in your database. Remember, everyone who has a copy of this book, or has ever looked at an Oracle database management book knows these passwords.

---

35. Create any additional tablespaces you require using the CREATE TABLESPACE command shown in Appendix B on the CD-ROM. Be sure to create a tablespace for ROLLBACK SEGMENTS.

TIP   For documentation purposes, and to save you from having to enter the commands over and over again, it is suggested you create a .SQL script to create these initial tablespaces. Look at the example scripts in Appendix C on the CD-ROM for guidelines on format for this script.

---

36. Using the CREATE ROLLBACK SEGMENTS command from Appendix B on the CD-ROM, add the rollback segments you require from step 10. (It is suggested that simple names be used, such as RBK1, RBK2, RBK3, etc.). Use the TABLESPACE option of the command to be sure they are placed in the ROLLBACK tablespace.

TIP   For documentation and for future use it is suggested you create a .SQL script to perform this function. An example script is located in Appendix C on the CD-ROM.

---

37. Once step 36 is complete, shut down the database and edit the INIT.ORA file to remove the rollback segment name added in step 34 from the ROLLBACK_SEGMENTS parameter and add the names of the rollback segments just created. Restart the instance.

38. Drop the now off-line rollback segment from step 34 using the DROP ROLLBACK SEGMENT command from Appendix B, or keep it for future maintenance of the other rollback segments.

39. Once the instance is created and operational, proceed with loading your toolset tables.

TIP   If you want the tools to be loaded in a different tablespace than the SYSTEM tablespace, use the SQLDBA program, connect internal, and issue an ALTER USER SYSTEM command to change the default tablespace for the SYSTEM user to the desired tools tablespace. You should also use the REVOKE command to remove the global RESOURCE privilege from the SYSTEM user. Use the GRANT command to grant resource on the new default tablespace to the SYSTEM user.

---

40. Type "ORACLEINS" at the command line. Once in the ORACLEINS procedure select the "Reconfigure Existing Products, Manage the Database, or Load Demo Tables" option from the menu.

41. From the "Oracle Product Installation and Upgrade" menu, select the "Build or Upgrade Database Tables Menu" option. When the list of products is displayed, select the ones to load the tables for and then exit the menu using the "E" option. The procedure will load all required tables, prompting you for any required data. Once this step is completed, the database is set up.

42. Shut down and cut a full backup of the Oracle installation. This is a base installation backup and should be saved.

TIP   Once a complete backup is taken, any archive logs accumulated during the install may be disposed of.

---

43. Consult the DBA guide for any SQL scripts, such as UTLMON.SQL, CATALOG.SQL, CATPROC.SQL, CATDBASYN.SQL, etc. that should be run against the SYSTEM user.

TIP   Once this step is complete, the database is fully operational.

---

44. Using the editor of your choice, create an .SQL script to add the users listed in step 18. UseCREATE USER user name IDENTIFIED BY password

DEFAULT TABLESPACE default tablespace name
TEMPORARY TABLESPACE temporary tablespace name
GRANT CREATE SESSION TO user name

as a template for creating this file. An example script with example names is shown in Appendix C on the CD-ROM.

Congratulations! If you have survived this far, your Oracle database is ready for business!

Installation of Oracle on UNIX

Unlike VMS, which is the same regardless of platform, the UNIX operating system varies considerably from platform to platform. This makes it difficult, if not impossible, to write a generic installation procedure for UNIX. It is strongly suggested that the DBA use the installation guide provided by Oracle for his or her own release of UNIX. The following procedure is just a general set of guidelines and is not intended to replace the installation procedures provided by Oracle.

1. Review all installation documents sent with the software.
2. Using the guides provided in the documentation, establish the proper operating system environment, coordinating changes to the shared memory parameters with the system manager.

Example changes to UNIX system Shared Memory and Semaphore parameters:

	HP-UX *Release 10.0*	*DYNIX / AT&T* *UNIX Sys V*	*SUN 4*
SHMMAX	0x4000000		20000000
SHMMNI	100		512
SHMSEG	12		
SHMMNS	128	140	128
SEMMNI	10	20	Depends
NOFILEEXT		65	
MAXNOFILE		65	
SEMMSL		85	Depends
SEMMNI			20
ULIMIT			2,097,152

3. Provide a detailed description of the Oracle DBA account requirements with explanations of the reasons behind requirements to the system manager and have the required account created.

T IP   The oracle account on UNIX must belong to the DBA group, as must the root account.

---

4. Have the system administrator review the available disks for space availability and speed of access.

5. Obtain from the system manager the disks, their speeds, and their available capacities. Using the charts provided for your system in the installation guide, determine your disk and memory requirements. Prepare an installation map showing file placement.

6. Write down how many users you are planning on.

7. Write down how many redo log groups you will need.

8. Write down how many rollback segments you will need.

9. Write down which disks you want to place the CONTROL files on.

10. Write down what you want to call your instance (SID). This can be up to six characters long.

11. Write down what you want to call your database. This can be up to eight characters long.

12. Write down the size for your SGA file (notify the SA that he or she may have to relink the UNIX kernel to accommodate this size).

13. Write down the number of data files will you need (remember, you will need at least five, with two additional for each application). What size should they be, in megabytes? Write it all down. Map out locations if you have more than one data disk. Do you have any large tables that might require their own tablespace area? If you are using RAW devices, map out placement.

14. Write down where you want your archive logs written to.

15. Write down where exports should go.

16. Make a list of your initial users and their default applications, and make note of any that require the ability to create files.

17. Once you have the required information gathered in one place, use the installation checklists for your system. Due to the differences for each release of UNIX that Oracle supports, it would be difficult and confusing to try and cover every possible combination in this procedure. Let's look at examples for SUN and SCO UNIX.

18. Most systems are going to a download or CDROM-based install, which greatly automates this procedure. For example, on the SUN Solaris Intel release:

    a. Either download the software for your platform from the demos available on http://www.oracle.com/ or place CD in CDROM drive.

    b. Log in as root.

    c. Start OpenWindows or Common Desktop environment on your system.

    d. Open an xterm window, verify your DISPLAY variable is set correctly, and change to the temporary directory where the downloaded server files(s) and the downloaded shell script is located. (Note: for CDROM-based installs, CD to the upper-level directory of your CD-ROM drive.)

e. If this load is from files downloaded from http://www.oracle.com/ then you must unbundle the compressed data sets with the command:

```
# sh ./runme[large/small].sh
```

where large or small tells Oracle what size files you downloaded (one large or many small).

f. If step e was required, then the installation script should start automatically. If you are loading from a CDROM drive, then there will be a readme file that tells you how to proceed, or, there will be instructions on the back of the sleeve in the CD jewel case. Generally there will be a setup.exe, install.exe, or some other obvious script or executable to run that starts the installation procedure.

g. Once the installation process is started you will be prompted for the following information:

  1. A password for the INTERNAL user; this defaults to either nothing, or ORACLE.

  2. The home directory $ORACLE_HOME location.

  3. The SID for your instance; this can be of varying lengths depending on the flavor of UNIX you are using.

  4. The national language and character set; for demo downloads you have a single choice each, U.S. English and US7ASCII.

  5. The host name for your system in the format "hostname.domainname."

  6. The installation process will now decompress all files and load the system. You may also get a prompt asking if you want a complete, minimal, or custom load. Unless you know exactly what is being asked here, do a complete load.

  7. This process may also either ask you if you want a demo database built, or it may just go ahead and build it. I usually say no to this prompt because it generally builds this demo database with everything in one place.

  8. Once the install is complete, if you installed from a demo download, you can now either back the source files off to tape and delete them or just delete them to save space (on the order of 110 megabytes for the Solaris Intel version).

For SCO UNIX:

  1. Log in as root

  2. Make sure the Desktop Manager is up and running, then open an xterm window.

  3. Insert the appropriate Oracle CD in your CDROM drive.

  4. Create a directory to mount the CDROM into via the following command:

```
# mkdir /cdrom
```

  5. Mount the CDROM by entering the following command:

```
# mount -f HS,lower /dev/cd0 /cdrom
```

6. Change your work directory to cdrom and execute the wgstart script:

```
# cd /cdrom
# ./wgstart
```

7. The installation process will prompt you for various bits of information such as SID, ORACLE_HOME location, and other data it needs to load the Oracle software. It may also ask for the type of install. I suggest complete unless you really know what you are doing. This will include a small example database.

19. Once the base install is complete, add control files, tablespaces, redo logs, and rollback segments. To start, a second rollback segment must be added.

   a. Log on as oracle. Log in to the SVRMGR program and use the CONNECT INTERNAL command to become the Oracle super user.

   b. Use the CREATE ROLLBACK SEGMENT command as specified in Appendix B on the CD-ROM to add a second rollback segment to the SYSTEM tablespace.

   c. Bring the second rollback segment on line using

   ```
   ALTER ROLLBACK SEGMENT name ONLINE:.
   ```

20. Add the additional tablespaces you require. This can be done from SVRMGR or from SQLPLUS.

TIP It is suggested that a script be created similar to the example script in Appendix B on the CD-ROM. This will provide documentation and reduce the possibility of error. The CREATE TABLESPACE command from Appendix B is used to create new tablespaces.

---

21. Once the additional tablespaces are created, add the required number of rollback segments, calculated by taking the PROCESSES value from the INIT.ORA file and fitting it into this equation:

PROCESSES * 1.1 / TRANSACTIONS_PER_ROLLBACK_SEGMENT
(1.1 * PROCESSES = TRANSACTIONS)

These rollback segments should be placed in their own tablespace.

22. Bring the new rollback segments on line using the ALTER command as you did with the second SYSTEM rollback segment. Edit the INIT.ORA file (located in the $ORACLE_HOME/dbs directory) to add the names of the new rollback segments.

23. If you want the tools tables in a separate tablespace from the SYSTEM tablespace, it may be required to export them from SYSTEM, alter the SYSTEM user so that they use the new tools tablespace as a default and only have resource on tools,

then import the tables into the tools tablespace. The tables can then be dropped from the SYSTEM area. (Note: It may be required to drop the export/import tables and reload them; refer to the DBA manual provided by Oracle for the name of the script to use for this.)

Installation on Windows NT 4.0

TIP   The server should be configured as an application server and not a file server or performance will not be acceptable. This is done at initial server setup and can be altered.

---

1. Review all installation documents sent with the software.
2. Using the guides provided in the documentation, establish the proper operating system environment. This will involve ensuring enough disk space is available on all drives that you will need to install Oracle and build your database.
3. Provide a detailed description of the Oracle DBA account to the system manager. In most cases, this will probably be you in an NT environment. Essentially the requirements are that the user be in the administrator's group and have share/write capabilities on all disks required for the installation.
4. Have the system administrator review the available disks for space availability, speed of access, and fragmentation status. If needed, have the system administrator defragment the disks.
5. Obtain from the system manager the disks, their speeds, and their available capacities. Prepare an installation map showing file placement.

   Disk space requirements for Oracle7 code:

   > Approximately 150 megabytes with 34 megabyte example database for basic installation (for example, the 60-day demo download from http:/www.oracle.com/).

   Disk space requirements for Oracle8 code:

   > The 8.0.2 code footprint on an NT 4.0 platform is 155 megabytes including a 36 megabyte example database.

6. Define the required directory structure on each disk. The structure should start with a generic top-level directory, such as Oracle7 or Oracle8 and then have subdirectories for each application. If desired, use the Oracle convention of DB_ followed by the SID name of the database to name these directories. Under these secondary directories it might be advisable to further subdivide the directory into file types if multiple file types will be stored there. Remember, if you have fewer than five disks available, you can still assign five or more subdirectories in preparation for the time when you may have more room to spread the files.

For example, on my NT server and on UNIX servers (if you ignore the disk speci-
fiers and make the \ a /) I have the following structure:

```
c:\oracle1\ORTEST1\
                        admin
                                bdump
                                udump
                                cdump
                                pfile
                                create
                        control
                        data
                        redo
d:\oracle2\ORTEST1\
                        control
                        data
                        redo
d:\oracle3\ORTEST1\
                        control
                        data
                        redo
                        exports
e:\oracle4\ORTEST1
                        data
                        arch

e:\oracle5\ORTEST1
                        data
```

7. Write down how many users you are planning on having.
8. Write down how many redo log groups and group members you will need.
9. Write down how many rollback segments you will need.
10. Write down which disks you want to place the CONTROL files on.
11. Write down what you want to call your instance (SID). This can be up to four char-
    acters long.
12. Write down what you want to call your database. This can be up to eight charac-
    ters long.
13. Write down the number of tablespaces you will need (remember, you will need at
    least five with two additional for each application.) What size should they be, in
    megabytes? Write it all down. Map out locations if you have more than one data
    disk. Do you have any large tables that might require their own tablespace area?
    It has been reported that Oracle prefers 500-meg datafiles. If your application is
    that large, use 500-meg datafiles to make up your large tablespaces. This is also
    an easier size to back up to tape and move from disk to disk if required.
14. Write down where you want your archive logs written. This should be on a drive
    with no redo logs assigned.
15. Write down where exports should go. Separate them from archive logs.

16. Make a list of your initial users and their default applications, and any that require the ability to create files.
17. Load the installation CD into your CDROM drive.
18. Log on as the administrator user created to own the Oracle system. On NT 3.51 open the file manager; on NT4.0 open the "My Computer" icon.
19. Select the drive which correlates to the CDROM, double click on SETUP.EXE.
20. The setup executive will ask you about language, company, and the Oracle Home directory (usually c:\orant; however, it can be on any drive that is always available to the NT box,—i.e., not a shared network drive).
21. Next, the Installation Type dialog box appears. Your choices will be:

    Oracle8 Server Products
    Oracle8 Client Products
    Programmer/2000

22. Since we are primarily concerned with the database (being DBAs) we will explain the Oracle8 Server Installation only. Select the line using your mouse for Oracle8 Server Products and then click on the OK icon.
23. You will be given the option to install a starter database. Oracle builds abysmal starter databases, putting everything in the c:\orant\databases directory. However, the create scripts and initialization scripts can be used to provide examples for your own databases. Unless you just want experience in deleting unwanted databases I would suggest choosing NONE and clicking on OK. Example scripts can be obtained from other sources.
24. You will be advised (if you selected NONE) that you will need to create your own database. A second dialog box will appear asking if you want documentation installed. Unless you are extremely short on disk space, go ahead and install the documentation by clicking on OK.

TIP The default password for the INTERNAL user (the user used to start up, shut down, and generally act as supreme commander of databases) is set to ORACLE by the startup. The SYS user, second in command, is set to the imaginative "change_on_install," and the lowly SYSTEM user, the general gofer and workman for system administration, is set to MANAGER. I suggest changing these as soon as possible.

If you have followed the installation guide provided by Oracle, and paid attention to the heads-up data provided so far, you should have a working Oracle installation. Congratulations!

CHAPTER 2

Administration
of ORACLE
(After the Bloom
Is Off the Rose . . .)

If you are at this point, one of three things has happened. You successfully installed your Oracle system using the guidelines in Chapter 1 and are anxiously awaiting further enlightenment; or, you didn't successfully install your Oracle system using the guidelines in Chapter 1 but are big-hearted enough to give this book another chance at proving that it's worth the purchase price; or, you either don't have Oracle yet, or have an existing system and just want to see what system administration tools this book can provide. In any case, the next few chapters are the heart of this book and are really what you paid for.

In this next chapter we will look at Oracle database-level administration and management in detail. We will cover the tools available to the DBA and administration of the physical database. In the following chapters we will examine object, space, and user administration, techniques for using the tools, tuning issues and solutions, backup and recovery, and security.

As the title of this chapter implies, Oracle administration isn't always a rose garden; sometimes it is the thorns. Hopefully, by using this book you can avoid some of the thorns that have gouged Oracle DBAs in the past. In writing this and subsequent chapters, use was made of the Oracle documentation set, articles from *Oracle* magazine, IOUG (International Oracle User's Group) presentations, *Oreview* magazine, *DBMS* magazine, Oracle CompuServe forums, Internet newsgroups, and real-life experiences of several Oracle database experts.

In order to make full use of this chapter, it is suggested that the DBA either load the Oracle Administrator Lite product from the companion disk (which contains all the scripts from the book), or load each by hand. The account used to run these scripts should have the DBA role under Oracle7, and have a default and temporary tablespace other than SYSTEM. The account should not be the SYSTEM account. It is suggested that a small (generally around 3 megabytes or less) tablespace be created to hold the temporary tables and permanent tables required to run the various utilities. The CATDBASYN.SQL or equivalent script should be run for this user so the DBA_ views are created and available. The UTLMONTR.SQL script (for pre-7.3 versions of Oracle) should also be run so the V$ views are available. (If it is desired that the views not be made available to the general user population, this script should be copied to a new location and modified accordingly.) On the companion disk, the file GRANTS.SQL script must be run from the SYS account to provide the needed direct grants and create some needed procedures for the abovementioned user. The CREA_TABS.SQL script will create the DBA tables and required views. Finally, the DBMS_REVEALNET.SQL script should be run to create some needed procedures and functions.

This chapter assumes that the DBA is familiar with basic SQL and SQL*Plus commands. As we move along, PL/SQL will also be used, so familiarity with these tools would be helpful. May I suggest Steve Feuerstein's excellent book on PL/SQL, *PL/SQL Programming*,, O'Reilly, 1995 from Osborne books, and the companion volume, *PL/SQL Advanced Programming.*,O'Reilly, 1996 None of the scripts is overly complex however, and even if you aren't an SQL virtuoso, you should be able to make some sense of them.

In any case, you should have the *SQL Language Reference Manual*, the *SQL*Plus Reference Manual*, the *Oracle Database Administrator's Guide*, the *PL/SQL Reference Guide*, the *Oracle RDBMS Performance Tuning Guide* and the appropriate installation and administration guide for your operating system or the equivalent Oracle7 server guides, handy when using this chapter. The document set provided by Oracle is detailed and provides excellent information, if you know where to find the data you need in all of the information provided. Wherever possible, this book will give references to the appropriate manual sections. The RevealNet Dictionary Lite product that is provided on the accompaning CD-ROM from RevealNet, Inc., should be installed and available as well.

The scripts and procedures presented in this chapter are being used at several sites to manage and administer Oracle databases. Each has been tested under Oracle7 and Oracle8 and under VMS, NT, Windows and UNIX implementations of Oracle databases. It is suggested that the scripts be called from a centralized menu, either an operating system script or Forms application. An example script for both DCL and HP-UX KORNE shell are shown in Appendix C on the CD-ROM. This provides for a single entry of your Oracle user name and password instead of having to invoke SQL*Plus each time you want to run a script. The scripts are kept simple to allow ease of understanding, and to ensure that those that may not have the transaction processing option or other advanced Oracle features implemented may still find this book of use. Only a few of the scripts use PL/SQL; every attempt has been made to follow the KISS principle (Keep it simple, stupid!).

2.1   GENERIC TOOLS AVAILABLE TO ALL DBAS

In almost every Oracle database, the DBA will have access to SQL, SQL*Plus and SQLDBA or SVRMGR. Almost all 7.2 and greater installations may also have the Oracle Enterprise Manager toolset. In some runtime versions of Oracle, such as is used with some CAD/CAM packages for drawing tracking, only SQLDBA or SVRMGR may be provided. The PL/SQL tool is always provided with all post-7.0 Oracle systems as well.

SQL: The Standard RDBMS Language

Structured Query Language (SQL) is the lingua franca of all RDBMS systems. The American National Standards Institute (ANSI) accepted SQL as the standard relational database language in October 1986 (ANSI X3.135-1986). SQL has also been accepted by the International Standards Organization (ISO standard 9075) as well as by the U.S. government in the Federal Information Processing Standard FIPS-127. A security enhancement has been added and is covered in ANSI SQL Addendum I and issued as X3.135-1989 and 9075-1989. SQL92 is the most recent standard and Oracle's implementation is entry-level-compliant and has numerous extensions that make it one of the best SQL implementations available.

SQL is considered to be a nonprocedural language; this is because of the way it processes sets of records and provides automatic data access, or navigation. SQL also uses query optimization, that is, the RDBMS kernel determines the optimum method to reach the desired data so you don't have to. Under Oracle7 and Oracle8, a cost-based or a rules-based approach can be used. SQL is designed to be simple to learn and use. Despite this simplicity, SQL provides a rich command set under which virtually any combination of data in a database can be retrieved and reported.

The major statement in SQL is the SELECT statement. SELECT allows the retrieval of data from the database. Multiple selects can be nested into a single statement, and, using SQL*NET version 2.x or NET8, selects can even span databases. SQL also allows insertion, update and deletion of data, as well as creation, modification, and deletion of database objects such as tables, sequences, indexes, and tablespaces. SQL provides for database security and consistency. Unlike other systems where entirely different command sets governed the different areas of database activities, SQL combines these functions into an integrated command set. Some of the SQL language is shown in Appendix B on the CD-ROM; refer to the appropriate reference manual for more details on the command usages.

SQL is also portable. If two RDBMS are ANSI compliant, then an SQL statement that works in one will work in the other, assuming the data structures are the same. This only applies to standard SQL commands; naturally, system-specific extensions won't transport to other systems. A good example of this is the Oracle storage clause.

If the DBA is not familiar with SQL, it is suggested that he or she look through the *SQL Language Reference Manual* and become familiar with the basic commands. The

SQL language is utilized through SQL*Plus, Oracle Administrator Toolbar SQL Worksheet, SVRMGR, or SQLDBA. In fact, with Oracle7 the SQLDBA and SVRMGR statement acceptance has been extended to make it easier to use it alone for DBA tasks.

Appendix B (on the CD-ROM) shows the general formats for all SQL commands referenced in this book. For more detailed explanations the DBA should refer to the *SQL Language Reference Manual* for the release of the Oracle database they are operating under.

SQL*Plus: An Oracle Extension to Standard SQL

The SQL*Plus program allows users to access SQL and the Oracle SQL extensions. This combination of commands, SQL, and the Oracle SQL extensions allows users and the DBA to access the database via standard SQL and to format input and output using the SQL*Plus extensions to the language.

SQL*Plus has a command buffer that stores the current command and allows the user to edit the command using the native system editor or via command line input. SQL*Plus also allows the user to store, retrieve, and execute SQL/SQL*Plus command scripts as well as PL/SQL command scripts. It allows use of abbreviated commands and calls to the host system command language. SQL*Plus allows local variables to be assigned as well as system variable control. The new SQL*Worksheet handles standard SQL well, but will not handle the formatting commands from the SQL*Plus extensions.

SQL*Plus can also be used to dynamically create command scripts that can then be used to perform en-mass changes to users, tables, or other Oracle objects. This is a very powerful feature that will be used in many of the example scripts. If DBAs are not familiar with SQL*Plus, it is suggested they review the SQL*Plus reference guide to acquaint themselves with the SQL*Plus commands.

SQL*Plus is accessed once the user has run the appropriate ORAUSER and instance-specific ORAUSER_instance files. On UNIX the appropriate system variables and path are set by use of the ". oraenv" command; however, the ORACLE_SID variable may have to be set in some environments to point to your database. The format for invoking SQL*Plus follows.

```
SQLPLUS  username/password@connect string  @command file
```

where:

   username/password—This is the user's Oracle username and password, which is usually different from the operating system username and password. If the user is assigned an autologin type of account, only the / is required.

   @connect string—This is a connect string that connects the user to other databases than the default database. It can be used with SQL*NET or NET8 over networks to access other systems.

@command file—This allows the user to specify an SQL command file that is run automatically.

If the DBA account is what is known as an OPS$ account (not recommended), the format would be as follows:

```
SQLPLUS /
```

Since an OPS$ account allows the user to get into the Oracle system without specifying a password if they are logging in from their normal account, the use of OPS$ accounts should be restricted to "captive" type users, that is, users who can only access the system via an appropriate secure menu system. Under Oracle7 and Oracle8 the OPS$ format is the default but the system manager can assign whatever prefix he or she desires by use of the OS_AUTHENT_PREFIX parameter in the INIT.ORA file.

SQLDBA and SVRMGR: A Database Administrator's Toolset

As their names imply, SQLDBA and SVRMGR (Server Manager) are designed for the DBA and only for the DBA. The SQLDBA and SVRMGR programs provide access to the database internals and allow access to all database objects. To use SQLDBA the user must have the ORA_DBA identifier in VMS or must belong to the DBA group under UNIX. The SVRMGR product has both a line command version and an X-windows implementation (SVRMGRL and SVRMGRM) on most operating systems where it is appropriate, such as VMS and UNIX.

In Oracle7, the use of SQLDBA is covered in the Oracle7 *Server Utilities User's Guide*. The use of SVRMGR is covered in the *Server Manager's User Guide*.

Monitor SQLDBA and SVRMGR also allow access to the Monitor utility. Monitor provides views of the database virtual performance tables. Monitor also allows the DBA to observe user processes as they interact with the Oracle system. Monitor is a very powerful tool for viewing database status. While the format and access have improved considerably in Oracle7, it appears that the plethora of data in the Monitor display screens that has plagued Oracle's Monitor displays since version 6 has not. In some of the screens, file and name filters are added; in the statistics windows, they have not been added. This still leaves dozens of parameters to sort through when the DBA is only interested in a few.

Changes Under Oracle8 Under version 7, SQLDBA was still command driven. Under Oracle8, the use of pull-down menus and fill-in screens has automated many of the more tedious administration tasks such as addition of data files, tablespaces, users, dealing with startup/shutdown, and dealing with various logs. With Oracle8, SVRMGR and Oracle enterprise monitor (OEM) have come a long way toward being the tools to use to administer a database. The addition of customizable monitor screens under the Oracle performance pack looks to be a big help. Unfortunately, one of the major limitations in SQLDBA under version 7, the lack of hard-copy reports, has not been addressed even in Oracle8. In fact, the SPOOL OUT option that allowed some reporting was removed; this is unfortunate. With some good, understandable reports SQLDBA and SVRMGR would be more powerful tools.

Operation of SVRMGR   To use SVRMGR, the DBA must have first run the appropriate ORAUSER procedure, usually located in the ORA_UTIL directory on VMS, or issued the .oraenv command on UNIX to set environmental variables. In addition, if the DBA wants to run SVRMGR against a specific instance, the ORAUSER_instance file in the directory specified by the ORA_INSTANCE logical on VMS must be run. Under UNIX this is taken care of by the oraenv program. For some commands, the user, under Oracle7, has the OSOPER and OSDBA roles assigned. These roles control the privileges granted thus allowing limited power to users who must use the CONNECT INTERNAL command under SVRMGR for shutdown and startup of the database but don't need other privileges. The SYS user must have run the utlmontr.sql script for users to access the Monitor screens. The SVRMGR command format follows.

```
SVRMGR (lowercase on UNIX)
```

Once the SVRMGR program is running, the DBA uses the CONNECT command to connect to the appropriate instance.

```
CONNECT username    or    CONNECT username/password
```

A special form of the CONNECT command can be used by DBAs from accounts with the proper privileges. This form allows the DBA to access all of the structures in the database, including those owned by SYS.

```
CONNECT INTERNAL
```

The DBA is allowed certain commands and privileges while in SVRMGR. These also depend on database status. The database status can be one of the following:

Database STATUS:	Allowed Commands:
CLOSED, not MOUNTED	SHUTDOWN, used for some maintenance activities.
CLOSED, MOUNTED	Used for some maintenance activities.
OPEN, MOUNTED, NORMAL EXCLUSIVE	Normal mode for nonparallel database.
OPEN, MOUNTED, DBA MODE	Used for maintenance.
OPEN, MOUNTED, PARALLEL	Used for parallel instance Oracle.

The DBA tasks include user administration, space administration (physical such as data files, and virtual such as tablespace usage), and tools administration. We will cover these tasks in the following sections.

PL/SQL: Procedural-Level Standard Query Language

The PL/SQL language extensions to SQL make doing complex programming tasks in SQL orders of magnitude easier. PL/SQL adds the capability to use cursors (predefined selects), loops, temporary tables, and a number of other high-level language features not available in standard SQL. Stored functions, procedures, packages, triggers, and methods are all built using PL/SQL. The Oracle-provided packages (DBMS_*, and, UTL*) are also built using PL/SQL and will become your good friends in the time to come as you use them to explore and conquer Oracle.

As a DBA you will have to become very familiar with PL/SQL. There are numerous examples in this book to help and I also suggest you keep handy the *PL/SQL User's Guide and Reference,* Release 3.0, Beta-2 (or most current), Part No. A50670-1, Feb. 1997. Another excellent reference is *PL/SQL Advanced Programming*, Steven Feuerstein, O'Reilly and Assoc., 1996, and nothing beats the RevealNet online references (PL/SQL for Developers, PLVision Lite, and PLVision Professional) available at http:/www.revealnet.com/ for sheer ease of use.

2.2   ADMINISTRATION OF THE DATABASE

A database consists of executables, global areas, and database files. Within the database files exist tables, indexes, sequences, views, clusters, and synonyms. The DBA will be involved in the creation, maintenance and deletion of these objects on a frequent basis. The commands, CREATE, ALTER and DROP, are fairly easy to master. A subset of the CREATE and ALTER command, the STORAGE clause, is also very important for the DBA to understand and use properly.

The Create Command

As its name implies, the CREATE statement is used to create databases, tablespaces, tables, clusters, database links, indexes, sequences, views, users, packages, procedures, functions, and rollback segments. It has this general format:

```
CREATE object_type object_name
create options,
STORAGE ( storage parameters).
```

The Storage Clause

The STORAGE clause specifies how an object uses the space that is allocated to it. Let's look at the format of the STORAGE clause.

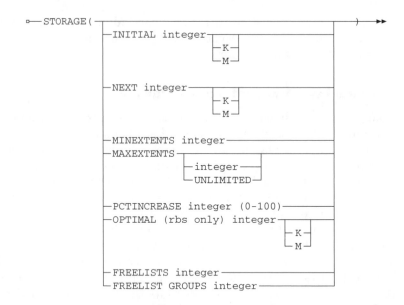

where:

INITIAL—This is the size in bytes of the initial extent of the object. The default is 10240 bytes. The minimum is 4096. The maximum is 4095 megabytes. All values are rounded to the nearest Oracle block size.

NEXT—This is the size for the next extent after the INITIAL is used. The default is 10240 bytes, the minimum is 2048, the maximum is 4095 megabytes. This is the value that will be used for each new extent if PCTINCREASE is set to 0.

MINEXTENTS—This is the number of initial extents for the object. Generally, except for rollback segments, it is set to 1. If a large amount of space is required, and there is not enough contiguous space for the table, setting a smaller extent size and specifying several extents may solve the problem.

MAXEXTENTS—This is the largest number of extents allowed the object. This defaults to the max allowed for your block size for Oracle7 and Oracle8. In addition, for Oracle8, if UNLIMITED is set, there is no upper limit.

PCTINCREASE—This parameter tells Oracle how much to grow each extent after the INITIAL and NEXT extents are used. A specification of 50 will grow each extent after NEXT by 50%, *for each subsequent extent*. This means that for a table created with one initial and a next extent, any further extents will increase in size by 50% over their predecessor. Under Oracle7 and Oracle8 this parameter is only applied against the size of the previous extent.

OPTIMAL—This is used only for rollback segments and specifies the value to which a rollback segment will shrink back after extending.

FREELIST GROUPS—This parameter specifies the number of freelist groups to maintain for a table or index.

FREELISTS—For objects other than tablespaces, specifies the number of free-lists for each of the freelist groups for the table, index, or cluster. The minimum value is 1 and the maximum is block size dependent.

Proper use of the STORAGE clause means that you will have to perform accurate estimates of table and index size before creation. This will be covered in the section on tables.

2.3   DATABASE CREATION, ALTERATION, AND DELETION

Like other objects under Oracle, databases themselves can be created, altered, and deleted. Let's look at these different processes.

Database Creation

To create a database, the CREATE command is run under SVRMGR.

1. First, the DBA must first connect to the Oracle internal user via the command:

   ```
   CONNECT INTERNAL
   ```

2. Next, the instance is started in an unmounted condition. This is accomplished with the following command.

   ```
   STARTUP NOMOUNT PFILE=filename
   ```

   where:

   PFILE=filename refers to the database initialization file (INIT.ORA) you will be using, unless it is located in the directory you are currently in; a path must also be provided.

3. Next, the database is created. The format would be:

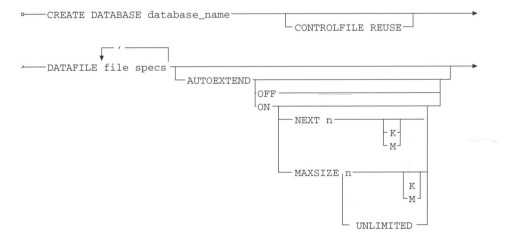

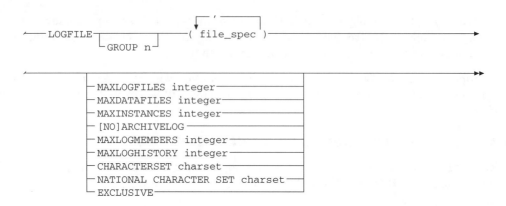

where:

Database name is the name of the database, maximum of eight characters long.

File specifications for data files are of the format: 'filename' SIZE integer K or M REUSE. K is for kilobytes, M is for Megabytes. REUSE specifies that if the file already exists, reuse it. New with later versions of Oracle7 is the AUTOEXTEND option, which is used to allow your datafiles to automatically extend as needed. Be very careful with this command as it can use up a great deal of disk space rather rapidly if a mistake is made during table builds or inserts.

File specifications for log files depend on the operating system.

The MAXLOGFILES, MAXDATAFILES, and MAXINSTANCES set hard limits for the database; these should be set to the maximum you ever expect.

MAXLOGMEMBERS and MAXLOGHISTORY are hard limits.

For Oracle7, CHARACTER SET determines the character set that data will be stored in; this value is operating system dependent.

If you need archive logging, set ARCHIVELOG; if you never will need it, set NOARCHIVELOG.

Databases are created in EXCLUSIVE mode. Databases are either EXCLUSIVE or PARALLEL. A database must be altered to PARALLEL mode after creation.

The CHARACTER_SET is for normal data. The NATIONALCHARACTER SET specifies the national character set used to store data in columns specifically defined as NCHAR, NCLOB, or NVARCHAR2. You cannot change the national character set after creating the database. If not specified, the national character set defaults to the database character set. The following character sets are allowed:

US7ASCII	ASCII 7-bit American
WE8DEC	DEC 8-bit West European
WE8HP	HP LaserJet 8-bit West European
US8PC437	IBM-PC Code Page 437 8-bit American
WE8EBCDIC37	EBCDIC Code Page 37 8-bit West European
WE8EBCDIC500	EBCDIC Code Page 500 8-bit West European
WE8EBCDIC285	EBCDIC Code Page 285 8-bit West European
WE8PC850	IBM-PC Code Page 850 8-bit West European
D7DEC	DEC VT100 7-bit German
F7DEC	DEC VT100 7-bit French
S7DEC	DEC VT100 7-bit Swedish
E7DEC	DEC VT100 7-bit Spanish
SF7ASCII	ASCII 7-bit Finnish
NDK7DEC	DEC VT100 7-bit Norwegian/Danish
I7DEC	DEC VT100 7-bit Italian
NL7DEC	DEC VT100 7-bit Dutch
CH7DEC	DEC VT100 7-bit Swiss (German/French)
YUG7ASCII	ASCII 7-bit Yugoslavian
SF7DEC	DEC VT100 7-bit Finnish
TR7DEC	DEC VT100 7-bit Turkish
IW7IS960	Israeli Standard 960 7-bit Latin/Hebrew
IN8ISCII	Multiple-Script Indian Standard 8-bit Latin/Indian Languages
WE8ISO8859P1	ISO 8859-1 West European
EE8ISO8859P2	ISO 8859-2 East European
SE8ISO8859P3	ISO 8859-3 South European
NEE8ISO8859P4	ISO 8859-4 North and North-East European
CL8ISO8859P5	ISO 8859-5 Latin/Cyrillic
AR8ISO8859P6	ISO 8859-6 Latin/Arabic
EL8ISO8859P7	ISO 8859-7 Latin/Greek
IW8ISO8859P8	ISO 8859-8 Latin/Hebrew
WE8ISO8859P9	ISO 8859-9 West European & Turkish
NE8ISO8859P10	ISO 8859-10 North European
TH8TISASCII	Thai Industrial Standard 620-2533 - ASCII 8-bit
TH8TISEBCDIC	Thai Industrial Standard 620-2533 - EBCDIC 8-bit
BN8BSCII	Bangladesh National Code 8-bit BSCII
VN8VN3	VN3 8-bit Vietnamese

WE8NEXTSTEP	NeXTSTEP PostScript 8-bit West European
AR8EBCDICX	EBCDIC XBASIC Server 8-bit Latin/Arabic
EL8DEC	DEC 8-bit Latin/Greek
TR8DEC	DEC 8-bit Turkish
WE8EBCDIC37C	EBCDIC Code Page 37 8-bit Oracle/c
WE8EBCDIC500C	EBCDIC Code Page 500 8-bit Oracle/c
IW8EBCDIC424	EBCDIC Code Page 424 8-bit Latin/Hebrew
TR8EBCDIC1026	EBCDIC Code Page 1026 8-bit Turkish
WE8EBCDIC871	EBCDIC Code Page 871 8-bit Icelandic
WE8EBCDIC284	EBCDIC Code Page 284 8-bit Latin American/Spanish
EEC8EUROASCI	EEC Targon 35 ASCI West European / Greek
EEC8EUROPA3	EEC EUROPA3 8-bit West European/Greek
LA8PASSPORT	German Government Printer 8-bit All-European Latin
BG8PC437S	IBM-PC Code Page 437 8-bit (Bulgarian Modification)
EE8PC852	IBM-PC Code Page 852 8-bit East European
RU8PC866	IBM-PC Code Page 866 8-bit Latin/Cyrillic
RU8BESTA	BESTA 8-bit Latin/Cyrillic
IW8PC1507	IBM-PC Code Page 1507/862 8-bit Latin/Hebrew
RU8PC855	IBM-PC Code Page 855 8-bit Latin/Cyrillic
TR8PC857	IBM-PC Code Page 857 8-bit Turkish
CL8MACCYRILLIC	Mac Client 8-bit Latin/Cyrillic
CL8MACCYRILLICS	Mac Server 8-bit Latin/Cyrillic
WE8PC860	IBM-PC Code Page 860 8-bit West European
IS8PC861	IBM-PC Code Page 861 8-bit Icelandic
EE8MACCES	Mac Server 8-bit Central European
EE8MACCROATIANS	Mac Server 8-bit Croatian
TR8MACTURKISHS	Mac Server 8-bit Turkish
IS8MACICELANDICS	Mac Server 8-bit Icelandic
EL8MACGREEKS	Mac Server 8-bit Greek
IW8MACHEBREWS	Mac Server 8-bit Hebrew
EE8MSWIN1250	MS Windows Code Page 1250 8-bit East European
CL8MSWIN1251	MS Windows Code Page 1251 8-bit Latin/Cyrillic
ET8MSWIN923	MS Windows Code Page 923 8-bit Estonian
BG8MSWIN	MS Windows 8-bit Bulgarian Cyrillic
EL8MSWIN1253	MS Windows Code Page 1253 8-bit Latin/Greek
IW8MSWIN1255	MS Windows Code Page 1255 8-bit Latin/Hebrew

LT8MSWIN921	MS Windows Code Page 921 8-bit Lithuanian
TR8MSWIN1254	MS Windows Code Page 1254 8-bit Turkish
WE8MSWIN1252	MS Windows Code Page 1252 8-bit West European
BLT8MSWIN1257	MS Windows Code Page 1257 8-bit Baltic
D8EBCDIC273	EBCDIC Code Page 273/1 8-bit Austrian German
I8EBCDIC280	EBCDIC Code Page 280/1 8-bit Italian
DK8EBCDIC277	EBCDIC Code Page 277/1 8-bit Danish
S8EBCDIC278	EBCDIC Code Page 278/1 8-bit Swedish
EE8EBCDIC870	EBCDIC Code Page 870 8-bit East European
CL8EBCDIC1025	EBCDIC Code Page 1025 8-bit Cyrillic
F8EBCDIC297	EBCDIC Code Page 297 8-bit French
IW8EBCDIC1086	EBCDIC Code Page 1086 8-bit Hebrew
CL8EBCDIC1025X	EBCDIC Code Page 1025 (Modified) 8-bit Cyrillic
N8PC865	IBM-PC Code Page 865 8-bit Norwegian
BLT8CP921	Latvian Standard LVS8-92(1) Windows/Unix 8-bit Baltic
LV8PC1117	IBM-PC Code Page 1117 8-bit Latvian
LV8PC8LR	Latvian Version IBM-PC Code Page 866 8-bit Latin/Cyrillic
BLT8EBCDIC1112	EBCDIC Code Page 1112 8-bit Baltic Multilingual
LV8RST104090	IBM-PC Alternative Code Page 8-bit Latvian (Latin/Cyrillic)
CL8KOI8R	RELCOM Internet Standard 8-bit Latin/Cyrillic
BLT8PC775	IBM-PC Code Page 775 8-bit Baltic
F7SIEMENS9780X	Siemens 97801/97808 7-bit French
E7SIEMENS9780X	Siemens 97801/97808 7-bit Spanish
S7SIEMENS9780X	Siemens 97801/97808 7-bit Swedish
DK7SIEMENS9780X	Siemens 97801/97808 7-bit Danish
N7SIEMENS9780X	Siemens 97801/97808 7-bit Norwegian
I7SIEMENS9780X	Siemens 97801/97808 7-bit Italian
D7SIEMENS9780X	Siemens 97801/97808 7-bit German
WE8GCOS7	Bull EBCDIC GCOS7 8-bit West European
EL8GCOS7	Bull EBCDIC GCOS7 8-bit Greek
US8BS2000	Siemens 9750-62 EBCDIC 8-bit American
D8BS2000	Siemens 9750-62 EBCDIC 8-bit German
F8BS2000	Siemens 9750-62 EBCDIC 8-bit French
E8BS2000	Siemens 9750-62 EBCDIC 8-bit Spanish
DK8BS2000	Siemens 9750-62 EBCDIC 8-bit Danish
WE8BS2000	Siemens EBCDIC.DF.04 8-bit West European

CL8BS2000	Siemens EBCDIC.EHC.LC 8-bit Cyrillic
WE8BS2000L5	Siemens EBCDIC.DF.04.L5 8-bit West European/Turkish
WE8DG	DG 8-bit West European
WE8NCR4970	NCR 4970 8-bit West European
WE8ROMAN8	HP Roman8 8-bit West European
EE8MACCE	Mac Client 8-bit Central European
EE8MACCROATIAN	Mac Client 8-bit Croatian
TR8MACTURKISH	Mac Client 8-bit Turkish
IS8MACICELANDIC	Mac Client 8-bit Icelandic
EL8MACGREEK	Mac Client 8-bit Greek
IW8MACHEBREW	Mac Client 8-bit Hebrew
US8ICL	ICL EBCDIC 8-bit American
WE8ICL	ICL EBCDIC 8-bit West European
WE8ISOICLUK	ICL special version ISO8859-1
WE8MACROMAN8	Mac Client 8-bit Extended Roman8 West European
WE8MACROMAN8S	Mac Server 8-bit Extended Roman8 West European
TH8MACTHAI	Mac Client 8-bit Latin/Thai
TH8MACTHAIS	Mac Server 8-bit Latin/Thai
HU8CWI2	Hungarian 8-bit CWI-2
EL8PC437S	IBM-PC Code Page 437 8-bit (Greek modification)
EL8EBCDIC875	EBCDIC Code Page 875 8-bit Greek
EL8PC737	IBM-PC Code Page 737 8-bit Greek/Latin
LT8PC772	IBM-PC Code Page 772 8-bit Lithuanian (Latin/Cyrillic)
LT8PC774	IBM-PC Code Page 774 8-bit Lithuanian (Latin)
EL8PC869	IBM-PC Code Page 869 8-bit Greek/Latin
EL8PC851	IBM-PC Code Page 851 8-bit Greek/Latin
CDN8PC863	IBM-PC Code Page 863 8-bit Canadian French
HU8ABMOD	Hungarian 8-bit Special AB Mod
AR8ASMO8X	ASMO Extended 708 8-bit Latin/Arabic
AR8NAFITHA711	Nafitha Enhanced 711 Server 8-bit Latin/Arabic
AR8SAKHR707	SAKHR 707 Server 8-bit Latin/Arabic
AR8MUSSAD768	Mussa'd Alarabi/2 768 Server 8-bit Latin/Arabic
AR8ADOS710	Arabic MS-DOS 710 Server 8-bit Latin/Arabic
AR8ADOS720	Arabic MS-DOS 720 Server 8-bit Latin/Arabic
AR8APTEC715	APTEC 715 Server 8-bit Latin/Arabic
AR8MSAWIN	MS Windows Code Page 1256 8-Bit Latin/Arabic

AR8MSWIN1256	MS Windows Code Page 1256 8-Bit Latin/Arabic
AR8NAFITHA721	Nafitha International 721 Server 8-bit Latin/Arabic
AR8SAKHR706	SAKHR 706 Server 8-bit Latin/Arabic
AR8ARABICMAC	Mac Client 8-bit Latin/Arabic
AR8ARABICMACS	Mac Server 8-bit Latin/Arabic
LA8ISO6937	ISO 6937 8-bit Coded Character Set for Text Communication
US8NOOP	No-op character set prohibiting conversions
JA16VMS	JVMS 16-bit Japanese
JA16EUC	EUC 16-bit Japanese
JA16SJIS	Shift-JIS 16-bit Japanese
JA16DBCS	IBM DBCS 16-bit Japanese
JA16EBCDIC930	IBM DBCS Code Page 290 16-bit Japanese
JA16MACSJIS	Mac client Shift-JIS 16-bit Japanese
KO16KSC5601	KSC5601 16-bit Korean
KO16DBCS	IBM DBCS 16-bit Korean
KO16KSCCS	KSCCS 16-bit Korean
ZHS16CGB231280	CGB2312-80 16-bit Simplified Chinese
ZHS16MACCGB231280	Mac client CGB2312-80 16-bit Simplified Chinese
ZHS16GBK	Windows95 16-bit PRC version Chinese character set
ZHS16DBCS	EBCDIC 16-bit Simplified Chinese character set
ZHT32EUC	EUC 32-bit Traditional Chinese
ZHT32SOPS	SOPS 32-bit Traditional Chinese
ZHT16DBT	Taiwan Taxation 16-bit Traditional Chinese
ZHT32TRIS	TRIS 32-bit Traditional Chinese
ZHT16DBCS	IBM DBCS 16-bit Traditional Chinese
ZHT16BIG5	BIG5 16-bit Traditional Chinese
ZHT16CCDC	HP CCDC 16-bit Traditional Chinese
AL24UTFFSS	Unicode UTF-8 character set
UTF8	Unicode 2.0 UTF-8 character set
JA16EUCFIXED	16-bit Japanese. A fixed-width subset of JA16EUC (contains only the 2-byte characters of JA16EUC). Contains no 7- or 8-bit ASCII characters
JA16SJISFIXED	SJIS 16-bit Japanese. A fixed-width subset of JA16SJIS (contains only the 2- byte characters of JA16JIS). Contains no 7- or 8-bit ASCII characters
JA16DBCSFIXED	16-bit only JA16DBCS. A fixed-width subset of JA16DBCS which has only 16-bit (double byte character set-DBCS) characters. Contains no 7- or 8-bit ASCII characters

AR8ASMO708PLUS	ASMO 708 Plus 8-bit Latin/Arabic
AR8XBASIC	XBASIC Right-to-Left Arabic Character Set
IW8MACHEBREWS	MAC Server 8-bit Hebrew
IW8MACHEBREW	MAC Client 8-bit Hebrew
AR8NAFITHA711T	Nafitha Enhanced 711 Client 8-bit Latin/Arabic
AR8SAKHR707T	SAKHR 707 Client 8-bit Latin/Arabic
AR8MUSSAD768T	Mussa'd Alarabi/2 768 Client 8-bit Latin/Arabic
AR8ADOS710T	Arabic MS-DOS 710 Client 8-bit Latin/Arabic
AR8ADOS720T	Arabic MS-DOS 720 Client 8-bit Latin/Arabic
AR8APTEC715T	APTEC 7 15 Client 8-bit Latin/Arabic
AR8NAFITHA721T	Nafitha International 721 Client 8-bit Latin/Arabic
AR8HPARABIC8T	HP ARABIC8 8-bit Latin/Arabic

Source List taken from *Oracle8 Server Reference,* Release 8.0, Beta-2, January 23, 1997.

What the system does when given a CREATE DATABASE command is easy. First, the system creates control, redo log, and database files. Next, the system creates the SYSTEM rollback segment in the SYSTEM tablespace, creates and loads data dictionary tables, and mounts and opens the database.

On NT the instance manager will help with creation of new instances. To access it use the *START* button and then choose the *PROGRAMS* menu item. From the list of *PROGRAMS* choose the *Oracle for Windows NT* folder. Inside the *Oracle for Windows NT* folder will be an icon for *NT Instance Manager v8.0* (or whatever version you are running). Selection of the *NT Instance manager v8.0* icon will start the instance manager, which will list the current (if any) instances of Oracle running on your platform. Select the *New* button from this display. You will be prompted for all required information to start a base installation of Oracle. The major limitation of this tool is that it only provides single line inputs for items that have multiple lines of values. However, be patient; it can be used once you are used to the way it works. Another painful part of its use is that if you make a mistake, it forgets everything you told it and you have to start over.

Alteration of Databases

Even the best-designed database eventually has to be changed. New log group member files may need to be added, data files may need to be renamed or moved, archive logging status changed, etc. These are all accomplished through the use of the ALTER DATABASE command. Let's look at its format and options.

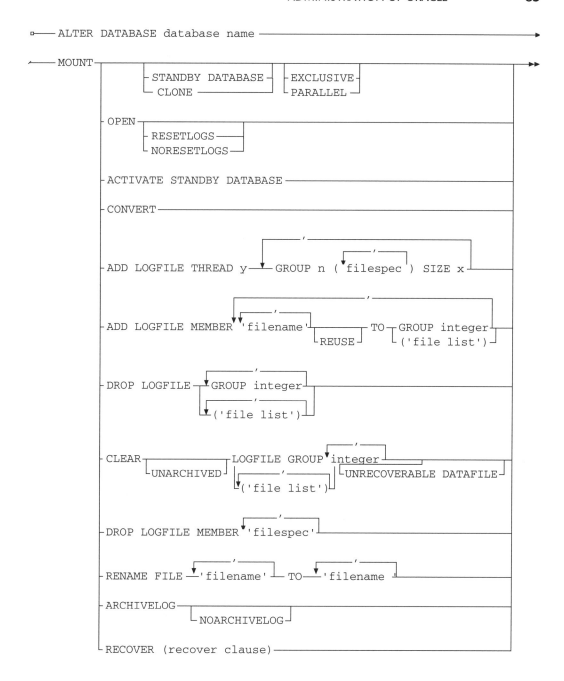

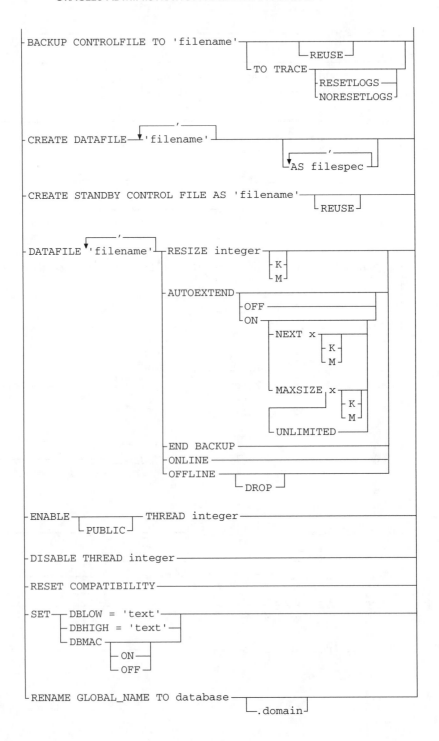

where:

database name is a maximum of 8 characters. If it is not specified, the value in the INIT.ORA file will be used.

filespec is a file specification in the format of 'filename' SIZE integer K or M REUSE, with filename an OS-specific full path name; K or M specifies integer as Kilobytes or megabytes; and REUSE specifies to reuse existing file if it exists. If SIZE isn't specified, 500K will be used. REUSE is optional.

filename is a full path file name.

MOUNT—Database is available for some DBA functions, but not normal functions. Either exclusive, which is default, or PARALLEL.

STANDBY DATABASE—With 7.3 and greater operates against a hot-standby database (see Backup, Chapter 17).

OPEN—Database is mounted and opened for general use. Either with RESET LOGS (default) or NORESET LOGS (see Backup, Chapter 17).

ACTIVATE STANDBY DATABASE—See Backup, Chapter 17.

ADD LOGFILE THREAD—Adds a thread or redo to a PARALLEL instance.

ADD LOGFILE MEMBER—Adds a logfile member to an existing group.

CLEAR—Reinitializes an on-line redo log and optionally does not archive the redo log. CLEAR LOGFILE is similar to adding and dropping a redo log except that the command may be issued even if there are only two logs for the thread and it also may be issued for the current redo log of a closed thread.

CLEAR LOGFILE cannot be used to clear a log needed for media recovery. If it is necessary to clear a log containing redo after the database checkpoint, then incomplete media recovery will be necessary. The current redo log of an open thread can never be cleared. The current log of a closed thread can be cleared by switching logs in the closed thread.

If the CLEAR LOGFILE command is interrupted by a system or instance failure, then the database may hang. If so, the command must be reissued once the database is restarted. If the failure occurred because of I/O errors accessing one member of a log group, then that member can be dropped and other members added.

UNARCHIVED must be specified if you want to reuse a redo log that was not archived. Note that specifying UNARCHIVED will make backups unusable if the redo log is needed for recovery.

UNRECOVERABLE DATAFILE must be specified if the tablespace has a datafile off-line and the unarchived log must be cleared to bring the tablespace online. If so, then the datafile and entire tablespace must be dropped once the CLEAR LOGFILE command completes.

DROP LOGFILE—Drops an existing log group.

DROP LOGFILE MEMBER—Drops an existing log member.

RENAME—Renames the specified database file.

ARCHIVELOG, NOARCHIVELOG—Turns archive logging on or off.

RECOVER—Puts database into recovery mode. The form of recovery is specified in the recovery clause. (See Chapter 17 on Backup.)

BACKUP CONTROLFILE—This can be used in two ways. First, to make a recoverable backup copy of the control file ("TO 'filename'") and second, to make a script to rebuild the control file (" TO TRACE").

CREATE DATAFILE—Creates a new datafile in place of an old one. You can use this option to recreate a datafile that was lost with no backup. The 'filename' must identify a file that was once a part of the database. The filespec specifies the name and size of the new datafile. If you omit the AS clause, ORACLE creates the new file with the same name and size as the file specified by 'filename'.

CREATE STANDBY CONTROLFILE—Creates a control file for use with the standby database.

DATAFILE—Allows you to perform manipulations against the datafiles in the instance such as resizing, turning autoextend on or off, and setting backup status.

ENABLE and DISABLE threads—Allows the enabling and disabling of redo log threads (only used for parallel databases).

RESET COMPATIBILITY—Marks the database to be reset to an earlier version of Oracle7 when the database is next restarted. This will render archived redo logs unusable for recovery.

TIP   This option will not work unless you have successfully disabled Oracle7 features that affect backward compatibility.

SET DBLOW I DBHIGH I DBMAC—Used with Secure Oracle.

RENAME GLOBAL_NAME TO—Changes the global name of the database. A rename will automatically flush the shared pool. It doesn't change data concerning your global name in remote instances, connect strings, or db links.

Some examples of the use of ALTER DATABASE are:

To mount a database PARALLEL:

```
ALTER DATABASE dbname MOUNT PARALLEL
```

To drop a logfile member:

```
ALTER DATABASE
    DROP LOGFILE '/oracle1/ORTEST1/redo/ORTEST1_redo31.log'
```

Re-creation of a Database

Periodically it may be required that a DBA recreate a database. Perhaps the block size was incorrectly specified, perhaps it has to be moved from one location to another, or perhaps a DBA has inherited a system and just wants to see how the database was created. I wish I could say there was an easy way to get this information from the database, but unfortunately unless you have some of the third-party tools, it just isn't so.

Hopefully, you are with a shop that has detailed information on the hows, whens, and whys databases were created. Unfortunately, most shops seem to do this in the SOTP mode (seat of the pants) so no actual documentation is available. The lesson to be learned here is to always use a script to create anything in the database that is permanent. Source 2.1 shows an example script to document a database create statement for an Oracle instance. Not documented in this script are the MAX set of parameters, the reason being that these are stored in the control file. To completely document the CREATE command, also document the control file with:

```
ALTER DATABASE BACKUP CONTROL FILE TO TRACE;
```

The file will be located in the background_dump_destination location specified in the v$parameter table. An example output from the ALTER DATABASE BACKUP CONTROLFILE TO TRACE is shown in Listing 2.2. Another item which must be documented is the initialization parameters for your database; these are located in the v$parameter virtual table. The script in Source 2.2 documents these for you in an almost-ready-for-prime-time format.

SOURCE 2.1   Script to recreate the database CREATE command for an instance.

```
REM FUNCTION: SCRIPT FOR CREATING DB
REM            This script must be run by a user with the DBA role.
REM            This script is intended to run with Oracle7 or 8.
REM            Running this script will in turn create a script to
REM            rebuild the database.  This created
REM            script, crt_db.sql,  is run by SQLDBA
REM            Only preliminary testing of this script was performed.
REM            Be sure to test it completely before relying on it.
REM M. Ault 3/29/96 TRECOM, REVELNET
REM
SET VERIFY OFF FEEDBACK OFF ECHO OFF PAGES 0
SET TERMOUT ON
PROMPT Creating db build script...
SET TERMOUT OFF;

CREATE TABLE db_temp
    (lineno NUMBER,  text VARCHAR2(255))
/
```

```
DECLARE
    CURSOR dbf_cursor IS
        SELECT
            file_name,bytes
        FROM
            dba_data_files
        WHERE
            tablespace_name='SYSTEM';
    CURSOR grp_cursor IS
        SELECT
            group#
        FROM
            v$log;
    CURSOR mem_cursor (grp_num number) IS
        SELECT
            a.member, b.bytes from v$logfile a, v$log b
        WHERE
            a.group#=grp_num
            AND a.group#=b.group#
        ORDER BY
            member;
    grp_member              v$logfile.member%TYPE;
    bytes               v$log.bytes%TYPE;
    db_name             VARCHAR2(8);
    db_string           VARCHAR2(255);
    db_lineno               NUMBER := 0;
    thrd            NUMBER;
    grp             NUMBER;
    filename                dba_data_files.file_name%TYPE;
    sz                  NUMBER;
    begin_count             NUMBER;
    max_group           NUMBER;
    PROCEDURE write_out(p_line INTEGER,
                    p_string VARCHAR2) IS
        BEGIN
            INSERT INTO db_temp (lineno,text)
                VALUES (db_lineno,db_string);
    END;
BEGIN
    SELECT MAX(group#) INTO max_group FROM v$log;
    db_lineno:=db_lineno+1;
    SELECT 'CREATE DATABASE '||name INTO db_string
        FROM v$database;
    write_out(db_lineno,db_string);
    db_lineno:=db_lineno+1;
    SELECT 'CONTROLFILE REUSE' INTO db_string
        FROM dual;
    write_out(db_lineno,db_string);
    db_lineno:=db_lineno+1;
    SELECT 'LOGFILE ' INTO db_string
```

```
     FROM dual;
     write_out(db_lineno,db_string);
COMMIT;
IF grp_cursor%ISOPEN
THEN
     CLOSE grp_cursor;
     OPEN grp_cursor;
ELSE
     OPEN grp_cursor;
END IF;
LOOP
     FETCH grp_cursor INTO grp;
     EXIT WHEN grp_cursor%NOTFOUND;
     db_lineno:=db_lineno+1;
     db_string:= ' GROUP '||grp||' (';
     write_out(db_lineno,db_string);
     IF mem_cursor%ISOPEN THEN
          CLOSE mem_cursor;
          OPEN mem_cursor(grp);
     ELSE
             OPEN mem_cursor(grp);
     END IF;
     db_lineno:=db_lineno+1;
     begin_count:=db_lineno;
     LOOP
          FETCH mem_cursor INTO grp_member, bytes;
          EXIT when mem_cursor%NOTFOUND;
          IF begin_count=db_lineno THEN
               db_string:=chr(39)||grp_member||chr(39);
               write_out(db_lineno,db_string);
               db_lineno:=db_lineno+1;
          ELSE
               db_string:=','||chr(39)||grp_member||chr(39);
               write_out(db_lineno,db_string);
               db_lineno:=db_lineno+1;
          END IF;
     END LOOP;
     db_lineno:=db_lineno+1;
     IF grp=max_group
     THEN
          db_string:=' ) SIZE '||bytes;
          write_out(db_lineno,db_string);
     ELSE
          db_string:=' ) SIZE '||bytes||',';
          write_out(db_lineno,db_string);
     END IF;
END LOOP;
IF dbf_cursor%ISOPEN THEN
     CLOSE dbf_cursor;
     OPEN dbf_cursor;
```

```
ELSE
     OPEN dbf_cursor;
END IF;
begin_count:=db_lineno;
LOOP
     FETCH dbf_cursor INTO filename, sz;
     EXIT WHEN dbf_cursor%NOTFOUND;
     IF begin_count=db_lineno THEN
db_string:='DATAFILE '||chr(39)||filename||chr(39)||' SIZE '||sz||' REUSE';
     ELSE
     db_string:=','||chr(39)||filename||chr(39)||' SIZE '||sz||' REUSE';
     END IF;
     db_lineno:=db_lineno+1;
     write_out(db_lineno,db_string);
END LOOP;
COMMIT;
SELECT DECODE(value,'TRUE','ARCHIVELOG','FALSE','NOARCHIVELOG')
     INTO db_string FROM v$parameter WHERE name='log_archive_start';
     db_lineno:=db_lineno+1;
     write_out(db_lineno,db_string);
SELECT ';' INTO db_string from  dual;
     db_lineno:=db_lineno+1;
     write_out(db_lineno,db_string);
CLOSE dbf_cursor;
CLOSE mem_cursor;
CLOSE grp_cursor;
COMMIT;
END;
/
rem The next section could be converted to use
rem UTLFILE so the entire anonymous PL/SQL section
rem and this report section would become a stored
rem procedure, but to keep it generic I will leave as
rem is.
COLUMN dbname NEW_VALUE db NOPRINT
SELECT name dbname FROM v$database;
SET HEADING OFF PAGES 0 VERIFY OFF RECSEP OFF
SPOOL rep_out\&db\crt_db.sql
COLUMN text FORMAT a80 WORD_WRAP
SELECT text
FROM db_temp
ORDER BY lineno;
SPOOL OFF
SET FEEDBACK ON VERIFY ON TERMOUT ON
DROP TABLE db_temp;
PROMPT Press enter to continue
SET VERIFY ON FEEDBACK ON PAGES 22 TERMOUT ON
CLEAR COLUMNS
```

SOURCE 2.2   Script to generate a listing of initialization parameters for your database.

```
REM
REM NAME         : init_ora_rct.sql
REM FUNCTION     : Recreate the instance init.ora file
REM USE          : GENERAL
REM Limitations : None
REM
SET NEWPAGE 0 VERIFY OFF
SET ECHO OFF FEEDBACK OFF TERMOUT OFF PAGES 300 LINES 80 HEADING OFF
COLUMN name  FORMAT a80 WORD_WRAPPED
COLUMN dbname NEW_VALUE db NOPRINT
SELECT name dbname FROM v$database;
DEFINE OUTPUT = 'rep_out\&db\init.ora'
DEFINE cr = chr(10)
SPOOL &OUTPUT
SELECT '# Init.ora file from v$parameter'||&&cr||
'# generated on:'||sysdate||&&cr||
'# script by MRA 11/7/95 REVEALNET'||&&cr||
'#' name FROM dual
UNION
SELECT name||' = '||value name  FROM V$PARAMETER
WHERE value IS NOT NULL;
SPOOL OFF
CLEAR COLUMNS
SET NEWPAGE 0 VERIFY OFF
SET TERMOUT ON PAGES 22 LINES 80 HEADING ON
SET TERMOUT ON
UNDEF OUTPUT
PAUSE Press enter to continue
```

LISTING 2.2   Example output from the ALTER DATABASE BACKUP CONTROL FILE command.

```
Dump file H:\ORAWIN\RDBMS71\trace\ORA14071.TRC
Sat Mar 30 10:05:53 1996
ORACLE V7.1.4.1.0 - Production.
vsnsta=0
vsnsql=a vsnxtr=3
MS-WINDOWS Version 3.10
Sat Mar 30 10:05:52 1996
Sat Mar 30 10:05:53 1996

*** SESSION ID:(5.3)
# The following commands will create a new control file and use it
# to open the database.
```

```
# No data other than log history will be lost. Additional logs may
# be required for media recovery of offline data files. Use this
# only if the current version of all online logs are available.
STARTUP NOMOUNT
CREATE CONTROLFILE REUSE DATABASE "ORACLE" NORESETLOGS NOARCHIVELOG
    MAXLOGFILES 32
    MAXLOGMEMBERS 2
    MAXDATAFILES 32
    MAXINSTANCES 16
    MAXLOGHISTORY 1600
LOGFILE
  GROUP 1 'H:\ORAWIN\DBS\wdblog1.ora'  SIZE 500K,
  GROUP 2 'H:\ORAWIN\DBS\wdblog2.ora'  SIZE 500K
DATAFILE
  'H:\ORAWIN\DBS\wdbsys.ora' SIZE 10M,
  'H:\ORAWIN\DBS\wdbuser.ora' SIZE 3M,
  'H:\ORAWIN\DBS\wdbrbs.ora' SIZE 3M,
  'H:\ORAWIN\DBS\wdbtemp.ora' SIZE 2M
;

# Recovery is required if any of the datafiles are restored backups,
# or if the last shutdown was not normal or immediate.
RECOVER DATABASE

# Database can now be opened normally.
ALTER DATABASE OPEN;
```

Database Startup and Shutdown

When the instance and database are created using ORACLEINS on VMS, the operating system command files START_EXCLUSIVE_sid.COM, START_PARALLEL_sid.COM, START_DBA_sid.COM, and STOP_sid.COM are created in the directory assigned to the ORA_INSTANCE logical on VMS and in the $ORACLE_HOME/bin/dbstart and $ORACLE_HOME/bin/dbshut files on UNIX.

On NT4.0, startup and shutdown are generally handled by the strt<SID>.cmd files located in (assuming your home drive is C:) C:/orant/database. The oradim7x (where x is the subversion) program is used to start, stop, and maintain the databases on NT4.0. By specifying command sets in the .CMD files different actions can be taken in regard to the Oracle database system. For example, the startdb.cmd file for an instance with a sid of TEST, an INTERNAL password of ORACLE, might look like this:

```
c:\orant\bin\oradim73    -startup -sid TEST -usrpwd ORACLE
                -pfile
C:\oracle1\ortest1\admin\pfile\initORTEST1.ora
                -starttype SRVC, INST
```

A shutdown script for the same instance would look like this:

```
c:\orant\bin\oradim73        -shutdown -sid TEST
                             -SURPWD ORACLE
                             -SHTTYPE  SRVC, INST
                             -SHUTMODE a
```

Startup The database is open and ready for use after being created. Once the operating system is shut down, or the database is shut down, it must be started before it can be accessed.

VMS Startup On VMS platforms the startup of the Oracle instances and databases can be automated by placing a call to the appropriate startup scripts in the SYSTARUP_Vx.COM procedure in the SYS$MANAGER directory. The script files are located in the ORA_INSTANCE directory for the instance. The full path name will have to be used in the startup command file since the ORA_INSTANCE logical is set by the procedures called by the startup script. As was stated above, these startup scripts are as follows:

START_EXCLUSIVE_sid.COM—This script starts up the database in the default mode, EXCLUSIVE.

START_PARALLEL_sid.COM—This script starts up the database in shared instance mode. More than one instance using the same database.

START_DBA_sid.COM—This script starts the database up in DBA only mode. Only users with the ORA_DBA or in the UNIX DBA group and with DBA privileges can access the database.

UNIX Startup On UNIX systems, the DBA has to perform the following steps to ensure the instance and database startup each time the system starts up.

1. Log in as root.
2. Edit the /etc/oratab file. Change the last field for your $ORACLE_SID to Y.
3. Add a line similar to the following to your /etc/rc file; be sure you use the full path to the dbstart procedure.

```
su - oracle_owner -c /users/oracle/bin/dbstart
```

Manual Startup On all systems manual startup is accomplished either via the supplied scripts or through the SVRMGR program. To startup a database using SVRMGR, use the following procedure. The command used is the STARTUP command; its format follows.

```
STARTUP  [RESTRICTED] [FORCE] [PFILE=filename]
         [EXCLUSIVE or PARALLEL]
         [MOUNT or OPEN] dbname
         [NOMOUNT]
         [RECOVER]
```

1. Log in to SVRMGR as INTERNAL.
2. Issue one of the following commands:
   a. STARTUP OPEN dbname PFILE=filename This command starts the instance, and opens the database named dbname using the parameter file specified by the filename following the PFILE= clause. This starts up the database in the default, EXCLUSIVE mode.
   b. STARTUP RESTRICT OPEN dbname PFILE=filename This command starts the instance, and opens the database named dbname using the parameter file specified by the filename following the PFILE= clause. This starts up the database in the restricted only mode (only users with RESTRICTED SESSION privilege can log in).
   c. STARTUP NOMOUNT This command starts the instance, but leaves the database dismounted and closed. Cannot be used with EXCLUSIVE, MOUNT, or OPEN.
   d. STARTUP MOUNT This command starts the instance and mounts the database, but leaves it closed.
   e. STARTUP OPEN dbname PARALLEL
      This command starts the instance, opens the database and puts the database in PARALLEL mode for multi-instance use in pre-Oracle8 versions. In Oracle8, simply setting the initialization parameter PARALLEL_SERVER to TRUE starts the instance in parallel server (shared) mode. PARALLEL is obsolete in Oracle8. It cannot be used with EXCLUSIVE or NOMOUNT or if the INIT.ORA parameter SINGLE_PROCESS is set to TRUE. The SHARED parameter is also obsolete in Oracle8.
   f. STARTUP OPEN dbname EXCLUSIVE
      This command is functionally identical to (a) above. Cannot be specified if PARALLEL or NOMOUNT is also specified in pre-Oracle8 versions. EXCLUSIVE is obsolete in Oracle8. If PARALLEL_SERVE is FALSE, the database defaults to EXCLUSIVE.
   g. The FORCE parameter can be used with any of the above options to force a shutdown and restart of the database into that mode. This is not normally done and is only used for debugging and testing.
   h. The RECOVER option can be used to immediately start recovery of the database on startup if desired.

Errors that can occur during a startup include missing files, improperly specified PFILE path or name, or corrupted file errors. If these occur, the database will immediately shut down. Using OEM (Oracle Enterprise Manager) you must log in as an account that has been assigned the SYSOPER or SYSDBA roles in order to start up or shut down an instance.

Shutdown The databases should be shut down before system shutdowns, before full backups and any time system operations require it to be shut down.

VAX Shutdown The VAX shutdown script is generally located in the SYS$MANAGER directory in a file named SYSHUTDOWN.COM. Just have the system manager add a call to the Oracle shutdown script to this file for each instance on the VAX node being shut down. The Oracle shutdown script is located in the ORA_INSTANCE location for VMS and will be named similar to SHUTDOWN_instance.COM.

UNIX Shutdown For UNIX there are several things that need to be done to ensure shutdown occurs. The following procedure, for the HP-UX version of UNIX, demonstrates these steps.

1. Log in as root.
2. Edit the /etc/oratab file. Make the last field a Y for the $ORACLE_SID you want shut down.
3. Add the following entry to your /etc/shutdown file. Be sure to use full path to the dbshut utility.

```
su - oracle_owner -c /usr/oracle/bin/dbshut
```

You should alter the shutdown scripts to do a SHUTDOWN IMMEDIATE. This allows IO operations to complete and then shuts down the database. If a normal SHUTDOWN is performed, the system politely waits for all users to log off of Oracle . . . if Joe is on vacation and left his terminal up in a form, you could have a long wait. The other shutdown, SHUTDOWN ABORT, should only be used for emergencies as it stops the database just as it is, with operations pending or not. A SHUTDOWN ABORT will require a recovery on startup.

The above provides for automatic shutdown when the operating system shuts down. For a normal shutdown, execute the dbshut procedure for UNIX, the SHUTDOWN_sid.COM procedure for VMS, where the sid is the SID for the database you want to shut down.

To perform a manual shutdown on either system, perform the following procedure.

1. Log in to SVRMGR as INTERNAL.
2. Issue the appropriate SHUTDOWN command.
   a. No option means SHUTDOWN NORMAL—The database waits for all users to disconnect, prohibits new connects, then closes and dismounts the database, then shuts down the instance.
   b. SHUTDOWN IMMEDIATE—Cancels current calls like a system interrupt, and closes and dismounts the database, then shuts down the instance. PMON gracefully shuts down the user processes. No instance recovery is required on startup.
   c. SHUTDOWN ABORT—This doesn't wait for anything. It shuts the database down now. Instance recovery will probably be required on startup. You should escalate to this by trying the other shutdowns first.

Killing Oracle User Processes

There are a number of reasons to kill Oracle user processes. By killing Oracle processes I mean killing nonessential database processes. These nonessential database processes usually consist of terminal sessions that are left connected after real work is accomplished. These active sessions result in problems when the database has to be shut down for either backup or maintenance operations. As long as there is an active session, a normal mode shutdown will hang. Coming in on Monday to discover that the database couldn't shut down, and thus couldn't be backed up, is a frustrating experience. Oracle has provided the immediate shutdown mode but this isn't always reliable and in some situations can result in an inconsistent backup. The abort shutdown option will shut down the database, but, you then have to restart and perform a normal shutdown before any backup operations or risk an inconsistent backup. Therefore it is important for the DBA to know how to kill these processes before operations of this type are accomplished.

Methods of Murder Other than the aforementioned abort option for the shutdown command, which after all is rather rude, what are the methods of killing these recalcitrant sessions? Essentially, you can issue an ALTER SYSTEM KILL SESSION or you can issue a manual process kill command such as the UNIX 'kill -9 pid' from the operating system side. You should do one or the other of these types of kill operation, but not both. If you kill both the Oracle process and the operating system process it can result in database hang situations where you will have to perform a shutdown abort.

Killing From the Oracle Side The DBA can either issue a series of ALTER SYSTEM commands manually or develop a dynamic SQL script to perform the operation for him or her. Source 2.3 shows a PL/SQL procedure to perform a kill of a process using the dynamic SQL package of procedures; DBMS_SQL.

SOURCE 2.3   kill_session procedure code.

```
CREATE OR REPLACE PROCEDURE kill_session ( session_id in varchar2,
serial_num in varchar2)
AS
cur INTEGER;
ret INTEGER;
string VARCHAR2(100);
BEGIN
 string :=
         'ALTER SYSTEM KILL SESSION
'||''''||session_id||','||serial_num||'''';
   cur := dbms_sql.open_cursor;
   dbms_sql.parse(cur,string,dbms_sql.v7);
   ret := dbms_sql.execute(cur)  ;
   dbms_sql.close_cursor(cur);
```

```
EXCEPTION
   WHEN OTHERS THEN
       raise_application_error(-20001,'Error in execution',TRUE);
       IF dbms_sql.is_open(cur) THEN
         dbms_sql.close_cursor(cur);
       END IF;
END;
/
```

Using the procedure from Source 2.3 the DBA can then create a quick SQL procedure to remove the nonrequired Oracle sessions from the Oracle side. An example of this procedure is shown in Source 2.4 An example of the output from ora_kill.sql (kill_all.sql) is shown in Listing 2.2.

SOURCE 2.4   ORA_KILL.SQL procedure for killing nonessential Oracle sessions.

```
REM
REM ORA_KILL.SQL
REM FUNCTION: Kills non-essential Oracle sessions (those that aren't owned
REM          : by SYS or "NULL"
REM DEPENDANCIES: Depends on kill_session procedure
REM MRA 9/12/96
REM
SET HEADING OFF TERMOUT OFF VERIFY OFF ECHO OFF
SPOOL kill_all.sql
SELECT 'EXECUTE kill_session('||chr(39)||sid||chr(39)||','||
chr(39)||serial#||chr(39)||');' FROM v$session
WHERE username IS NOT NULL
OR username <> 'SYS'
/
SPOOL OFF
START kill_all.sql
```

LISTING 2.4   Example kill.sql script (output from ora_kill.sql).

```
EXECUTE kill_session('10','212');
EXECUTE kill_session('13','1424');
```

Once a session is killed, its status in the V$SESSION view goes to "KILLED" and users will receive an error if they try to reactivate the session. The session entry will not be removed until the user attempts to reconnect. Shutdown immediate and shutdown normal are supposed to be able to handle killed sessions properly but there have been some reports of problems up to version 7.3.2 on some platforms.

Killing From the Operating System Side The other method of removing these unwanted sessions is to kill them from the operating system side. In UNIX environments this is accomplished with the "kill -9' command executed from a privileged user. In other operating systems there are similar commands. Source 2.5 shows a UNIX shell command script that will remove the nonessential Oracle sessions for all currently active Oracle databases on the UNIX server.

The ora_kill.sh script in Source 2.5 employs a technique used in the dbshut and dbstart shell scripts. This technique uses the /etc/oratab file to determine what databases should be operating. An alternative to using the oratab file would be to do "ps -ef | grep smon" redirecting output into a file and using awk to strip out the SID names (similar to the technique used below). Each operating instance will have one "smon" process, so this makes a logical string value to grep out of the "ps -ef" process list.

Killing the sessions from the operating system side will remove their entries from the V$SESSION view. An example of the output from ora_kill.sh (kill.lis) is shown in Listing 2.5.

SOURCE 2.5   Shell script to kill nonessential Oracle processes from the server side.

```
#!/bin/ksh
ORATAB=/etc/oratab
trap 'exit' 1 2 3
# Set path if path not set (if called from /etc/rc)
case $PATH in
    "")     PATH=/bin:/usr/bin:/etc
    export PATH ;;
esac
rm kill.lis
rm proc.lis
touch kill.lis
touch proc.lis
#
# Loop for every entry in oratab
#
cat $ORATAB | while read LINE
do
    case $LINE in
     \#*)             ;;      #comment-line in oratab
     *)
     ORACLE_SID='echo $LINE | awk -F: '{print $1}' -'
    if [ "$ORACLE_SID" = '*' ] ; then
         ORACLE_SID=""
    fi
     esac
```

```
      if [ "$ORACLE_SID" <> '*' ] ; then

          proc_name='oracle'$ORACLE_SID
          ps -ef|grep $proc_name>>proc.lis
      fi
done
cat proc.lis | while read LINE2
do
     command='echo $LINE2 | awk -F: 'BEGIN { FS = ",[ \t]*|[ \t]+" }
                          { print $2}' -'
        test_it='echo $LINE2 | awk -F: 'BEGIN { FS = ",[ \t]*|[ \t]+" }
                          { print $8}' -'
     if [ "$test_it" <> 'grep' ] ; then
          command='kill -9 '$command
          echo $command>>kill.lis
     fi
done
rm proc.lis
chmod 755 kill.lis
kill.lis
rm kill.lis
```

LISTING 2.5   Example output from the ora_kill.sh script (kill.lis).

```
kill -9 11240
kill -9 11244
kill -9 11248
kill -9 11252
kill -9 11256
kill -9 9023
kill -9 9025
kill -9 9028
kill -9 9030
```

It may be required to terminate nonessential Oracle sessions if these sessions are "abandoned" by their users, or a shutdown must be accomplished regardless of database activity. This termination can be accomplished with one of three methods: a shutdown with the abort option, use of the ALTER SYSTEM kill option, or use of the operating system process killer.

Database Deletion

Databases are deleted by shutting them down and then removing all of their associated files from the system. There is no command to perform this provided by Oracle.

There are several files that contain data concerning the database and the instance. If deletion is required of both, it is suggested that a VMS "SEARCH" command, or a UNIX "grep" or "find" command, be used to locate the files that contain the instance or database name. The name and related data must be removed from these files, or the files deleted, if the user wishes to reuse the instance name. Generally the files on UNIX are related to SQLNET, such as the tnsnames.ora, sqlnet.ora, listener.ora, and tnsnames.ora files, and of course the oratab file. In many cases the files will be either in the /etc directory or will be located (in the case of the network files) in $ORACLE_HOME/netword/admin. If only the database needs to be deleted and then recreated, edit the CREATE script and rerun it under SVRMGR with the database shut down. This will reinitialize the database.

Changing the "dbname" for a Database

1. At the operating system command line enter:

```
% svrmgrl
```

2. Once the server manager command line appears, enter:

```
connect internal
```

3. When the server manager indicates that you are connected, enter the command:

```
alter database backup controlfile to trace resetlogs;
```

This will write in a trace file, the "CREATE CONTROLFILE" command that would recreate the control file as it currently exists. This trace file will be located in the user_dump_dest location specified in the v$parameter table.

4. Exit and go to the directory where your trace files are located. They are usually in the $ORACLE_HOME/rdbms/log directory if you haven't explicitly set the location in your initialization file. If user_dump_dest is set in the init<SID>.ora, then go to the directory listed in the user_dump_dest variable. The trace file will have the form "ora_NNNN.trc with NNNN being a number that will correspond (either in decimal or hexadecimal) to your system process id.

5. Get the "CREATE CONTROLFILE" command from the trace file and put it in a new file called something like crt_cf.sql.

6. Edit the "crt_cf.sql" file and modify the "CREATE CONTROLFILE" command. Change the word "REUSE" to "SET",and "NORESETLOGS" to "RESETLOGS", and modify the "dbname".

Old line:

```
CREATE CONTROLFILE REUSE DATABASE "old_name" NORESETLOGS ...
```

New line:

```
CREATE CONTROLFILE set DATABASE "new_name"  RESETLOGS ...
```

Then save the "crt_cf.sql" file.

7. Rename the old control files for backup purposes and so they are not in the way of creating the new ones.
8. Edit initSID.ora so that db_name="new_name".
9. At the operating system prompt type:

```
% svrmgrl
```

10. Once the server manager prompt appears, enter:

```
connect internal
```

11. Once you are connected as INTERNAL enter:

```
startup nomount
```

12. Type:

```
@crt_cf
```

13. Once the file stops executing, enter:

```
alter database open;
```

14. Verify that the database is functional, and you can check that the database name has been reset with the command:

```
select name from v$database;
```

15. Shut down and back up the database.

Other Database Administration Tasks

Let's look at some of the other operations that may need to be performed against a database.

Addition of Log Groups and Log Member Files The number of redo logs is directly related to the number, size, and length of transactions that are performed in the database. Each transaction that alters the database is recorded in the redo log files. The size of redo logs is governed by the amount of data a database can afford to lose. If a database supports noncritical data, where loss of a few hours' worth of data is not important, then very large redo logs can be used. In a database where each piece of data is critical and loss of even minuscule portions of data could be catastrophic, then a very small redo log is in order. If you have larger redo logs, fewer are needed; if you have small redo logs, many may be needed. Under Oracle7, two groups of at least one redo log each are required; again, three are suggested. Having multiple group members allows shadowing of log files on multiple drives, thus making redo-log-loss-type failures almost impossible.

Under Oracle7 and Oracle8, redo logs are members of groups, each group should be located on a separate drive, and each group can be associated with a single thread of the multithread server. In addition, Oracle7 allows redo log mirroring, where a redo log can be simultaneously copied to two disks at the same time by the LGWR process. This ensures that loss of a group of log files will not affect operation. Groups are archived together. The MAXLOGMEMBERS parameter in the create database statement determines the maximum number of redo logs in a group. The MAXLOGFILES parameter in the create database statement determines the maximum number of groups.

Another factor is whether or not you are using archive logging. While a redo log (or log group) is being archived, it cannot be used. If a log switch goes to a redo log (or log group) that is being archived, the database stops. This is why three is the minimum number of logs or log groups recommended for an archive situation: one in-use, one waiting to be used, and one archiving. Generally, it is suggested that several be available for use. In several installations where the logs were archived to disk, during heavy-use periods the disk filled, causing archiving to be suspended. Once the available logs filled, the database stopped.

With multiple logs or log groups, you can have time to respond to this type of situation before the database has to be stopped. This also points out that you should keep a close eye on disk space usage for your archive destination. If the redo logs or groups are archived to tape, ensure the log sizes are such that an equal number will fit on a standard tape to avoid wasting space and time. For example, if you have redo logs that are 1 megabyte in size on a version 6 database, and your tape is 90 megabytes' capacity, then 90 will fit on the tape (approximately) with little wastage. For Oracle7 the entire group is archived as a unit with a size equal to that of one of the members.

After operating for a while, DBAs get a feel for how often their databases generate logs. This will tell them how many they will require and what size they will need to be. Unfortunately there is no convenient formula for determining this; each DBA must determine this for his or her own database(s). To add a redo log, the following command is used:

```
ALTER DATABASE database name
ADD LOGFILE  THREAD y GROUP n (file specification, file specification) SIZE x;
```

or:

```
ALTER DATABASE database name
ADD LOGFILE  MEMBER 'file specification'  REUSE TO GROUP n;
```

or:

```
ALTER DATABASE database name
     ADD LOGFILE  MEMBER 'file specification'  REUSE TO
          ('file specification', 'file specification');
```

where:

n is the group number. If the GROUP n clause is left out, a new group will be added that consists of the specified log files.

x is the size for all members of the group.

y is the tread number to which the group is assigned.

file specification is a system-specific full path file name:

UNIX:

```
'/etc/usr/ora_redo1.rdo'  SIZE 1M REUSE
```

(For Oracle7 the size parameter is not with the file specification.)

VMS:

```
'DUA1:[M_ORACLE_1.DB_EXAMPLE]ORA_REDO1.RDO' SIZE 1M
     REUSE
```

The SIZE clause specifies the size of the new log (it should be the same size as all of the other redo logs). M means megabytes, K is kilobytes, and no specification, just a number, means bytes. REUSE tells Oracle if the file exists, reuse it.

Dropping Log Files   The alter command is also used to drop redo logs:

```
ALTER DATABASE database name
    DROP LOGFILE   GROUP n —OR—('filename', 'filename');
```

or:

```
ALTER DATABASE database name
    DROP LOGFILE  MEMBER 'filename';
```

where 'filename' is just the file name, no SIZE or REUSE clause.

Addition of Rollback Segments   Another database structure is the ROLLBACK segment. ROLLBACK segments can be placed in any tablespace, but it is suggested that they be placed in a tablespace that only contains other rollback segments. This makes administration easier. Rollback segments can be PUBLIC, which means that for a multi-instance database, any instance can use the rollback segment, or PRIVATE, which means only the instance which has the rollback segments named in the ROLLBACK SEGMENTS clause of its INIT.ORA file can use the rollback segment. Rollback segments are created using the CREATE command. The format for this command follows.

```
CREATE [PUBLIC] ROLLBACK SEGMENT rollback name
    TABLESPACE tablespace name
    STORAGE storage clause;
```

where:

Rollback name is the name for the rollback segment; this name must be unique.

Tablespace name is the name of the tablespace where the segment is to be created.

Storage clause specifies the required storage parameters for the rollback segment. It is strongly suggested that the following guidelines be used:

> **INITIAL = NEXT**
>
> **MINEXTENTS = 2** (default on CREATE ROLLBACK)
>
> **MAXEXTENTS** is a calculated maximum based on size of the rollback segment tablespace, size of rollback segments extents, and number of rollback segments.
>
> **OPTIMAL**—This parameter reflects the size that the system will restore the rollback segment to after it has been extended by a large transaction.

When a rollback segment is created it is not on-line. To be used, it must be brought on-line using the ALTER ROLLBACK SEGMENT name ONLINE; command, or, the database must be shut down, the INIT.ORA parameter ROLLBACK_SEGMENTS modified, and the database restarted. In any case, the INIT.ORA file parameter should be altered if the rollback segment is to be used permanently or else it will not be acquired when the database is shut down and restarted.

Altering a Rollback Segment The rollback segment can be altered using the ALTER command. However, this can result in mismatched extent sizes and is not recommended. You cannot alter a rollback segment from public to private or private to public; it must be dropped and recreated for this type of change. The format of the command follows.

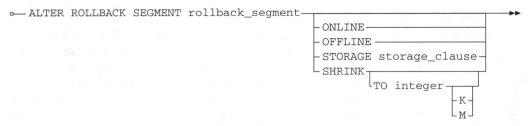

where:

ONLINE brings the rollback segment on-line.

OFFLINE takes the rollbacks segment off-line (after any transactions it has are completed).

STORAGE—Storage clause cannot contain new values for INITIAL, MINEXTENTS, or PCTINCREASE (which is not allowed for rollback segments).

Dropping a Rollback Segment Periodically it will be required that the DBA drop a rollback segment. This is required when the rollback segment has overextended due to a large transaction, has too many extents in general, or a larger size is desired for all rollback segments. This is accomplished through the DROP command. The format of this command follows.

```
o── DROP ──┬────────┬── ROLLBACK SEGMENT rollback name ──────────►►
           └─PUBLIC─┘
```

A rollback segment must not be in use or on-line, or it cannot be dropped. Once dropped, it must be removed from the INIT.ORA - ROLLBACK SEGMENT clause or the database cannot be restarted.

Moving Database Files Periodically, DBAs will need to move database files, such as the SYSTEM tablespace datafiles or redo logs, from one location to another. This is accomplished through the following procedure:

1. Shut down the database.
2. Use the operating system to copy the file(s) to their new location. (On UNIX, don't move them with the mv command; use cp or dd.)
3. Using SVRMGR, issue the CONNECT INTERNAL command to connect to the database.
4. Using SVRMGR, MOUNT the database, but don't OPEN it.
5. Issue the ALTER DATABASE command to rename the file.

```
ALTER DATABASE database name
    RENAME DATAFILE 'OLD FILE NAME' TO 'NEW FILE NAME';
```

6. Shut down and restart the database.
7. Use SVRMGR or SQLPLUS to look at the view DBA_DATA_FILES to be sure the file is renamed.
8. Delete the old file via the appropriate operating system command. (Be sure the database is started before you delete the file; if the database is running it will prevent you from deleting files that are still active on VMS and NT. On UNIX use the "fuser" command against the file to see if it is active.)

2.4   USE OF THE ALTER SYSTEM COMMAND

The ALTER SYSTEM command is used to dynamically alter the Oracle instance under an Oracle7 or Oracle8 database. The ALTER SYSTEM command allows the following system-level items to be modified:

Resource limits.

Create or terminate shared server or dispatcher processes.

Switch redo log groups.

Perform a checkpoint.

Verify datafile access.

Restrict login to users with RESTRICTED SESSION privilege (replaces DBA mode).

Perform distributed recovery in single process environment.

Disable distributed recovery.

Manually archive redo logs or enable or disable automatic archiving.

Clear the shared pool in the SGA.

Terminate a session.

The ALTER SYSTEM command allows the DBA much greater control over the Oracle environment than was possible in previous releases.

ALTER SYSTEM Command Format

The ALTER SYSTEM command's format follows.

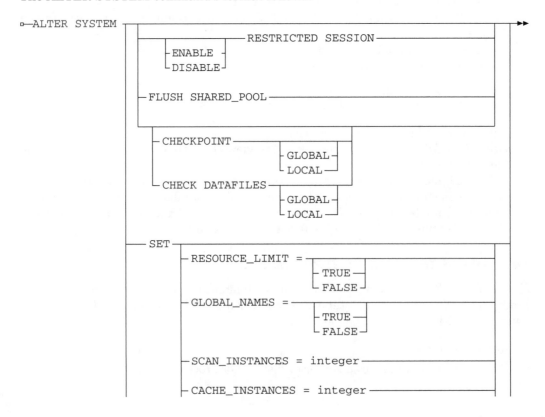

```
          ┌─ MTS_SERVERS = integer ──────────────────────────────┐
          │                                          ┌─OPTIONS─┐  │
          ├─ MTS_DISPATCHERS = '(protocol = protocol)┴─────────┴─,┤
          │                    (ADDRESS = address                 │
          │                     DESCRIPTION = description)         │
          ├─ LICENSE_MAX_SESSIONS = integer ─────────────────────┤
          │                                                       │
          ├─ LICENSE_SESSIONS_WARNING = integer ─────────────────┤
          │                                                       │
          ├─ LICENSE_MAX_USERS = integer ────────────────────────┤
          │                                                       │
          └─ REMOTE_DEPENDENCIES_MODE = ──────┬──────────────────┤
                                              ├─ TIMESTAMP ─┤
                                              └─ SIGNATURE ─┘
└─ SWITCH LOGFILE ──────────────────────────────────────────────┐
  ──────────────┬───────── DISTRIBUTED RECOVERY ────────────────
     ┌─ ENABLE ─┤
     └─ DISABLE ┘
┌─ ARCHIVE LOG archive_log-clause ──────────────────────────────┐
│                                                                │
├─ KILL SESSION 'integer1, integer2' ───────────────────────────┤
│                                                                │
├─ DISCONNECT SESSION  'integer1, integer2' POST_TRANSACTION ────┤
│                                                                │
├─ ALLOW_PARTIAL_SN_RESULTS = ──┬───────────────────────────────┤
│                               ├─ TRUE ──┤
│                               └─ FALSE ─┘
│                                                                │
├─ BACKUP_DISK_10_SLAVES = integer ──── DEFERRED ────────────────┤
│                                                                │
├─ BACKUP_TAPE_10_SLAVES = ──┬──────────── DEFERRED ─────────────┤
│                            ├─ TRUE ──┤
│                            └─ FALSE ─┘
│                                                                │
├─ CONTROLFILE_RECORD_KEEP_TIME = integer ─── DEFERRED ──────────┤
│                                                                │
├─ DB_BLOCK_CHECKPOINT_BATCH = integer ─────────────────────────┤
│                                                                │
├─ DB_BLOCK_CHECKSUM = ──┬───────────────────────────────────────┤
│                        ├─ TRUE ──┤
│                        └─ FALSE ─┘
│                                                                │
├─ DB_BLOCK_MAX_DIRTY_TARGET = integer ─────────────────────────┤
```

```
─ DB_FILE_MULTIBLOCK_READ_COUNT = integer ──────────────────────────────

─ FIXED_DATE = ' ┬ DD_MM_YY ─────────────────────── ' ──
                └ YYY_MM_DD_HH24_MI_SS ────────────┘

─ FREEZE_DB_FOR_FAST_INSTANCE_RECOVERY = ┬───────────────────────────
                                         │           ┌ DEFERRED ┐
                                         ├ TRUE ─┤
                                         └ FALSE ┘

─ GC_DEFER_TIME = integer ──────────────────────────────────────────

─ HASH_MULTI_BLOCK_10_COUNT = integer ──────────────────────────────

─ LOG_ARCHIVE_DUPLEX_DEST = 'text' ─────────────────────────────────

─ LOG_ARCHIVE_MIN_SUCCEED_DEST = integer ───────────────────────────

─ LOG_CHECKPOINT_INTERNAL = integer ────────────────────────────────

└ LOG_CHECKPOINT_TIMEOUT = integer ─────────────────────────────────


─ LOG_SMALL_ENTRY_MAX_SIZE = integer ───────────────────────────────

                                               ┌ DEFERRED ┐
─ MAX_DUMP_FILE_SIZE = ┬──────────────────────┤
                       ├ SIZE ─────────┐
                       └ 'UNLIMITED' ─┘

                                                   ┌ DEFERRED ┐
─ OBJECT_CACHE_MAX_SIZE_PERCENT = integer ─────────┤

                                                 ┌ DEFERRED ┐
─ OBJECT_CACHE_OPTIMAL_SIZE = integer ───────────┤

─ OPS_ADMIN_GROUP = 'text' ─────────────────────────────────────────

─ PARALLEL_INSTANCE_GROUP = 'text' ─────────────────────────────────

─ PARALLEL_TRANSACTION_RESOURCE_TIMEOUT = integer ──────────────────

                                              ┌ DEFERRED ┐
─ PLSQL_VZ_COMPATIBILITY ┬────────────────────┤
                         ├ TRUE ─┐
                         └ FALSE ┘

                                       ┌ DEFERRED ┐
─ SORT_AREA_SIZE = integer ────────────┤
```

```
                                                    ┌─DEFERRED─┐
─SORT_AREA_RETAINED_SIZE = integer──────────────────┴──────────┴──────

                                          ┌─DEFERRED─┐
─SORT_DIRECT_WRITES =─┬─TRUE──┬───────────┴──────────┴────────────────
                      ├─AUTO──┤
                      └─FALSE─┘

                                   ┌─DEFERRED─┐
─SORT_READ_TAC = integer───────────┴──────────┴──────────────────────

                                      ┌─DEFERRED─┐
─SORT_WRITE_BUFFERS = integer─────────┴──────────┴───────────────────

                                           ┌─DEFERRED─┐
─SORT_WRITE_BUFFER_SIZE = integer──────────┴──────────┴──────────────

                              ┌─DEFERRED─┐
─SPIN_count = integer─────────┴──────────┴───────────────────────────
```

```
                             ┌─DEFERRED─┐
─TEXT ENABLE >───────────────┴──────────┴────────────────────────────
             ├─TRUE──┤
             └─FALSE─┘

─TIME STATISTICS =───────────────────────────────────────────────────
                   ├─TRUE──┤
                   └─FALSE─┘

─TIMED_OS_STATISTICS = integer───────────────────────────────────────

                                  ┌─DEFERRED─┐
─TRANSACTIONAL AUDITING =─────────┴──────────┴───────────────────────
                          ├─TRUE──┤
                          └─FALSE─┘

─USER_DUMP DEST = 'dir_name'─────────────────────────────────────────
```

```
┌(───────────────────────────────────────────────────────────────)┐

─DISPATCHERS = integer───────────────────────────────────────────

─SESSIONS = integer──────────────────────────────────────────────

─CONNECTIONS = integer───────────────────────────────────────────

─TICKS = seconds─────────────────────────────────────────────────
```

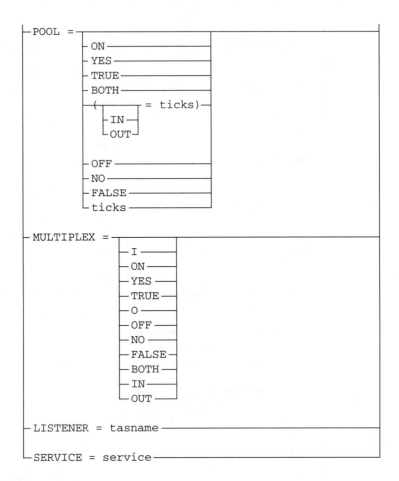

where:

RESOURCE_LIMIT—This either enables (TRUE) or disables (FALSE) the use of resource limits.

GLOBAL_NAMES—This either enables (TRUE) or disables (FALSE) the use of global names in database links.

MTS_SERVERS—The n specifies the number of shared server process to enable, up to the value of the MAX_SERVERS parameter.

MTS_DISPATCHERS—The protocol specifies the network protocol for the dispatcher(s), then specifies the number of dispatchers for the specified protocols up to the value of MAX_DISPATCHERS (as a sum of all dispatchers under all protocols).

SWITCH LOGFILE—This switches the active log file groups.

CHECKPOINT—This performs either a GLOBAL (all open instances on the database) or LOCAL (current instance) checkpoint.

CHECK DATAFILES—This verifies access to data files. If GLOBAL is specified, all data files in all instances accessing the database are verified accessible. If LOCAL is specified only the current instance's data files are verified.

ENABLE RESTRICTED SESSION—This only allows users with RESTRICTED SESSION privilege to log on to the database.

DISABLE RESTRICTED SESSION—This allows any user to log on to the instance.

ENABLE RESTRICTED RECOVERY—This enables distributed recovery.

DISABLE RESTRICTED RECOVERY—This disables distributed recovery.

ARCHIVE LOG—Manually archives redo log files or enables or disables automatic archiving depending on the clause specified.

ARCHIVE LOG clauses:

```
THREAD n
  [SEQ n] [TO 'location']
  [CHANGE n] [TO 'location']
  [CURRENT] [TO 'location']
  [GROUP n] [TO 'location']
  [LOGFILE 'filename'] [TO 'location']
  [NEXT] [TO 'location']
  [ALL] [TO 'location']
  [START] [TO 'location']
  [STOP]
```

A Detailed Look at ARCHIVE LOG Clauses

For Oracle7 the command is removed from SQLDBA and SVRMGR (except for the pull-down display) and is placed under the ALTER SYSTEM command (shown above). The new command has additional clauses to handle the more complex archive log scheme under Oracle7 and Oracle8. The new syntax handles the threads and groups associated with the new archive logs. The new syntax follows.

```
ALTER SYSTEM ARCHIVE LOG clause;

ARCHIVE LOG clauses:
      THREAD n
        [SEQ n] [TO 'location']
        [CHANGE n] [TO 'location']
        [CURRENT] [TO 'location']
        [GROUP n] [TO 'location']
        [LOGFILE 'filename'] [TO 'location']
        [NEXT] [TO 'location']
        [ALL] [TO 'location']
        [START] [TO 'location']
        [STOP]
```

where:

THREAD—This specifies the particular redo log thread to affect. If this isn't specified then the current instance redo log thread is affected.

SEQ—This archives the redo log group that corresponds to the integer specified by the integer given as the argument.

CHANGE—This corresponds to the SCN (system *change* number) for the transaction you want to archive. It will force archival of the log containing the transaction with the SCN that matches the integer given as the argument to the CHANGE argument.

GROUP—This manually archives the redo logs in the specified group. If both THREAD and GROUP are specified, the group must belong to the specified thread.

CURRENT—This causes all nonarchived redo log members of the current group to be archived.

LOGFILE—This manually archives the group that contains the file specified by 'filespec'. If thread is specified the file must be in a group contained in the thread specified.

NEXT—This forces manual archival of the next on-line redo log that requires it. If no thread is specified, Oracle archives the earliest available unarchived redo log.

ALL—This archives all on-line archive logs that are part of the current thread that haven't been archived. If no thread is specified then all unarchived logs from all threads are archived.

START—Starts automatic archiving of redo log file groups. This only applies to thread assigned to the current instance.

TO—This specifies the location to archive the logs to. This must be a full path specification.

STOP—This disables automatic archiving of redo file log groups. This applies to your current instance.

2.5   THE INIT<sid>.ORA (INITIALIZATION FILE) PARAMETERS

It should be obvious that the most important file regarding database setup and operation is probably the INIT<sid>.ORA, or initialization file. This file contains the assignments for the database initialization parameters.

For Oracle7, version 7.3, there are 154 initialization parameters, for Oracle8, version 8.0.2, there are 184. Table 2.1 is a list of the Oracle7 and Oracle8 INIT.ORA parameters, their default values, and descriptions.

TABLE 2.1   Oracle7 and Oracle8 initialization parameters.

NAME	VALUE	DESCRIPTION
spin_count	2000	Amount to spin waiting for a latch
processes	50	user processes
sessions	60	user and system sessions
timed_statistics	FALSE	maintain internal timing statistics
timed_os_statistics*	off	maintain internal os statistics
resource_limit	FALSE	master switch for resource limit
license_max_sessions	0	maximum number of non-system user sessions allowed
license_sessions_warning	0	warning level for number of non-system user sessions
lm_procs*	72	number of client processes configured for the lock manager
lm_ress*	6000	number of resources configured for the lock manager
lm_locks*	12000	number of locks configured for the lock manager
parallel_transaction_resource_timeout*	300	global parallel transaction resource deadlock timeout in seconds
cpu_count	1	number of cpu's for this instance
instance_groups*		list of instance group names
event		debug event control - default null string
shared_pool_size	6500000	size in bytes of shared pool
shared_pool_reserved_size	325000	size in bytes of reserved area of shared pool
shared_pool_reserved_min_alloc	5K	minimum allocation size in bytes for reserved area of shared pool
large_pool_size*	0	size in bytes of the large allocation pool
large_pool_min_alloc*	16K	minimum allocation size in bytes for the large allocation pool

continued

TABLE 2.1   (Continued)

NAME	VALUE	DESCRIPTION
pre_page_sga	FALSE	pre-page sga for process
lock_name_space*		lock name space used for generating lock names for standby/clone
enqueue_resources	155	resources for enqueues
nls_language	AMERICAN	NLS language name
nls_territory	AMERICA	NLS territory name
nls_sort		NLS linguistic definition name
nls_date_language		NLS date language name
nls_date_format		NLS Oracle date format
nls_currency		NLS local currency symbol
nls_numeric_characters		NLS numeric characters
nls_iso_currency		NLS ISO currency territory name
disk_asynch_io	TRUE	Use asynch I/O for random access devices
tape_asynch_io*	TRUE	Use asynch I/O requests for tape devices
dbwr_io_slaves*	0	DBWR I/O slaves
lgwr_io_slaves*	0	LGWR I/O slaves
arch_io_slaves*	0	ARCH I/O slaves
backup_io_slaves*	0	BACKUP I/O slaves
io_min_servers*	2	minimum IO slaves per instance
control_files		control file names list
db_file_name_convert		datafile name convert pattern and
db_file_standby_name_convert V7)		string for standby/clone database
log_file_name_convert		logfile name convert pattern and
(log_file_standby_name_convert V7)		string for standby/clone database
db_block_buffers	200	Number of database blocks cached in memory
db_block_checksum	FALSE	store checksum in db blocks and check during reads
db_block_size	2048	Size of database block in bytes
db_block_checkpoint_batch	8	Max number of blocks to checkpoint in a DB Writer IO
db_block_lru_statistics	FALSE	Maintain buffer cache LRU hits-by-position statistics (slow)

continued

TABLE 2.1   (Continued)

NAME	VALUE	DESCRIPTION
db_block_lru_extended_statistics	0	Maintain buffer cache LRU statistics for last N blocks discarded
db_block_lru_latches	1	number of lru latches
max_commit_propagation_delay	90000	Max age of new snapshot in .01 seconds
compatible	8.0.0.0	Database will be completely compatible with this software version
compatible_no_recovery		Database will be compatible unless crash or media recovery is needed
log_archive_start	FALSE	start archival process on SGA initialization
log_archive_buffers	4	Number of buffers to allocate for archiving
log_archive_buffer_size	127	Size of each archival buffer in log file blocks
log_archive_dest	%RDBMS80%\	archival destination text string
log_archive_duplex_dest*		duplex archival destination text string
log_archive_min_succeed_dest*	1	minimum number of archive destinations that must succeed
log_archive_format	ARC%S.%T	archival destination format
log_buffer	8192	redo circular buffer size
log_checkpoint_interval	10000	redo blocks checkpoint threshold
log_checkpoint_timeout	0	Maximum time interval between checkpoints in seconds
log_block_checksum	FALSE	calculate checksum for redo blocks when writing
log_small_entry_max_size	80	redo entries larger than this will acquire the redo copy latch
log_simultaneous_copies	2	number of simultaneous copies into redo buffer of copy latches
db_files	1024	max allowable # db files
db_file_simultaneous_writes	1	max simultaneous (overlaped) writes per db file

continued

TABLE 2.1   (Continued)

NAME	VALUE	DESCRIPTION
db_file_multiblock_read_count	8	db block to be read each IO
log_files	255	max allowable log files
parallel_server*	FALSE	if TRUE startup in parallel server mode
gc_lck_procs	1	number of background parallel server lock processes to start
gc_releasable_locks	0	releasable locks (DFS)
gc_rollback_locks		undo locks (DFS)
gc_files_to_locks		mapping between file numbers and hash buckets (DFS)
thread	0	Redo thread to mount
freeze_DB_for_fast_instance_recovery*	FALSE	freeze database during instance recovery
checkpoint_process	FALSE	create a separate checkpoint process
log_checkpoints_to_alert	FALSE	log checkpoint begin/end to alert file
recovery_parallelism	0	number of server processes to use for parallel recovery
control_file_record_keep_time*	7	control file record keep time in days
temporary_table_locks	60	temporary table locks
dml_locks	100	dml locks - one for each table modified in a transaction
row_locking	always	use row-locking
serializable	FALSE	serialize transactions
delayed_logging_block_cleanouts	TRUE	turn on delayed-logging block cleanouts feature
instance_number	0	instance number
spread_extents*	TRUE	should extents be spread across files in the tablespace
max_rollback_segments	30	max. number of rollback segments in SGA cache
transactions	66	max. number of concurrent active transactions
transactions_per_rollback_segment	11	number of active transactions per rollback segment
rollback_segments		undo segment list
cleanup_rollback_entries	20	no. of undo entries to apply per transaction cleanup

continued

TABLE 2.1   (Continued)

NAME	VALUE	DESCRIPTION
transaction_auditing*	TRUE	transaction auditing records generated in the redo log
discrete_transactions_enabled	FALSE	enable OLTP mode
sequence_cache_entries	10	number of sequence cache entries
sequence_cache_hash_buckets	10	number of sequence cache hash buckets
row_cache_cursors	10	number of cached cursors for row cache management
os_roles	FALSE	retrieve roles from the operating system
max_enabled_roles	20	max number of roles a user can have enabled
remote_os_authent	FALSE	allow non-secure remote clients to use auto-logon accounts
remote_os_roles	FALSE	allow non-secure remote clients to use os roles
O7_DICTIONARY_ACCESSIBILITY*	TRUE	Version 7 Dictionary Accessibility Support
remote_login_passwordfile	SHARED	password file usage parameter
dblink_encrypt_login	FALSE	enforce password for distributed login always be encrypted
license_max_users	0	maximum number of named users that can be created in the database
db_domain	WORLD	directory part of global database name stored with CREATE DATABASE
global_names	FALSE	enforce that database links have same name as remote database
distributed_lock_timeout	60	number of seconds a distributed transaction waits for a lock
distributed_transactions	16	max. number of concurrent distributed transactions
max_transaction_branches	8	max. number of branches per distributed transaction
distributed_recovery_connection_hold_time*	200	number of seconds RECO holds outbound connections open

continued

TABLE 2.1 **(Continued)**

NAME	VALUE	DESCRIPTION
commit_point_strength*	1	Bias this node has toward not preparing in a two-phase commit
mts_service*		service supported by dispatchers
mts_dispatchers		specifications of dispatchers
mts_servers*	0	number of servers to start
upmts_max_servers*	0	max number of servers
mts_max_dispatchers	0	max number of dispatchers
mts_listener_address	(address=(protocol=ipc)(key=%s))	address(es) of network listener
mts_multiple_listeners	FALSE	Are multiple listeners enabled?
open_links	4	max # open links per session
open_links_per_instance*	4	max # open links per instance
close_cached_open_cursors	FALSE	close cursors cached by PL/SQL at each commit
fixed_date		fixed SYSDATE value
audit_trail	NONE	enable system auditing
sort_area_size	655326	size of in-memory sort work area
sort_area_retained_size	0	size of in-memory sort work area retained between fetch calls
sort_direct_writes	AUTO	use direct write
sort_write_buffers	2	number of sort direct write buffers
sort_write_buffer_size	32768	size of each sort direct write buffer
sort_spacemap_size	512	size of sort disk area space map
sort_read_fac	20	multi-block read factor for sort
db_name		database name specified in CREATE DATABASE
open_cursors	50	max # cursors per process
ifile		include file in init.ora
sql_trace	FALSE	enable SQL trace
os_authent_prefix	OPS$	prefix for auto-logon accounts
optimizer_mode	CHOOSE	optimizer mode (Either RULE or CHOOSE)
sql92_security	FALSE	require select privilege for searched update/delete

continued

TABLE 2.1   (Continued)

NAME	VALUE	DESCRIPTION
blank_trimming	FALSE	blank trimming semantics parameter
always_anti_join	NESTED_LOOPS	always use this anti-join when possible
partition_view_enabled	FALSE	enable/disable partitioned views
b_tree_bitmap_plans*	FALSE	enable the use of bitmap plans for tables w. only B-tree indexes
star_transformation_enabled*	FALSE	enable the use of star transformation
serial_reuse*	DISABLE	reuse the frame segments
cursor_space_for_time	FALSE	use more memory in order to get faster execution
session_cached_cursors	0	number of cursors to save in the session cursor cache
text_enable	FALSE	enable text searching
remote_dependencies_mode	TIMESTAMP	remote-procedure-call dependencies mode parameter
utl_file_dir		utl_file accessible directories list
plsql_v2_compatibility*	FALSE	PL/SQL version 2.x compatibility flag
job_queue_processes	0	number of job queue processes to start
job_queue_interval	60	Wakeup interval in seconds for job queue processes
job_queue_keep_connections	FALSE	Keep network connections between execution of jobs
snapshot_refresh_processes	1	number of job queue processes to start
snapshot_refresh_interval	60	Wakeup interval in seconds for job queue processes
snapshot_refresh_keep_connections	FALSE	Keep network connections between execution of jobs
optimizer_percent_parallel	0	optimizer percent parallel
optimizer_search_limit	5	optimizer search limit
parallel_min_percent	0	minimum percent of threads required for parallel query
parallel_default_max_instances	0	default maximum number of instances for parallel query
cache_size_threshold	80	maximum size of table or piece to be cached (in blocks)

continued

TABLE 2.1   (Continued)

NAME	VALUE	DESCRIPTION
create_bitmap_area_size	8388608	size of create bitmap buffer for bitmap index
bitmap_merge_area_size	1048576	maximum memory allow for BITMAP MERGE
parallel_min_servers	0	minimum parallel query servers per instance
parallel_max_servers	5	maximum parallel query servers per instance
parallel_server_idle_time	5	idle time before parallel query server dies
allow_partial_sn_results*	FALSE	allow partial results when processing gv$ views
parallel_instance_group*		instance group to use for all parallel operations
ops_admin_group*		instance group to use for global v$ queries
hash_join_enabled	TRUE	enable/disable hash join
hash_area_size	0	size of in-memory hash work area
hash_multiblock_io_count	8	number of blocks hash join will read/write at once
background_dump_dest	%RDBMS80%\trace	Detached process dump directory
user_dump_dest	%RDBMS80%\trace	User process dump directory
max_dump_file_size	102400	Maximum size (blocks) of dump file
oracle_trace_enable	FALSE	Oracle TRACE instance wide enable/disable
oracle_trace_facility_path	%OTRACE80%\ADMIN\FDF\	Oracle TRACE facility path
oracle_trace_collection_path	%OTRACE80%\ADMIN\CDF\	Oracle TRACE collection path
oracle_trace_facility_name	oracled	Oracle TRACE default facility name
oracle_trace_collection_name		Oracle TRACE default collection name
oracle_trace_collection_size	5242880	Oracle TRACE collection file max. size
object_cache_optimal_size	102400	optimal size of the user session's object cache in bytes
object_cache_max_size_percent*	10	percentage of maximum size over optimal of the user session's ob
session_max_open_files*	0	maximum number of open files allowed per session
aq_tm_processes*	0	number of AQ Time Managers to start

* — New for Oracle8

The Oracle7 initialization parameters shown in Table 2.2 are invalid for use with Oracle8:

TABLE 2.2   Invalid initialization parameters for use with Oracle8.

NAME	VALUE	DESCRIPTION
gc_segments	10	# Segment headers
gc_tablespaces	5	# tablespaces
gc_rollback_segments	20	# Undo Segments
gc_db_locks	200	# DB locks (DFS)
gc_save_rollback_locks	20	# Save Undo locks in (DFS)
gc_freelist_groups	50	# freelist groups locks in (DFS)

The DBA should review the applicable administrator's and tuning guides before modifying any INIT.ORA parameters.

The Undocumented Initialization Parameters ("_*")

In addition to the Oracle-documented initialization parameters, there are varying numbers of undocumented initialization parameters in every version of Oracle. These undocumented initialization parameters are usually only used in emergencies and should only be used under the direction of a senior DBA or Oracle support. Source 2.6 shows a script for getting the undocumented initialization parameters out of an Oracle 7.2 instance and then out of a 7.3 or 8.0.2 instance.

SOURCE 2.6   **Script for documenting undocumented initialization parameters (pre-7.3 and post-7.3).**

```
REM Script for getting undocumented init.ora
REM parameters from a 7.2 instance
REM MRA - Revealnet 2/23/97
REM
COLUMN parameter FORMAT a40
COLUMN value FORMAT a30
COLUMN ksppidf HEADING 'Is|Default'
SET FEEDBACK OFF VERIFY OFF PAGES 55
START title80 'Undocumented Init.ora Parameters'
SPOOL rep_out/&db/undoc
SELECT  ksppinm "Parameter",
  ksppivl "Value",
  ksppidf
FROM x$ksppi
WHERE ksppinm LIKE '/_%' escape '/'
/
SPOOL OFF
TTITLE OFF
```

```
REM Script for getting undocumented init.ora
REM parameters from a 7.3 or 8.0.2 instance
REM MRA - Revealnet 4/23/97
REM
COLUMN parameter               FORMAT a37
COLUMN description       FORMAT a30 WORD_WRAPPED
COLUMN "Session Value"        FORMAT a10
COLUMN "Instance Value" FORMAT a10
SET LINES 100
SET PAGES 0
SPOOL undoc.lis
SELECT
     a.ksppinm  "Parameter",
     a.ksppdesc "Description",
     b.ksppstvl "Session Value",
     c.ksppstvl "Instance Value"
FROM
     x$ksppi a,
     x$ksppcv b,
     x$ksppsv c
WHERE
     a.indx = b.indx
     AND a.indx = c.indx
     AND a.ksppinm LIKE '/_%' escape '/'
/
SPOOL OFF
SET LINES 80 PAGES 20
CLEAR COLUMNS
```

The output for an Oracle 7.2 database looks like Listing 2.6.

LISTING 2.6   Undocumented initialization parameters for Oracle 7.2 not included in Oracle 7.3 and 8.0.2.

```
Date: 03/04/97
Page:   1
Time: 03:47 PM                     Undocumented Init.ora Parameters
SYS
                                      ORCNETD1 database

Is
Parameter                          Value
Default
--------------------------------------------------------------------------------
_latch_spin_count (7.3 - _spin_count)  100                              TRUE
_trace_instance_termination            FALSE                           TRUE
_wakeup_timeout                        100                             TRUE
_lgwr_async_write                      TRUE                            TRUE
```

The undocumented parameters for 7.3 are listed in Listing 2.7. Note that the descriptions for the parameters are available starting with Oracle 7.3. The undocumented parameters new for Oracle8 are shown in Listing 2.8.

LISTING 2.7   Undocumented initialization parameters for Oracle 7.3 not included in 8.0.2.

Parameter Name	Parameter Description	Default Value
_standby_lock_name_space	lock name space used for generating lock names for standby datab	
_enable_dba_locking	enable persistent locking	FALSE

LISTING 2.8   Undocumented initialization parameters for 8.0.2.

Parameter Name	Description	Default	Instance
_trace_files_public	Create publicly accessible trace files	FALSE	FALSE
_max_sleep_holding_latch	max time to sleep while holding a latch	4	4
_max_exponential_sleep	max sleep during exponential backoff	0	0
_latch_wait_posting	post sleeping processes when free latch	1	1
_latch_recovery_alignment	align latch recovery structures	80	80
_session_idle_bit_latches	one latch per session or a latch per group of sessions	0	0
_lm_dlmd_procs*	number of background lock manager daemon processes to start	1	1
_lm_xids*	number of transaction IDs configured for the lock manager	79	79
_lm_groups*	number of groups configured for the lock manager	20	20
_lm_domains*	number of groups configured for the lock manager	2	2
_lm_non_fault_tolerant*	disable lock manager fault-tolerance mode	FALSE	FALSE
_lm_statistics*	enable lock manager statistics collection	FALSE	FALSE
_single_process	run without detached processes	FALSE	FALSE
_number_cached_attributes	maximum number of cached attributes per instance	10	10
_debug_sga	debug sga	FALSE	FALSE
_test_param_1	test parameter 1	25	25
_test_param_2	test parameter 2		

_test_param_3	test parameter 3		
_messages	message queue resources - dependent on # processes & # buffers	200	200
_enqueue_locks	locks for managed enqueues	1481	1481
_enqueue_hash	enqueue hash table length	265	265
_enqueue_debug_multi_instance	debug enqueue multi instance	FALSE	FALSE
_enqueue_hash_chain_latches	enqueue hash chain latches	2	2
_trace_buffers_per_process	trace buffers per process	0	0
_trace_block_size	trace block size	2048	2048
_trace_archive_start	start trace process on SGA initialization	FALSE	FALSE
_trace_flushing	TRWR should try to keep tracing buffers clean	FALSE	FALSE
_trace_enabled	Should tracing be enabled at startup	TRUE	TRUE
_trace_events	turns on and off trace events		
_trace_archive_dest	trace archival destination	%RDBMS80%\ TRACE.DAT	%RDBMS80%\ TRACE.DAT
_trace_file_size	trace file size	10000	10000
_trace_write_batch_size	trace write batch size	32	32
_io_slaves_disabled*	Do not use I/O slaves	FALSE	FALSE
_open_files_limit*	Limit on number of files opened by I/O subsystem	4294967294	4294967294
_controlfile_enqueue_timeout	control file enqueue timeout in seconds	900	900
_db_block_cache_protect	protect database blocks (true only when debugging)	FALSE	FALSE
_db_block_hash_buckets	Number of database block hash buckets	2000	2000
_db_block_no_idle_writes	Disable periodic writes of buffers when idle	FALSE	FALSE
_db_handles	System-wide simultaneous buffer operations	420	420
_db_handles_cached	Buffer handles cached each process	3	3
_wait_for_sync	wait for sync on commit MUST BE ALWAYS TRUE	TRUE	TRUE
_db_block_max_scan_cnt	Maximum number of buffers to inspect when looking for free	0	0
_db_writer_scan_depth	Number of LRU buffers for dbwr to scan when looking for dirty	0	0
_db_writer_scan_depth_increment	Add to dbwr scan depth when dbwr is behind	0	0
_db_writer_scan_depth_decrement	Subtract from dbwr scan depth when dbwr is working too hard	0	0
_db_large_dirty_queue	Number of buffers which force dirty queue to be written	0	0
_db_block_write_batch	Number of blocks to group in each DB Writer IO	0	0
_db_block_cache_clone	Always clone data blocks on get (for debugging)	FALSE	FALSE
_db_block_cache_map*	Map / unmap and track reference counts on blocks (for debugging)	0	0

_db_block_max_cr_dba	Maximum Allowed Number of CR buffers per dba	10	10
_db_block_low_priority_batch_size*	Percentage of write batch used for low priority ckpts	20	20
_db_block_med_priority_batch_size*	Percentage of write batch used for medium priority ckpts	40	40
_db_block_med_priority_batch_size*	Percentage of write batch used for high priority ckpts	40	40
_minimum_giga_scn	Minimum SCN to start with in 2^30 units	0	0
_log_checkpoint_recovery_check	# redo blocks to verify after checkpoint	0	0
_log_io_size	automatically initiate log write if this many redo blocks in buf	0	0
_log_buffers_debug	debug redo buffers (slows things down)	FALSE	FALSE
_log_debug_multi_instance	debug redo multi instance code	FALSE	FALSE
_log_entry_prebuild_threshold	redo entries larger than this will be prebuilt before getting la	0	0
_disable_logging	Disable logging	FALSE	FALSE
_db_no_mount_lock	do not get a mount lock	FALSE	FALSE
_cr_deadtime*	global cache lock CR deadlock timeout in seconds	6	6
_gc_class_locks*	set locks for the minor classes (DFS)	0	0
_defer_pings*	if TRUE, defer pings (DFS)	FALSE	FALSE
_upconvert_from_ast*	if TRUE, attempt to up-convert from an AST (DFS)	FALSE	FALSE
_save_escalates*	if TRUE, save escalates from basts (DFS)	TRUE	TRUE
_defer_time*	how long to defer a ping (DFS)	100	100
_log_blocks_during_backup	log block images when changed during backup	TRUE	TRUE
_allow_resetlogs_corruption	allow resetlogs even if it will cause corruption	FALSE	FALSE
_corrupt_blocks_on_stuck_recovery	number of times to corrupt a block when media recovery stuck	0	0
_log_space_errors	should we report space errors to alert log	TRUE	TRUE
_bump_highwater_mark_count	how many blocks should we allocate per free list on advancing HW	0	0
_rollback_segment_initial	starting undo segment number	1	1
_rollback_segment_count	number of undo segments	0	0
_offline_rollback_segments	offline undo segment list		
_corrupted_rollback_segments	corrupted undo segment list		
_small_table_threshold	threshold level of table size for forget-bit enabled during scan	160	160
_release_insert_threshold	maximum number of unusable blocks to unlink from freelist	5	5
_walk_insert_threshold	maximum number of unusable blocks to walk across freelist	0	0

_reuse_index_loop	number of blocks being examine for index block reuse	5	5
_row_cache_instance_locks	number of row cache instance locks	100	100
_row_cache_buffer_size	size of row cache circular buffer	200	200
_kgl_multi_instance_lock	whether KGL to support multi-instance locks	TRUE	TRUE
_kgl_multi_instance_pin	whether KGL to support multi-instance pins	TRUE	TRUE
_kgl_multi_instance_invalidation	whether KGL to support multi-instance invalidations	TRUE	TRUE
_kgl_latch_count	number of library cache latches	0	0
_kgl_bucket_count	index to the bucket count array	0	0
_passwordfile_enqueue_timeout	password file enqueue timeout in seconds	900	900
_mts_load_constants	server load balancing constants (S,P,D,I)	3,0.75,0.2 5,0.1	3,0.75,0.2 5,0.1
_mts_fastpath	dispatcher network fastpath	TRUE	TRUE
_mts_listener_retry	listener connection retry rate (secs)	120	120
_all_shared_dblinks*	treat all dblinks as shared		
_init_sql_file	File containing SQL statements to execute upon database creation	%RDBMS80%\ ADMIN\SQL. BSQ	%RDBMS80%\ ADMIN\SQL. BSQ
_shared_session_sort_fetch_buffer	size of in-memory merge buffer for mts or xa fetch calls	0	0
_optimizer_undo_changes	undo changes to query optimizer	FALSE	FALSE
_sql_connect_capability_table	SQL Connect Capability Table (testing only)		
_sql_connect_capability_override	SQL Connect Capability Table Override	0	0
_always_star_transformation*	always favor use of star transformation	FALSE	FALSE
_parallel_server_sleep_time	sleep time between dequeue timeouts (in 1/100ths)	10	10
_dynamic_stats_threshold*	delay threshold (in 1/100ths) between sending statistics message	6000	6000
_parallel_min_message_pool	minimum size of shared pool memory to reserve for pq servers	64440	64440
_affinity_on*	enable/disable affinity at run time	TRUE	TRUE
_cursor_db_buffers_pinned*	additional number of buffers a cursor can pin at once	78	78
_disable_ntlog_events*	Disable logging to NT event log	FALSE	FALSE
_oracle_trace_events	Oracle TRACE event flags		
_oracle_trace_facility_version	Oracle TRACE facility version		
_no_objects*	no object features are used	FALSE	FALSE

* Indicates that this parameter is Oracle8 only.

You will note that each undocumented parameter begins with an underscore (_) character. For those of you who have been around awhile, you will also notice some of these "undocumented" parameters used to be documented. Some you may have seen used, such as "_offline_rollback_segments" (whose use I document in the backup and recovery Chapter 17); others you will never use or see used. However, you should be aware that there are more parameters than those listed in a user's manual. You may need to prompt Oracle support if you see one (such as "_corrupted_rollback_ segments") that may just be helpful in a sticky situation. Another set of parameters that may be useful are events. Let's discuss events a bit.

The Initializaion File Event Settings

The SET EVENTS command in an init<SID>.ora file have generally been placed there at the command of Oracle support to perform specific functions. Usually these alerts turn on more advanced levels of tracing and error detection than are commonly available. Source 2.7 lists some of the more common events.

SOURCE 2.7   Example uses of Oracle event codes.

```
To enable block header and trailer checking to detect corrupt blocks:
event="10210 trace name context forever, level 10"  — for tables
event="10211 trace name context forever, level 10"  — for indexes

and to go with these the undocumented parameter setting:
 _db_block_cache_protect=TRUE

Which will prevent corruption from getting to your disks (at the cost of a
database crash)

For tracing of a MAX_CURSORS exceeded error:

event="1000 trace name ERRORSTACK level 3"

To get an error stack related to a SQLNET ORA-03120 error:

event="3120 trace name error stack"

To turn on bitmapped indexes  in 7.3.2:

event="10111 trace name context forever"
event="10112 trace name context forever"
event="10114 trace name context forever"

and…set the initialization parameter COMPATIBLE to 7.3.2

To work around a space leak problem:

event="10262 trace name context forever, level 1024"
```

```
To trace memory shortages:

event="10235 trace name context forever, level 4"
event="600 trace name heapdump, level 4"

Events are also used as the SESSION level:

alter session set events '10046 trace name context forever level NN'
    where NN:
            1 - same as a regular trace
            4 - also dump bind variables
            8 - also dump wait information
            12 - dump both bind and wait information

To coalesce freespace in a tablespace pre-7.3:

alter session set events 'immediate trace name coalesce level XX'
    where XX:
                the value of ts# from ts$ table for the tablespace
```

As with the undocumented initialization parameters, these should only be used under the direction of a senior-level DBA or Oracle support.

2.6   FURTHER DBA READING

For further reading, the DBA should look at the following references.

Oracle8 Server Administrator's Guide, Release 8.0, Beta-2 (or most current release), Part No. A50648-1, Copyright © 1989, 1997, Oracle Corporation.

Oracle8 Server SQL Reference, Release 8.0, Beta-2 (or most current release), Part No. A50605-1, Copyright © 1989, 1997, Oracle Corporation.

Oracle8 Server Reference, Part No. A50665-1, Copyright © 1997, Oracle Corporation.

Oracle7 Server Administrator's Guide, Part No. 6694-70-1292, Dec. 1992, Oracle Corporation.

Oracle7 Server SQL Language Reference Manual, Part No. 778-70-1292, Dec. 1992, Oracle Corporation.

CHAPTER 3

Tablespace Administration

Tablespaces take the place of disks if we carry through with the analogy that Oracle is an operating system. Only with this disk, you, the DBA, can specify its size and how it will create and store data (via the DEFAULT STORAGE clause) in its files (tables).

3.1 TABLESPACE CREATION

Let's look at the command for creating a tablespace.

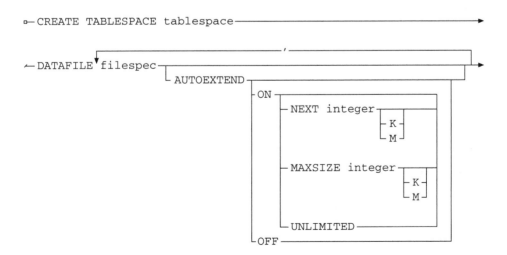

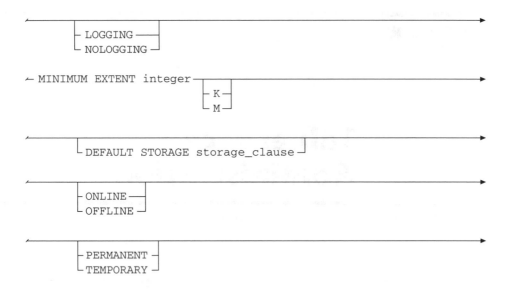

Keywords and Parameters

tablespace—The name of the tablespace to be created.

DATAFILE—Specifies the datafile or files to comprise the tablespace.

MINIMUM EXTENT integer—Controls freespace fragmentation in the tablespace by ensuring that every used and/or free extent size in a tablespace is at least as large as,and is a multiple of, integer.

AUTOEXTEND—Enables or disables the automatic extension of datafile.

OFF—Disables autoextend if it is turned on. NEXT and MAXSIZE are set to zero. Values for NEXT and MAXSIZE must be respecified in further ALTER TABLE-SPACE AUTOEXTEND commands.

ON—Enables autoextend.

NEXT—Disk space to allocate to the datafile when more extents are required.

MAXSIZE—Maximum disk space allowed for allocation to the datafile.

UNLIMITED—Set no limit on allocating disk space to the datafile.

LOGGING,NOLOGGING—Specifies the default logging attributes of all tables, index, and partitions within the tablespace. LOGGING is the default.

If NOLOGGING is specified, no undo and redo logs are generated for operations that support the NOLOGGING option on the tables, index, and partitions within the tablespace.

The tablespace-level logging attribute can be overridden by logging specifications at the table, index, and partition levels.

DEFAULT—Specifies the default storage parameters for all objects created in the tablespace.

ONLINE—Makes the tablespace available immediately after creation to users who have been granted access to the tablespace.

OFFLINE—Makes the tablespace unavailable immediately after creation. If you omit both the ONLINE and OFFLINE options, Oracle creates the tablespace on-line by default. The data dictionary view DBA_TABLESPACES indicates whether each tablespace is on-line or off-line.

PERMANENT—Specifies that the tablespace will be used to hold permanent objects. This is the default.

TEMPORARY—Specifies that the tablespace will only be used to hold temporary objects, for example, segments used by implicit sorts to handle ORDER BY clauses.

3.2   ALTERATION OF TABLESPACES

Periodically, a tablespace may need to have its default storage changed, require addition of data files to increase its storage volume, require a name change, require to be taken off-line for maintenance, need to have autoextend turned off or on, be made temporary or converted to permanent, or may require to be placed in backup status for a hot backup. The command used for all of these functions is the ALTER command. Let's look at its format.

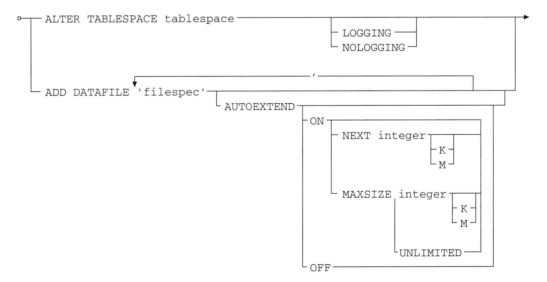

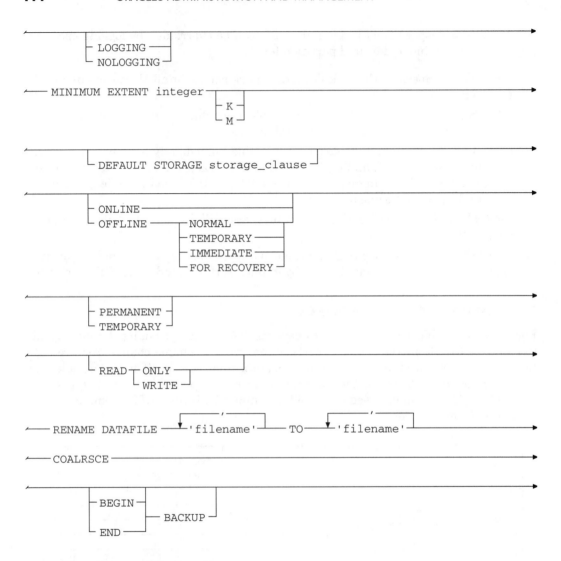

Keywords and Parameters

tablespace—The name of the tablespace to be altered.

LOGGING, NOLOGGING—Specifies that the creation and logging attributes of all tables, index, and partitions within the tablespace are logged in the redo log file. LOGGING is the default.The tablespace-level logging attribute can be over-ridden by logging specifications at the table, index, and partition levels.

When an existing tablespace logging attribute is changed by an ALTER TABLESPACE statement, all tables, indexes, and partitions created after the statement will have the new logging attribute; the logging attributes of existing objects are not changed.

If the database is run in ARCHIVELOG mode, media recovery from a backup will recreate the table (and any indices required because of constraints). When running in NOARCHIVELOG mode, all operations that can execute without logging will not generate log entries even if LOGGING is specified.

ADD DATAFILE—Adds the datafile specified by filespec to the tablespace. See the syntax description of filespec. You can add a datafile while the tablespace is on-line or off-line. Be sure that the datafile is not already in use by another database.

AUTOEXTEND—Enables or disables the autoextending of the size of the datafile in the tablespace.

OFF—Disables autoextend if it is turned on. NEXT and MAXSIZE are set to zero. Values for NEXT and MAXSIZE must be respecified in further ALTER TABLE-SPACE AUTOEXTEND commands.

ON—Enables autoextend.

NEXT—The size in bytes of the next increment of disk space to be automatically allocated to the datafile when more extents are required. You can also use K or M to specify this size in kilobytes or megabytes. The default is one data block.

MAXSIZE—Maximum disk space allowed for automatic extension of the datafile.

UNLIMITED—Set no limit on allocating disk space to the datafile.

RENAME DATAFILE—Renames one or more of the tablespace's datafile. Take the tablespace off-line before renaming the datafile. Each 'filename' must fully specify a datafile using the conventions for filenames on your operating system.

This clause only associates the tablespace with the new file rather than the old one. This clause does not actually change the name of the operating system file. You must change the name of the file through your operating system.

COALESCE—For each datafile in the tablespace, coalesce all contiguous free extents into larger contiguous extents.

TIP   COALESCE cannot be specified with any other command option.

DEFAULT STORAGE—Specifies the new default storage parameters for objects subsequently created in the tablespace. See the STORAGE clause.

MINIMUM EXTENT integer—Controls freespace fragmentation in the tablespace by ensuring that every used and/or free extent size in a tablespace is at least as large as, and is a multiple of, integer.

ONLINE—Brings the tablespace on-line.

OFFLINE—Takes the tablespace off-line and prevents further access to its segments.

NORMAL—Performs a checkpoint for all datafiles in the tablespace. All of these datafiles must be on-line. You need not perform media recovery on this tablespace before bringing it back on-line. You must use this option if the database is in noarchivelog mode.

TEMPORARY—Performs a checkpoint for all on-line datafiles in the tablespace but does not ensure that all files can be written. Any off-line files may require media recovery before you bring the tablespace back on-line.

IMMEDIATE—Does not ensure that tablespace files are available and does not perform a checkpoint. You must perform recovery on the tablespace before bringing it back on-line.

The default is NORMAL.

If you are taking a tablespace off-line for a long time, you may want to alter any users who have been assigned the tablespace as either a default or temporary tablespace to use some other tablespace for these purposes. When the tablespace is off-line, these users cannot allocate space for objects or sort areas in the tablespaces that are off-line. You can reassign users new default and temporary tablespaces with the ALTER USER command.

BEGIN BACKUP—Signifies that an on-line backup is to be performed on the datafiles that comprise this tablespace. This option does not prevent users from accessing the tablespace. You must use this option before beginning an on-line backup. You cannot use this option on a read-only tablespace.

While the backup is in progress, you cannot:

- Take the tablespace off-line normally.
- Shut down the instance.
- Begin another backup of the tablespace.

END BACKUP—Signifies that an on-line backup of the tablespace is complete. Use this option as soon as possible after completing an on-line backup. If a tablespace is left in BACKUP mode the database will think it needs recovery the next time the database is shut down and started and you may not be able to recover. You cannot use this option on a read-only tablespace.

READ ONLY—Signifies that no further write operations are allowed on the tablespace.

READ WRITE—Signifies that write operations are allowed on a previously read only tablespace.

PERMANENT—Specifies that the tablespace is to be converted from a temporary to a permanent one. A permanent tablespace is one where permanent database objects are stored. This is the default when a tablespace is created.

TEMPORARY—Specifies that the tablespace is to be converted from a permanent to a temporary one. A temporary tablespace is one where no permanent database objects can be stored.

READ ONLY | WRITE—This allows you to specify that a tablespace is read only; the normal default value is READ WRITE. A read only tablespace doesn't generate redo, rollback, or require backup (after its initial backup just after its creation).

At least one of the lines following the ALTER command must be supplied (or else why issue the command?). The definitions for most of the arguments are the same as for the CREATE command. The addition of the COALESCE clause is very welcome in that for those tablespaces SMON doesn't choose to cleanup freespace in (i.e., any with a default storage pctincrease of zero) the command option forces a scavenge of free segments. There are now three options for the OFFLINE clause: NORMAL (meaning wait for users to finish with it), TEMPORARY (which means do a checkpoint of all of its datafiles), and IMMEDIATE (which means *Now, darn it!*)

Another addition is the READ ONLY and READ WRITE options. As their name implies, READ ONLY makes a tablespace read only in nature; this means no redo will be generated as will no rollback against this tablespace, and of course, you cannot write to it. The READ WRITE is the normal mode and returns a READ ONLY to full service.

The PERMANENT and TEMPORARY do the same as in the CREATE, that is, PERMANENT means objects such as tables, indexes, and clusters can be assigned to this tablespace, while TEMPORARY means only temporary segments can be placed here.

One thing to note is the RENAME DATAFILE option. This option is used when you need to: (A) alter the name of a datafile, or (B) relocate a datafile. Option A is obvious, but B needs some explanation. The procedure for moving a datafile is:

1. Using the ALTER TABLESPACE command, take the tablespace that uses the datafile off-line.

```
ALTER TABLESPACE tablespace OFFLINE;
```

2. Using the operating system command appropriate for your system, copy the data file to the new location (don't move it in UNIX "mv", it needs to exist in both locations until renamed).

3. Using the ALTER TABLESPACE command, rename the datafile.

```
ALTER TABLESPACE tablespace
RENAME DATAFILE 'old name' TO 'new name';
```

where old and new names are full path names.

4. Using the ALTER TABLESPACE command, bring the tablespace back on-line.

```
ALTER TABLESPACE tablespace ONLINE;
```

5. Remove the extra copy of the datafile from its old location using the appropriate operating system command (rm on UNIX, DELETE on VMS).

The OFFLINE qualifiers apply to how user processes are treated as the tablespace is taken OFFLINE. NORMAL tells Oracle to wait for user processes to finish with the tablespace. IMMEDIATE tells the system to take the tablespace off-line regardless of who is using it.

When using ALTER to place a tablespace in BEGIN BACKUP, be sure that the backup procedure backs up all the redo and archive logs as well. Immediately after the backup concludes, bring the tablespace back to normal with the END BACKUP command or the redo logs will get out of sync and the file will not be recoverable should you be required to recover it due to a problem.

3.3   DELETION OF TABLESPACES

At one time or another, such as when consolidating a rollback segment tablespace, the DBA will have to remove, or drop, a tablespace from the Oracle database system. Removing tablespaces is done through the DROP command. Its format follows.

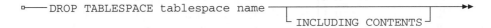

```
DROP TABLESPACE tablespace name
                                  INCLUDING CONTENTS
```

The INCLUDING CONTENTS clause is optional, but if it isn't included, the tablespace must be empty of tables or other objects. If it is included, the tablespace will be dropped regardless of its contents unless it contains an on-line rollback segment. The SYSTEM tablespace cannot be dropped.

TIP   This doesn't remove the physical data files from the system; you must use operating-system-level commands to remove the physical files.

3.4   RECREATING TABLESPACES

There may be times when the DBA has to drop and recreate tablespaces. For instance, if the physical drive that the tablespaces are on has been damaged, the DBA will have to recreate the tablespaces on another volume, or recover from a backup and apply redo logs. If the DBA has good documentation of what the database physical structure was before the incident, there is no problem. If the DBA has inherited a legacy system, or the system has grown substantially without good documentation, the DBA could have his or her hands full with rebuilding it. The script in Source 3.1 can be used to document existing tablespaces and their data files.

SOURCE 3.1   Script to create rebuild script for tablespaces.

```
REM TBSP_RCT.SQL
REM
REM FUNCTION: SCRIPT FOR CREATING TABLESPACES
REM
REM FUNCTION: This script must be run by a user with the DBA role.
REM
REM This script is intended to run with Oracle7 or 8.
REM
REM FUNCTION: Running this script will in turn create a script to build
REM           all the tablespaces in the database.  This created script,
REM           crt_tbls.sql, can be run by any user with the DBA role
REM           or with the 'CREATE TABLESPACE' system privilege.
REM
REM Only preliminary testing of this script was performed.  Be sure to
REM test it completely before relying on it.
REM
REM
SET VERIFY OFF TERMOUT OFF FEEDBACK OFF ECHO OFF PAGESIZE 0
SET TERMOUT ON

PROMPT 'Creating tablespace build script...'
SET TERMOUT OFF;
rem
rem The following view needs to be created in SYS with a public
rem  select grant and synonym or this script will not work
rem create or replace view dba_file_data as
rem select
rem a.name tablespace,a.dflminext min_extents, a.dflmaxext max_extents,
rem a.dflinit init,a.dflincr next,a.dflextpct pct_increase, d.name
rem datafile,
rem b.blocks datafile_size, c.maxextend max_extend, c.inc ext_incr
rem from sys.ts$ a, sys.file$ b, sys.filext$ c, v$dbfile d
rem where
rem a.ts#=b.ts# and
rem b.file#=c.file#(+) and
rem b.file#=d.file#(+)
rem /
CREATE TABLE ts_temp (lineno NUMBER, ts_name VARCHAR2(30),
                 text VARCHAR2(800))
/
DECLARE
   CURSOR ts_cursor IS
     SELECT   tablespace_name,
              initial_extent,
```

```
                    next_extent,
                    min_extents,
                    max_extents,
                    pct_increase,
                    0,
                    status
                FROM    sys.dba_tablespaces
                WHERE tablespace_name != 'SYSTEM'
                    AND status != 'INVALID'
                ORDER BY tablespace_name;
        CURSOR df_cursor (c_ts VARCHAR2) IS
            SELECT
                    file_name,
                    bytes
            FROM        sys.dba_data_files
            WHERE       tablespace_name = c_ts
                    and tablespace_name != 'SYSTEM'
            ORDER BY file_name;
        CURSOR get_auto (df_nm VARCHAR2) IS
            SELECT
                    max_extend, ext_incr
                    ext_incr
            FROM
                    dba_file_data
            WHERE
                    datafile=df_nm;
        lv_max_extend           dba_file_data.max_extend%TYPE;
        lv_ext_incr             dba_file_data.ext_incr%TYPE;
        lv_tablespace_name      sys.dba_tablespaces.tablespace_name%TYPE;
        lv_initial_extent       sys.dba_tablespaces.initial_extent%TYPE;
        lv_next_extent          sys.dba_tablespaces.next_extent%TYPE;
        lv_min_extents          sys.dba_tablespaces.min_extents%TYPE;
        lv_max_extents          sys.dba_tablespaces.max_extents%TYPE;
        lv_pct_increase         sys.dba_tablespaces.pct_increase%TYPE;
        lv_status               sys.dba_tablespaces.status%TYPE;
        lv_file_name            sys.dba_data_files.file_name%TYPE;
        lv_bytes                sys.dba_data_files.bytes%TYPE;
        lv_first_rec            BOOLEAN;
        lv_string               VARCHAR2(800);
        lv_lineno               NUMBER := 0;
        lv_min_extlen           NUMBER := 0;
        sub_strg                VARCHAR2(20);
        PROCEDURE write_out(p_line INTEGER, p_name VARCHAR2,
                    p_string VARCHAR2) is
        BEGIN
            INSERT INTO ts_temp (lineno, ts_name, text)
            VALUES (p_line, p_name, p_string);
        END;
BEGIN
    OPEN ts_cursor;
```

```
LOOP
   FETCH ts_cursor INTO lv_tablespace_name,
                        lv_initial_extent,
                        lv_next_extent,
                        lv_min_extents,
                        lv_max_extents,
                        lv_pct_increase,
                        lv_min_extlen,
                        lv_status;
   EXIT WHEN ts_cursor%NOTFOUND;
   lv_lineno := 1;
   lv_string := ('CREATE TABLESPACE '||lower(lv_tablespace_name));
   lv_first_rec := TRUE;
   write_out(lv_lineno, lv_tablespace_name, lv_string);
   OPEN df_cursor(lv_tablespace_name);
   LOOP
      FETCH df_cursor INTO lv_file_name,
                           lv_bytes;
      EXIT WHEN df_cursor%NOTFOUND;
      IF (lv_first_rec) THEN
         lv_first_rec := FALSE;
         lv_string := 'DATAFILE ';
      ELSE
         lv_string := lv_string || ',';
      END IF;
      lv_string:=lv_string||''''||lv_file_name||''''||
                  ' SIZE '||to_char(lv_bytes) || ' REUSE';
      OPEN get_auto(lv_file_name);
      FETCH get_auto INTO lv_max_extend, lv_ext_incr;
      IF lv_max_extend=0 THEN
            sub_strg:='MAXSIZE UNLIMITED';
   ELSE
       sub_strg:=' MAXSIZE '||TO_CHAR(lv_max_extend);
   END IF;
      IF lv_ext_incr != 0 THEN
      lv_string:=lv_string||chr(10)||' AUTOEXTEND ON NEXT '||
      to_char(lv_ext_incr)||sub_strg;
         CLOSE get_auto;
      END IF;
  IF get_auto%ISOPEN THEN
 CLOSE get_auto;
  END IF;
  IF lv_min_extlen != 0 THEN
 lv_string:=lv_string||chr(10)||
      'MINIMUM EXTENT '||TO_CHAR(lv_min_extlen);
  END IF;
  END LOOP;
  CLOSE df_cursor;
     lv_lineno := lv_lineno + 1;
     write_out(lv_lineno, lv_tablespace_name, lv_string);
```

```
                lv_lineno := lv_lineno + 1;
                lv_string := (' DEFAULT STORAGE (INITIAL ' ||
                              TO_CHAR(lv_initial_extent) ||
                              ' NEXT ' || lv_next_extent);
            write_out(lv_lineno, lv_tablespace_name, lv_string);
                lv_lineno := lv_lineno + 1;
                lv_string := (' MINEXTENTS ' ||
                              lv_min_extents ||
                              ' MAXEXTENTS ' || lv_max_extents);
            write_out(lv_lineno, lv_tablespace_name, lv_string);
                lv_lineno := lv_lineno + 1;
                lv_string := (' PCTINCREASE ' ||
                              lv_pct_increase || ')');
            write_out(lv_lineno, lv_tablespace_name, lv_string);
                lv_string := ('     '||lv_status);
            write_out(lv_lineno, lv_tablespace_name, lv_string);
                lv_lineno := lv_lineno + 1;
                lv_string:='/';
            write_out(lv_lineno, lv_tablespace_name, lv_string);
                lv_lineno := lv_lineno + 1;
                lv_string:='
';
            write_out(lv_lineno, lv_tablespace_name, lv_string);
    END LOOP;
    CLOSE ts_cursor;
END;
/
COLUMN dbname NEW_VALUE db NOPRINT
SELECT name dbname FROM v$database;
SPOOL rep_out\&db\crt_tbsp.sql
SET HEADING OFF
COLUMN text FORMAT a80 WORD_WRAP
SELECT    text
FROM      ts_temp
ORDER BY ts_name, lineno;
SPOOL OFF;
DROP TABLE ts_temp;
SET VERIFY ON RECSEP ON TERMOUT ON HEADING ON FEEDBACK ON
SET PAGESIZE 22 LINES 80
CLEAR COLUMNS
```

Some things to notice in the script in Source 3.1 is that the cursor ts_cursor selects a 0 (zero) out of the file for the variable lv_min_extlen. For Oracle7 this selection is required since there is no equivalent to the minimum extent specification, so, for Oracle7 the script works as is (that is, for 7.3 and above); for Oracle8, replace the zero with MIN_EXTLEN. Also, the view shown in the comments is not needed since the data for the autoextend feature can be obtained from dba_data_files as MAXBYTES and INCREMENT_BY, thus eliminating the need for the GET_AUTO cursor. Just select these values in the DF_CURSOR and place them into the variables just as with the other items selected in the cursor.

3.5 PERIODIC TABLESPACE MAINTENANCE

Periodic tablespace maintenance includes consolidation of extents, reorganization to push all the freespace in the file to the front, and exports to ensure recoverability. Let's look at these topics.

Consolidation of Extents

As tables, indexes, and clusters are created and dropped in a tablespace, extents are dynamically assigned and deassigned to the objects. Like a disk system which dynamically assigns space to files, this causes fragmentation. Fragmentation results in objects being stored all over the tablespace, requiring more head moves to recover the information to fill users' queries. This reduces response time and makes the system slow. Unless you can exactly specify the required storage and sizing information for each and every table in each tablespace, some of this internal fragmentation will occur. The SMON process automatically consolidates contiguous free extents into single large extents for tablespaces whose default value for the pctincrease storage parameter is greater than zero. This reduces but doesn't eliminate the problem. So, how do you correct it? There are two methods. Let's look at each of them.

Method 1: Use of Export and Import This method will consolidate all freespace, and will consolidate all tables into single extents. However, the database won't be available and for large systems, the time required could be extensive.

1. Perform an export on all objects in the tablespace. Remember that you must export each owner's objects for all users who own objects in the tablespace.
2. Drop the tablespace using the INCLUDING CONTENTS clause.
3. Recreate the tablespace. (If you created a script to create the tablespace, you can just rerun the script; be sure to include all active data files. It might be desirable to delete all of a tablespaces' datafiles and consolidate them into one large datafile at this time.)
4. Import all of the exports generated in step 1.

Another major problem with this method is it won't work on the SYSTEM tablespace.

Method 2: Use of Events (pre 7.3) or Commands (7.3) For version 7 up to version 7.3 you can use one of two methods. The first method is just to temporarily set the pctincrease to one and await SMON's automatic cleanup. This can take several minutes. The second method involves issuing an event command against the specific tablespace where the fragmentation is happening:

```
alter session
set events 'immediate trace name coalesce level ts#';
```

where ts# is the tablespace number as specified in the ts$ table.

If you create a view against the DBA_FREE_SPACE view that summarizes the fragmentation state of all the tablespaces, a simple procedure can be created that defragments the database on command. For example:

```
rem Name:     view.sql
rem FUNCTION: Create free_space view for use by freespc reports
rem
CREATE VIEW free_space
        (tablespace, file_id, pieces, free_bytes, free_blocks,
         largest_bytes,largest_blks) as
SELECT tablespace_name, file_id, COUNT(*),
    SUM(bytes), SUM(blocks),
    MAX(bytes), MAX(blocks) FROM sys.dba_free_space
GROUP BY tablespace_name, file_id;
```

The SQL procedure becomes:

```
rem
rem NAME: defrag7.sql
rem FUNCTION: Uses the "set events" command to manually coalesce
rem FUNCTION: any tablespace with greater than 1 fragment. You
rem FUNCTION: may alter to exclude the temporary tablespace.
rem FUNCTION: The procedure uses the FREE_SPACE view which is a
rem FUNCTION: summarized version of the DBA_FREE_SPACE view.
rem FUNCTION: This procedure must be run from a DBA user id.
rem HISTORY:
rem WHO          WHAT          WHEN
rem Mike Ault    Created       1/4/96
rem
DEFINE cr='CHR(10)'
SET HEADING OFF FEEDBACK OFF ECHO OFF TERMOUT OFF
SPOOL def.sql
SELECT
     'ALTER SESSION SET EVENTS '||&&cr||
     'IMMEDIATE TRACE NAME COALESCE LEVEL '||ts#||&&cr||';'
FROM
     sys.ts$,
     free_space
WHERE
     ts#=file_id-1 AND pieces>1;
SPOOL OFF
```

```
@def.sql
HOST rm def.sql
```

The script above has been used successfully on numerous databases with no reported problems. Part two of method 2 involves a command new to version 7.3 of Oracle. The command is an addition to the ALTER TABLESPACE command; the COALESCE clause for this command now takes the place of the SET EVENT commands used for pre-7.3 instances. To coalesce a tablespace named ACCOUNTS the command would be:

```
ALTER TABLESPACE ACCOUNTS COALESCE;
```

The automated procedure shown above will become:

```
rem
rem NAME: defrg73.sql
rem FUNCTION: Uses the coalesce command to manually coalesce
rem FUNCTION: any tablespace with greater than 1 fragment. You
rem FUNCTION: may alter to exclude the temporary tablespace.
rem FUNCTION: The procedure uses the FREE_SPACE view which is a
rem FUNCTION: summarized version of the DBA_FREE_SPACE view.
rem FUNCTION: This procedure must be run from a DBA user id.
rem HISTORY:
rem WHO            WHAT            WHEN
rem Mike Ault      Created         1/4/96
rem
CLEAR COLUMNS
CLEAR COMPUTES
DEFINE cr='chr(10)'
TTITLE OFF
SET HEADING OFF FEEDBACK OFF ECHO OFF TERMOUT OFF
SPOOL def.sql
SELECT
     'ALTER TABLESPACE '||tablespace||' COALESCE;'||&&cr||
     'COMMIT;'
FROM
     free_space
WHERE
     pieces>1;
SPOOL OFF
@def.sql
HOST rm def.sql
SET HEADING ON FEEDBACK ON TERMOUT ON
TTITLE OFF
```

If there is Swiss cheese fragmentation, the DBA needs to find which objects are bound by freespace in order to plan for the rebuild of these objects. The script in Source 3.2 can be run to determine the bound objects in your database.

SOURCE 3.2   Script to determine bound objects.

```
rem    ****************************************************************
rem    NAME:       BOUND_OB.sql
rem    FUNCTION: Show objects with extents bounded by freespace
rem****************************************************************
START title80 "Objects With Extents Bounded by Free Space"
SPOOL rep_out\&db\b_ob..lis
COLUMN e FORMAT a15        HEADING "TABLE SPACE"
COLUMN a FORMAT a6         HEADING "OBJECT|TYPE"
COLUMN b FORMAT a30        HEADING "OBJECT NAME"
COLUMN c FORMAT a10        HEADING "OWNER ID"
COLUMN d FORMAT 99,999,999 HEADING "SIZE|IN BYTES"
BREAK ON e SKIP 1 ON c
SET FEEDBACK OFF
SET VERIFY OFF
SET TERMOUT OFF
COLUMN bls NEW_VALUE block_size NOPRINT
SELECT blocksize bls
FROM sys.ts$
WHERE name='SYSTEM';

SELECT h.name e, g.name c, f.object_type a, e.name b,
       b.length*&&block_size d
 FROM sys.uet$ b, sys.fet$ c, sys.fet$ d, sys.obj$ e,
      sys.sys_objects f,sys.user$ g, sys.ts$ h
 WHERE b.block# = c.block# + c.length
   AND b.block# + b.length = d.block#
   AND f.header_file = b.segfile#
   AND f.header_block = b.segblock#
   AND f.object_id = e.obj#
   AND g.user# = e.owner#
   AND b.ts# = h.ts#
 ORDER BY 1,2,3,4
/

CLEAR COLUMNS
SET FEEDBACK ON
SET VERIFY ON
SET TERMOUT ON
TTITLE ''
TTITLE OFF
SPOOL OFF
CLEAR BREAKS
```

Bound objects need to be exported, dropped, and rebuilt after a consolidation of freespace. Many times you will have a number of objects, not just one, that are bound because of extensive dynamic extension in the tablespace being monitored. If this is the case, a reorganization of the entire tablespace is in order, which could involve a tablespace-specific export. The script in Source 3.3 can be used to generate a tablespace-specific export script.

SOURCE 3.3   Example script to generate tablespace-level export script for UNIX.

```
rem******** RevealNet Oracle Administration *****************
rem  File: tbsp_exp.sql
rem  Part of the RevealNet Oracle Administration library.
rem  Copyright (C) 1996-97 RevealNet, Inc.
rem  All rights reserved.
rem  For more information, call RevealNet at 1-800-REVEAL4
rem  or check out our Web page: www.revealnet.com
rem  Modifications (Date, Who, Description)
rem FUNCTION: Creates a shell script to perform tablespace level
rem FUNCTION: exports for a database
rem FUNCTION: Each tablespace has its own export that handles
rem FUNCTION: its tables, related indexes, grants and contraints
rem NOTE: Only preliminary testing of this script is done,
rem NOTE: test this script throughly before production use.
rem ***********************************************************
rem
SET VERIFY OFF ECHO OFF TERMOUT ON FEEDBACK OFF
PROMPT ...creating tablespace level export script
SET TERMOUT OFF
DROP TABLE exp_temp;
CREATE TABLE
exp_temp (file# NUMBER, line_no NUMBER, line_txt long);
DECLARE
CURSOR count_tabs (tbsp IN VARCHAR2) IS
     SELECT count(*)
     FROM dba_tables
     WHERE tablespace_name=tbsp;
CURSOR get_tbsp IS
     SELECT tablespace_name
     FROM dba_tablespaces
     WHERE tablespace_name != 'SYSTEM';
CURSOR get_owners ( tbsp IN VARCHAR2 ) IS
     SELECT DISTINCT(owner)
     FROM dba_tables
     WHERE tablespace_name=tbsp;
cursor get_tabs ( tbsp IN VARCHAR2, owner in VARCHAR2 ) IS
     SELECT table_name
     FROM dba_tables
     WHERE tablespace_name=tbsp
           AND owner=owner;
row_cntr           INTEGER:=0;
tablespace_nm      dba_tablespaces.tablespace_name%TYPE;
owner              dba_tables.owner%TYPE;
table_nm           dba_tables.table_name%TYPE;
```

```
ln_txt              exp_temp.line_txt%TYPE;
own_cnt             INTEGER;
tab_cnt             INTEGER;
file_no             INTEGER;
tab_count           INTEGER;
dbname              v$database.name%TYPE;
PROCEDURE insert_tab (
file_no NUMBER, row_cntr NUMBER, ln_txt VARCHAR2) IS
BEGIN
    INSERT INTO exp_temp (file#,line_no, line_txt)
    VALUES (file_no,row_cntr,ln_txt);
END;
BEGIN
/* initialize various counters */
row_cntr    :=0;
tab_count   :=0;
file_no     :=1;
/* Get database name */
SELECT name INTO dbname FROM v$database;
ln_txt:='# Tablespace level export for instance: '||dbname;
row_cntr:=row_cntr+1;
insert_tab (file_no, row_cntr, ln_txt);
/* Set command in script to set SID */
ln_txt:='ORACLE_SID='||LOWER(dbname);
row_cntr:=row_cntr+1;
insert_tab (file_no, row_cntr, ln_txt);
/* First run to build export script header
 Get all tablespace names other than system */
IF get_tbsp%ISOPEN THEN
    CLOSE get_tbsp;
    OPEN get_tbsp;
ELSE
    OPEN get_tbsp;
END IF;
LOOP
    FETCH get_tbsp INTO tablespace_nm;
    EXIT WHEN get_tbsp%NOTFOUND;
/* See if tablespace has tables */
    IF count_tabs%ISOPEN THEN
        CLOSE count_tabs;
        OPEN count_tabs(tablespace_nm);
    ELSE
        OPEN count_tabs(tablespace_nm);
    END IF;
    FETCH count_tabs INTO tab_count;
    IF tab_count=0 THEN
        GOTO end_loop1;
    END IF;
    row_cntr:=row_cntr+1;
    ln_txt:='#';
```

```
    insert_tab (file_no, row_cntr, ln_txt);
    row_cntr:=row_cntr+1;
    ln_txt:='#';
    insert_tab (file_no, row_cntr, ln_txt);
    SELECT
       '# Tablespace: '||tablespace_nm INTO ln_txt FROM dual;
    row_cntr:=row_cntr+1;
    insert_tab (file_no, row_cntr, ln_txt);
    SELECT '#   Export DMP file name:
'||tablespace_nm||'_'||trunc(sysdate)||'.dmp' INTO ln_txt
    FROM dual;
    row_cntr:=row_cntr+1;
    insert_tab (file_no, row_cntr, ln_txt);
    row_cntr:=row_cntr+1;
    ln_txt:='#   Owners for '||tablespace_nm;
    insert_tab (file_no, row_cntr, ln_txt);
    SELECT '' into ln_txt FROM dual;
    own_cnt:=0;
/* Get tablespace table owners */
    IF get_owners%ISOPEN THEN
        CLOSE get_owners;
        OPEN get_owners(tablespace_nm);
    ELSE
        open get_owners(tablespace_nm);
    END IF;
    tab_cnt:=0;
    LOOP
        FETCH get_owners INTO owner;
        EXIT WHEN get_owners%NOTFOUND;
/* Get tablespace tables */
        ln_txt:='#   Tables for tablespace: '||tablespace_nm;
        row_cntr:=row_cntr+1;
        insert_tab (file_no, row_cntr, ln_txt);
        ln_txt:='';
        IF get_tabs%ISOPEN THEN
            CLOSE get_tabs;
            OPEN get_tabs(tablespace_nm,owner);
        ELSE
            OPEN get_tabs(tablespace_nm, owner);
        END IF;
        LOOP
            FETCH get_tabs INTO table_nm;
            EXIT WHEN get_tabs%NOTFOUND;
            tab_cnt:=tab_cnt+1;
            IF tab_cnt=1 THEN
                ln_txt:='/* '||ln_txt||owner||'.'||table_nm;
            ELSE
                ln_txt:=ln_txt||', '||owner||'.'||table_nm;
            END IF;
        END LOOP;
```

```
      CLOSE get_tabs;
      row_cntr:=row_cntr+1;
      ln_txt:=ln_txt||' */';
      insert_tab (file_no, row_cntr, ln_txt);
      END LOOP;
      CLOSE get_owners;
<<end_loop1>>
NULL;
END LOOP;
close get_tbsp;
ln_txt:='###### End of Header - Start of script ########';
row_cntr:=row_cntr+1;
insert_tab (file_no, row_cntr, ln_txt);
ln_txt:='set -x ';
row_cntr:=row_cntr+1;
insert_tab (file_no, row_cntr, ln_txt);
select 'script tablespace_exp_'||sysdate||'.log' into ln_txt
from dual;
row_cntr:=row_cntr+1;
insert_tab (file_no, row_cntr, ln_txt);
/* Now build actual export command sets */
/* Get all tablespace names other than system */
IF get_tbsp%ISOPEN THEN
      CLOSE get_tbsp;
      OPEN get_tbsp;
ELSE
      OPEN get_tbsp;
END IF;
LOOP
      FETCH get_tbsp INTO tablespace_nm;
      EXIT WHEN get_tbsp%NOTFOUND;
/* See if tablespace has tables */
      IF count_tabs%ISOPEN THEN
          CLOSE count_tabs;
          OPEN count_tabs(tablespace_nm);
      ELSE
          OPEN count_tabs(tablespace_nm);
      END IF;
      FETCH count_tabs into tab_count;
      IF tab_count=0 THEN
          GOTO end_loop;
      END IF;
      row_cntr:=row_cntr+1;
      ln_txt:='#';
      insert_tab (file_no, row_cntr, ln_txt);
      row_cntr:=row_cntr+1;
      ln_txt:='#';
      insert_tab (file_no, row_cntr, ln_txt);
      SELECT '# Export script for tablespace '||tablespace_nm
        INTO ln_txt FROM dual;
```

```
    row_cntr:=row_cntr+1;
    insert_tab (file_no, row_cntr, ln_txt);
    SELECT '# created on '||sysdate into ln_txt FROM dual;
    row_cntr:=row_cntr+1;
    insert_tab (file_no, row_cntr, ln_txt);
    ln_txt:='if ( -r  '||tablespace_nm||'.par'||' ) then';
    row_cntr:=row_cntr+1;
    insert_tab (file_no, row_cntr, ln_txt);
     ln_txt:='   rm '||tablespace_nm||'.par';
    row_cntr:=row_cntr+1;
    insert_tab (file_no, row_cntr, ln_txt);
    ln_txt:='end if';
    row_cntr:=row_cntr+1;
    insert_tab (file_no, row_cntr, ln_txt);
    ln_txt:='touch '||tablespace_nm||'.par';
    row_cntr:=row_cntr+1;
    insert_tab (file_no, row_cntr, ln_txt);
/* Set up basic export commands */
    SELECT
    'echo '||chr(39)||
    'grants=y indexes=y constraints=y compress=y'||chr(39)||
    '>>'||tablespace_nm||'.par'
    INTO ln_txt
    FROM dual;
    row_cntr:=row_cntr+1;
    insert_tab (file_no, row_cntr, ln_txt);
    SELECT '' INTO ln_txt FROM dual;
    own_cnt:=0;
    ln_txt:='echo
'||chr(39)||'tables=('||chr(39)||'>>'||tablespace_nm||'.par';
    row_cntr:=row_cntr+1;
    insert_tab (file_no, row_cntr, ln_txt);
/*  Get tablespace table owners */
    IF get_owners%ISOPEN THEN
        CLOSE get_owners;
        OPEN get_owners(tablespace_nm);
    ELSE
        OPEN get_owners(tablespace_nm);
    END IF;
    tab_cnt:=0;
    LOOP
        FETCH get_owners INTO owner;
        EXIT WHEN get_owners%NOTFOUND;
/* Get tablespace tables */
        IF get_tabs%ISOPEN THEN
            CLOSE get_tabs;
            OPEN get_tabs(tablespace_nm,owner);
        ELSE
            OPEN get_tabs(tablespace_nm,owner);
        END IF;
```

```
        LOOP
            FETCH get_tabs INTO table_nm;
            EXIT WHEN get_tabs%NOTFOUND;
            tab_cnt:=tab_cnt+1;
            IF tab_cnt=1 THEN
             ln_txt:='echo '||chr(39)||
             owner||'.'||table_nm||chr(39)||
             '>>'||tablespace_nm||'.par';
            ELSE
            ln_txt:='echo '||chr(39)||',
            '||owner||'.'||table_nm||chr(39)||
            '>>'||tablespace_nm||'.par';
            END IF;
            row_cntr:=row_cntr+1;
            insert_tab (file_no, row_cntr, ln_txt);
        END LOOP;
        CLOSE get_tabs;
     END LOOP;
     CLOSE get_owners;
     ln_txt:='echo '||chr(39)||
      ')'||chr(39)||'>>'||tablespace_nm||'.par';
     row_cntr:=row_cntr+1;
     insert_tab (file_no, row_cntr, ln_txt);
/*Set file name for export file*/
     SELECT
         'echo '||chr(39)||
         'file='||tablespace_nm||'_'||TRUNC(sysdate)||
         '.dmp'||chr(39)||'>>'||tablespace_nm||'.par'
     INTO ln_txt
     FROM dual;
     row_cntr:=row_cntr+1;
     insert_tab (file_no, row_cntr, ln_txt);
     SELECT
         'exp system/angler parfile='||tablespace_nm||'.par'
     INTO ln_txt
     FROM dual;
     row_cntr:=row_cntr+1;
     insert_tab (file_no, row_cntr, ln_txt);
     SELECT
        'compress '||tablespace_nm||'_'||TRUNC(sysdate)||'.dmp '
     INTO ln_txt
     FROM dual;
     row_cntr:=row_cntr+1;
     insert_tab (file_no, row_cntr, ln_txt);
     file_no:=file_no+1;
<<end_loop>>
NULL;
END LOOP;
CLOSE get_tbsp;
COMMIT;
```

```
END;
/
SET HEADING OFF FEEDBACK OFF LONG 4000 LINES 80 PAGES 0
SET RECSEP OFF EMBEDDED ON ECHO OFF TERMOUT OFF VERIFY OFF
COLUMN      file#       NOPRINT
COLUMN      line_no     NOPRINT
COLUMN      line_txt    FORMAT a80      WORD_WRAPPED
SPOOL tablespace_export.sh
SELECT *  FROM exp_temp
ORDER BY file#,line_no;
SPOOL OFF
SET HEADING ON FEEDBACK ON LONG 2000 LINES 80 PAGES 22 VERIFY ON
SET RECSEP ON EMBEDDED OFF ECHO OFF TERMOUT ON
CLEAR COLUMNS
PROMPT  Procedure completed
```

The problem with the script generated in Source 3.3 is that it may exceed the limit for the size of an export parfile if you have a large number of tables under one owner in a single tablespace. The way to correct for this would be to place a counter on the table loop and just export a fixed number of tables per parfile.

CHAPTER 4

Administration Relational Database Tables

With Oracle8 the number and complexity of database objects has increased substantially. In Oracle7 we had two types of tables, standard and clustered; in Oracle8 we have standard, partitioned, object, index only, nested, and clustered tables. We also have a new basic building block for objects in Oracle8, the TYPE. A TYPE can be just a structure of scalar datatypes, an object type, a nested table type, or a VARRAY. In this chapter we will cover the "standard" relational table, clusters, and triggers. In the next chapter we will look at the new object extensions to tables. Let's get started.

4.1   THE CONCEPT OF ROWIDS IN ORACLE7 AND ORACLE8

Oracle used the concept of the ROWID in Oracle7 and earlier releases to uniquely identify each row in each table in the database. This was represented as the pseudo-column ROWID in Oracle7 and earlier releases. Hence, unknown to many DBAs and developers, even third-normal-form-violating nonunique identified tables always had a unique identifier that could be used for removal of duplicates and other unique-identifier-required operations, the ROWID column. Of course, views don't have ROWIDs. In Oracle8 the concept of ROWID is still with us, but, the format has been expanded. In Chapter 10 we discuss the DBMS_ROWID set of Oracle-provided packages that provide for ROWID manipulation between the old and new formats and piecing out as well as building ROWIDs. But what does a ROWID contain? In this chapter we will examine the Oracle7 ROWID concepts and will expand in the next chapter (covering Oracle8 types, tables, and such) into the Oracle8 ROWID.

Oracle7 ROWID Format

The ROWID in Oracle7 is a varchar2 representation of a binary value shown in hexadecimal format. It is displayed as:

bbbbbbbb.ssss.ffff

where:

bbbbbbbb is the block ID.

ssss is the sequence in the block.

ffff is the file ID.

As was stated in the introduction, this ROWID is a pseudo- (meaning the DESCRIBE command won't show it) column in each table (and cluster). The ROWID is always unique except in the case of cluster tables that have values stored in the same block. This makes it handy for doing entry comparisons in tables that may not have a unique key, especially when you want to eliminate or show duplicates before creating a unique or primary key. In *Oracle Performance Tuning* from O'Reilly & Associates by Mark Gurry and Peter Corrigan, 1996 a simple query for determining duplicates using the ROWID is shown:

```
DELETE FROM emp E
WHERE E.rowid > ( SELECT MIN (x.rowid)
               FROM emp X
               WHERE X.emp_no = E.emp_no );
```

And of course, any operation where you can do a select, update, or delete based on exact ROWID values will always outperform virtually any other similar operation using standard column value logic. The file id portion of the ROWID points to the file with that number, which happens to be the same number as is given the data file in the DBA_DATA_FILES view. In the sections to follow a script called ACT_SIZE.SQL makes use of the ROWID to determine the actual number of blocks used by a table. The ROWID pseudocolumn is one that any DBA should be aware of and use to advantage. ORACLE has expanded the ROWID in Oracle8. The next chapter (Administration of Oracle8 Object Tables) discusses these changes and their implications.

4.2   RELATIONAL TABLE ADMINISTRATION

Tables are the primary storage division in Oracle. All data is stored in tables. Sequences and indexes support tables. Synonyms point to tables. Types and VARRAYS are stored in tables. Tables make Oracle work. The next sections describe the administration and maintenance of standard relational database tables in detail.

Creation of Relational Tables

Tables are owned by users. You may hear them referred to as schemas and see this in the Oracle documentation, but as with previous Oracle versions, whether you call them schemas or users makes little difference—the two terms are synonymous. For a given application it is suggested that its tables reside in a single dedicated tablespace or group of tablespaces. This leads to the corollary that all of an application's tables should be owned by a single user, or if you prefer, reside in a single schema. This makes further maintenance such as exports, imports, synonym creation, table creates, and drops easier to deal with. As with the other database objects, tables are built using the CREATE command. This command has changed significantly since early versions of Oracle7. Let's look at this command's format when used to create simple relational tables.

Relational Table CREATE Command Definition

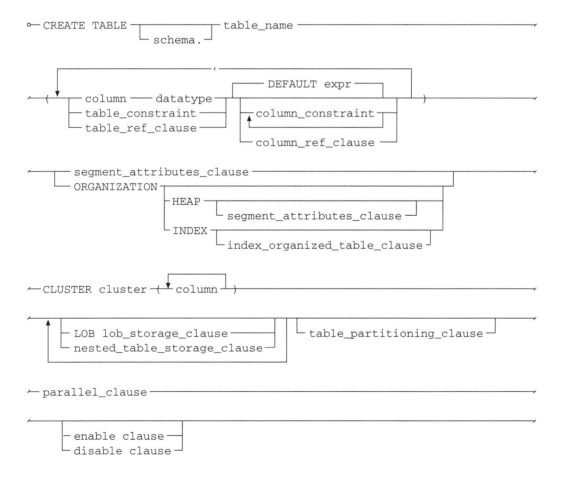

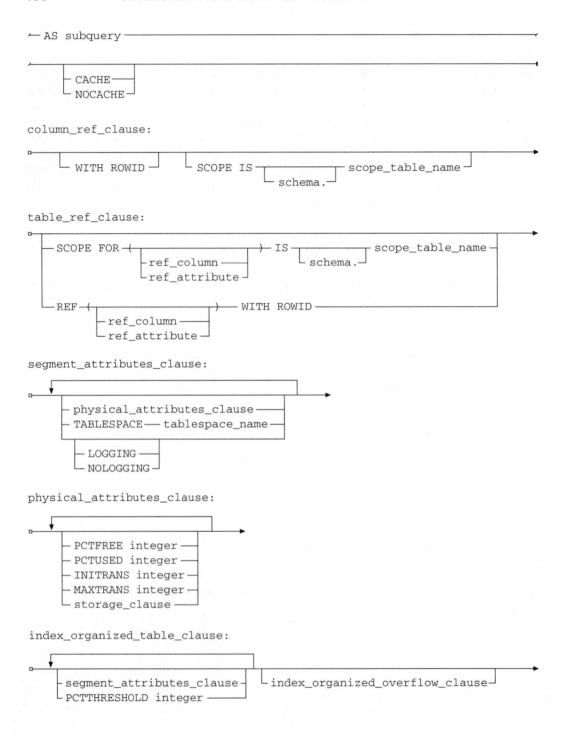

column_ref_clause:

table_ref_clause:

segment_attributes_clause:

physical_attributes_clause:

index_organized_table_clause:

index_organized_overflow_clause:

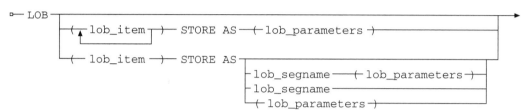

LOB lob_storage_clause:

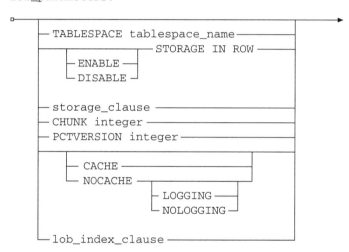

lob_parameters:

lob_index_clause:

INDEX
    ┌ lob_index_name (lob_index_parameters) ┐
    ├ lob_index_name ┤
    └ (lob_index_parameters) ┘

nested_table_storage_clause:

NESTED TABLE — nested_item — STORE AS — storage_table

```
table_partition_clause:
```

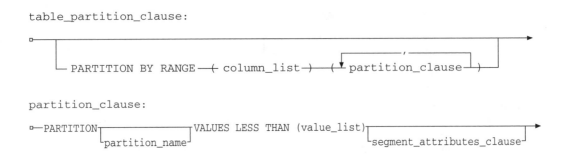

```
partition_clause:
```

The Keywords and Parameters for CREATE TABLE Commands The CREATE TABLE commands have the following parameter definitions in Oracle8:

Schema—This is the schema to contain the table. If you omit schema, Oracle creates the table in your own schema.

Table—This is the name of the table (or object table) to be created. A partitioned table cannot be a clustered table or an object table.

OF object_type—This explicitly creates an object table of type object_type. The columns of an object table correspond to the top-level attributes of type object_type. Each row will contain an object instance and each instance will be assigned a unique, system-generated object identifier (OID) when a row is inserted. Object tables cannot be partitioned. Of course, relational tables cannot be object tables.

Column—This specifies the name of a column of the table. A table can have up to 1000 columns in Oracle8. You may only omit column definitions when using the AS subquery clause.

Attribute—Specifies the qualified column name of an item in an object.

Datatype—This is the datatype of a column. You can omit the datatype only if the statement also designates the column as part of a foreign key in a referential integrity constraint. Oracle automatically assigns the column the datatype of the corresponding column of the referenced key of the referential integrity constraint. Object types, REF object_type, VARRAYs, and nested tables are valid datatypes.

DEFAULT—Specifies a value to be assigned to the column if a subsequent INSERT statement omits a value for the column. The datatype of the expression must match the datatype of the column. The column must also be enough to hold this expression. A DEFAULT expression cannot contain references to other columns, the pseudocolumn CURRVAL, NEXTVAL, LEVEL, and ROWNUM, or date constants that are not fully specified.

WITH ROWID—Stores the ROWID and the REF value in column or attribute. Storing a REF value with a ROWID can improve the performance of dereferencing operations, but will also use more space. Default storage of REF values is without ROWIDs.

SCOPE IS scope_table_name—This restricts the scope of the column REF values to scope_table_name. The REF values for the column must come from REF values obtained from the object table specified in the clause. You can only specify one scope table per REF column.

The scope_table_name is the name of the object table in which object instances (of the same type as the REF column) are stored. The values in the REF column point to objects in the scope table.

You must have SELECT privileges on the table or SELECT ANY TABLE system privileges.

SCOPE FOR (ref_column_name) IS scope_table_name—This restricts the scope of the REF values in ref_column_name to scope_table_name. The REF values for the column must come from REF values obtained from the object table specified in the clause.

The ref_column_name is the name of a REF column in an object table or an embedded REF attribute within an object column of a relational table. The values in the REF column point to objects in the scope table.

REF (ref_column_name)—This is a reference to a row in an object table. You can specify either a REF column name of an object or relational table or an embedded REF attribute within an object column as ref_column_name.

OIDINDEX—Specifies an index on the hidden object identifier column and/or the storage specification for the index. Either index or storage_specification must be specified.

Index—The name of the index on the hidden object identifier column. If not specified, a name is generated by the system.

column_constraint—Defines an integrity constraint as part of the column definition.

table_constraint—Defines an integrity constraint as part of the table definition.

ORGANIZATION INDEX—Specifies that table is created as an index-only table. In an index-only table, the data rows are held in an index defined on the primary key for the table.

ORGANIZATION HEAP—Specifies that the data rows of table are stored in no particular order. This is the default.

PCTTHRESHOLD—This specifies the percentage of space reserved in the index block for index-only table row. Any portion of the row that exceeds the specified threshold is stored in the area. If OVERFLOW is not specified, then rows exceeding the THRESHOLD limit are rejected. PCTTHRESHOLD must be a value from 0 to 50.

INCLUDING column_name—This specifies a column at which to divide an index-only table row into index and overflow portions. All columns which follow column_name are stored in the overflow data segment. A column_name is either the name of the last primary key column or any nonprimary key column.

PCTFREE—This specifies the percentage of space in each of the table's, OIDINDEX, or partition's data blocks reserved for future updates to the table's rows. The value of PCTFREE must be a value from 0 to 99. A value of 0 allows the entire block to be filled by inserts of new rows. The default value is 10. This value reserves 10% of each block for updates to existing rows and allows inserts of new rows to fill a maximum of 90% of each block.

PCTFREE has the same function in the PARTITION description clause and in the commands that create and alter clusters, indexes, snapshots, and snapshot logs. The combination of PCTFREE and PCTUSED determines whether inserted rows will go into existing data blocks or into new blocks.

For nonpartitioned tables, the value specified for PCTFREE is the actual physical attribute of the segment associated with the table.

For partitioned tables, the value specified for PCTFREE is the default physical attribute of the segments associated with the table. The default value of PCTFREE applies to all partitions specified in the CREATE statement (and on subsequent ALTER TABLE ADD PARTITION statements) unless you specify PCTFREE in the PARTITION description clause.

PCTUSED—This specifies the minimum percentage of used space in each data block of the table, object table OIDINDEX, or index-only table overflow data segment that Oracle can use for inserts. A block becomes a candidate for row insertion when its used space falls below PCTUSED. PCTUSED is specified as a positive integer from 1 to 99 and defaults to 40.

PCTUSED has the same function in the PARTITION description clause and in the commands that create and alter clusters, snapshots, and snapshot logs.

For nonpartitioned tables, the value specified for PCTUSED is the actual physical attribute of the segment associated with the table.

For partitioned tables, the value specified for PCTUSED is the default physical attribute of the segments associated with the table partitions. The default value of PCTUSED applies to all partitions specified in the CREATE statement (and on subsequent ALTER TABLE ADD PARTITION statements) unless you specify PCTUSED in the PARTITION description clause.

PCTUSED is not a valid table storage characteristic when creating an index-only table (ORGANIZATION INDEX).

The sum of PCTFREE and PCTUSED must be less than 100. You can use PCTFREE and PCTUSED together to use space within a table more efficiently.

INITRANS—This specifies the initial number of transaction entries allocated within each data block allocated to the table, object table OIDINDEX, partition, LOB index segment, or overflow data segment. This value can range from 1 to 255 and defaults to 1. In general, you should not change the INITRANS value from its default.

Each transaction that updates a block requires a transaction entry in the block. The size of a transaction entry depends on your operating system.

This parameter ensures that a minimum number of concurrent transactions can update the block and helps avoid the overhead of dynamically allocating a transaction entry.

The INITRANS parameter serves the same purpose in the PARTITION description clause and in clusters, indexes, snapshots, and snapshot logs as in tables. The minimum and default INITRANS value for a cluster or index is 2, rather than 1.

For nonpartitioned tables, the value specified for INITRANS is the actual physical attribute of the segment associated with the table.

For partitioned tables, the value specified for INITRANS is the default physical attribute of the segments associated with the table partitions. The default value of INITRANS applies to all partitions specified in the CREATE statement (and on subsequent ALTER TABLE ADD PARTITION statements) unless you specify INITRANS in the PARTITION description clause.

MAXTRANS—This specifies the maximum number of concurrent transactions that can update a data block allocated to the table, object table OIDINDEX, partition, LOB index segment, or index-only overflow data segment. This limit does not apply to queries. This value can range from 1 to 255 and the default is a function of the data block size. You should not change the MAXTRANS value from its default.

If the number of concurrent transactions updating a block exceeds the INITRANS value, Oracle dynamically allocates transaction entries in the block until either the MAXTRANS value is exceeded or the block has no more free space. The MAXTRANS parameter serves the same purpose in the PARTITION description clause, clusters, snapshots, and snapshot logs as in tables.

For nonpartitioned tables, the value specified for MAXTRANS is the actual physical attribute of the segment associated with the table.

For partitioned tables, the value specified for MAXTRANS is default physical attribute of the segments associated with the table partitions. The default value of MAXTRANS applies to all partitions specified in the CREATE statement (and on subsequent ALTER TABLE ADD PARTITION statements) unless you specify MAXTRANS in the PARTITION description clause.

TABLESPACE—This specifies the tablespace in which Oracle creates the table, object table OIDINDEX, partition, LOB storage, LOB index segment, or index-only table overflow data segment. If you omit this option, then Oracle creates the table, partition, LOB storage, LOB index segment, or partition in the default tablespace of the owner of the schema containing the table.

For nonpartitioned tables, the value specified for TABLESPACE is the actual physical attribute of the segment associated with the table.

For partitioned tables, the value specified for TABLESPACE is the default physical attribute of the segments associated with the table partitions. The default value of TABLESPACE applies to all partitions specified in the CREATE statement (and on subsequent ALTER TABLE ADD PARTITION statements) unless you specify TABLESPACE in the PARTITION description clause.

STORAGE—This specifies the storage characteristics for the table, object table OIDINDEX, partition, LOB storage, LOB index segment, or index-only table overflow data segment. This clause has performance ramifications for large tables. Storage should be allocated to minimize dynamic allocation of additional space.

For nonpartitioned tables, the value specified for STORAGE is the actual physical attribute of the segment associated with the table.

For partitioned tables, the value specified for STORAGE is the default physical attribute of the segments associated with the table partitions. The default value of STORAGE applies to all partitions specified in the CREATE statement (and on subsequent ALTER TABLE ADD PARTITION statements) unless you specify STORAGE in the PARTITION description clause.

OVERFLOW—Specifies that index-only table data rows exceeding the specified threshold are placed in the data segment listed in this clause.

LOGGING—This specifies that the creation of the table, (and any indices required because of constraints), partition, or LOB storage characteristics will be logged in the redo log file. LOGGING also specifies that subsequent operations against the table, partition, or LOB storage are logged in the redo file. This is the default.

If the database is run in ARCHIVELOG mode, media recovery from a backup will recreate the table (and any indices required because of constraints). You cannot specify LOGGING when using NOARCHIVELOG mode.

For nonpartitioned tables, the value specified for LOGGING is the actual physical attribute of the segment associated with the table.

For partitioned tables, the value specified for LOGGING is the default physical attribute of the segments associated with the table partitions. The default value of LOGGING applies to all partitions specified in the CREATE statement (and on subsequent ALTER TABLE ADD PARTITION statements) unless you specify LOGGING in the PARTITION description clause.

TIP   In future versions of Oracle, the LOGGING keyword will replace the RECOVERABLE option. RECOVERABLE is still available as a valid keyword in Oracle when creating nonpartitioned tables, however, it is not recommended. You must specify LOGGING when creating a partitioned table.

RECOVERABLE—See LOGGING above. RECOVERABLE is not a valid keyword for creating partitioned tables or LOB storage characteristics.

NOLOGGING—This specifies that the creation of the table (and any indexes required because of constraints), partition, or LOB storage characteristics will not be logged in the redo log file. NOLOGGING also specifies that subsequent operations against the table or LOB storage are not logged in the redo file. As a result, media recovery will not recreate the table (and any indices required because of constraints).

For nonpartitioned tables, the value specified for NOLOGGING is the actual physical attribute of the segment associated with the table.

For partitioned tables, the value specified for NOLOGGING is the default physical attribute of the segments associated with the table partitions. The default value of NOLOGGING applies to all partitions specified in the CREATE statement (and on subsequent ALTER TABLE ADD PARTITION statements) unless you specify NOLOGGING in the PARTITION description clause. Using this keyword makes table creation faster than using the LOGGING option because redo log entries are not written.

NOLOGGING is not a valid keyword for creating index-only tables.

TIP   In future versions of Oracle, the NOLOGGING keyword will replace the UNRECOVERABLE option. UNRECOVERABLE is still available as a valid keyword in Oracle when creating nonpartitioned tables, however, it is not recommended. You must specify NOLOGGING when creating a partitioned table.

UNRECOVERABLE—See NOLOGGING above. This keyword can only be specified with the AS subquery clause. UNRECOVERABLE is not a valid keyword for creating partitioned or index-only tables.

LOB—This specifies the LOB storage characteristics.

lob_item—This is the LOB column name or LOB object attribute for which you are explicitly defining tablespace and storage characteristics that are different from those of the table.

STORE AS lob_segname—This specifies the name of the LOB data segment. You cannot use lob_segname if more than one lob_item is specified.

CHUNK integer—This is the unit of LOB value allocation and manipulation. Oracle allocates each unit of LOB storage as CHUNK integer. You can also use K or M to specify this size in kilobytes or megabytes. The default value of integer is 1 K and the maximum is 32 K. For efficiency, use a multiple of the Oracle block size.

PCTVERSION integer—This is the maximum percentage of overall LOB storage space used for creating new versions of the LOB. The default value is 10, meaning that older versions of the LOB data are not overwritten until 10% of the overall LOB storage space is used.

INDEX lob_index_name—This the name of the LOB index segment. You cannot use lob_index_name if more than one lob_item is specified.

NESTED TABLE nested_item STORE AS storage_table—This specifies storage_table as the name of the storage table in which the rows of all nested_item values reside. You must include this clause when creating a table with columns or column attributes whose type is a nested table.

The nested_item is the name of a column or a column-qualified attribute whose type is a nested table.

The storage_table is the name of the storage table. The storage table is created in the same schema and the same tablespace as the parent table.

CLUSTER—This specifies that the table is to be part of the cluster. The columns listed in this clause are the table columns that correspond to the cluster's columns. Generally, the cluster columns of a table are the column or columns that comprise its primary key or a portion of its primary key.

Specify one column from the table for each column in the cluster key. The columns are matched by position, not by name. Since a clustered table uses the cluster's space allocation, do not use the PCTFREE, PCTUSED, INITRANS, or MAXTRANS parameters, the TABLESPACE option, or the STORAGE clause with the CLUSTER option.

PARALLEL parallel_clause—This specifies the degree of parallelism for creating the table and the default degree of parallelism for queries on the table once created.

This is not a valid option when creating index-only tables.

PARTITION BY RANGE—This specifies that the table is partitioned on ranges of values from column_list.

column_list—This is an ordered list of columns used to determine in which partition a row belongs. You cannot specify more than 16 columns in column_list. The column_list cannot contain the ROWID pseudocolumn or any columns of datatype ROWID or LONG.

PARTITION partition_name—This specifies the physical partition clause. If partition_name is omitted, Oracle generates a name with the form SYS_Pn for the partition. The partition_name must conform to the rules for naming schema objects and their parts.

VALUES LESS THAN—This specifies the noninclusive upper bound for the current partition.

value_list—This is an ordered list of literal values corresponding to column_list in the PARTITION BY RANGE clause. You can substitute the keyword MAXVALUE for any literal in value_list. Specifying a value other than MAXVALUE for the highest partition bound imposes an implicit integrity constraint on the table.

MAXVALUE—This specifies a maximum value that will always sort higher than any other value, including NULL.

ENABLE—This enables an integrity constraint.

DISABLE—This disables an integrity constraint.

Constraints specified in the ENABLE and DISABLE clauses of a CREATE TABLE statement must be defined in the statement. You can also enable and disable constraints with the ENABLE and DISABLE keywords of the CONSTRAINT clause. If you define a constraint but do not explicitly enable or disable it, Oracle enables it by default.

You cannot use the ENABLE and DISABLE clauses in a CREATE TABLE statement to enable and disable triggers.

AS subquery—This inserts the rows returned by the subquery into the table upon its creation.

The number of columns in the table must equal the number of expressions in the subquery. The column definitions can only specify column names, default values, and integrity constraints, not datatypes. Oracle derives datatypes and lengths from the subquery. Oracle also adheres to the following rules for integrity constraints:

Oracle automatically defines any NOT NULL constraints on columns in the new table that existed on the corresponding columns of the selected table if the subquery selects the column rather than an expression containing the column.

A CREATE TABLE statement cannot contain both AS clause and a referential integrity constraint definition.

If a CREATE TABLE statement contains both the AS clause and a CONSTRAINT clause or an ENABLE clause with the EXCEPTIONS option, Oracle ignores the EXCEPTIONS option. If any rows violate the constraint, Oracle does not create the table and returns an error message.

If all expressions in the subquery are columns, rather than expressions, you can omit the columns from the table definition entirely. In this case, the names of the columns of table are the same as the columns in the subquery.

CACHE—This specifies that the data will be accessed frequently; therefore the blocks retrieved for this table are placed at the most recently used end of the LRU list in the buffer cache when a full table scan is performed. This option is useful for small lookup tables.

CACHE as a parameter in the LOB storage clause specifies that Oracle preallocates and retains LOB data values in memory for faster access. CACHE is the default for index-only tables.

NOCACHE—This specifies that the data will not be accessed frequently; therefore the blocks retrieved for this table are placed at the least recently used end of the LRU list in the buffer cache when a full table scan is performed. For LOBs, the LOB value is not placed in the buffer cache.

This is the default behavior except when creating index-only tables. This is not a valid keyword when creating index-only tables.

NOCACHE as a parameter in the LOB storage clause specifies that LOB values are not preallocated in memory. This is the LOB storage default.

Section 5.5 in Chapter 5 shows an example port of an application fragment from Oracle7 syntax to Oracle8 using table objects, varrays, types, and nested tables.

The Oracle7 CREATE TABLE Command Format In contrast to the complex Oracle8 CREATE TABLE commands listed above, here is the Oracle7 (7.3.2) CREATE TABLE command:

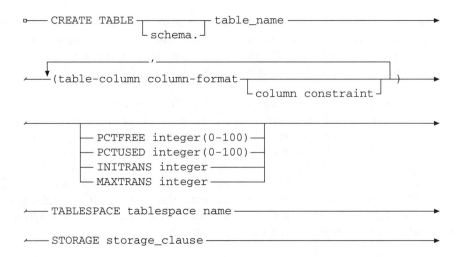

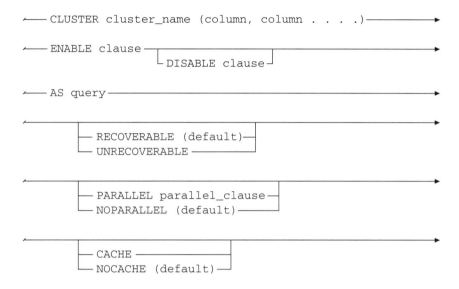

where:

Table-name—This is formatted either user.name or just the name, defaulting to the current user. This must be a unique name by user. This unique name applies to tables, views, synonyms, clusters and indexes. For uniqueness, the user portion counts.

Column-name—This is a unique name by table. The column name can be up to 30 characters long and cannot contain a quotation, slash, or character other than A-Z, 0-9, _, $, and #. A column name must not duplicate an Oracle reserved word (see the SQL manual for a list of these words). To use mixed case, include the mixed case portion in quotation marks.

For example:

- EMPNAME
- DOG
- AULT.EXPENSE

"SELECT" (Even though select is a reserved word, if it is enclosed in quotes it is okay to use.)

"NIP AND TUCK" (Even spaces are allowed with quotes.)

Names should be meaningful, not a bunch of symbols like A, B, C, etc. The Oracle CASE products always pluralize the names of tables; if you will be using CASE you might want to follow this convention.

Column-format—This is one of the allowed SQL data types. They are listed in the SQL manual. A brief list is:

CHAR(size)—Character type data, max size 255. Under Oracle7 this is replaced by VARCHAR2. Under Oracle7 CHAR will be right-side padded to specified length.

VARCHAR2—Variable-length character up to 2000.

DATE—Date format, from 1/1/4712 BC to 12/31/4712 AD. Standard Oracle format is (10-APR-93).

LONG—Character, up to 65,535 long. Only one LONG per table; 2 gig under Oracle7.

RAW(size)—Raw binary data, max of 255 size in version 6; 2000 under Oracle7.

LONG RAW—Raw binary data in hexadecimal format, 65,535 long; 2 gig under Oracle7.

ROWID—Internal data type, not user definable, used to uniquely identify table rows.

NUMBER(p,s)—Numeric data with p being precision and s being scale. Defaults to 38 p, null s.

DECIMAL(p,s)—Same as numeric.

INTEGER—Defaults to NUMBER(38), no scale.

SMALLINT—Same as INTEGER.

FLOAT—Same as NUMBER(38).

FLOAT(b)—NUMBER with precision of 1 to 126.

REAL—NUMBER(63).

DOUBLE PRECISION—Same as NUMBER(38).

No scale specification means floating point.

Column-Constraint—This is used to specify constraints. Constraints are limits placed either on a table or column. Oracle version 6 supports the format of constraints and stores constraint definitions but does not enforce them. It is a statement of the format:

```
CONSTRAINT name constraint type
```

Constraints also may be of the form:

```
NULL  CONSTRAINT constraint_type
NOT NULL CONSTRAINT constraint_type
PRIMARY KEY CONSTRAINT constraint_type
UNIQUE CONSTRAINT constraint_type
CHECK condition CONSTRAINT constraint_type
```

```
REFERENCES    table name (column name) CONSTRAINT constraint_type
                    DEFAULT default_value_clause
```

In the above formats the "CONSTRAINT constraint_type" is optional. Tables may also have the additional constraints:

```
FOREIGN KEY (column, column)
        REFERENCES table name (column, column)
        CONSTRAINT constraint_type
```

The foreign key constraint IS enforced. However, no index is automatically generated. It is suggested that indexes be maintained on foreign keys or else excessive full table scans may result.

PCTFREE—This parameter tells Oracle how much space to leave in each Oracle block for future updates. This defaults to 10. If a table will have a large number of updates, a larger value is needed; if the table will be static, a small value can be used. This is very table and table usage specific. Improper specification can result in chaining or improper space usage and performance degradation.

PCTUSED—This parameter tells Oracle the minimum level of space in a block to maintain. PCTUSED defaults to 40. A block becomes a candidate for updates if its storage falls below PCTUSED. The sum of PCTFREE and PCTUSED may not exceed 100. A high PCTUSED value results in more efficient space utilization but higher overhead as Oracle must work harder to maintain the free block list.

INITRANS—This option specifies the initial number of transactions that are allocated within each block.

MAXTRANS—This option species the maximum number of transactions that can update a block concurrently.

TABLESPACE—This specifies the tablespace, if other than the user's default.

STORAGE—This specifies the storage options for the table.

CLUSTER—This specifies the table is to be part of the specified cluster through the specified columns. PCTFREE, PCTUSED, and TABLESPACE options will produce errors when used with the CLUSTER clause.

ENABLE, DISABLE—This enables or disables constraints for an Oracle7 database.

RECOVERABLE, UNRECOVERABLE—This determines if the operation that creates the table should generate redo/rollback data or simply fail in the event of a problem.

PARALLEL parallel_clause, NOPARALLEL—This sets the default parallelism of the table (for a parallel query situation, sets how may processes will be used.)

CACHE, NOCACHE—this tells Oracle whether to cache the table in the SGA or not.

Let's look at a full example of an Oracle7 CREATE TABLE command with both column and table constraints. Afterward, we will examine the Oracle8 command usage as well.

```
CREATE TABLE purchase_order
      (po_number        INTEGER NOT NULL,
       line_no          INTEGER NOT NULL,
       line_description CHAR(60),
       part_no          CHAR(30),
       no_items         NUMBER,
       unit_cost        FLOAT,
       line_comment     LONG,
    PRIMARY KEY (po_number, line_no) CONSTRAINT
       po_lno_pk,
    FOREIGN KEY (part_no)
     REFERENCES (po_dba.part_list) CONSTRAINT po_pn_fk,
      CHECK (line_no > 0) CONSTRAINT po_ck1,
      CHECK (no_items >0) CONSTRAINT po_ck2 )
      UNRECOVERABLE
      PARALLEL DEGREE 4
      NOCACHE
```

This command creates the table purchase_orders with the columns po_number, line_no, line_description, part_no, no_items, unit_cost and line_comment. The primary key, or unique identifier is a concatenation of po_number and line_no. Part_no references another table, called part_list, that is owned by the user PO_DBA. No values can be entered into part_no unless they also exist in part_list. No values less than zero can be entered in either line_no or no_items. Po_number cannot be null, neither can line_no. The table is to be created with no recovery available should the operation fail, with a parallelism of 4 and not cached in the SGA.

Notice that all of the constraints are named. If you allow the system to provide default names, it will punish you by making them very cryptic. Since they may need to be enabled, disabled, dropped, or rebuilt, it will make your life easier if you name them explicitly.

Example Creation of Partitioned Tables A partitioned table has to be a straight relational table. A partitioned table is used to split up a table's data into separate physical as well as logical areas. This gives the benefits of being able to break up a large table in more manageable pieces and allows the Oracle8 kernel to more optimally retrieve values. Remember, you cannot (yet) put types, objects, varrays or nested tables into a partitioned table. Let's look at a quick example. We have a sales entity that will store results from sales for the last twelve months. This type of table is a logical candidate for partitioning because:

1. Its values have a clear separator (months).
2. It has a sliding range (the last year).
3. We usually access this type of date by sections (months, quarters, years).

The DDL for this type of table would look like this:

```
CREATE TABLE sales (
acct_no                  NUMBER(5),
sales_person             VARCHAR2(32),
sales_month              NUMBER(2),
amount_of_sale           NUMBER(9,2),
po_number                VARCHAR2(10))
PARTITION BY RANGE (sales_month)
    PARTITION sales_mon_1 VALUES LESS THAN (2),
    PARTITION sales_mon_2 VALUES LESS THAN (3),
    PARTITION sales_mon_3 VALUES LESS THAN (4),
         ...
    PARTITION sales_mon_12 VALUES LESS THAN (13),
    PARTITION sales_bad_mon VALUES LESS THAN (MAXVALUE));
```

In the above example we created the sales table with 13 partitions, one for each month plus an extra to hold improperly entered months (values >12). Always specify a last partition to hold MAXVALUE values for your partition values.

Oracle7 Table Sizing To estimate a table's size for the storage clause, use the following procedures.

Case 1: You have a test database available

If you have a test database available, perform the following to determine the required size for your production table:

1. Calculate the Block Header size using:

   Block Header = $57 + (23 \times \text{INITRANS}) + (4 \times \text{T}) + (2 \times \text{RPB})$

   where:

   T = Number of tables in cluster (1 for single table)

TIP   You can't figure RPB yet so you get some integer plus $2 \times \text{RPB}$.

---

2. Issue the following query against your test database:

```
SELECT AVG(NIL(VSIZE(col1), 1)) +
       AVG(NIL(VSIZE(col2), 1)) +
       ... +
       AVG(NIL(VSIZE(coln), 1)) "Average Data Length (ADL)"
       FROM Table name
```

where:

col1, col2, . . . coln are the names of the columns in the table.
Table name is the name of the table to be sized.

3. Calculate the Average Row Length (ARL).

ARL = row header + TLB1b + TLB3b + ADL

where:

row header = 3 for each row in a nonclustered table

TLB1b = total length bytes of all columns with 1-byte column lengths
  (CHAR, NUMBER, DATE, ROWID)
    TLB1b = (1 × # of 1 byte records)

TLB3b = total length bytes of all columns with 3-byte column lengths
  (LONG, RAW, LONG RAW)
    TLB3b = (3 × # of 3 byte records)

4. Now calculate RPB (substitute and solve for RPB).

RPB = (Data space in block / average row length (or 9 whichever is larger))

5. Now calculate the total amount of Blocks needed for the table.

Total table space = Estimated # rows/RPB

6. Finally, calculate bytes.

Space required in bytes = (Bytes/block) × (# of blocks)

If an example table exists that contains enough test data to be an accurate representation of the final table, the script in Source 4.1 can be used to estimate the size of the final table's average row length.

If the table exists in a test database, use the ANALYZE command to calculate the tables statistics, then simply look at the DBA_TABLES view to find average row length.

SOURCE 4.1   Script used to determine the average row length for a table.

```
rem   ***********************************************************
rem   NAME: TB_RW_SZ.sql
rem   HISTORY:
rem   Date            Who                 What
rem   --------        ----------------    -------------------
rem   01/20/93        Michael Brouillette    Creation
rem   FUNCTION:  Compute the average row size for a table.
rem   NOTES:  Currently requires DBA.
```

```
rem  INPUTS:
rem        tname  = Name of table.
rem        towner = Name of owner of table.
rem        cfile  = Name of output SQL Script file
rem  *********************************************************
COLUMN dum1        NOPRINT
COLUMN rsize       FORMAT 99,999.99
COLUMN rcount      FORMAT 999,999,999 newline
ACCEPT tname  PROMPT 'Enter table name: '
ACCEPT towner PROMPT 'Enter owner name: '
ACCEPT cfile  PROMPT 'Enter name for output SQL file: '
SET PAGESIZE 999 HEADING OFF  VERIFY OFF   TERMOUT OFF
SET FEEDBACK OFF  SQLCASE UPPER  NEWPAGE 3
SPOOL &cfile..sql
SELECT 0 dum1,
      'SELECT Table '||'&towner..&tname'||
      ' has '',COUNT(*) rcount,'' rows of '', ('
FROM dual
UNION
SELECT column_id,
      'SUM(NVL(VSIZE('||column_name||'),0)) + 1 +'
FROM dba_tab_columns
 WHERE table_name = '&tname' AND owner = '&towner'
   AND column_id <> (SELECT MAX(column_id)
                     FROM dba_tab_columns
              WHERE table_name = '&tname'
                AND owner = '&towner')
UNION
SELECT column_id,
      'SUM(NVL(VSIZE('||column_name||'),0)) + 1)'
FROM  dba_tab_columns
WHERE table_name = '&tname' AND owner = '&towner'
      AND column_id = (SELECT MAX(column_id)
                       FROM dba_tab_columns
              WHERE table_name = '&tname'
                AND owner = '&towner')
UNION
SELECT 997,  '/ COUNT(*) + 5 rsize, '' bytes each.'''
FROM dual
UNION
SELECT 999,  'from &towner..&tname.;'  FROM dual;
SPOOL OFF
SET TERMOUT ON  FEEDBACK 15   PAGESIZE 20
SET SQLCASE MIXED   NEWPAGE 1
START &cfile
CLEAR COLUMNS
UNDEF cfile
UNDEF tname
UNDEF towner
```

Case 2: You don't have a test database

If you don't have a test database, or the test database has an insignificant amount of data in it (you need at least enough data to provide good averages) then you will need to manually calculate the average data length (ADL).

1. Calculate the block header size using:

   Block Header = $57 + (23 \times \text{INITRANS}) + (4 \times T) + (2 \times \text{RPB})$

   where:

   T = Number of tables in cluster (1 for single table)

$\mathbf{T}$IP   You can't figure RPB yet so you get some integer plus $2 \times$ RPB.

---

2. Calculate the data space available in the block (BLOCK SIZE is set on database creation, usually 2048).

   Data space in block = (block size – total block header) $(1 - \text{PCTFREE})$

3. Calculate the average data length per row (ADL).

   ADL = (total char. in fixed records + avg. char in var. length records)

   where:

   Total char. in fixed records = (total of CHAR types + $(7 \times$ #of date fields))
   Total char in var. length records = $((\text{ave\_prec}/2+1) + (\text{ave\_prec}/2+1) + ...)$

4. Calculate the average row length (ARL).

   ARL = row header + TLB1b + TLB3b + ADL

   where:

   row header = 3 for each row in a nonclustered table
   TLB1b = total length bytes of all columns with 1-byte column lengths
       (CHAR, NUMBER, DATE, ROWID)
       TLB1b = $(1 \times$ # of 1 byte records)
   TLB3b = total length bytes of all columns with 3-byte column lengths
       (LONG, RAW, LONG RAW)
       TLB3b = $(3 \times$ # of 3-byte records)

5. Now calculate RPB (substitute and solve for RPB).

   RPB = (data space in block / average row length (or 9 whichever is larger))

6. Now calculate the total amount of blocks needed for the table.

Total table space = estimated # rows/RPB

7. Finally, calculate bytes.

Space required in bytes = (bytes/block) × (# of blocks)

The ANALYZE command can be used on an example table to give the data to get accurate size estimates. The format of this command follows.

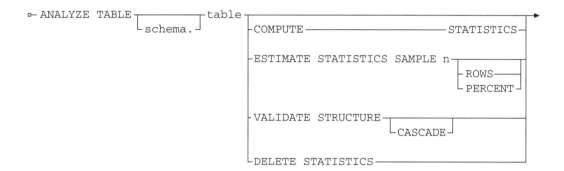

where:

COMPUTE STATISTICS—Calculates statistics based on all rows.

ESTIMATE STATISTICS—Calculates an estimate of the statistics based on "n" ROWS or PERCENT of rows in table.

VALIDATE STRUCTURE—Validates that the table and its indexes are consistent and not corrupted.

CASCADE—For clusters, validates all tables in cluster.

DELETE STATISTICS—Removes current statistics.

The results for statistics appear in the DBA_TABLES view.

Sizing an Oracle8 Nonclustered Table The procedures in this section describe how to estimate the total number of data blocks necessary to hold data inserted into a nonclustered table. No allowance is made for changes to pctfree or pctused due to insert, delete, or update activity.

T IP   This is a best-case scenario only when users insert rows without performing deletes or updates.

Typically, the space required to store a set of rows that experience updates, deletes, and inserts will exceed this calculated value. The actual space required for complex workloads is best determined by analysis of an existing table, and then scaled by the projected number of future rows in the production table. In general, increasing amounts of concurrent activity on the same data block results in additional overhead (for transaction records), so it is important that you take into account such activity when scaling empirical results.

To calculate space required by nonclustered tables is a five-step process:

1. Calculate the total block header size.
2. Calculate the available data space per data block.
3. Calculate the space used per row.
4. Calculate the total number of rows that will fit in a data block.
5. With the rows/block data, calculate the total number of data blocks and convert to kilo- or megabytes.

Let's take a more detailed look at the steps.

■ Step 1: Calculate the total block header size.
The space required by the data block header is the result of the following formula:

Space after headers (hsize) =

DB_BLOCK_SIZE – KCBH – UB4 – KTBBH – ((INITRANS – 1) * KTBIT) – KDBH

where:

DB_BLOCK_ SIZE—This is the database block size the database was created with. It can be viewed in the V$PARAMETER view by selecting:

```
SELECT value FROM v$parameter WHERE name = 'db_block_size';
```

KCBH, UB4, KTBBH, KTBIT, KDBH—These are constants whose sizes you can obtain by selecting from entries in the V$TYPE_SIZE view.

KCBH is the block common header; on NT with a 4 K block size this is 20.

UB4 is "either byte 4"; on NT with a 4 K block size this is 4.

KTBBH is the transaction fixed header length; on NT with a 4 K block size this is 48.

KTBIT is transaction variable header; on NT with a 4 K block size this is 24.

KDBH is the data header; on NT with a 4 K block size this is 14.

INITRANS—This is the initial number of transaction entries allocated to the table.

So, for an NT4.0 platform with a 4 K block size and an INITRANS value of 5 the calculation would be:

DB_BLOCK_SIZE – KCBH – UB4 – KTBBH – ((INITRANS – 1) * KTBIT) – KDBH
hsize = 4192 – 20 – 4 – 48 – ((5 – 1)*24) – 14 = 4192 – 182 = 4010 bytes

- Step 2: Calculate the available data space per data block.
  The space reserved in each data block for data, as specified by PCTFREE, is calculated as follows:

available data space (availspace) =
CEIL(hsize * (1 – PCTFREE/100)) – KDBT

where:

CEIL—Round fractional result to the next highest integer.

PCTFREE—This is the percentage of space reserved for updates in the table.

KDBT—This is a constant corresponding to the Table Directory Entry size whose size you can obtain by selecting the entry from the V$TYPE_SIZE view. For an NT4.0 platform with a 4-K block size this is 4.

$\rm T$IP   If you are unable to locate the value of KDBT, use the value of UB4 instead.

So, to carry on our example assuming a PCTFREE of 20 for our table:

CEIL(hsize * (1 – PCTFREE/100)) – KDBT
CEIL(4010* (1 – 20/100)) – 4 = CEIL((4010*.8) – 4) = CEIL(3208 – 4) = 3204

- Step 3: Calculate the space used per row.
  Calculating the amount of space used per row is a multistep task. First, you must calculate the column size, including byte lengths:

Column size including byte length =
column size + (1, if column size < 250, else 3)

I suggest using estimated averages for all variable-length fields such as numeric, varchar, and raw. Remember that number data types are stored at a 2 to 1 ratio in the database (i.e., a NUMBER(30) takes up 15 bytes of storage if each place is filled). The maximum for a NUMBER is 21 bytes. The size for a DATE is 7 bytes. ROWID takes 10 bytes for the extended and 6 bytes for the restricted type of ROWID. CHAR always takes its full specified length, VARCHAR2, RAW and other variable-length fields will only use the space they actually take up.

TIP You can also determine column size empirically, by selecting avg(vsize(colname)) for each column in the table.

For example, I have a table TEST with a single VARCHAR2(50) column that has 8 rows of various lengths. The return from the select "SELECT AVG(VSIZE(TEST1)) FROM TEST;" is:

```
AVG(VSIZE(TEST1))
---------------------------------
                29
```

The table also has a number column TEST2:

```
AVG(VSIZE(TEST2))
---------------------------------
                 7
```

Then, calculate the row size:

Rowsize =

row header (3 * UB1) + sum of column sizes including length bytes

UB1 is "UNSIGNED BYTE 1" and is 1 on NT4.0 with a 4 K block size.

Rowsize =

$(3*1) + (8 + 30) = 41$

Of course, if you have an example table the quickest way to get average row size is just to analyze it and then select average row size from USER_TABLES:

```
SQL> analyze table test1 compute statistics;
Table analyzed.
SQL> select avg_row_len from user_tables where table_name='TEST1';

AVG_ROW_LEN
-----------
         41
```

Finally, you can calculate the space used per row:

Space used per row (rowspace) =

MIN(UB1 * 3 + UB4 + SB2, rowsize) + SB2

where:

UB1, UB4, SB2—These are constants whose size can be obtained by selecting entries from the V$TYPE_SIZE view.

UB1 is "unsigned byte 1" and is set to 1 for NT4.0 with a 4 K block size.

UB4 is "unsigned byte 4" and is set to 4 for NT4.0 with a 4 K block size.

SB2 is "signed byte 2" and is set to 2 for NT4.0 with a 4 K block size.

So this becomes MIN((1*3) + 4 + 2, 41) + 2, or, 41 + 2 = 43.

MIN—Take the lesser of either UBI *3 + UB4 + SB2 or the calculated rowsize value.

If the space per row exceeds the available space per data block, but is less than the available space per data block without any space reserved for updates (for example, available space with PCTFREE=0), each row will be stored in its own block.

When the space per row exceeds the available space per data block without any space reserved for updates, rows inserted into the table will be chained into two or more pieces; hence, this storage overhead will be higher.

- Step 4: Calculate the total number of rows that will fit in a data block.
  You can calculate the total number of rows that will fit into a data block using the following equation:

Number of rows in block =
FLOOR(availspace / rowspace)

where:

FLOOR—Round fractional result to the next lowest integer.

So for our example this becomes:

FLOOR(3204/43) = 74

Step 5: Calculate the total blocks required.

Total blocks =
(total table rows) / (rows per block)

Total kilobytes =
CEIL((total blocks * block size) / 1024)

Total megabytes =
CEIL((total blocks * block size) / 1048576)   -- (1024^2)

For our example we approximate we will have 42,000 rows in this table over the next year. So, the calculation becomes:

((42000/74)*4192)/1024 = 2324k or 3m (rounding up)

Table Alteration

Face it, none of us is perfect. No one designs perfect applications. This means we some-times have to change things. For tables this means adding, changing, or dropping columns, adding constraints, or even deleting all of the rows from the table. Let's look at how to accomplish these table changes.

Functions of the Oracle8 ALTER TABLE command

- Adding a column
- Adding an integrity constraint
- Redefining a column (datatype, size, default value)
- Modification of the storage characteristics or other parameters
- Modification of the real storage attributes of a nonpartitioned table or the default attributes of a partitioned table
- Enabling, disabling, or dropping of an integrity constraint or trigger
- Explicit allocation of an extent
- Explicit deallocation of the unused space of a table
- Allowing or disallowing writes to a table
- Modification of the degree of parallelism for a table
- Modification of the LOGGING/NOLOGGING attributes
- Addition, modification, splitting, moving, dropping, or truncation of table partitions
- Renaming of a table or a table partition
- Addition or modification of index-only table characteristics
- Addition or modification of LOB columns
- Addition or modification of object type, nested table type, or VARRAY type column for a table
- Addition of integrity constraints to object type columns

In order to use the ALTER TABLE command in Oracle8 the following must be true:

1. The table must be in your own schema or you must have ALTER privilege on the table or you must have ALTER ANY TABLE system privilege.
2. To use an object type in a column definition when modifying a table, either that object must belong to the same schema as the table being altered, or you must have either the EXECUTE ANY TYPE system or the EXECUTE schema object privilege for the object type.
3. If you are using Trusted Oracle in DBMS MAC mode, your DBMS label must match the table's creation label or you must satisfy one of the following criteria:
4. If the table's creation label is higher than your DBMS label, you must have READUP and WRITEUP system privileges.
5. If the table's creation label is lower than your DBMS label, you must have WRITEDOWN system privilege.
6. If the table's creation label and your DBMS label are not comparable, you must have READUP, WRITEUP, and WRITEDOWN system privileges.

The syntax of the ALTER TABLE Command for Oracle8

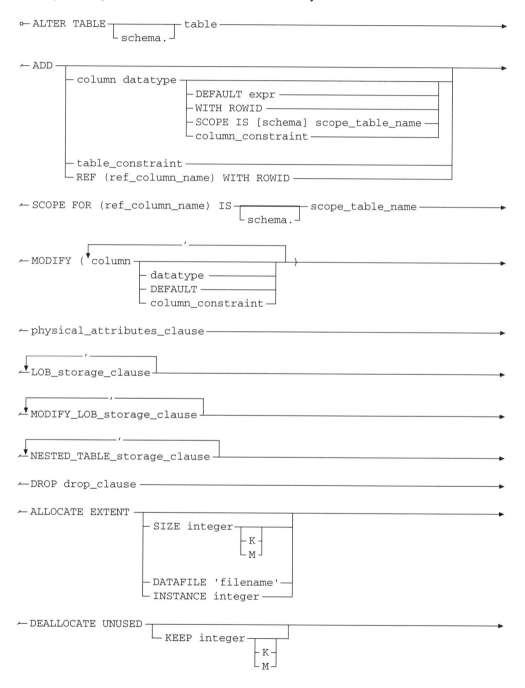

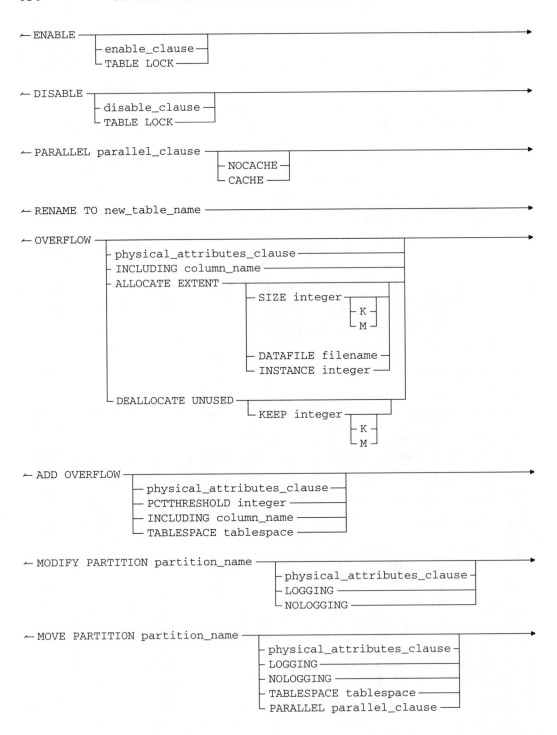

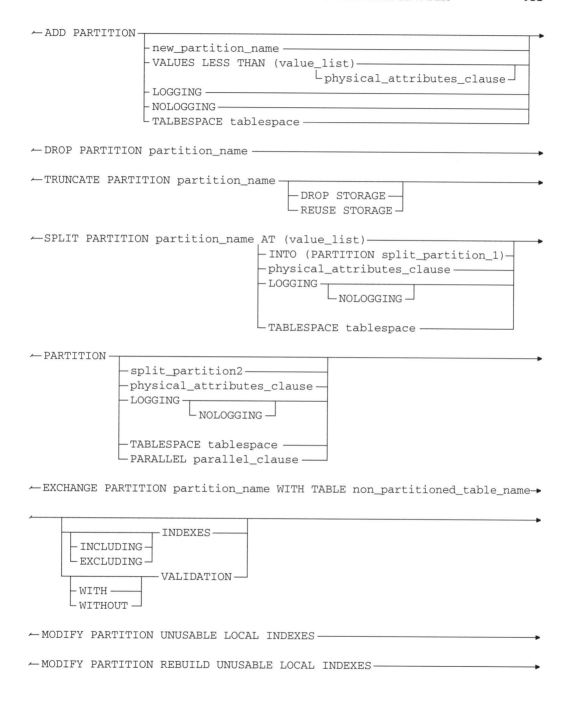

The physical_attributes_clause contains zero, and one or more of the following:

PCTFREE integer
PCTUSED integer
INITRANS integer
MAXTRANS integer
STORAGE storage_clause
The LOB_storage_clause has the following format:

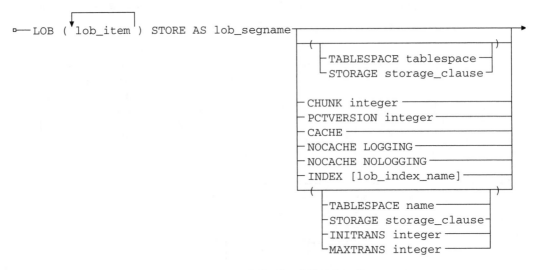

The MODIFY_LOB_storage_clause has the following format:

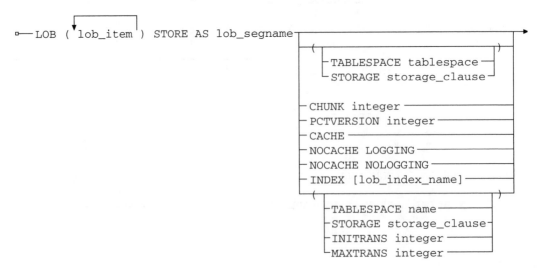

The NESTED_TABLE_storage_clause has the simple format:

```
NESTED TABLE nested_item STORE AS storage_table
```

The Keywords and Parameters for the Oracle8 Commands and Clauses

schema—This is the schema containing the table. If you omit schema, Oracle assumes the table is in your own schema.

table—This is the name of the table to be altered. You can alter the definition of an index-only table.

ADD—This adds a column or integrity constraint.

MODIFY—This modifies the definition of an existing column. If you omit any of the optional parts of the column definition (datatype, default value, or column constraint), these parts remain unchanged.

column—This is the name of the column to be added or modified.

datatype—This specifies a datatype for a new column or a new datatype for an existing column.

You can only omit the datatype if the statement also designates the column as part of the foreign key of a referential integrity constraint. Oracle automatically assigns the column the same datatype as the corresponding column of the referenced key of the referential integrity constraint.

DEFAULT—This specifies a default value for a new column or a new default for an existing column. Oracle assigns this value to the column if a subsequent INSERT statement omits a value for the column. The datatype of the default value must match the datatype specified for the column. The column must also be long enough to hold the default value. A DEFAULT expression cannot contain references to other columns, the pseudocolumns CURRVAL, NEXTVAL, LEVEL, and ROWNUM, or date constants that are not fully specified.

column_constraint—This adds or removes a NOT NULL constraint to or from an existing column.

table_constraint—This adds an integrity constraint to the table.

PCTFREE, PCTUSED, INITRANS, MAXTRANS—These change the value of specified parameters for the table, partition, or the overflow data segment, or the default characteristics of a partitioned table. See the PCTFREE, PCTUSED, INITRANS, and MAXTRANS parameters of the CREATE TABLE command.

STORAGE—This changes the storage characteristics of the table, partition, or overflow data segment.

PCTTHRESHOLD—This specifies the percentage of space reserved in the index block for an index-only table row. Any portion of the row that exceeds the specified threshold is stored in the overflow area. If OVERFLOW is not specified, then rows exceeding the THRESHOLD limit are rejected. PCTTHRESHOLD must be a value from 0 to 50.

The subclause for the PCTTRESHOLD clause is:

INCLUDING column_name—This specifies a column at which to divide an index-only table row into index and overflow portions. All columns which follow column_name are stored in the overflow data segment. A column_name is either the name of the last primary key column or any nonprimary key column.

LOB—This specifies the LOB storage characteristics.

lob_item—This is the LOB column name or LOB object attribute for which you are explicitly defining tablespace and storage characteristics that are different from those of the table.

The subclauses for the LOB clause are:

STORE AS

lob_segname—This specifies the name of the LOB data segment. You cannot use lob_segname if more than one lob_item is specified.

CHUNK integer—This is the unit of LOB value allocation and manipulation. Oracle allocates each unit of LOB storage as CHUNK integer. You can also use K or M to specify this size in kilobytes or megabytes. The default value of integer is 1 K and the maximum is 32 K. For efficiency, use a multiple of the Oracle block size.

PCTVERSION integer—This is the maximum percentage of overall LOB storage space used for creating new versions of the LOB. The default value is 10, meaning that older versions of the LOB data are not overwritten until 10% of the overall LOB storage space is used.

INDEX lob_index_name—This is the name of the LOB index segment. You cannot use lob_index_name if more than one lob_item is specified.

MODIFY LOB (column)—This modifies the physical attributes of the LOB storage column. You can only specify one LOB column for each MODIFY LOB clause.

NESTED TABLE nested_item STORE AS storage_table—This specifies storage_table as the name of the storage table in which the rows of all nested_item values reside. You must include this clause when modifying a table with columns or column attributes whose type is a nested table.

The nested_item is the name of a column or a column-qualified attribute whose type is a nested table.

The storage_table is the name of the storage table. The storage table is modified in the same schema and the same tablespace as the parent table.

DROP—This drops an integrity constraint.

ALLOCATE EXTENT—This explicitly allocates a new extent for the table, the overflow data segment, the LOB data segment, or the LOB index.

The subclauses for the ALLOCATE EXTENT clause are:

SIZE—This specifies the size of the extent in bytes. You can use K or M to specify the extent size in kilobytes or megabytes. If you omit this parameter, Oracle determines the size based on the values of the table's overflow data segment's, or LOB index's STORAGE parameters.

DATAFILE—This specifies one of the data files in the table's, overflow data segment's, LOB data's, or LOB index's tablespace to contain the new extent. If you omit this parameter, Oracle chooses the data file.

INSTANCE—This makes the new extent available to the freelist group associated with the specified instance. If the instance number exceeds the maximum number of freelist groups, the former is divided by the latter, and the remainder is used to identify the freelist group to be used. An instance is identified by the value of its initialization parameter INSTANCE_NUMBER. If you omit this parameter, the space is allocated to the table, but is not drawn from any particular freelist group.

Rather the master freelist is used, and space is allocated as needed. Only use this parameter if you are using Oracle with the Parallel Server option in parallel mode.

Explicitly allocating an extent with this clause does affect the size for the next extent to be allocated as specified by the NEXT and PCTINCREASE storage parameters.

DEALLOCATE UNUSED—This explicitly deallocates unused space at the end of the table, overflow data segment, LOB data segment, or LOB index and makes the space available for other segments. You can free only unused space above the high-water mark. If KEEP is omitted, all unused space is freed.

The DEALLOCATE UNUSED subclause has the definition:

KEEP—This specifies the number of bytes above the high-water mark that the table, overflow data segment, LOB data segment, or LOB index will have after deallocation. If the number of remaining extents are less than MINEXTENTS, then MINEXTENTS is set to the current number of extents. If the initial extent becomes smaller than INITIAL, then INITIAL is set to the value of the current initial extent.

OVERFLOW—This specifies the overflow data segment physical storage attributes to be modified for the index-only table. Parameters specified in this clause are only applicable to the overflow data segment. See the CREATE TABLE command.

ADD OVERFLOW—This adds an overflow data segment to the specified index-only table.

ENABLE enable_clause—This enables a single integrity constraint or all triggers associated with the table.

ENABLE TABLE LOCK—This enables DML and DDL locks on a table in a parallel server environment.

DISABLE disable_clause—This disables a single integrity constraint or all triggers associated with the tables.

Integrity constraints specified in DISABLED clauses must be defined in the ALTER TABLE statements or in a previously issued statement. You can also enable and disable integrity constraints with the ENABLE and DISABLE keywords of the CONSTRAINT clause. If you define an integrity constraint but do not explicitly enable or disable it, Oracle enables it by default.

DISABLE TABLE LOCK—This disables DML and DDL locks on a table to improve performance in a parallel server environment.

PARALLEL parallel_clause—This specifies the degree of parallelism for the table. PARALLEL is not a valid option for index-only tables.

CACHE—This specifies that the data is accessed frequently; therefore the blocks retrieved for this table are placed at the most recently used end of the LRU list in the buffer cache when a full table scan is performed. This option is useful for small lookup tables.

CACHE is not a valid option for index-only tables.

NOCACHE—This specifies that the data is not accessed frequently; therefore the blocks retrieved for this table are placed at the least recently used end of the LRU list in the buffer cache when a full table scan is performed. For LOBs, the LOB value is not placed in the buffer cache. This is the default behavior.

NOCACHE is not a valid option for index-only tables.

LOGGING—LOGGING specifies that subsequent operations against the table, partition, or LOB storage that can execute without logging are logged in the redo file.

If the table is partitioned, only the default table attributes are affected.

If the database is run in ARCHIVELOG mode, media recovery from a backup will recreate the table (and any indexes required because of constraints).

The logging attribute of the base table is independent of that of its indexes.

NOLOGGING—specifies that altering the table (and any indexes required because of constraints), partition, or LOB storage characteristics will not be logged in the redo log file. NOLOGGING also specifies that subsequent operations against the table or LOB storage are not logged in the redo file. As a result, media recovery will not recreate the table (and any indexes required because of constraints).

When running in NOARCHIVELOG mode, all operations that can execute without logging will not generate log entries even if LOGGING is specified for the table.

Using this keyword makes table modifications faster than using the LOGGING option because redo log entries are not written.

NOLOGGING is not a valid keyword for altering index-only tables.

RENAME TO new_table_name—This renames table to new_table_name.

MODIFY PARTITION partition_name—This modifies the real physical attributes of a table partition. You can specify any of the following as new physical attributes for the partition:

Logging attribute

PCTFREE

PCTUSED

INITRANS

MAXTRANS

STORAGE

RENAME PARTITION partition_name TO new_partition_name—This renames table partition partition_name to new_partition_name.

MOVE PARTITION partition_name—Moves table partition partition_name to another segment. You can move partition data to another tablespace, recluster data to reduce fragmentation, or change a create-time physical attribute.

ADD PARTITION new_partition_name—Adds a new partition new_partition_name to the "high" end of a partitioned table. You can specify any of the following as new physical attributes for the partition:

Logging attribute

PCTFREE

PCTUSED

INITRANS

MAXTRANS

STORAGE

VALUES LESS THAN (value_list)—This specifies the upper bound for the new partition. The value_list is a comma-separated, ordered list of literal values corresponding to column_list. The value_list must collate greater than the partition bound for the highest existing partition in the table.

DROP PARTITION partition_name—This removes partition partition_name, and the data in that partition, from a partitioned table.

TRUNCATE PARTITION partition_name—This removes all rows from a partition in a table.

TRUNCATE PARTITION clauses:

DROP STORAGE—This specifies that space from the deleted rows be deallocated and made available for use by other schema objects in the tablespace.

REUSE STORAGE—This specifies that space from the deleted rows remains allocated to the partition. The space is subsequently only available for inserts and updates to the same partition.

SPLIT PARTITION partition_name_old—This creates two new partitions, each with a new segment and new physical attributes, and new initial extents. The segment associated with the old partition is discarded.

SPLIT PARTITION clauses:

AT (value_list)—This specifies the new noninclusive upper bound for split_partition_1. The value_list must compare less than the presplit-partition bound for partition_name_old and greater than the partition bound for the next lowest partition (if there is one).

INTO—This describes the two partitions resulting from the split.

PARTITION split_partition_1,

PARTITION split_partition_2

This specifies the names and physical attributes of the two partitions resulting from the split.

EXCHANGE PARTITION partition_name—This converts partition partition_name into a nonpartitioned table, and a nonpartitioned table into a partition of a partitioned table by exchanging their data (and index) segments.

EXCHANGE PARTITION clauses:

WITH TABLE table—This specifies the table with which the partition will be exchanged.

INCLUDING INDEXES—This specifies that the local index partitions be exchanged with the corresponding regular indexes.

EXCLUDING INDEXES—This specifies that all the local index partitions corresponding to the partition and all the regular indexes on the exchanged table are marked as unusable.

WITH VALIDATION—This specifies that any rows in the exchanged table that do not collate properly return an error.

WITHOUT VALIDATION—This specifies that the proper collation of rows in the exchanged table are not checked.

UNUSABLE LOCAL INDEXES—This marks all the local index partitions associated with partition_name as unusable.

REBUILD UNUSABLE LOCAL INDEXES—This rebuilds the unusable local index partitions associated with the specified partition_name.

Adding Columns If you use the ADD clause to add a new column to the table, then the initial value of each row for the new column is null. You can add a column with a NOT NULL constraint only to a table that contains no rows.

If you create a view with a query that uses the asterisk (*) in the select list to select all columns from the base table and you subsequently add columns to the base table, Oracle will not automatically add the new column to the view. To add the new column to the view, you can recreate the view using the CREATE VIEW command with the OR REPLACE option.

Operations performed by the ALTER TABLE command can cause Oracle to invalidate procedures and stored functions that access the table.

Modifying Column Definitions You can use the MODIFY clause to change any of the following parts of a column definition:

Datatype

Size

Default value

NOT NULL column constraint

The MODIFY clause need only specify the column name and the modified part of the definition, rather than the entire column definition.

Datatypes and Sizes You can change:

- A CHAR column to VARCHAR2 (or VARCHAR).

  A VARCHAR2 (or VARCHAR) to CHAR only if the column contains nulls in all rows or if you do not attempt to change the column size.

  Any column's datatype or decrease any column's size if all rows for the column contain nulls. However, you can always increase the size of a character or raw column or the precision of a numeric column.

Default Values A change to a column's default value only affects rows subsequently inserted into the table. Such a change does not change default values previously inserted.

Integrity Constraints The only type of integrity constraint that you can add to an existing column using the MODIFY clause with the column constraint syntax is a NOT NULL constraint. However, you can define other types of integrity constraints (UNIQUE, PRIMARY KEY, referential integrity, and CHECK constraints) on existing columns using the ADD clause and the table constraint syntax.

You can define a NOT NULL constraint on an existing column only if the column contains no nulls.

Allocation of Extents The following statement allocates an extent of 5 kilobytes for the EMP table and makes it available to instance 4:

```
ALTER TABLE emp
  ALLOCATE EXTENT (SIZE 5K INSTANCE 4);
```

Because this command omits the DATAFILE parameter, Oracle allocates the extent in one of the data files belonging to the tablespace containing the table.

LOB Columns You can add a LOB column to a table, modify a LOB index, or modify the LOB index storage characteristics.

The following statement adds CLOB column REFERENCES to the EMP table:

```
ALTER TABLE emp ADD (references CLOB)
  LOB (references) STORE AS references_seg (TABLESPACE references_ts);
```

To modify the LOB column RESUME to use caching, enter the following statement:

```
ALTER TABLE emp MODIFY LOB (references) (CACHE);
```

Nested Table Columns You can add a nested table type column to a table. Specify a nested table storage clause for each column added. The following example adds the nested table column ABILITIES to the EMP table:

```
ALTER TABLE emp ADD (abilities ability_list)
  NESTED TABLE abilities STORE AS abilitiesv8;
```

You can also modify a nested table's storage characteristics. Use the name of the storage table specified in the nested table storage clause to make the modification. You cannot query or perform DML statements on the storage table; only use the storage table to modify the nested table column storage characteristics.

The following example creates table CARSERVICE with nested table column CLIENT and storage table CLIENTV8. Nested table CARSERVICE is modified to specify constraints and modify a column length by altering nested storage table CLIENT_LIST:

```
CREATE TABLE carservice (mech_name VARCHAR2(30),
                         client   client_list);
  NESTED TABLE client STORE AS clientv8;
```

```
ALTER TABLE clientv8 ADD UNIQUE (ssn);

ALTER TABLE clientv8 MODIFY (mech_name VARCHAR2(35));
```

The following statement adds a UNIQUE constraint to nested table ABILITY_LIST:

```
ALTER TABLE ABILITY_LIST ADD UNIQUE (a);
```

Scoped REFs A REF value is a reference to a row in an object table. A table can have top-level REF columns or it can have REF attributes embedded within an object column. In general, if a table has a REF column, each REF value in the column could reference a row in a different object table. A SCOPE clause restricts the scope of references to a single table. In the real world I would say 99% of applications will use scoped REFs; I can envision few applications where you would want to access multiple tables from the same column of a single table.

Use the ALTER TABLE command to add new REF columns or to add REF clauses to existing REF columns. You can modify any table, including named inner nested tables (storage tables). If a REF column is created WITH ROWID or with a scope table, you cannot modify the column to drop these options. However, if a table is created without any REF clauses, you can add them later with an ALTER TABLE statement.

TIP   You can only add a scope clause to existing REF columns of a table if the table is empty. The scope_table_name must be in your own schema or you must have SELECT privilege on the table, or the SELECT ANY TABLE system privilege. This privilege is only needed while altering the table with the REF column.

In the following example an object type DEPT_T has been previously defined. Now assume that table EMP is created as follows:

```
CREATE TABLE emp
   (name    VARCHAR(100),
    salary       NUMBER,
    dept    REF dept_t) AS OBJECT;
```

An object table DEPARTMENTS is created as:

```
CREATE TABLE departments OF dept_t AS OBJECT;
```

If the DEPARTMENTS table contains all possible departments, the DEPT column in EMP can only refer to rows in the DEPARTMENTS table. This can be expressed as a scope clause on the DEPT column as follows:

```
ALTER TABLE emp
    ADD (SCOPE FOR (dept) IS departments);
```

Note that the above ALTER TABLE statement will succeed only if the EMP table is empty.

Modifying Table Partitions You can modify a table or table partition in any of the following ways. You cannot combine partition operations with other partition operations or with operations on the base table in one ALTER TABLE statement.

ADD PARTITION Use ALTER TABLE ADD PARTITION to add a partition to the high end of the table (after the last existing partition). If the first element of the partition bound of the high partition is MAXVALUE, you cannot add a partition to the table. You must split the high partition.

You can add a partition to a table even if one or more of the table indexes or index partitions are marked UNUSABLE.

You must use the SPLIT PARTITION clause to add a partition at the beginning or the middle of the table.

The following example adds partition JAN98 to tablespace YR98:

```
ALTER TABLE sales
  ADD PARTITION jan98 VALUES LESS THAN( '980201' )
  TABLESPACE yr98;
```

DROP PARTITION ALTER TABLE DROP PARTITION drops a partition and its data. If you want to drop a partition but keep its data in the table, you must merge the partition into one of the adjacent partitions.

If you drop a partition and later insert a row that would have belonged to the dropped partition, the row will be stored in the next higher partition. However, if you drop the highest partition, the insert will fail because the range of values represented by the dropped partition is no longer valid for the table.

This statement also drops the corresponding partition in each local index defined on table. The index partitions are dropped even if they are marked as unusable.

If there are global indexes defined on table, and the partition you want to drop is not empty, dropping the partition marks all the global, nonpartitioned indexes and all the partitions of global partitioned indexes as unusable.

When a table contains only one partition, you cannot drop the partition. You must drop the table.

The following example drops partition JAN96:

```
ALTER TABLE sales DROP PARTITION jan96;
```

EXCHANGE PARTITION This form of ALTER TABLE converts a partition to a non-partitioned table and a table to a partition by exchanging their data segments. You must have ALTER TABLE privileges on both tables to perform this operation.

The statistics of the table and partition, including table, column, index statistics, and histograms, are exchanged. The aggregate statistics of the partitioned table are recalculated. The logging attribute of the table and partition is exchanged.

The following example converts partition FEB97 to table SALES_FEB97:

```
ALTER TABLE sales
  EXCHANGE PARTITION feb97 WITH TABLE sales_feb97
  WITHOUT VALIDATION;
```

MODIFY PARTITION Use the MODIFY PARTITION options of ALTER TABLE to

- Mark local index partitions corresponding to a table partition as unusable.
- Rebuild all the unusable local index partitions corresponding to a table partition.
- Modify the physical attributes of a table partition.

The following example marks all the local index partitions corresponding to the APR96 partition of the procurements table UNUSABLE:

```
ALTER TABLE procurements MODIFY PARTITION apr96
  UNUSABLE LOCAL INDEXES;
```

The following example rebuilds all the local index partitions which were marked UNUSABLE:

```
ALTER TABLE procurements MODIFY PARTITION jan98
  REBUILD UNUSABLE LOCAL INDEXES;
```

The following example changes MAXEXTENTS for partition KANSAS_OFF:

```
ALTER TABLE branch MODIFY PARTITION kansas_off
  STORAGE(MAXEXTENTS 100) LOGGING;
```

MOVE PARTITION This ALTER TABLE option moves a table partition to another segment. MOVE PARTITION always drops the partition's old segment and creates a new segment, even if you do not specify a new tablespace.

If partition_name is not empty, MOVE PARTITION marks all corresponding local index partitions and all global nonpartitioned indexes and all the partitions of global partitioned indexes as unusable.

ALTER TABLE MOVE PARTITION obtains its parallel attribute from the PARALLEL clause, if specified. If not specified, the default PARALLEL attributes of the table, if any, are used. If neither is specified, it performs the move without using parallelism.

The PARALLEL clause on MOVE PARTITION does not change the default PARALLEL attributes of table.

The following example moves partition STATION3 to tablespace TS097:

```
ALTER TABLE trains
   MOVE PARTITION station3 TABLESPACE ts097 NOLOGGING;
```

MERGE PARTITION While there is no explicit MERGE statement, you can merge a partition using either the DROP PARTITION or EXCHANGE PARTITION clauses. You can use either of the following strategies to merge table partitions.

If you have data in partition PART1, and no global indexes or referential integrity constraints on the table, PARTS, you can merge table partition PART1 into the next highest partition, PART2.

To merge partition PART1 into partition PART2:

1. Export the data from PART1.
2. Issue the following statement:

```
ALTER TABLE PARTS DROP PARTITION PART1;
```

3. Import the data from step 1 into partition PART2.

TIP   The corresponding local index partitions are also merged.

Here is another way to merge partition PART1 into partition PART2:

1. Exchange partition PART1 of table PARTS with "dummy" table PARTS_DUMMY.
2. Issue the following statement:

```
ALTER TABLE PARTS DROP PARTITION PART1;
```

3. Insert as SELECT from the "dummy" tables to move the data from PART1 back into PART2.

SPLIT PARTITION The SPLIT PARTITION option divides a partition into two partitions, each with a new segment, new physical attributes, and new initial extents. The segment associated with the old partition is discarded.

This statement also performs a matching split on the corresponding partition in each local index defined on table. The index partitions are split even if they are marked unusable.

With the exception of the TABLESPACE attribute, the physical attributes of the LOCAL index partition being split are used for both new index partitions. If the parent LOCAL index lacks a default TABLESPACE attribute, new LOCAL index partitions will reside in the same tablespace as the corresponding newly created partitions of the underlying table.

If you do not specify physical attributes (PCTFREE, PCTUSED, INITRANS, MAXTRANS, STORAGE) for the new partitions, the current values of the partition being split are used as the default values for both partitions.

If partition_name is not empty, SPLIT PARTITION marks all affected index partitions as unusable. This includes all global index partitions as well as the local index partitions which result from the split.

The PARALLEL clause on SPLIT PARTITION does not change the default PARALLEL attributes of table.

The following example splits the old partition STATION5 creating a new partition for STATION9:

```
ALTER TABLE trains
  SPLIT PARTITION STATION5 AT ( '50-001' )
  INTO (
    PARTITION station5 TABLESPACE train009 (MINEXTENTS 2),
    PARTITION station9 TABLESPACE train010 )
  PARALLEL ( DEGREE 9 );
```

TRUNCATE PARTITION Use TRUNCATE PARTITION to remove all rows from a partition in a table. Freed space is deallocated or reused depending on whether DROP STORAGE or REUSE STORAGE is specified in the clause.

This statement truncates the corresponding partition in each local index defined on table. The local index partitions are truncated even if they are marked as unusable. The unusable local index partitions are marked valid, resetting the UNUSABLE indicator.

If there are global indexes defined on table, and the partition you want to truncate is not empty, truncating the partition marks all the global nonpartitioned indexes and all the partitions of global partitioned indexes as unusable.

If you want to truncate a partition that contains data, you must first disable any referential integrity constraints on the table. Alternatively, you can delete the rows and then truncate the partition.

The following example deletes all the data in the part_17 partition and deallocates the freed space:

```
ALTER TABLE shipments
  TRUNCATE PARTITION part_17 DROP STORAGE;
```

RENAME Use the RENAME option of ALTER TABLE to rename a table or to rename a partition. The following example renames a table:

```
ALTER TABLE emp RENAME TO employee;
```

In the following example, partition EMP3 is renamed:

```
ALTER TABLE employee RENAME PARTITION emp3 TO employee3;
```

The Oracle7 ALTER TABLE Command Format

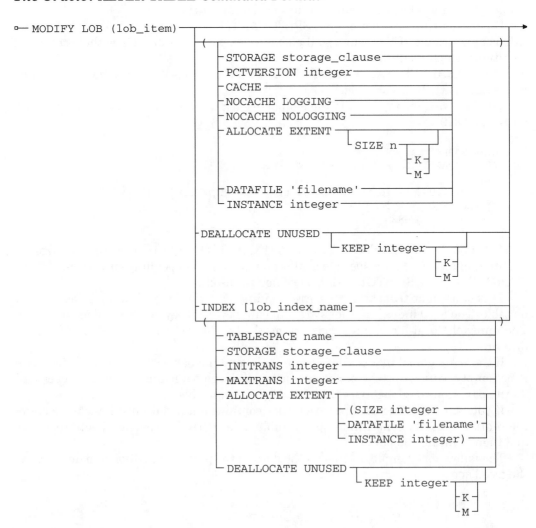

Here are some notes on the Oracle7 ALTER TABLE command.

Things you can do:

1. Add columns that can have NULL values to any table.
2. Modify columns to a larger size.
3. Modify columns that have all null values to be shorter, or to a different data type.
4. Alter the PCTFREE, PCTUSED, INITRANS or MAXTRANS for any table.
5. Alter the storage clause for any table.
6. Tell the data dictionary that the table has been backed up as of the date of the ALTER command by use of BACKUP clause.
7. Change or remove the PARALLELism of a table.
8. Specify if a table is to be cached or not.

Things you cannot do:

1. Modify a column that has values to be shorter or to a different data type.
2. Add a NOT NULL column to a table that has rows.
3. Alter a column to NOT NULL if it has rows with NULL values in that column.
4. Drop a column.
5. Rename a column.
6. Change a column's data type to a noncompatible datatype.

Table Statistics and Validity—The ANALYZE Command

To help a DBA determine if a table's data and indexes have integrity and to calculate the statistics used by the cost-based optimizer, Oracle7 and Oracle8 provide the ANALYZE command that can be used to analyze the structure of a table and its indexes. The schema object to be analyzed must be in your own schema or you must have the ANALYZE ANY system privilege.

If you want to list chained rows of a table or cluster into a list table, the list table must be in your own schema or you must have INSERT privilege on the list table or you must have INSERT ANY TABLE system privilege.

If you want to validate a partitioned table, you must have INSERT privilege on the table into which you list analyzed ROWIDS, or you must have INSERT ANY TABLE system privilege.

The Oracle8 Syntax for ANALYZE

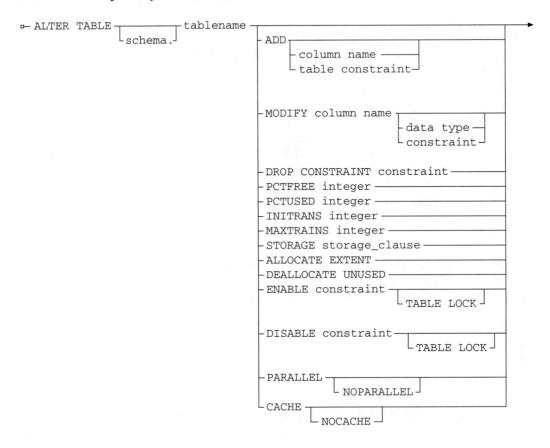

Here is the format for the FOR clause (used for HISTOGRAM option):

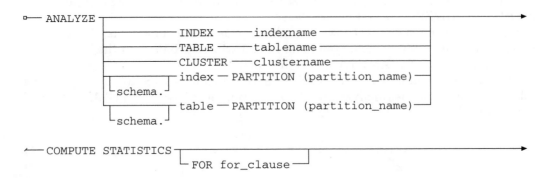

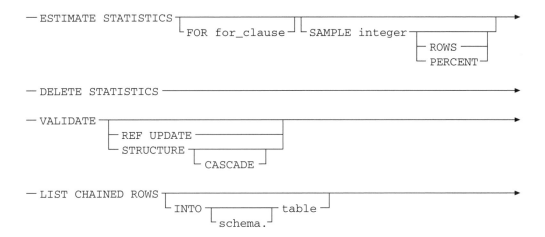

The Keywords and Parameters for the Oracle8 ANALYZE Command

attribute—This specifies the qualified column name of an item in an object.

INDEX—This identifies an index to be analyzed (if no FOR clause is used). If you omit schema, Oracle assumes the index is in your own schema.

TABLE—Identifies a table to be analyzed. If you omit schema, Oracle assumes the table is in your own schema. When you collect statistics for a table, Oracle also automatically collects the statistics for each of the table's indexes, provided that no FOR clauses are used.

PARTITION (partition_name)—This specifies that statistics will be gathered for (partition_name). You cannot use this option when analyzing clusters.

CLUSTER—This identifies a cluster to be analyzed. If you omit schema, Oracle assumes the cluster is in your own schema. When you collect statistics for a cluster, Oracle also automatically collects the statistics for all the cluster's tables and all their indexes, including the cluster index.

VALIDATE REF UPDATE—This validates the REFs in the specified table, checks the ROWID portion in each REF, compares it with the true ROWID, and corrects, if necessary. You can only use this option when analyzing a table.

COMPUTE STATISTICS—Computes exact statistics about the analyzed object and stores them in a data dictionary.

ESTIMATE STATISTICS—This estimates statistics about the analyzed object and stores them in the data dictionary.

The clauses for ESTIMATE STATISTICS are:

SAMPLE—Specifies the amount of data from the analyzed object Oracle samples to estimate statistics. If you omit this parameter, Oracle samples 1064 rows. If you specify more than half of the data, Oracle reads all the data and computes the statistics.

ROWS—This causes Oracle to sample integer rows of the table or cluster or integer entries from the index. The integer must be at least 1.

PERCENT—Causes Oracle to sample integer percent of the rows from the table or cluster or integer percent of the index entries. The integer can range from 1 to 99.

The following HISTOGRAM clauses only apply to the ANALYZE TABLE version of this command:

FOR TABLE—Collect table statistics for the table.

FOR ALL COLUMNS—Collect column statistics for all columns and scalar attributes.

FOR ALL INDEXED COLUMNS—Collect column statistics for all indexed columns in the table.

FOR COLUMNS—Collect column statistics for the specified columns and scalar object attributes.

FOR ALL INDEXES—All indexes associated with the table will be analyzed.

FOR ALL LOCAL INDEXES—Specifies that all local index partitions are analyzed. You must specify the keyword LOCAL if the PARTITION (partition_name) clause and the index option are specified.

SIZE—This specifies the maximum number of partitions in the histogram. The default value is 75, minimum value is 1, and maximum value is 254.

DELETE STATISTICS—Delete any statistics about the analyzed object that are currently stored in the data dictionary.

VALIDATE STRUCTURE—This validates the structure of the analyzed object. If you use this option when analyzing a cluster, Oracle automatically validates the structure of the cluster's tables.

INTO—This specifies a table into which Oracle lists the rowids of the partitions whose rows do not collate correctly. If you omit schema, Oracle assumes the list is in your own schema. If you omit this clause altogether, Oracle assumes that the table is named INVALID_ROWS. According to Oracle documentation, the SQL script used to create this table is UTLVALID.SQL, however as of 7.3.2 and 8.0.2 there is no trace of this file to be found.

CASCADE—This validates the structure of the indexes associated with the table or cluster. If you use this option when validating a table, Oracle also validates the table's indexes. If you use this option when validating a cluster, Oracle also validates all the clustered tables' indexes, including the cluster index.

LIST CHAINED ROWS—This identifies migrated and chained rows of the analyzed table or cluster. You cannot use this option when analyzing an index.

INTO—This specifies a table into which Oracle lists the migrated and chained rows. If you omit schema, Oracle assumes the list table is in your own schema. If you omit this clause altogether, Oracle assumes that the table is named CHAINED_ROWS. The script used to create this table is UTLCHAIN.SQL. The list table must be on your local database.

The structure under Oracle8 for the table is:

```
CREATE TABLE chained_rows (
owner_name           varchar2(30),
table_name           varchar2(30),
cluster_name         varchar2(30),
partition_name       varchar2(30),
head_rowid           rowid,
analyze_timestamp    date);
```

The structure under Oracle7 for the table is:

```
CREATE TABLE chained_rows (
owner_name           varchar2(30),
table_name           varchar2(30),
cluster_name         varchar2(30),
head_rowid           rowid,
timestamp            date);
```

To analyze index-only tables, you must create a separate chained rows table for each index-only table created to accommodate the primary key storage of index-only tables. Use the SQL scripts DBMSIOTC.SQL and PRVTIOTC.PLB to define the DBMS_IOT package with the BUILD_CHAIN_ROWS_TABLE(owner VARCHAR2, iot_name VARCAHR2, chainrow_table_name VARCHAR2) procedure and then execute this procedure to create an IOT_CHAINED_ROWS table for an index-only table. The IOT_CHAINED_ROWS table has the structure:

```
CREATE TABLE iot_chained_rows (
owner_name               varchar2(30),
table_name               varchar2(30),
cluster_name             varchar2(30),
partition_name           varchar2(30),
head_rowid               rowid,
timestamp                date,
test1           varchar2(6) <<-- This is the primary key
);                            from the table being analyzed
```

Collecting Statistics You can collect statistics about the physical storage characteristics and data distribution of an index, table, column, or cluster and store them as histograms in the data dictionary. For computing or estimating statistics computation always provides exact values, but can take longer than estimation and requires large amounts of temporary tablespace (up to four times the size of your largest table). Estimation is often much faster than computation and the results are usually nearly exact. You cannot compute or estimate histogram statistics for the following column types:

REFs

VARRAYs

Nested tables

LOBs

LONGs

Object types

Use estimation, rather than computation, unless you feel you need exact values. Some statistics are always computed exactly, regardless of whether you specify computation or estimation. If you choose estimation and the time saved by estimating a statistic is negligible, Oracle computes the statistic exactly.

If the data dictionary already contains statistics for the analyzed object, Oracle updates the existing statistics with the new ones.

Deletion of a Table's Data

Deletion of a table's data can be done by two methods. Method one uses the DELETE command and can be conditional. A DELETE is also able to be rolled back if you decide, before you commit, that you goofed. The second method is the TRUNCATE command. The TRUNCATE is a DDL and not DML command, is not conditional (it's all or nothing), and cannot be rolled back (yes, you will be there for days reentering data if you goof). Let's look at these commands and their options.

The DELETE Command You can selectively delete data or delete all of a table's data using the DELETE command. The format for this command follows.

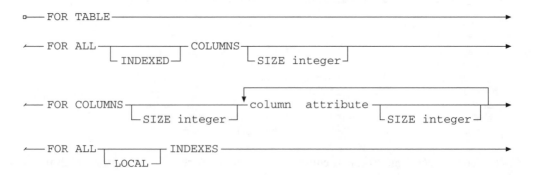

where the clauses have the following definitions:

schema—This is the schema or owner of the table, view, or partition being deleted from. If it is left off, the user's default schema is used.

table or view—This is the name of the table or view to be deleted from.

dblink—If the table, view, or partition is in a remote database, this is the dblink to that database.

PARTITION(partition name)—This deletes from a specified (partition_name) subpartition of a partitioned table.

THE—This is used to flatten nested tables. The subquery following the THE clause tells Oracle how the flattening should occur.

subquery—Used to tell Oracle how to delete from the table or nested table. If deletion is from a nested table the THE clause must be included.

alias—Used when a correlated subquery is used to denote table hierarchy in the query/delete commands.

WHERE condition—The condition each deleted row must meet or fail.

TIP   You can use hints in a DELETE statement to optimize delete subquery processing.

The table name can include an alias; if the WHERE clause is left out, all of the rows in the table are deleted. Four examples follow.

```
DELETE FROM PER_DBA.JOBS A WHERE A.JOB_STATUS = 'COMPLETE';
```

This command would delete all rows with the data value COMPLETE in the column JOB_STATUS from the JOBS table owned by the PER_DBA user.

```
DELETE PER_DBA.OLD_JOBS
```

This command would remove all rows from the table OLD_JOBS that belongs to the schema PER_DBA.

To delete specific rows from a nested table, the THE clause is specified (I like to think 'FROM THE SET' when I see THE):

```
DELETE THE (SELECT addresses
 FROM clientsv8 c
 WHERE c.customer_name = 'Joes Bar and Grill, Inc.')
 AS a
WHERE a.addrtype=1;
```

Deleting from a single partition is accomplished by use of the PARTITION clause:

```
DELETE FROM trains PARTITION (roundhouse1)
WHERE
service_date < to_date('01-Jan-1956 00:00:00,
'DD-Mon-YYYY hh24:mi:ss');
```

The TRUNCATE TABLE Command There is also a way to avoid the use of roll-back and make deletions much faster. The command is the TRUNCATE command. One good feature of this command is that it can be used to reclaim the space used by the data that was in the table. As was said in the introduction to this section, the TRUNCATE is a DDL command and once issued, the data is gone. A TRUNCATE cannot be rolled back. The format for this command follows.

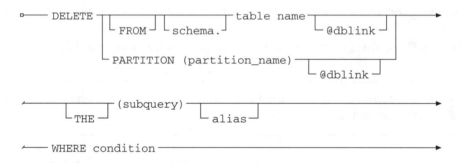

The DROP/REUSE STORAGE option allows you to shrink the table back to its high-water mark or leave the table at its current size. Both DROP and REUSE qualifiers also apply to whatever index space is regained.

For tables, PRESERVE or PURGE SNAPSHOT options allow control over a table's snapshot logs as well.

The truncate command is faster than the delete command because it is a DDL command and generates no rollback data. When using truncate on a clustered table, the data must be removed from the entire cluster, not just the one table. Any referential integrity constraints on a table must be disabled before it can be truncated. Like a table DROP, a truncation is not recoverable. If a table is truncated you cannot rollback if you made a mistake. Use TRUNCATE carefully.

Dropping a Table

To completely remove a table from the tablespace, use the DROP TABLE command. This command's format follows.

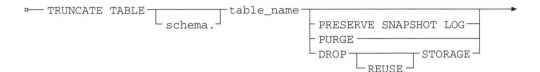

Oracle will drop the table regardless of its contents. The only time a drop will fail is when a table's primary key is referenced by another table's foreign key via a restraint clause. The DBA can check for this situation by looking at the DBA_ CONSTRAINTS and the DBA_CONS_COLUMNS views. A view called USER_ CROSS_REFS provides this information on a user-by-user basis. Using the CASCADE CONSTRAINTS clause will force a CASCADE DELETE to occur in all child tables.

Rebuilding Tables

The DBA may have to rebuild a table or tables after maintenance, after a physical disk crash, or, the leading cause, due to operational stupidity. If the application designers were thoughtful enough to provide a build script, there is no problem. However, for legacy systems, systems that have been modified and not redocumented, or systems created on-the-fly, there may be no current build scripts, if there were any to begin with. In this case, the DBA is in trouble. How can this situation be prevented? Require build scripts for each application and keep them up to date. For existing, undocumented systems, the script in Source 4.2 will create a build script for existing tables. It must be run before any loss has occurred. Due to the added complexity of Oracle8 it is doubtful many systems will be created on-the-fly that make use of the complex options and types. Unfortunately, the script shown in Source 4.2 cannot handle complex type schemes in Oracle8. Over time I will be revising it to handle the more complex Oracle8 structures and newer versions will be made available at the RevealNet website http://www.revealnet.com/.

SOURCE 4.2   Script to create a table-rebuild script for undocumented systems.

```
REM tab_rct.sql
REM
REM FUNCTION: SCRIPT FOR CREATING TABLES
REM
REM          This script can be run by any user .
REM          This script is intended to run with Oracle7.
REM          Running this script will in turn create a script to
REM          build all the tables owner by the user in the database.
REM          This created
REM          script, crt_tab.sql, can be run by any user with the
REM          'CREATE TABLE' system privilege.
```

```
REM NOTE:      The script will NOT include constraints on tables.  This
REM            script will also NOT capture tables created by user 'SYS'.
REM Only preliminary testing of script was performed.  Be sure to test
REM it completely before relying on it.
REM
SET VERIFY OFF FEEDBACK OFF TERMOUT OFF ECHO OFF PAGESIZE 0
SET TERMOUT ON
SELECT 'Creating table build script...' FROM dual;
SET TERMOUT OFF

CREATE TABLE t_temp
    (lineno NUMBER, tb_owner VARCHAR2(30), tb_name VARCHAR2(30),
     text VARCHAR2(2000))
/


DECLARE
   CURSOR tab_cursor IS
     SELECT   table_name, pct_free,
              pct_used,ini_trans,
              max_trans,tablespace_name,
              initial_extent,next_extent,
              min_extents,max_extents,
              pct_increase,freelists,
              freelist_groups
     FROM       user_tables
     ORDER BY   table_name;
   CURSOR col_cursor (c_tab VARCHAR2) IS
     SELECT
       column_name,data_type,
       data_length,data_precision,
       data_scale,nullable
     FROM       user_tab_columns
     WHERE     table_name = c_tab
     ORDER BY column_id;
   lv_table_name        user_tables.table_name%TYPE;
    lv_pct_free         user_tables.pct_free%TYPE;
   lv_pct_used          user_tables.pct_used%TYPE;
   lv_ini_trans         user_tables.ini_trans%TYPE;
   lv_max_trans         user_tables.max_trans%TYPE;
   lv_tablespace_name   user_tables.tablespace_name%TYPE;
   lv_initial_extent    user_tables.initial_extent%TYPE;
   lv_next_extent       user_tables.next_extent%TYPE;
   lv_min_extents       user_tables.min_extents%TYPE;
   lv_max_extents       user_tables.max_extents%TYPE;
   lv_pct_increase      user_tables.pct_increase%TYPE;
   lv_column_name       user_tab_columns.column_name%TYPE;
   lv_data_type         user_tab_columns.data_type%TYPE;
   lv_data_length       user_tab_columns.data_length%TYPE;
   lv_data_precision    user_tab_columns.data_precision%TYPE;
   lv_data_scale        user_tab_columns.data_scale%TYPE;
```

```
    lv_nullable          user_tab_columns.nullable%TYPE;
    lv_freelists         user_tables.freelists%TYPE;
    lv_freelist_groups   user_tables.freelist_groups%TYPE;
    lv_first_rec         BOOLEAN;
    lv_lineno            NUMBER := 0;
    lv_string            VARCHAR2(2000);
    nul_cnt              NUMBER;
    PROCEDURE write_out(p_line INTEGER,  p_name VARCHAR2,
          p_string VARCHAR2) is
    BEGIN
       INSERT INTO t_temp (lineno, tb_name, text)
          VALUES (p_line,p_name,p_string);
    END;

BEGIN
    OPEN tab_cursor;
    LOOP
       FETCH tab_cursor INTO     lv_table_name,lv_pct_free,
                   lv_pct_used,lv_ini_trans,
                   lv_max_trans,lv_tablespace_name,
                   lv_initial_extent,lv_next_extent,
                   lv_min_extents,lv_max_extents,
                   lv_pct_increase,lv_freelists,
                   lv_freelist_groups;
      EXIT WHEN tab_cursor%NOTFOUND;
      lv_lineno := 1;
      lv_string := 'DROP TABLE '|| lower(lv_table_name)||';';
      write_out(lv_lineno,  lv_table_name, lv_string);
      lv_lineno := lv_lineno + 1;
      lv_first_rec := TRUE;
      lv_string := 'CREATE TABLE '|| lower(lv_table_name)||' (';
      write_out(lv_lineno,  lv_table_name, lv_string);
      lv_lineno := lv_lineno + 1;
       lv_string := null;
       OPEN col_cursor(lv_table_name);
       nul_cnt:=0;
       LOOP
       FETCH col_cursor INTO  lv_column_name,lv_data_type,
               lv_data_length,lv_data_precision,
               lv_data_scale,lv_nullable;
      EXIT WHEN col_cursor%NOTFOUND;
      IF (lv_first_rec) THEN
         lv_first_rec := FALSE;
      ELSE
         lv_string :=  ',';
      END IF;
      IF ((lv_data_type = 'NUMBER') AND (lv_data_precision>0))
      THEN
        lv_string := lv_string || lower(lv_column_name) ||
           ' ' || lv_data_type ||'('||lv_data_precision||','||
```

```
      NVL(lv_data_scale,0)||')';
ELSIF ((lv_data_type = 'FLOAT') AND (lv_data_precision>0))
THEN
 lv_string := lv_string || lower(lv_column_name) ||
      ' ' || lv_data_type ||'('||lv_data_precision||')';
ELSE
 lv_string := lv_string || lower(lv_column_name) ||
          ' ' || lv_data_type;
END IF;
 IF ((lv_data_type = 'CHAR') or (lv_data_type = 'VARCHAR2'))
THEN
    lv_string := lv_string || '(' || lv_data_length || ')';
 END IF;
 IF (lv_nullable = 'N') THEN
    nul_cnt:=nul_cnt+1;
  lv_string := lv_string||
' CONSTRAINT ck_'||lv_table_name||'_'||nul_cnt||' NOT NULL';
END IF;
write_out(lv_lineno, lv_table_name, lv_string);
lv_lineno := lv_lineno + 1;
END LOOP;
CLOSE col_cursor;
lv_string := ')';
write_out(lv_lineno, lv_table_name, lv_string);
lv_lineno := lv_lineno + 1;
lv_string := null;
lv_string := 'PCTFREE ' || TO_CHAR(lv_pct_free) ||
'   PCTUSED ' || TO_CHAR(lv_pct_used);
write_out(lv_lineno, lv_table_name, lv_string);
lv_lineno := lv_lineno + 1;
lv_string := 'INITRANS ' || TO_CHAR(lv_ini_trans) ||
  ' MAXTRANS ' || TO_CHAR(lv_max_trans);
write_out(lv_lineno, lv_table_name, lv_string);
lv_lineno := lv_lineno + 1;
lv_string := 'TABLESPACE ' || lv_tablespace_name;
write_out(lv_lineno, lv_table_name, lv_string);
lv_lineno := lv_lineno + 1;
lv_string := 'STORAGE (';
write_out(lv_lineno, lv_table_name, lv_string);
lv_lineno := lv_lineno + 1;
lv_string := 'INITIAL ' || TO_CHAR(lv_initial_extent) ||
     ' NEXT ' || TO_CHAR(lv_next_extent);
write_out(lv_lineno, lv_table_name, lv_string);
lv_lineno := lv_lineno + 1;
lv_string := 'FREELISTS ' || TO_CHAR(lv_freelists) ||
 ' FREELIST GROUPS ' || TO_CHAR(lv_max_trans);
write_out(lv_lineno, lv_table_name, lv_string);
lv_lineno := lv_lineno + 1;
lv_string := 'MINEXTENTS ' || TO_CHAR(lv_min_extents) ||
 ' MAXEXTENTS ' || TO_CHAR(lv_max_extents) ||
```

```
            ' PCTINCREASE ' || TO_CHAR(lv_pct_increase) || ')';
        write_out(lv_lineno,  lv_table_name, lv_string);
        lv_lineno := lv_lineno + 1;
        lv_string := '/';
        write_out(lv_lineno,  lv_table_name, lv_string);
        lv_lineno := lv_lineno + 1;
        lv_string:='                                          ';
        write_out(lv_lineno,  lv_table_name, lv_string);
    END LOOP;
    CLOSE tab_cursor;
END;
/
SET HEADING OFF
SPOOL rep_out\crt_tabs.sql
SELECT    text
FROM      T_temp
ORDER BY  tb_name, lineno;
SPOOL OFF
DROP TABLE t_temp;
SET VERIFY ON FEEDBACK ON TERMOUT ON
SET PAGESIZE 22
```

A similar script is provided for indexes in Chapter 6. This script will rebuild straight Oracle7 and Oracle8 relational tables only. It will not rebuild tables with types, objects, nested tables, or varrays

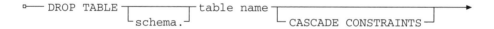

CHAPTER 5

Administration of Oracle8 Object Tables

As was discussed at the opening of Chapter 4, Oracle8 has introduced a number of new tables for DBAs to worry about. Probably the most basic of these is the straight object table. Also introduced are the nested tables, varray types, REF values, and the entire concept of types. In this chapter we will discuss these new Oracle8 tables and the types used to build them.

5.1   THE ROWID CONCEPT IN ORACLE8

Under Oracle8, the concept of OBJECTS is introduced. These OBJECTS have identifiers which now are added to the ROWID, giving an EXTENDED ROWID format which is 10 bytes long versus the 6 bytes that was the norm in Oracle7. The Oracle8 ROWID is a varchar2 representation of a base 64 number (remember that base 64 starts at B, not A; A is used to designate zero). The ROWID is displayed as follows:

OOOOOO.FFF.BBBBBB.SSS

where:

OOOOOO is the data object number.
FFF is the relative file number.
BBBBBB is the block number.
SSS is the slot number.

An example of the new ROWID would be:

AAAAVJAAEAAAABEAAA

where:

AAAAVJ is the data object number.
AAE is the relative file number.
AAAABE is the block number.
AAA is the slot number.

The new parts of the ROWID are the object number and the relative file number. Multiple files can have the same relative file number because Oracle assigns the number based on tablespace. This means that these numbers are only unique per table-space, which indicates that you cannot derive an absolute address directly from the new ROWID. This means that the new ROWID addressing schema is tablespace relative.

The new ROWID contains the data object number which increments when an object's version changes. An object's version changes whenever a table is truncated or a partition is moved. The data object number is not related to the object ID.

The ROWID can be easily manipulated with the DBMS_ROWID package shown in Chapter 10. If you have used ROWID in your Oracle7 application (something that Oracle has repeatedly said not to do, but some people never listen . . .) then you will have to familiarize yourself with this package. The only "application" type use I have put ROWID to is the aforementioned ACT_SIZE.SQL script, of which I show you the new version in the following sections.

Old ROWIDs (called restricted ROWIDs) will be automatically converted to the new format if:

1. You use export/import to move data.
2. You use the migration utility.

If you have used ROWIDs in your application and store them as columns in other tables then these columns will have to be manually changed to the new format using the DBMS_ROWID package. If a column in a table has been designated as a datatype of ROWID it will be altered to accept the new format during migration, but this will not affect the data in the column.

5.2   THE CONCEPT OF OBJECT IDENTIFIERS (OID) IN ORACLE8

Oracle8 introduces us to the concept of objects as they apply to Oracle8. Each object in Oracle8 (i.e., table, cluster, etc.) has a 16-byte object identifier. This object identifier (OID) is guaranteed to be globally unique across all databases in your environment. It is a 16-byte, base-64 number that allows for a ridiculously high number of objects to be identified (in the peta-region of countability—a petillion?—the maximum is: $2^{**}128$ (340,283,266,920,938,463,463,374,607,431,768,211,456)).

The object ID is used to construct REFs for nested tables. In some statements involving nested tables, if you don't specifically tell Oracle to bring back the UNREF value (i.e., translate the OID and get the data) you will get a 42- to 46-byte REF number returned, as useful as that sounds. The number itself is simply an identifier and contains no "intelligence" such as would be in a ROWID. The REF value can vary in size between 42 and 46 bytes of internal storage.

5.3 ORACLE8 OBJECT TYPES

Before we can begin to discuss objects in Oracle8, we need to discuss object types. As their name implies, an object type is used to define an object. To bridge the gulf between Oracle7 and Oracle8 you can think of an object type as a predefined row that you can then use to build Oracle8 objects.

Before you can build an object table in Oracle8 you will need to define its types. A table can consist of single columns, types, or a mix as well as varrays (we will discuss varrays later). There are TYPEs and object TYPEs; to create an object TYPE the "AS OBJECT" (added in 8.0.2) clause must be added to the TYPE command. Let's look at a simple type definition and how it would be used to build an Oracle8 object table. The only time the AS OBJECT clause is not used is with VARRAY, TABLE or incomplete type specified.

Suppose we want to define a real-world situation such as a collection of pictures. What are the attributes of pictures? How about topic, date and time taken, photographer, negative number, and bfile location? Let's look at the type required to implement this structure:

```
CREATE TYPE picture_t AS OBJECT  (topic         varchar2(80),
                                  date_taken    date,
                                  photographer  person_t,
                                  negative#     number,
                                  picture       bfile) AS OBJECT;
```

Notice something odd? What are these person_t and bfile columns? The person_t is another type definition, "person type," that includes:

```
CREATE TYPE person_t AS OBJECT ( first_name  varchar2(32),
                                 last_name   varchar2(32),
                                 middle_init varchar2(3)
                                   DEFAULT 'NMN',
                                 sex         char(1),
                                 address     address_t);
```

The type address_t is:

```
CREATE TYPE address_t AS OBJECT (address_line1    varchar2(80),
                                 address_line2    varchar2(80),
                                 street_name      varchar2(30),
                                 street_number    number,
                                 city             varchar2(30),
                                 state_or_province varchar2(2),
                                 zip              number(5),
                                 zip_4            number(4),
                                 country_code     varchar2(20));.
```

See the value of these type definitions (and the nightmare)? The bfile definition is a new BLOB (binary large object) definition that specifies it as stored external to the database. Anyway, back to the example: now we want to create our picture object. This becomes:

```
CREATE TABLE pictures OF picture_t;
```

One of the nice things about this concept of types is that it allows us to create these type primitives such as person_t and then use them to define objects. If we need to, say, add an attribute to the primitive such as a "married" indicator, all that we must do is add it to the primitive definition and it will be carried through to any object that uses the type in its own definition. This will allow the collapse of some of the more complex designs of databases into a more manageable real-world view. We will take a deeper look at types when we discuss tables, nested tables, and varrays later in this chapter. Types can be: incomplete, complete, varray, or nested table or a combination of complete, varray, and nested table. A varray cannot contain another varray or nested table and a nested table cannot contain another nested table or varray.

The Incomplete TYPE

The command to create an incomplete type is shown below. Incomplete types are required for circular reference situations. Incomplete types specify no attributes.

```
o──── CREATE ──┬──────────┬── TYPE ──┬──────────┬── type_name ──┬──────────────┬── ; ──►
               └─OR REPLACE─┘          └─schema.─┘                └─AS OBJECT ─┘
```

An incomplete type would be used in the situation where a type referenced a second type which referenced the first type (a circular reference such as emp-supervisor). This allows the incomplete type to be referenced before it is completed. However, before a table can be constructed from an incomplete type it must be completed.

The VARRAY Type

VARRAYs are used for small sets of related items. For example, a house has several rooms, and each room has measurements. You could assume that a house of a certain square footage couldn't have more than 10 rooms. A VARRAY to hold this room data would be sized at a limit of 10. The type from which a VARRAY is constructed cannot contain a VARRAY or a nested table.

The command to create a VARRAY type would be:

```
o──── CREATE ────────── TYPE ────── type_name AS VARRAY(n) ────────────── OF dtype;──►
          └─OR REPLACE─┘ └─schema.──┘                      └─VARYING ARRAY(n) ──┘
```

A VARRAY should be used when the number of items to be stored in the type is:

1. Known and fixed.
2. Small (this is a relative term; remember the data is stuffed into a RAW and stored in line with the rest of the type's data).

A VARRAY cannot be used in a partitioned table. In early release (i.e., up to and including 8.0.3) varrays take up an inordinate amount of space. I suggest using nested tables as the overall storage requirements are lower and the limitations are the same.

The Nested Table Type

A nested table is used in situations where the same data is repeated for a given entity an unknown number of times, such as the one-to-many relationships between parent and children. In applications where storage is at a premium a nested table may actually be more efficient (at least in early 8.0 releases) than a VARRAY. If you have the time, check both types of object for storage usage before committing your design to one or the other.

The command to create a NESTED TABLE type would be:

```
CREATE ─────────────── TYPE ────────── type_name AS TABLE OF dtype;
         └─ OR REPLACE ─┘       └─ schema.─┘
```

A NESTED TABLE should be used when:

1. The number of items is large or unknown.
2. The storage of the items needs to be managed.

A NESTED TABLE is stored in a STORE TABLE which must be specified in the CREATE TABLE command for each NESTED TABLE type used. The NESTED TABLE type cannot be used in partition tables. In some early documentation releases it states that Oracle itself specifies the store table name; this is incorrect. Nested tables cannot contain VARRAYs or other nested tables.

Object Types

If you will be using the type to build an object table that will be REFed by a second table, it must be constructed as an OBJECT type and thus include an object ID (OID). Nested tables and VARRAYs are limited in the types of types they can store; a second OBJECT table is not. In cases where the ERD shows a series of one-to-many type relationships, OBJECT tables will have to be used to show this relationship structure under the object-oriented paradigm in Oracle8.

The command to create an OBJECT type would be:

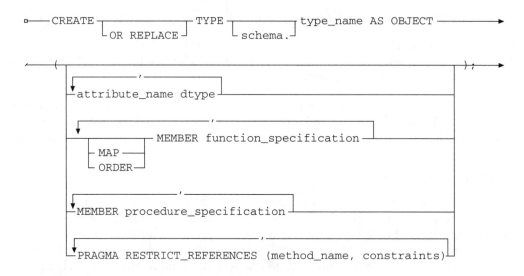

The constraints for the PRAGMA line are:

RNDS—Reads no database state.
WNDS—Writes no database state.
RNPS—Reads no package state.
WNPS—Writes no package state.

Note that these can be specified in any order, but no duplicates are allowed.

TIP   Object types cannot be used in partition tables.

The possible dtype specifications are:

REF schema.object_type_name
schema.type_name
VARCHAR2(size)
NUMBER (precision, scale)
DATE
RAW(size)
CHAR(size)
CHARACTER(size)

CHAR(size)
CHARACTER VARYING(size)
CHAR VARYING(size)
VARCHAR(size)

The following data types are provided for compatibility, but are treated internally the same as NUMBER:

NUMERIC(precision, scale)
DECIMAL(precision, scale)
DEC(precision, scale)
INTEGER
INT
SMALLINT
FLOAT(size)
DOUBLE PRECISION
REAL

The following are Large Object Data types:

BLOB
CLOB
BFILE

TIP The NCLOB datatype is also a LOB but cannot be used for TYPE definitions.

Keywords and Parameters for the TYPE Commands

OR REPLACE—This recreates the type if it already exists. You can use this option to change the definition of an existing type without first dropping it. Users previously granted privileges on the recreated object type can use and reference the object type without being granted privileges again.

schema—This is the schema to contain the type. If this is omitted, Oracle creates the type in the user's default schema.

type_name—This is the name of an object type, a nested table type, or a VARRAY type.

AS OBJECT—This creates the type as a user-defined object type. The variables that form the data structure are called attributes. The member procedures and functions that define the object's behavior are called methods.

TIP   AS OBJECT is new for Oracle version 8.0.2 and is now required when creating an object type.

AS TABLE—This creates a named nested table of type datatype. When datatype is an object type, the nested table type describes a table whose columns match the name and attributes of the object type. When datatype is a scalar type, then the nested table type describes a table with a single, scalar type column called "column_value".

AS VARRAY(limit)—This creates the type as an ordered set of elements, each of which has the same datatype. You must specify a name and a maximum limit of zero or more. The array limit must be an integer literal. Only variable-length arrays are supported. Oracle does not support anonymous VARRAYs. The type name for the objects contained in the VARRAY must be one of the following:

> A scalar datatype
>
> A REF
>
> An object type, including an object with VARRAY attributes

The type name for the objects contained in the VARRAY cannot be any of the following:

> An object type with a nested table attribute
>
> A VARRAY type
>
> A TABLE type
>
> A LOB data type

The (limit) value is an unsigned integer in the range of 1 to 2^{31} (2,147,483,647). Of course, since the VARRAY is stored in line with the other data in a table as a RAW value, specifications of extremely large limits would be foolish since it would cause chaining and performance degradation. For a large number of elements, use a NESTED TABLE instead.

OF dtype—This is the name of any Oracle built-in datatype or library type. ROWID, LONG, and LONG RAW are not valid datatypes.

REF object_type_name—This associates an instance of a source type with an instance of the target object. A REF logically identifies and locates the target object. The target object must have an object identifier.

type_name—This is the name of user-defined object type, nested table type, or a VARRAY type.

attribute_name—This is an object attribute name. Attributes are data items with a name and a type specifier that form the structure of the object.

MEMBER—This specifies a function or procedure subprogram method associated with the object type which is referenced as an attribute. You must specify a corresponding method body in the object type body for each procedure or function specification.

procedure_specification—This is the specification of a procedure subprogram.

function_specification—This is the specification of a function subprogram.

MAP MEMBER function_specification—This specifies a member function (map method) that returns the relative position of a given instance in the ordering of all instances of the object. A map method is called implicitly and induces an ordering of object instances by mapping them to values of a predefined scalar type. PL/SQL uses the ordering to evaluate Boolean expressions and to perform comparisons.

A scalar value is always manipulated as a single unit. Scalars are mapped directly to the underlying hardware. An integer, for example, occupies 4 or 8 contiguous bytes of storage, in memory or on disk.

An object specification can contain only one map method, which must be a function. The resulting type must be a predefined SQL scalar type, and the map function can have no arguments other than the implicit SELF argument.

You can define either MAP method or ORDER method in a type specification, but not both. If a MAP or an ORDER method is not specified, only comparisons for equality or inequality can be performed and thus the object instances cannot be ordered. No comparison method needs to be specified to determine the equality of two object types.

ORDER MEMBER function_specification—This specifies a member function (ORDER method) that takes an instance of an object as an explicit argument and the implicit SELF argument and returns either a negative, zero, or positive integer. The negative, positive, or zero indicates that the implicit SELF argument is less than, equal to, or greater than the explicit argument.

When instances of the same object type definition are compared in an ORDER BY clause, the order method function_specification is invoked.

An object specification can contain only one ORDER method, which must be a function having the return type INTEGER.

You can either declare a MAP method or an ORDER method, but not both. If you declare either method, you can compare object instances in SQL. If you do not declare either method, you can only compare object instances for equality or inequality. Note that instances of the same type definition are equal only if each pair of their corresponding attributes is equal. No comparison method needs to be specified to determine the equality of two object types.

PRAGMA RESTRICT_REFERENCES—This is a compiler directive that denies member functions read/write access to database tables, packaged variables, or both, and thereby helps to avoid side effects. The arguments for this directive are:

method_name—This is the name of the MEMBER function or procedure to which the pragma is being applied.

WNDS—This specifies function writes no database state (does not modify database tables).

WNPS—This specifies function writes no package state (does not modify packaged variables).

RNDS—This specifies function reads no database state (does not query database tables).

RNPS—This specifies function reads no package state (does not reference packages variables).

5.4 CREATION OF OBJECT TABLES

Object tables differ from relational tables in that an object table has an object identifier that is system generated and maintained.

Object Table CREATE Command Definition

Oracle8 allows creation of an OBJECT table as well. An object table is a table made up of object types or a combination of standard and object types. An object table cannot be partitioned. Object tables have object IDs and can be used for a REF call. To use a relational table in a REF it must be masked with an Object View.

The command to create an object table is:

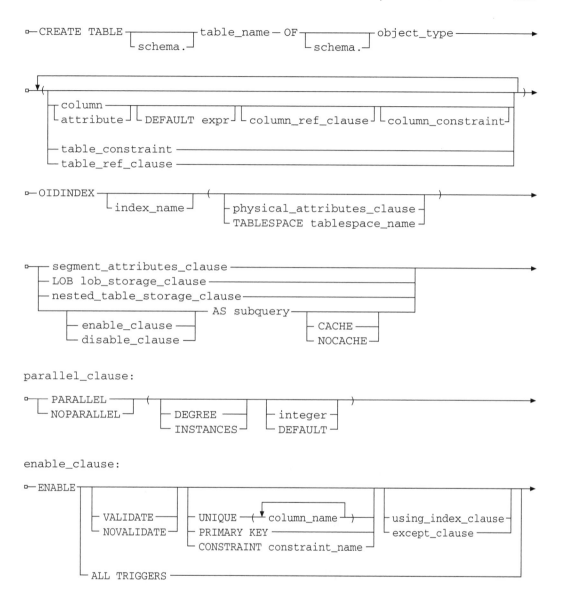

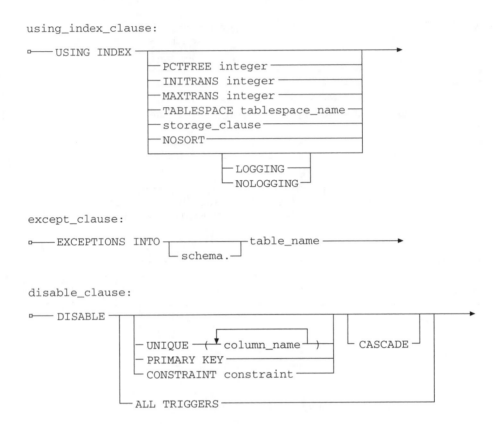

```
using_index_clause:

□── USING INDEX ──────────────────────────────────────────▶
                  ├─ PCTFREE integer ─────────┤
                  ├─ INITRANS integer ────────┤
                  ├─ MAXTRANS integer ────────┤
                  ├─ TABLESPACE tablespace_name ┤
                  ├─ storage_clause ──────────┤
                  └─ NOSORT ──────────────────┘
                            ├─ LOGGING ──┐
                            └─ NOLOGGING ┘
```

```
except_clause:

□── EXCEPTIONS INTO ──┬─────────────┬── table_name ──────────▶
                      └─ schema. ───┘
```

```
disable_clause:

□── DISABLE ──┬───────────────────────────────────┬─────────────▶
             │  ┌─ UNIQUE ──┬─( column_name )─┐  ┌─ CASCADE ─┐
             │  ├─ PRIMARY KEY ───────────────┤  └───────────┘
             │  └─ CONSTRAINT constraint ─────┘
             └─ ALL TRIGGERS ──────────────────────────────┘
```

The Keywords and Parameters for CREATE TABLE Commands

The CREATE TABLE commands have the following parameter definitions in Oracle8:

schema—This is the schema to contain the table. If you omit schema, Oracle creates the table in your own schema.

table—This is the name of the table (or object table) to be created. A partitioned table cannot be a clustered table or an object table.

OF object_type—This explicitly creates an object table of type object_type. The columns of an object table correspond to the top-level attributes of type object_type. Each row will contain an object instance and each instance will be assigned a unique, system-generated object identifier (OID) when a row is inserted. If you omit schema, Oracle creates the object table in your own schema. Object tables cannot be partitioned.

Column—This specifies the name of a column of the table. A table can have up to 1000 columns. You may only omit column definitions when using the AS subquery clause.

Attribute—This specifies the qualified column name of an item in an object.

Datatype—This is the datatype of a column. You can omit the datatype only if the statement also designates the column as part of a foreign key in a referential integrity constraint. Oracle automatically assigns the column the datatype of the corresponding column of the referenced key of the referential integrity constraint.

Object types, REF object_type, VARRAYs, and nested tables are valid datatypes.

DEFAULT—This specifies a value to be assigned to the column if a subsequent INSERT statement omits a value for the column. The datatype of the expression must match the datatype of the column. The column must also be enough to hold this expression. A DEFAULT expression cannot contain references to other columns, the pseudocolumns CURRVAL, NEXTVAL, LEVEL, and ROWNUM, or date constants that are not fully specified.

WITH ROWID—This stores the ROWID and the REF value in column or attribute. Storing a REF value with a ROWID can improve the performance of dereferencing operations, but will also use more space. Default storage of REF values is without ROWIDs.

SCOPE IS scope_table_name—This restricts the scope of the column REF values to scope_table_name. The REF values for the column must come from REF values obtained from the object table specified in the clause. You can only specify one scope table per REF column.

The scope_table_name is the name of the object table in which object instances (of the same type as the REF column) are stored. The values in the REF column point to objects in the scope table.

You must have SELECT privileges on the table or SELECT ANY TABLE system privileges.

SCOPE FOR (ref_column_name) IS scope_table_name—This restricts the scope of the REF values in ref_column_name to scope_table_name. The REF values for the column must come from REF values obtained from the object table specified in the clause.

The ref_column_name is the name of a REF column in an object table or an embedded REF attribute within an object column of a relational table. The values in the REF column point to objects in the scope table.

REF (ref_column_name)—This is a reference to a row in an object table. You can specify either a REF column name of an object or relational table or an embedded REF attribute within an object column as ref_column_name.

OIDINDEX—This specifies an index on the hidden object identifier column and/or the storage specification for the index. Either index or storage_specification must be specified.

Index—This is the name of the index on the hidden object identifier column. If not specified, a name is generated by the system.

column_constraint—This defines an integrity constraint as part of the column definition.

table_constraint—This defines an integrity constraint as part of the table definition.

ORGANIZATION INDEX—This specifies that table is created as an index-only table. In an index-only table, the data rows are held in an index defined on the primary key for the table.

ORGANIZATION HEAP—This specifies that the data rows of table are stored in no particular order. This is the default.

PCTTHRESHOLD—This specifies the percentage of space reserved in the index block for index-only table row. Any portion of the row that exceeds the specified threshold is stored in the area. If OVERFLOW is not specified, then rows exceeding the THRESHOLD limit are rejected. PCTTHRESHOLD must be a value from 0 to 50.

INCLUDING column_name—This specifies a column at which to divide an index-only table row into index and overflow portions. All columns which follow column_name are stored in the overflow data segment. A column_name is either the name of the last primary key column or any nonprimary key column.

PCTFREE—This specifies the percentage of space in each of the table's, object table's OIDINDEX, or partition's data blocks reserved for future updates to the table's rows. The value of PCTFREE must be a value from 0 to 99. A value of 0 allows the entire block to be filled by inserts of new rows. The default value is 10. This value reserves 10% of each block for updates to existing rows and allows inserts of new rows to fill a maximum of 90% of each block.

PCTFREE has the same function in the PARTITION description clause and in the commands that create and alter clusters, indexes, snapshots, and snapshot logs. The combination of PCTFREE and PCTUSED determines whether inserted rows will go into existing data blocks or into new blocks.

For nonpartitioned tables, the value specified for PCTFREE is the actual physical attribute of the segment associated with the table.

For partitioned tables, the value specified for PCTFREE is the default physical attribute of the segments associated with the table. The default value of PCTFREE applies to all partitions specified in the CREATE statement (and on subsequent ALTER TABLE ADD PARTITION statements) unless you specify PCTFREE in the PARTITION description clause.

PCTUSED—This specifies the minimum percentage of used for each data block of the table, object table OIDINDEX, or index-only table overflow data segment. A block becomes a candidate for row insertion when its used space falls below PCTUSED. PCTUSED is specified as a positive integer from 1 to 99 and defaults to 40.

PCTUSED has the same function in the PARTITION description clause and in the commands that create and alter clusters, snapshots, and snapshot logs.

For nonpartitioned tables, the value specified for PCTUSED is the actual physical attribute of the segment associated with the table.

For partitioned tables, the value specified for PCTUSED is the default physical attribute of the segments associated with the table partitions. The default value of PCTUSED applies to all partitions specified in the CREATE statement (and on subsequent ALTER TABLE ADD PARTITION statements) unless you specify PCTUSED in the PARTITION description clause.

PCTUSED is not a valid table storage characteristic when creating an index-only table (ORGANIZATION INDEX).

The sum of PCTFREE and PCTUSED must be less than 100. You can use PCTFREE and PCTUSED together to use space within a table more efficiently.

INITRANS—This specifies the initial number of transaction entries allocated within each data block allocated to the table, object table OIDINDEX, partition, LOB index segment, or overflow data segment. This value can range from 1 to 255 and defaults to 1. In general, you should not change the INITRANS value from its default.

Each transaction that updates a block requires a transaction entry in the block. The size of a transaction entry depends on your operating system.

This parameter ensures that a minimum number of concurrent transactions can update the block and helps avoid the overhead of dynamically allocating a transaction entry.

The INITRANS parameter serves the same purpose in the PARTITION description clause and in clusters, indexes, snapshots, and snapshot logs as in tables. The minimum and default INITRANS value for a cluster or index is 2, rather than 1.

For nonpartitioned tables, the value specified for INITRANS is the actual physical attribute of the segment associated with the table.

For partitioned tables, the value specified for INITRANS is the default physical attribute of the segments associated with the table partitions. The default value of INITRANS applies to all partitions specified in the CREATE statement (and on subsequent ALTER TABLE ADD PARTITION statements) unless you specify INITRANS in the PARTITION description clause.

MAXTRANS—This specifies the maximum number of concurrent transactions that can update a data block allocated to the table, object table OIDINDEX, partition, LOB index segment, or index-only overflow data segment. This limit does not apply to queries. This value can range from 1 to 255 and the default is a function of the data block size. You should not change the MAXTRANS value from its default.

If the number of concurrent transactions updating a block exceeds the INITRANS value, Oracle dynamically allocates transaction entries in the block until either the MAXTRANS value is exceeded or the block has no more free space. The MAXTRANS parameter serves the same purpose in the PARTITION description clause, clusters, snapshots, and snapshot logs as in tables.

For nonpartitioned tables, the value specified for MAXTRANS is the actual physical attribute of the segment associated with the table.

For partitioned tables, the value specified for MAXTRANS is default physical attribute of the segments associated with the table partitions. The default value of MAXTRANS applies to all partitions specified in the CREATE statement (and on subsequent ALTER TABLE ADD PARTITION statements) unless you specify MAXTRANS in the PARTITION description clause.

TABLESPACE—This specifies the tablespace in which Oracle creates the table, object table OIDINDEX, partition, LOB storage, LOB index segment, or index-only table overflow data segment. If you omit this option, then Oracle creates the table, partition, LOB storage, LOB index segment, or partition in the default tablespace of the owner of the schema containing the table.

For nonpartitioned tables, the value specified for TABLESPACE is the actual physical attribute of the segment associated with the table.

For partitioned tables, the value specified for TABLESPACE is the default physical attribute of the segments associated with the table partitions. The default value of TABLESPACE applies to all partitions specified in the CREATE statement (and on subsequent ALTER TABLE ADD PARTITION statements) unless you specify TABLESPACE in the PARTITION description clause.

STORAGE—This specifies the storage characteristics for the table, object table OIDINDEX, partition, LOB storage, LOB index segment, or index-only table overflow data segment. This clause has performance ramifications for large tables. Storage should be allocated to minimize dynamic allocation of additional space.

For nonpartitioned tables, the value specified for STORAGE is the actual physical attribute of the segment associated with the table.

For partitioned tables, the value specified for STORAGE is the default physical attribute of the segments associated with the table partitions. The default value of STORAGE applies to all partitions specified in the CREATE statement (and on subsequent ALTER TABLE ADD PARTITION statements) unless you specify STORAGE in the PARTITION description clause.

OVERFLOW—This specifies that index-only table data rows exceeding the specified threshold are placed in the data segment listed in this clause.

LOGGING—This specifies that the creation of the table (and any indices required because of constraints), partition, or LOB storage characteristics will be logged in the redo log file. LOGGING also specifies that subsequent operations against the table, partition, or LOB storage are logged in the redo file. This is the default.

If the database is run in ARCHIVELOG mode, media recovery from a backup will recreate the table (and any indices required because of constraints). You cannot specify LOGGING when using NOARCHIVELOG mode.

For nonpartitioned tables, the value specified for LOGGING is the actual physical attribute of the segment associated with the table.

For partitioned tables, the value specified for LOGGING is the default physical attribute of the segments associated with the table partitions. The default value of LOGGING applies to all partitions specified in the CREATE statement (and on subsequent ALTER TABLE ADD PARTITION statements) unless you specify LOGGING in the PARTITION description clause.

TIP   In future versions of Oracle, the LOGGING keyword will replace the RECOVERABLE option. RECOVERABLE is still available as a valid keyword in Oracle when creating nonpartitioned tables; however, it is not recommended. You must specify LOGGING when creating a partitioned table.

RECOVERABLE—See LOGGING above. RECOVERABLE is not a valid keyword for creating partitioned tables or LOB storage characteristics.

NOLOGGING—This specifies that the creation of the table (and any indices required because of constraints), partition, or LOB storage characteristics will not be logged in the redo log file. NOLOGGING also specifies that subsequent operations against the table or LOB storage are not logged in the redo file. As a result, media recovery will not recreate the table (and any indices required because of constraints).

For nonpartitioned tables, the value specified for NOLOGGING is the actual physical attribute of the segment associated with the table.

For partitioned tables, the value specified for NOLOGGING is the default physical attribute of the segments associated with the table partitions. The default value of NOLOGGING applies to all partitions specified in the CREATE statement (and on subsequent ALTER TABLE ADD PARTITION statements) unless you specify NOLOGGING in the PARTITION description clause. Using this keyword makes table creation faster than using the LOGGING option because redo log entries are not written.

NOLOGGING is not a valid keyword for creating index-only tables.

TIP   In future versions of Oracle, the NOLOGGING keyword will replace the UNRECOVERABLE option. UNRECOVERABLE is still available as a valid keyword in Oracle when creating nonpartitioned tables; however, it is not recommended. You must specify NOLOGGING when creating a partitioned table.

UNRECOVERABLE—See NOLOGGING above. This keyword can only be specified with the AS subquery clause. UNRECOVERABLE is not a valid keyword for creating partitioned or index-only tables.

LOB—This specifies the LOB storage characteristics.

lob_item—This is the LOB column name or LOB object attribute for which you are explicitly defining tablespace and storage characteristics that are different from those of the table.

STORE AS lob_segname—This specifies the name of the LOB data segment. You cannot use lob_segname if more than one lob_item is specified.

> **CHUNK integer**—This is the unit of LOB value allocation and manipulation. Oracle allocates each unit of LOB storage as CHUNK integer. You can also use K or M to specify this size in kilobytes or megabytes. The default value of integer is 1 K and the maximum is 32 K. For efficiency, use a multiple of the Oracle block size.
>
> **PCTVERSION integer**—This is the maximum percentage of overall LOB storage space used for creating new versions of the LOB. The default value is 10, meaning that older versions of the LOB data are not overwritten until 10% of the overall LOB storage space is used.
>
> **INDEX lob_index_name**—This is the name of the LOB index segment. You cannot use lob_index_name if more than one lob_item is specified.

NESTED TABLE nested_item STORE AS storage_table—This specifies storage_table as the name of the storage table in which the rows of all nested_item values reside. You must include this clause when creating a table with columns or column attributes whose type is a nested table.

The nested_item is the name of a column or a column-qualified attribute whose type is a nested table.

The storage_table is the name of the storage table. The storage table is created in the same schema and the same tablespace as the parent table.

CLUSTER—This specifies that the table is to be part of the cluster. The columns listed in this clause are the table columns that correspond to the cluster's columns. Generally, the cluster columns of a table are the column or columns that comprise its primary key or a portion of its primary key.

Specify one column from the table for each column in the cluster key. The columns are matched by position, not by name. Since a clustered table uses the cluster's space allocation, do not use the PCTFREE, PCTUSED, INITRANS, or MAXTRANS parameters, the TABLESPACE option, or the STORAGE clause with the CLUSTER option.

PARALLEL parallel_clause—This specifies the degree of parallelism for creating the table and the default degree of parallelism for queries on the table once created. This is not a valid option when creating index-only tables.

PARTITION BY RANGE—This specifies that the table is partitioned on ranges of values from column_list.

column_list—This is an ordered list of columns used to determine in which partition a row belongs. You cannot specify more than 16 columns in column_list. The column_list cannot contain the ROWID pseudocolumn or any columns of datatype ROWID or LONG.

PARTITION partition_name—This specifies the physical partition clause. If partition_name is omitted, Oracle generates a name with the form SYS_Pn for the partition. The partition_name must conform to the rules for naming schema objects and their parts.

VALUES LESS THAN—This specifies the noninclusive upper bound for the current partition.

value_list—This is an ordered list of literal values corresponding to column_list in the PARTITION BY RANGE clause. You can substitute the keyword MAXVALUE for any literal in value_list. Specifying a value other than MAXVALUE for the highest partition bound imposes an implicit integrity constraint on the table.

MAXVALUE—This specifies a maximum value that will always sort higher than any other value, including NULL.

ENABLE—This enables an integrity constraint.

DISABLE—This disables an integrity constraint.

Constraints specified in the ENABLE and DISABLE clauses of a CREATE TABLE statement must be defined in the statement. You can also enable and disable constraints with the ENABLE and DISABLE keywords of the CONSTRAINT clause. If you define a constraint but do not explicitly enable or disable it, Oracle enables it by default.

You cannot use the ENABLE and DISABLE clauses in a CREATE TABLE statement to enable and disable triggers.

AS subquery—This inserts the rows returned by the subquery into the table upon its creation. The number of columns in the table must equal the number of expressions in the subquery. The column definitions can only specify column names, default values, and integrity constraints, not datatypes. Oracle derives datatypes and lengths from the subquery. Oracle also abides by the following rules for integrity constraints:

Oracle automatically defines any NOT NULL constraints on columns in the new table that existed on the corresponding columns of the selected table if the subquery selects the column rather than an expression containing the column.

A CREATE TABLE statement cannot contain both AS clause and a referential integrity constraint definition.

If a CREATE TABLE statement contains both the AS clause and a CONSTRAINT clause or an ENABLE clause with the EXCEPTIONS option, Oracle ignores the EXCEPTIONS option. If any rows violate the constraint, Oracle does not create the table and returns an error message.

If all expressions in the subquery are columns, rather than expressions, you can omit the columns from the table definition entirely. In this case, the names of the columns of table are the same as the columns in the subquery.

CACHE—This specifies that the data will be accessed frequently; therefore the blocks retrieved for this table are placed at the most recently used end of the LRU list in the buffer cache when a full table scan is performed. This option is useful for small lookup tables.

CACHE as a parameter in the LOB storage clause specifies that Oracle preallocates and retains LOB data values in memory for faster access. CACHE is the default for index-only tables.

NOCACHE—This specifies that the data will not be accessed frequently; therefore the blocks retrieved for this table are placed at the least recently used end of the LRU list in the buffer cache when a full table scan is performed. For LOBs, the LOB value is not placed in the buffer cache.

This is the default behavior except when creating index-only tables. This is not a valid keyword when creating index-only tables.

NOCACHE as a parameter in the LOB storage clause specifies that LOB values are not preallocated in memory. This is the LOB storage default.

5.5   EXAMPLE CONVERSION FROM ORACLE7 TO ORACLE8

You may soon be faced with the prospect of not only migration from Oracle7 to Oracle8 but conversion from the Oracle7 relational table and data structure into the new object-based format for Oracle8.

If you don't intend on taking advantage of the Oracle8 object extensions then this section isn't for you. You see, the conversion from Oracle7 to Oracle8, if you are doing a straight port relational to relational, is simply a matter of migration. Even adding partitions to tables or indexes or converting partition views to partition tables is

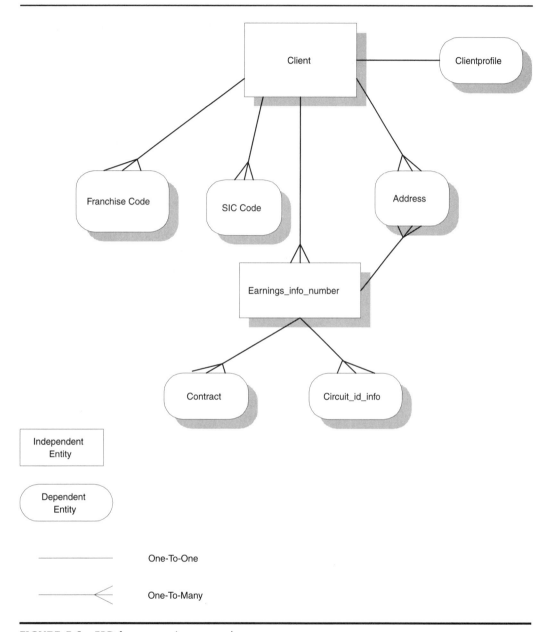

FIGURE 5.1 ERD for conversion example.

pretty straightforward. In fact, if you intend on using partitions then you cannot use Oracle object types such as nested tables, varrays, or REFs as they are not supported for use in partitioned tables.

However, if you are jumping into the deep end with Oracle8 and doing a full conversion into the new object-oriented structure, then by all means read on.

A Concrete Example

Let's look at a small example application fragment and see how we can map it from Oracle7 relational table format into Oracle8 types and objects. I have removed the storage and physical attributes since they are not germane to this example. The application fragment is from a telecommunications application and provides for the tracking of clients, their assigned client numbers, phone numbers, contracts, and related data.

The Oracle7 structure to be converted consists of eight tables, eight primary keys, and eleven foreign keys with supporting indexes for the primary and foreign keys. The entity relational diagram for this structure is shown in Figure 5.1 on the previous page. The actual table definitions are shown in Source 5.1. This structure shows that the client entity, and thus clients table and the clients_info_number entity and thus clients_info_numbers table are the two main entities; all of the other entities are dependent upon these two controlling entities. This will evolve under Oracle8 into two objects, CLIENTS and CLIENTS_INFO_NUMBERS, which will absorb the other entities into a hierarchical object structure. This is shown in Source 5.2.

SOURCE 5.1   Oracle7 creation script for application fragment.

```
DROP TABLE clients CASCADE CONSTRAINTS;

CREATE TABLE clients (
        clients_id              INTEGER         NOT NULL,
        customer_name           VARCHAR2(35)    NOT NULL,
        active_flag             VARCHAR2(1),
        fax                     VARCHAR2(20),
        lookup_no               VARCHAR2(9)     NOT NULL,
        phone                   VARCHAR2(20),
        corporate_name          VARCHAR2(30),
        lookup_parent           VARCHAR2(9),
        lookup_str_adrs         VARCHAR2(25),
        lookup_city             VARCHAR2(20),
        lookup_state            VARCHAR2(2),
        lookup_zip              VARCHAR2(5),
        lookup_zip_ext          VARCHAR2(4),
        lookup_type             CHAR(2),
        lookup_parent_flag      CHAR(1),
        creation_ts             DATE,
```

```
        creation_sy_user       INTEGER,
        spp_rating             CHAR(2),
        rating_date            DATE,
        competitor_loss        INTEGER,
        note                   VARCHAR2(250),
        last_contact_ts        DATE,
        delete_status          CHAR(1),
        name_soundex           CHAR(4),
        sales_volume           VARCHAR2(15),
        sales_volume_code      CHAR(1),
        total_employees        VARCHAR2(9),
        line_of_bus            VARCHAR2(19),
        pct_growth_sales       VARCHAR2(4),
        territory_covered      CHAR(1),
        ceo_first_name         VARCHAR2(13),
        ceo_last_name          VARCHAR2(15),
        ceo_middle_initial     VARCHAR2(1),
        ceo_suffix             VARCHAR2(3),
        ceo_prefix             VARCHAR2(10),
        ceo_title              VARCHAR2(30),
        mrc                    VARCHAR2(4),
        sub_indctr             CHAR(1),
         CONSTRAINT PK_clients
           PRIMARY KEY (clients_id)
               USING INDEX
              TABLESPACE APPL_INDEX
)
TABLESPACE APPL_DATA
;

DROP TABLE clientprofiles CASCADE CONSTRAINTS;

CREATE TABLE clientprofiles (
        clientprofiles_id      INTEGER NOT NULL,
        clients_id             INTEGER NOT NULL ,
        revnum                 INTEGER,
        created_by             INTEGER,
        creation_ts            DATE,
        delta_sy_user          INTEGER,
        delta_ts               DATE,
        industry               INTEGER,
        business_descrip       VARCHAR2(160),
        primary_contact        INTEGER,
        num_locations          SMALLINT,
        equipment              INTEGER,
        equipment_brand        VARCHAR2(32),
        year_equip_installed   INTEGER,
        voice_network          INTEGER,
        business_strategy      VARCHAR2(160),
        bell_perception        INTEGER,
```

```
        lan_info                    VARCHAR2(160),
        long_dist_carrier           INTEGER,
        revenue                     NUMBER(9,2),
        internet_flag               CHAR(1),
        isp                         VARCHAR2(32),
        home_page                   VARCHAR2(50),
        cust_market_info            VARCHAR2(160),
        co_type                     INTEGER,
        msa_flag                    CHAR(1),
        msa_term                    SMALLINT,
        csa_flag                    CHAR(1),
        maint_provider              VARCHAR2(32),
        telecom_budget              NUMBER(9,2),
        fiscal_end                  DATE,
        equip_vendor                VARCHAR2(32),
        long_dist_bill              NUMBER(10,2),
        contact_frequency           INTEGER,
        video_flag                  CHAR(1),
  CONSTRAINT PK_clientprofiles
   PRIMARY KEY (clientprofiles_id)
       USING INDEX
      TABLESPACE APPL_INDEX,
   CONSTRAINT fk_clientprofiles_1
   FOREIGN KEY (clients_id)
      REFERENCES clients
)
TABLESPACE APPL_DATA
;

CREATE INDEX Fk_clientprofiles_1 ON clientprofiles
(
      clients_id
)
TABLESPACE APPL_INDEX
;

DROP TABLE clients_info_nmbrs CASCADE CONSTRAINTS;

CREATE TABLE clients_info_numbers (
      clients_info_nmbrs_id       INTEGER NOT NULL ,
      userid                      INTEGER,
      clients_id                  INTEGER,
      listing_name                VARCHAR2(100),
      clients_number              CHAR(13),
      service_class               VARCHAR2(5),
      installed_lines             NUMBER(4),
      restrict_code_1             VARCHAR2(14),
      restrict_code_2             VARCHAR2(14),
      restrict_code_3             VARCHAR2(14),
      restrict_code_4             VARCHAR2(14),
```

```
      restrict_code_5          VARCHAR2(14),
      billing_name             VARCHAR2(40),
      phone                    VARCHAR2(10),
      disconnect_reason        CHAR(2),
      disconnect_date          DATE,
      btn                      CHAR(13),
      old_clients_number       CHAR(13),
      service_address          VARCHAR2(100),
      con_ctrl_number          CHAR(15),
      term_agreement           CHAR(13),
      shared_tenant_svcs       VARCHAR2(10),
      installation_date        DATE,
 CONSTRAINT pk_clients_info_nmbrs
  PRIMARY KEY (clients_info_nmbrs_id)
     USING INDEX
     TABLESPACE APPL_INDEX,
      CONSTRAINT fk_clients_info_nmbrs_1
  FOREIGN KEY (userid)
     REFERENCES users,
 CONSTRAINT fk_clients_info_nmbrs_2
  FOREIGN KEY (clients_id)
     REFERENCES clients
)
TABLESPACE APPL_DATA
;

CREATE INDEX Fk_clients_info_nmbrs_2 ON clients_info_nmbrs
(
     clients_id
)
 TABLESPACE APPL_INDEX
;

CREATE INDEX FK_clients_info_nmbrs_1 ON clients_info_nmbrs
(
     userid
)
TABLESPACE APPL_INDEX
;

DROP TABLE addresses CASCADE CONSTRAINTS;

CREATE TABLE addresses (
     addresses_id             INTEGER NOT NULL ,
     addrtype                 INTEGER NOT NULL ,
     clients_info_nmbrs_id    INTEGER,
     clients_id               INTEGER,
     address1                 VARCHAR2(80),
     address2                 VARCHAR2(80),
     address3                 VARCHAR2(80),
```

```
     address4                 VARCHAR2(80),
     address5                 VARCHAR2(80),
     address6                 VARCHAR2(80),
     address7                 VARCHAR2(80),
     address8                 VARCHAR2(80),
     address9                 VARCHAR2(80),
     address10                VARCHAR2(80),
     address11                VARCHAR2(80),
     address12                VARCHAR2(80),
     address13                VARCHAR2(80),
     address14                VARCHAR2(80),
     address15                VARCHAR2(80),
 CONSTRAINT pk_addresses
  PRIMARY KEY (addresses_id)
     USING INDEX
     TABLESPACE APPL_INDEX
 CONSTRAINT fk_addresses_1
  FOREIGN KEY (userid)
     REFERENCES users,
 CONSTRAINT fk_addresses_2
  FOREIGN KEY (clients_id)
     REFERENCES clients(clients_id),
 CONSTRAINT fk_addresses_3
  FOREIGN KEY (clients_info_nmbrs_id)
     REFERENCES clients_info_nmbrs
)
TABLESPACE APPL_DATA
;

CREATE INDEX FK_addresses_3 ON addresses
(
     clients_info_nmbrs_id
)
TABLESPACE APPL_INDEX
;

CREATE INDEX FK_addresses_2 ON addresses
(
     clients_id
)
TABLESPACE APPL_INDEX
;

CREATE INDEX Fk_addresses_1 ON addresses
(
     userid
)
TABLESPACE APPL_INDEX
;
```

```
DROP TABLE circuit_id_info CASCADE CONSTRAINTS;

CREATE TABLE circuit_id_info (
    circuit_id_info_id          INTEGER NOT NULL,
    clients_info_nmbrs_id       INTEGER,
    connect_type                CHAR(1),
    connected_number            VARCHAR2(36) NOT NULL,
 CONSTRAINT PK_circuit_id_info
  PRIMARY KEY (circuit_id_info_id)
     USING INDEX
     TABLESPACE APPL_INDEX,
 CONSTRAINT fk_circuit_id_info_1
  FOREIGN KEY (clients_info_nmbrs_id)
   REFERENCES clients_info_nmbrs
)
TABLESPACE APPL_DATA
;

DROP TABLE sub_codes CASCADE CONSTRAINTS;

CREATE TABLE sub_codes (
    sub_codes_id            INTEGER NOT NULL,
    sub_code                VARCHAR2(8) NOT NULL,
    clients_id              INTEGER NOT NULL,
 CONSTRAINT PK_sub_codes
  PRIMARY KEY (clients_id,sub_codes_id)
     USING INDEX
     TABLESPACE APPL_INDEX,
 CONSTRAINT fk_sub_codes
  FOREIGN KEY (clients_id)
    REFERENCES clients
)
TABLESPACE APPL_DATA
;

CREATE INDEX FK_sub_codes_1 ON sub_codes
(
    clients_id
)
TABLESPACE APPL_INDEX
;

DROP TABLE ftx_codes CASCADE CONSTRAINTS;

CREATE TABLE ftx_codes (
    ftx_codes_id        INTEGER NOT NULL,
    ftx_code            CHAR(8) NOT NULL,
    clients_id          INTEGER,
    ftx_code_desc       VARCHAR2(32),
    primary_ftx_code_ind CHAR(1),
```

```
   CONSTRAINT PK_ftx_codes
    PRIMARY KEY (clients_id,ftx_codes_id)
       USING INDEX
       TABLESPACE APPL_INDEX,
  CONSTRAINT fk_ftx_codes
    FOREIGN KEY (clients_id)
       REFERENCES clients
  )
  TABLESPACE APPL_DATA
  ;

  CREATE INDEX FK_ftx_codes_1 ON ftx_codes
  (
   clients_id
  )
  TABLESPACE APPL_INDEX
  ;

  DROP TABLE contracts CASCADE CONSTRAINTS;

  CREATE TABLE contracts (
       contacts_id              INTEGER NOT NULL,
       clients_info_nmbrs_id    INTEGER,
       contract_no              CHAR(15),
  CONSTRAINT PK_contracts
    PRIMARY KEY (clients_info_nmbrs_id,contacts_id)
       USING INDEX
       TABLESPACE APPL_INDEX,
  CONSTRAINT fk_contracts_1
    FOREIGN KEY (clients_info_nmbrs_id)
       REFERENCES clients_info_nmbrs
  )
  TABLESPACE APPL_DATA
  ;

  CREATE INDEX Fk_contracts_1 ON contracts
  (
   clients_info_nmbrs_id
  )
  TABLESPACE APPL_INDEX
  ;
```

I realize that many of the structures above violate third normal form; unfortunately, certain design restrictions (i.e., much of this was from a third-party application and therefore verboten to touch) forced this design. If I would have had the freedom to design the structure from the ground up, it would have been better normalized.

In order to convert this relational structure into an object-relational structure we have to know the dependencies. In this case we are working against the following business rules:

1. Clients and clients_info_numbers can have independent existence, but usually for every one client there may be many or no clients_info_number records.
2. A clients_info_number can be created without a parent client.
3. A ftx_code and/or sub_code entities are dependent (i.e., can't exist without the parent) on clients.
4. A contract and/or circuit_id_info are dependent on clients_info_number.
5. In some cases the records in address are dependent on clients, and sometimes they are dependent on clients_info_number.
6. There can be no more than six franchise codes and no more than three ftx_codes per client.
7. There are up to three addresses that can tie to a clients_info_number but only one that ties to the client.
8. A single clients_info_number can be tied to multiple contracts.
9. A single clients_info_number can be tied to multiple circuit/phone numbers.
10. A restrict_code indicator (up to 5) is used on a per clients_info_number basis to restrict access to that number's information (this promulgates back up to any client information as well).
11. A client may have one client profile.

Under Oracle8 relationships are shown by use of REF statements. REF relationships are one-to-one. Since we can't make clients_info_number dependent on client (see rule 1 below), we need the two main object structures CLIENTS and CLIENTS_INFO_NUMBERS. CLIENTS and CLIENTS_INFO_NUMBERS will relate by a REF from CLIENTS_INFO_NUMBERS to CLIENTS. All of the other dependent entities will roll up into one of: a type, a nested table, or VARRAY internal object.

For dependent entities whose behavior is limited to a fixed number of occurrences per parent record, Oracle suggests the use of VARRAYS which are stored in line with the parent records in RAW format. However, in tests it appears this wastes space and a nested table may be more efficient. For multiple relations where the ultimate number is unknown or is extremely high or the size of the resulting RAW would be too long (like any time in early releases), I suggest using a nested table. For related one-to-one data, such as the RESTRICT_CODE data and the client profile data, I suggest using a type specification.

These are some rules for using types:

1. A VARRAY or nested table cannot contain a VARRAY or nested table as an attribute.
2. When using nested tables you must specify a store table in which to store their records.

3. Store tables inherit the physical attributes of their parent table.
4. Default values cannot be specified for VARRAYs.
5. Constraints (even NOT NULL) cannot be used in type definitions (they must be specified using an ALTER TABLE command).
6. A table column specified as a VARRAY cannot be indexed.
7. A table using varrays or nested tables cannot be partitioned.
8. VARRAYs cannot be directly compared in SQL.
9. Incomplete types (forward typing) is allowed, but an incomplete type cannot be used in a CREATE TABLE command until it is complete.
10. The scalar parts of a type can be indexed directly in the parent table object.
11. VARRAY and nested table subattributes cannot be indexed directly on a parent table object.
12. Nested table store table attributes can be indexed.

Let's take a look at how this maps into the CREATE TYPE, VARRAY, and NESTED TABLEs of Oracle8. Look at Source 5.2, the code to implement the structure as remapped to Oracle8.

SOURCE 5.2   Oracle8 code to implement application fragment.

```
rem
rem First drop then create the types, varrays and nested table
rem definitions.
rem Order is important you cannot delete a type with dependent
rem types, varrays or nested tables.
rem
DROP TABLE clients_info_numbersv8;
DROP TYPE clients_info_t force;
DROP TABLE clientsv8;
DROP TYPE client_t force;
DROP TYPE sub_v force;
DROP TYPE ftx_v force;
DROP TYPE ceo_t force;
DROP TYPE restrict_code_t force;
DROP TYPE address_list force;
DROP TYPE address_t force;
DROP TYPE contract_list force;
DROP TYPE contract_t force;
DROP TYPE circuit_list force;
DROP TYPE circuit_t force;
rem
rem There can be multiple contracts so lets
rem make it a nested table
rem
CREATE TYPE circuit_t AS OBJECT (
     connect_type                    CHAR(1),
     connected_number                VARCHAR2(36)
```

```
);

CREATE OR REPLACE TYPE circuit_list AS TABLE OF circuit_t;
rem
rem There can be multiple contracts, lets make it a
rem nested table
rem
CREATE OR REPLACE TYPE contract_t AS OBJECT (
     contract_number          CHAR(15)
);
CREATE OR REPLACE TYPE contract_list AS TABLE OF contract_t;
rem
rem There was a fixed number of franchise codes allowed and it was small
rem so use a VARRAY
rem
CREATE OR REPLACE TYPE sub_t AS OBJECT (
     sub_code          VARCHAR2(8)
);
rem
rem sub_v is aVARRAY of 10 elements
rem
CREATE OR REPLACE TYPE sub_v AS VARRAY(10) OF sub_t;
rem
rem There is a fixed number of SIC codes and it is small
rem so use a VARRAY
rem
CREATE OR REPLACE TYPE ftx_t AS OBJECT (
     ftx_code                     CHAR(8) ,
     ftx_code_desc                VARCHAR2(32),
     primary_ftx_code_ind         CHAR(1)
);
rem
rem ftx_v is a VARRAY of 6 elements
rem
CREATE OR REPLACE TYPE ftx_v AS VARRAY(6) OF ftx_t;
rem
rem The LOOKUP information is a one-to-one type
rem data set so use a type definition directly into the object
rem
CREATE OR REPLACE TYPE lookup_t AS OBJECT (
     lookup_no                    VARCHAR2(9) ,
     lookup_parent                VARCHAR2(9),
     lookup_str_adrs              VARCHAR2(25),
     lookup_city                  VARCHAR2(20),
     lookup_state                 VARCHAR2(2),
     lookup_zip                   VARCHAR2(5),
     lookup_zip_ext               VARCHAR2(4),
     lookup_type                  CHAR(2),
     lookup_parent_flag           CHAR(1)
);
```

```
rem
rem The address information is fairly long, so even though
rem it is a fixed number of values, lets put it in a nested table.
rem This data is from a legacy system, addresses can have from
rem 5 to 15 lines of data.
rem
CREATE OR REPLACE TYPE address_t AS OBJECT (
        addrtype            INTEGER ,
        address1            VARCHAR2(80),
        address2            VARCHAR2(80),
        address3            VARCHAR2(80),
        address4            VARCHAR2(80),
        address5            VARCHAR2(80),
        address6            VARCHAR2(80),
        address7            VARCHAR2(80),
        address8            VARCHAR2(80),
        address9            VARCHAR2(80),
        address10           VARCHAR2(80),
        address11           VARCHAR2(80),
        address12           VARCHAR2(80),
        address13           VARCHAR2(80),
        address14           VARCHAR2(80),
        address15           VARCHAR2(80)
);
rem
rem address_list is a nested table definition
rem
CREATE OR REPLACE TYPE address_list AS TABLE OF address_t;
rem
rem The restrict_code data is a one-to-one type relation
rem so lets use a type definition directly into the object.
rem
CREATE OR REPLACE TYPE restrict_code_t AS OBJECT (
        restrict_code_1               VARCHAR2(14),
        restrict_code_2               VARCHAR2(14),
        restrict_code_3               VARCHAR2(14),
        restrict_code_4               VARCHAR2(14),
        restrict_code_5               VARCHAR2(14)
);
rem
rem The CEO data is a one-to-one relationship so just use
rem a type definition directly into the object.
rem
CREATE OR REPLACE TYPE ceo_t AS OBJECT (
        ceo_first_name      VARCHAR2(13),
        ceo_last_name       VARCHAR2(15),
        ceo_middle_initial  VARCHAR2(1),
        ceo_suffix          VARCHAR2(3),
        ceo_prefix          VARCHAR2(10),
        ceo_title           VARCHAR2(30)
```

```
);
rem
rem The client table is the master in this set. Now that
rem the dependent types, VARRAYs, Nested Tables and
rem REF table have been created, go ahead and create it.
rem
CREATE OR REPLACE TYPE client_t as object (
      clients_id              INTEGER ,
      addresses               address_list,
      customer_name           VARCHAR2(35) ,
      active_flag             VARCHAR2(1),
      fax                     VARCHAR2(20),
      lookups                 lookup_t ,
      phone                   VARCHAR2(20),
      corporate_name          VARCHAR2(30),
      creation_ts             DATE,
      creation_sy_user        NUMBER(38),
      spp_rating              CHAR(2),
      rating_date             DATE,
      competitor_loss         INTEGER,
      last_contact_ts         DATE,
      delete_status           CHAR(1),
      name_soundex            CHAR(4),
      sales_volume            VARCHAR2(15),
      sales_volume_code       CHAR(1),
      total_employees         VARCHAR2(9),
      line_of_bus             VARCHAR2(19),
      pct_growth_sales        VARCHAR2(4),
      territory_covered       CHAR(1),
      mrc                     VARCHAR2(4),
      ceo                     ceo_t,
      sub_indctr              CHAR(1),
      ftx_codes               ftx_v,
      sub_codes               sub_v,
      MEMBER PROCEDURE do_soundex(id IN integer, nor_val IN varchar2)
);
rem
rem Now create the object clients which contains
rem nested tables, types and normal attributes
rem
CREATE TABLE clientsV8 OF client_t
OIDINDEX oid_clientsV8 (TABLESPACE APPL_INDEX)
NESTED TABLE addresses STORE AS addressesv8
      PCTFREE 10
      PCTUSED 80
      INITRANS 5
      MAXTRANS 255
      TABLESPACE APPL_DATA
      STORAGE (
            INITIAL 20m
```

```
                    NEXT 10m
                    MINEXTENTS 1
                    MAXEXTENTS 10
                    PCTINCREASE 0
            )
;
ALTER TABLE clientsV8 ADD
        CONSTRAINT PK_clientsv8
                PRIMARY KEY (clients_id)
        USING INDEX
                PCTFREE 20
                INITRANS 5
                MAXTRANS 255
                TABLESPACE APPL_INDEX
                STORAGE (
                        INITIAL 10m
                        NEXT 10m
                        MINEXTENTS 1
                        MAXEXTENTS 121
                        PCTINCREASE 0
                        FREELISTS 5
                )
;
ALTER TABLE clientsV8 MODIFY
      customer_name NOT NULL;
CREATE OR REPLACE TYPE BODY client_t IS
MEMBER PROCEDURE do_soundex(id IN integer, nor_val IN varchar2) IS
sx_val integer;
begin
      sx_val:=soundex(nor_val);
      update clientsv8 set name_soundex=sx_val where clients_id=id;
end;
END;
/
rem
rem The clients_info_data is an independent one-to-many
rem from clientsv8. We will REF client_t and CLIENTSV8
rem
CREATE OR REPLACE TYPE clients_info_t as object (
      clients_info_nmbrs_id       INTEGER,
      clients_id_r                REF client_t,
      listed_name                 VARCHAR2(100),
      earning_number              CHAR(13),
      service_class               VARCHAR2(5),
      restrict_code               restrict_code_t,
      no_of_lines                 NUMBER(4),
      disconnect_date             DATE,
      disconnect_reason           CHAR(2),
      billing_name                VARCHAR2(40),
      phone                       VARCHAR2(10),
```

```
      btn                        CHAR(13),
      old_clients_number         CHAR(13),
      service_address            VARCHAR2(100),
      con_ctrl_number            CHAR(15),
      term_agreement             CHAR(13),
      shared_tenant_svcs         VARCHAR2(10),
      installation_date          DATE,
      contracts                  contract_list,
      circuits                   circuit_list,
MEMBER PROCEDURE get_client_id_ref
(client_id IN integer, earning_id IN integer)
);
rem
rem clients_info_numbers is a table definition
rem
CREATE TABLE  clients_info_numbersV8 OF clients_info_t
      (clients_id_r WITH ROWID
      SCOPE IS tele_dba.clientsv8)
      OIDINDEX oid_clients_info_nmbrsV8 (TABLESPACE APPL_INDEX)
      NESTED TABLE contracts STORE AS contractsV8
      NESTED TABLE circuits STORE AS circuitsV8
      PCTFREE 10
        PCTUSED 80
        INITRANS 5
        MAXTRANS 255
        TABLESPACE APPL_DATA
        STORAGE (
              INITIAL 20m
              NEXT 10m
              MINEXTENTS 1
              MAXEXTENTS 10
              PCTINCREASE 0
        )
;
ALTER TABLE clients_info_numbersV8 ADD
      CONSTRAINT PK_clients_info_numbersV8
            PRIMARY KEY (clients_info_nmbrs_id)
      USING INDEX
            PCTFREE 20
            INITRANS 5
            MAXTRANS 255
            TABLESPACE APPL_INDEX
            STORAGE (
                  INITIAL 10m
                  NEXT 10m
                  MINEXTENTS 1
                  MAXEXTENTS 121
                  PCTINCREASE 0
                  FREELISTS 5
            )
```

```
;
CREATE TYPE BODY clients_info_t AS
MEMBER PROCEDURE get_client_id_ref
(client_id IN integer, earning_id IN integer)
IS
begin
        update CLIENTS_INFO_NUMBERSV8 z
   set z.clients_id_r =
   (SELECT REF(x) FROM clientsv8 x
        WHERE x.clients_id=client_id)
   WHERE z.clients_info_nmbrs_id=earning_id;
end;
END;
/
```

One thing to notice in the above code is the use of the following coding conventions:

1. All TYPES end in "_t".
2. All VARRAYs end in "_v" (I use "_vw" for views).
3. All NESTED TABLES end in "_list".
4. When used in a DDL statement native datatypes are capitalized while user-defined types are lowercase.
5. The entities are singular while the tables or objects that they become are plural or are a plural or neutral form.
6. All REF columns end in "_r".
7. All primary keys have the prefix "PK_" followed by the table name.
8. All foreign keys have the prefix "FK_" followed by the table name and arbitrary integer.
9. All lookup keys have the prefix "LU_" followed by the table name and arbitrary integer.
10. All unique value keys have the prefix "UK_" followed by the table name and an arbitrary integer.
11. All object ID indexes (OID) have the prefix "OID_" followed by the table name.

Also notice that each section is remarked (in the new code) to tell what is going on and why. These are good practices and should be emulated (I don't say this is the best way or the only way; you should develop a methodology that makes sense to your environment).

If I would have included the storage and physical attributes for the standard relational Oracle7 code, it would have been 12 pages long. The object relational Oracle8 code (with storage clauses) is only 5 pages. The Oracle7 DDL must have the primary tables created first and then the related tables (or, all tables, then the constraints). The Oracle8 code must have all types, VARRAYs, and nested tables, as well as related tables before the primary tables are defined. If methods used in the type bodies are dependent on specific tables existing, then those tables must be created before the type bodies. This indicates that the Oracle8 system will require more analysis on the front end to build properly. If this analysis is not done properly the rebuilding is more complex than with an Oracle7 database structure.

Notice that the number of indexes drops from nineteen to four. This is because as tables are made into nested tables Oracle8 adds another column (SETID$) that is in the structure of their store tables. This SETID$ value is added to the applicable indexes to establish the proper relations. This is done under the covers and DBAs need not concern themselves with it. The store tables inherit the physical attributes of their master table. The store tables can be modified just as regular tables can be modified; thus, if required, you can add performance-enhancing indices as well as alter storage parameters.

Again, the order is critical. Notice that the type bodies come after the table created with the types (for client_t and clients_info_t). This is because the methods included in the bodies are dependent on the clients and clients_info_numbers tables to be valid. Also, see that the clients table is created prior to the clients_info_numbers table. This is required because the column clients_id_r references the clients table. (Note that a REF can only refer to one entry in a referenced object; therefore references always go from the dependent table to the controlling table, from the many side of the relation to the one side.)

In the table definition for the clients_info_numbers table examine the first couple of lines that follow the CREATE line. These commands:

```
clients_id_r WITH ROWID
SCOPE IS tele_dba.clientsv8
```

"finish" the REF command that was started in the type declaration. Due to a type being generic in nature, you cannot limit the scope of a REF value inside a type declaration. Instead, you must restrict the value at point of use, in this case, the table creation. These commands allow the ROWID pseudocolumn to be stored with the OID from the REFed object table, This storing of the ROWID and OID speeds any UNREF activities. The SCOPE command restricts all REFs from this column to the specified table; this also reduces the space requirements for the REF column value and speeds access.

The OIDINDEX clause in both CREATE TABLE commands creates an index on the Object Identifier that can then be used to speed REF type queries against the tables. In this situation the clients_info_numbersV8 object table will be REFing the clientsv8 object table, so placing the clientsv8 OIDs into an index is a performance-enhancing idea. The OIDINDEX on clients_info_numbersV8 is just good form.

Summary

What can be summarized from the above conversion example? Let's put down a few conversion guidelines:

1. Attribute sets that are one-to-one with the main object should be placed in a TYPE definition and used directly.
2. Attribute sets that have a low, fixed number of occurrences should be placed into VARRAYs (this may not be true if constraints or direct comparisons are required).
3. Attribute sets with many occurrences or that require constraints and value-to-value comparison should be placed in nested tables.
4. If a type is to be used in a REFable object, the object must be created using the AS OBJECT clause.
5. REF clauses in a TYPE declaration must be finished via an ALTER TABLE command on the final object table if scoping or ROWID storage is required.
6. Use of WITH ROWID and OIDINDEX clauses should be encouraged to speed access and in some cases reduce storage requirements.
7. Analysis of dependencies is critical to success.

Oracle8 will require a great deal more front-end analysis in order to prevent recoding. In order to pull together the above example I had to use the DBA, Application Developer, Server Concepts, PL/SQL, and SQL reference manuals (Oracle8 beta2 copies) and my class handouts from the Oracle8 beta2 week-long training class. Even with references it still took two days of testing to get clean builds of the above code (hence the drop commands at the top of the script). Oracle8 is a new view of the world and you will have to change your perception of how the database works in order to fully utilize the provided features.

The DBA should read the SQL reference manual sections concerning constraints, table creation, and use of storage parameters before creating tables.

5.6   EXAMPLE OF AN INDEX-ONLY TABLE

In many cases, such as with lookup tables, we end up having a one- or two-column table and an index for that table. This wastes space. Oracle8 allows us to create an index-only table that is stored in B-tree format based on the value of the primary keys. Since the table is stored as an index there are no ROWIDs and all access is through the primary key. This reduces space needs and makes access to the table much faster. This should be used for small tables and low update/insert tables. Index-only tables cannot contain LOB or LONG columns and the following operations are not allowed:

- Creation of an index-only table with a subquery clause
- Indexing an index-only table
- UNIQUE constraints on values in an index-only table
- Partitioning an index-only table

The following is an example of the creation of an index-only table:

```
CREATE TABLE look_ups (
```

```
lookup_code            INTEGER NOT NULL,
lookup_value           VARCHAR2(10),
lookup_descr           VARCHAR2(80),
CONSTRAINT pk_look_ups PRIMARY KEY (lookup_code)
ORGANIZATION INDEX TABLESPACE sales_ts
PCTTHRESHOLD 20 INCLUDING lookup_value
OVERFLOW TABLESPACE sales_ts;
```

You can convert INDEX ONLY tables to regular tables using the Oracle IMPORT/EXPORT utilities. To convert an INDEX ONLY table to a regular table:

1. Export the INDEX ONLY table data using conventional path.
2. Create a regular table definition with the same definition.
3. Import the INDEX ONLY table data, making sure IGNORE = y (ensures that object exists error is ignored).

After an INDEX ONLY table is converted to a regular table, it can be exported and imported using pre-Oracle 8 EXPORT/IMPORT utilities.

5.7   SIZING AN ORACLE8 NONCLUSTERED TABLE

The procedures in this section describe how to estimate the total number of data blocks necessary to hold data inserted into a nonclustered table. No allowance is made for changes to pctfree or pctused due to insert, delete, or update activity.

TIP   This is a best-case scenario only when users insert rows without performing deletes or updates.

Typically, the space required to store a set of rows that experience updates, deletes, and inserts will exceed this calculated value. The actual space required for complex workloads is best determined by analysis of an existing table, and then scaled by the projected number of future rows in the production table. In general, increasing amounts of concurrent activity on the same data block results in additional overhead (for transaction records), so it is important that you take into account such activity when scaling empirical results.

To calculate space required by nonclustered tables is a five-step process:

1. Calculate the total block header size.
2. Calculate the available data space per data block.
3. Calculate the space used per row.
4. Calculate the total number of rows that will fit in a data block.
5. With the rows/block data, calculate the total number of data blocks and convert to kilo- or megabytes.

A Simple Example of Sizing

Let's take a more detailed look at the steps.

- Step 1: Calculate the total block header size.
  The space required by the data block header is the result of the following formula:

  Space after headers (hsize) =
  DB_BLOCK_SIZE – KCBH – UB4 – KTBBH – ((INITRANS – 1) * KTBIT) – KDBH

where:

> **DB_BLOCK_ SIZE**—This is the database block size the database was created with. It can be viewed in the V$PARAMETER view by selecting:
>
> > SELECT value FROM v$parameter WHERE name = 'db_block_size';
>
> **KCBH, UB4, KTBBH, KTBIT, KDBH**—These are constants whose sizes you can obtain by selecting from entries in the V$TYPE_SIZE view.
>
> > **KCBH** is the block common header; on NT with a 4-K block size this is 20.
> >
> > **UB4** is "either byte 4"; on NT with a 4-K block size this is 4.
> >
> > **KTBBH** is the transaction fixed header length; on NT with a 4-K block size this is 48.
> >
> > **KTBIT** is transaction variable header; on NT with a 4-K block size this is 24.
> >
> > **KDBH** is the data header; on NT with a 4-K block size this is 14.
>
> **INITRANS**—This is the initial number of transaction entries allocated to the table. So, for an NT4.0 platform with a 4-K block size and an INITRANS value of 5 the calculation would be:

> > DB_BLOCK_SIZE – KCBH – UB4 – KTBBH – ((INITRANS – 1) * KTBIT) – KDBH
> >
> > hsize = 4192 – 20 – 4 – 48 – ((5–1)*24) – 14 = 4192 – 182 = 4010 bytes

- Step 2: Calculate the available data space per data block.
  The space reserved in each data block for data, as specified by PCTFREE, is calculated as follows:

  available data space (availspace) =
  CEIL(hsize * (1 – PCTFREE/100)) – KDBT

where:

> **CEIL**—Round fractional result to the next highest integer.
>
> **PCTFREE**—This is the percentage of space reserved for updates in the table.

KDBT—This is a constant corresponding to the Table Directory Entry size whose size you can obtain by selecting the entry from the V$TYPE_SIZE view. For an NT4.0 platform with a 4-K block size this is 4.

TIP   If you are unable to locate the value of KDBT, use the value of UB4 instead.

So, to carry on our example assuming a PCTFREE of 20 for our table:

CEIL(hsize * (1 − PCTFREE/100)) − KDBT

CEIL(4010*(1 − 20/100)) − 4 = CEIL((4010*.8) − 4) = CEIL(3208 − 4) = 3204

- Step 3: Calculate the space used per row.
  Calculating the amount of space used per row is a multistep task. First, you must calculate the column size, including byte lengths:

Column size including byte length =

column size + (1, if column size < 250, else 3)

I suggest using estimated averages for all variable-length fields such as numeric, varchar2, and raw. Remember that number data types are stored at a 2 to 1 ratio in the database (i.e., a NUMBER(30) takes up 15 bytes of storage if each place is filled). The maximum for a NUMBER is 21 bytes. The size for a DATE is 7 bytes. ROWID takes 10 bytes for the extended and 6 bytes for the restricted type of ROWID. CHAR always takes its full specified length; VARCHAR2, RAW, and other variable length will only use the space they actually take up.

TIP   You can also determine column size empirically, by selecting avg(vsize(colname)) for each column in the table.

For example, I have a table TEST with a single VARCHAR2(50) column that has 8 rows of various lengths. The return from the select "SELECT AVG(VSIZE(TEST1)) FROM TEST;" is:

```
AVG(VSIZE(TEST1))
---------------------------------
               29
```

The table also has a number column TEST2:

```
AVG(VSIZE(TEST2))
---------------------------------
                7
```

Then, calculate the row size:

Rowsize =

row header (3 * UB1) + sum of column sizes including length bytes

UB1 is "UNSIGNED BYTE 1" and is 1 on NT4.0 with a 4-K block size, so:

Rowsize =

(3*1) + (8 + 30) = 41

Of course, if you have an example table the quickest way to get average row size is just to analyze it and then select average row size from USER_TABLES:

```
SQL> analyze table test1 compute statistics;
Table analyzed.
SQL> select avg_row_len from user_tables
  2 where table_name='TEST1';

AVG_ROW_LEN
---------------------
               41
```

Finally, you can calculate the space used per row:

Space used per row (rowspace) =

MIN(UB1 * 3 + UB4 + SB2, rowsize) + SB2

where:

UB1, UB4, SB2—These are constants whose size can be obtained by selecting entries from the V$TYPE_SIZE view.

UB1 is "unsigned byte 1" and is set to 1 for NT4.0 with a 4-K block size.

UB4 is "unsigned byte 4" and is set to 4 for NT4.0 with a 4-K block size.

SB2 is "signed byte 2" and is set to 2 for NT4.0 with a 4-K block size.

So this becomes MIN((1*3) + 4 + 2, 41) + 2, or, 41 + 2 = 43.

MIN—Take the lesser of either UBI *3 + UB4 + SB2 or the calculated rowsize value. If the space per row exceeds the available space per data block, but is less than the available space per data block without any space reserved for updates (for example, available space with PCTFREE = 0), each row will be stored in its own block.

When the space per row exceeds the available space per data block without any space reserved for updates, rows inserted into the table will be chained into 2 or more pieces; hence, this storage overhead will be higher.

■ Step 4: Calculate the total number of rows that will fit in a data block.
You can calculate the total number of rows that will fit into a data block using the following equation:

Number of rows in block =
FLOOR(availspace / rowspace)

where:

FLOOR—Round fractional result to the next lowest integer.

So for our example this becomes:

FLOOR(3204/43) = 74

■ Step 5: Calculate the total blocks required.
total blocks =
(Total Table Rows) / (Rows Per Block)

Total Kilobytes =
CEIL((total blocks * block size) / 1024)

Total Megabytes =
CEIL((total blocks * block size) / 1048576)   --(1024^2)

For our example we approximate we will have 42,000 rows in this table over the next year. So, the calculation becomes:

((42000/74)*4192) / 1024 = 2324 K or 3 M (rounding up)

For each nested table type this calculation must also be done and the table storage altered accordingly. Remember to add the SETID$ column length of 16 to each row length calculated for a nested table. The size of the RAW required for in-line storage of a varray can vary between 2.5 and over 6 times the size of the combined row length times the number of elements. A nested table reference pointer is usually a RAW(36) value. A REF value will vary between 42 and 46 bytes of system storage.

A More Complex Sizing Example

Let's do a complex example and then move on. From our example of conversion we have the following example of an Oracle8 complex object:

```
SQL> DESC CLIENTSV8
 Name                              Null?     Type
 ------------------------------- --------- ------------
 CLIENTS_ID                      NOT NULL NUMBER(38)
 ADDRESSES                                RAW(36)
 CUSTOMER_NAME                            VARCHAR2(35)
 ACTIVE_FLAG                              VARCHAR2(1)
 FAX                                      VARCHAR2(20)
 LOOKUPS                                  NAMED TYPE
 PHONE                                    VARCHAR2(20)
 CORPORATE_NAME                           VARCHAR2(30)
 CREATION_TS                              DATE
 CREATION_SY_USER                         NUMBER(38)
 SPP_RATING                               CHAR(2)
 RATING_DATE                              DATE
 COMPETITOR_LOSS                          NUMBER(38)
 LAST_CONTACT_TS                          DATE
 DELETE_STATUS                            CHAR(1)
 NAME_SOUNDEX                             CHAR(4)
 SALES_VOLUME                             VARCHAR2(15)
 SALES_VOLUME_CODE                        CHAR(1)
 TOTAL_EMPLOYEES                          VARCHAR2(9)
 LINE_OF_BUS                              VARCHAR2(19)
 PCT_GROWTH_SALES                         VARCHAR2(4)
 TERRITORY_COVERED                        CHAR(1)
 MRC                                      VARCHAR2(4)
 CEO                                      NAMED TYPE
 SUB_INDCTR                               CHAR(1)
 FTX_CODES                                RAW(676)
 SUB_CODES                                RAW(560)
```

In this object we have normal attributes, named types, varrays, and a nested table. The named types are: look_ups and ceo. The nested table is addresses and the varrays are ftx_codes and sub_codes. The first step is to size the nested tables and named types. The nested table is called address_list and consists of:

```
setid$          RAW(16)
addrtype        INTEGER
address1        VARCHAR2(80)
address2        VARCHAR2(80)
address3        VARCHAR2(80)
address4        VARCHAR2(80)
address5        VARCHAR2(80)
address6        VARCHAR2(80)
address7        VARCHAR2(80)
address8        VARCHAR2(80)
address9        VARCHAR2(80)
address10       VARCHAR2(80)
address11       VARCHAR2(80)
address12       VARCHAR2(80)
address13       VARCHAR2(80)
```

```
address14        VARCHAR2(80)
address15        VARCHAR2(80)
```

The address1-15 fields will always be filled with two records, one with 5 fields (average of 10 characters each) plus a single integer value for addrtype and a second with up to 15 fields (average of 7 with 10 characters each) and a single integer value for addrtype. This yields the following row lengths:

$$16 + 1 + (10 * 5) + (1 * 7) = 75$$
$$16 + 1 + (10 * 7) + (1 * 9) = 96$$

We have a 4-K block size and this is on NT4.0 so the following calculation from step 1 is still good assuming we use an INITRANS of 5:

DB_BLOCK_SIZE − KCBH − UB4 − KTBBH − ((INITRANS − 1) * KTBIT) − KDBH

$$hsize = 4192 − 20 − 4 − 48 − ((5−1) * 24) − 14 = 4192 − 182 = 4010 \text{ bytes}$$

The calculation from step 2 is also still valid:

CEIL(hsize * (1 − PCTFREE / 100)) − KDBT
$$\text{CEIL}(4010 * (1 − 20 / 100)) − 4 = \text{CEIL}((4010 * .8) − 4) = \text{CEIL}(3208 − 4) = 3204$$

- Step 3:

    Rowsize =
    row header (3 * UB1) + sum of column sizes including length bytes
    $$3 + 75 = 78$$
    $$3 + 96 = 99$$

At this point let's average these to a single row size and double the expected count (since we will have X occurrences of two rows, if we average the row size we will have 2X of the average size): average = $(78 + 99) / 2 = 177/2 = 89$ (rounding up).

- Step 4:

    Rows per block: =
    $$3204 / 89 = 36$$

- Step 5:
    We estimate 2.5 million rows, so let's calculate in megabytes only:

    $$((2500000 / 36) * 4196) / 1048576) = 278 \text{ meg}$$

This should be the amount of storage required for our nested table store table.
    Next, we do the named types. The named types are LOOK_UPS and CEO.

Here is CEO:

```
ceo_first_name          VARCHAR2(13),
ceo_last_name           VARCHAR2(15),
ceo_middle_initial      VARCHAR2(1),
ceo_suffix              VARCHAR2(3),
ceo_prefix              VARCHAR2(10),
ceo_title               VARCHAR2(30)
```

with a total length of 72 plus 7 length bytes, for a grand total of 79.

Here is LOOK_UPS:

```
lookup_no               VARCHAR2(9) ,
    lookup_parent       VARCHAR2(9),
    lookup_str_adrs     VARCHAR2(25),
    lookup_city         VARCHAR2(20),
    lookup_state        VARCHAR2(2),
    lookup_zip          VARCHAR2(5),
    lookup_zip_ext      VARCHAR2(4),
    lookup_type         CHAR(2),
    lookup_parent_flag  CHAR(1)
```

with a total length of 77 plus 9 length bytes, for a total of 86.

Now we have the data required to finish the calculation:

$$3 + (35 + 17 + 1 + 20 + 86 + 20 + 10 + 7 + 3 + 2 + 7 + 3 + 7 + 1 + 4 + 7 + 2 + 10 + 3 + 1 + 4 + 79 + 1 + 676 + 560) + (1 * 25) =$$
$$1700$$

TIP   Some values (most of the VARCHAR2s) were averaged. The number values all correspond to integers that won't exceed 6 places (6 / 2 = 3) and DATEs are always 7 bytes.

So now we have the 3204 available space calculation and the 1700 row size which indicates we will have 1 row per block with a 4-K block size. If we changed the VARRAYs into NESTED TABLE, this requirement would drop by 1166 and push us down to a row size of 534 and a rows per block of 3204/534 or 6, decreasing the storage requirements by a factor of 6 for the primary object table. Since we are talking a much smaller row size in the nested table store tables than would be required with varrays, we would also reduce the overall storage requirements and make better use of available resources.

5.8   TABLE ALTERATION AND TRUNCATION

The ALTER TABLE command is covered in Chapter 4 under the relational table section. The commands for dropping and truncating tables are also covered in Chapter 4.

CHAPTER 6

Administration of Indexes

Indexes can make or break an application. A nonindexed query that takes tens of minutes can be made to return values within seconds if indexes are done properly. The placement, create, sizing, and maintenance of the normal, bitmapped, and partition indexes available in Oracle8 is a critical subset of the DBA's tasks.

Oracle8 offers new functionality in the form of partitioned, bitmapped, and reversed key indexes. Partitioned indexes allow the spread of index data automatically by data value range across multiple partitions that can be placed on several disk arrays or platters. Bitmapped indexes allow for indexing of low-cardinality data, a feature which actually came about in 7.3.2.3 and is continued with Oracle8. Bitmapped indexes map data values as binary integers allowing low-cardinality data to be quickly accessed with sometimes almost quantum decreases in access speed. For some specialized types of query a reverse key index can improve data access speeds.

Indexes allow queries to rapidly retrieve data, with proper implementation. Single columns, or groups of columns, are indexed. A DBA can specify whether or not an index is unique. Remember: for proper table design each table must have a unique identifier. A unique index is automatically created when a unique or primary key constraint clause is used in a create or ALTER TABLE command.

Indexes speed the search for queries when approximately 10 to 15% of the table or less is being retrieved. For large retrievals, insert and updates to index columns, and deletes, indexes slow response. An exception to this is if you use a bitmapped index for low-cardinality data.

The way columns are indexed will affect their efficiency. The way order columns are specified should reflect the way a select will retrieve them. Put the column expected to be accessed most often first. Remember the leading portion of the index is used to speed queries. A composite index can be created on up to 16 columns. Columns of type LONG and LONG RAW cannot be indexed.

6.1   CREATION OF INDEXES

With Oracle8 the concept of partitioned, bitmapped (available in 7.3.2), and reversed indexes are introduced. We will first cover the Oracle8 command for index creation and then look at the Oracle7 command. You should specify the INITRANS and MAXTRANS when an index is created or you will have to drop and recreate the index to change them. If you are loading data, create indexes last as it is usually more efficient to load data and then create indexes rather than update multiple disks concurrently during the load process. If a table is fairly static then a large number of indexes may be good; however, if you have a table with a large number of inserts and updates then multiple indexes can be a performance hit.

The value for PCTFREE should be set according to how much update activity you expect on the table. The space specified as PCTFREE (a percent of each block) will never be used unless there is update activity against the columns in an index. Therefore, for primary keys where you expect the values to never be updated, set PCTFREE low. For foreign key or lookup indexes, set PCTFREE higher to allow for expected update activity.

When creating an index always specify the tablespace where it is to be placed. If the location is not specified, it goes in your default tablespace, which is probably the location of the table you are indexing as well! Not specifying the tablespace can result in instant contention for disk resources and poor performance. I once saw an application where the indexes were in with the tables improve query speeds by 300% just by placing the indexes in their proper location. The DBA before me had dropped and recreated the primary keys for each of the tables by simply using the disable/enable clause of the ALTER TABLE without specifying the storage clause.

If you use parallel server to create your index remember to set your extent sizes to X/N bytes where X is the calculated size for the index (max expected size) and N is the number of query servers to be used. Each parallel query server takes an extent to do its work in above the high-water mark; this is true for table creations and loads in parallel as well.

To further speed index builds, specify the UNRECOVERABLE option so that the index doesn't generate any redo. Remember to immediately back up since the creation will not be logged. Use this for large index creations since it does little good for small indexes.

The Oracle8 CREATE INDEX Command Syntax

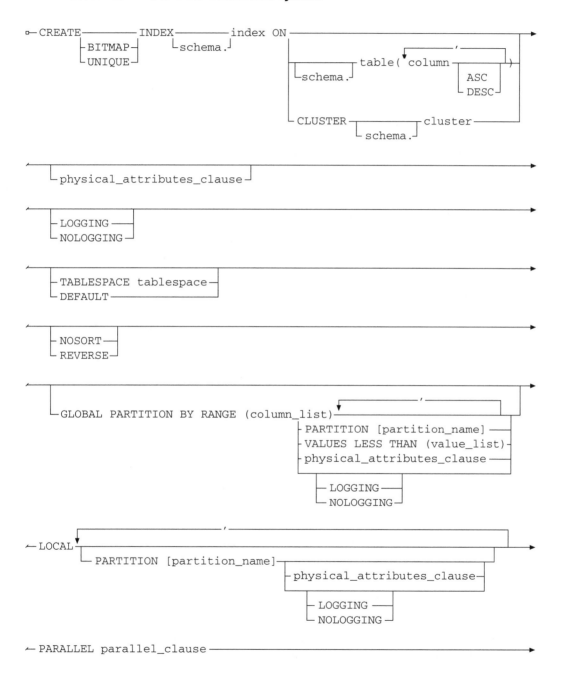

The physical_attributes_clause contains zero, and one or more of the following:

PCTFREE integer
PCTUSED integer
INITRANS integer
MAXTRANS integer
STORAGE storage_clause

The keywords and parameters for the Oracle8 CREATE INDEX clauses are:

UNIQUE—This specifies that the value of the column (or group of columns) in the table to be indexed must be unique.

If the index is local nonprefixed (see LOCAL clause below), then the index columns must contain the partitioning columns.

BITMAP—This specifies that index is to be created as a bitmap, rather than as a B-tree. You cannot use this keyword when creating a global partitioned index.

schema—This is the schema to contain the index. If you omit schema, Oracle creates the index in your own schema.

index—This is the name of the index to be created. An index can contain several partitions. You cannot range partition a cluster index or an index defined on a clustered table.

table—This is the name of the table for which the index is to be created. If you do not qualify table with schema, Oracle assumes the table is contained in your own schema.

If the index is LOCAL, then table must be partitioned.
You cannot create an index on an index-only table.
You can create an index on a nested table storage table.

column—This is the name of a column in the table. An index can have up to 16 columns. A datatype of LONG or LONG RAW cannot be used for indexing.

You can create an index on a scalar object (non-VARRAY) attribute column or on the system-defined NESTED_TABLE_ID column of the nested table storage table. If an object attribute column is specified, the column name must be qualified with the table name. If a nested table column attribute is specified, then it must be qualified with the outermost table name, the containing column name, and all intermediate attribute names leading to the nested table column attribute.

ASC and **DESC**—These are allowed for DB2 syntax compatibility, although indexes are always created in ascending order. Indexes on character data are created in ascending order of the character values in the database character set.

CLUSTER schema.cluster—This specifies the cluster for which a cluster index is to be created. If you do not qualify cluster with schema, Oracle assumes the cluster is contained in your current schema. You cannot create a cluster index for a hash cluster.

INITRANS and **MAXTRANS**—These establish values for these parameters for the index. See the INITRANS and MAXTRANS parameters of the CREATE TABLE command.

TABLESPACE tablespace—This is the name of the tablespace to hold the index or index partition. If this option is omitted, Oracle creates the index in the default tablespace of the owner of the schema containing the index. This causes immediate contention if the table, and its index, are both contained in the default tablespace of the schema owner.

For a partitioned index, this is the tablespace name.

For a LOCAL index, you can specify the keyword DEFAULT in place of a tablespace name. New partitions added to the LOCAL index will be created in the same tablespace(s) as the corresponding partition(s) of the underlying table.

STORAGE—This establishes the storage characteristics for the index.

PCTFREE—This is the percentage of space to leave free for updates and insertions within each of the index's data blocks.

NOSORT—This indicates to Oracle that the rows are stored in the database in ascending order and therefore Oracle does not have to sort the rows when creating the index. You cannot specify REVERSE with this option. If the rows are not in ascending order when this clause is used, an ORA-01409 error is returned and no index is created.

REVERSE—This stores the bytes of the index block in reverse order, excluding the ROWID. You cannot specify NOSORT with this option.

LOGGING—This specifies that the creation of the index will be logged in the undo and redo log and redo and log data will be recorded on activity in this index.

If index is nonpartitioned, this is the logging attribute of the index.

If index is partitioned, this is the default logging attribute of the index partitions created. If index is LOCAL, this value is used as the default attribute for index partitions created when new partitions are added to the base table of the index.

If the [NO]LOGGING clause is omitted, the logging attribute of the index defaults to the logging attribute of the tablespace in which it resides.

If the database is run in NOARCHIVELOG mode, index creation is not logged in the undo and redo log file, even if LOGGING is specified. Media recovery from backup will not recreate the index.

If the database is run in ARCHIVELOG mode, media recovery from a backup will recreate the index.

NOLOGGING—This specifies that the creation of the index *will not* be logged in the undo and redo log file. As a result, media recovery will not recreate the index.

If index is nonpartitioned, this is the logging attribute of the index.

If index is partitioned, this is the default logging attribute of the index partitions created. If index is LOCAL, this value is used as the default attribute for index partitions created when new partitions are added to the base table of the index.

If the [NO]LOGGING clause is omitted, the logging attribute of the index defaults to the logging attribute of the tablespace in which it resides.

Using this keyword makes index creation faster than using the LOGGING option because undo and redo log entries are not written.

GLOBAL—This specifies that the partitioning of the index is user-defined and is not equipartitioned with the underlying table. By default, nonpartitioned indexes are global indexes.

PARTITION BY RANGE specifies that the global index is partitioned on the ranges of values from the columns specified in column_list. You cannot specify this clause for a LOCAL index.

(column_list)—This is the name of the column(s) of a table on which the index is partitioned. The column_list must specify a left prefix of the index column list.

You cannot specify more than 16 columns in column_list and the columns cannot contain the ROWID pseudocolumn or a column of type ROWID.

LOCAL—This specifies that the index is range partitioned on the same columns, with the same number of partitions, and the same partition bounds as the underlying partitioned table. Oracle automatically maintains LOCAL index partitioning as the underlying table is repartitioned.

PARTITION partition_name—This names the individual partitions. The number of PARTITION clauses determines the number of partitions. If the index is local, the number of index partitions must be equal to the number, and will correspond to the order of the table partitions.

The partition_name is the name of the physical index partition. If partition_name is omitted Oracle punishes you by generating a name with the form SYS_Pn where n is some arbitrary value from a SYS-maintained sequence. Name your partitions!

For LOCAL indexes, if partition_name is omitted Oracle generates a name that is consistent with the corresponding table partition. If the name conflicts with an existing index partition name, the form SYS_Pn is used.

VALUES LESS THAN (value_list)—This specifies the (noninclusive) upper bound for the current partition in a global index. This means that if the value specified is 10 then everything less than 10, *but not including 10*, will be stored in this partition. The value_list is a comma-separated, ordered list of literal values corresponding to column_list in the PARTITION BY RANGE clause. Always specify MAXVALUE as the value_list of the last partition. You cannot specify this clause for a local index.

PARALLEL—This specifies the degree of parallelism for creating the index.

Indexes and Their Usage

Indexes store column values in either B-tree or binary format. The B-tree format is used for high-cardinality data (data with many unique values such as last name, date of birth, part number, etc.). The binary index is used for low-cardinality data (sex, true/false, race, etc.). Indexes improve the performance of queries sometimes one-hundredfold. Indexes are especially useful for:

- Searching for rows with specified index column values
- Accessing tables in index column order

When you initially insert a great number of rows into a new table, such as with import or sqlloader, it is generally faster to create the table, insert the rows, and then create the index. If you create the index before inserting the rows, Oracle must update the index for every row inserted. However, if you are inserting using a PL/SQL routine from a flat database table into a more normal structure, indexes can speed the process considerably.

Oracle recommends that you do not explicitly define UNIQUE indexes on tables; uniqueness is strictly a logical concept and should be associated with the definition of a table. Therefore, define UNIQUE integrity constraints on the desired columns. Oracle enforces UNIQUE integrity constraints by automatically defining a unique index on the unique key. Exceptions to this recommendation are usually performance related. For example, using a CREATE TABLE . . . AS SELECT with a UNIQUE constraint is very much slower than creating the table without the constraint and then manually creating the UNIQUE constraint via an ALTER TABLE command.

If indexes contain NULLs, the NULLs are considered distinct values. There is, however, one exception: if all the non-NULL values in two or more rows of an index are identical, the rows are considered identical; therefore, UNIQUE indexes prevent this from occurring. This does not apply if there are no non-NULL values—in other words, if the rows are entirely NULL.

Use of Normal Unique and Nonunique Indexes

For most situations a normal index (i.e., not a bitmapped or reverse key) will be used. This type of index can be monolithic (all in one index, albeit with multiple extents) or partitioned (divided automatically by Oracle8 into several different identically structured indexes with different data ranges).

A normal index can be unique, which enforces uniqueness on the column it is based on (primary key and unique indexes are of this type), or nonunique. If the primary key constraint, unique constraint, or UNIQUE command option is not specified either during CREATE or ALTER tables or CREATE INDEX, then the index is nonunique.

If an index is being used for high cardinality (few related table rows for a single value) or to enforce uniqueness (primary key or unique index) then it should be a normal index. Normal indexes should also be used when enforcing a normal relational-type primary-foreign key relationship.

Normal indexes are subject to index browning, a condition where deletes from the underlying tables have caused leaf nodes to not be filled, resulting in long search times as Oracle walks the tree to find good values. Generally, this can be determined by analyzing the indexes for a table and examining the DBA_INDEXES or INDEX_STATS views. The DBA_INDEXES view has one row for each index in the database; the INDEX_STATS view has one row, for the most recently analyzed index. I suggest use of a code fragment like the one shown in Source 6.1 to populate a temporary table so all of a table's indexes can be examined at once for problems.

SOURCE 6.1   Code fragment to analyze all of an owner's table's indexes.

```
ACCEPT owner PROMPT 'Enter table owner name: '
ACCEPT table PROMPT 'Enter table name: '
SET HEADING OFF FEEDBACK OFF VERIFY OFF ECHO OFF RECSEP OFF PAGES 0
DEFINE cr = 'chr(10)'
SPOOL index_sz.sql
SELECT 'CREATE TABLE stat_temp AS SELECT * FROM index_stats;'||&&cr||
'TRUNCATE TABLE stat_temp;'
FROM dual;
SELECT
'ANALYZE INDEX '||owner||'.'||index_name||' VALIDATE STRUCTURE;'||&&cr||
'INSERT INTO stat_temp SELECT * FROM index_stats;'||&&cr||
'COMMIT;'
FROM dba_indexes
WHERE owner=upper('&owner')
AND table_name=upper('&table');
SPOOL OFF
@index_sz.sql
```

Once a table's indexes have been analyzed, you can query the stat_temp table to find the ratio between del_lf_rows_len and the sum of lf_rows_len and del_lf_rows_len. If this ratio exceeds 0.3 (i.e., 30% of the leaf rows are probably empty) then you more than likely have a browning problem. The report in Source 6.2 can be run against the stat_temp table to determine this and other data that will help determine index state.

SOURCE 6.2   Browning report for indexes.

```
rem
rem browning.sql
rem purpose: Generate browning report from stat_temp
rem
rem MRA RevealNet/TreCom  5/28/97
rem
COLUMN del_lf_rows_len FORMAT 999,999,999 HEADING 'Deleted Bytes'
COLUMN lf_rows_len FORMAT 999,999,999 HEADING 'Filled Bytes'
COLUMN browning FORMAT 999.90 HEADING 'Percent|Browned'
SPOOL browning.lst
SELECT name,del_lf_rows_len,lf_rows_len,
(del_lf_rows_len/
((lf_rows_len+del_lf_rows_len),0,1,lf_rows_len+del_lf_rows_len))*100 browning
FROM stat_temp;
SPOOL OFF
```

Bitmapped Index Usage*

A bitmapped index is used for low-cardinality data such as sex, race, hair color, and so on. If a column to be indexed has a selectivity of greater than 30 to 40% of the total data then it is probably a good candidate for bitmap indexing.

Bitmap indexing is not suggested for high-cardinality, high-update, or high-delete-type data as in these type situations bitmap indexes may have to be frequently rebuilt.

There are three things to consider when choosing an index method:

- Performance
- Storage
- Maintainability

The major advantages for using bitmapped indexes are: performance impact for certain queries, and their relatively small storage requirements. Note, however, that bitmapped indexes are not applicable to every query and bitmapped indexes, like B-tree indexes, can impact the performance of insert, update, and delete statements.

Bitmapped indexes can provide very impressive performance improvements. Under test conditions the execution times of certain queries improved by several orders of magnitude. The queries that benefit the most from bitmapped indexes have the following characteristics:

- The WHERE-clause contains multiple predicates on low-cardinality columns.

---

*Extracted from Bitmapped Indexes in Oracle7, Oracle Warehouse, an Oracle White Paper, Oct. 1995 Part #10406.

- The individual predicates on these low-cardinality columns select a large number of rows.
- Bitmapped indexes have been created on some or all of these low-cardinality columns.
- The tables being queried contain many rows.

An advantage of bitmapped indexes is that multiple bitmapped indexes can be used to evaluate the conditions on a single table. Thus, bitmapped indexes are very useful for complex ad hoc queries that contain lengthy WHERE-clauses involving low-cardinality data.

Bitmapped indexes incur a small storage cost and have a significant storage savings over B-tree indexes. A bitmapped index can require 100 times less space than a B-tree index for a low-cardinality column.

Remember that a strict comparison of the relative sizes of B-tree and bitmapped indexes is not an accurate measure for selecting bitmapped over B-tree indexes. Because of the performance characteristics of bitmapped indexes and B-tree indexes, you should continue to maintain B-tree indexes on your high-cardinality data. Bit-mapped indexes should be considered primarily for your low-cardinality data.

The storage savings are so large because bitmapped indexes replace multiple-column B-tree indexes. In addition, single bit values replace possibly long columnar type data. When using only B-tree indexes, you must anticipate the columns that will commonly be accessed together in a single query and then create a multicolumn B-tree index on those columns. Not only does this B-tree index require a large amount of space, but it will also be ordered; that is, a B-tree index on (MARITAL_STATUS, RACE, SEX) is use-less for a query that only accesses RACE and SEX. To completely index the database, you are forced to create indexes on the other permutations of these columns. In addition to an index on (MARITAL_STATUS, RACE, SEX), there is a need for indexes on (RACE, SEX, MARITAL_STATUS), (SEX, MARITAL_STATUS, RACE), etc. For the simple case of three low-cardinality columns, there are six possible concatenated B-tree indexes. What this means is that you are forced to decide between disk space and performance when determining which multiple-column B-tree indexes to create.

With bitmapped indexes, the problems associated with multiple-column B-tree indexes is solved because bitmapped indexes can be efficiently combined during query execution. Three small single-column bitmapped indexes are a sufficient functional replacement for six three-column B-tree indexes. Note that while the bitmapped indexes may not be quite as efficient during execution as the appropriate concatenated B-tree indexes, the space savings provided by bitmapped indexes can often more than justify their utilization.

The net storage savings will depend upon a database's current usage of B-tree indexes:

- A database that relies on single-column B-tree indexes on high-cardinality columns will not observe significant space savings (but should see significant performance increases).

- A database containing a significant number of concatenated B-tree indexes could reduce its index storage usage by 50% or more, while maintaining similar performance characteristics.
- A database that lacks concatenated B-tree indexes because of storage constraints will be able to use bitmapped indexes and increase performance with minimal storage costs.

Bitmapped indexes are best for read-only or light OLTP environments. Because there is no effective method for locking a single bit, row-level locking is not available for bitmapped indexes. Instead, locking for bitmapped indexes is effectively at the block level which can impact heavy OLTP environments. Note also that like other types of indexes, updating bitmapped indexes is a costly operation.

Although bitmapped indexes are not appropriate for databases with a heavy load of insert, update, and delete operations, their effectiveness in a data warehousing environment is not diminished. In such environments, data is usually maintained via bulk inserts and updates. For these bulk operations, rebuilding or refreshing the bitmapped indexes is an efficient operation. The storage savings and performance gains provided by bitmapped indexes can provide tremendous benefits to data warehouse users.

In preliminary testing of bitmapped indexes, certain queries ran up to 100 times faster. The bitmapped indexes on low-cardinality columns were also about ten times smaller than B-tree indexes on the same columns. In these tests, the queries containing multiple predicates on low-cardinality data experienced the most significant speedups. Queries that did not conform to this characteristic were not assisted by bitmapped indexes.

Example Index Scenarios

The following sample queries on the CUSTOMERS table demonstrate the variety of query-processing techniques that are necessary for optimal performance.

Example #1: Single predicate on a low-cardinality attribute.

select * from customers where gender = 'male';

   Best approach: parallel table scan.
   This query will return approximately 50% of the data. Since we will be accessing such a large number of rows, it is more efficient to scan the entire table rather than use either bitmapped indexes or B-tree indexes. To minimize elapsed time, the Server should execute this scan in parallel.

Example #2: Single predicate on a high-cardinality attribute.

select * from customers where customer# = 101;

Best approach: conventional unique index.

This query will retrieve at most one record from the employee table. A B-tree index or hash cluster index is always appropriate for retrieving a small number of records based upon criteria on the indexed columns.

Example #3: Multiple predicates on low-cardinality attributes.

select * from customers where gender = 'male' and region in ('central','west') and marital_status in ('married', 'divorced');

Best approach: bitmapped index.

Though each individual predicate specifies a large number of rows, the combination of all three predicates will return a relatively small number of rows. In this scenario, bitmapped indexes provide substantial performance benefits.

Example #4: Multiple predicates on both high-cardinality and low-cardinality attributes.

select * from customers

where gender = 'male' and customer# < 100;

Best approach: B-tree index on CUSTOMER#.

This query returns a small number of rows because of the highly selective predicate on CUSTOMER#. It is more efficient to use a B-tree index on CUSTOMER# than to use a bitmapped index on GENDER.

In each of the previous examples, the Oracle cost-based optimizer transparently determines the most efficient query-processing technique if the tables and indexes have representative statistics present in the database.

The Oracle7 CREATE INDEX Command

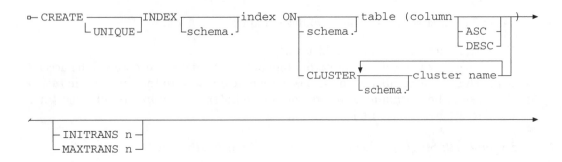

```
├── TABLESPACE tablespace name ───
├── STORAGE storage clause ────────
├── PCTFREE n ─────────────────────
├── NOSORT──────────────────────────
└── RECOVERABLE──────────
                └── UNRECOVERABLE ─┘
```

```
        └── PARALLEL clause ─┘
```

where:

> **Index name**—This is a user unique index name.

> **Table name**—This is the name of the table to be indexed; the table must exist.

> **Column**—This is the name of the column to include in the index, maximum of 16.

> The order of a concatenated key is important. Only queries that access columns in this order will use the index. For example, table EXAMPLE has 16 columns. The first three are used as the concatenated index. Only queries that contain columns 1,2,3 or 1,2 or 1 will use the index.

> **Tablespace name**—This is the name of the tablespace in which to store the index.

> **Storage clause**—This is a standard storage clause.

> **NOSORT**—This tells Oracle to not sort the index, since the table is already loaded into Oracle in ascending order.

> **RECOVERABLE** or **UNRECOVERABLE**—This is used to tell Oracle whether to generate redo/rollback information. For large index creates, it is suggested that the unrecoverable option be used to speed index creation.

> The UNIQUE clause causes Oracle to enforce uniqueness of the entire key. If UNIQUE is left out, the index is nonunique. In Oracle7 the primary key and unique key constraints automatically generate the required indexes.

The BITMAP clause (7.3.2 and above) causes the index to be stored as a bitmap and should only be used for low-cardinality data such as sex, race, and so on. The option is only available as beta in pre-7.3.2.2 releases (7.3 only) and is bundled with the parallel query option. There are several initialization parameters and event settings that are required to use the option in earlier versions of 7.3:

Initialization parameters (must be set regardless of version):

```
COMPATIBLE set to 7.3.2 or higher
V733_PLANS_ENABLED set to TRUE
```

Events (must be set prior to 7.3.2.3):

```
event = "10111 trace name context forever"
event = "10112 trace name context forever"
event = "10114 trace name context forever"
```

An Example Creation of a Partitioned Index

New with Oracle8 is the concept of a partitioned index. A partitioned index goes hand-in-hand with partitioned tables. In fact, usually a partitioned table will have partitioned indexes by default. A prefixed index is defined as an index whose leftmost columns correspond exactly with those of the partition key. In the arena of partitioned indexes the concept of prefixed indexes is important because:

- Unique prefixed indexes guarantee that you only need to access one index partition to get the data.
- Nonunique prefixed indexes still guarantee you only need one index partition if you provide the full partition key as part of the where clause. The caveat to this is that if you only provide part of the partition key all partitions will be scanned.

Let's look at two quick examples.

```
CREATE TABLE sales
     (acct_no                NUMBER(5) NOT NULL,
     sales_person_id         NUMBER(5) NOT NULL,
     po_number               VARCHAR2(10) NOT NULL,
     po_amount               NUMBER(9,2),
     month_no                NUMBER(2) NOT NULL)
     PARTITION BY RANGE (month_no)
          PARTITION first_qtr     VALUES LESS THAN (4),
          PARTITION sec_qtr       VALUES LESS THAN (7),
          PARTITION thrd_qtr      VALUES LESS THAN(10),
          PARTITION frth_qtr      VALUES LESS THAN(13),
          PARTITION bad_qtr       VALUES LESS THAN (MAXVALUE));
     CREATE INDEX pt_sales
     ON sales (month_no, sales_person_id,acct_no,po_number)
          LOCAL;
```

Notice in this example that we didn't have to specify the index partitions themselves. This is because we used the LOCAL clause which tells Oracle to use the same partition logic as the master table. A suitable prefix is added to differentiate the indexes. One problem is that the indexes, if the location is not specified, will be placed in the same tablespace as the table partitions. A better form to use would be:

```
CREATE INDEX pt_lc_sales
ON sales (month_no, sales_person_id,acct_no,po_number)
      LOCAL(
      PARTITION i_first_qtr        TABLESPACE part_ind_tbsp1,
      PARTITION i_sec_qtr          TABLESPACE part_ind_tbsp2,
      PARTITION i_thrd_qtr         TABLESPACE part_ind_tbsp3,
      PARTITION i_frth_qtr         TABLESPACE part_ind_tbsp4,
      PARTITION i_bad_qtr          TABLESPACE part_ind_tbsp5);
```

The other choice is to use a GLOBAL index; this is a partitioned index that doesn't use the same partitioning as the base table. Let's look at an example:

```
CREATE INDEX pt_gl_sales
ON sales (month_no, sales_person_id,acct_no,po_number)
GLOBAL
      PARTITION BY RANGE (month_no)
(PARTITION i_gl_sales1 VALUES LESS THAN (6)
      TABLESPACE sales_index1,
          PARTITION i_gl_sales2 VALUES LESS THAN (MAXVALUE)
      TABLESPACE sales_index2));
```

Here are some guidelines for use of partitioned indexes:

- Use local prefixed indexes whenever possible.
- It is more expensive to scan a nonprefixed index due to more index probes required.
- Unique local nonprefixed indexes are not supported.
- DML operations on global unique indexes are not supported in parallel update.
- Global prefixed indexes can minimize number of index probes.

Estimating an Index's Size

To estimate the size of an index for the storage clause, use the following procedure.

1. Calculate the required database Block Header Size (BHS).

   BHS = fixed header + variable transaction header

   where:

   Fixed header = 113

   variable transaction header = $24 \times$ INITRANS

2. Calculate Available Data Space (ADS).

   ADS = ((Block size - BHS) $\times$ (PCTFREE/100))

3. Calculate the Average Data Length per row (ADL).

Same as step three in the table-sizing section. However, only size for those columns in the index.

4. Calculate the Average Row Length (ARL).

bytes/entry = entry header + ROWID length + F + V + D

entry header = 2

ROWID = 6

F = Total length bytes of all columns that store 127 bytes or less—one header byte per column.

V = Total length bytes of all columns that store more than 127 bytes—two header bytes per column.

For UNIQUE indexes the entry header is 0.

5. Calculate number of blocks for index.

\# of Blocks = 1.05 * (((\# of NOT NULL rows) / (ADS) / ARL))

The 1.05 factor allows for branch space and is an empirically (SWAG) derived value.

6. Calculate the number of bytes required.

Size in bytes = BLOCK SIZE × number of blocks

If the table that the index is based on exists, the script in Source 6.3 is used to estimate the size of the index that is generated from a given list of columns. The DBA enters the table name, the table owner name, and a list of columns, and the procedure does the rest.

6.2   ANALYZING INDEXES

For Oracle7 and Oracle8 the ANALYZE command can be used to get the average index size from an example index. The format of this command follows. Other statistics are also generated, but these will be covered in Chapter 12.

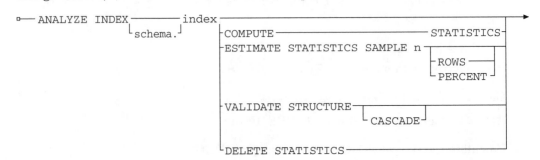

where:

> **COMPUTE STATISTICS**—Calculates statistics based on all rows.
>
> **ESTIMATE STATISTICS**—Calculates an estimate of the statistics based on n ROWS or PERCENT of rows in table.
>
> **VALIDATE STRUCTURE**—Validates that the table and its indexes are consistent and not corrupted.
>
> **CASCADE**—For clusters validates all tables in cluster.
>
> **DELETE STATISTICS**—Removes current statistics.

The results appear in the INDEX_STATS view. One thing to remember is that unlike the DBA_TABLES view only one row at a time is saved in the INDEX_STATS view, the row for the last index analyzed.

The script in Source 6.3 estimates index sizes.

SOURCE 6.3   Script to calculate index space requirements for a proposed index.

```
rem    ******************************************************
rem    NAME:  IN_ES_SZ.sql
rem    HISTORY:
rem    Date                Who                  What
rem    --------            -------------------  ----------------
rem    01/20/93       Michael Brouillette    Creation
rem    FUNCTION:  Compute the space used by an entry for an
rem     existing index.
rem    NOTES:  Currently requires DBA.
rem    INPUTS:
rem          tname   = Name of table.
rem          towner  = Name of owner of table.
rem          clist   = List of columns enclosed in quotes.
rem                    i.e 'ename', 'empno'
rem          cfile   = Name of output SQL Script file
rem    ******************************************************
COLUMN name        NEW_VALUE      db NOPRINT
COLUMN dum1        NOPRINT
COLUMN isize       FORMAT 99,999.99
COLUMN rcount      FORMAT 999,999,999 NEWLINE
ACCEPT tname  PROMPT 'Enter table name: '
ACCEPT towner PROMPT 'Enter table owner name: '
ACCEPT clist  PROMPT 'Enter column list: '
ACCEPT cfile  PROMPT 'Enter name for output SQL file: '
SET PAGESIZE 999 HEADING OFF VERIFY OFF TERMOUT OFF
SET FEEDBACK OFF SQLCASE UPPER
 SET NEWPAGE 3
SELECT name FROM v$database;
SPOOL rep_out/&db/propindx
```

```
SELECT -1 dum1,
       'SELECT ''Proposed Index on table ''||' FROM dual
UNION
SELECT 0,
       '''&towner..&tname'||' has '',COUNT(*)
rcount,'' entries of '', ('  FROM dual UNION
SELECT column_id,
     'SUM(NIL(vsize('||column_name||'),0)) + 1 +'
FROM dba_tab_columns
WHERE table_name = '&tname'
   AND owner = '&towner'
   AND column_name in (&clist)
   AND column_id <> (SELECT MAX(column_id)
                     FROM dba_tab_columns
                       WHERE table_name = '&tname'
                         AND owner = '&towner'
                         AND column_name IN (&clist))
UNION
SELECT column_id,
       'SUM(NIL(VSIZE('||column_name||'),0)) + 1)'
 FROM dba_tab_columns
 WHERE table_name = '&tname'
   AND owner = '&towner' AND column_name IN (&clist)
   AND column_id = (SELECT MAX(column_id)
                     FROM dba_tab_columns
                       WHERE table_name = '&tname'
                         AND owner = '&towner'
                         AND column_name IN (&clist))
UNION
SELECT 997, '/ COUNT(*) + 11 isize, '' bytes each.'''
FROM dual
UNION
SELECT 999,
       'FROM &towner..&tname.;'  FROM dual;
SPOOL OFF
SET TERMOUT ON FEEDBACK 15 PAGESIZE 20 SQLCASE MIXED
SET NEWPAGE 1
START &cfile
CLEAR COLUMNS
```

6.3   ALTERATION OF INDEXES

If the DBA suspects that an index's storage clause is improper, the script in Source 6.4 is run to show the space used for the average entry in the index. This data can then be input into the space calculation formula to get a more accurate sizing estimate. The DBA can then use the ALTER INDEX command to alter the indexes storage clause for future extents, or drop and recreate the index with better parameters.

Indexes can be altered to change their storage clauses, and in version 7.3.x, they can be rebuilt on the fly. The alteration will only affect the storage allocations of future extents. To alter rows used in the index, unique versus nonunique, or all of the storage extents for an existing index, it must be dropped and recreated. To alter the storage within an existing index, use the ALTER INDEX command.

SOURCE 6.4   Script to calculate average length of an index entry.

```
rem     *********************************************************
rem
rem     NAME:  IN_CM_SZ.sql
rem
rem     HISTORY:
rem     Date            Who                  What
rem     --------        -------------------  ------------------------
rem     01/20/93  Michael Brouillette  Creation
rem
rem     FUNCTION:  Compute the space used by an entry for an
rem        existing index.
rem
rem     NOTES:  Currently requires DBA.
rem
rem     INPUTS:
rem          tname  = Name of table.
rem          towner = Name of owner of table.
rem          iname  = Name of index.
rem          iowner = Name of owner of index.
rem          cfile  = Name of output file SQL Script.
rem     *********************************************************
COLUMN dum1        NOPRINT
COLUMN isize       FORMAT 99,999.99
COLUMN rcount      FORMAT 999,999,999 NEWLINE
ACCEPT tname  PROMPT 'Enter table name: '
ACCEPT towner PROMPT 'Enter table owner name: '
ACCEPT iname  PROMPT 'Enter index name: '
ACCEPT iowner PROMPT 'Enter index owner name: '
ACCEPT cfile  PROMPT 'Enter name for output SQL file: '
SET PAGESIZE 999 HEADING OFF VERIFY OFF TERMOUT OFF
SET FEEDBACK OFF
SET SQLCASE UPPER NEWPAGE 3
SPOOL &cfile..sql
SELECT -1 dum1,
      'SELECT ''Index '||'&iowner..&iname'||' on table '
  FROM dual
UNION
SELECT 0,
      '&towner..&tname'||' has '',
      COUNT(*) rcount,'' entries of '', ('
  FROM dual
UNION
```

```
SELECT column_id,
       'SUM(NIL(vsize('||column_name||'),0)) + 1 +'
  FROM dba_tab_columns
 WHERE table_name = '&tname'
   AND owner = '&towner' AND column_name IN
                     (SELECT column_name FROM dba_ind_columns
                       WHERE table_name = '&tname'
                         AND table_owner = '&towner'
                         AND index_name = '&iname'
                         AND index_owner = '&iowner')
                         AND column_id <> (select max(column_id)
                                             FROM dba_tab_columns
                                            WHERE table_name = '&tname'
                                            AND owner = '&towner'
                                            AND column_name IN
                     (SELECT column_name FROM dba_ind_columns
                       WHERE table_name = '&tname'
                         AND table_owner = '&towner'
                         AND index_name = '&iname'
                         AND index_owner = '&iowner'))
UNION
SELECT column_id,
       'SUM(NIL(vsize('||column_name||'),0)) + 1)'
  FROM dba_tab_columns
  WHERE table_name = '&tname' AND owner = '&towner'
   AND column_name IN
                     (SELECT column_name FROM dba_ind_columns
                       WHERE table_name = '&tname'
                         AND table_owner = '&towner'
                         AND index_name = '&iname'
                         AND index_owner = '&iowner')
   AND column_id = (SELECT MAX(column_id)
                       FROM dba_tab_columns
                      WHERE table_name = '&tname'
                       AND owner = '&towner'
                       AND column_name IN
                       (SELECT column_name FROM dba_ind_columns
                         WHERE table_name = '&tname'
                           AND table_owner = '&towner'
                           AND index_name = '&iname'
                           AND index_owner = '&iowner'))
UNION
SELECT 997,
       '/ COUNT(*) + 11 isize, '' bytes each.'''  from dual
UNION
SELECT 999,  'FROM &towner..&tname.;'  FROM dual;
SPOOL OFF
SET TERMOUT ON FEEDBACK 15 PAGESIZE 20 SQLCASE MIXED
SET NEWPAGE 1
START &cfile
```

```
CLEAR columns
UNDEF tname
UNDEF towner
UNDEF iname
UNDEF iowner
UNDEF cfile
```

The ALTER INDEX Command Syntax for Oracle8

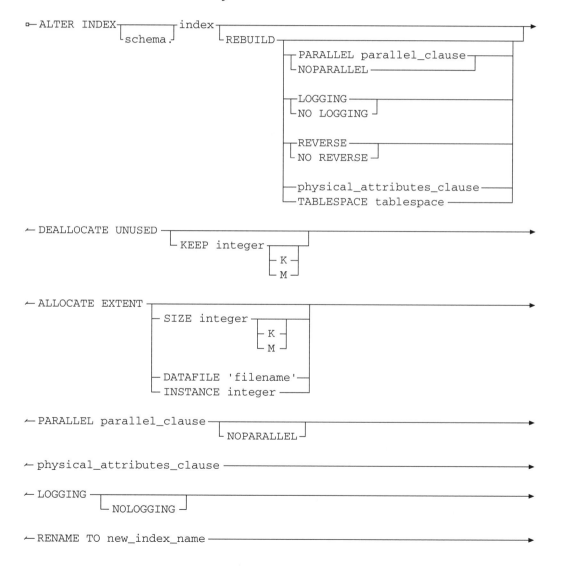

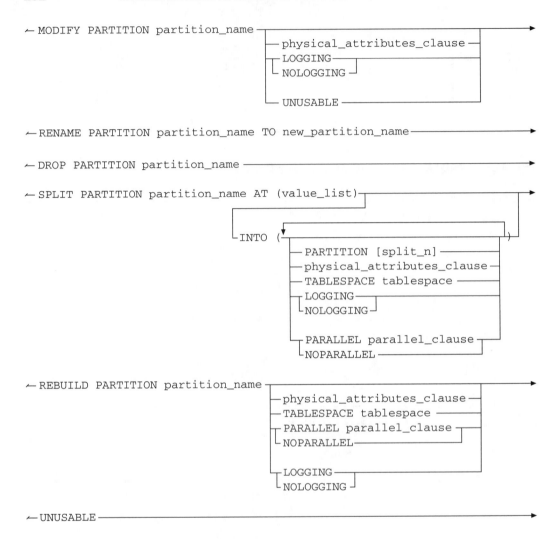

The physical_attributes_clause of the Oracle8 ALTER INDEX command consists of zero, and one or more of the following:

PCTFREE integer

INITRANS integer

MAXTRANS integer

STORAGE storage_clause

Keywords and Parameters

schema—This is the schema containing the index. If you omit schema, Oracle assumes the index is in your own schema.

index—This is the name of the index to be altered. The following operations can only be performed on partitioned global indexes:

Drop partition

Split partition

Rename partition

Rebuild partition

Modify partition

partition_name—This is the name of the index partition to be altered. It must be a partition in index.

PCTFREE, INITRANS, MAXTRANS—These change the value of these parameters for the index or index partition. See the PCTFREE, INITRANS and MAXTRANS parameters of the CREATE TABLE command for more information.

STORAGE—This changes the storage parameters for the index.

ALLOCATE EXTENT—This explicitly allocates a new extent for the index. The subclauses for the ALLOCATE EXTENT clause are:

SIZE—This specifies the size of the extent in bytes. You can use K or M to specify the extent size in kilobytes or megabytes. If you omit this parameter, Oracle determines the size based on the values of the index's STORAGE parameters.

DATAFILE—specifies one of the data files in the index's tablespace to contain the new extent. If you omit this parameter, it chooses the data file.

INSTANCE—This makes the new extent available to the specified instance. An instance is identified by the value of its initialization parameter.

INSTANCE_NUMBER—If you omit this parameter, the extent is available to all instances. This parameter is valid only if you are using Oracle with the parallel server option in parallel mode.

Explicitly allocating an extent with this clause does affect the size for the next extent to be allocated as specified by the NEXT and PCTINCREASE storage parameters.

DEALLOCATE UNUSED—This explicitly deallocates unused space at the end of the index and makes the freed space available for other segments. Only unused space above the high-water mark can be freed. If KEEP is omitted, all unused space is freed.

The subclause for the DEALLOCATE UNUSED clause is:

KEEP—This specifies the number of bytes above the high-water mark that the index will have after deallocation. If the number of remaining extents are less than MINEXTENTS, then MINEXTENTS is set to the current number of extents. If the initial extent becomes smaller than INITIAL, then INITIAL is set to the value of the current initial extent.

REBUILD—This clause is used to recreate an existing index. The subclauses for the REBUILD clause are:

REVERSE—This stores the bytes of the index block in reverse order, excluding the ROWID, when the index is rebuilt.

NOREVERSE—This stores the bytes of the index block without reversing the order when the index is rebuilt. Rebuilding a REVERSE index without the NOREVERSE keyword produces a rebuilt, reverse-keyed index.

PARALLEL parallel_clause, NOPARALLEL—This specifies that rebuilding the index, or some queries against the index or the index partition is performed either in serial or parallel execution.

LOGGING—This specifies that the rebuilding of the index or index partition will be logged in the undo and redo log file. LOGGING further specifies that subsequent operations against the index or index partition will be logged in the undo and redo log file. This is the default.

If the database is run in ARCHIVELOG mode, media recovery from a backup will recreate the index. You cannot specify LOGGING when using NOARCHIVELOG mode.

TIP   In future versions of Oracle, the LOGGING keyword will replace the RECOVERABLE option. RECOVERABLE is still available as a valid keyword in Oracle when altering or rebuilding nonpartitioned indexes, however, it is not recommended. You must specify LOGGING when altering or rebuilding a partitioned index.

RECOVERABLE—See LOGGING above. You cannot use RECOVERABLE for partitioned indexes or index partitions.

NOLOGGING—This specifies that the rebuilding of the index or index partition will not be logged in the undo and redo log file. NOLOGGING further specifies that subsequent operations against the index or index partition that can execute without logging will not be logged in the redo log file. As a result, media recovery will not recreate the index.

When this option is used, index creation is faster than the LOGGING option because no redo log entries are written.

TIP   In future versions of Oracle, the NOLOGGING keyword will replace the UNRECOVERABLE option. UNRECOVERABLE is still available as a valid keyword in Oracle when altering or rebuilding non-partitioned indexes, however, it is not recommended. You must specify NOLOGGING when altering or rebuilding a partitioned index.

UNRECOVERABLE—See NOLOGGING above. You cannot use UNRECOVERABLE for partitioned indexes or index partitions.

TABLESPACE—This specifies the tablespace where the rebuilt index will be stored. The default is the default tablespace of the user issuing the command.

RENAME—This renames index to new_index_name. The new_index_name is a single identifier and does not include the schema name.

RENAME PARTITION—This renames index partition_name to new_partition_name.

MODIFY PARTITION—This modifies the real physical attributes, logging option, or storage characteristics of index partition partition_name.

UNUSABLE—This marks the index or index partition(s) as unusable. An unusable index must be rebuilt, or dropped and recreated before it can be used. While one partition is marked unusable, the other partitions of the index are still valid, and you can execute statements that require the index if the statements do not access the unusable partition. You can also split or rename the unusable partition before rebuilding it.

REBUILD PARTITION—This rebuilds one partition of an index. You can also use this option to move an index partition to another tablespace or to change a create-time physical attribute.

DROP PARTITION—This removes a partition and the data in it from a partitioned global index. Dropping a partition of a global index marks the index's next partition as unusable. You cannot drop the highest partition of a global index.

SPLIT PARTITION—This splits a global partitioned index into two partitions, adding a new partition to the index. Splitting a partition marked as unusable results in two partitions, both marked as unusable. The partitions must be rebuilt before using them.

Splitting a usuable partition results in two partitions populated with data that are both marked as usable.

The subclauses for the PARTITION SPLIT clause are:

AT (value_list)—This specifies the new noninclusive upper bound for split_1. The value_list must compare less than the presplit partition bound for partition_name and greater than the partition bound for the next lowest partition (if there is one).

INTO—This describes the two partitions resulting from the split.

PARTITION split_1, PARTITION split_2—These specify the names and physical attributes of the two partitions resulting from the split.

MERGE PARTITION—While there is no explicit MERGE statement, you can merge a partition using either the DROP PARTITION or EXCHANGE PARTITION clauses. The only way to merge partitions in a local index is to merge partitions in the underlying table.

If the index partition BULLDOGS is empty, you can merge global index partition BULLDOGS into the next highest partition, GOGSU, by issuing the following statement:

```
ALTER INDEX UGAS DROP PARTITION BULLDOGS;
```

If the index partition BULLDOGS contains data, issue the following statements:

```
ALTER INDEX UGAS DROP PARTITION BULLDOGS;
ALTER INDEX UGAS REBUILD PARTITION GOGSU;
```

While the first statement marks partition GOGSU unusable, the second makes it valid again.

The Oracle7 ALTER INDEX Command

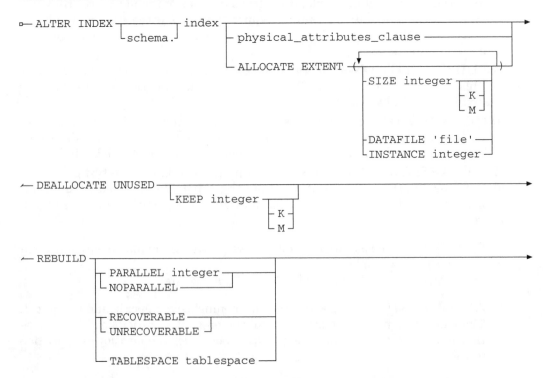

The parameters for the physical_attributes_clause are zero, one, or more of the following:

> PCTFREE integer
>
> INITRANS integer
>
> MAXTRANS integer
>
> STORAGE storage_clause

where the parameters are as described in the CREATE TABLE command with the exception of the REBUILD clause. The REBUILD clause allows rebuild of the specified index on the fly in 7.3.x and greater databases.

6.4   REBUILDING INDEXES

Occasionally, the DBA may be required to drop and recreate indexes. In Oracle version 7.3 and Oracle8 the ALTER INDEX . . . REBUILD command can be used to rebuild indexes on the fly. In earlier versions (pre-7.3) the indexes are rebuilt using drop and recreate scripts. If the scripts used to initially create the system are available, this is a relatively simple matter. If the scripts used to build the indexes are not available, or were never created in the first place, the script in Source 6.5 can be run to create a script that will recreate existing indexes when run. The script will not recreate bitmapped or partition indexes. The script can be modified to create bitmapped indexes by utilizing the INDEX_TYPE column of the USER_INDEXES or DBA_INDEXES views. The recreate script can also flag partition indexes by utilization of the PARTITIONED column of the USER_INDEXES or DBA_INDEXES views. To also rebuild partitioned indexes the USER_IND_PARTITIONS, USER_PART_KEY_COLUMNS or DBA_IND_PARTITIONS and DBA_PART_KEY_COLUMNS views would have to be queried.

The DBA can use the ANALYZE command to validate an index's structures. The format of this command follows. This data can help the DBA determine if a specific index has become corrupted and must be rebuilt.

```
ANALYZE INDEX [schema.]index
VALIDATE STRUCTURE;
```

The results are supplied to the DBA on-screen and are placed in a view called index_stats, which is dropped upon session exit.

SOURCE 6.5   Script to create rebuild script for indexes.

```
REM
REM in_rct.sql
REM
```

```
REM FUNCTION: SCRIPT FOR CREATING INDEXES
REM
REM            This script must be run by a user with the DBA role.
REM
REM            This script is intended to run with Oracle7 or Oracle8.
REM
REM            Running this script will in turn create a script to
REM            build all the indexes in the database.  This created
REM            script, create_index.sql, can be run by any user with
REM            the DBA role or with the 'CREATE ANY INDEX' system
REM            privilege.
REM
REM            The script will NOT capture the indexes created by
REM            the user 'SYS' or partitioned indexes.
REM
REM NOTE:      Indexes automatically created by table CONSTRAINTS will
REM            also be INCLUDED in the create_index.sql script.  It may
REM            cause a problem to create an index with a system assigned
REM            name such as SYS_C00333.
REM
REM            Only preliminary testing of this script was performed.
REM            Be sure to test it completely before relying on it.
REM


SET VERIFY OFF TERMOUT OFF FEEDBACK OFF ECHO OFF PAGES 0
SET TERMOUT ON
SELECT 'Creating index build script...' FROM dual;
SET TERMOUT OFF;

CREATE table i_temp
      (lineno NUMBER, id_name VARCHAR2(30),
       text VARCHAR2(2000)) STORAGE (INITIAL 100k NEXT 100k)
/


DECLARE
    CURSOR ind_cursor IS
     SELECT
        index_name,
        table_owner,
        table_name,
        uniqueness,
        tablespace_name,
        ini_trans,
        max_trans,
        initial_extent,
        next_extent,
        min_extents,
        max_extents,
        pct_increase,
```

```
       pct_free
     FROM
      user_indexes
     ORDER BY
      index_name;
   CURSOR col_cursor ( c_ind VARCHAR2, c_tab VARCHAR2) IS
     SELECT
     column_name
      FROM
     user_ind_columns
      WHERE
     index_name = c_ind
     AND table_name = c_tab
      ORDER BY
     column_position;

   lv_index_name          user_indexes.index_name%TYPE;
   lv_table_owner         user_indexes.table_owner%TYPE;
   lv_table_name          user_indexes.table_name%TYPE;
   lv_uniqueness          user_indexes.uniqueness%TYPE;
   lv_tablespace_name     user_indexes.tablespace_name%TYPE;
   lv_ini_trans           user_indexes.ini_trans%TYPE;
   lv_max_trans           user_indexes.max_trans%TYPE;
   lv_initial_extent      user_indexes.initial_extent%TYPE;
   lv_next_extent         user_indexes.next_extent%TYPE;
   lv_min_extents         user_indexes.min_extents%TYPE;
   lv_max_extents         user_indexes.max_extents%TYPE;
   lv_pct_increase        user_indexes.pct_increase%TYPE;
   lv_pct_free            user_indexes.pct_free%TYPE;
   lv_column_name         user_ind_columns.column_name%TYPE;
   lv_first_rec           BOOLEAN;
   lv_string              VARCHAR2(2000);
   lv_lineno              NUMBER := 0;

   PROCEDURE write_out(p_line INTEGER, p_name VARCHAR2,
               p_string VARCHAR2) IS
   BEGIN
     INSERT INTO i_temp (lineno,id_name,text)
         VALUES  (p_line,p_name,p_string);
   END;

BEGIN
   OPEN ind_cursor;
   LOOP
     FETCH ind_cursor INTO
     lv_index_name,
     lv_table_owner,
     lv_table_name,
     lv_uniqueness,
     lv_tablespace_name,
```

```
                  lv_ini_trans,
                  lv_max_trans,
                  lv_initial_extent,
                  lv_next_extent,
                  lv_min_extents,
                  lv_max_extents,
                  lv_pct_increase,
                  lv_pct_free;
                 EXIT WHEN ind_cursor%NOTFOUND;
                 lv_lineno := 1;
                 lv_first_rec := TRUE;
                 if (lv_uniqueness = 'UNIQUE') THEN
                 lv_string:= 'CREATE UNIQUE INDEX '||LOWER(lv_index_name);
                 write_out(lv_lineno, lv_index_name, lv_string);
                 lv_lineno := lv_lineno + 1;
                 ELSE
                 lv_string:= 'CREATE INDEX ' || LOWER(lv_index_name);
                 write_out(lv_lineno,  lv_index_name, lv_string);
                 lv_lineno := lv_lineno + 1;
                 END IF;
                 OPEN col_cursor(lv_index_name,lv_table_name);
                 LOOP
                 FETCH col_cursor INTO  lv_column_name;
                 EXIT WHEN col_cursor%NOTFOUND;
                 IF (lv_first_rec) THEN
                     lv_string := '   ON '|| LOWER(lv_table_owner) || '.' ||
                     lower(lv_table_name)||' (';
                 lv_first_rec := FALSE;
                 ELSE
                     lv_string := lv_string || ',';
                 END IF;
                 lv_string := lv_string || LOWER(lv_column_name);
                 END LOOP;
                 CLOSE col_cursor;
                 lv_string := lv_string || ')';
                 write_out(lv_lineno,  lv_index_name, lv_string);
                 lv_lineno := lv_lineno + 1;
                 lv_string := NULL;
                 lv_string := 'PCTFREE ' || TO_CHAR(lv_pct_free);
                 write_out(lv_lineno,  lv_index_name, lv_string);
                 lv_lineno := lv_lineno + 1;
                 lv_string := 'INITRANS ' || TO_CHAR(lv_ini_trans) ||
                     ' MAXTRANS ' || TO_CHAR(lv_max_trans);
                 write_out(lv_lineno,  lv_index_name, lv_string);
                 lv_lineno := lv_lineno + 1;
                 lv_string := 'TABLESPACE ' || lv_tablespace_name || ' STORAGE (';
                 write_out(lv_lineno,  lv_index_name, lv_string);
                 lv_lineno := lv_lineno + 1;
                 lv_string := 'INITIAL ' || TO_CHAR(lv_initial_extent) ||
```

```
                ' NEXT ' || TO_CHAR(lv_next_extent);
        write_out(lv_lineno,  lv_index_name, lv_string);
        lv_lineno := lv_lineno + 1;
        lv_string := 'MINEXTENTS ' || TO_CHAR(lv_min_extents) ||
        ' MAXEXTENTS ' || TO_CHAR(lv_max_extents) ||
        ' PCTINCREASE ' || TO_CHAR(lv_pct_increase) || ')';
        write_out(lv_lineno,  lv_index_name, lv_string);
        lv_lineno := lv_lineno + 1;
        lv_string := '/';
        write_out(lv_lineno,  lv_index_name, lv_string);
        lv_lineno := lv_lineno + 1;
        lv_lineno := lv_lineno + 1;
        lv_string:='                                                          ';
        write_out(lv_lineno,  lv_index_name, lv_string);
    END LOOP;
    CLOSE ind_cursor;
END;
/
COLUMN dbname NEW_VALUE db NOPRINT;
SELECT name dbname FROM v$database;
SPOOL rep_out\&db\crt_indx.sql
SET HEADING OFF
SET RECSEP OFF
COL text FORMAT A80 WORD_WRAP

SELECT
    text
FROM
    I_temp
ORDER BY
    id_name, lineno;
rem
SPOOL OFF
rem
DROP TABLE i_temp;
SET VERIFY ON TERMOUT ON FEEDBACK ON ECHO ON PAGES 22
CLEAR COLUMNS
```

6.5   DROPPING INDEXES

Indexes occasionally have to be dropped. Sometimes they are built incorrectly or shouldn't have been built at all. Other times, especially in early Oracle7 releases (prior to 7.3), in order to rebuild an index it had to be dropped first. Finally, dropping an index may be required to speed import or sqlloader during large data loads.

The DROP INDEX Command

The DROP INDEX command has the following format:

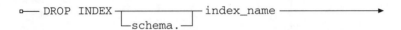

Of course, you must own the index or have the DROP ANY INDEX privilege to drop an index.

Administration of Other Database Objects

In Chapters 4, 5, and 6, we covered the administration of database tables and indexes. In Chapter 7 we will discuss the administration of the other database objects such as synonyms, sequences, views, and so on. For Oracle8 we also add DIRECTORY and LIBRARY objects.

7.1 ADMINISTRATION OF SYNONYMS

Synonyms are a database shorthand. They allow the specifications of long or complex object names to be shortened. This is especially useful for shared tables or views. In addition, use of DATABASE LINKS in synonyms allows transparent access to other databases on other nodes or even other entire systems halfway around the globe. Synonyms are a very powerful feature of Oracle and other SQL-compliant relational database systems.

Creation of Synonyms

Synonyms are created using the CREATE SYNONYM command. Synonyms can be either PRIVATE (the default) or PUBLIC. Private synonyms can only be used by the user creating them. You must have a specific grant or one of the special ROLES assigned to you before you can create synonyms. Only users with appropriate privileges (usually DBAs) can create PUBLIC synonyms. Since only the owner can use them, PRIVATE synonyms are more secure.

The format of the CREATE SYNONYM command follows.

where:

> **Synonym**—This is an allowed name. (It cannot be the name of an existing object for this user. For purposes of uniqueness, the schema name is considered as a part of the name for an object.)
>
> **Schema.object**—This is an existing table, view, package, procedure, function, or sequence name.
>
> **Database link**—This is an existing database link (covered later).

Synonyms provide both data independence and location transparency. With proper use and assignment, they allow an application to function regardless of table ownership, location, or even database.

Alteration of Synonyms

Synonyms cannot be altered. To change a synonym's definition it must be dropped and recreated.

Dropping Synonyms

Synonyms are dropped via the DROP command.

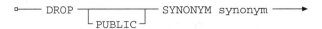

Recreating Synonyms

It is sometimes handy to have a script lying around to rebuild your existing synonyms. The script in Source 7.1 will create a synonym rebuild script for you from your data dictionary.

SOURCE 7.1   Script to generate synonym rebuild script.

```
REM FUNCTION: SCRIPT FOR CREATING SYNONYMS
REM    This script must be run by a user with the DBA role.
REM    This script is intended to run with Oracle7 or Oracle8.
REM    Running this script will in turn create a script to build
REM    all the synonyms in the database. The created script,
REM    create_synonyms.sql, can be run by any user with the DBA
REM    role or with the 'CREATE ANY SYNONYM' and 'CREATE PUBLIC
REM    SYNONYM' system privileges.
REM NOTE: This script does not capture synonyms for tables owned
REM    by the 'SYS' user.
REM    Only preliminary testing of this script was performed. Be
```

```
REM     sure to test it completely before relying on it.
REM
SET VERIFY OFF FEEDBACK OFF TERMOUT OFF ECHO OFF PAGESIZE 0
SET TERMOUT ON
SELECT 'Creating synonym build script...' FROM dual;
SET TERMOUT OFF
COLUMN dbname NEW_VALUE db NOPRINT
SELECT name dbname FROM v$database;
DEFINE cr='chr(10)'
SPOOL rep_out\&db\crt_syns.sql

SELECT 'CREATE '|| DECODE(owner,'PUBLIC','PUBLIC ',NULL) ||
       'SYNONYM '|| DECODE(owner,'PUBLIC',NULL, owner || '.') ||
       LOWER(synonym_name) || ' FOR ' || LOWER(table_owner) ||
       '.' || LOWER(table_name) ||
       DECODE(db_link,NULL,NULL,'@'||db_link) || ';'
  FROM sys.dba_synonyms
  WHERE table_owner != 'SYS'
  ORDER BY owner
/
SPOOL OFF
SET VERIFY ON FEEDBACK ON TERMOUT ON PAGESIZE 22
CLEAR COLUMNS
UNDEF cr
```

7.2   ADMINISTRATION OF SEQUENCES

Sequences are special database objects that provide numbers in sequence for input to a table. They are useful for providing generated primary key values, input of number type columns such as purchase order, employee number, sample number, and sales order number, where the input must be unique and in some form of numerical sequence.

Creation of Sequences

Sequences are created by use of the CREATE SEQUENCE command. The command's format follows.

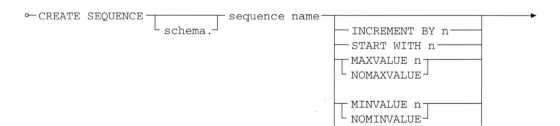

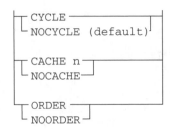

where:

Sequence name—This is the name you want the sequence to have. This may include the user name if created from an account with DBA privilege.

n—This is an integer, positive or negative.

INCREMENT BY—This tells the system how to increment the sequence. If it is positive the values are ascending; negative,descending.

START WITH—This tells the system what integer to start with.

MINVALUE—This tells the system how low the sequence can go. For ascending sequences it defaults to 1, for descending the default value is 10e27-1.

MAXVALUE—This tells the system the highest value that will be allowed.For descending sequences the default is 1, for ascending sequences the default is 10e27-1.

CYCLE—This option causes the sequence to automatically recycle to minvalue when maxvalue is reached for ascending sequences; for descending sequences it will cause recycle from minvalue back to maxvalue.

CACHE—This option will cache the specified number of sequence values into the buffers in the SGA. This speeds access , but all cached numbers are lost when the database is shut down. Default value is 20, maximum value is maxvalue-min-value.

ORDER—This option forces sequence numbers to be output in order of request. In cases where they are used for time stamping, this may be required. In most cases, the sequence numbers will be in order anyway and ORDER is not required.

Sequences avoid the performance problems associated with sequencing numbers generated by application triggers of the form:

```
DECLARE
     TEMP_NO NUMBER;
BEGIN
     LOCK TABLE PO_NUM IN EXCLUSIVE MODE NOWAIT;
     SELECT MAX(PO_NUM)+1 INTO TEMP_NO FROM SALES ;
END;
```

If the application requires numbers that are exactly in sequence (e.g., 1,2,3 . . .) then the trigger shown above may be your only recourse since if a statement that references a sequence is rolled back (canceled) that sequence number is lost. Likewise, any cached sequence numbers are lost each time a database is shut down.

If a sequence already exists in a test or development instance, the script in Source 7.2 can be used to build a script to transfer or document the structure of the sequence.

SOURCE 7.2   Script to create a sequence rebuild script.

```
REM
REM     FUNCTION: SCRIPT FOR RE-CREATING DATABASE SEQUENCES
REM
REM          This script must be run by a user with select
REM          grant on DBA_SEQUENCES
REM          This script is intended to run with Oracle7 or 8.
REM
REM     Running this script will in turn create a script to
REM     build all the sequences in the database.  This created
REm     script is called 'crt_seq.sql'.
REM
REM     This script will start the sequence (start with value)
REM     at the last value of the sequence at the time the
REM     script is run (LAST_NUMBER).
REM
REM
REM Only preliminary testing of this script was performed. Test
REM it completely before relying on it.
REM


SET VERIFY OFF FEEDBACK OFF TERMOUT OFF ECHO OFF PAGESIZE 0
SET TERMOUT ON
SELECT 'Creating sequence build script...' FROM dual;
SET TERMOUT OFF

CREATE TABLE seq_temp (grantor_owner varchar2(30),
text VARCHAR2(255))
/
DECLARE
   CURSOR seq_cursor IS
    SELECT
      sequence_owner,
      sequence_name,
      min_value,
      max_value,
      increment_by,
      DECODE(cycle_flag,'Y','CYCLE','NOCYCLE'),
      DECODE(order_flag,'Y','ORDER','NOORDER'),
      DECODE(to_char(cache_size),'0','NOCACHE',
```

```
'CACHE '||to_char(cache_size)),
     last_number
   FROM
     dba_sequences
   WHERE
     sequence_owner not in ('SYS','SYSTEM')
   ORDER BY
     sequence_owner;
     seq_owner        dba_sequences.sequence_owner%TYPE;
     seq_name         dba_sequences.sequence_name%TYPE;
     seq_min          dba_sequences.min_value%TYPE;
     seq_max          dba_sequences.max_value%TYPE;
     seq_inc          dba_sequences.increment_by%TYPE;
     seq_order        VARCHAR2(7);
     seq_cycle        VARCHAR2(7);
     seq_cache        VARCHAR2(15);
     seq_lnum         dba_sequences.last_number%TYPE;
     seq_string       VARCHAR2(255);
   PROCEDURE write_out(p_string VARCHAR2) is
   BEGIN
      INSERT INTO seq_temp (grantor_owner,text)
               VALUES (seq_owner,p_string);
   END;

BEGIN
   OPEN seq_cursor;
   LOOP
      FETCH seq_cursor INTO
                     seq_owner,
                     seq_name,
                     seq_min,
                     seq_max,
                     seq_inc,
                     seq_order,
                     seq_cycle,
                     seq_cache,
                     seq_lnum;
      EXIT WHEN seq_cursor%NOTFOUND;
      seq_string:=('CREATE SEQUENCE '||seq_owner||
                  '.'||seq_name||'
                     INCREMENT BY '||seq_inc||'
                     START WITH '||seq_lnum||'
                     MAXVALUE '||seq_max||'
                     MINVALUE '||seq_min||'
                     '||seq_cycle||'
                     '||seq_cache||'
                     '||seq_order||';');
write_out(seq_string);
   END LOOP;
```

```
    CLOSE seq_cursor;
END;
/
COLUMN dbname new_value db NOPRINT
SELECT name dbname FROM v$database;
SPOOL rep_out\&db\crt_seq.sql
BREAK ON downer SKIP 1
COLUMN text FORMAT a60 WORD_WRAP
COLUMN downer NOPRINT
SELECT
    grantor_owner downer,
    text
FROM
    seq_temp
ORDER BY
    downer
/
SPOOL OFF
rem
DROP TABLE seq_temp;
SET TERMOUT ON VERIFY ON FEEDBACK ON
CLEAR COLUMNS
CLEAR BREAKS
PROMPT Finished build
```

Alteration of Sequences

There may be times when a sequence must be altered, such as when a maximum or minimum value is reached. The ALTER SEQUENCE command is used to accomplish this. The format of the command follows.

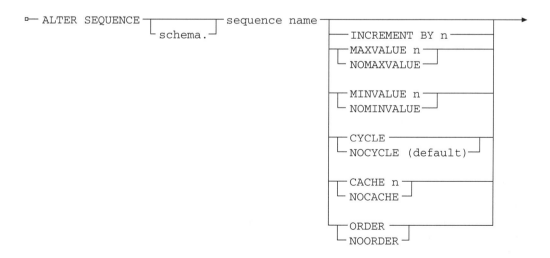

Only future sequence numbers are affected by this statement. To alter the START WITH clause, the sequence must be dropped and recreated. For ascending sequences, the MAXVALUE cannot be less than the current sequence value. For descending sequences, the MINVALUE cannot be greater than the current sequence value.

Dropping a Sequence

Sequences are dropped using the DROP SEQUENCE command. The format of this command follows.

If triggers and procedures reference the sequence, these triggers and procedures will fail if the sequence is dropped. It may be advisable to add an exception that will perform the trigger in Creation of Sequences in this situation.

Use of Sequences

Sequences are used by selecting using the sequence name and the parameters CURRVAL AND NEXTVAL. For example:

```
INSERT INTO purchase_orders (po_num, po_date, originator)
VALUES (po_seq.NEXTVAL, SYSDATE, USER) FROM dual;
```

In the above example, po_seq is the name of a sequence. The above INSERT would update the po_num, po_date and originator fields of the purchase_orders table with the next sequence value from po_seq, the current system date, and the current user name.

CURRVAL will retrieve the same value into multiple fields in the same session. CURRVAL cannot be used unless the NEXTVAL for the sequence has already been referenced in the current session.

The following are uses and restrictions of NEXTVAL and CURRVAL.

Uses

- Used with the VALUES clause on an INSERT command
- Used with the SELECT subclause of a SELECT command
- Used in the SET clause of an UPDATE command

Restrictions

- Neither one can be used in a subquery.
- Neither can be used in a view or snapshot query.
- Neither can be used with a DISTINCT clause.

- Neither can be used with GROUP BY or ORDER BY.

  Neither can be used in a SELECT command in combination with another SELECT using UNION, MINUS, or INTERSECT.

- Neither can be used in the WHERE clause.

  Neither can be used in the DEFAULT column value in a CREATE TABLE or ALTER TABLE command.

- Neither can be used in a CHECK in a constraint.

Sequences and Import, Export, and SQLLOADER

Sequences are ignorant objects. Sequences know nothing about the tables or clusters they service and furthermore they don't care that they don't know. This puts the onus on the DBA of ensuring that sequence values and table values are synchronized after the use of imports, manual data insertion, or use of SQLLOADER to load values into tables whose key values depend on sequences.

IMPORT Scenario A database is being used for testing. The test plan calls for the database to be periodically purged of data by use of combined deletion and truncation of key data tables. After the first test cycle it is decided that a larger data set is required. A larger, second test database is exported and its data values are imported with the IGNORE=Y option. What will happen?

In this scenario the sequences will be out of sync with the tables. The sequences will have a lesser value than the key fields in the database. Any attempted insert will most likely result in a duplicate key error being returned. So, what can you do to correct it? Actually, the solution is quite simple:

1. Determine the affected tables by doing simple

   SELECT COUNT(primary key field) FROM table;

   type selects and comparing that to known data counts before the drop occurred, or by comparing to a:

   SELECT last_number FROM dba_sequences WHERE
   sequence_name='affected_sequence';

2. Determine the difference between the affected sequences and the row count of the tables they support.

3. Adjust the sequence parameter INCREMENT_BY to this difference plus one:

   ALTER SEQUENCE affected_sequence INCREMENT BY difference+1;

4. Select the NEXTVAL from the sequence:

SELECT affected_sequence.NEXTVAL FROM dual;

5. Reset the INCREMENT_BY value to 1 (or whatever it is supposed to be).

ALTER SEQUENCE affected_sequence INCREMENT BY 1;

For example: table clients in phase one of testing has 1.2 million rows. The table is truncated and reloaded with 2.5 million rows. The clients_seq sequence shows its LAST_VALUE to be 1,200,000 and any attempted inserts generate the duplicate primary key error. To fix this:

```
SQL>ALTER SEQUENCE clients_seq INCREMENT BY 1300001;
SQL>SELECT clients_seq.NEXTVAL FROM dual;

clients_seq.NEXTVAL
----------------------------
                   25000001
one row returned.

SQL>ALTER SEQUENCE clients_seq INCREMENT BY 1;
```

7.3   ADMINISTRATION OF DATABASE LINKS

Database links allow users to access tables in other databases, even other databases on other computers running different operating systems. To use database links, the systems involved must have the SQL*NET product installed. All systems need to have network links as well.

Creation of Database Links

Database links are created with the CREATE DATABASE LINK command. The Oracle7 and Oracle8 format of this command follows.

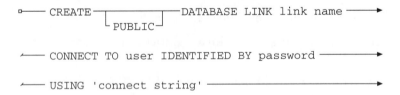

where:

database link—Under version 6 this was a user-specified name. Under Oracle7 this is the GLOBAL db_name and the DB_DOMAIN.

DBLINKS are schema independent.

PUBLIC—This is specified for database links that are to be used by all users. The user must have DBA privilege to specify a PUBLIC link.

CONNECT TO—This clause is used to force connection to a specific database user at the database being connected to. This allows the DBA to restrict access to confidential or sensitive information for one user instead of all users. If this clause isn't specified, the user's user name and password will be used in its place.

'connect string'—This is the protocol specific connection command. For a version 2 SQLNET or NET8 connection the string would be:

```
sid|alias.domain
```

where:

sid | alias—This is either the actual SID for the database or the alias entered in the tnsnames.ora file for the platform or names server.

domain—This is the domain to which the instance belongs.

Connect strings are very system specific and DBAs should read all documentation provided by Oracle on their system's SQL*Net version before attempting to use them.

The database link would be used in the following manner:

```
SELECT * FROM emp@link;
```

The combination of table name and link can be placed into a single synonym for ease of use:

```
CREATE PUBLIC SYNONYM BOS_EMP FOR EMP@ORPERDB.BOSTON;
```

(assuming ORPERDB.BOSTON is a defined database link alias in the tnsnames.ora file).

To document existing database links the script in Source 7.3 can be run to create a database link rebuild script.

SOURCE 7.3   Example script to recreate database links.

```
REM
REM NAME:         link_rct.sql
REM
REM FUNCTION:     SCRIPT FOR RE-CREATING DATABASE LINKS
REM
REM         This script must be run by users with select
REM         grant on dba_db_links.
REM
REM         This script is intended to run with Oracle7 or 8.
REM
```

```
REM Running this script will creates a script to build all the
REM database links in the database.  This script is called
REM 'crt_dbls.sql'.
REM
REM A DBA cannot create a private database link for a user.
REM This script will contain connect clauses before each create
REM statement. For the database links to be created under
REM the correct schema, must connect as that User. Therefore,
REM before executing the script, add each user's password to
REM the connect clause.  Duplicate clauses can be eliminated by
REM ensuring the database link is created under the correct
REM schema.
REM
REM PUBLIC database links require a connect as 'SYS'. However, REM username
can be changed to user with the DBA role or with REM the 'CREATE PUBLIC
DATABASE LINK' system privilege.
REM
REM The output is ordered by the link owner, a PUBLIC database
REM link has 'PUBLIC' as its owner.
REM
REM Only preliminary testing of this script was performed. Test
REM it completely before relying on it.
REM

SET VERIFY OFF FEEDBACK OFF TERMOUT OFF ECHO OFF PAGES 0

SET TERMOUT ON
SELECT 'Creating database link build script...' FROM dual;
SET TERMOUT OFF

CREATE TABLE dl_temp (lineno NUMBER, grantor_owner VARCHAR2(20),
text VARCHAR(255));

DECLARE
   CURSOR link_cursor IS
     SELECT
         u.name,
         l.name,
         l.userid,
         l.password,
         l.host
      FROM
         sys.link$ l,
         sys.user$ u
      WHERE
         l.owner# = u.user#
      ORDER BY
         l.name;
   lv_owner      sys.user$.name%TYPE;
   lv_db_link    sys.link$.name%TYPE;
```

```
   lv_username    sys.link$.userid%TYPE;
   lv_password    sys.link$.password%TYPE;
   lv_host        sys.link$.host%TYPE;
   lv_string      VARCHAR2(255);
   lv_user        VARCHAR2(255);
   lv_connect     VARCHAR2(255);
   lv_text        VARCHAR2(500);

   PROCEDURE write_out(p_string VARCHAR2) IS
   BEGIN
      INSERT INTO dl_temp (grantor_owner,text)
      VALUES (lv_owner,p_string);
   END;

BEGIN
   OPEN link_cursor;
   LOOP
      FETCH link_cursor INTO lv_owner,
                             lv_db_link,
                             lv_username,
                             lv_password,
                             lv_host;
      EXIT WHEN link_cursor%NOTFOUND;
IF (lv_owner = 'PUBLIC') THEN
      lv_string := ('CREATE PUBLIC DATABASE LINK '||
              LOWER(REPLACE(lv_db_link,'.WORLD','')));
ELSE
      lv_string := ('CREATE DATABASE LINK '||
              LOWER(REPLACE(lv_db_link,'.WORLD','')));
END IF;
      IF (lv_username IS NOT NULL) THEN
         lv_user := ('CONNECT TO '||LOWER(lv_username)||
                   ' IDENTIFIED BY '||LOWER(lv_password));
      END IF;
      IF (lv_host IS NOT NULL) THEN
         lv_connect := ('USING '''||lv_host||''''||';');
      END IF;
   lv_text := lv_string || ' ' || lv_user || ' ' || lv_connect;
   write_out(lv_text);
   lv_user := ' ';
   lv_connect := ' ';
   END LOOP;
   CLOSE link_cursor;
END;
/
DEFINE cr = CHR(10)
COLUMN dbname NEW_VALUE db NOPRINT
SELECT name dbname FROM v$database;
SPOOL rep_out\&db\crt_dbls.sql
BREAK ON downer SKIP 1
```

```
COLUMN text FORMAT A60 WORD_WRAP

SELECT
    'CONNECT '||DECODE(grantor_owner,'PUBLIC','SYS',grantor_owner)
||'/'||
DECODE(grantor_owner,'PUBLIC','SYS',grantor_owner) downer||
&&cr||
RTRIM(text)
FROM
    dl_temp
ORDER BY
    downer
/
SPOOL OFF
SET VERIFY ON FEEDBACK ON TERMOUT ON PAGES 22
CLEAR COLUMNS
DROP TABLE dl_temp;
```

Alteration of Database Links

Database links cannot be altered. To modify a database link, it must be dropped and recreated.

Dropping Database Links

Database links are dropped via the DROP DATABASE LINK command. For public database links the word public must be inserted after DROP. Only DBAs can drop public database links. The format of the DROP command follows.

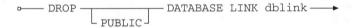

7.4   ADMINISTRATION OF VIEWS

Views are virtual looks at tables. They don't exist until queried except as a specification statement stored in the database. A single view can be very efficient, but the "stacking" of views, that is, views that reference views that reference views, will show a performance problem. Views allow the DBA to restrict access to certain columns within a table or tables. Views can act as preprocessing for reports. Views can be used to perform calculations and display the results alongside of the data as if the results were stored in a table. Views can also be used to "filter" data. A view can be constructed from virtually any SELECT statement. Depending upon how a view is constructed, updates and inserts can be done through them.

Creation of Views

Creation of views is accomplished with the CREATE VIEW command. Let's look at this command.

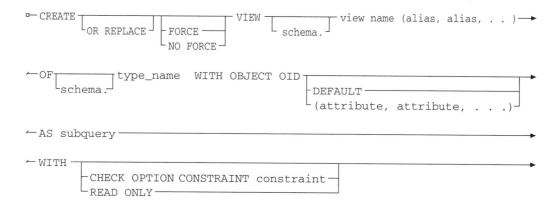

where:

> **view name**—This is the name for the view.
>
> **alias**—This is a valid column name; it isn't required to be the same as the column it is based on. If aliases aren't used, the names of the columns are used. If a column is modified by an expression, it must be aliased. If four columns are in the query, there must be four aliases.
>
> **subquery**—This is any valid SELECT statement that doesn't include an ORDER BY or FOR UPDATE clause.
>
> **WITH CHECK**—This clause specifies that inserts and updates through the view must be selectable from the view. This can be used in a view based on a view.
>
> **READ ONLY**—This specifies that the view is READ ONLY and cannot be updated.
>
> **CONSTRAINT**—This specifies the name associated with the WITH CHECK constraint.
>
> **FORCE**—This specifies that the view be created even if all permissions or objects it specifies as part of the view aren't available. Before the view can be used the permissions or objects must be in the database and accessible.
>
> **NO FORCE (default)**—This means all objects and permissions must be in place before the view can be created.
>
> **OF object_type**—This explicitly creates an object view of type object_type. The columns in the object view are the same as the top-level attributes of the specified object_type. Each row will have an assigned OID.

WITH OBJECT OID—This specifies the attributes of the row that will be used as a key to uniquely identify each row of the object view. These should correspond to the primary key of the base table. If the base object has an OID already you can specify DEFAULT. This is only for Oracle8.

A view can usually be used in the following commands:

COMMENT

DELETE

INSERT

LOCK TABLE

UPDATE

SELECT

A view's select statement in the subquery cannot select a CURVAL or NEXTVAL from a sequence or directly access ROWID, ROWNUM, or LEVEL pseudocolumns. To use the pseudocolumns for a table a view select must alias them.

A view is just a window to data; it can't store data itself. Views can be used in a SQL statement just like a table, with the following exceptions:

You can't update a view if:

- It contains a join.
- It contains a GROUP BY, CONNECT BY, or START WITH clause.
- It contains a DISTINCT clause, or expressions like "AMOUNT+10" in the column list.

It doesn't reference all NOT NULL columns in the table (all "not nulls" must be in the view and assigned a value by the update).

You can update a view that contains pseudocolumns or columns modified by expressions if the update doesn't affect these columns. A new trigger, called an INSTEAD-OF trigger, can be used to update the underlying tables in a view that can't be directly updated.

You can query the view USER_UPDATABLE_COLUMNS to find out if the columns in a join view are updatable. Generally speaking, as long as all of the NOT-NULLs and key columns are included in a join view for a table, then that table may be updatable through the view.

A join view can have the commands INSERT, UPDATE, and DELETE used against it under these circumstances:

- The DML affects only one of the tables in the join.

  If the command is UPDATE, then all of the columns updated are extracted from a key preserved table. In addition if the view has a CHECK OPTION constraint, join columns and columns taken from tables that are referenced more than once in the view are shielded from update.

If the statement is DELETE, then there is one and only one key-preserved table in the join and that table can be present more than once if there is no CHECK OPTION constraint on the view.

If the statement is INSERT, then all of the columns are from a key-preserved table and the view doesn't have a CHECK OPTION constraint.

Partition Views

Under Oracle7 version 7.3, a new type of view called the partition view is allowed. This view joins several tables that have identical structure into a single entity that can be queried as if all of the component parts were actually in one table. The purpose for a partition view is to allow physical partitioning of data into several table partitions (this is pre-8 and shouldn't be confused with actual partition tables, which aren't available until Oracle8). These table partitions are hand built by the DBA to spread data across several disk volumes and to separate data by a preset algorithm that is application controlled (instead of like Oracle8, which is specified at the table's creation). An example would be an application that breaks sales data down by month and stores it in independent monthly sales tables. A partitioned view could be created to join all of the monthly sales tables in quarterly, yearly, or whatever views of all sales for that period.

The steps to create a partition view are as follows:

1. CREATE the tables that will comprise the view or ALTER existing tables.
2. Give each table a constraint that limits the values that may be stored in the table.
3. Create an index on the constrained columns of each table.
4. Create the partition view as a series of select statements that are combined using the UNION ALL join. The view should select all underlying columns from all tables (i.e., there should be identical columns in all of the tables making up the view).
5. If parallel query is available, specify that the view is parallel so all tables in the view are scanned in parallel rather than serially. This is accomplished by one or more of the following:
    a. Specify parallel for all underlying tables.
    b. Give a "parallel" hint in the select statement for the view.

There is no special syntax or partition clause for the CREATE VIEW to create a partition view, Oracle7 and Oracle8 interprets a UNION ALL of several tables, each of which have identical local indexes on the same columns, as a partition view.

Converting a Partition View into a Partitioned Table   This procedure delineates the method to convert a partition view (also called "manual partition") into a partitioned table. If you use the MIG80 routine to migrate from Oracle7 to Oracle8 it is supposed to convert these automatically but I haven't personally confirmed this is the truth. The partition view in this example conversion is defined as follows:

```
CREATE VIEW sales
        SELECT * FROM sales_jan96
            UNION ALL
        SELECT * FROM sales_feb96
            UNION ALL
            ...
        SELECT * FROM sales_dec96;
```

To incrementally migrate the partition view to a partitioned table:

1. Initially, only the two most recent partitions, SALES_NOV96 and SALES_DEC96, will be migrated from the view to the table by creating the partition table, with each partition getting a temporary segment of two blocks (assuming a 2-K block size) as a placeholder.

```
CREATE TABLE sales_new (...)
        TABLESPACE ts_temp STORAGE (INITIAL 4098)
          PARTITION BY RANGE (sales_date)
           (PARTITION jan96 VALUE LESS THAN ('960201'),
               ...
            PARTITION dec96 VALUE LESS THAN ('970101'));
```

2. Reset the default tablespace and storage parameters associated with the SALES_NEW table to more reasonable settings.

3. Use the EXCHANGE command to migrate the tables to the corresponding partitions.

```
ALTER TABLE sales_new
        EXCHANGE PARTITION nov96 WITH TABLE
        sales_96 WITH VALIDATION;
ALTER TABLE sales_new
        EXCHANGE PARTITION dec96 WITH TABLE
        sales_dec96 WITH VALIDATION;
```

So now the placeholder data segments associated with the NOV96 and DEC96 partitions have been exchanged with the data segments associated with the SALES_NOV95 and SALES_DEC95 tables.

4. Redefine the SALES view.

```
CREATE OR REPLACE VIEW sales
        SELECT * FROM sales_jan95
            UNION ALL
```

```
SELECT * FROM sales_feb_95
      UNION ALL
      ...
      UNION ALL
SELECT * FROM sales_new PARTITION (nov96)
      UNION ALL
SELECT * FROM sales_new PARTITION (dec96);
```

5. Drop the SALES_NOV96 and SALES_DEC96 tables, which own the placeholder segments that were originally attached to the NOV96 and DEC96 partitions.

6. After all the tables in the UNION ALL view are converted into partitions, drop the view and the partitioned table that was renamed as the view.

```
DROP VIEW sales;
RENAME sales_new TO sales;
```

Object Views

In order to take advantage of the benefits of the new object paradigm in Oracle8, a common relational table can be made into a pseudoobject table by creating what is known as an object view that is directly based on the relational table. The object ID is not system generated but based on columns that you specify.

An example using the EMP table would be:

```
CREATE TYPE emp_t AS OBJECT (
empno     NUMBER(5),
ename     VARCHAR2(20),
salary    NUMBER(9,2),
job       VARCHAR2(20));

CREATE TABLE emp(
empno     NUMBER(5),
ename     VARCHAR2(20),
salary    NUMBER(9,2),
job       VARCHAR2(20)
CONSTRAINT pk_emp PRIMARY KEY (empno));

CREATE VIEW emp_man OF emp_t
WITH OBJECT OID (empno) AS
SELECT emp_T(empno, ename, salary, job)
FROM emp
WHERE job='MANAGER';
```

This creates an object view of EMP_T (type) objects corresponding to the employees from the EMP table who are managers, with EMPNO, the primary key of EMP, as the object identifier.

Example Views

An example view that uses aliases and expressions to modify columns is shown in Source 7.4.

SOURCE 7.4   **Example of a view with expressions.**

```
CREATE VIEW free_space
    (tablespace, file_id, pieces, free_bytes, free_blocks,
     largest_bytes,largest_blks) AS
SELECT tablespace_name, file_id, COUNT(*),
    SUM(bytes), SUM(blocks),
    MAX(bytes), MAX(blocks) FROM sys.dba_free_space
GROUP BY tablespace_name, file_id;
```

In Source 7.4 the SUM, MAX, and COUNT expressions (functions) are used to provide summary data on space usage. This view could not be updated. Further reading will show it is also based upon a view DBA_FREE_SPACE that is based on several data dictionary tables owned by the SYS user. An example of a view that performs calculations and filters the data provided is shown in Source 7.5.

SOURCE 7.5   **View using expressions and filtering.**

```
REM      and the percent of GETMISSES/GETS
REM USE     : Use as a selectable table only
REM Limitations   : User must have access to V$ views.
REM Revisions:
REM   Date  Modified By Reason For change
REM   4/28/93    Mike Ault   Initial Creation
REM
CREATE VIEW dd_cache
AS SELECT parameter,gets,getmisses,
getmisses/gets*100 percent
,count,usage
FROM v$rowcache
WHERE gets > 100 AND getmisses > 0;
```

To create a script to document and allow rebuild of existing views, the script in Source 7.6 can be used.

SOURCE 7.6   Script to rebuild views.

```
REM
REM NAME        :view_rct.sql
REM FUNCTION:recreate database views by owner
REM USE             :Generate a report on database views
REM Limitations :If your view definitions are greater than 5000
REM             characters then increase the set long. This can be
REM             determined by querying the DBA_VIEWS table's
REM             text_length column for the max value: select
REM             max(text_length) from dba_views;
REM
SET PAGES 59 LINES 79 FEEDBACK OFF ECHO OFF VERIFY OFF
DEFINE cr='chr(10)'
COLUMN text        FORMAT a80 word_wrapped
COLUMN view_name       FORMAT a20
COLUMN dbname NEW_VALUE db NOPRINT
UNDEF owner_name
UNDEF view_name
SELECT name dbname from v$database;
SET LONG 5000 HEADING OFF
SPOOL rep_out\&db\cre_view.sql
SELECT
'rem Code for view: '||v.view_name||'Instance: '||&&db||&&cr||
'CREATE OR REPLACE VIEW '||v.owner||'.'||v.view_name||' AS '
    ||&&cr,
    v.text
FROM
    dba_views v
WHERE
    v.owner LIKE UPPER('%&&owner_name%')
    AND view_name LIKE UPPER('%&&view_name%')
ORDER BY
    v.view_name;
SPOOL OFF
SET HEADING ON PAGES 22 LINES 80 FEEDBACK ON
CLEAR COLUMNS
TTITLE OFF
PAUSE Press enter to continue
```

Alteration of Views

Under Oracle7 and Oracle8 there is only a single option for the ALTER VIEW command; this is the COMPILE option. If a view's underlying views or tables are marked as invalid or changed, the view is marked as invalid and must be recompiled. This can be done automatically when the view is next called, or it can be done explicitly with the ALTER VIEW command. It is best to do this explicitly so that any problems are found before the user's attempt to use the view. The format for the ALTER VIEW command follows.

Dropping Views

Views are dropped with the DROP VIEW command. Its format follows.

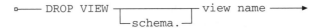

TIP   Altering or dropping a view will result in invalidation of any dependent packages, functions, or procedures. Be sure to check dependencies before performing these operations.

7.5   ADMINISTRATION OF TRIGGERS IN ORACLE7

Database triggers are PL/SQL procedures stored in the database and associated with specific actions on a database level. Under Oracle8, a new type of trigger called an INSTEAD-OF trigger can be created exclusively for views. Never depend on the order in which triggers fire. This is not guaranteed to always be identical.

Creation of Database Triggers

Database triggers are created using the CREATE TRIGGER command. There are three basic types of triggers in Oracle7: BEFORE, AFTER, and FOR EACH ROW. Under Oracle8 a fourth is added: the INSTEAD OF trigger for views. Since the FOR EACH ROW clause can be combined with the other two, this gives four types of triggers: before and after statement triggers and before and after row triggers. In addition, each of the four types can be tied to the three basic actions, DELETE, INSERT, and UPDATE, giving twelve possible triggers per table. A view can only have a INSTEAD OF trigger (under Oracle8 only). A trigger is ENABLED when it is created. This command's format follows.

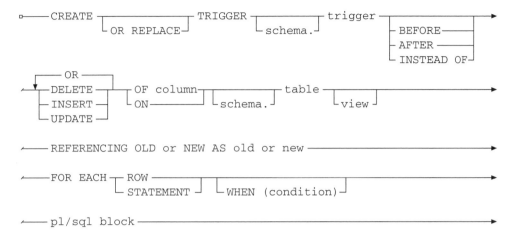

where:

> **OR REPLACE**—This replaces the trigger if it exists, and can be used to change the definition of a trigger without dropping it first.
>
> **schema**—This takes the place of the owner.
>
> **trigger**—This is the trigger's name.
>
> **BEFORE**—This specifies the trigger is fired before the specified action.
>
> **AFTER**—This indicates the trigger is fired after the specified action.
>
> **INSTEAD OF**—This statement indicates that for this view the action specified in the trigger be taken instead of the specified action.
>
> **DELETE / INSERT / UPDATE**—These are the specified actions, only one per trigger.
>
> **OF**—This limits the action response to the listed columns.
>
> **ON**—This specifies the table name of the table the trigger is for.
>
> **REFERENCING**—This deals with correlation names. This allows specification of old and new values for a column.
>
> **FOR EACH ROW**—This forces the trigger to fire on each affected row or STATEMENT, making it a row trigger. The trigger is fired for each row that is affected by the trigger and that meets the WHEN clause constraints. If STATEMENT is used, it makes it a statement-level trigger.
>
> **WHEN**—This specifies any constraints on the trigger. This is a trigger restriction clause. This contains a standard SQL clause.
>
> **PL/SQL Block**—This is the trigger body and is in the standard PL/SQL format.

Database triggers are complex and if you do not save the creation script, it is very difficult to readily recall the exact command used in many cases. The script in Source 7.7 can be used to retrieve trigger definitions for the database.

SOURCE 7.7   Example script to recreate triggers.

```
REM  trig_rct.sql
REM
REM     FUNCTION: SCRIPT FOR RE-CREATING DATABASE TRIGGERS
REM This script can be run by users with access to dba_ triggers
REM      This script is intended to run with Oracle7.
REM      Running this script will in turn create a script to
REM      build all the triggers in the database.  This created
REM      script is called 'create_triggers.sql'.
REM       Only preliminary testing of this script was performed.
REM       Be sure to test it completely before relying on it.
SET VERIFY OFF FEEDBACK OFF TERMOUT OFF ECHO OFF PAGES 0
SET LONG 4000 TERMOUT ON ARRAYSIZE 1
SELECT 'Creating trigger build script...' from dual;
SET TERMOUT OFF
CREATE TABLE trig_temp (owner        VARCHAR2(30),
                 trigger_name        VARCHAR2(30),
                 trigger_type        VARCHAR2(16),
                 triggering_event    VARCHAR2(26),
                 table_owner         VARCHAR2(30),
                 table_name          VARCHAR2(30),
                 referencing_names   VARCHAR2(87),
                 when_clause         VARCHAR2(2000),
                 trigger_body        LONG,
                 trigger_columns     VARCHAR2(400)) ;

DECLARE
   CURSOR trig_cursor IS
      select owner,
        trigger_name,
        trigger_type ,
        triggering_event,
        'ON '||table_owner,
        table_name,
        referencing_names,
      'WHEN '||when_clause,
        trigger_body
   FROM
        dba_triggers
   WHERE
        owner NOT IN ('SYS','SYSTEM')
   ORDER BY
        owner;
   CURSOR trig_col ( owner VARCHAR2, name VARCHAR2 ) IS
     SELECT
           trigger_owner,
           trigger_name,
           column_name
```

```
    FROM
        dba_trigger_cols
    WHERE
        trigger_owner = owner AND
        trigger_name = name;

    trig_owner      dba_triggers.owner%TYPE;
    trig_name       dba_triggers.trigger_name%TYPE;
    trig_type       dba_triggers.trigger_type%TYPE;
    trig_event      dba_triggers.triggering_event%TYPE;
    trig_towner     dba_triggers.table_owner%TYPE;
    trig_tname      dba_triggers.table_name%TYPE;
    trig_rnames     dba_triggers.referencing_names%TYPE;
    trig_wclause    dba_triggers.when_clause%TYPE;
    trig_body       dba_triggers.trigger_body%TYPE;
    trig_col_own    dba_trigger_cols.trigger_owner%TYPE;
    trig_col_nam    dba_trigger_cols.trigger_name%TYPE;
    trig_column     dba_trigger_cols.column_name%TYPE;
    all_columns     VARCHAR2(400);
    counter         INTEGER:=0;

BEGIN
  OPEN trig_cursor;
  LOOP
    FETCH trig_cursor INTO    trig_owner,
                    trig_name,
                    trig_type,
                    trig_event,
                    trig_towner,
                    trig_tname,
                    trig_rnames,
                    trig_wclause,
                    trig_body;
    EXIT WHEN trig_cursor%NOTFOUND;
    all_columns :='';
    counter := 0;
    OPEN trig_col(trig_owner,trig_name);
    LOOP
        FETCH trig_col INTO
                    trig_col_own,
                    trig_col_nam,
                    trig_column;
        EXIT WHEN trig_col%NOTFOUND;
            counter := counter+1;
            IF counter = 1 THEN
            all_columns := ' OF '||all_columns||trig_column;
            ELSE
            all_columns := all_columns||', '||trig_column;
        END IF;
```

```
        END LOOP;
        CLOSE trig_col;
        IF trig_rnames = 'REFERENCING NEW AS NEW OLD AS OLD' THEN
            trig_rnames := '';
        END IF;
        IF trig_wclause = 'WHEN ' THEN
            trig_wclause := '';
        END IF;
        INSERT INTO trig_temp VALUES (trig_owner,
                        trig_name,
                        trig_type,
                        trig_event,
                        trig_towner,
                        trig_tname,
                        trig_rnames,
                        trig_wclause,
                        trig_body,
                        all_columns);
    END LOOP;
    CLOSE trig_cursor;
    COMMIT;
END;
/
COLUMN dbname NEW_VALUE db NOPRINT
SELECT name dbname FROM v$database;
DEFINE cr='CHR(10)'
SPOOL rep_out\&db\crt_trgs.sql
SET HEADING OFF
SET RECSEP OFF PAGES 0

SELECT '/'||&&cr||&&cr||'CREATE OR REPLACE TRIGGER '||
  owner||'.'||trigger_name||&&cr||
DECODE(trigger_type,'BEFORE EACH ROW','BEFORE ',
     'AFTER EACH ROW','AFTER ',trigger_type)||
triggering_event||&&cr||
trigger_columns||&&cr||
table_owner||'.'||table_name||' '||referencing_names||&&cr||
DECODE(trigger_type,'BEFORE EACH ROW','FOR EACH ROW',
         'AFTER EACH ROW','FOR EACH ROW','')||&&cr||
when_clause,
trigger_body
FROM trig_temp
ORDER BY owner;
SPOOL OFF
DROP TABLE trig_temp;
SET VERIFY ON FEEDBACK ON TERMOUT ON PAGESIZE 22
SET HEADING ON RECSEP ON
CLEAR COLUMNS
```

Before Oracle version 7.3, triggers were compiled at runtime. After 7.3 they are stored in the database as Pcode. This provides significant performance benefits over earlier versions since the overhead of reparsing the trigger for each firing is eliminated. This allows larger and more complex triggers to be created without fear of performance degradation caused by reparsing large sections of code.

Conditional Predicates New to Oracle8 is the concept of a conditional predicate for a trigger that tells the trigger why it is being fired. These conditional predicates are of the form:

INSERTING—Evaluates to true if an insert operation fired the trigger.

DELETING—Evaluates to true if a delete operation fired the trigger.

UPDATING—Evaluates to true if an update operation fired the trigger.

UPDATING(column)—Evaluates to true if the operation is an update and the specified column is updated.

LOB Trigger Limitations You can reference object, VARRAY, nested table, LOB, and REF columns inside triggers but you cannot modify their values. Triggers based on actions against these types of attributes can be created.

Triggers and Mutating Tables One recurring problem with triggers is when a trigger tries to reference the table for which it is fired (for example, to check a date range). This self-referencing results in "ORA-04091 table 'table_name' is mutating, trigger/function may not see it." Usually this situation can be remedied by using a temporary PL/SQL table to hold values, by use of a temporary table to hold values, or by use of a view. The key here is to remove the values to be selected against away from the table before you attempt the operation and then refer to this remote source for any value checking. It might also be possible to create an index that any selects will reference. Any solution that moves the data from the table to a secondary source that can then be used in place of the table itself should correct this problem.

Alteration of Triggers

As was stated in "Creation of Database Triggers," the CREATE command has the OR REPLACE option to allow a trigger to be recreated without being dropped. A recently added feature is the COMPILE [DEBUG] option that allows recompilation and debug of a trigger that has become invalidated. To alter the contents of a trigger, this create or replace option is used. A trigger has one of two possible states, either ENABLED or DISABLED.

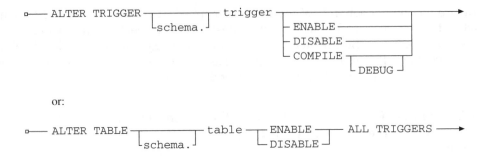

or:

One limit on the usefulness of the ALTER TABLE in either disabling or enabling triggers is that it is an all-or-nothing proposition. It is better to use the ALTER TRIGGER command unless you want all of the triggers on the table enabled or disabled at one time.

The DEBUG option instructs the PL/SQL compiler to generate and store the code for use by the PL/SQL debugger.

Dropping a Trigger

Triggers are dropped using the DROP TRIGGER command.

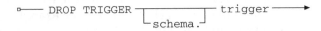

TIP Careful consideration should be given to all triggers created in Oracle8. Could its function be better accomplished with a method? If so, use a method. Check for trigger dependencies before dropping a trigger or significantly altering a trigger's actions.

7.6   ADMINISTRATION OF FUNCTIONS AND PROCEDURES

New to Oracle8 is the advance typing that allows a PL/SQL table in functions and procedures to be multidimensional. Before, in Oracle7 a PL/SQL table had to be scalar (a single datatype). Oracle8 also offers object support and external procedure and function calls.

Functions and procedures under Oracle7 and Oracle8 are virtually identical. The major exceptions are that functions always return a single value, while procedures may return one, many, or no values. This leads to the second difference: the procedure can use the OUT and IN OUT arguments in the create command while the function can't. In fact, the function doesn't have to specify the IN argument since input to a function is required.

Why Use Functions and Procedures?

The benefits are numerous. Functions and procedures provide a consistent means of accessing, altering, and deleting database information. They allow enhanced security by giving the DBA the ability to grant access to the procedures and functions instead of the actual tables or views. The procedure or functions can have elevated privileges that are in effect while the procedure or function is active, but go away when it completes.

Functions and procedures enhance productivity by allowing a given process to be coded once and then referenced by all developers. Instead of each form requiring coded triggers for data access, the stored procedures and functions can be referenced instead. This drives consistency down to the database level instead of requiring it from each developer.

Performance is enhanced by allowing multiple users to access the same shared image. Since the procedures and functions are loaded into the cached memory area, only one I/O is required for each procedure or function to be available to all users. In network situations a function or procedure can be called with a single network call; the function or procedure can then trigger a multitude of database actions and then return, via another single call, the results, thus greatly reducing network traffic.

TIP   If a function or procedure affects only one table, then perhaps in Oracle8 it should be made into a method. Methods should be used for any internal PL/SQL objects that affect only one table or are used to obtain values from only one table. Using a method instead of a procedure or function will utilize the concept of encapsulation in these cases.

Let's look at administration of functions and procedures.

Creation of Functions and Procedures

Before a function or procedure can be created the DBA must have run the CATPROC. SQL script. The CATPROC.SQL script is usually run at database creation and, unless you upgrade, you shouldn't have to run it again. The user creating the function or procedure must have CREATE PROCEDURE to create a procedure or function in their own schema or CREATE ANY PROCEDURE system privilege.

Any tables, clusters, or views used in creation of functions and procedures must have direct grants against them issued to the developer who creates the function or procedure. If this is not the case, the errors returned can either be as informative as stating that you can't create a stored object with privileges granted through a role, or be the rather frustrating "ORA-0942—Table or View doesn't exist."

A new entity known as an external function is available under Oracle8. The CREATE FUNCTION command is also used to register this new entity to the database. External functions are 3GL code functions stored in a shared library which can be called from either SQL or PL/SQL. To call an external function you must have EXECUTE privileges on the callout library where it resides (this is an external operating system file and OS-level execute permission, not Oracle internal level).

Functions and procedures are created using the CREATE command. The format for each differs slightly.

CREATE FUNCTION Command For functions the format is:

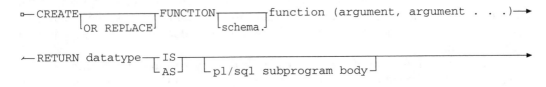

An argument has the form:

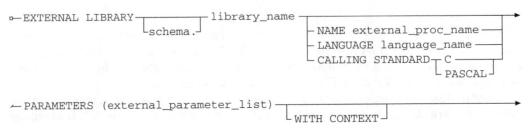

where:

argument_name—This is the name given to this argument and can be any valid variable name.

argument_type—This is the type of argument, IN, OUT, or IN OUT, and specifies how the argument is to be treated (strictly input, strictly output, or both). This is optional and will default to IN if not specified.

argument datatype—This is the datatype of the argument and can be any valid scalar datatype.

The external_body has the form:

```
o—EXTERNAL LIBRARY——————library_name—
              └schema.┘              ├ NAME external_proc_name ─┤
                                     ├ LANGUAGE language_name ──┤
                                     └ CALLING STANDARD─┬ C ────┘
                                                        └ PASCAL┘

╰— PARAMETERS (external_parameter_list) ──────────────────────────
                                        └ WITH CONTEXT ┘
```

The external_parameter_list has the form:

```
{{parameter_name [PROPERTY] | RETURN prop } [BY REF] [extern_datatype] | CONTEXT}
```

with the above repeated as many times as is needed. prop has the values:

INDICATOR, LENGTH, MAXLEN, CHARSETID, or, CHARSETFORM

The command for creating a procedure is almost identical except there is no required RETURN clause. The CREATE PROCEDURE command can be used to create either internal standalone procedures or procedures that register calls to external procedures.

CREATE PROCEDURE Command For procedures the CREATE command format is:

```
□─ CREATE────────────── PROCEDURE ─────── procedure (argument, argument . . .) ─→
        └OR REPLACE┘          └schema.┘

┌─IS─────────┐
┴─AS─┘   ┌─pl/sql subprogram body─┐
         └external_body───────────┘
```

An argument has the form:

```
  ┌──── argument_name ──────────────┬─ argument_datatype ─→
                   └─ argument_type ─┘
```

where:

argument_name—This is the name given to this argument and can be any valid variable name.

argument_type—This is the type of argument, IN, OUT, or IN OUT, and specifies how the argument is to be treated (strictly input, strictly output, or both).

argument_datatype—This is the datatype of the argument and can be any valid scalar datatype.

The external_parameter_list has the form:

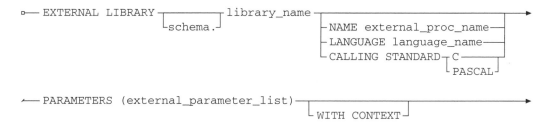

```
{{parameter_name [PROPERTY] | RETURN prop } [BY REF] [extern_datatype] | CONTEXT}
```

with the above repeated as many times as is needed.

prop has the values:

INDICATOR, LENGTH, MAXLEN, CHARSETID, or, CHARSETFORM

For both procedures and functions the command arguments are listed below.

OR REPLACE—This optional statement specifies that if the procedure or function exists, replace it; if it doesn't exist, create it.

schema—This is the schema to place the procedure or function into. If other than the user's default schema, the user must have CREATE ANY PROCEDURE system privilege.

procedure or function—This is the name of the procedure or function being created.

argument(s)—This is the argument to the procedure or function; it may be more than one of these.

IN—This specifies that the argument must be specified when calling the procedure or function. For functions, an argument must always be provided.

OUT—This specifies the procedure passes a value for this argument back to the calling object. Not used with functions.

IN OUT—This specifies both the IN and OUT features are in effect for the procedure. This is not used with functions.

datatype—This is the data type of the argument. Precision, length, and scale cannot be specified; they are derived from the calling object.

PL/SQL body—This is an SQL, PL/SQL body of statements.

IS or AS—The documentation states that these are interchangable, but one or the other must be specified. However, Oracle didn't tell this to some of their tools so if you get an error using one, try the other.

It is suggested that each function and procedure be created under a single owner for a given application. This makes administration easier and allows ease of use of dynamic SQL to create packages. It is also suggested that the procedure or function be created as a text file for documentation and later ease of update. The source files for related procedures and functions should be stored under a common directory area.

Alteration of Procedures and Functions

To alter the logic or variables of a procedure or function, the CREATE OR REPLACE form of the command in the previous subsection should be used. The only option for the ALTER command for functions and procedures is the COMPILE option. This option recompiles the procedure or function after a modification to their referenced objects has occurred. The format of this command follows.

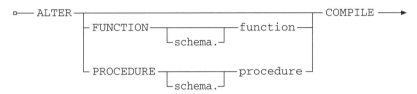

If a function or procedure is called that has been invalidated by a change to a table, view, or other referenced procedure or function, it is automatically recompiled. Whenever possible, explicit recompilation via the ALTER command should be used. This will pinpoint any problems before the users find them for you. The script in Source 7.8 will provide a list of invalid database objects upon execution. Use this script to pinpoint which packages, procedures, functions, or views need to be recompiled.

SOURCE 7.8   Example script to check on database object status.

```
rem Name: inv_obj.sql
rem Purpose: Show alll invalid objects in database
rem Mike Ault 7/2/96 TreCom/RevealNet
rem
COLUMN object_name    FORMAT A30 HEADING 'Object|Name'
COLUMN owner          FORMAT a10 HEADING 'Object|Owner'
COLUMN last_time      FORMAT a20 HEADING 'Last Change|Date'
SET LINES 80 FEEDBACK OFF PAGES 0 VERIFY OFF
START title80 'Invalid Database Objects'
SPOOL rep_out/&db/inv_obj
SELECT
    owner,
    object_name,
    object_type,
    TO_CHAR(last_ddl_time,'DD-MON-YY hh:mi:ss') Last_time
FROM
    dba_objects
WHERE
    status='INVALID'
/
PAUSE Press enter to continue
SET LINES 80 FEEDBACK ON PAGES 22 VERIFY ON
CLEAR COLUMNS
TTITLE OFF
```

Dropping Procedures or Functions

Periodically it may be required for a DBA to remove a function or procedure from the database. This is accomplished with the DROP command. The format of this command follows.

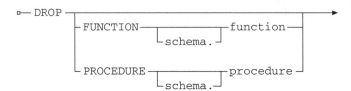

This will invalidate any related functions or procedures and they will have to be recompiled before use.

7.7   ADMINISTRATION OF PACKAGES

Under Oracle7 and Oracle8, packages are collections of related functions, variables, procedures, and external calls to functions and procedures. All of the functions and procedures for a specific application can be grouped under one or more packages and handled as units. A package is loaded into shared memory whenever one of its parts is referenced. The package stays in memory until the least recently used algorithm (LRU) determines it hasn't been recently used. You as DBA can force an object to stay in the SGA by "pinning" it. We will discuss pinning of objects under the tuning section. This determination of use is for all database users, not just the originating user.

Packages allow public and private functions, procedures, and variables. Public functions, procedures, and variables are named in the package definition and are available to all users with the privilege to access the package. Private procedures, functions, and variables are not referenced in the package definition but are contained in the package body. Private procedures, functions, and variables are only referenced by the package internal objects. External functions and procedures are new with Oracle8.

As is hinted at above, the package consists of two possible parts: a definition and a body. Each of the parts of a package is created separately. In the case of a package that has no private functions, procedures, or variables, no package body is required. However, each of the referenced public objects must exist.

Not using private objects allows the DBA and developers to maintain the individual objects separately instead of as a single entity. If a package has private objects, it must have a body.

The package definition contains the names of all public functions, procedures, and variables. The package body contains the PL/SQL and SQL code for all of the public and private package objects.

If the DBA has enforced use of script files to create database functions and procedures, creating the package body involves simply concatenating the various scripts together and making minor changes to the syntax of the statements. By use of the DBA_SOURCE view, the DBA can use dynamic SQL to create script listings. An example of this is shown in Source 7.9.

SOURCE 7.9   Example script to rebuild function and procedure objects.

```
rem   **********************************************************
rem   NAME:  FPRC_RCT.sql
rem   HISTORY:
rem   Date       Who                    What
rem   --------   -------------   ---------------------
rem   05/22/93  Michael Ault        Created
rem   FUNCTION:  Build a script to re-create functions,
rem                  procedures, packages or package bodies.
rem   **********************************************************
SET VERIFY OFF   FEEDBACK OFF LINES 80 PAGES 0 HEADING OFF
SPOOL cre_fprc.sql
SELECT 'CREATE '||s1.type||' '||s1.owner||'.'||s1.name,
     substr(s2.text,1,80)||';'
FROM
     dba_source s1,
     dba_source s2
WHERE
     s1.type = UPPER('&object_type') AND
     s1.owner = UPPER('&object_owner') AND
     s1.type = s2.type AND
     s1.owner = s2.owner AND
     s1.name = UPPER('&object_name') AND
     s1.name = s2.name
GROUP BY
     s1.owner,
     s1.name
ORDER BY
     s2.line;
rem
SPOOL OFF
```

This will create one large file with all of the type of objects that the DBA specifies for a specific owner. This script can also be used to document existing package definitions and package bodies.

Let's look at the processes and commands used to administer packages.

Creation of Packages

Package creation involves up to two steps. The first step, creation of the package definition (or header), is required for all packages. The second step, creation of the package body, is required only for those packages that have private components. If use of functions stored in a package is required from outside the package, the functions' purity level must be explicitly stated using the PRAGMA RESTRICT_REFERENCES call. This call is documented in Chapter 10. The command for creating package definitions follows.

TIP   You can insert the PRAGMA RESTRICT_REFERENCES call into Oracle provided package headers for functions that you need to use outside of those packages; however, it may not always work and is not supported by Oracle.

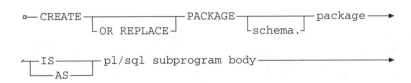

where:

OR REPLACE—This is used when the user wishes to create or replace a package. If the package definition exists, it is replaced; if it doesn't exist, it is created.

schema—This is the schema the package is to be created in. If this is not specified the package is created in the user's default schema.

package—This is the name of the package to be created.

PL/SQL package specification—This is the list of procedures, functions, or variables that make up the package. All components listed are considered to be public in nature.

Example:

```
CREATE PACKAGE admin.employee_package
    AS
FUNCTION new_emp(ename CHAR, position CHAR, supervisor NUM,
                    catagory NUM, hiredate DATE)
            RETURN NUMBER;
FUNCTION fire_them(ename CHAR, reason VARCHAR2, term_date DATE)
            RETURN DATE;
PROCEDURE new_dept(ename CHAR, dept CHAR, new_dept CHAR,
                    date_of_change DATE);
  bad_catagory EXCEPTION;
  bad_date EXCEPTION;
END employee_package
```

This example creates the package employee_package. The package contains the functions new_emp and fire_them, the procedure new_dept, and the exceptions bad_catagory and bad_date. All of the objects are available to whoever has privileges on employee_package.

Creation of the Package Body The package body contains all of the SQL and PL/SQL scripts that make up the procedures, functions, exceptions, and variables used by the package. If the package only contains public items, a package body may not be required. The format for the CREATE PACKAGE BODY command follows.

```
CREATE [OR REPLACE] PACKAGE BODY [schema.]package
IS—or—AS PL/SQL package body;
```

where:

> **OR REPLACE**—When this is used, if the package body exists it is replaced; if it doesn't exist, it is created.

> **schema**—This specifies the schema to create the package in. If this is not specified, the package body is created in the user's default schema.

> **PL/SQL package body**—This is the collection of all of the SQL and PL/SQL text required to create all of the objects in the package.

Source 7.10 is an example use of the CREATE PROCEDURE BODY command. The exceptions listed in the package definition are contained within the procedures.

SOURCE 7.10   Example format for package body.

```
CREATE OR REPLACE PROCEDURE BODY admin.employee_package AS
FUNCTION new_emp(ename CHAR, position CHAR, supervisor NUM,
catagory NUM, hiredate DATE)
     RETURN NUMBER IS
     emp_number number(5);
     BEGIN
     .
     .
     .
     END;

FUNCTION fire_them(
     ename CHAR,reason VARCHAR2,term_date DATE)
     RETURN NUMBER AS
     years_of_service NUMBER (4,2);
     BEGIN
     .
     .
     .
     END;
```

```
PROCEDURE new_dept(ename CHAR, dept CHAR, new_dept CHAR,
date_of_change DATE)
    IS
    BEGIN
    .

    .
    END;

    END  employee_package
```

Alteration of the Package

It will be required for the DBA to alter a package when the tables, views, sequences, and so on that the package procedures and functions reference change. This is accomplished through use of the CREATE OR REPLACE PACKAGE [BODY] form of the CREATE PACKAGE command. The format for the command is identical to the CREATE PACKAGE [BODY] command. Remember that all procedures, variables, and functions referenced in the CREATE PACKAGE command must be present in the CREATE OR REPLACE PACKAGE BODY command. If you just use the command with a single procedure or function you want altered, that will be the only object left in the body when you are finished. Perhaps with a future release we will see the ability to use the package definition as a link list and this won't be required. There is also an ALTER PACKAGE BODY command that is used only to recompile the package body. The format of the ALTER command follows.

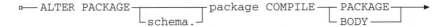

Dropping a Package

Even such wonderful things as packages have limited lifetimes. Applications are replaced or are no longer needed; entire database practices are rethought and changed. This leads to the requirement to be able to drop packages that are no longer needed. This is accomplished through the DROP PACKAGE command. The format of this command follows.

```
□── DROP PACKAGE ─┬───────┬─┬────────┬─ package ──▶
                  └─ BODY ─┘ └ schema. ┘
```

Exclusion of the keyword BODY results in the drop of both the definition and the body. Inclusion of BODY drops just the package body, leaving the definition intact.

When a package is dropped, all dependent objects are invalidated. If the package is not recreated before one of the dependent objects is accessed, Oracle7 tries to recompile the package; this will return an error and cause failure of the command.

7.8 ADMINISTRATION OF SNAPSHOTS

Another feature of Oracle that needs administration is the snapshot. Snapshots are copies of either an entire single table or set of its rows (simple snapshot) or a collection of tables, views, or their rows using joins, grouping, and selection criteria (complex snapshots). Snapshots are very useful in a distributed environment where remote locations need a queriable copy of a table from the master database. Instead of paying the penalty for using the network to send out the query and get back the data, the query is against a local table image and is thus much faster. With later versions of Oracle7 and in Oracle8, snapshots can be made updatable.

Snapshots are asynchronous in nature; they reflect a table's or a collection's state at the time the snapshot was taken. A simple snapshot can be periodically refreshed by either use of a snapshot log containing only the changed rows for the snapshot (fast refresh), or a totally new copy (complete refresh). In most cases, the fast refresh is quicker and just as accurate. A fast refresh can only be used if the snapshot has a log, and that log was created prior to the creation or last refresh of the snapshot. For a complex snapshot, a complete refresh is required. It is also possible to allow the system to decide which to use, either a fast or complete refresh.

One problem with a snapshot log is that it keeps a copy of each and every change to a row. Therefore, if a row undergoes 200 changes between one refresh and the next, there will be 200 entries in the snapshot log that will be applied to the snapshot at refresh. This could lead to the refresh of the snapshot taking longer than a complete refresh. Each snapshot should be examined for the amount of activity it is seeing and if this is occurring with any of them, the snapshot log should be eliminated or the refresh mode changed to COMPLETE.

Since the snapshot log must be created prior to the snapshot itself for a simple snapshot, let's examine the administration of snapshot logs first.

Creation of Snapshot Logs

A snapshot log is created for the master table of a snapshot. In the case of a simple snapshot, there is only one table. Creation of a snapshot log for a complex snapshot does no good since a complex snapshot requires a complete refresh that doesn't use a snapshot log. The user creating the snapshot must have the CREATE TRIGGER privilege on the table the log is being created for.

The CREATE SNAPSHOT LOG command is used to create a snapshot log. The format of the command follows.

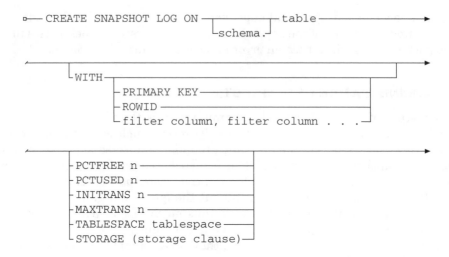

where:

> **schema**—This is the schema in which to store the log; if not specified, this will default to the user's own schema.
>
> **table**—This is the table name to create the snapshot log for.
>
> **WITH**—This specifies what is recorded about the source table in the log, PRIMARY KEY, ROWID, or both. The columns listed as filter columns are used to tell Oracle that changes to these columns should be recorded.
>
> **PCTFREE, PCTUSED, INITRANS**, **MAXTRANS**—These are the values for these creation parameters to use for the created log file.
>
> **TABLESPACE**—This specifies the tablespace in which to create the snapshot log. This will default to the user's default tablespace if not specified.
>
> **STORAGE**—This is a standard storage clause.

Here is an example use of the CREATE SNAPSHOT LOG command:

```
CREATE SNAPSHOT LOG ON  admin.personnel
    PCTFREE 10
    PCTUSED 70
    TABLESPACE remote_admin_data
    STORAGE ( INITIAL 50K NEXT 50K
            MINEXTENTS 1 MAXEXTENTS 50
            PCTINCREASE 0);
```

As was noted above, the CREATE SNAPSHOT LOG command creates an additional after-row trigger on the affected table.

Alteration of Snapshot Logs

Periodically, snapshot logs may need to be altered. Storage needs may change or the storage dynamics may need to be altered on a snapshot log. These are accomplished by use of the ALTER SNAPSHOT LOG command. The format for this command follows.

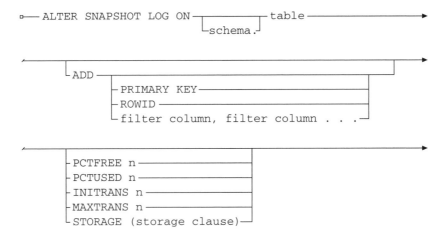

where:

> **schema**—This is the schema in which to store the log; if not specified, this will default to the user's own schema.

> **table**—This is the table name to alter the snapshot log for.

> **ADD**—This adds additional logging options such as ROWID or additional filter columns to the snapshot log profile.

> **PCTFREE, PCTUSED, INITRANS, MAXTRANS**—These are the values for these creation parameters to use for the created log file.

> **STORAGE**—This is a standard storage clause.

To change a snapshot log's location either an export/import or a drop/create of the snapshot log is required.

Dropping a Snapshot Log

A snapshot log is dropped using the DROP SNAPSHOT LOG command. The format for the command follows.

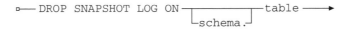

Creation of Snapshots

Once any required snapshot logs are created, the snapshots themselves can be created. This is accomplished through the CREATE SNAPSHOT command. Snapshots can be either simple or complex. A simple snapshot consists of either an entire single table, or a simple select of rows from a single table. A complex snapshot consists of joined tables, views, and grouped or complex select statement queries. Snapshots are built using the CREATE SNAPSHOT command.

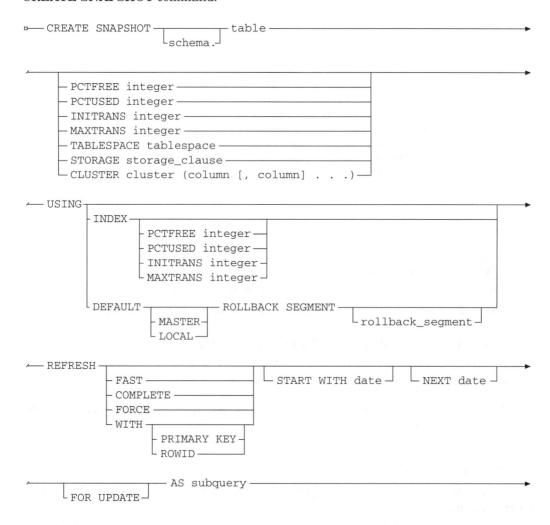

The keywords and parameters for the CREATE SNAPSHOT command are as follows:

schema—This is the schema to contain the snapshot. If you omit schema, Oracle creates the snapshot in your schema.

snapshot—This is the name of the snapshot to be created.

Oracle chooses names for the table, views, and index used to maintain the snapshot by adding a prefix and suffix to the snapshot name. To limit these names to 30 bytes and allow them to contain the entire snapshot name, it is recommended that you limit your snapshot names to 19 bytes.

PCTFREE, PCTUSED, INITRANS, MAXTRANS—These establish values for the specified parameters for the internal table Oracle uses to maintain the snapshot's data. For information on the PCTFREE, PCTUSED, INITRANS, and MAXTRANS parameters, see the CREATE TABLE command.

TABLESPACE—This specifies the tablespace in which the snapshot is to be created. If you omit this option, Oracle creates the snapshot in the default tablespace of the owner of the snapshot's schema.

STORAGE—This establishes storage characteristics for the table Oracle uses to maintain the snapshot's data.

CLUSTER—This creates the snapshot as part of the specified cluster. Since a clustered snapshot uses the cluster's space allocation, do not use the PCTFREE, PCTUSED, INITRANS, MAXTRANS, TABLESPACE, or STORAGE parameters with the CLUSTER option.

USING INDEX—This specifies parameters for the index Oracle creates to maintain the snapshot. You can choose the values of the INITRANS, MAXTRANS, TABLESPACE, STORAGE, and PCTFREE parameters. For information on the PCTFREE, PCTUSED, INITRANS, and MAXTRANS parameters, see the CREATE TABLE command.

ROLLBACK SEGMENT—This specifies the local snapshot and/or remote master rollback segments to be used during snapshot refresh.

rollback_segment—This is the name of the rollback segment to be used.

DEFAULT—This specifies that Oracle will choose which rollback segment to use.

MASTER—This specifies the rollback segment to be used at the remote master for the individual snapshot .

LOCAL—This specifies the rollback segment to be used for the local refresh group that contains the snapshot.

If you do not specify MASTER or LOCAL, Oracle uses LOCAL by default. If you do not specify rollback_segment, Oracle chooses the rollback segment to be used, automatically. If you specify DEFAULT, you cannot specify rollback_ segment.

REFRESH—This specifies how and when Oracle automatically refreshes the snapshot:

FAST—This specifies a fast refresh, or a refresh using only the updated data stored in the snapshot log associated with the master table.

COMPLETE—This specifies a complete refresh, or a refresh that reexecutes the snapshot's query.

FORCE—This specifies a fast refresh if one is possible or complete refresh if a fast refresh is not possible. Oracle decides whether a fast refresh is possible at refresh time.

If you omit the FAST, COMPLETE, and FORCE options, Oracle uses FORCE by default.

START WITH—This specifies a date expression for the first automatic refresh time.

NEXT—This specifies a date expression for calculating the interval between automatic refreshes.

Both the START WITH and NEXT values must evaluate to a time in the future. If you omit the START WITH value, Oracle determines the first automatic refresh time by evaluating the NEXT expression when you create the snapshot. If you specify a START WITH value but omit the NEXT value, Oracle refreshes the snapshot only once. If you omit both the START WITH and NEXT values, or if you omit the REFRESH clause entirely, Oracle does not automatically refresh the snapshot.

WITH PRIMARY KEY—This specifies that primary key snapshots are to be created. Primary key snapshots allow snapshot master tables to be reorganized without impacting the snapshot's ability to continue to fast refresh. Primary key snapshots can also be defined as simple snapshots with subqueries.

WITH ROWID—This specifies that ROWID snapshots are to be created. ROWID snapshots provide backward compatibility with Oracle7 release 7.3 masters.

If you omit both WITH PRIMARY KEY and WITH ROWID, Oracle creates primary key snapshots by default.

FOR UPDATE—This allows a simple snapshot to be updated. When used in conjunction with the Replication Option, these updates will be propagated to the master.

AS subquery—This specifies the snapshot query. When you create the snapshot, it executes this query and places the results in the snapshot. The select list can contain up to 1000 expressions. The syntax of a snapshot query is described with the syntax description of subquery. The syntax of a snapshot query is subject to the same restrictions as a view query. For a list of these restrictions, see the CREATE VIEW command.

Snapshot Usage

Source 7.11 shows the use of the CREATE SNAPSHOT command for a simple snapshot. Source 7.12 shows use of the CREATE SNAPSHOT command with a complex snapshot. The sizing considerations should mirror those for the source table. If the source table is stable, a large initial extent with smaller subsequent extents should be used. Since snapshots will most likely be on slow growth tables, set pctincrease to zero in most cases.

SOURCE 7.11   Example of the CREATE SNAPSHOT command for a simple snapshot.

```
CREATE SNAPSHOT new_drugs
PCTFREE 10 PCTUSED 70
TABLESPACE clinical_tests
STORAGE (INITIAL 50K NEXT 50K PCTINCREASE 0)
REFRESH
     START WITH ROUND(SYSDATE + 7) + 2/24
     NEXT NEXT_DAY(TRUNC(SYSDATE, 'TUESDAY') + 2/24
AS select * from appl_dba.test_drugs@kcgc;
```

In the snapshot in Source 7.11 the entire test_drugs table is used to create a snapshot from its location at a remote database identified in the kcgc connect string into the tablespace clinical_trials in the current database. It will be first refreshed in seven days at two o'clock in the morning and subsequently at seven-day intervals on every Tuesday thereafter at two o'clock in the morning. Since no refresh mode is specified, if the table has a snapshot log, the fast mode will be used since it is a simple snapshot. If no snapshot log is available, then the complete mode will be used. If you specify the FORCE option it will always try to do a FAST first.

SOURCE 7.12   Script to produce a complex snapshot.

```
CREATE SNAPSHOT trial_summary
PCTFREE 5 PCTUSED 60
TABLESPACE clinical_tests
STORAGE (INITIAL 100K NEXT 50K PCTINCREASE 0)
REFRESH COMPLETE
     START WITH ROUND(SYSDATE + 14) + 6/24
     NEXT NEXT_DAY(TRUNC(SYSDATE, 'FRIDAY') + 19/24
AS
select td.drug_name, s.trial_number, dr.doctor_id,
 s.comment_line,s.comment
from
     appl_dba. test_drugs@kcgc td,
     appl_dba.trial_doctors@kcgc dr,
     appl_dba.trial_summaries@kcgc s
```

```
where
     td.drug_id = s.drug_id and
     s.trial_id = dr.trial_id and
     s.doctor_id = dr.doctor_id;
```

The script in Source 7.12 produces a complex snapshot called trail_summary with data from the test_drugs, trial_doctors, and trial_summaries tables in the database specified in the connect string kcgc. The snapshot is refreshed using the complete mode since it is a complex query and is created in the clinical_tests tablespace of the local database.

Altering a Snapshot

A snapshot is altered using the ALTER SNAPSHOT command. The user may alter such items as storage and space usage parameters and type and frequency of refresh. The format for this command follows.

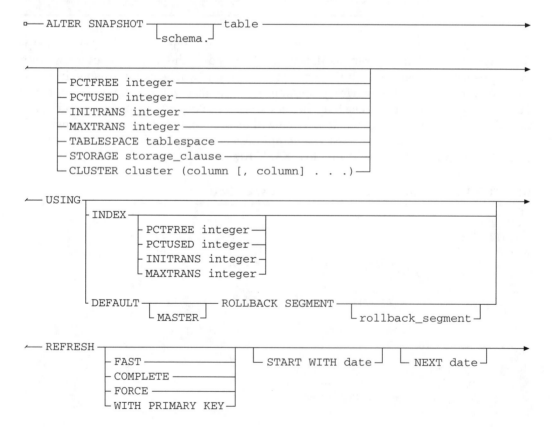

where:

> **schema**—This is the schema in which to store the log; if not specified, this will default to the user's own schema.
>
> **table**—This is the table name to create the snapshot log for.
>
> **PCTFREE, PCTUSED, INITRANS, MAXTRANS**—These are the values for these creation parameters to use for the created log file.
>
> **STORAGE**—This is a standard storage clause.
>
> **REFRESH**—This specifies the refresh mode, either FAST, COMPLETE or FORCE. FAST uses a SNAPSHOT LOG; COMPLETE reperforms the subquery and is the only valid mode for a complex snapshot. FORCE causes the system to first try a FAST and if this is not possible, then a COMPLETE. FAST is the default mode.
>
> **START WITH**—This specifies the date for the first refresh.
>
> **NEXT**—This specifies either a date or a time interval for the next refresh of the snapshot.

Start with and next values are used to determine the refresh cycle for the snapshot. If just start with is specified only the initial refresh is done.If both are specified, the first is done on the start with date and the next is evaluated against the start with to determine future refreshes. If just the next value is specified it computes based on the date the snapshot is created. If neither is specified, the snapshot is not automatically refreshed.

Dropping a Snapshot

A snapshot is dropped using the DROP SNAPSHOT command. The command's format follows.

When a snapshot is dropped, if it has a snapshot log associated with it, only the rows required for maintaining that snapshot are dropped. Dropping a master table upon which a snapshot is based doesn't drop the snapshot. However, any subsequent refreshes will fail.

7.9   ADMINISTRATION OF SCHEMAS

An Oracle7 and Oracle8 feature that has been mentioned but not explained in the previous sections is the feature known as SCHEMAS. Those DBAs familiar with other database systems may already be familiar with this concept as it has been used in other systems such as INFORMIX for several years. However, the concept schemas were introduced to Oracle as of Oracle7.

A schema is a logical grouping of related database objects; it roughly compares to the owner of the objects. Objects in a given schema do not have to be in the same table-space. In fact, each user has a default schema that corresponds to his user name in Oracle. A user may only create objects in his or her own schema (that schema named the same as the user he or she is logged in under). Schemas can be populated via the CREATE SCHEMA command or by using individual object CREATE commands.

Creation of Schemas

The CREATE SCHEMA statement can include the creation commands for tables, views, and grants. The user issuing the command must have the appropriate privileges to create each of the objects mentioned in the CREATE SCHEMA command. The format of this command follows.

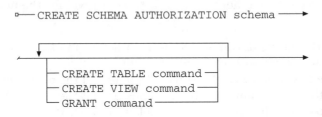

where:

schema—This is the user's schema; it must be his or her user name.

command—This corresponds to the appropriate CREATE object command.

The individual create commands are not separated with a command terminator; the terminator is placed at the end of the entire create sequence of commands for the schema. Schemas cannot be altered or dropped; only individual schema objects can be altered or dropped.

7.10 ADMINISTRATION OF LIBRARY OBJECTS

Under Oracle8 a new type of schema object known as a library has been introduced. A library is a schema object that represents an operating system shared library from which calls can be made by SQL and PL/SQL to external functions and procedures.

To create a library you must have CREATE ANY LIBRARY internal Oracle system privilege. To use the functions and procedures stored in the library, you must have execute privilege at the operating system level on the shared library that is referenced. Libraries are only able to be used on operating systems that allow shared libraries and dynamic linking.

The file specified as the source for the shared library is not verified to exist when the library is initially specified; it is only verified at runtime.

The syntax for the CREATE LIBRARY command is:

```
□── CREATE ──┬─────────────┬── LIBRARY ──┬──────────┬── library ──┬─ IS ─┬── 'filename' ──→
             └─ OR REPLACE ─┘             └─ schema. ─┘            └─ AS ─┘
```

where:

> **schema**—This is the schema in which the library is to reside. If not specified it defaults to the user's default schema.

> **library name**—This is the name for the schema object and must comply with object naming standards.

> **filename**—This is the existing operating system shared library that is to correspond to the internal library name.

Example Use of CREATE LIBRARY

The following is an example of the creation of a library.

```
CREATE LIBRARY dev_c_lib IS '/users/oracle/c/lib/sharedlibs.so.1.0';
```

Once a library link to an external shared library is created, the functions and procedures inside can be referenced for use from SQL and PL/SQL:

```
CREATE FUNCTION bitand (
left IN BINARY_INTEGER, right IN BINARY_INTEGER)
RETURN BINARY_INTEGER
IS
EXTERNAL
    NAME "bitand"
    LIBRARY dev_c_lib
    PARAMETERS (
        left INT,
        left INDICATOR long,
        right INT,
        right INDICATOR short,
        RETURN INDICATOR short);
```

An external procedure call is similar:

```
CREATE OR REPLACE PROCEDURE factorial (
input_number IN INTEGER,
number_factorial OUT INTEGER)
IS
EXTERNAL NAME "factorial"
LIBRARY "dev_c_lib"
```

```
PARAMETERS  (
      input_number INDICATOR short,
      input_number INT,
      output_factorial INDICATOR long,
      output_factorial INT,
      RETURN INDICATOR short);
```

Libraries are not physical schema objects; they are stored pointers to physical operating system shared library files. Available libraries can be viewed via queries to the DBA_LIBRARIES, ALL_LIBRARIES, and USER_LIBRARIES views.

Altering Libraries

The command for altering libraries is ALTER LIBRARY and has the following syntax:

```
□── ALTER LIBRARY ──┬──────────┬── lib_alias ──┬─ IS ─┬── 'filename' ──▶
                    └─schema.─┘               └─ AS ─┘
```

where:

lib_alias—This is the library name created with the CREATE LIBRARY command.

filename—This is the new file name for the shared library to be associated with this alias.

This command allows a library alias to be associated with a different source library. This does not invalidate dependencies. This command may not be available until later versions of Oracle8. Although it appeared in certain documentation it was not available as of 8.0.2 for NT4.0.

Dropping a Library

A library is dropped via the DROP LIBRARY command. The command has the following format:

```
□── DROP LIBRARY ──┬──────────┬── lib_alias ──▶
                   └─schema.─┘
```

The drop command only removes the library alias at the database level and does not affect the status of the operating system shared library.

7.11   ADMINISTRATION OF DIRECTORIES

A directory is an internal Oracle8 database pointer to a physical operating system directory where database objects of type BFILE are stored. BFILEs are large binary objects such as video segments which would be impractical to store within the database structure itself. An internal Oracle directory is an alias that points to the external physical directory.

A directory in Oracle has no size or space requirements other than that for a table entry in the data dictionary. You must have the CREATE ANY DIRECTORY system privilege to create a directory alias in Oracle. The operating system directory must have the proper access permissions (read) to allow the Oracle process access.

A BFILE column in a database table contains a locator that has the directory alias as specified in a CREATE DIRECTORY command and a file name. The locator maintains the directory alias and filename.

A directory is created inside a single namespace and is not owned by a schema. Therefore directory names have to be unique across the entire database. You grant access to the BFILEs in a specific directory by granting READ access to the users or roles that require access. When a directory is created by a user, that user automatically receives the READ grant with the admin option so it can be regranted to others.

A directory is created with the CREATE DIRECTORY command; its syntax follows:

```
□── CREATE ┬──────────────┬ DIRECTORY ── directory ── AS ── 'path name' ──→
           └─ OR REPLACE ─┘
```

Example Use of the CREATE DIRECTORY Command

```
CREATE OR REPLACE DIRECTORY g_vid_lib AS '/video/library/g_rated';
```

The above command associates the directory internal Oracle alias g_vid_lib with the directory '/video/library/g_rated'.

The path name must be a full path and not use any system logicals or symbols. The directory's existence is not validated until the directory alias is referenced by Oracle.

Altering Directories

Under Oracle8 there are no current plans to allow altering of existing directory entries. To change them you must drop and recreate them.

Dropping Oracle8 Directories

When a directory is no longer needed it should be dropped with the DROP DIRECTORY command. You must have the DROP ANY DIRECTORY command to drop a directory. The syntax for this command is:

```
□── DROP DIRECTORY directory_alias ──→
```

Once a directory is dropped all BFILEs in that directory location become inaccessible.

7.12   THE STORAGE CLAUSE

The STORAGE clause is used in table, cluster, index, rollback segment, snapshot, snapshot log, and tablespace creation commands as well as in their respective ALTER commands. Let's look at this clause, as DBAs must become intimately familiar with all aspects of the STORAGE clause.

The syntax for the STORAGE clause is:

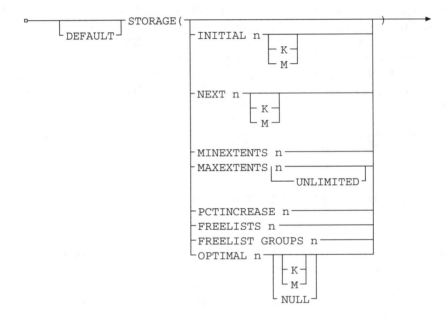

Definitions for the STORAGE Parameters

INITIAL—This sets the size in bytes, kilobytes, or megabytes for the initial extent for the object. This should be set to hold the first year of expected data. If you will be loading data using sqlloader parallel inserts, set the initial extent to the size expected for one year divided by the number of parallel processes and set NEXT to the same value. This is suggested because parallel insert processes all insert into their own extents. The Oracle process will round up to the next multiple of data block size for sizes smaller than five data blocks. The minimum size is two data blocks. The maximum size is operating-system specific.

NEXT—This sets the value for the next extent of the file. It is specified in bytes, kilobytes, or megabytes. The default value is five data blocks. The minimum is one data block. Oracle rounds up to the next whole block size for sizes less than five blocks. The maximum size is operating-system specific. For sizes over five blocks Oracle will resize to minimize fragmentation if possible.

PCTINCREASE—This value is from 0-100 and sets the amount each extension after NEXT will increase in size over the size of NEXT. This factor is applied to the last extent created and not calculated based on the size of NEXT after the first extension after NEXT. The default is 50. If you properly size your tables this should be set to zero. This factor cannot be set for rollback segments. For rollback segments this factor will be set to zero.

MINEXTENTS—This sets how many initial extents Oracle will create for a specified object. Generally this is set to the default of 1 (2 for rollback segments). If you use parallel insert processes you may want to adjust INITIAL, NEXT, PCTINCREASE, and MINEXTENTS to set the size of initial extents to the size corresponding to calculated table size divided by number of insert processes, and the MINEXTENTS to the number of insert processes. The value for the sizes of the extents is calculated based on INITIAL, NEXT, and PCTINCREASE.

MAXEXTENTS—This value determines the maximum number of extents allowed a specific object. The minimum value is 1 and the maximum is determined by the size of your data block size.

UNLIMITED setting for this parameter means the object can grow until it runs out of space. This setting is not suggested for use with rollback segments.

FREELIST GROUPS—This parameter is used for objects other than tablespaces to set up the number of groups of FREELISTS. The default and minimum for this parameter is 1. Only use this parameter with the parallel server set in parallel mode. This parameter is only used in tables and clusters.

FREELISTS—This parameter is used for objects other than tablespaces. The default is 1 and the maximum is dependent on your data block size. If multiple processes will be updating the same data block this parameter should be set higher. This parameter is only used in tables, indexes, and clusters.

OPTIMAL—This parameter is only used with rollback segments and sets the size in bytes, kilobytes, or megabytes for the optimal size of a rollback segment. This is the size that the rollback segment will shrink to when it has expanded because of a large transaction. This cannot be set to less than the amount of space used by the rollback segment via the INITIAL, NEXT, and MINEXTENTS values.

The High-Water Mark

To view an object's high-water mark, you can use the DBMS_SPACE package, which contains a procedure (UNUSED_SPACE) that returns information about the position of the high-water mark and the amount of unused space in a segment.

Some operations such as parallel inserts will only insert into space above the high-water mark. It may be smart to reduce space used to the absolute minimum and then reset NEXT and PCTINCREASE before a large parallel insert.

Within a segment, the high-water mark indicates the amount of used space. You cannot release space below the high-water mark (even if there is no data in the space you wish to deallocate). However, if the segment is completely empty, you can release space using the TRUNCATE object DROP STORAGE statement.

7.13   FURTHER DBA READING

The DBA should consult the following references for more detailed information.

Oracle8 Server Administrator's Guide, Release 8.0, Beta-2, Part# A50648-1,Feb. 1997 (or most current release).

Oracle8 Server SQL Reference, Release 8.0, Beta-2, Part# A50605-1, Feb. 1997 (or most current release).

Oracle8 PL/SQL User's Guide and Reference, Release 3.0, Beta-2, Part# A50670-1, Feb. 1997 (or most current release).

Oracle8 Application Developer's Guide, Release 8.0, Beta-2, Part# A50659-1, Feb. 1997 (or most current release).

Oracle8 Server Concepts, Volume 1, Release 8.0, Beta-2, Part# A50654-1, Feb. 1997 (or most current release).

Oracle8 Server Reference Manual, Release 8.0, Beta-2, Part#A50665-1, Jan. 1997 (or most current release).

Oracle8: New Features For Developers, Student Guide, Feb. 1997 DRAFT copy.

Oracle8:New Features for Administrators, Instructor's Guide, Beta version, Mar. 1997.

Oracle Administrator on-line reference, RevealNet, Inc. version 97-2. www.revealnet .com/.

Modeling With Oracle8, IOUG-A Alive 97 presentation proceedings, Bob Navarro, Boeing ISS, April 1997.

Bitmapped Indexes In Oracle7, Oracle Warehouse, Oracle White Paper, Oct. 1995, Part# 10406.

ORACLE7 Server Administrator's Guide, Release 7.3, Part# A14538-16, June 1996, Oracle Corp. (CD-ROM).

ORACLE7 Server SQL Language Reference Manual, Release 7.3 Part# A14538-16, June 1996, Oracle Corp. (CD-ROM).

CHAPTER 8

Administration of
Table Clusters

A cluster can be used when several tables store a row that is of the same data type and size in the same location. This reduces storage requirements and in some cases can speed access to data. The major drawback is that in operations involving updates, inserts, and deletes there can be performance degradation. The DBA should look at the expected mix of transaction types on the tables to be clustered and only cluster those that are frequently joined and don't have numerous updates, inserts, and deletes.

Clusters store shared data values in the same physical blocks (the cluster key values). For tables that are frequently joined this can speed access; for tables frequently accessed separately joining is not the answer. An exception is when a single table is clustered. A single table cluster forces the key values for that table into a single set of blocks, thus speeding up accesses of that table. Usually this single table clustering also uses a HASH structure to further improve access times.

Under Oracle7 there was an additional cluster feature added, the ability to specify a HASH cluster. A HASH cluster uses a HASH form of storage and no index rather than the normal B-tree type index. Hash structures should only be used for static tables. Hashing is the process where a value, either of a unique or nonunique row, is used to generate a hash value. This hash value is used to place the row into the hashed table. To retrieve the row, the value is simply recalculated. Hashes can only be used for equality operations.

Oracle8 did not add any further functionality to clusters. Clusters may not be partitioned.

8.1   CREATION OF CLUSTERS

Cluster creation is actually a two-step process. The first step is to specify the cluster using the CREATE CLUSTER command. Before any tables in the cluster can be accessed, the cluster index must also be created. Let's look at this process.

1. First create the cluster. The syntax for the CREATE CLUSTER command for both Oracle7 and Oracle8 is:

```
□─CREATE CLUSTER  cluster name (column datatype, column datatype, . . .)→
              └─schema.─┘
```

```
┌──────────────────────────────────────────────────────────────────────────►
│   ┌─PCTUSED n─────────────┐
│   ├─PCTFREE n─────────────┤
│   ├─SIZE n─┬──────────────┤
│   │        ├─K─┐          │
│   │        └─M─┘          │
│   │                       │
│   ├─INITRANS n────────────┤
│   ├─MAXTRANS n────────────┤
│   ├─TABLESPACE tablespace──┤
│   ├─STORAGE storage────────┤
│   ├─INDEX──────────────────┤
│   └─HASHKEYS n─┬───────────┘
│                └─HASH IS expr─┘
```

```
┌─ PARALLEL ─┬──────────────────────────────────────────────────────────────►
│            └─ NOPARALLEL ─┘
```

```
┌─ CACHE ─┬─────────────────────────────────────────────────────────────────►
│         └─ NOCACHE ─┘
```

where:

cluster name—This is the name for the cluster; if the user has DBA privilege, a user name may be specified (user.cluster).

(column datatype, column datatype . . .)—This is a list of columns and their data types, called the cluster key. The names for the columns do not have to match the table column names, but the data types, lengths, and precisions do have to match.

n—This is an integer (not all of the n's are the same value; n is just used for convenience).

SIZE—This is the expected size of the average cluster. This is calculated by:

$$19 + (\text{sum of column lengths}) + (1 \times \text{num of columns})$$

SIZE should rounded up to the nearest equal divisor of your block size. For example, if your block size is 2048 and the cluster length is 223, round up to 256.

storage—This storage clause will be used as the default for the tables in the cluster.

INDEX—This specifies to create an indexed cluster (default).

HASH IS—This specifies to create a HASH cluster. The specified column must be a zero precision number.

HASHKEYS—This creates a hash cluster and specifies the number (n) of keys. The value is rounded up to the nearest prime number.

The other parameters are the same as for the CREATE TABLE command.

2. Create the cluster index:

```
CREATE  INDEX index name ON CLUSTER cluster name
```

Note that you don't specify the columns; this is taken from the CREATE CLUSTER command that was used to create the named cluster.

3. Create the tables that will be in the cluster:

```
CREATE TABLE cluster table
    ( column list)
    CLUSTER cluster name (cluster column(s))
```

where:

cluster table—This is a table name for a table that will be a part of the cluster.

Column list—This is a list of columns for the table, specified identically to the CREATE TABLE command's normal format.

Remember: the cluster columns don't have to have the same name, but must be the same data type, size, and precision and must be specified in the same order as the columns in the CREATE CLUSTER command.

8.2   ESTIMATING SPACE REQUIRED BY CLUSTERS

The following procedure shows how to estimate the initial amount of space required by a clustered set of tables. This procedure only estimates the initial amount of space required for a cluster. When using these estimates, note that the following factors can affect the accuracy of estimations:

- Trailing nulls are not stored, nor is a length byte.

  Inserts, updates, and deletes of rows, as well as tables containing rows or columns larger than a single data block, can cause chained row pieces. Therefore, the following estimates may tend to be lower than the actual space required if significant row chaining occurs.

Once you figure an estimate for a table's size using the following procedure, you should add about 10 to 20% additional space to calculate the initial extent size for a working table.

To estimate space required by clusters, perform the following general steps:

1. Calculate total block header size and space available for table data.
2. Calculate the combined average column lengths of the rows per cluster key.
3. Calculate the average row size of all clustered tables.
4. Calculate the average cluster block size.
5. Calculate the total number of blocks required for the cluster.

Let's look at a more detailed example.

- Step 1: Calculate total block header size and space available for table data. The following formula returns the amount of available space in a block:

TIP   Several calculations are required to obtain a final estimate, and several of the constants (indicated by *) provided are operating system specific. Your estimates should not significantly differ from actual values. See your operating system-specific Oracle documentation for any substantial deviations from the constants provided in the following procedure:

```
space left in block after headers (hspace)
hspace =  BLOCKSIZE -( KCBH - UB4 - KTBBH - (KTBIT*(INITTRANS - 1)) - KDBH)
```

where the sizes of KCBH, KTBBH, KTBIT, KDBH, and UB4 can be obtained by selecting * from v$type_size table.

Then use the following formula to calculate the space available (s_avail) for table data:

s_avail = (hspace*(1 – PCTFREE/100)) – (4*(NTABLES + 1) * ROWSINBLOCK)

where:

BLOCKSIZE—This is the size of a data block.

INITTRANS—This is the initial number of transaction entries for the object.

PCTFREE—This is the percentage of space to reserve in a block for updates.

NTABLES—This is the number of tables in the cluster.

ROWS IN BLOCK—This is the number of rows in a block.

- Step 2: Calculate space required by a row.

  Use Step 3 from the procedure for "Estimating Space Required by Nonclustered Tables" from Chapter 5 to calculate this number. Make note of the following caveats:

  Calculate the data space required by an average row for each table in the cluster. For example, in a cluster that contains tables T1 and T2, calculate the average row size for both tables.

  Do not include the space required by the cluster key in any of the above calculations. However, make note of the space required to store an average cluster key value for Step 5. For example, calculate the data space required by an average row in table T1, not including the space required to store the cluster key.

  Do not include any space required by the row header (that is, the length bytes for each column); this space is accounted for in the next step.

For example, assume two clustered tables are created with the following statements:

```
CREATE TABLE t1 (a CHAR(6), b DATE, c NUMBER(9,2))
            CLUSTER t1_t2 (c);
CREATE TABLE t2 (c NUMBER(9,2), d CHAR(6))
            CLUSTER t1_t2 (c);
```

Notice that the cluster key is column C in each table.

Considering these example tables, the space required for an average row (D1) of table T1 and the space required for an average row (D2) of table T2 is:

D1 (space/average row) = (a + b) = (9 + 6) bytes = 15 bytes
D2 (space/average row) = (d) = 9 bytes

- Step 3: Calculate total average row size.
  You can calculate the minimum amount of space required by a row in a clustered table according to the following equation:

  Sn bytes/row = row header + Fn + Vn + Dn

where:

row header—This is 4 bytes per row of a clustered table.

Fn—Total length bytes of all 250 bytes or less. The number of length bytes required by each column of this type is 1 byte.

Vn—Total length bytes of all columns in table n that store more than 250 bytes. The number of length bytes required by each column of this type is 3 bytes.

Dn—Combined data space of all columns in table n (from Step 3).

TIP   Do not include the column length for the cluster key in variables F or V for any table in the cluster. This space is accounted for in Step 5.

For example, the total average row size of the clustered tables T1 and T2 is as follows:

S1 = (4 + (1 * 2) + (3 * 0) + 15) bytes = 21 bytes
S = (4 + (1 * 1) + (3 * 0) + 9) bytes = 14 bytes

TIP   The absolute minimum row size of a clustered row is 10 bytes, and is operating system specific. Therefore, if your calculated value for a table's total average row size is less than these absolute minimum row sizes, use the minimum value as the average row size in subsequent calculations.

- Step 4: Calculate average cluster block size .
  To calculate the average cluster block size, first estimate the average number of rows (for all tables) per cluster key. Once this is known, use the following formula to calculate average cluster block size:

  avg. cluster block size (bytes) = ((R1*S1) + (R2*S2) + .. + (Rn*Sn)) + key header + Ck + Sk + 2Rt

where:

Rn—This is the average number of rows in table n associated with a cluster key.

Sn—This is the average row size in table n (see Step 4).

key header—This is 19.

Ck—This is the column length for the cluster key.

Sk—This is the space required to store average cluster key value.

Rt—This is the total number of rows associated with an average cluster key (R1 + R2 ... + Rn). This accounts for the space required in the data block header for each row in the block.

For example, consider the cluster that contains tables T1 and T2. An average cluster key has one row per table T1 and 20 rows per table T2. Also, the cluster key is of datatype NUMBER (column length is 1 byte), and the average number is 4 digits (3 bytes). Considering this information and the previous results, the average cluster key size is:

SIZE = ((1 * 21) + (20 * 14) + 19 + 1 + 3 + (2 * 21)) bytes = 368 bytes

Specify the estimated SIZE in the SIZE option when you create the cluster with the CREATE CLUSTER command. This specifies the space required to hold an average cluster key and its associated rows; Oracle uses the value of SIZE to limit the number of cluster keys that can be assigned to any given data block. After estimating an average cluster key SIZE, choose a SIZE somewhat larger than the average expected size to account for the space required for cluster keys on the high side of the estimate.

To estimate the number of cluster keys that will fit in a database block, use the following formula, which uses the value you calculated in Step 2 for available data space, the number of rows associated with an average cluster key (Rt), and SIZE:

cluster keys per block = FLOOR(available data space + 2R / SIZE + 2Rt)

For example, with SIZE previously calculated as 400 bytes (calculated as 368 earlier in this step and rounded up), Rt estimated at 21, and available space per data block (from Step 2) calculated as 1742 – 2R bytes, the result is as follows:

cluster keys per block = FLOOR((1936 – 2R + 2R) / (400 + 2 * 21))

= FLOOR(1936 / 442) = FLOOR(4.4) = 4

FLOOR means round down.

- Step 5: Calculate total number of blocks.
  To calculate the total number of blocks for the cluster, you must estimate the number of cluster keys in the cluster. Once this is estimated, use the following formula to calculate the total number of blocks required for the cluster:

blocks = CEIL(# cluster keys / # cluster keys per block)

CEIL means round up.

TIP   If you have a test database, you can use statistics generated by the ANALYZE command to determine the number of key values in a cluster key.

For example, assume that there are approximately 500 cluster keys in the T1_T2 cluster:

blocks T1_T2 = CEIL(500/3) = CEIL(166.7) = 167

To convert the number of blocks to bytes, multiply the number of blocks by the data block size.

This procedure provides a reasonable estimation of a cluster's size, but not an exact number of blocks or bytes. Once you have estimated the space for a cluster, you can use this information when specifying the INITIAL storage parameter (size of the cluster's initial extent) in your corresponding CREATE CLUSTER statement.

Space Requirements for Clustered Tables in Use

Once clustered tables are created and in use, the space required by the tables is usually higher than the estimate given by the previous section. More space is required due to the method Oracle uses to manage free space in the database.

8.3   ESTIMATING SPACE REQUIRED BY HASH CLUSTERS

As with index clusters, it is important to estimate the storage required for the data in a hash cluster. Use the procedure described in Section 8.2 ("Estimating Space Required by Clusters") with the following additional notes:

A subgoal of the procedure is to determine the SIZE of each cluster key. However, for hash clusters, the corresponding subgoal is to determine the SIZE of each hash key. Therefore, you must consider not only the number of rows per cluster key value, but also the distribution of cluster keys over the hash keys in the cluster.

In Step 3, make sure to include the space required by the cluster key value. Unlike an index cluster, the cluster key value is stored with each row placed in a hash cluster.

In Step 5, you are calculating the average hash key size, not cluster key size. Therefore, take into account how many cluster keys map to each hash value. Also, disregard the addition of the space required by the cluster key value, Ck. This value has already been accounted for in Step 3.

8.4   ALTERATION OF CLUSTERS

Clusters are altered via the ALTER CLUSTER command. Only the sizing and storage parameters may be altered. No additional columns may be added to the cluster, or removed, using the ALTER CLUSTER command. The format of the command follows.

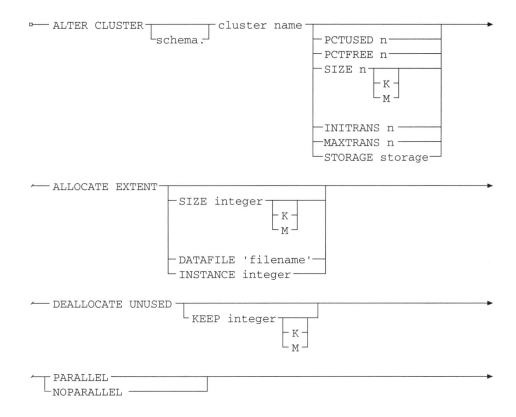

The definitions for the above parameters are the same as for the CREATE TABLE, CREATE CLUSTER, and storage clause definitions.

In Oracle7 the structure of a cluster and its associated index and tables can be analyzed for consistency and for sizing data using the ANALYZE CLUSTER command. The format of this command follows.

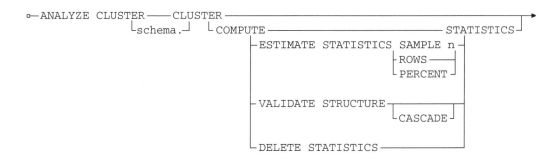

where:

COMPUTE STATISTICS—Calculates statistics based on all rows.

ESTIMATE STATISTICS—Calculates an estimate of the statistics based on "n" ROWS or PERCENT of rows in table.

VALIDATE STRUCTURE—Validates that the table and its indexes are consistent and not corrupted.

CASCADE—For clusters, validates all tables in cluster.

DELETE STATISTICS—Removes current statistics.

The results appear in the DBA_CLUSTERS view.

To verify a cluster's integrity, the following version of the ANALYZE command is used.

```
ANALYZE CLUSTER [schema.]cluster
VALIDATE STRUCTURE  [CASCADE]
```

The CASCADE option forces analysis of all indexes and tables in the cluster.

8.5   DROPPING A CLUSTER

As with the creation of clusters, dropping a cluster is a multistep function. The first step is to drop the tables in the cluster using the DROP TABLE command. Next, the cluster is dropped with the DROP CLUSTER command. There is an INCLUDING TABLES clause that will allow the DBA to drop both the cluster and tables at the same time. The format of the command follows.

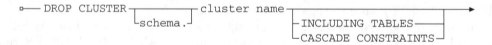

8.6   DECLUSTERING TABLES

Rather than dropping a cluster's tables completely, it may be desirable to decluster them and then just drop the cluster and cluster index with the DROP CLUSTER command. The procedure to decluster a table follows.

1. Create a new table that is a mirror of the existing clustered table, only of course, it isn't clustered.

```
CREATE TABLE new table
AS SELECT * FROM cluster table
```

> **T**IP   Remember that "new table" is a different name from "cluster table".

2. Drop the clustered table.

```
DROP TABLE cluster table
```

3. Rename the replacement table.

```
RENAME new table TO cluster table
```

4. Regrant all grants; create required indexes and constraints.

> **T**IP   In the example SQL scripts there is a dynamic SQL script that will create a grant script for a specified database object. The script must of course be run before the object is dropped.

CHAPTER 9

Oracle Provided Packages DBMS_*

In Oracle7, Oracle Corporation first introduced us to the DBMS_* utilities. Known collectively as the Oracle Provided Packages and Procedures, these form a powerful set of database-level utilities that all DBAs and developers should be aware of and make use of. In Oracle8 these have been expanded to include advanced queuing support and external procedure call support as well as extensions to existing packages.

In addition to the packages, Oracle has included since version 6 multiple utility scripts to address index selection, lock problems, and object dependencies. These scripts usually begin with "utl" and are standard SQL code scripts. These are documented in Chapter 11.

The scripts used to build the DBMS_* utility packages are stored under the RDBMS directory in the admin subdirectory on all the platforms I have worked on in the last several years. For example, on UNIX they are located in $ORACLE_HOME/rdbms/admin. On NT, assuming you have it installed on the C: drive, the path for Oracle8 would be C:\orant\rdbms80\admin, and on VMS, if memory serves me correctly, it would be ORA_HOME:[rdbms.admin]. The DBMS_* utilities are built using two scripts each (generally): one to create the header, which is user readable, and one to create the package body, which has been "wrapped" (i.e., converted to HEX). For example, the DBMS_SHARED_POOL package has the header file dbmspool.sql and the wrapped body script prvtpool.plb. Generally, a wrapped script supplied by Oracle Corporation will have the ".plb" suffix. Both scripts must be run from the SYS user on Oracle8 or the INTERNAL user for Oracle7. If the scripts are not run from the proper user they will not function. Virtually all of the packages will be built if the catproc.sql script is executed when the database is built. I have tried to cover all of the "extra" scripts in Chapter 11. Tables 9.1 and 9.2 show all of the scripts and whether they are executed via the catproc.sql script.

When using a package for the first time you should review the header file. Virtually all of the data in this section came directly or indirectly from the header files themselves. In fact, if you look at Oracle documentation for the scripts it is also virtually identical to the documentation in the header files. When you get a new release you should review both the readme files and the header files for any changes which could affect the operation of any of the packages you use in your application.

All of the data used for this section came from either Oracle8 documentation, Oracle8 utility header files, or the most up-to-date papers dealing with the particular utility available. What this means is that if you are on an earlier release some of the utilities covered may not be available on your system.

TABLE 9.1   The SQL Procedures Used to Build the Procedural Option in Oracle7

Procedure	Purpose	Run By
CATPROC.SQL	Builds procedural option	Database creation SQL script
CATPRC.SQL	Builds procedural tables	CATPROC.SQL
CATSNAP.SQL	Builds snapshot views	CATPROC.SQL
CATRPC.SQL	Builds views used by remote databases to access databases with procedural option	CATPROC.SQL
STANDARD.SQL	Builds required datatypes and prams for PL/SQL	CATPROC.SQL
DBMSSTDX.SQL	Provides kernel extensions for STANDARD.SQL	CATPROC.SQL
DBMSSSYER.SQL	Returns errors to DBMS packages. DBMS_SYS_ERROR	CATPROC.SQL
PIPIDL.SQL	Package Portable IDL definitions and procedures	CATPROC.SQL
PIDIAN.SQL	Provides definitions for DIANA functions and constants	CATPROC.SQL
DIUTIL.SQL	DIANA utilities	CATPROC.SQL
PISTUB.SQL	Subprogram stub generator package	CATPROC.SQL
DBMSLOCK.SQL	Lock tables and Locking routines from Oracle (DBMS_LOCK package.) Allows procedures to detect deadlocks, do lock conversion, create, control and use locks	CATPROC.SQL
DBMSPIPE.SQL	Procedures for process communication	CATPROC.SQL
DBMSALRT.SQL	Tables and Procedures for named event monitoring (user-alerts) (DBMS_ALERT package)	CATPROC.SQL
DBMSOTPT.SQL	Procedures used with the 'set serveroutput on' command (DBMS_OUTPUT package)	CATPROC.SQL

continued

TABLE 9.1 (Continued)

Procedure	Purpose	Run By
DBMSDESC.SQL	Procedures to describe stored procedures and packages (DBMS_DESCRIBE package)	CATPROC.SQL
DBMSMAIL.SQL ORA*MAIL	Procedures for ORA*MAIL	Manually to install
DBMSPOOL.SQL	Procedures for Shared Pool management DBMS_SHARED_POOL	Manually
DBMSUTIL.SQL	Contains various utility packages: DBMS_TRANSACTION DBMS_SESSION DBMS_DDL DBMS_UTILITY DBMS_APPLICATION_INFO DBMS_SYSTEM DBMS_SPACE DBMS_ROWID	CATPROC.SQL
DBMSSQL.SQL*	Allows use of Dynamic SQL from PL/SQL DBMS_SQL	CATPROC.SQL
DBMSDEFR.SQL	Allows replicated deferred remote procedure calls via sub-packages: DBMS_DEFER DBMS_DEFER_QUERY DBMS_DEFER_SYS	CATREP.SQL
DBMSDFRD.SQL*	DBMS_DEFER_DUMMY	CATPROC.SQL
DBMSJOB.SQL*	Allows use of queues from PL/SQL DBMS_JOB	Manually
DBMSOFLN.SQL	Used by snapshots for offline instantiation DBMS_OFFLINE_SCHEMA	Manually
DBMSGEN.SQL	Used by the replication manager to generate shadow tables, triggers and packages for table replication DBMS_DEFERGEN DBMS_REPUTIL	CATREP.SQL
DBMSPEXP.SQL	Provides procedural extensions to the export process DBMS_EXPORT_EXTENSION	CATPROC.SQL
DBMSREPC.SQL	Creates the replication catalog packages DBMS_REPCAT DBMS_REPCAT_AUTH DBMS_REPCAT_ADMIN	CATREP.SQL

Additional package definitions for Oracle8 are shown in Table 9.2.

TABLE 9.2   Oracle8 Packages

Procedure	Purpose	Run By
PLITBLM.SQL	Package to allow index-table operations Functions: COUNT, FIRST, LAST, EXISTS, PRIOR NEXT, LIMIT Procedures: DELETE, TRIM, EXTEND	catproc.sql
UTILFIL.SQL	Creates the UTL_FILE OS file IO package. Functions: FOPEN, IS_OPEN Procedures: FCLOSE, FCLOSE_ALL,GET_LINE PUT, NEW_LINE, PUTF, FFLUSH	catproc.sql
DBMSAPIN.SQL	DBMS_APPLICATION_INFO package (moved out of DBMS_UTILITIES)	catproc.sql
CATQUEUE.SQL	Creates tables, views, packages for advanced queue feature.	catproc.sql
DBMSPB.SQL	Package used by the PROBE pl/sql debugger	catproc.sql
CATPITR.SQL	Creates views used by point in time recovery	catproc.sql
DBMSPITR.SQL	This package contains procedures which get called during the import phase and export phase of point-in-time recovery (PITR).	catproc.sql
DBMSLOB.SQL	DBMS package specification for Oracle8 Large Objects (DBMS_LOB).	catproc.sql
DBMSAQ.PLB	DBMS package specification for advanced queueing operations (DBMS_AQ). Procedures: ENQUEUE, DEQUEUE	catqueue.sql
DBMSAQAD.SQL	DBMS package specification for advanced queueing operations administration (DBMS_AQADM) Procedures: CREATE_QTABLE, CREATE_Q, DROP_Q, DROP_QTABLE, START_Q, STOP_Q, ALTER_Q, TEST_AC_DDL Package: DBMS_AQ_IMPORT_INTERNAL Functions: AQ_TABLE_EXPORT_CHECK, AQ_EXPORT_CHECK	catqueue.sql

continued

TABLE 9.2   (Continued)

Procedure	Purpose	Run By
	Procedures: AQ_TABLE_DEFN_UPDATE, AQ_DEFN_UPDATE	
CATAUDIT.SQL	Builds the auditing views	catalog.sql
CATEXP.SQL	Builds the export views	catalog.sql
CATLDR.SQL	Builds the loader views	catalog.sql
CATSVRMG.SQL	Builds the server manager views	catalog.sql
CATPART.SQL	Builds the partitioning views	catalog.sql
CATADT.SQL	Builds the data type views	catalog.sql
CATRMAN.SQL	Builds recovery manager tables	
CATSNMP.SQL	Builds role and tables for SNMP agent	

As you can see, there is a lot of material in all of these packages; fortunately many of them are used strictly by the ORDBMS internals and you will probably never deal with them. The rest of this chapter will address the packages and utilities that the DBA should be aware of and know how to use if required.

One quick note about the Oracle provided functions. One universal complaint that I have heard over and over is that many useful functions, such as "is_role_enabled" from DBMS_SESSION, aren't available outside of their own packages (i.e., can't be used in callouts from other packages). This is caused by Oracle failing to assert the purity level of the function (purity level assures Oracle internals that you won't do forbidden things with the function, such as changing database or package state). Oracle has not asserted their purity level via the pragma restrict_references statement; thus they can only be used in their parent packages or from the command line. However, you can add this statement (use other function statements with purity asserted as an example) and recompile the packages that contain the functions you want to use to get around this. On the line immediately following the function declaration for "is_role_enabled" I added:

```
pragma restrict_references(is_role_enabled,WNDS, RNDS, WNPS);
```

to the package header file dbmsutil.sql. The package compiled cleanly and I was able to call the function from outside the package. This can be done with other useful functions that Oracle neglected to make universally available as well.

I have endeavored to cover all of the packages that I believe a DBA or user should have a use for in this section. I didn't cover those that are strictly internal use. An example would be the replication and recovery manager packages. If I covered the packages that you shouldn't mess with, someone would and then this book would get

the blame. If you feel you just can't live without using some of the functions and procedures contained in these "forbidden" packages, then go ahead and read the headers
and whatever documentation is available and go at it. . . . But don't post questions to
me on CompuServe asking how to undo whatever you end up doing to your system!

9.1   DBMS_EXPORT_EXTENSION

The DBMS_EXPORT_EXTENSION package is used to load the pre- and post-action
tables used by export and import to define actions taken either before a table is exported or after a table is exported. The package utilizes the expact$ table, which has
the structure shown in Table 9.3.

TABLE 9.3   Structure of the expact$ Table (Oracle7 and Oracle8)

Column Name	Column Null?	Column Type	Purpose
Structure of the Oracle 7.3 sys.expact$ Table			
OWNER	NOT NULL	VARCHAR2(30)	owner of table
NAME	NOT NULL	VARCHAR2(30)	name of table
FUNC_SCHEMA	NOT NULL	VARCHAR2(30)	schema function runs under
FUNC_PACKAGE	NOT NULL	VARCHAR2(30)	package name
FUNC_PROC	NOT NULL	VARCHAR2(30)	procedure name
CODE	NOT NULL	NUMBER	pretable or posttable
CALLORDER		NUMBER	

Column Name	Column Null?	Column Type	Purpose
Structure of the Oracle8 sys.expact$ Table			
OWNER	NOT NULL	VARCHAR2("M_IDEN")	owner of object
NAME	NOT NULL	VARCHAR2("M_IDEN")	name of object
FUNC_SCHEMA	NOT NULL	VARCHAR2("M_IDEN")	schema func runs under
FUNC_PACKAGE	NOT NULL	VARCHAR2("M_IDEN")	package name
FUNC_PROC	NOT NULL	VARCHAR2("M_IDEN")	procedure name
CODE	NOT NULL	NUMBER	pretable or posttable
CALLORDER		NUMBER	
CALLARG		VARCHAR2(1)	whether this function takes arguments or not. Null—no arguments; Y—pass arguments
OBJ_TYPE	NOT NULL	NUMBER	type of object to be exported
USER_ARG		VARCHAR2(2000)	user arguments for pkg, proc, func

The DBA has to prebuild a procedure that performs the desired action against the table(s) and then makes an entry into the sys.expact$ table giving the information for the procedure they have created. The DBA must also specify a function code (shown in Table 9.4). The row-level action codes that are listed are not supported as of version 8.0.2. The pre_table and post_table procedures are called automatically via the export and import programs; no DBA action, other than loading sys.expact$ with data about the procedures to be executed, is required. Actually, I have never heard of anyone using this feature of Oracle. It is used internally by Oracle with five preloaded pretable expact$ entries in Oracle version 7.3.2 and even six/six split between pre- and post-table actions for a total of twelve entries in Oracle version 8.0.2. For an example of how it can be used look at these entries and their associated procedures.

TABLE 9.4   expact$ Table Function Codes and Their Meaning

Function Code Variable	Code Value	Code Meaning
func_pre_table	1	execute before loading table
func_post_tables	2	execute after loading all tables
func_pre_row	3	execute before loading row (future)
func_post_row	4	execute after loading row (future)
func_row	5	execute in lieu of loading row (future)

The procedures and functions in this package are intended to be called from the export process and thus are not DBA callable. They are listed here for reference purposes only.

PRE_TABLE

The first function in the package is the "pre_table" function. As its name implies, it inserts calls to the pre-table procedures listed as such in the expact$ table into the export stream. The function accepts two varchar2 arguments: table_schema and table_name, which, as their names imply, refer to the table schema and name of the table to have actions taken upon. The calls to this function are recursive until a null return is generated for a specific table. Note that these procedure calls are placed in the export stream and are applied upon import, not against the existing table in the instance being exported from. The function does not assert purity so it may not be used in packages other than the parent package.

POST_TABLE

The second function in the package is the "post_table" function. As its name implies, it inserts calls to the post-table procedures listed as such in the expact$ table into the export stream. The function accepts two varchar2 arguments, the table_schema and table_name, which, as their names imply, refer to the table schema and name of the table to have actions taken upon. The calls to this function are recursive until a null return is generated for a specific table. Note that these procedure calls are placed in the export stream and are applied upon import, not against the existing table in the instance being exported from. The function does not assert purity so it cannot be used in packages external to the parent function.

9.2   DBMS_LOCK

The DBMS_LOCK package allows for users to create, hold, drop, and in general control their own locks for their applications. This package can create and manipulate locks with lockids in the range of 1073741824 to 1999999999. The procedures create named locks, which should be easier to deal with than attempting to deal with lockids. The package, when built, creates the DBMS_LOCK_ALLOCATED table, which has the structure shown in Table 9.5 for both Oracle7 and Oracle8.

This package was designed for use by developers who needed to create and manage locks from within applications. This package is used extensively by many third-party vendors and developers. The locks generated are managed by the rdbms lock management services. User generated locks are prefixed with UL so they won't conflict with system-generated locks. This means that deadlock detection and elimination will be performed against these locks. As with regular locks, these locks are released when a session terminates. Developers should take care to carefully coordinate the creation and use of user-defined locks. I suggest assigning ranges of lockids to each developer or application. The first call to allocate_unique inserts a row into the DBMS_LOCK_ALLOCATED table with the name and lockid. Any subsequent calls against this lock name will return the assigned lockid. After the expiration time (specified in seconds) has passed, the lockid is released; however, the entry remains in the table. This means that if you use DBMS_LOCK you should periodically review the size of DBMS_LOCK_ALLOCATED and purge any expired lock entries. If no expiration time is set it will default to 10 days. If allocate_unique is called from a procedure, one important thing to remember is that it performs a commit so any assigned rollback segment will be released and will have to be reassigned. If a deadlock is detected when a user requests a user-generated lock, a sleep procedure is provided to cause the second caller to sleep until the lock becomes available or the specified interval is reached, whichever comes first. This package is not designed to provide thousands of locks; it doesn't manage more than a hundred or so locks per session.

TABLE 9.5   Structure of Table sys.dbms_lock_allocated

Column Name	Null?	Column Type
NAME	NOT NULL	VARCHAR2(128)
LOCKID		NUMBER(38)
EXPIRATION		DATE

Your operating system may have limits on the maximum number of locks available. You need to take this into consideration when using user-allocated locks, or making this package available to developers. A way to control how this package is used is to create a cover package for this package which limits those locks used. Then, instead of granting execute on DBMS_LOCK package to public, grant execute on the cover package only to specific users. Source 9.1 shows the suggested cover package from the DBMSLOCK.SQL header script.

SOURCE 9.1   Example procedure to limit access to the DBMS_LOCK package.

```
create package lock_100_to_200 is
nl_mode   constant integer := 1;
ss_mode   constant integer := 2;
sx_mode   constant integer := 3;
s_mode    constant integer := 4;
ssx_mode  constant integer := 5;
x_mode    constant integer := 6;
maxwait   constant integer := 32767;
function request(id in integer,
                 lockmode in integer default x_mode,
                 timeout in integer default maxwait,
               release_on_commit in boolean default FALSE
    return integer;
  function convert(id in integer;
                 lockmode in integer,
                 timeout in number default maxwait)
    return integer;
  function release(id in integer) return integer;
end;
create package body lock_100_to_200 is
begin
  function  request(id in integer,
                 lockmode in integer default x_mode,
                 timeout in integer default maxwait,
                 release_on_commit in boolean default FALSE)
    return integer is
  begin
    if id < 100 or id > 200 then
    raise_application_error(-20000,'Lock id out of range');
    endif;
    return dbms_lock.request(id, lockmode, timeout,
      release_on_commit);
  end;
  function convert(id in integer,
                 lockmode in integer,
                 timeout in number default maxwait)
    return integer is
  begin
    if id < 100 or id > 200 then
```

```
      raise_application_error(-20000,'Lock id out of range');
      endif;
      return dbms_lock.convert(id, lockmode, timeout);
   end;
   function release(id in integer) return integer is
   begin
      if id < 100 or id > 200 then
      raise_application_error(-20000,'Lock id out of range');
      endif;
      return dbms_lock.release(id);
   end;
end;
```

According to the header script it is suggested that you grant execute on the lock_100_to_200 package to those users who are allowed to use locks in the 100-200 range. This means that you don't have to grant execute on package dbms_lock to anyone; you just grant them execute on the cover package. The lock_100_200 package should be created from the SYS user.

The dbms_lock package also defines some special constants for use when converting locks; these constants are as follows:

Constant	Value	
nl_mode	1	
ss_mode	2	—Also called 'Intended Share'
sx_mode	3	—Also called 'Intended Exclusive'
s_mode	4	
ssx_mode	5	
x_mode	6	

These constants correspond to the various lock modes:

Prefix	Meaning
nl	Null
ss	Sub Shared
sx	Sub eXclusive
s	Shared
ssx	Shared Sub eXclusive
x	eXclusive

The concept of a "sub" lock needs a bit of explanation. A sub-share lock can be used on an aggregate object to indicate that share locks are being acquired on subparts of the object. Similarly, a subexclusive lock can be used on an aggregate object to indicate that exclusive locks are being acquired on subparts of the object. A share-subexclusive lock indicates that the entire aggregate object has a share lock, but some of the subparts may additionally have exclusive locks. For the convert functions there are certain lock compatibility rules that must be followed. These are listed in Table 9.6.

Lock Compatibility Rules Table 9.6 shows what happens when you try to get a lock of type:

TABLE 9.6   Lock Compatibility Chart

Lock held	NL	SS	SX	S	SSX	X
NL	SUCC	SUCC	SUCC	SUCC	SUCC	SUCC
SS	SUCC	SUCC	SUCC	SUCC	SUCC	fail
SX	SUCC	SUCC	SUCC	fail	fail	fail
S	SUCC	SUCC	fail	SUCC	fail	fail
SSX	SUCC	SUCC	fail	fail	fail	fail
X	SUCC	fail	fail	fail	fail	fail

The functions and procedures provided by DBMS_LOCK are as follows:

allocate_unique—Allocate a unique lock given a name.

request—Request a lock of given mode.

convert—Convert lock from one mode to another.

release—Release the lock.

sleep—Sleep for the specified time.

ALLOCATE_UNIQUE

The procedure allocate_unique has the input parameters: lockname (varchar2), and expiration_secs (integer which defaults to 864000). The function returns the lockhandle as a varchar2. Given a name, the procedure generates a unique lockid for this lock and inserts a record into the DBMS_LOCK_ALLOCATED table. This procedure always performs a 'commit'. The input and output parameters have the following characteristics:

lockname—This is the name of lock for which to generate a unique lockid. If this name already has been assigned a lockid, then allocate_unique returns a handle to that lockid. If the name doesn't exist, generate a new lockid and return a handle to it.

T IP   Do not use locknames beginning with 'ORA$'; these names are reserved for products supplied by Oracle Corporation. The name can be up to 128 bytes, and is case sensitive.

---

expiration_secs—This input parameter is the number of seconds after an 'allocate_unique' is last performed on this lockname that this lock is subject to cleanup (i.e., deleting from the dbms_lock_allocated table). This cleanup is not automatic. It defaults to 10 days.

lockhandle—This is the only output for allocate_unique. The actual lockid is not returned; rather a handle to it is returned. Use this handle in subsequent calls to the request, convert, and release packages. Up to 128 bytes are returned. A handle is used to reduce the chance that a programming error can accidentally create an incorrect but valid lockid. This provides better isolation between different applications that are using the DBMS_LOCK package.

Some caveats for using DBMS_LOCK.ALLOCATE_UNIQUE are as follows:

1. All sessions using a lockhandle returned by a call to allocate_unique using the same name will be referring to the same lock. Different sessions may have different lockhandles for the same lock, so lockhandles should not be passed from one session to another.
2. The lockids generated by allocate_unique are between 1073741824 and 1999999999, inclusive.
3. This routine will always do a commit.

The DBMS_LOCK.ALLOCATE_UNIQUE procedure will raise the following exception:

```
---20000, ORU-10003: Unable to find or insert lock <lockname> into catalog
        dbms_lock_allocated.
```

REQUEST

The function request has the following input parameters: id or lockhandle (integer or varchar2), lockmode (integer with a default of x_mode), timeout (integer with a default of maxwait), and release_on_commit (boolean with a default of FALSE). The function returns an integer value. The request function will request a specified lock with the given mode. Note that this routine is overloaded (can take inputs of various types) based on the type of its first argument. The appropriate routine is used based on how it is called. If a deadlock is detected, then an arbitrary session that is involved in the deadlock is chosen to receive deadlock status.

TIP   When running both multithreaded server (dispatcher) and parallel server, a multithreaded "shared server" will be bound to a session during the time that any locks are held. Therefore the "shared server" will not be shareable during this time.

The details of the input parameters for the function DBMS_LOCK.REQUEST are as follows:

id—From 0 to 1073741823. All sessions that use the same number will be referring to the same lock. Lockids from 2000000000 to 2147483647 are exempted by this routine. Do not use these as they are reserved for products supplied by Oracle Corporation.

lockhandle—Can be used instead of the id; it corresponds to the handle returned by call to allocate_unique.

lockmode—See lockmodes and lock compatibility chart (Table 9.6).

timeout—Timeout in seconds. If the lock cannot be granted within this time period then the call returns a value of 1. Deadlock detection is performed for all "nonsmall" values of timeout.

release_on_commit—If TRUE, then release on commit or rollback; otherwise keep until explicitly released or until end-of-session. If a transaction has not been started, it will be.

The function's return value is defined as follows:

0—success

1—timeout

2—deadlock

3—parameter error

4—already own lock specified by 'id' or 'lockhandle'

5—illegal lockhandle

CONVERT

The function convert has the following input parameters: id or lockhandle(integer, varchar2), lockmode (integer), and timeout (number with a default of maxwait). The function returns an integer value that denotes the status of your lock request. The convert function is used to convert a lock from one mode to another. Note that this routine is overloaded based on the type of its first argument. The appropriate routine is used based on how it is called. If a deadlock is detected, then an arbitrary session involved in this transaction is chosen to receive deadlock status.

The detailed definitions of the input parameters are as follows:

id—This is an integer from 0 to 1073741823.

lockhandle—This is a handle returned by a call to allocate_unique.

lockmode—See lockmodes and lock compatibility in Table 9.6.

timeout—This is the value for lock conversion timeout in seconds. If the lock cannot be converted within this time period then the call returns a value of 1. Deadlock detection is performed for all "nonsmall" values of timeout.

The return value is defined as:

0—success

1—timeout

2—deadlock

3—parameter error

4—session doesn't own lock specified by 'id' or 'lockhandle'

5—illegal lockhandle

The function does not assert purity, so you may have problems using it in packages outside of its parent package.

RELEASE

The function release has the input parameter id (integer) or lockhandle(varchar2) and returns an integer. The purpose of the release function is to release a lock previously acquired by 'request'. Note that this routine is overloaded based on the type of its argument. The appropriate routine is used based on how it is called.

The detailed definitions of the input parameters are as follows:

id—This is an integer from 0 to 1073741823.

lockhandle—This is a handle returned by a call to allocate_unique.

The return value has the following meanings:

0—success

3—parameter error

4—session doesn't own lock specified by 'id' or 'lockhandle'

5—illegal lockhandle

The function does not assert purity, so you may have trouble using it in packages outside of its parent package.

SLEEP

The procedure sleep has an input value of seconds(number). The purpose of sleep, as its name implies, is to suspend the session for the specified period of time. This procedure is also useful for watching pipes for data values in a loop situation.

The input parameter for sleep is:

seconds—This is the input wait period in seconds, currently the maximum resolution is in hundreths of a second (e.g., 1.00, 1.01, .99 are all legal and distinct values).

9.3 DBMS_PIPE

The DBMS_PIPE package allows for interprocess communication. The communication is asynchronous and is nonblocking in nature. This means one process loads data into a message buffer known as a pipe and another process can read from the pipe at any time. The data is not, however, persistent in nature; it is held in the SGA memory shared pool area until it is either read or flushed or the database is shut down.

Oracle pipes are similar to UNIX pipes. You can do the following:

```
dbms_pipe.send_message(<pipename>)
dbms_pipe.receive_message(<pipename>)
```

which will cause a message to be sent or received. You can do:

```
dbms_pipe.pack_message(<varchar2>|<number>|<date>)
```

to pack an item into a static buffer (which will then be sent with the "send_message" call), and

```
dbms_pipe.unpack_message(<varchar2>|<number>|<date>)
```

to get an item out of the static buffer (which is filled by the "receive_message" call).

Oracle pipes can be private to a user-id—this will only allow sessions connected under the same user-id or using a stored procedure owned by the user-id to read or write to the pipe. Pipes can also be public—and all database users with execute privilege on dbms_pipe and knowledge of the pipe can read or write to a public pipe.

Oracle pipes operate independently of transactions. They also operate asynchronously. There can be multiple readers and writers of the same pipe. Pipes only operate between sessions in the same instance.

Oracle pipes are explicitly created using dbms_pipe.create_pipe(<pipename>) and explicitly created pipes must be removed using dbms_pipe.remove_pipe(<pipename>). A pipe created using the explicit CREATE command should be removed using the REMOVE function. A pipe can also be created implicitly.

Implicit pipes automatically come into existence the first time they are referenced via packages and procedures using the DBMS_PIPE package. Implicitly created pipes effectively disappear when they contain no more data (some overhead remains in the SGA until it gets aged out). Explicitly created pipes take up space in the SGA (see "maxpipesize" parameter to "send_message") until removed. If multiple processes are using pipes, ensure each has its own uniquely named pipe; only one process at a time can retrieve a message from a pipe and once retrieved, a message is gone from the pipe and unavailable for other processes to read.

So, what can we use Oracle pipes for?

- **External service interface.** You can provide the ability to communicate with (user-written) services that are external to the RDBMS. This can be done in an effectively multithreaded manner so that several instances of the service can be executing simultaneously. Additionally, the services are available asynchronously, which means that the requestor of the service need not block awaiting a reply. The requestor can check (with or without timeout) at a later time. The service can be written in any of the 3GL languages that ORACLE supports, not just C.

- **Independent transactions.** The pipe can be used to communicate to a separate session which can perform an operation in an independent transaction (such as logging an attempted security violation detected by a trigger).

  Alerters (nontransactional). You can post another process without requiring the waiting process to poll. If an "after-row" or "after-statement" trigger were to alert an application, then the application would treat this alert as an indication that the data probably changed. The application would then go read the data to get the current value. Since this is an "after" trigger, the application would want to do a "select for update" to make sure it read the correct data.

- **Debugging.** Triggers and/or stored procedures can send debugging information to a pipe. Another session can keep reading out of the pipe and displaying it on the screen or writing it out to a file.

- **Concentrator.** Useful for multiplexing large numbers of users over fewer network connections, or improving performance by concentrating several user transactions into one dbms transaction.

DBMS_PIPEs security can be achieved by selective use of 'grant execute' on the dbms_pipe package, granting execute to only those users who need it, or by creating a pipe using the 'private' parameter in the create function, or by writing cover packages that only expose particular features or pipe names to particular users or roles.

The DBMS_PIPE package sets up a single special constant called maxwait. This is an integer value set to 86400000, which corresponds to 1000 days and translates into the maximum time to wait in attempting to send or receive a message.

PACK_MESSAGE

The first procedure in the package is the pack_message procedure, which has a single input value that due to the package being overloaded can accept varchar2, number, and date datatypes. The procedure pack_message_raw is functionally the same but accepts raw input and pack_message_rowid is functionally the same but accepts rowid values as input.

The purpose of the pack_message series of procedures is to pack an item into the message buffer. If your item exceeds 4092 bytes in length for an implicit pipe you will get an exception based on an ORA-06558. The actual size of an implicit pipe buffer is 4096 bytes but each item in the buffer takes one byte for the type, two bytes for the length, plus the actual data. In addition there is also one byte needed to terminate the message.

UNPACK_MESSAGE

The next procedure is the unpack_message procedure, which has a single output value that due to the package being overloaded can generate varchar2, number, and date datatypes. The procedure unpack_message_raw is functionally the same but gives raw output and unpack_message_rowid is functionally the same but outputs rowid values. The purpose of the upack_message series of procedures is to unpack an item from the message buffer. If your item is of the incorrect type or there are no more items in the buffer, then ORA-06559 or 06556 is generated.

NEXT_ITEM_TYPE

The function next_item_type returns an integer that corresponds to the type of the next item in the buffer. The return integer translates as follows:

Return value:

    0—no more items

    6—number

    9—varchar2

    11—rowid

    12—date

    23—raw

The function asserts purity so it can be used in packages external to the parent package.

CREATE_PIPE

The next function, create_pipe, is used to create explicit pipes. The function takes the arguments: pipename (varchar2), maxpipesize (integer with a default of 8192), and private (boolean with a default of TRUE). The function returns an integer.

The function has the following argument definitions:

pipename—Name of pipe to be created.

T**IP**   Do not use pipe names beginning with 'ORA$'. These are reserved for use by procedures provided by Oracle Corporation. The pipename should not be longer than 128 bytes, and is case insensitive. At this time, the name cannot contain NLS characters.

---

maxpipesize—Maximum allowed size for the pipe. The total size of all the messages on the pipe cannot exceed this amount. The maxpipesize for a pipe becomes part of the pipe and persists for the lifetime of the pipe. Callers of send_message with larger values will cause the maxpipesize to be increased. Callers with a smaller value will just use the larger value. The specification of maxpipesize here allows us to avoid its use in future send_message calls.

private—Boolean, indicating whether the pipe will be private—and for the use of the creating user-id—or public. A private pipe can be used directly through calls to this package by sessions connected to the database as the same user as the one that created the pipe. It can also be used via stored procedures owned by the user that created the pipe. The procedure may be executed by anyone with execute privilege on it. A public pipe can be accessed by anyone who has knowledge of it and execute privilege on dbms_pipe.

Return values:

0—Success—This is returned even if the pipe had been created in a mode that permits its use by the user executing the create call. If a pipe already existed, it is not emptied.

Exceptions:

Null pipe name, Permission error—There is a pipe with the same name that already exists and you are not allowed to use it.

The function asserts purity so it can be used in packages external to the parent package.

REMOVE_PIPE

The next function is called remove_pipe and it accepts the argument pipename (varchar2) and returns an integer value. The purpose of this function, as its name implies, is to remove an explicitly named pipe.

The remove_pipe function has a single input parameter: pipename—Which is the name of pipe to remove. The function has one return value: 0—Success. Calling remove on a pipe that does not exist returns 0. The function handles the following exceptions:

Null pipe name—You get this if you have insufficient privilege to remove the pipe.

Permission error—The pipe was created and is owned by someone else.

The function asserts purity so it can be used in packages external to the parent package.

SEND_MESSAGE

The next function is the send_message function, which has the input arguments pipename (varchar2), timeout (integer with a default value of maxwait), and maxpipesize (integer with a default value of 8192). The function returns an integer value. The function is used to send a message on the named pipe. The message is contained in the local message buffer which was filled with calls to 'pack_message'. The pipe could have been created explicitly using 'create_pipe', or it will be created implicitly.

The detailed definition of the input parameters follows:

pipename—This is the name of the pipe to place the message in. The message is copied from the local buffer which can be filled by the "pack_message" routine.

TIP Do not use pipe names beginning with 'ORA$'. These names are reserved for use by procedures provided by Oracle Corporation. Pipename should not be longer than 128 bytes, and is case insensitive. At this time, the name cannot contain NLS characters.

---

timeout—This is the time to wait while attempting to place a message on a pipe, in seconds (see return codes below).

maxpipesize—This is the maximum allowed size for the pipe. The total size of all the messages on the pipe cannot exceed this amount. If this message exceeds this amount the call will block. The maxpipesize for a pipe becomes part of the pipe and persists for the lifetime of the pipe. Callers of send_message with larger values will cause the maxpipesize to be increased. Callers with a smaller value will just use the larger value. The specification of maxpipesize here allows us to avoid the use of a "open_pipe" call.

The function's return value has the following meanings:

0—success

1—timed out (either because can't get lock on pipe or pipe stays too full)

3—interrupted

The function handles the following exceptions:

Null pipe name—This means you have insufficient privilege to write to the pipe.

Permission error—This indicates that the pipe is private and owned by someone else.

The function asserts purity so it can be used in packages external to the parent package.

RECEIVE_MESSAGE

The next function is the receive_message function and has the input values pipename (varchar2), and timeout (integer with a default value of maxwait), and returns an integer value. The purpose of the function is to receive a message from the named pipe and copy the message into the local message buffer. Use 'unpack_message' to access the individual items in the message. The pipe can be created explicitly using the 'create_pipe' function or it will be created implicitly if it doesn't already exist.

The detailed definition of the input parameters follows:

pipename—The name of the pipe from which to retrieve a message. The message is copied into a local buffer which can be accessed by the "unpack_message" routine.

WARNING   Do not use pipe names beginning with 'ORA$'. These names are reserved for use by procedures provided by Oracle Corporation. Pipename should not be longer than 128 bytes, and is case insensitive. At this time the name cannot contain NLS characters.

---

timeout—This is the time to wait for a message. A timeout of 0 allows you to read without blocking.

The function's return values have the following meaning:

0—success

1—timed out

2—record in pipe too big for buffer (should not happen)

3—interrupted

The function handles the following exceptions:

Null pipe name—This means you have insufficient privilege to remove the record from the pipe.

Permission error—The pipe is private or is owned by someone else.

The function asserts purity so it can be used in packages external to the parent package.

RESET_BUFFER

The next procedure is reset_buffer. This procedure has no arguments and is used to reset the pack and unpack positioning indicators to 0. Generally this routine is not needed.

PURGE

The next procedure is the purge procedure, which has a single input argument: pipename (varchar2). The purpose of this procedure is to empty out the named pipe. An empty pipe is a candidate for LRU removal from the SGA; therefore 'purge' can be used to free all memory associated with a pipe.

The detailed definition for the purge input parameter follows:

pipename—This is the name of the pipe from which to remove all messages. The local buffer may be overwritten with messages as they are discarded. Pipename should not be longer than 128 bytes, and is case insensitive.

The purge procedure handles the following exception:

Permission error—This means the pipe belongs to another user.

UNIQUE_SESSION_NAME

The final function is unique_session_name, which has no inputs but returns a varchar2 value. This function is used to get a name that is unique among all sessions currently connected to this database. Multiple calls to this routine from the same session will always return the same value. The return value will always be a unique name. The returned name can be up to 30 bytes. The function asserts purity so it can be used in packages external to the parent package.

9.4 DBMS_ALERT

The DBMS_ALERT package provides for a process to either post or wait for alerts. Alerts are asynchronous and blocking in nature. This means that if a process is waiting for an alert it cannot be used for other processing. Alerts are excellent for event-based processing.

An example of the use of alerts would be a graphics tool that is displaying a graph of some data from a database table. The graphics tool can, after reading and graphing the data, wait on a database alert ('dbms_alert.waitone') covering the data just read. The tool will automatically wake up when the data is changed by any other user. All that is required is that a trigger be placed on the database table which then performs a signal ('dbms_alert.signal') whenever the trigger is fired. The alert would trigger a reread of the data and a reposting of the graph to the screen. Once the graph was updated, the tool would loop back into a wait state for the alert signal. Alerts are transaction based. This means that the waiting session does not get alerted until the transaction signaling the alert commits. There can be any number of concurrent signalers of a given alert, and there can be any number of concurrent waiters on a given alert.

With alerts being transaction based and blocking in nature, a waiting application will be blocked in the database and cannot do any other work. This is great for event-based processing.

One thing to remember is that most of the calls in the package, except for 'signal', do commits. So any transaction that depends on a specific rollback segment will have to have that rollback segment reassigned after calls to this package.

An example of the use of this package (taken from the package header file dbmsalrt.sql) would be when an application wishes to graph average salaries, say by department, for all employees. So the application needs to know whenever 'emp' is changed. The application would look like this:

```
    dbms_alert.register('emp_table_alert');
readagain:
  <read the emp table and graph it>
  dbms_alert.waitone('emp_table_alert', :message, :status);
  if status = 0 then goto readagain; else <error condition>
```

The 'emp' table would have a trigger similar to the following:

```
create trigger emptrig after insert or update or delete on emp
  begin
    dbms_alert.signal('emp_table_alert', 'message_text');
  end;
```

When the application is no longer interested in the alert, it does this:

```
dbms_alert.remove('emp_table_alert');
```

This is important since it reduces the amount of work required by the alert signaler.

If a session exits (or dies) while there exist registered alerts, they will eventually be cleaned up by future users of this package.

The above example guarantees that the application will always see the latest data, although it may not see every intermediate value.

The application can register for multiple events and can then wait for any of them to occur using the 'waitany' call. An application can also supply an optional 'timeout' parameter to the 'waitone' or 'waitany' calls. A 'timeout' of 0 returns immediately if there is no pending alert. The signaling session can optionally pass a message which will be received by the waiting session.

Alerts may be signaled more often than the corresponding application 'wait' calls. In such cases the older alerts are discarded. The application always gets the latest alert (based on transaction commit times).

If the application does not require transaction-based alerts, then the 'dbms_pipe' package may provide a useful alternative. If the transaction is rolled back after the call to 'dbms_alert.signal', no alert will occur.

It is possible to receive an alert, read the data, and find that no data has changed. This is because the data changed after the *prior* alert, but before the data was read for that *prior* alert.

In applications using DBMS_ALERT, in most cases the implementation is event-driven (i.e., there are no polling loops.) There are two cases where polling loops will occur:

1. Parallel mode. If your database is running in parallel mode then a polling loop is required to check for alerts from another instance. The polling loop defaults to one second and is settable by the 'set_defaults' call.
2. Waitany call. If you use the 'waitany' call, and a signaling session does a signal but does not commit within one second of the signal, then a polling loop is required so that this uncommitted alert does not camouflage other alerts. The polling loop begins at a one-second interval and exponentially backs off to 30-second intervals.

The DBMS_ALERT package uses the dbms_lock package (for synchronization between signalers and waiters) and the dbms_pipe package (for asynchronous event dispatching).

When using DBMS_ALERT with the parallel server *and* multithreaded server, a multithreaded (dispatcher) "shared server" will be bound to a session (and therefore not shareable) during the time a session has any alerts "registered," or from the time a session "signals" an alert until the time the session commits. Therefore, applications which register for alerts should use "dedicated servers" (be launched from the local server environment) rather than connecting through the dispatcher (to a "shared server"), since registration typically lasts for a long time, and applications which cause "signals" should use relatively short transactions so as not to tie up "shared servers" for too long.

Security on DBMS_ALERT may be controlled by granting execute on this package to just those users or roles that you trust. You can also write a cover package on top of this one which restricts the alertnames used. Execute privilege on this cover package can then be granted rather than direct grants on DBMS_ALERT.

The DBMS_ALERT uses one database pipe and two locks for each alert a session has registered. The package sets up a single special constant called "maxwait" which is set to 86400000 seconds (1000 days) and corresponds to the default maximum time to wait for an alert (essentially forever).

SET_DEFAULTS

The first procedure is called set_defaults and has a single input parameter: sensitivity (number). This procedure is used to set various defaults for DBMS_ALERT. The sensitivity setting is used in case a polling loop is required and is the time to sleep between polls. The sensitivity default is five seconds.

REGISTER

The next procedure is called register and has a single input parameter name: (varchar2). The procedure is used to register interest in an alert. A session may register interest in an unlimited number of alerts. Alerts should be deregistered when the session no longer has any interest (see section on REMOVE). This deregistering is important to reduce the load on the alerters. This call always performs a 'commit' so if rollback segment usage is important remember to reassign your rollback segment after a call to the register procedure.

The register procedure has one input parameter: name, which is the name of the alert in which this session is interested.

W ARNING   Alert names beginning with 'ORA$' are reserved for use for products provided by Oracle Corporation. Name must be 30 bytes or less. The name is case insensitive.

REMOVE

The next procedure is called remove and has a single input parameter: name (varchar2). The procedure remove is used to remove alert from the registration list. You should always do this when the session is no longer interested in an alert. Removing an alert is important since it will reduce the amount of work done by signalers of the alert. If a session dies without removing the alert, that alert will eventually (but not immediately) be cleaned up. This call to remove an alert always performs a commit so any rollback assignments will have to be redone.

The register procedure has one input parameter name which is the name of the alert to be removed from registration list. The name is case insensitive.

REMOVEALL

The removeall procedure has no inputs and is used to remove all alerts for a session from registration list. Do this when the session is no longer interested in any alerts. Removing alerts is important since it will reduce the amount of work done by the signalers of the alert. If a session dies without removing all of its alerts, the alerts will eventually (but not immediately) be cleaned up. This call always performs a commit, so be sure to reassign any rollback segments.

This procedure is called automatically upon first reference to DBMS_ALERT during a session. Therefore no alerts from prior sessions which may have terminated abnormally can affect the session.

WAITANY

The next procedure is called waitany and has one input parameter: timeout (number which defaults to maxwait); and several output parameters: name (varchar2), message (varchar2), and status (integer). The purpose of waitany is to wait for an alert to occur for any of the alerts for which this session is registered. Although probably unusual, the same session that waits for the alert may also first signal the alert. In this case remember to commit after the signal and prior to the wait. Otherwise a lock request exception (status 4) will occur. This call always performs a commit so be sure to reassign any rollback segments if required.

The waitany input parameter timeout is the maximum time to wait for an alert. If no alert occurs before timeout seconds, then this call will return with status of 1. The waitany output parameters are defined as:

name—This is the name of the alert that occurred, in uppercase.

message—This is any message associated with the alert. This is the message provided by the 'signal' call. Note that if multiple signals on this alert occurred before the waitany call, then the message will correspond to the most recent signal call. Messages from prior signal calls will be discarded.

status—This has the following values:

0—alert occurred

1—timeout occurred

The following error will be raised if you don't register for an alert or alerts before calling waitany:

```
-20000, ORU-10024: there are no alerts registered.
```

WAITONE

The next procedure is called waitone, with two input and two output parameters. The input parameters are: name (varchar2) and timeout (number with a default value of maxwait). The output parameters are message (varchar2) and status (integer). The purpose of waitone is to wait for a specified alert to occur, unlike waitany, which waits for any registered alert. If waitone is used, only a single alert can be registered and waited on. The session is blocked while it waits for a signal. If the alert was signaled since the register or last waitone/waitany, then this call will return immediately. The same session that waits for the alert may also first signal the alert. In this case you must commit after the call to the signal procedure and prior to the wait, otherwise a lock request exception (status 4) will occur. This call always performs a commit so remember to reassign any required rollback segment.

The procedure's input parameters are defined as follows:

name—This is the name of the alert to wait for. The name is case insensitive.

timeout—This is the maximum time to wait for this alert. If no alert occurs before timeout number of seconds, then this call will return with status of 1. This defaults to 1000 days, so remember to explicitly set it to a shorter time period.

If the alert named in the call to waitone has not been registered, then this call will return after the timeout period expires. Remember, this defaults to 1000 days so be sure to register your alert first or explicitly set the timeout value to a shorter period.

The waitone output parameters are defined as follows:

message—The message associated with the alert. This is the message provided by the 'signal' call. Note that if multiple signals on this alert occurred before the waitone call, then the message will correspond to the most recent signal call. Messages from prior signal calls will be discarded. The message may be up to1800 bytes.

status—The possible status returns are:

  0—alert occurred

  1—timeout occurred

SIGNAL

The last procedure in the package is called signal and has two input parameters: name (varchar2), and message (varchar2). The signal procedure is used to signal an actual alert. Remember to commit after the call to signal since it doesn't automatically commit and the alert will not be signaled if no commit is done. In fact, if a rollback occurs no alert will be signaled at all.

The signal procedure's input parameters are defined as follows:

name—This is the name of the alert to signal. The effect of the signal call only occurs when the transaction in which it is made commits. If the transaction rolls back, then the effect of the signal call is as if it had never occurred. All sessions that have registered interest in this alert will be notified. If the interested sessions are currently waiting, they will be awakened. If the interested sessions are not currently waiting, then they will be notified the next time they do a wait call. Multiple sessions may concurrently perform signals on the same alert. However the first session will block concurrent sessions until the first session commits. Name must be 30 bytes or less. It is case insensitive. This call does not perform a commit.

message—This parameter is used to send a message to associate with this alert. This will be passed to the waiting session. The waiting session may be able to avoid reading the database after the alert occurs by using the information in this message. The message must be 1800 bytes or less.

9.5   DBMS_OUTPUT

The DBMS_OUTPUT package is used to allow a PL/SQL routine to send output to the screen. However, this is not "live time" output, but is queued in a buffer area until the procedure ends or aborts for some reason. However, in spite of this limitation it is very useful for procedure troubleshooting. If this package is disabled, then all calls to this package are simply ignored. This way, these routines are only active when the client is one that is able to deal with the information. This is good for debugging, or stored procedures that want to display messages or reports to svrmgr or SQL*plus (like 'describing procedures', etc.). The default buffer size is 2000 bytes. The minimum is 2000 and the maximum is 1,000,000.

A simple example of the use of this package is taken from the dbmsotpt.sql header file for the DBMS_OUTOUT package. A trigger might want to print out some debugging information. If so, the trigger would do this:

```
dbms_output.put_line('I got here:'||:new.col||' is the new value');
```

If the client had enabled the dbms_output package, then this put_line would be buffered and the client could, after executing the statement (presumably some insert, delete, or update that caused the trigger to fire), execute:

```
execute dbms_output.get_line(:buffer, :status);
```

to get the line of information back. It could then display the buffer on the screen. The client would repeat calls to get_line until status came back as nonzero. For better performance, the client would use calls to get_lines, which can return an array of lines.

In the case of SVRMGR and SQL*Plus, for instance, users can implement the following command:

```
'SET SERVEROUTPUT ON BUFFER xxxx'
```

where xxxx is the buffer size in bytes.

This command is implemented so that users know whether to make calls to get_line(s) after issuing insert, update, delete, or anonymous PL/SQL calls (these are the only ones that can cause triggers or stored procedures to be executed). This command will place the buffer contents onto the user's screen when the transaction completes or terminates, but not before.

The dbmsotpt script creates a public synonym (dbms_output) and execute permission on this package is granted to public when the script is run.

ENABLE

The first procedure is called enable and has a single input parameter: buffer_size (integer with a default value of 20,000 on Oracle8). The enable procedure is used to enable calls to put, put_line, new_line, get_line, and get_lines. According to the header file, calls to these procedures are noops if the package has not been enabled. However, if the package is being used from SVRMGR or SQL*Plus, the SET SERVEROUTPUT BUFFER xxx command, where xxx is the size buffer to use, also enables the package. Personally, I have never used enable. The input value of buffer_size is used to set the default amount of information to buffer. A call to enable will also clean up data buffered from any dead sessions. Multiple calls to enable are allowed. The enable procedure is not needed with SVRMGR or SQL*Plus.

The enable input parameter is defined as follows:

buffer_size—Amount of information, in bytes, to buffer. Varchar2, number, and date items are stored in their internal representation. The information is stored in the SGA. An error is raised if the buffer size is exceeded. If there are multiple calls to enable, then the buffer_size is generally the largest of the values specified, and will always be greater than or equal to (>=) the smallest value specified. Currently a more accurate determination is not possible. The maximum size is 1,000,000; the minimum is 2000.

DISABLE

The next procedure, disable, has no inputs or outputs. The purpose of disable, as its name implies, is to disable all calls to put, put_line, new_line, get_line, and get_lines. The call to the disable procedure also purges the buffer of any remaining information. This procedure is only used for disabling internal input and output inside a PL/SQL script and is not needed for SVRMGR or SQL*Plus.

PUT

The next procedure is called put and it has one input parameter, a, which is overloaded to accept varchar2, number, and date values. Put is used to put a piece of information in the buffer. When retrieved by get_line(s), the number and date items will be formatted with to_char using the default formats. If you want another format, then format it explicitly and use the put(<varchar2>) call.

PUT_LINE

The next procedure is called put_line and it has one input parameter, a, that is over-loaded to accept varchar2, number, or date (but not mixed) values. If you need to mix values on the same input line you will need to use the TO_CHAR function to explicitly convert the noncharacter values into characters. The put_line procedure is use to put a piece of information in the buffer followed by an end-of-line marker. When retrieved by get_line(s), the number and date items will be formatted with to_char using the default formats. If you want another format then format it explicitly and use the put_line(<varchar2>) call. The procedure get_line(s) returns "lines" as delimited by "newlines". So every call to put_line or new_line will generate a line that will be returned by get_line(s). The procedure will raise the following errors if either the buffer size or line size (255 characters) are exceeded:

```
-20000, ORU-10027: buffer overflow, limit of <buf_limit> bytes.
-20000, ORU-10028: line length overflow, limit of 255 bytes per line.
```

NEW_LINE

The next procedure, new_line, has no arguments. It is used to add a newline character to the buffer. This newline acts as an end-of-line marker. get_line(s) return "lines" as delimited by "newlines". So every call to put_line or new_line will generate a line that will be returned by get_line(s). The new_line procedure will generate the following errors:

```
-20000, ORU-10027: buffer overflow, limit of <buf_limit> bytes.
-20000, ORU-10028: line length overflow, limit of 255 bytes per line.
```

GET_LINE

The next procedure is called get_line and has two output parameters: line (varchar2), and status (integer). The purpose of the get_line procedure is to get a single line back that has been buffered. The lines are delimited by calls to put_line or new_line. The line will be constructed taking all the items up to a newline, converting all the items to varchar2, and concatenating them into a single line. If the client fails to retrieve all lines before the next put, put_line, or new_line, the nonretrieved lines will be dis-carded. This is so if the client is interrupted while selecting back the information, there will not be junk left over which would look like it was part of the *next* set of lines. The output parameters have the following definitions:

line—This line will hold the line; it may be up to 255 bytes long.

status—This will be 0 upon successful completion of the call. 1 means that there are no more lines.

GET_LINES

The next procedure, get_lines, has a single input and a single output parameter: lines. The output is actually a PL/SQL type that corresponds to a scalar array of varchar2(255). The single input, numlines (integer), also doubles as an input so you can pass in however many lines you want the procedure to fetch and it passes back however many it got out of the buffer. The lines are delimited by calls to put_line or new_line. The line will be constructed taking all the items up to a newline, converting all the items to varchar2, and concatenating them into a single line. Once get_lines is executed, the client should continue to retrieve all lines because the next put, put_line, or new_line will first purge the buffer of leftover data. This is so if the client is interrupted while selecting back the information, there will not be junk values left over.

The get_lines procedure has the following input parameters:

numlines—This is the maximum number of lines that the caller is prepared to accept. The get_lines procedure will not return more than this number of lines.

The get_lines procedure has two outputs, one of which is actually a scalar array:

lines—This array will hold the lines; they may be up to 255 bytes long each. The array is indexed beginning with 0 and increases sequentially. From a 3GL host program the array begins with whatever is the convention for that language.

numlines—This will be the number of lines actually returned. If it is less than the value passed in, then there are no more lines.

9.6   DBMS_DESCRIBE

The DBMS_DESCRIBE package has one procedure: DBSM_DESCRIBE. This procedure is used by OCI calls to get data about procedures and functions. It is used internally to get the arguments required by procedures and functions. For more information, look at the Oracle OCI manual.

9.7   DBMS_MAIL

The DBMS_MAIL package is only used by ORACLE*MAIL and allows Oracle mail users to communicate with other Oracle mail users. For more information, look in the Oracle*Mail documentation. The package has one procedure: send. The header of the package (dbmsmail.sql) has fairly complete instructions for the installation of the mail option.

9.8   DBMS_SHARED_POOL

The DBMS_SHARED_POOL package gives the DBA the ability to look into the shared pool and extract data about cursors, packages, procedures, and such that currently reside there. In addition, the package allows a DBA to "keep" or pin packages so they don't get aged out of the pool by the LRU algorithm. The package also allows for the "unpinning" of package and procedures as well. Supposedly this option is no longer needed in version 7.3 and greater versions of the database; however, Oracle still ships it with the Oracle8 product and for those who are on earlier versions its use is still valid.

I have seen several questions as to how to determine the size of objects in the shared pool, and how to keep the LRU algorithm from forcing objects out of the shared pool. The DBMS_SHARED_POOL package provides procedures to facilitate these actions.

SIZES

The procedure sizes accepts a single argument: minsize (number). The purpose of sizes is to show objects in the shared_pool that are larger than the specified size. The name of the object is also given, which can be used as an argument to either the 'keep' or 'unkeep' calls below. You should issue the SVRMGR or SQLPLUS 'set serveroutput on size xxxxx' (where xxxxx is size of the buffer you want to use) command prior to using this procedure so that the results will be displayed. The package uses the DBMS_OUTPUT package to display its results. The input argument minsize specifies the size, in kilobytes, an object must be larger than that which is in the shared pool, in order for it to be displayed.

KEEP

The procedure keep accepts two input parameters: name (varchar2), and flag (char(1) with a default value of 'P'). The purpose of keep is to flag an object to be kept in the shared pool. Once an object has been "keeped" in the shared pool, it is not subject to LRU aging out of the pool. This is useful for certain semifrequently used large objects since when large objects are brought into the shared pool, a larger number of other objects (much more than the size of the object being brought in, may need to be aged out in order to create a contiguous area that's large enough.

W̲ARNING   This procedure may not be supported in the future when and if automatic mechanisms are implemented to make this unnecessary.

The procedure keep has the following input arguments:

name—This is the name of the object to keep. There are two types of objects: PL/SQL objects, which are specified by name, and SQL cursor objects, which are specified by a two-part number (indicating a location in the shared pool). For example:

```
dbms_shared_pool.keep('scott.hispackage')
```

will keep package HISPACKAGE, owned by SCOTT. The names for PL/SQL objects follow SQL rules for naming objects (i.e., delimited identifiers, multibyte names, etc. are allowed).

A cursor can be keeped by:

```
dbms_shared_pool.keep('0034CDFF, 20348871')
```

The complete hexadecimal address must be in the first 8 characters. The value for this identifier is the concatenation of the 'address' and 'hash_value' columns from the v$sqlarea view. This is displayed by the 'sizes' call above.

Currently, 'TABLE' and 'VIEW' objects may not be keeped.

flag—This is an optional parameter. If the parameter is not specified, the package assumes that the first parameter is the name of a package and will resolve the name. It can also be set to 'P' or 'p' to fully specify that the input is the name of a package. In case the first argument is a cursor address and hash-value, the parameter should be set to any character except 'P' or 'p'.

The procedure can handle the following exception:

An exception will be raised if the named object cannot be found.

UNKEEP

The next procedure in the package is the unkeep procedure. The unkeep procedure has the following input parameters: name (varchar2), and flag (char(1) with a default value of 'P'). The purpose of the unkeep procedure is to unkeep the named object that has been previously kept by issuing a call to keep against it.

W ARNING   This procedure may not be supported in the future when and if automatic mechanisms are implemented to make this obsolete.

The unkeep input arguments are as follows:

name—This is the name of the object to unkeep. See description of the name object for the keep procedure.

flag—This is the flag that tells Oracle if this is a kept procedure or cursor. See description for the keep procedure.

The unkeep procedure has the following exception:

An exception will be raised if the named object cannot be found.

ABORTED_REQUEST_THRESHOLD

The last procedure in the package is aborted_request_threshold, which has a single input parameter: threshold_size (number). This package is used to set aborted request threshold for the shared pool. The input argument threshold_size specifies the size in bytes of a request which will not try to free unpinned (not "unkeep-ed") memory within the shared pool. The range of threshold_size is 5000 to ~2 GB inclusive.

Let's discuss the actual purpose of this procedure in a bit more detail. Usually, if a request cannot be satisfied based on the SGA free list, the RDBMS will try to reclaim memory by freeing objects from the SGA LRU list and checking periodically to see if the request can be fulfilled. After finishing this step, the RDBMS has performed a near equivalent of an alter system flush shared_pool. As this flush operation impacts all users on the system, this procedure "localizes" the impact to the process failing to find a piece of shared pool memory of size greater than threshold_size.

The procedure raises the following exception:

An exception will be raised if threshold is not in the valid range.

Views

DBA_KEEPSIZES The DBMS_SHARED_POOL creation script create a single view called DBA_KEEPSIZES, which has the following structure:

ColumnColumn Name	Null?	Type
TOTSIZE	NUMBER	
OWNER	NOT NULL	VARCHAR2(30)
NAME	NOT NULL	VARCHAR2(30)

9.9   DBMS_SNAPSHOT

The DBMS_SNAPSHOT package allows DBAs to control the snapshot processes. With this package you can force refreshes on single or all snapshots that need it, purge log files, and in general maintain snapshots. The functionality provided via DBMS_SNAPSHOT and DBMS_REFRESH (both of which are created by DBMSSNAP.SQL and UTILSNAP.SQL) includes:

purge_log—Purge log of unnecessary rows.

refresh—Refresh a given snapshot.

refresh_all—Refresh all snapshots that are due to be refreshed.

drop_snapshot—Drop a given snapshot.

set_up—Prepare master site to refresh a snapshot.

wrap_up—Record a refresh at the master site.

get_log_age—Find oldest date entry in log.

testing—Test snapshots (currently null).

I_am_a_refresh flag—Used to let triggers identify refreshes.

None of the functions in either package assert purity, so if you have a need to use them in other packages you will have to modify the appropriate header files to insert pragma calls, as was shown at the beginning of this chapter.

Let's take a more detailed look at DBMS_SNAP and DBMS_REFRESH, starting with DBMS_SNAP.

DBMS_SNAP Procedures and Functions

The procedure purge_log has the input parameters: master (VARCHAR2), num (BINARY_INTEGER with a DEFAULT of 1), and flag (VARCHAR2 with a DEFAULT of 'NOP'). The purpose of this procedure is to purge a snapshot log of unnecessary rows.

The procedure input parameter definitions are as follows:

master—This is the name of the master table for the snapshot.

num—This is the number of the least recently refreshed snapshots whose rows you want to remove from the snapshot log. Here is the command to delete the rows needed to refresh at least the three least recently refreshed snapshots:

```
EXECUTE dbms_snapshot.purge_log('master name', 3);
To do all of the rows, make num an outlandishly high value:
EXECUTE dbsm_snapshot.puge_log('master name',999999);
```

A simple snapshot whose rows have been purged from its log will have to have the COMPLETE refresh method used the next time it is refreshed.

flag—Normally this is set to NOP; it can also be set to 'DELETE', which will delete all rows from the snapshot log for the least recently refreshed snapshot with dependent rows in the snapshot log, for example:

```
EXECUTE dbms_snapshot.puge_log('master name', 0, 'DELETE');
```

REFRESH The procedure refresh has the input parameters:

list	VARCHAR2
method	VARCHAR2 with a DEFAULT of NULL
rollback_seg	VARCHAR2 with a DEFAULT of NULL
push_deferred_rpc	BOOLEAN with a DEFAULT of TRUE
refresh_after_errors	BOOLEAN with a DEFAULT of FALSE
execute_as_user	BOOLEAN with a DEFAULT of FALSE

The procedure's purpose is to perform a transaction-consistent refresh of an array of snapshots. The snapshots are refreshed atomically and consistently.

- Atomically: all snapshots are refreshed or none are.
- Consistently: all integrity constraints that hold among master tables will hold among the snapshot tables.

The procedure's input values are defined as follows:

list—This is a comma-separated list of snapshots to refresh. No synonyms are allowed. The snapshots in the list can have different schemas and master tables but all must be in the current database. The procedure is overloaded so you can also use a PL/SQL table of type DBMS_UTILITY.UNCL_ARRAY where each table entry is a snapshot name.

method—This string (not required) should contain a letter for each of the snapshots in the array according to the following codes:

'**?**'—Use fast refresh when possible.

'**F**'—Use fast refresh or raise an error if not possible.

'**C**'—Perform a complete refresh, copying the entire snapshot from the master.

The default method for refreshing a snapshot is the method stored for that snapshot in the data dictionary. The maximum number of snapshots that can be consistently refreshed is 100.

Rollback_seg—This is the name of the rollback segment to use while refreshing snapshots.

Push_deferred_rpc—If set to TRUE, pushes changes from an updatable snapshot to its associated master before refreshing the snapshot. Otherwise, these changes may appear to be temporarily lost.

Refresh_after_errors—If TRUE, will allow the refresh to proceed even if there are outstanding conflicts logged in the DefError table for the snapshot's master.

Execute_as_user—If set to TRUE, the execution of deferred RPCs is authenticated at the remote system using the authentication context of the session user. If

FALSE, the execution of deferred RPCs is authenticated at the remote system using the authentication contexts of the users that originally queued the deferred RPCs (indicated in the origin_user column of the deftran table).

REFRESH_ALL The procedure refresh_all has no arguments. The purpose of the procedure is to force a refresh of all snapshots due to be refreshed. The user calling the procedure must have the ALTER ANY SNAPSHOT privilege.

SET_I_AM_A_REFRESH The procedure set_i_am_a_refresh has one input parameter value (BOOLEAN). The purpose of the procedure is to disable all local replication triggers for snapshots at the current site. An example of how to do this is:

```
SQL> EXECUTE dbms_snapshot.set_i_am_a_refresh(value=> TRUE);
```

To reenable the local replication triggers, issue the above with a value of FALSE.

I_AM_A_REFRESH The function i_am_a_refresh has no inputs and returns a boolean value of TRUE or FALSE depending upon whether SET_I_AM_A_REFRESH has been run and has set REP$WHAT_AM_I.I_AM_A_SNAPSHOT to TRUE or FALSE. For example, assuming that ref_stat is defined as a boolean:

```
SQL> declare
2      ref_stat boolean;
3      begin
4      begin
5      ref_stat := dbms_snapshot.i_am_refresh;
6      end;
7      /
```

DROP_SNAPSHOT The procedure drop_snapshot has the following input values:

mowner	varchar2
master	varchar2
snapshot	date

The purpose of this procedure is to drop a given data snapshot. The procedure's input variables are defined as:

mowner—This is the master table owner.

master—This is the name of the master table.

snapshot—This is the date of the snapshot refresh to drop.

SET_UP The procedure set_up has the following input and output variables:

Input:
mowner   varchar2
master   varchar2

Both input and output:

log   varchar2
snapshot   date
snaptime   date

This is an internal-use-only procedure. The purpose of this procedure is to prepare a master site to refresh a snapshot. You as a DBA will never use this procedure.

WRAP_UP The procedure wrap_up has the following input parameters:

mowner   varchar2
master   varchar2
sshot   date
stime   date

This is an internal-use-only procedure. The procedure's purpose is to record a refresh at the master site. As a DBA you will never use this procedure directly.

GET_LOG_AGE The procedure get_log_age has the following input/output parameters:
Both input and output:

oldest   date

Input:
mow   VARCHAR2

This internal-use procedure finds the oldest date entry in the snapshot log specified. As a DBA you will never use this procedure directly.

DBMS_REFRESH Procedures and Functions

The dbms_refresh package is the interface for administering refresh groups.

MAKE The procedure make has the following input variables:

name	varchar2
list	varchar2 or as tab and a dbms_utility.uncl_array
next_date	date
interval	varchar2
implicit_destroy	boolean default FALSE
lax	boolean default FALSE
job	binary_integer default 0
rollback_seg	varchar2 default NULL
push_deferred_rpc	boolean default TRUE
refresh_after_errors	boolean default FALSE

The procedure's function is to make a new refresh group. The procedure's input variables are defined as:

name—The unique name used to identify the refresh group. Use the same naming conventions as for tables.

list or tab—This is the comma-separated list of snapshots to include in the group. This can also be a PL/SQL table of type DBMS_UTILITY.UNCL_ARRAY.

next_date—This is the next date you want this group to be refreshed.

interval—This is the function used to calculate the next time to refresh the group. The field is used with the NEXT_DATE value. For example, if the value is specified to be:

```
NEXT_DAY(SYSDATE+1,"MONDAY")
```

and the value you entered for next date was a Monday then you will refresh every Monday.

implicit_destroy—Set this flag if you want the group dropped once it has no members. The flag is only checked when the SUBTRACT procedure is run. This allows the creation of empty groups if needed.

lax—This is used when a snapshot is moved from one group to another. A snapshot is not allowed to exist in more than one group. Setting this parameter to TRUE allows the creation of the other group entry and Oracle will automatically remove the laxed entry.

job—This value is used but the import utility always sets it to its default value of 0 (zero).

rollback_seg—This is the name of the rollback segment to use for this refresh group.

push_defferred_rpc—This is used by updatable snapshots only. Use the default value, TRUE, to push changes from the snapshot to its master before a refresh is performed.

refresh_after_errors—This is used by updatable snapshots only. TRUE allows refreshes even if defError has registered conflicts for the snapshots' masters.

ADD The procedure add has the following input parameters:

name	varchar2
list	varchar2
lax	boolean with a default value of FALSE

The procedure's purpose is to add snapshots to a specified refresh group. The procedure's input parameters are defined as follows:

name—This is the name of the refresh group you want to add members to.

list or tab—This is the comma-separated list, or PL/SQL table of the type DBMS_UTILITY.UNCL_ARRAY of snapshots to add to the group.

lax—To move a snapshot from one group to another, specify this as TRUE.

SUBTRACT The procedure subtract has the following input parameters:

name	varchar2
list or tab	varchar2 or DBMS_UTILITY.UNCL_ARRAY
lax	boolean with a default of FALSE

The purpose of subtract is to remove some refreshable objects from a refresh group. The parameters have the same definition as in the ADD procedure. The exception is that lax now determines if you get an error if the requested snapshot to be removed isn't a member of the refresh group. Setting lax to FALSE will give you the error if this situation occurs.

DESTROY The procedure destroy has one input parameter: name (varchar2). This procedure removes all the snapshots from the specified group and destroys the group. The group is specified as an input via the name parameter.

CHANGE The procedure change has the same input parameters as the make procedure with the exception that no list or tab values can be specified. The procedure is used to change any changeable pieces of the job that does the refresh.

REFRESH The procedure refresh accepts one input parameter: name (varchar2). The procedure atomically and consistently refreshes all objects in the named refresh group immediately and clears the BROKEN flag for the job if the refresh succeeds.

USER_EXPORT The procedure user_export accepts a single input parameter, rg# (binary_integer), and produces an output of mycall (varchar2). The purpose of this procedure is to produce the text of a call for recreating the given group. The parameter rg# is the number of the refresh group that is to be exported.

USER_EXPORT_CHILD The procedure user_export_child accepts the following input parameters:

myowner	varchar2
myname	varchar2
mytype	varchar2

and produces the following output:

mycall	varchar2

The purpose of the procedure is to produce the text of a call for recreating the given group item.

9.10 DBMS_SQL

In my opinion, the DBMS_SQL package is one of the most useful for DBAs and developers. The DBMS_SQL package allows the use of dynamic SQL from within PL/SQL. This allows generic procedures and functions to be created that are dynamic; that is, you can specify their logic or variables at runtime. One problem with the package is that none of its functions assert purity, so you may want to modify the header file to include pragma calls, as was shown at the beginning of this chapter.

Before we look at the individual procedures, let's look at an extract of the rules and limitations on the use of the DBMS_SQL procedures and functions as set down in the package header:

1. Bind variables of a SQL statement are identified by their names.
2. When binding a value to a bind variable, the string identifying the bind variable in the statement may optionally contain the leading colon. For example, if the parsed SQL statement is:

```
"SELECT ENAME FROM EMP WHERE SAL > :X"
```

on binding the variable to a value, it can be identified using either of the strings ':X' and 'X'.
3. Columns of the row being selected in a SELECT statement are identified by their relative positions (1, 2, 3, . . .) as they appear on the select list from left to right. Columns and their alias value count as one position.

4. Privileges are associated with the caller of the procedures/functions in this package as follows:

   a. If the caller is an anonymous PL/SQL block, the procedures/functions are run using the privileges of the current user.

   b. If the caller is a stored procedure, the procedures/functions are run using the privileges of the owner of the stored procedure.

WARNING   Using the package to dynamically execute DDL statements can result in the program hanging. For example, a call to a procedure in a package will result in the package being locked until the execution returns to the user side. Any operation that results in a conflicting lock, such as dynamically trying to drop the package before the first lock is released, will result in a hang. Use the dbms_utility.execute_ddl procedure instead.

The flow of procedure calls will typically look like Figure 9.1.

The parse procedure requires the following constants to be defined. These are automatically set up by the header script when it is executed by CATPROC.SQL. The value of the constant tells DBMS_SQL what level of SQL to expect.

Constant	*Value*
v6	0
native	1
v7	2

OPEN_CURSOR

The function open_cursor has no input parameters and returns an integer value that equates to the handle for the opened cursor location. This handle will be used in all subsequent operations involved with this cursor.

When the cursor created with open_cursor is no longer needed, the cursor must be closed explicitly by calling the procedure "close_cursor." This function doesn't assert its purity so there may be difficulty in using it in other packages.

IS_OPEN

The function is_open has one input parameter: c. The parameter c is an integer value corresponding to the return from the open_cursor function. The is_open function returns a boolean value (TRUE or FALSE) that corresponds to whether or not the referenced cursor is open or closed respectively. This function is used to perform an iden-

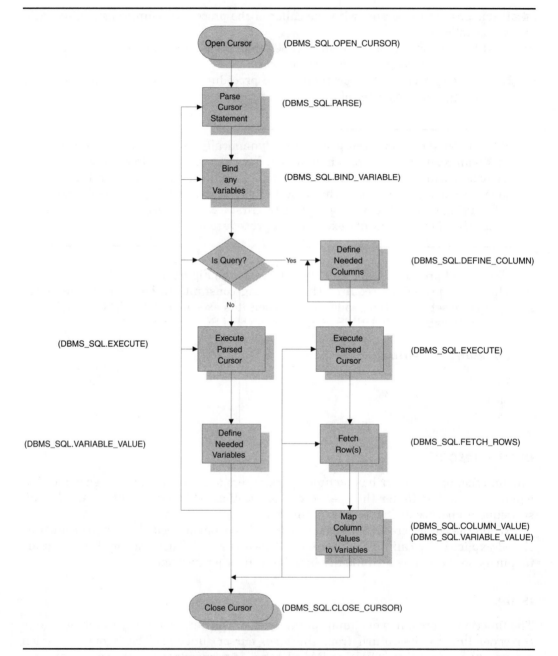

FIGURE 9.1 DBMS_SQL Process Flow.

tical check to that done by the %ISOPEN cursor variable but for the cursors handled by DBMS_SQL only. This function doesn't assert its purity, so there may be difficulties using it in other packages.

CLOSE_CURSOR

The procedure close_cursor uses the parameter c as both an input and output integer value. The purpose of the procedure is to close the given cursor. The input parameter c corresponds to the cursor id number of the cursor to close. On successful closure, c will be nulled.

PARSE

The procedure parse accepts three input parameters: c (integer), statement (varchar2), and language_flag (integer). The purpose of the procedure is to parse the given statement in the given cursor.

WARNING Parsing and executing ddl statements can cause hangs! Use the DBMS_UTILITY.EXECUTE_DDL procedure instead.

Currently, the deferred parsing feature of the Oracle Call Interface is not used. As a result, statements are parsed immediately. In addition, DDL statements are executed immediately when parsed. However, this behavior may change in the future so that the actual parsing (and execution of DDL statement) does not occur until the cursor is executed with "execute." *Do not rely on the current timing of the actual parsing!* The procedure input parameters are defined as follows:

c—This is the cursor id number of the cursor in which to parse the statement (from DBMS_SQL.OPEN_CURSOR).

statement—This is the statement to parse. *Do not include a trailing semi_colon (;).*

language_flag—Specifies behavior for statement. Valid values are v6, v7, and NATIVE; v6 and v7 specify behavior according to version 6 and Oracle7, respectively. NATIVE specifies behavior according to the version of the database the program is connected to. Under Oracle7 I always use DBMS_SQL.V7; for Oracle8 use DBMS_SQL.NATIVE.

BIND_VARIABLE

The procedure bind_variable has three input parameters: c (integer), name (varchar2), and value (number, varchar2, integer, date, mlslabel). Note that the value parameter is overloaded to accept multiple input data types. The procedure also has several clones that allow input of other datatypes. These clones are:

bind_variable_char(c in integer, name in varchar2, value in char, out_value_size in integer);

bind_variable_raw(c in integer, name in varchar2, value in raw, out_value_size in integer);

bind_variable_rowid(c in integer, name in varchar2, value in rowid);

(Note the addition of the "out_value_size" input parameter for the bind_variable_char and bind_variable_raw procedures.)

The purpose of the procedure is to bind the given value to the variable identified by its name in the parsed statement in the given cursor. If the variable is an in or in/out variable, the given bind value should be a valid one. If the variable is an out variable, the given bind value is ignored.

The procedure's input parameters are defined as follows:

c—This is the cursor id number of the cursor to bind.

name—This is the name of the variable *in the statement*.

value—This is the value to bind to the variable *in the cursor*. If the variable is an out or in/out variable, its type is the same as the type of the value being passed in for this parameter.

out_value_size—This is the maximum expected out value size in bytes for the varchar2 out or in/out variable. If it is not given for the varchar2 out or in/out variable, the size is the length of the current "value".

DEFINE_COLUMN

The procedure define_column accepts up to four input parameters depending on the type of column being defined: c (integer), position (integer), column (number, varchar2, date, mlslabel), and for varchar2 columns, column_size (integer). The procedure also has several clones for other data types:

define_column_char(c in integer, position in integer, column in char, column_size in integer);

define_column_raw(c in integer, position in integer, column in raw, column_size in integer);

define_column_rowid(c in integer, position in integer, column in rowid);

define_column_long(c in integer, position in integer);

The purpose of this procedure is to define a column to be selected from the given cursor; so this procedure is applicable only to SELECT cursors (see Figure 9.1). The column being defined is identified by its relative position as it appears on the select list in the statement in the given cursor. The type of the column to be defined is the type of the value being passed in for parameter "column".

The procedure's input parameters are defined as follows:

c—This is the cursor id number of the cursor to define the row to be selected (returned from the DBMS_SQL.OPEN_CURSOR call).

position—Position of the column in the row being defined. Note that a column and its alias count as one position.

column—The type of the local variable value being passed in for this parameter is the type of the column to be defined.

column_size—This is the maximum expected size of the value in bytes for the varchar2, raw or char column.

EXECUTE

The function execute accepts one input parameter, c (integer), and returns an integer that corresponds to the number of rows acted upon by the execute call. The purpose of the function is to execute the given cursor and return the number of rows processed for INSERT, DELETE, or UPDATE statements; for other types of statements, the return value is undefined and should be ignored. The single input value is the value returned from the DBMS_SQL.OPEN_CURSOR call and used in the subsequent call to DBMS_SQL.PARSE. Only cursors which have opened and parsed can be executed (see Figure 9.1).

FETCH_ROWS

The function fetch_rows accepts a single input parameter, c (integer), and returns an integer value that corresponds to the number of rows fetched. The purpose of the function is to fetch rows from the given cursor. The function tries to fetch a row as long as "fetch_rows" is able to fetch a row; it can be called repeatedly to fetch additional rows. If no row was actually fetched, "fetch_rows" cannot be called to fetch additional rows. Use the return value from DBMS_SQL.FETCH_ROWS to control the number of fetches performed. The DBMS_SQL.EXECUTE_AND_FETCH function can take the place of the first call to the execute and fetch functions.

EXECUTE_AND_FETCH

The function execute_and_fetch accepts two input parameters: c (integer) and exact (boolean with a default value of false). The function returns an integer value that corresponds to the number of rows actually fetched.

The purpose of the function is to execute the given cursor and fetch rows. It gives the same functionality as a call to "execute" followed by a call to "fetch_rows". However, this function can potentially cut down on the number of message round-trips compared to calling "execute" and "fetch_rows" separately.

The function's input parameters are defined as follows:

c—This is the cursor id from DBMS_SQL.OPEN_CURSOR, which is the number of the cursor to execute and fetch.

exact—If set to TRUE, will raise an exception if the number of rows matching the query differs from 1.

COLUMN_VALUE

The procedure column_value accepts up to five input and output parameters:

Input:

c	integer
position	integer

Output:

value	number, varchar2, date, mlslabel
column_error	number
actual_length	integer

The procedure also has several clones to support other data types:

column_value_char(c in integer, position in integer, value out char);

column_value_raw(c in integer, position in integer, value out raw);

column_value_rowid(c in integer, position in integer, value out rowid);

column_value_long(c in integer, position in integer, length in integer, offset in integer, value out varchar2, value_length out integer);

The clones also support the additional output parameters column_error and actual_length as needed.

The purpose of the procedure is to get the value of the column identified by the given position in the specified cursor. This procedure is used to access the data retrieved by "fetch_rows".

The procedure's input parameters are defined as follows:

c—This is the cursor id number returned by the DBMS_SQL.OPEN_CURSOR call and corresponds to the number of the cursor from which to get the value.

position—This is the position of the column from which to get the value. A column and its alias take one position only.

The procedure's output parameters are defined as follows:

value—This is the value of the column.

column_error—This is any column error code associated with "value".

actual_length—This is the actual length of "value" in the table before any truncation that may have occured during the fetch.

The procedure may raise the following exception:

inconsistent_type (ORA-06562)

This is raised if the type of the given out parameter value is different from the actual type of the value. This type was the given type when the column was defined by calling procedure dbms_sql.define_column.

VARIABLE_VALUE

The procedure variable_value has the following input and output parameters :

Input:

c	integer
name	varchar2,

Output:

value	number, varchar2, date, mlslabel, char, rowid, raw

The purpose of the procedure is to get a value or values of the variable identified by the name and the given cursor value. The procedure dbms_sql.bind_variable must have been run against the variable and column specifications for the cursor id number in order for calls to this procedure to be valid.

The procedure's input parameters are defined as follows:

c—This is the cursor id number defined by the call to DBMS_SQL.OPEN_CURSOR of the cursor from which to get the value.

name—This is the name of the variable for which to get the value.

The procedure's output parameter is defined as:

value—This is the value of the returned variable.

The procedure may raise the following exception:

inconsistent_type (ORA-06562)

This is raised if the type of the given out parameter "value" is different from the actual type of the value. This type was the given type when the variable was bound by calling procedure "bind_variable".

Miscellaneous Cursor Functions

The DBMS_SQL package has the following cursor-related functions:

last_error_position—This returns an integer that corresponds to the position in the parsed statement where the last error occured.

last_sql_function_code—This returns an integer value that corresponds to the code that corresponds to the last SQL function executed.

last_row_count—This returns an integer value that corresponds to the number of rows operated on by the last SQL call.

last_row_id—This returns the rowid of the last row operated on by the cursor.

These functions all get various information for the last-operated cursor in the session. To ensure that the information relates to a particular cursor, the functions should be called after an operation on that cursor and before any other operation on any other cursor. None of these functions have purity asserted, so they are only applicable to the current package (DBMS_SQL) and may cause errors if you attempt to use them in other packages. You can get around this by adding the appropriate pragma calls to the package header for each function.

The return values for each function are defined as follows:

last_error_position—This returns the relative position in the statement when the error occurs.

last_sql_function_code—This returns the SQL function code of the statement. See the list in Table 9.7.

last_row_count—This returns the cumulative count of rows fetched.

last_row_id—This returns the rowid of the last processed row.

TABLE 9.7   Codes and SQL Functions

Code	SQL Function	Code	SQL Function
1	CREATE TABLE	11	ALTER INDEX
2	INSERT	12	DROP TABLE
3	SELECT	13	CREATE SEQUENCE
4	CREATE CLUSTER	14	ALTER SEQUENCE
5	ALTER CLUSTER	15	ALTER TABLE
6	UPDATE	16	DROP SEQUENCE
7	DELETE	17	GRANT
8	DROP CLUSTER	18	REVOKE
9	CREATE INDEX	19	CREATE SYNONYM
10	DROP INDEX	20	DROP SYNONYM

continued

TABLE 9.7 (Continued)

Code	SQL Function	Code	SQL Function
21	CREATE VIEW	63	ANALYZE INDEX
22	DROP VIEW	64	ANALYZE CLUSTER
23	VALIDATE INDEX	65	CREATE PROFILE
24	CREATE PROCEDURE	66	DROP PROFILE
25	ALTER PROCEDURE	67	ALTER PROFILE
26	LOCK TABLE	68	DROP PROCEDURE
27	NO OPERATION	69	(NOT USED)
28	RENAME	70	ALTER RESOURCE COST
29	COMMENT	71	CREAT SNAPSHOT LOG
30	AUDIT	72	ALTER SNAPSHOT LOG
31	NOAUDIT	73	DROP SNAPSHOT LOG
32	CREATE DATABASE LINK	74	CREATE SNAPSHOT
33	DROP DATABASE LINK	75	ALTER SNAPSHOT
34	CREATE DATABASE	76	DROP SNAPSHOT
35	ALTER DATABASE	77	CREATE TYPE
36	CREATE ROLLBACK SEGMENT	78	DROP TYPE
37	ALTER ROLLBACK SEGMENT	79	ALTER ROLE
38	DROP ROLLBACK SEGMENT	80	ALTER TYPE
39	CREATE TABLESPACE	81	CREATE TYPE BODY
40	ALTER TABLESPACE	82	ALTER TYPE BODY
41	DROP TABLESPACE	83	DROP TYPE BODY
42	ALTER SESSION	84	DROP LIBRARY
43	ALTER USER	85	TRUNCATE TABLE
44	COMMIT	86	TRUNCATE CLUSTER
45	ROLLBACK	87	CREATE BITMAPFILE
46	SAVEPOINT	88	ALTER VIEW
47	PL/SQL EXECUTE	89	DROP BITMAPFILE
48	SET TRANSACTION	90	SET CONSTRAINTS
49	ALTER SYSTEM SWITCH LOG	91	CREATE FUNCTION
52	CREATE ROLE	92	ALTER FUNCTION
53	DROP USER	93	DROP FUNCTION
54	DROP ROLE	94	CREATE PACKAGE
55	SET ROLE	95	ALTER PACKAGE
56	CREATE SCHEMA	96	DROP PACKAGE
57	CREATE CONTROL FILE	97	CREATE PACKAGE BODY
58	ALTER TRACING	98	ALTER PACKAGE BODY
59	CREATE TRIGGER	99	DROP PACKAGE BODY
60	ALTER TRIGGER	157	CREATE DIRECTORY
61	DROP TRIGGER	158	DROP DIRECTORY
62	ANALYZE TABLE	159	CREATE LIBRARY

9.11   DBMS_JOB

The DBMS_JOB package allows control of the Oracle job queues. Oracle job queues allow DBAs to schedule, execute, and eliminate jobs from within Oracle itself independent of the operating system queuing mechanisms. The job queue:

1. Runs user-defined routines from background processes (or directly in the user's process).
2. Runs the jobs at user-defined times (or reasonably soon afterwards).
3. Runs a given job repeatedly at user-defined intervals (or just once, then the job deletes itself).
4. Runs the jobs in the same environment they were submitted in (except with the user's default roles and privileges).
5. Reports errors, and does exponential backoff.
6. Allows the user to identify and administer these jobs.

DBMS_JOB and DBMS_IJOB are the only interface for manipulating jobs. Queries against the catalog should be used for examining jobs. The catalog views dba_jobs and dba_jobs_running are in catjobq.sql (run from catproc.sql). Out of all these routines, only dbms_job.run and dbms_ijob.run have implicit commits.

There are no kernel privileges associated with jobs. The right to execute dbms_job or dbms_ijob takes their place. The dbms_job package does not allow users to touch any jobs but their own.

1. See the parameter WHAT in the specification for dbms_job for a description of legal jobs.

The background processes are specified by initialization parameters in the init<SID>.ora file; the parameters that control the job queue processes are (values shown are for example only):

```
job_queue_processes=3    #for three background processes
job_queue_interval=30    #wake up every 30 seconds
job_queue_keep_connections=TRUE  #sleep, don't disconnect
```

2. See NEXT_DATE in the specification for dbms_job.
3. See INTERVAL in the specification for dbms_job.
4. All the parameters that can be set with ALTER SESSION are stored when a job is created (or when WHAT is changed), and they are restored when the job is run. See the view definition for dba_jobs in Table 9.8.
5. When dbms_job.run( ) or dbms_ijob.run( ) encounters an error, the complete errorstack is dumped to a trace file and an alert file. If dbms_ijob.run( ) was used, the number of jobs that ran with errors is reported to the user.
6. Jobs are identified by job number. Jobs can be exported and imported again, and the job number will remain the same.

TABLE 9.8   Description of view dba_ jobs

Name	Null?	Type	Description
JOB	NOT NULL	NUMBER	Identifier of the job. Export/import nor repeat executions change it.
LOG_USER	NOT NULL	VARCHAR2(30)	User who was logged in when job was submitted.
PRIV_USER	NOT NULL	VARCHAR2(30)	User whose default privileges apply to job.
SCHEMA_USER	NOT NULL	VARCHAR2(30)	Schema job executes in.
LAST_DATE		DATE	Last successful execution.
LAST_SEC		VARCHAR2(8)	Same as last_date.
THIS_DATE		DATE	Date this job started (null if job isn't executing).
THIS_SEC		VARCHAR2(8)	Same as this_date.
NEXT_DATE	NOT NULL	DATE	Next execution date.
NEXT_SEC		VARCHAR2(8)	Same as next_date.
TOTAL_TIME		NUMBER	Total clock time spent executing this job last time it was executed.
BROKEN		VARCHAR2(1)	If Y, don't execute.
INTERVAL	NOT NULL	VARCHAR2(200)	A date function that determines next_date.
FAILURES		NUMBER	How many failures since last successful execute.
WHAT		VARCHAR2(2000)	Body of anonymous PL/SQL that this job executes.
CURRENT_SESSION_LABEL		RAW MLSLABEL	Trusted Oracle label of current job session.
CLEARANCE_HI		RAW MLSLABEL	Highest level of clearance available to the job.
CLEARANCE_LO		RAW MLSLABEL	Lowest level of clearance available to the job.
NLS_ENV		VARCHAR2(2000)	Alter session parameters describing the nls environment of the job.
MISC_ENV		RAW(32)	A versioned raw maintained by the kernel to track other session parameters.

ISUBMIT

The procedure isubmit has the following input parameters:

job	binary_integer
what	varchar2
next_date	varchar2
interval	varchar2 with a default of 'null'
no_parse	boolean with a default of FALSE.

The purpose of ISUBMIT is to create a job with the given job number. The procedure's input parameters are defined as follows:

job—This is the number of the job being executed.

what—This is the PL/SQL procedure to execute.The job must always be a single call to a procedure. The routine may take any number of hardcoded parameters. Always remember the trailing semicolon. Some legal values of WHAT (assuming the routines exist) are:

'myproc("10-JAN-82", next_date, broken);'

'scott.emppackage.give_raise("JENKINS", 30000.00);'

'dbms_ job.remove(job);'

broken—This is in the form of in/out, is the job broken. The IN value is FALSE.

next_date—This is the date at which the job will next be automatically run, assuming there are background processes attempting to run it.

interval—This is a date function, evaluated immediately before the job starts executing. If the job completes successfully, this new date is placed in next_date. interval is evaluated by plugging it into the statement select interval into next_date from dual; interval must evaluate to a time in the future. legal intervals include:

'sysdate + 7'—Execute once a week.

'next_day(sysdate,"tuesday")'—Execute once every Tuesday.

'null'—Only execute once.

If interval evaluates to null and a job completes successfully, then the job is automatically deleted from the queue.

no_parse—This is either a TRUE or FALSE value. If NO_PARSE is set to FALSE (the default), Oracle parses the procedure associated with the job. If NO_PARSE is set to TRUE, Oracle parses the procedure associated with the job the first time that the job is executed. If, for example, you want to submit a job before you have created the tables associated with the job, set NO_PARSE to TRUE.

SUBMIT

The procedure submit is virtually identical with ISUBMIT except that SUBMIT pulls the value of JOB from the sequence JOBSEQ, whereas you must submit a value for JOB to ISUBMIT. The procedure has these input and output parameters:

Output:

job	binary_integer

Input:

what	varchar2 (Always end WHAT with a semi colon)
next_date	date with a default of sysdate
interval	varchar2 with a default of 'null'
no_parse	boolean with a default of FALSE

The purpose of the procedure is to submit a new job. Unlike ISUBMIT, SUBMIT chooses JOB from the sequence sys.jobseq. For example,

```
SQL> variable x number;
SQL> execute
dbms_job.submit(:x,'pack.proc(''arg1'');',sysdate,'sysdate+1');
```

The :x definition is required because JOB is defined as IN OUT.

With the difference in JOB being as noted, the definitions for the SUBMIT parameters are identical to those for ISUBMIT.

REMOVE

The procedure remove has a single input parameter: job (binary_integer). The purpose of the procedure is to remove an existing job from the job queue. As of Oracle version 8.0.2 this procedure does not stop a running job. An example of its use, assuming the job number is 16975, would be:

```
SQL> execute dbms_job.remove(16975);
```

The job number can be found by querying the DBA_JOBS view (Table 9.8). For example, let's say you want to delete all jobs with a status of broken (a value of "Y" in broken tells Oracle not to attempt to run the job; something may be wrong with it— i.e., it is broken):

```
SQL> select job from dba_jobs where broken='Y';
```

Then you would take the listed job numbers and submit them into the remove procedure. Of course, if you really want to get tricky you can use dynamic SQL via the DBMS_SQL package to do all of the calls automatically.

CHANGE

The procedure change has the following input parameters:

job	binary_integer
what	varchar2
next_date	date
interval	varchar2.

The purpose of the procedure is to change any of the user-settable fields in a job. If what, next_date, or interval is null, leave that value as is. An example of the use of this procedure would be:

```
SQL> execute dbms_job.change( 16795, null, null, 'sysdate+2');
```

The procedure's input parameters are defined identically to those in ISUBMIT.

WHAT

The procedure what has two input parameters: job (binary_integer) and what (varchar2). The procedure's purpose is to change what an existing job does, and replace its environment. You specify an existing job and with a change to "what" point the job number at a different procedure to be executed.

NEXT_DATE

The procedure next_date has two input parameters: job (binary_integer) and next_date (date). The procedure is used to change when an existing job will next execute by simply specifying a new future date in the "next_date" input location.

INTERVAL

The procedure interval accepts two input parameters: job (binary_integer) and interval (varchar2). The purpose of the procedure is to change how often a job executes. Example values for interval are:

'sysdate + 7'	execute once a week
'next_day(sysdate,"tuesday")'	execute once every Tuesday
'null'	only execute once

BROKEN

The procedure broken has three input parameters: job (binary_integer), broken (boolean), and next_date (date with a default of SYSDATE). The purpose of the procedure is to set the broken flag. Broken jobs are never run. A value of TRUE for the broken parameter equates to an entry of "Y" in the DBA_JOBS view.

RUN

The procedure run has a single input parameter: job (binary_integer). The purpose of the procedure is to run the specified job now. This will force a run of the specified job even if it is broken. Running the job will recompute next_date (see the section on view user_jobs). An example of the use of this procedure would be:

```
SQL> execute dbms_job.run(16795);
```

W̶ARNING   This will reinitialize the current session's packages.

USER_EXPORT

The procedure user_export accepts a single input parameter, job (binary_integer), and produces a single output, mycall (varchar2). The purpose of the procedure is to produce the text of a call to recreate the given job.

CHECK_PRIVS

The procedure check_privs accepts a single input parameter: job (binary_integer). This is an internal-use procedure that checks the privileges used by the submitted job.

9.12   FURTHER DBA READING

Oracle8 Server Application Developer's Guide, Release 8.0, Beta2, Feb. 1997, Oracle Corp. (or latest release).

Advanced Oracle PL/SQL Programming With Packages, Steven Feuerstein, O'Reilly and Associates, Inc., 1996 .

Oracle Performance Tuning, 2nd Edition, Mark Gurry, Peter Corrigan, O'Reilly and Associates, Inc. 1996.

Building Intelligent Databases With Oracle PL/SQL, Triggers & Stored Procedures, Kevin T. Owens, 1996, Prentice Hall.

DBMS*.SQL package headers, most current release of Oracle.

CHAPTER **10**

The DBMS_UTILITY Series of Packages

The DBMS_UTILITIES set of packages provides several different types of utilities for use by the DBA and developers. See each section below for a discussion of each set of packaged procedures. All of the packages described below run with the privileges of calling user, rather than the package owner ('sys').

The procedures dbms_ddl.alter_compile and dbms_ddl.analyze_object commit the current transaction, perform the compilation, and then commit again.

The dbms_utility package is run-as-caller only for its name_resolve, compile_schema, and analyze_schema procedures. This package is not run-as-caller so that the SQL works correctly (runs as SYS). The privileges are checked via dbms_ddl.

10.1   DBMS_TRANSACTION

The DBMS_TRANSACTION package allows for transaction-level commands to be issued from within a PL/SQL routine. None of the functions in this package assert purity. If you need to use these functions in other packages, alter the package header as is shown at the beginning of this chapter.

READ_ONLY

The first procedure, read_only, has no arguments and is the PL/SQL equivalent of the SQL command:

```
SET TRANSACTION READ ONLY
```

READ_WRITE

The next procedure, read_write, has no arguments and is the PL/SQL equivalent of the SQL command:

```
SET TRANSACTION READ WRITE
```

ADVISE_ROLLBACK

The next procedure, advise_rollback, has no arguments and is the PL/SQL equivalent of the SQL command:

```
ALTER SESSION ADVISE ROLLBACK
```

ADVISE_NOTHING

The next procedure, advise_nothing, has no arguments and is the PL/SQL equivalent of the SQL command:

```
ALTER SESSION ADVISE NOTHING
```

ADVISE_COMMIT

The next procedure, advise_commit, has no arguments and is the PL/SQL equivalent of the SQL command:

```
ALTER SESSION ADVISE COMMIT
```

USE_ROLLBACK_SEGMENT

The next procedure, use_rollback_segment, has a single input parameter: rb_name (varchar2). The procedure is the PL/SQL equivalent of the SQL command:

```
SET TRANSACTION USE ROLLBACK SEGMENT <rb_seg_name>
```

The procedure has the input argument:

rb_name—This is the name of the rollback segment to use.

You may have to respecify this procedure call after calls to other DBMS_* utilities that perform commits. You should issue a commit just before calling this procedure or it won't take effect until you commit.

COMMIT_COMMENT

The procedure commit_comment has a single input parameter: cmnt (varchar2). This procedure is the PL/SQL equivalent of the SQL command:

```
COMMIT COMMENT <text>
```

where text would be the value of the cmnt argument. The procedure has the following input argument:

cmnt—This is the comment to associate with this commit.

COMMIT_FORCE

The procedure commit_force has two input parameters: xid (varchar2) and scn (varchar2, which defaults to null). The procedure is the PL/SQL equivalent of the SQL command:

```
COMMIT FORCE <text>, <number>
```

The procedure's input arguments are defined as follows:

xid—This is the local or global transaction id.
scn—This is the system change number.

COMMIT

The procedure commit has no arguments and is equivalent to the SQL command: COMMIT. The procedure is included here for completeness. This command is already implemented as part of PL/SQL.

SAVEPOINT

The procedure savepoint accepts a single input variable savept (varchar2). The procedure is the PL/SQL equivalent of the SQL command: SAVEPOINT <savepoint_name>. This is included here for completeness since this command is already implemented as part of PL/SQL.

The procedure has the following input argument:

savept—This is the savepoint identifier.

ROLLBACK

The procedure rollback has no arguments and is the PL/SQL equivalent of the SQL command: ROLLBACK . This procedure is here for completeness, since this command is already implemented as part of PL/SQL.

ROLLBACK_SAVEPOINT

The procedure rollback_savepoint has a single input parameter: savept (varchar2). The procedure is the PL/SQL equivalent of the SQL command:

```
ROLLBACK TO SAVEPOINT <savepoint_name> .
```

The procedure is here for completeness, since this command is already implemented as part of PL/SQL. The procedure has the following input argument:

savept—This is the savepoint identifier.

BEGIN_DISCRETE_TRANSACTION

The procedure begin_discrete_transaction has no parameters. The purpose of the procedure is to set discrete transaction mode for this transaction. The procedure will generate the following exceptions:

ORA-08175—This will be generated if a transaction attempts an operation which cannot be performed as a discrete transaction. If this exception is encountered, roll back and retry the transaction.

ORA-08176—This will be generated if a transaction encounters data changed by an operation that does not generate rollback data: create index, direct load, or discrete transaction. If this exception is encountered, retry the operation that received the exception.

PURGE_MIXED

The procedure purge_mixed has a single input parameter: xid (varchar2). To understand what this procedure does, you need to understand two-phase-commits (2PCs) and distributed transactions. Let's discuss this for a moment.

When in-doubt transactions (transactions participating in a 2PC that can't finish) are forced to commit or roll back (instead of letting automatic recovery resolve their outcomes), there is a possibility that a transaction can have a mixed outcome: some sites commit, and others roll back. Such inconsistency cannot be resolved automatically by Oracle; however, Oracle will flag entries in the DBA_2PC_PENDING table by setting the MIXED column to a value of "yes." Oracle won't automatically delete information about a mixed outcome transaction. When the application or DBA is sure all inconsistencies that might have arisen as a result of the mixed transaction have been resolved, this procedure can be used to delete the information about a given mixed outcome transaction.

The procedure's input argument is as follows:

xid—This must be set to the value of the LOCAL_TRAN_ID column in the DBA_2PC_PENDING table.

PURGE_LOST_DB_ENTRY

The procedure purge_lost_db_entry has a single input parameter: xid (varchar2). This procedure is used to help resolve distributed transaction failures. When a failure occurs during commit processing, automatic recovery will consistently resolve the results at all sites involved in the transaction. However, if the remote database is destroyed or recreated before recovery completes, then the entries used to control recovery in DBA_2PC_PENDING and associated tables will never be removed, and recovery will periodically retry to resolve them. Procedure purge_lost_db_entry allows removal of such transactions from the local site.

WARNING purge_lost_db_entry should only be used when the other database is lost or has been recreated. Any other use may leave the other database in an unrecoverable or inconsistent state.

Before automatic recovery runs, the transaction may show up in DBA_2PC_PENDING as state collecting, committed, or prepared. If the DBA has forced an indoubt transaction to have a particular result by using commit force or rollback force, then states forced commit or forced rollback may also appear.

Automatic recovery will normally delete entries in any of these states. The only exception is when recovery finds a forced transaction which is in a state inconsistent with other sites in the transaction; in this case, the entry will be left in the table and the MIXED column will have a value of "yes."

However, under certain conditions, it may not be possible for automatic recovery to run. For example, a remote database may have been permanently lost. Even if it is recreated, it will get a new database id, so that recovery cannot identify it (a possible symptom of this is ORA-02062). In this case, the DBA may use the procedure purge_lost_db_entry to clean up the entries in any state other than prepared. The DBA does not need to be in any particular hurry to resolve these entries, since they will not be holding any database resources.

The following table shows what the various states indicate about the transaction and what the DBA's actions should be:

State Column	State of Global Transaction	State of Local Transaction	Normal DBA Action	Alternative DBA Action
collecting	rolled back	rolled back	none	purge_lost_db_entry (1)
committed	committed	committed	none	purge_lost_db_entry (1)
prepared	unknown	prepared	none	force commit or rollback
forced commit	unknown	committed	none	purge_lost_db_entry (1)
forced rollback	unknown	rolled back	none	purge_lost_db_entry (1)

continued

State Column	State of Global Transaction	State of Local Transaction	Normal DBA Action	Alternative DBA Action
forced commit (mixed)	mixed	committed	(2)	
forced rollback (mixed)	mixed	rolled back	(2)	

(1): Use only if significant reconfiguration has occurred so that automatic recovery cannot resolve the transaction. Examples are: total loss of the remote database, reconfiguration in software resulting in loss of two-phase commit capability, or loss of information from an external transaction coordinator such as a TP Monitor.

(2): Examine and take any manual action to remove inconsistencies, then use the procedure purge_mixed.

The procedure has the following input argument:

xid—This must be set to the value of the LOCAL_TRAN_ID column in the DBA_2PC_PENDING table.

LOCAL_TRANSACTION_ID

The function local_transaction_id has the input parameter: create_transaction (BOOLEAN with the default value FALSE) and returns a VARCHAR2. The purpose of this function is to return to the local instance a unique identifier for current transaction or to return null if there is no current transaction.

The function's input parameter is defined as follows:

create_transaction—If true, start a transaction if one is not currently active.

STEP_ID

The function step_id has no input parameters but returns a number value. The purpose of this function is to return to the local transaction a unique positive integer that orders the DML operations of a transaction.

10.2   DBMS_SESSION

The DBMS_SESSION package provides access to the ALTER SESSION type command options at the PL/SQL routine level.

SET_ROLE

The procedure set_role has the input parameter: role_cmd (varchar2). The procedure is the PL/SQL equivalent to the SQL command "SET ROLE ...." The input argument role_cmd is appended to the SET ROLE command and executed. Therefore, it can be as simple as a role name, or it can include the role name and the "IDENTIFIED BY pword" clause as well.

SET_SQL_TRACE

The procedure set_sql_trace has a single boolean argument (TRUE or FALSE): sql_trace. This procedure is the PL/SQL equivalent of the SQL command:

```
ALTER SESSION SET SQL_TRACE ... .
```

The only input, sql_trace, is set either to TRUE to turn tracing on or FALSE to turn it off.

SET_NLS

The procedure set_nls has two input parameters: param (varchar2), and value (varchar2). This procedure is the PL/SQL equivalent to the SQL command:

```
ALTER SESSION SET <nls_parameter> = <value>
```

The input arguments are defined as follows:

param—This is the NLS parameter to change for the session. The parameter name must begin with 'NLS' and of course be a valid NLS parameter.

Valid parameters are as follows:

Parameter Name	*Description*
nls_language	NLS language name
nls_territory	NLS territory name
nls_sort	NLS linguistic definition name
nls_date_language	NLS date language name
nls_date_format	NLS Oracle date format
nls_currency	NLS local currency symbol
nls_numeric_characters	NLS numeric characters
nls_iso_currency	NLS ISO currency territory name

value—This is the value to set the parameter to. If the parameter is a text literal then it will need embedded single-quotes. For example set_nls('nls_date_format','''DD-MON-RRRR'''). A better way would be to prebuild the entry and use chr(39) to embed the quotes:

```
nls_parm:=chr(39)||'DD-MON-RRRR'||chr(39);
        set_nls('nls_date_format',nls_parm);
```

CLOSE_DATABASE_LINK

The procedure close_database_link has one input parameter: dblink (varchar2). The procedure is the PL/SQL equivalent of the SQL command:

```
ALTER SESSION CLOSE DATABASE LINK <dblink> .
```

The procedure's input argument is defined as follows:

name—This is the name of the database link to close.

SET_LABEL

The procedure set_label is used with Trusted Oracle7 and has one input parameter: lbl (varchar2). The procedure is the PL/SQL equivalent of the SQL command:

```
ALTER SESSION SET LABEL <label specification> .
```

The procedure's input argument is defined as follows:

lbl—Set to either 'DBHIGH', 'DBLOW', or a text literal.

SET_MLS_LABEL_FORMAT

The procedure set_mls_label_format is used with Trusted Oracle7 and has a single input parameter: fmt (varchar2). The procedure is equivalent to the SQL command:

```
ALTER SESSION SET MLS_LABEL_FORMAT <format> .
```

The procedure's input argument is defined as follows:

fmt—This is the format specification for the label.

RESET_PACKAGE

The procedure reset_package has no input or output variables. The package is used to deinstantiate all packages in this session. In other words, free all package state. This is the situation at the beginning of a session.

UNIQUE_SESSION_ID

This function, unique_session_id, returns a varchar2 value. The purpose of the function is to return an identifier that is unique among all sessions currently connected to this database. Multiple calls to this function during the same session will always return the same result. This function asserts purity so it can be used in packages external to its parent package.

The function's return value is defined as follows:

unique_session_id—This can return up to 24 bytes of character data.

IS_ROLE_ENABLED

The function is_role_enabled has a single input parameter, rolename (varchar2), and returns a boolean TRUE or FALSE. The purpose of the function is to determine if the named role is enabled for this session. The function does not assert purity so using it in packages external to its parent package may be difficult.

The function's input argument is rolename, which is the name of the role to test. The output arguments from is_role_enabled will be TRUE or FALSE depending on whether the role is enabled.

SET_CLOSE_CACHED_OPEN_CURSORS

The procedure set_close_cached_open_cursors has a single input argument: close_cursors, which is a boolean TRUE/FALSE. This procedure is the PL/SQL equivalent of the SQL command:

```
ALTER SESSION SET CLOSE_CACHED_OPEN_CURSORS ...
```

The procedure's input argument is defined as follows:

close_cursors—This can only be set to TRUE or FALSE, which turns close_cached_open_cursors on or off respectively.

FREE_UNUSED_USER_MEMORY

The procedure free_unused_user_memory has no input or output parameters. The procedure is used to reclaim unused memory after performing operations requiring large amounts of memory (where large is >100 K). Note that this procedure should only be used in cases where memory is at a premium.

Some examples of operations that use lots of memory are:

- Large sorts, where entire sort_area_size is used and sort_area_size is megabytes in size
- Compiling large PL/SQL packages/procedures/functions
- Storing hundreds of kilobytes of data within PL/SQL indexed tables

You can monitor user memory by tracking the statistics session uga memory and session pga memory in the v$sesstat/v$statname fixed views. Monitoring these statistics will also show how much memory this procedure has freed. The select to get this information would be:

```
select sid, name, value
from v$sesstat a, v$statname b
where a.statistic#=b.statistic#
and b.name in ('session uga memory','session pga memory');
```

(This select works in both Oracle7 and Oracle8.)

The behavior of this procedure depends upon the configuration of the server operating on behalf of the client:

- If dedicated server—it returns unused PGA memory to the OS.
- If MTS server—it returns unused session memory to the shared_pool.

In order for this procedure to free memory, the memory can't be in use. Once an operation allocates memory, only the same type of operation can reuse the allocated memory. For example, once memory is allocated for sort, even once the sort is complete and the memory is no longer in use, only another sort from this session can reuse the sort-allocated memory. For both sort and compilation, after the operation is complete, the memory is no longer in use and the user can invoke this procedure to free the unused memory.

A PL/SQL table implicitly allocates memory to store values assigned to the PL/SQL table's elements. Thus, the more elements in a PL/SQL table, the more memory the RDBMS allocates to the PL/SQL table. As long as there are elements within the PL/SQL table, the memory associated with a PL/SQL table is in use.

The scope of PL/SQL tables determines how long their memory is in use. PL/SQL tables declared globally are declared in packages or package bodies. They allocate memory from session memory. For a PL/SQL table declared globally, the memory will remain in use for the lifetime of a user's login (lifetime of a user's session), and is freed after the user disconnects from Oracle.

PL/SQL tables declared locally are indexed tables declared within functions, procedures, or anonymous blocks. These PL/SQL tables allocate memory from PGA memory. For a PL/SQL table declared locally, the memory will remain in use for as long as the user is still executing the procedure, function, or anonymous block in which the PL/SQL table is declared. After the procedure, function, or anonymous block is finished executing, the memory is then available for other locally declared PL/SQL tables to use (i.e., the memory is no longer in use).

Assigning an uninitialized, empty, PL/SQL table to an existing PL/SQL table is a method to explicitly reinitialize the PL/SQL table and the memory associated with the PL/SQL table. After this operation, the memory associated with the PL/SQL table will no longer be in use, making it available to be freed by calling this procedure. This method is particularly useful on PL/SQL tables declared globally, which can grow during the lifetime of a user's session, as long as the user no longer needs the contents of the table.

The memory rules associated with an indexed table's scope still apply; this method and this procedure, however, allow users to intervene and to explicitly free the memory associated with a PL/SQL table.

The PL/SQL fragment below illustrates the method and the use of procedure free_unused_user_memory.

```
create package example_proc
   type number_idx_tbl is table of number
    indexed by binary_integer;
   -
      store1_table  number_idx_tbl;     - PL/SQL indexed table
      store2_table  number_idx_tbl;     - PL/SQL indexed table
      store3_table  number_idx_tbl;     - PL/SQL indexed table
   -     ... processing commands
   end;             - end of example_proc

   declare
   -    ... misc. declares
empty_table number_idx_tbl;  - uninitialized ( empty ) version
   -
    begin
      for i in 1..1000000 loop
       store1_table(i) := i;        - load data
      end loop;
      ...
   store1_table := empty_table; -  truncate  the indexed table
    ...
      -
   dbms_session.free_unused_user_memory;  - give memory back
   -
      store1_table(1) := 100;  - index tables still declared;
      store2_table(2) := 200;         - but truncated.
      ...
    end;
```

This procedure is designed for memory-poor environments and should be used infrequently and judiciously.

10.3   DBMS_SYSTEM

The DBMS_SYSTEM package allows for turning on and off tracing at the PL/SQL routine level. In pre-Oracle8, it was part of the DBMS_UTIL family, in Oracle8 it has actually been moved in its entirety to prvtutil.plb and thus its header is no longer in DBMSUTIL.SQL.

SET_SQL_TRACE_IN_SESSION

The procedure set_sql_trace_in_session has three input parameters: sid (number), serial# (number) and sql_trace (boolean). The purpose of the procedure is to turn SQL tracing on and off from within PL/SQL and is equivalent to the SQL command:

```
ALTER SESSION SET SQL_TRACE...
```

The procedure's input parameter's detailed definitions are as follows:

sid—This is the sid of the session to be traced (from v$session).

serial#—This is the serial# of the session to be traced (from v$session).

sql_trace—This is set to TRUE to turn on tracing and FALSE to turn off tracing.

Functions

All of the functions in DBMS_SYSTEM are for internal use only.

10.4   DBMS_UTILITY

The DBMS_UTILITY package holds several very useful packages and functions. The packages and functions in DBMS_UTILITY allow you to analyze an entire schema, compile an entire schema, resolve names, and adjust output from comma to non-comma delimited. Several useful functions for dealing with time, getting addresses, and getting error stacks are also provided in DBMS_UTILITY.

COMPILE_SCHEMA

The procedure compile_schema takes one input parameter: schema (varchar2). The purpose of the procedure is to compile all procedures, functions, and packages in the specified schema. After calling this procedure you should select from view DBA_OBJECTS for items with status of 'INVALID' to see if all objects were successfully compiled. You may use the SVRMGR command SHOW ERRORS <type> <schema>.<name> to see the errors associated with 'INVALID' objects.

The procedure's single input argument has the value:

schema—This is the name of the schema to be compiled.

The procedure generates the following exception:

ORA-20000: Insufficient privileges for some object in this schema.

ANALYZE_SCHEMA

The procedure analyze_schema has the following input parameters:

schema	varchar2
method	varchar2
estimate_rows	number with a default of null
estimate_percent	number with a default of null
method_opt	varchar2 with a default of null

The purpose of the procedure analyze_schema is to analyze all the tables, clusters, and indexes in a specified schema. The procedure's input arguments are defined as follows:

schema—This is the name of the schema. You should never analyze the SYS schema or deadlocks will occur.

method, estimate_rows, estimate_percent, method_opt—See the descriptions above in dbms_ddl.analyze.object.

The procedure generates the following exception:

ORA-20000: Insufficient privileges for some object in this schema.

ANALYZE_DATABASE

The procedure analyze_database has the following input parameters:

method	varchar2
estimate_rows	number with the default of null
estimate_percent	number with the default of null
method_opt	varchar2 with the default of null

The purpose of the procedure is to analyze all the tables, clusters, and indexes in a database with the exception of those owned by SYS. The procedure's input arguments are defined as follows:

method, estimate_rows, estimate_percent, method_opt—See the descriptions above in dbms_ddl.analyze.object.

The procedure generates the following exception:

ORA-20000: Insufficient privileges for some object in this database.

FORMAT_ERROR_STACK

The function format_error_stack returns a varchar2 (up to 4000 characters in Oracle8, and 2000 in Oracle7). This function is for internal package use only since it doesn't assert purity via the pragma restrict_references command. The purpose of this function is to format the current error stack. This can be used in exception handlers to look at the full error stack. The function does not assert purity, so using the function in packages outside of its parent package may be difficult.

The function has output consisting of as much of the error stack as will fit into a varchar2 return variable (4000 bytes for Oracle8 and 2000 for Oracle7).

FORMAT_CALL_STACK

The function format_call_stack has a return variable of varchar2 (4000 bytes for Oracle8 and 2000 for Oracle7). The purpose of the function is to format the current call stack. This can be used on any stored procedure or trigger within this package to access the call stack. This can be useful for debugging. Since this function doesn't assert purity it may not be accessible from packages outside of its parent package.

The function's output consists of as much of the call stack for the current object as will fit into a varchar2 variable (4000 bytes for Oracle8 and 2000 for Oracle7).

IS_PARALLEL_SERVER

The function is_parallel_server returns a boolean TRUE or FALSE value. The purpose of the function is to allow the current process to find out if this database is running in parallel server mode. Since this function doesn't assert purity it may not be accessible to packages outside of its parent package.

GET_TIME

The function get_time has a single return (number) that corresponds to hundredths of seconds from some arbitrary starting point. This number can wrap and, on some platforms, has shown up as a negative number. This function doesn't assert purity so it may not be available to packages other than its parent package. Use a select against the v$timer dynamic performance table for the same effect.

GET_PARAMETER_VALUE

The function get_parameter_value has three parameters: parnam, an input only varchar2; intval, an input or output binary_integer; and strval, a second input varchar2. The function returns a binary_integer. The purpose of this function is to get the value of a specified parameter. The function does not assert purity, so using the function in packages outside of its parent package may be difficult.

The detailed definition of the input and output arguments for get_parameter_value follow:

parnam—This is the parameter name of interest.

intval—This is the integer parameter value or value length of a string parameter.

strval—This is the string parameter value.

This function returns parameter type.

NAME_RESOLVE

The procedure name_resolve has the following input/output parameters:

Input:

name	varchar2
context	number

Output:

schema	varchar2
part1	varchar2
part2	varchar2
dblink	varchar2
part1_type	number
object_number	number

This procedure's purpose is to resolve the given name. The procedure can do synonym translation if necessary. The procedure will also do authorization checking. The procedure's input arguments have the following definitions:

name—This is the name of the object. This can be of the form [[a.]b.]c[@d] where a,b,c are SQL identifiers and d is a dblink. No syntax checking is performed on the dblink. If a dblink is specified, if the name resolves to something with a dblink, then the object itself is not resolved, but the schema, part1, part2, and dblink out arguments are filled in. a,b, and c may be delimited identifiers, and may contain NLS characters (single and multibyte).

context—This value is not currently used, but must be set to 1 for future compatibility.

The procedure's output arguments are defined as follows:

schema—This is the schema of the object. If no schema is specified in 'name' then the schema is determined by resolving the name.

part1—This is the first part of the name. The type of this name is specified part1_type (synonym, procedure or package).

part2—If this is nonnull, then this is a procedure name within the package indicated by part1.

dblink—If this is nonnull then a database link was either specified as part of 'name' or 'name' was a synonym which resolved to something with a database link. In this latter case, part1_type will indicate a synonym.

part1_type—The type of part1 is:

    5—synonym

    7—procedure (top level)

    8—function (top level)

    9—package

If a synonym, it means that 'name' is a synonym that translates to something with a database link. In this case, if further name translation is desired, then you must call the dbms_utility.name_resolve procedure on this remote node.

object_number—If nonnull then 'name' was successfully resolved and this is the object number to which the name resolved.

The procedure generates the following exceptions:

All errors are handled by raising exceptions. A wide variety of exceptions are possible, based on the various syntax errors that are possible when specifying object names.

NAME_TOKENIZE

The procedure name_tokenize has the following input and output procedures:

Input:

| name | varchar2 |

Output:

a	varchar2
b	varchar2
c	varchar2
dblink	varchar2
nextpos	binary_integer

This procedure calls the parser to parse the given name as a [. b [. c]][@ dblink] . The parser will strip doublequotes, or convert to uppercase if there are no quotes. The parser will ignore comments of all sorts. The parser does no semantic analysis and will leave any missing values as null.

The procedure, for each of a, b, c, and dblink, tells where the following token starts in anext, bnext, cnext, and dnext respectively.

COMMA_TO_TABLE

The procedure comma_to_table has the following input and output parameters:

Input:

| list | varchar2 |

Output:

| tablen | binary_integer |
| tab | uncl_array |

The purpose of this procedure is to convert a comma-separated list of names into a PL/SQL table of names. This uses the name_tokenize procedure to figure out what are names and what are commas.

TABLE_TO_COMMA

The procedure table_to_comma has the following input and output variables:

Input:
tab   uncl_array

Output:
tablen   binary_integer
list   varchar2

The purpose of the procedure is to convert a PL/SQL table of names into a comma-separated list of names. This is the inverse procedure from comma_to_table.

PORT_STRING

The function port_string returns a varchar2 value. The function asserts purity so it can be used external to the parent package. The purpose of the function is to return a string that uniquely identifies the version of Oracle and the port (operating system). EG VAX/VMX-7.1.0.0 maximum length is port specific. This function asserts purity so it can be used in packages external to its parent package.

DB_VERSION

The procedure db_version has two output variables: version (varchar2), and compatibility (varchar2). The purpose of the procedure is to return the actual version of the database and the setting of the compatibility initialization parameter. The detailed definitions of the output parameters follow:

version—A string which represents the internal software version of the database (e.g., 8.0.2.0.0). The length of this string is variable and is determined by the database version.

compatibility—The compatibility setting of the database determined by the compatible init.ora parameter. If the parameter is not specified in the init.ora file, NULL is returned.

MAKE_DATA_BLOCK_ADDRESS

The function make_data_block_address accepts two number arguments, file and block, and returns number that corresponds to a data block address. The function asserts purity so it can be used external to the parent package. The purpose of this function is to create a data block address given a file# and a block#. A data block address is the internal structure used to identify a block in the database. This function is useful when accessing certain fixed tables that contain data block addresses.

The function's input arguments are defined as follows:

file—The number of the file that contains the block (from sys.file$).

block—The offset of the block within the file in terms of block increments (for example, block# from out of sys.tab$).

The output from the function is a dba, the data block address.

DATA_BLOCK_ADDRESS_FILE

The function data_block_address_file accepts one number input, dba, and returns a number value. The function asserts purity so that it can be used outside of the parent package. The purpose of the function is to get the block number part of a data block address.

The function's input argument corresponds to a dba (a data block address). In return for this input, the function's output is a block number, the block offset of the block.

GET_HASH_VALUE

The function get_hash_value accepts a varchar2 value, name, and two number values, base and hash_size number. The function returns a number value. The function asserts purity so it can be used outside of its parent procedure. The purpose of the function is to compute a hash value for the given string.

The function's input arguments are defined as follows:

name—This is the string to be hashed.

base—This is a base value for the returned hash value to start at.

hash_size—This is the desired size of the hash table.

The function returns a hash value based on the input string.

For example, to get a hash value on a string where the hash value should be between 1000 and 3047, use 1000 as the base value and 2048 as the hash_size value. Using a power of 2 for the hash_size parameter works best.

ANALYZE_PART_OBJECT

The procedure analyze_part_object has the following input parameters:

schema	varchar2 with a default of null
object_name	varchar2 with a default of null

object_type   char with a default of 'T'

command_type   char with a default of 'E'

command_opt   varchar2 with a default of null

sample_clause   varchar2 with a default of 'sample 5 percent'

The procedure allows PL/SQL to analyze partition objects. This procedure is equivalent to the SQL command:

```
ANALYZE TABLE|INDEX [<schema>.]<object_name>
PARTITION <pname> [<command_type>] [<command_opt>] [<sample_clause>]
```

For each partition of the object, the procedure will run in parallel using job queues. The package will submit a job for each partition. It is the user's responsibility to control the number of concurrent jobs by setting the INIT parameter JOB_QUEUE_PROCESSES correctly. There is minimal error checking for correct syntax. Any error will be reported in the SNP trace files.

The procedure's input arguments are defined as follows:

schema—This is the schema that owns the object_name.

object_name—This is the name of object to be analyzed; it must be a partitioned object.

object_type—This is the type of the object: it must be T(able) or I(ndex).

command_type—This must be one of the following:

C(ompute statistics)

E(stimate statistics)

D(elete statistics)

V(alidate structure)

command_opt—These are the other options for the command type:

For C, E, it can be FOR table, FOR all LOCAL indexes, FOR all columns or a combination of some of the 'for' options of analyze statistics (table).

For V, it can be 'CASCADE' when object_type is T.

sample_clause—This specifies the sample clause to use when command_type is E.

EXEC_DDL_STATEMENT

The procedure exec_ddl_statement accepts the input parameter parse_string (varchar2). This procedure will execute the DDL statement in parse_string. The argument's detailed definition is:

parse_string—This is the DDL statement to be executed.

10.5   DBMS_DDL

The DBMS_DDL package allows the compilation and analysis of single objects from within PL/SQL routines.

ALTER_COMPILE

The procedure alter_compile accepts three input parameters: type (varchar2), schema (varchar2), and name (varchar2). This procedure is equivalent to the SQL command:

```
ALTER PROCEDURE|FUNCTION|PACKAGE [<schema>.]<name> COMPILE [BODY].
```

If the named object is this package, or any packages upon which it depends (currently standard or dbms_standard) then the procedure simply returns (since these packages are clearly successfully compiled).

The procedure's input arguments are defined as follows:

type—This must be one of the allowed Oracle objects: PROCEDURE, FUNCTION, PACKAGE, or PACKAGE BODY.

schema—This is the schema name where the object resides. If schema is NULL then the procedure will use the current schema. This value is case sensitive.

name—This is the name of the object. This value is case sensitive.

The procedure generates the following exceptions:

ORA-20000: Insufficient privileges or object does not exist.

ORA-20001: Remote object, cannot compile.

ORA-20002: Bad value for object type. Should be one of PACKAGE, PACKAGE BODY, PROCEDURE, or FUNCTION.

ANALYZE_OBJECT

The procedure analyze_object has the following input parameters:

type	varchar2
schema	varchar2
name	varchar2
method	varchar2
estimate_rows	number with a default of null
estimate_percent	number with a default of null
method_opt	varchar2 with a default of null

This procedure is the PL/SQL equivalent to the SQL command:

```
ANALYZE TABLE|CLUSTER|INDEX [<schema>.]<name>
[<method>] STATISTICS [SAMPLE <n> [ROWS|PERCENT]]
```

The procedure's input arguments are defined as follows:

type—This is one of 'TABLE', 'CLUSTER' or 'INDEX'. If none of these, the procedure just returns.

schema—This is the schema of the object to analyze. NULL means current schema. This value is case sensitive.

name—This is the name of the object to analyze. This value is case sensitive.

method—NULL or 'ESTIMATE'. If 'ESTIMATE' then either estimate_rows or estimate_percent must be nonzero, but not both.

estimate_rows—This sets the number of rows to estimate.

estimate_percent—This establishes the percentage of rows to estimate. If estimate_rows is specified, then ignore this parameter.

method_opt—This specifies the method options of the following format:

```
[ FOR TABLE ]
[ FOR ALL [INDEXED] COLUMNS] [SIZE n]
[ FOR ALL INDEXES ]
```

The procedure generates the following exceptions:

ORA-20000: Insufficient privileges or object does not exist.

ORA-20001: Bad value for object type. Should be one of TABLE, INDEX, or CLUSTER.

ALTER_TABLE_REFERENCEABLE

The procedure alter_table_referenceable has the following input parameters:

table_name	varchar2
table_schema	varchar2 with a default of null
affected_schema	varchar2 with a default of null

The purpose of the procedure is to alter the given object table table_schema.table_name so it becomes the referenceable table for the given schema affected_schema. This would be equivalent to the SQL command:

```
ALTER TABLE [<table_schema>.]<table_name>
REFERENCEABLE FOR <affected_schema>
```

but this command is not currently supported or available as a DDL statement.

When you create an object table, it automatically becomes referenceable, unless you use the OID AS clause when creating the table. The OID AS clause allows you to create an object table and to assign to the new table the same EOID as another object table of the same type. After you create a new table using the OID AS clause, you end up with two object tables with the same EOID. The new table is not referenceable; the original one is. All references that used to point to the objects in the original table still reference the same objects in the same original table.

If you execute this procedure on the new table, it will make the new table the referenceable table, replacing the original one; thus, those references now point to the objects in the new table instead of the original table.

For example, the following steps recreate an object table that needs to be reorganized for various reasons:

```
SQL> CREATE TABLE EMP_NEW OF EMPLOYEE OID AS EMP;
SQL> INSERT INTO EMP_NEW (SYS_NC_OID$, EMP_NEW)
     2 SELECT SYS_NC_OID$, EMP FROM EMP;
SQL> EXECUTE DBMS_DDL.ALTER_TABLE_REFERENCEABLE('EMP_NEW');
```

In this example the table_schema defaults to NULL; and therefore Oracle uses the current schema. The affected_schema also defaults to NULL; therefore Oracle will use the PUBLIC schema, which means all schemas will be affected:

```
SQL> RENAME EMP TO EMP_OLD;
SQL> RENAME EMP_NEW TO EMP;
```

The affected schema can be PUBLIC or a particular schema. If it is PUBLIC, all schemas are affected. If it is a particular schema, only that schema is affected. The user that executes this procedure must own the new table (i.e., the schema is the same as the user), and the affected schema must be the same as the user or PUBLIC. If the affected schema is PUBLIC, then the user must own the old mapping table for PUBLIC as well.

If the user executing this procedure has ALTER ANY TABLE and SELECT ANY TABLE and DROP ANY TABLE privileges, the user doesn't have to own the tables, and the affected schema can be any valid schema or PUBLIC.

The procedure uses the following input arguments:

table_name—This is the name of the table to be altered. This cannot be a synonym and must not be NULL. The value is case sensitive.

table_schema—This is the name of the schema owning the table to be altered. If the value is NULL then the current schema is used. The value is case sensitive.

affected_schema—This is the name of the schema affected by this alteration. If the value is NULL then PUBLIC (equivalent to all schemas) is used. This value is case sensitive.

The procedure generates the following exception:

ORA-20000: Insufficient privileges, invalid schema name or table does not exist.

ALTER_TABLE_NOT_REFERENCEABLE

The procedure alter_table_not_referenceable has the following input parameters:

table_name	varchar2
table_schema	varchar2 with a default of null
affected_schema	varchar2 with a default of null

The procedure's purpose is to alter the given object table table_schema.table_name so it becomes not the default referenceable table for the schema affected_schema. This would be equivalent to the SQL command:

```
ALTER TABLE [<table_schema>.]<table_name>
NOT REFERENCEABLE FOR <affected_schema>
```

but this is currently not supported or available as a DDL statement. This procedure simply reverts the affected schema and table to nonreferenceable for PUBLIC (i.e., it simply undoes the previous alter_table_referenceable call for this specific schema).

- The affected schema must be a particular schema (cannot be PUBLIC).

  The user that executes this procedure must own the table (i.e., the schema is the same as the user), and the affected schema must be the same as the user.

  If the user executing this procedure has ALTER ANY TABLE and SELECT ANY TABLE and DROP ANY TABLE privileges, the user doesn't have to own the table and the affected schema can be any valid schema.

  The procedure's input arguments are defined as follows:

  table_name—This is the name of the table to be altered. This value cannot be a synonym and must not be NULL. This value is case sensitive.

  table_schema—This is the name of the schema owning the table to be altered. If the value is NULL, then the current schema is used. This value is case sensitive.

  affected_schema—This is the name of the schema affected by this alteration. If the value is NULL, then the current schema is used. This value is case sensitive.

  The procedure generates the following exception:

  ORA-20000: Insufficient privileges, invalid schema name or table does not exist.

10.6   DBMS_SPACE

This package provides segment space information not currently available through the standard views. When the package is built, the execution privilege is granted to PUBLIC. Procedures in this package run under the caller's security (grants). The user must have ANALYZE privilege on the object for which space information is desired.

UNUSED_SPACE

The procedure unused_space has the following input and output parameters:

Input:

segment_owner	varchar2
segment_name	varchar2
segment_type	varchar2

Output:

total_blocks	number
total_bytes	number
unused_blocks	number
unused_bytes	number
last_used_extent_file_id	number
last_used_extent_block_id	number
last_used_block	number

As its name implies, the procedure returns information about unused space in an object (table, index, or cluster).

The procedure's input argument definitions follow:

segment_owner—This is the schema name of the segment to be analyzed.

segment_name—This is the object name of the segment to be analyzed.

segment_type—This is the type of the segment to be analyzed (TABLE, INDEX, or CLUSTER).

The procedure's output argument definitions are as follows:

total_blocks—This is the total number of blocks in the segment.

total_bytes—This is the same as above, expressed in bytes.

unused_blocks—This is the number of blocks which are not used.

unused_bytes—This is the same as above, expressed in bytes.

last_used_extent_file_id—This is the file ID of the last extent which contains data.

last_used_extent_block_id—This is the block ID of the last extent which contains data.

last_used_block—This is the last block within this extent which contains data.

FREE_BLOCKS

The procedure free_blocks has the following input and output parameters:

Input:
segment_owner	varchar2
segment_name	varchar2
segment_type	varchar2
freelist_group_id	number
scan_limit	number with a default of NULL

Output:
free_blks	number

This procedure returns information about free blocks in an object (table, index, or cluster). The procedure's input arguments are defined as follows:

segment_owner—This is the schema name of the segment to be analyzed.

segment_name—This is the name of the segment to be analyzed.

segment_type—This is the type of the segment to be analyzed (TABLE, INDEX, or CLUSTER).

freelist_group_id—This is the freelist group (instance) whose freelist size is to be computed.

scan_limit (optional)—This is the maximum number of free blocks to read.

The procedure's output argument is defined as follows:

free_blks—This is the count of free blocks for the specified group.

10.7   DBMS_APPLICATION_INFO

The dbms_application_info package provides a mechanism for registering the name of the application module that is currently running with the rdbms. Registering the name of the module allows DBAs to monitor how the system is being used, and do performance analysis and resource accounting by module. The name that is registered through this package will appear in the 'module' and 'action' columns of the v$session virtual table. It will also appear in the 'module' and 'action' columns in v$sqlarea.

The MODULE name is normally set to a user-recognizable name for the program that is currently executing. For example, this could be the name of the form that is executing, or it could be the name of the script that is being executed by SQL*Plus. The idea is to be able to identify the high level function that is being performed. For instance, you can tell that a user is in the 'order entry' form instead of just telling that he or she is running Oracle*forms. Oracle would like application tool vendors to automatically set this value whenever an application is executed. Of course, since they don't talk much about this (or many of the other utilities), people don't know it exists.

The ACTION name is normally set to a specific action that a user is performing within a module. For instance, a user could be 'reading mail' or 'entering a new customer'. This is meant to more specifically identify what a user is currently doing. The action should normally be set by the designer of a specific application. It should not automatically be set by the application tool.

If the local DBA would like to gather his or her own statistics based on module, then the DBA can implement a wrapper around this package by writing a version of this package in another schema that first gathers statistics and then calls the sys version of the package. The public synonym for dbms_application_info can then be changed to point to the DBA's version of the package.

SET_MODULE

The procedure set_module accepts two input parameters: module_name (varchar2) and action_name (varchar2). The purpose of this procedure is to set the name of the module that is currently running to a new module. When the current module terminates, this should be called with the name of the new module if there is one, or null if there is not a new module. Passing null for either of these values is equivalent to passing a zero length string.

The procedure's input arguments are defined as follows:

module_name—This is the name of the module that will now be running. The maximum length of the module name is 48 bytes. Longer names will be truncated.

action_name—This is the name of the action that will now be running. The maximum length of the action_name is 32 bytes. Longer names will be truncated. If the action name is not being specified, then null should be passed for this value.

SET_ACTION

The procedure set_action accepts a single input parameter, action_name (varchar2). The purpose of the procedure is to set the name of the current action within the current module. When the current action terminates, this should be called with the name of the new action if there is one, or null if there is no new action. Passing null for this value is equivalent to passing a zero length string.

The procedure's input argument is defined as follows:

action_name—This is the name of the action that will now be running. The maximum length of the action_name is 32 bytes. Longer names will be truncated.

READ_MODULE

The procedure read_module returns two values to the caller: module_name (varchar2) and action_name (varchar2). The purpose of this procedure is to read the current values of the module and action fields of the calling session.

The procedure's output arguments are defined as follows:

module_name—This is the last value that the module name was set to using the set_module procedure.

action_name—This is the last value that the action name was set to using the set_module or set_action procedures.

SET_CLIENT_INFO

The procedure set_client_info accepts the parameter client_info (varchar2). The purpose of this procedure is to set the client info field of the v$session dynamic performance table for the calling session. The client info field is provided for the use of individual applications. The Oracle system does not use this field for any purpose. After being set, the client info field can be queried from v$session.

The procedure's input argument is defined as follows:

client_info—This is any character data that the client wishes to store, up to a maximum of 64 bytes. Longer values will be truncated. Passing a null is equivalent to passing a zero length string.

READ_CLIENT_INFO

The procedure read_client_info produces one output field, client_info (varchar2). The procedure reads the value of the client_info field of the current session.

The procedure's output argument is defined as follows:

client_info—This is the last value that the client_info field was set to using the set_client_info procedure.

10.8   DBMS_ROWID

The package dbms_rowid provides procedures to create ROWIDs and to interpret their contents between the change from Oracle7 format to Oracle8 format. Execution privilege is granted to PUBLIC for DBMS_ROWID. Procedures in this package run under the caller's security. Beginning with Oracle8 there are two types of ROWID:

RESTRICTED—Restricted ROWID (Oracle7 and earlier)

EXTENDED—Extended ROWID (Oracle8 and later)

These are equated to two constants for use in identifying specific operations in this package:

rowid_type_restricted   0

rowid_type_extended   1

For verification purposes, two additional constants are defined for use when verifying ROWID state:

rowid_is_valid   0

rowid_is_invalid   1

ROWID_CREATE

The function rowid_create constructs a ROWID from its constituents:

rowid_type	—type (restricted/extended) number.
object_number	—data object number (rowid_object_undefined for restricted) number.
relative_fno	—relative file number -- number.
block_number	—block number in this file -- number.
file_number	—file number in this block -- number.

The function returns a valid rowid. The function asserts purity so it can be used in packages outside of its parent package.

ROWID_INFO

The procedure rowid_info breaks a specified ROWID into its components and returns them. The procedure has the following input and output parameters:

Input:

rowid_in	—ROWID to be interpreted -- rowid

Output:

rowid_type	—type (restricted/extended) -- number
object_number	—data object number (rowid_object_undefined for restricted) -- number
relative_fno	—relative file number -- number
block_number	—block number in this file -- number
file_number	—file number in this block -- number.

This procedure asserts purity.

ROWID_TYPE

The function rowid_type accepts a single input parameter: row_id (ROWID). The function returns the type of a ROWID (number corresponding to restricted/extended). The input is defined as follows:

row_id—This is the ROWID to be interpreted.

The function's number return is defined as follows:

rowid_type_restricted   0
rowid_type_extended   1

The function asserts purity so it can be used in packages outside of its parent package.

ROWID_OBJECT

The function rowid_object accepts a single input parameter: row_id (ROWID). The function extracts the data object number from the input ROWID and returns it as a number. The function will return a status corresponding to ROWID_OBJECT_UNDEFINED for restricted rowids.

The function asserts purity so it can be used in packages other than its parent package.

ROWID_RELATIVE_FNO

The function rowid_relative_fno accepts a single input parameter: row_id (ROWID). The function extracts the relative file number from this ROWID and returns it as a number. The function asserts purity so it can be used in packages outside of its parent package.

ROWID_BLOCK_NUMBER

The function rowid_block_number accepts a single input parameter: row_id (ROWID). The function extracts the block number from this ROWID and returns it as a number. The function asserts purity so it can be called from a package external to its parent package.

ROWID_ROW_NUMBER

The function rowid_row_number accepts a single input parameter: row_id (ROWID). The function extracts the row number from this ROWID and returns a number. The function asserts purity so it can be called from packages outside of its parent package.

ROWID_TO_ABSOLUTE_FNO

The function rowid_to_absolute_fno accepts three input parameters: row_id (ROWID), schema_name (varchar2), and object_name (varchar2). The function extracts the relative file number from this data and returns a number. The function asserts purity so it can be used in packages outside of its parent package.

ROWID_TO_EXTENDED

The function rowid_to_extended accepts the following input parameters:

old_rowid	rowid
schema_name	varchar2
object_name	varchar2
conversion_type	integer

The parameters have the following definitions:

old_rowid—This is the ROWID to be converted.

schema_name—This is the name of the schema which contains the table (OPTIONAL).

object_name—This is the table name (OPTIONAL).

conversion_type—This is rowid_convert_internal/external_convert_external (whether old_rowid was stored in a column of ROWID type, or the character string).

The function translates the restricted ROWID which addresses a row in a given table to the extended format. The function asserts purity so it can be used in packages outside of its parent package.

ROWID_TO_RESTRICTED

The function rowid_to_restricted accepts two input parameters: old_rowid (ROWID) and conversion_type (NUMBER). These parameters are defined as follows:

old_rowid—This is the ROWID to be converted.

conversion_type—This is internal/external (IN) where:

> **conversion_type**—rowid_convert_internal/external_convert_external (whether returned rowid will be stored in a column of ROWID type, or the character string).

This function translates the extended ROWID into a restricted format and returns it as a rowid.

ROWID_VERIFY

The function rowid_verify accepts the following input parameters:

rowid_in	rowid
schema_name	varchar2
object_name	varchar2
conversion_type	integer.

The function verifies the ROWID. It returns rowid_valid or rowid_invalid value depending on whether a given ROWID is valid or not. The function's input parameters are defined as follows:

rowid_in—This is the ROWID to be verified.

schema_name—This is the name of the schema which contains the table.

object_name—This is the table name.

conversion_type—This is rowid_convert_internal/external_convert_external (whether old_rowid was stored in a column of ROWID type, or the character string).

The function asserts purity so it can be used in packages outside of its parent package.

CHAPTER 11

Utility Procedures and Other Scripts

There is no one manual that lists all of the available scripts and utilities located in the $ORACLE_HOME/rdbms/admin directory (on UNIX) or its equivalent on other operating systems. Even this book doesn't get them. The reason for this is that most of them, like migrate.sql, catalog5.sql, and catalog6.sql are special-use only; most DBAs will never have a use for them and, if they ever need them, they will probably be using them under Oracle's guidance. I have endeavored to document the truly useful scripts. This chapter covers some of the new scripts and packages such as UTL_FILE, DBMS_AQ, and so on, and some old ones like CATALOG.SQL.

11.1 UTL_FILE

The UTL_FILE package was introduced with Oracle version 7.3. The package allows input and output from operating system files into and out of PL/SQL. This package brings PL/SQL very close to being a true programming language. However, the functions in this package do not assert purity so they cannot be used in packages outside of the parent package.

The package defines a special type to use to assign the file handle, appropriately called FILE_TYPE. Before a file can be read from or written into, it must be assigned a file handle of this type.

The package also uses several generic exceptions. These are as follows:

invalid_path—This is raised if the value for utl_file_dir is set incorrectly in the init<SID>.ora file.

invalid_mode—This is raised if an operation is attempted that is invalid for the current file mode, such as attempting to write to a read mode file.

invalid_filehandle—This is raised if an invalid file handle is used, for example, if you attempt to specify the file handle without using the package's built-in procedures.

invalid_operation—This indicates an invalid operation, such as writing into a read-only file, was attempted.

read_error—This is raised if for some reason the packages cannot read from a file.

write_error—This is raised if for some reason a package cannot write to a file.

internal_error—This is raised if an internal error not covered above is caused by one of the procedures.

FOPEN

The function fopen is used to open a file. The function has three input parameters: location (varchar2), filename (varchar2), and open_mode (varchar2). This function doesn't assert purity so use of this function in packages outside of the parent package may be difficult.

The procedure's input parameters are defined as follows:

Location—This is the directory location of the file.

filename—This is the file name (including extension) of the file to open.

open_mode—This is the open mode for the file: 'r' (read), 'w' (write), 'a' (append).

The file must be opened using the file_type handle. The file will generate the following exceptions:

invalid_path—The file location or name was invalid.

invalid_mode—The open_mode string was invalid.

invalid_operation—The file could not be opened as requested.

IS_OPEN

The function is_open is used to test if the file corresponding to the referenced file handle is open. The function has the input parameter file (file_type). The function returns a boolean value TRUE or FALSE. A true return shows the file handle is open or valid. This function doesn't assert purity so use of this function in packages outside of the parent package may be difficult.

FCLOSE

The procedure fclose is used to close a file opened with fopen. The procedure has a single input parameter: file (file_type). The file must be open. The procedure will generate the following exceptions:

invalid_filehandle—Not a valid file handle.

write_error—The OS error occurred during the write operation.

FCLOSE_ALL

The procedure fclose_all is used for emergency cleanup of fopened files. The procedure will close all open files for this session. The FILE_TYPE handles will not be cleared (IS_OPEN will still indicate they are valid). The procedure will accept a single argument, file (file_type), in open status. The procedure generates the following exception:

write_error—The OS error occurred during the write operation.

GET_LINE

The procedure get_line gets (reads) a line of text from the file opened with the file handle which is passed to get_line. The one input parameter is the file (file_type) file handle. The file must be open in read mode in order to use get_line against it. The procedure places the line of text into buffer (varchar2). Under Oracle7 the varchar2 is limited to 2000 bytes; under Oracle8 this increases to 4000 bytes. The procedure will generate the following exceptions:

no_data_found—Reached the end of the file.

value_error—The line is too long to store in the buffer.

invalid_filehandle—Not a valid file handle.

invalid_operation—The file is not open for reading.

read_error—The OS error occurred during the read.

PUT

The put procedure is used to put (write) text to the file opened by fopen in write or append mode. The procedure has two input parameters: file (file_type) and buffer (varchar2). You are limited to 2000 bytes of input in Oracle7 and this limit should increase to 4000 bytes for Oracle8. The procedure will generate the exceptions:

invalid_filehandle—Not a valid file handle.

invalid_operation—The file is not open for writing/appending.

write_error—The OS error occurred during the write operation.

NEW_LINE

The procedure new_line is used to write line terminators to a file. The procedure has two input parameters: file (file_type) and lines (integer with a default of 1). The file referenced by the passed file handle must be open in append or write mode. Although the default value for lines is 1 (one) you can append as many as you desire. The procedure will generate the following exceptions:

invalid_filehandle—Not a valid file handle.

invalid_operation—The file is not open for writing/appending.

write_error—The OS error occurred during the write operation.

PUT_LINE

The procedure put_line is used to put (write) a line to the file referenced by the file handle. The procedure has two input parameters: file (file_type) and buffer (varchar2). The limit on buffer size is set at the maximum size for a varchar2 data type (2000 bytes for Oracle7 and 4000 bytes for Oracle8). The file referenced by the file parameter (a file handle) must be open for append or write. The procedure will generate the following exceptions:

invalid_filehandle—Not a valid file handle.

invalid_operation—The file is not open for writing/appending.

write_error—The OS error occurred during the write operation.

PUTF

The procedure putf is used to put (write) formatted text into the file referenced by the passed file handle. The procedure accepts three input parameters: file (file_type), format (varchar2), and arg1 (varchar2). The file must be open in write or append mode in order to use putf. The text passed by this routine must use the following format string special characters:

'%s'—Substitute with next argument.

'\n'—newline (line terminator).

The definitions for the input parameters are as follows:

file—File handle (open in write/append mode) (file_type).

format—Formatting string (varchar2).

arg1—Substitution argument #1 (varchar2 that defaults to null).

arg2—Substitution argument #2 (varchar2 that defaults to null).

arg3—Substitution argument #3 (varchar2 that defaults to null).

arg4—Substitution argument #4 (varchar2 that defaults to null).

arg5—Substitution argument #5 (varchar2 that defaults to null).

The procedure will generate the following exceptions:

invalid_filehandle—Not a valid file handle.

invalid_operation—The file is not open for writing/appending.

write_error—The OS error occurred during the write operation.

FFLUSH

The procedure fflush is used to force a physical write of buffered output to the file. The procedure has a single input parameter: file (file_type). The file referenced by the handle "file" must be open in append or write mode. The procedure generates the following exceptions:

invalid_filehandle—Not a valid file handle.

invalid_operation—The file is not open for writing/appending.

write_error—The OS error occurred during the write operation.

11.2 DBMS_LOB

The DBMS_LOB package is new with Oracle8. The package adds utility procedures and functions for dealing with large objects (LOBS). In Oracle8, LOBS are of several types: BLOB (binary large object), CLOB(character large object), NCLOB (national character large object), and BFILE (binary externally stored file—read only).

Other than for BFILE type, Oracle8 SQL supports the definition, creation, deletion, and complete updates of LOBs. The main bulk of the LOB operations are provided by this package.

According to the header file for the DBMS_LOB package (dbmslob.sql), the following rules apply in the specification of functions and procedures in this package:

1. The LENGTH and OFFSET parameters for routines operating on BLOBs and BFILEs are to be specified in terms of bytes.
2. LENGTH and OFFSET parameters for routines operating on CLOBs are to be specified in terms of characters.
3. A function/procedure will raise an INVALID_ARGVAL exception if the following restrictions are not adhered to in specifying values for parameters (unless otherwise specified):
   a. Only positive, absolute OFFSETs from the beginning of LOB data are allowed. Negative offsets from the tail of the LOB are not allowed.
   b. Only positive, nonzero values are allowed for the parameters that represent size and positional quantities such as AMOUNT, OFFSET, NEWLEN, NTH, etc.
   c. The value of OFFSET, AMOUNT, NEWLEN, NTH must not exceed the value lobmaxsize (which is (4 GB − 1) in Oracle 8.0) in any DBMS_LOB procedure or function.

    d. For CLOBs consisting of fixed-width multibyte characters, the maximum value for these parameters must not exceed (lobmaxsize/character_width_in_bytes) characters. For example, if the CLOB consists of 2-byte characters such as JA16SJISFIXED, then the maximum amount value should not exceed 4294967295 ÷ 2 = 2147483647 characters.

4. PL/SQL language specifications stipulate an upper limit of 32767 bytes (not characters) for RAW and VARCHAR2 parameters used in DBMS_LOB routines.

5. If the value of AMOUNT+OFFSET exceeds 4 GB (i.e., lobmaxsize + 1) for BLOBs and BFILEs, and (lobmaxsize/character_width_in_bytes) + 1 for CLOBs in calls to update routines (i.e., APPEND, COPY, TRIM, and WRITE routines), access exceptions will be raised. Under these input conditions, read routines such as READ, COMPARE, INSTR, SUBSTR, will read until End of LOB/File is reached. For example, for a READ operation on a BLOB or BFILE, if the user specifies an offset value of 3 GB, and an amount value of 2 GB, READ will read only ((4GB − 1) − 3 GB) bytes.

6. Functions with NULL or invalid input values for parameters will return a NULL. Procedures with NULL values for destination LOB parameters will raise exceptions.

7. Operations involving patterns as parameters, such as COMPARE, INSTR, and SUBSTR do not support regular expressions or special matching characters (such as % in the LIKE operator in SQL) in the PATTERN parameter or substrings.

8. The End of LOB condition is indicated by the READ procedure using a NO_DATA_FOUND exception. This exception is raised only upon an attempt by the user to read beyond the end of the LOB/FILE. The READ buffer for the last read will contain 0 bytes.

9. For consistent LOB updates, the user is responsible for locking the row containing the destination LOB before making a call to any of the procedures (mutators) that modify LOB data.

10. For BFILEs, the routines COMPARE, INSTR, READ, SUBSTR, will raise exceptions if the file is not already opened using FILEOPEN.

The security of the DBMS_LOB package establishes that privileges are associated with the caller of the procedures/functions in this package as follows:

- If the caller is an anonymous PL/SQL block, the procedures/functions are run with the privilege of the current user.
- If the caller is a stored procedure, the procedures/functions are run using the privileges of the owner of the stored procedure.

The package establishes the following constants for use by the procedures and functions it controls:

    file_readonly—This is a binary integer with a value of 0 (zero).

lobmaxsize—This is an integer with a value of 4294967295 (4 gig – 1).

The package uses the following exceptions:

invalid_argval—This will have the value 21560 and will display the message:

"argument %s is null, invalid, or out of range"

and will be caused by an argument that is expecting a nonnull, valid value but the argument value that was passed in is null, invalid, or out of range. Examples include when the LOB/FILE positional or size argument has a value outside the range 1 through (4 GB – 1), or when an invalid open mode is used to open a file, etc.

If you get this exception you should check your program and correct the caller of the routine to not pass a null, invalid, or out-of-range argument value.

The package also enables the access_error exception with error 22925. The error message associated with this exception is: "operation would exceed maximum size allowed for a lob." The cause of this exception is a process trying to write too much data to the lob. Lob size is limited to 4 gigabytes – 1. The action to correct this exception is to either start writing at a smaller lob offset or write less data to the lob.

The next exception the package may generate is noexist_directory. This will display an error number 22285 and display the message "%s failed—directory does not exist." The cause of this exception is that the directory leading to the file does not exist. If you get this exception you should ensure that an Oracle system object corresponding to the specified directory exists in the database dictionary.

The next exception that the package may generate is nopriv_directory. This exception will display an error number 22286 and the message: "%s failed—insufficient privileges on directory." The cause of this exception is that the user does not have the necessary access privileges on the directory alias and/or the file for the operation. The action required to correct this is to ask the database/system administrator to grant the required privileges on the directory alias and/or the file.

The next exception generated by the package is invalid_directory, which will display the error number 22287 and the message: "%s failed—invalid or modified directory." The cause of this exception is that the directory alias used for the current operation is not valid if being accessed for the first time, or has been modified by the DBA since the last access. The corrective action for this exception is that if you are accessing this directory for the first time, provide a valid directory name. If you have been already successful in opening a file under this directory before this error occurred, then first close the file, then retry the operation with a valid directory alias as modified by your DBA. Oracle strongly recommends that any changes to directories and/or their privileges should be done only during quiescent periods of database operation.

The next exception this package generates is invalid_operation, which displays an error code of 22288 and the message: "%s operation failed." The cause of this exception is that the operation attempted on the file failed. The suggested action is to check if the file is available, and has the necessary privileges set for the mode of your operation. If they are okay and the error still persists, report the error to the DBA—there is some problem with the file.

The next exception that the package generates is unopened_file, which displays an error number 22289 and the message: "cannot perform %s operation on an unopened file." As the message states, the cause of this exception is that the file is not open for the required operation to be performed. The action suggested for this exception is to check that the current operation is preceded by a successful file open operation.

The next exception generated by the package is open_too many, with an error number of 22290 and the message: "%s failed—max limit reached on number of open files." The cause of this exception is that the process has opened its maximum limit of open files. The suggested action to overcome this exception is to close some of your open files, and retry the operation for your current session. To increase the database-wide limit on number of open files allowed per session, contact your DBA.

APPEND

The procedure append accepts two input parameters: dest_lob (BLOB or CLOB), and src_lob (BLOB or CLOB). The purpose of the procedure is to append the BLOB or CLOB specified in the src_lob parameter to the BLOB or CLOB specified in the dest_ lob parameter.

The procedure generates the following exception:

VALUE_ERROR

if either the source or the destination LOB is null.

COMPARE

The function compare accepts five input arguments: lob_1 (BLOB), lob_2 (BLOB), amount (INTEGER with a default of 4294967295), offset_1 (integer with a default of 1), and offset_2 (integer with a default of 1). The function returns an integer value that corresponds to the following:

zero if the comparison succeeds, nonzero if not.
NULL, if:
    amount < 1
    amount > LOBMAXSIZE
    offset_1 or offset_2 < 1
    offset_1 or offset_2 > LOBMAXSIZE.

The function asserts purity so that it may be used in packages outside of its parent package.

The function's input parameters are defined as follows:

dest_lob—This is the LOB locator of the copy target.

src_lob—This is the LOB locator of source for the copy.

amount—This is the number of bytes or characters to copy.

offset_1—This is the offset in bytes or characters in the destination LOB (origin: 1) for the start of the compare.

offset_2—This is the offset in bytes or characters in the source LOB (origin: 1) for the start of the compare.

The procedure generates the following exceptions for BFILE operations:

UNOPENED_FILE, if the file is not opened

NOEXIST_DIRECTORY, if the directory does not exist

NOPRIV_DIRECTORY, if you do not have privileges for the directory

INVALID_DIRECTORY, if the directory has been invalidated after the file was opened

INVALID_OPERATION, if the file does not exist, or if you do not have access privileges on the file

COPY

The procedure copy has five input parameters: dest_lob (BLOB,CLOB), src_lob (BLOB, CLOB), amount (INTEGER), dest_offset (INTEGER with a default of 1), src_offset (INTEGER with a default of 1). The purpose of this procedure is to copy the source (src_lob) BLOB or CLOB into the destination (dest_lob) BLOB or CLOB beginning at the specified offset values (dest_offset, src_offset).

The procedure's input parameters are defined as follows:

dest_lob—This is the LOB locator of the copy target.

src_lob—This is the LOB locator of source for the copy.

amount—This is the number of bytes or characters to copy.

dest_offset—This is the offset in bytes or characters in the destination LOB (origin: 1) for the start of the copy.

src_offset—This is the offset in bytes or characters in the source LOB (origin: 1) for the start of the copy.

The procedure generates the following exceptions:

VALUE_ERROR, if any of the input parameters are NULL or invalid.

INVALID_ARGVAL, if:

    src_offset or dest_offset < 1

    src_offset or dest_offset > LOBMAXSIZE

    amount < 1

    amount > LOBMAXSIZE

ERASE

The procedure erase has three input parameters: lob_loc (BLOB, CLOB), amount (INTEGER), and offset (INTEGER which has a default of 1). The purpose of the procedure is to erase the BLOB or CLOB specified by the value lob_loc by the specified amount starting at the specified offset.

The procedure generates the following exceptions:

VALUE_ERROR, if any input parameter is NULL.

INVALID_ARGVAL, if:

    AMOUNT < 1 or AMOUNT > LOBMAXSIZE

    OFFSET < 1 or OFFSET > LOBMAXSIZE

FILECLOSE

The bfile procedure fileclose has a single input parameter: file_loc (BFILE). The purpose of this procedure is to close the specified bfile.

The procedure generates the following exceptions:

VALUE_ERROR, if NULL input value for file_loc

UNOPENED_FILE if the file is not opened

NOEXIST_DIRECTORY if the directory does not exist

NOPRIV_DIRECTORY if you do not have privileges for the directory

INVALID_DIRECTORY if the directory has been invalidated after the file was opened

INVALID_OPERATION if the file does not exist, or you do not have access privileges on the file

FILECLOSEALL

The bfile procedure filecloseall has no inputs. The purpose of this procedure is to close all opened bfiles.

The procedure generates the following exception:

UNOPENED_FILE

if the file is not opened.

FILEEXISTS

The bfile function fileexists has a single input parameter: file_loc (BFILE). The purpose of the procedure is to determine if the file pointed to by the value of file_loc exists. The function returns an integer value that has the following possible values depending on outcome of the file check:

1 if the physical file exists

0 if the physical file does not exist

NULL, if:

file_loc is NULL

file_loc does not have the necessary directory and OS privileges

file_loc cannot be read because of an OS error.

The function asserts purity so it can be used outside of its parent package in other package procedures and functions.The function raises the following exceptions:

NOEXIST_DIRECTORY if the directory does not exist

NOPRIV_DIRECTORY if you do not have privileges for the directory

INVALID_DIRECTORY if the directory has been invalidated after the file was opened

FILEGETNAME

The bfile procedure filegetname has one input parameter: file_loc (BFILE), and two output parameters: dir_alias (VARCHAR2), and filename (VARCHAR2). The purpose of the procedure is to accept a file locator value and return the files directory alias and file name values. This function only indicates the directory alias name and filename assigned to the locator, not if the physical file or directory actually exists. Maximum value for the dir_alias buffer is 30, and for the entire pathname is 2000.

The procedure raises the following exceptions:

VALUE_ERROR, if any of the input parameters are NULL or invalid

INVALID_ARGVAL, if dir_alias or filename are NULL

FILEISOPEN

The bfile function fileisopen accepts a single input parameter, file_loc (BFILE), and returns an integer value that has the following possible values:

1—File is open

0—File is not open

The function raises the following exceptions:

NOEXIST_DIRECTORY if the directory does not exist

NOPRIV_DIRECTORY if you do not have privileges for the directory

INVALID_DIRECTORY if the directory has been invalidated after the file was opened

INVALID_OPERATION if the file does not exist, or you do not have access privileges on the file

FILEOPEN

The bfile procedure fileopen accepts two input parameters: file_loc (BFILE) and open_mode (BINARY_INTEGER which defaults to the value for file_readonly). The purpose of the procedure is to open a BFILE type file for reading. Currently, BFILE type files can only be opened for reading.

The procedure raises the following exceptions:

VALUE_ERROR, if file_loc or open_mode is NULL

INVALID_ARGVAL, if open_mode is not equal to FILE_READONLY

OPEN_TOOMANY, if the number of open files in the session exceeds SESSION_MAX_OPEN_FILES init<SID>.ora parameter value

NOEXIST_DIRECTORY, if the directory does not exist

INVALID_DIRECTORY, if the directory has been invalidated after the file was opened

INVALID_OPERATION, if the file does not exist, or you do not have access privileges on the file

GETLENGTH

The function getlength accepts one overloaded input parameter: lob_loc (BLOB, CLOB, BFILE). The purpose is to return the length of the specified BLOB, CLOB or BFILE in the units appropriate for the type. The function asserts purity so it may be used external to its parent package (in other packages). The function returns an integer value that corresponds to the following:

The length of the LOB in bytes or characters is an INTEGER

NULL is returned if the input LOB is null

NULL is returned in the following cases for BFILEs:

lob_loc is NULL

lob_loc is not a valid open file

lob_loc does not have the necessary directory and OS privileges

lob_loc cannot be read because of an OS read error

The function raises no exceptions.

INSTR

The function instr has four input parameters: lob_loc (BLOB, CLOB, BFILE), pattern (RAW), offset (INTEGER which defaults to 1), and nth (INTEGER with a default value of 1). You can call the INSTR function to return the matching position of the nth occurrence of the pattern in the LOB, starting from the offset you specify. For CLOBs, the VARCHAR2 buffer (the PATTERN parameter) and the LOB value must be from the same character set (single byte or fixed-width multibyte). For BFILEs, the file has to be already opened using a successful FILEOPEN() operation for this operation to succeed. The function asserts purity so it can be used in packages outside of the parent package.

The function's input parameters are defined as follows:

lob_loc—This is the locator for the LOB to be examined.

pattern—This is the pattern to be tested for. The pattern is a group of RAW bytes for BLOBS, and a character string (VARCHAR2) for CLOBs.

offset—This is the absolute offset in bytes (BLOBs) or characters (CLOBs) at which the pattern matching is to start.

nth—This is the occurrence number, starting at 1.

The return integer has the following possible values:

The integer value of the offset of the start of the matched pattern, in bytes or characters. It returns 0 if the pattern is not found.

A NULL is returned if:

Any one or more of the IN parameters was null or invalid

OFFSET < 1 or OFFSET > LOBMAXSIZE

nth < 1

nth > LOBMAXSIZE

The function will generate the following exceptions for BFILEs:

UNOPENED_FILE, if the file is not opened

NOEXIST_DIRECTORY, if the directory does not exist

NOPRIV_DIRECTORY, if you do not have privileges for the directory

INVALID_DIRECTORY, if the directory has been invalidated after the file was opened

INVALID_OPERATION, if the file does not exist, or if you do not have access privileges on the file

READ

The procedure read accepts three input parameters: lob_loc (BLOB, CLOB, BFILE), amount (BINARY_INTEGER), and offset (INTEGER). The procedure has one output parameter: buffer (RAW, VARCHAR2). The size of the output buffer is limited by the specification for RAW: 32767 bytes; and for VARCHAR2: 4000 bytes.

The procedure's parameters are defined as follows:

Input:

lob_loc—This is the locator for the LOB to be read.

amount—This is the number of bytes or characters to be read.

offset—This is the offset in bytes (for BLOBs) or characters (for CLOBs) from the start of the LOB (origin: 1).

Output:

buffer—The output buffer for the read operation.

The procedure generates the following exceptions:

VALUE_ERROR, if any of LOB_LOC, AMOUNT, or OFFSET parameters are null

INVALID_ARGVAL, if:

    AMOUNT < 1

    AMOUNT > MAXBUFSIZE

    OFFSET < 1

    OFFSET > LOBMAXSIZE

    AMOUNT is greater, in bytes or characters, than the capacity of BUFFER

NO_DATA_FOUND, if the end of the LOB is reached and there are no more bytes or characters to read from the LOB. AMOUNT has a value of 0.

For BFILEs operations:

UNOPENED_FILE, if the file is not opened

NOEXIST_DIRECTORY, if the directory does not exist

NOPRIV_DIRECTORY, if you do not have privileges for the directory

INVALID_DIRECTORY, if the directory has been invalidated after the file was opened

INVALID_OPERATION, if the file does not exist, or if you do not have access privileges on the file

SUBSTR

The function substr accepts three input parameters: lob_loc (BLOB, CLOB, BFILE), amount (INTEGER with a default of 32767), and offset (INTEGER with a default of 1); the function returns a RAW. The function asserts purity so it can be used in packages outside of the parent package.

The function's input parameters are defined as follows:

lob_loc— This is the locator for the LOB to be read.

amount—This is the number of bytes or characters to be read.

offset—This is the offset in bytes (for BLOBs) or characters (for CLOBs) from the start of the LOB (origin: 1).

The function's return parameter is defined as follows:

RAW, for the function overloading that has a BLOB or BFILE in parameter

VARCHAR2, for the CLOB version

NULL, if:

Any input parameter is null

AMOUNT < 1

AMOUNT > 32767

OFFSET < 1

OFFSET > LOBMAXSIZE

The function raises the following exceptions for BFILE operations:

UNOPENED_FILE, if the file is not opened

NOEXIST_DIRECTORY, if the directory does not exist

NOPRIV_DIRECTORY, if you do not have privileges for the directory

INVALID_DIRECTORY, if the directory has been invalidated after the file was opened.

INVALID_OPERATION, if the file does not exist, or if you do not have access privileges on the file

TRIM

The procedure trim accepts the two input parameters: lob_loc (BLOB, CLOB), and newlen (INTEGER). The purpose of the procedure is to trim the BLOB or CLOB to the specified length (newlen).

The procedure's input parameters are defined as follows:

lob_loc—This is the locator for the LOB whose length is to be trimmed.

newlen—This is the new, trimmed length of the LOB value in bytes for BLOBs or characters for CLOBs.

The function will generate the following exceptions:

VALUE_ERROR, if lob_loc is null
INVALID_ARGVAL, if:
    NEW_LEN < 0
    NEW_LEN > LOBMAXSIZE

WRITE

The procedure write has the following input parameters:

lob_loc	BLOB or CLOB
amount	BINARY_INTEGER (also an OUT parameter)
offset	INTEGER
buffer	RAW or VARCHAR2.

As its name implies, the purpose of the write procedure is to write a specified AMOUNT of data into a LOB, starting from an absolute OFFSET from the beginning of the LOB. The data is written from the BUFFER parameter. WRITE replaces (overwrites) any data that already exists in the LOB at the offset, for the length you specify. The actual number of bytes or characters written is returned in the AMOUNT parameter.

The procedure's parameters have the following definitions:

lob_loc—This is the locator for the LOB to be written to.

amount—This is the number of bytes or characters to write, or that were written.

offset—This is the offset in bytes (for BLOBs) or characters (for CLOBs) from the start of the LOB (origin: 1) for the write operation.

buffer—This is the input buffer for the write.

The procedure generates the following exceptions:

VALUE_ERROR, if any of LOB_LOC, AMOUNT, or OFFSET parameters are null, out of range, or invalid

INVALID_ARGVAL, if:

> AMOUNT < 1
>
> AMOUNT > MAXBUFSIZE
>
> OFFSET < 1
>
> OFFSET > LOBMAXSIZE

11.3 DBMS_AQ

New in Oracle8 is the advanced queuing option. This option allows database requests to be funneled through queues from remote databases to local databases and of course back the other way. This allows a "store-and-forward" transaction processing model to be implemented. For example, an order taker can take an order and post it to a remote database, then go right back to posting the next order, even if the remote server is temporarily not available. The order is placed into the queue and patiently waits until the other server is available and then is processed. This is known as the deferred or disconnected execution model. Oracle8 is the first database to offer this type of advanced queuing technology without the use of third-party transaction monitoring systems.

The advanced queuing model is based on the concept of messages. Messages consist of user data and control information and are generally the smallest unit of work processed by a single transaction. This queuing is supported through the use of physical database tables, not memory structures, which means advanced queuing is persistent. These queue tables are created using the DBMS_AQADM package (covered in the next section).

Advanced queuing should be used where the following items are important:

- Ordering of messages (transactions, i.e., a comes before b which comes before c)
- Sequence deviation
- Correlation of discrete message events
- Time constraints on processing (a must be done before time z or not at all)
- Retention of messages is required (which transactions happened when)
- Message replies need to be queued/deferred
- Exceptions need to be queued
- The environment contains both transactional and nontransactional requests. The browsing of transactions (messages) may be required (has the Smith transaction processed yet?).

This advanced queuing model allows a better OLTP modeling of real-world processes. Central to this concept is the DBMS_AQ package, which allows the queuing to take place. For security reasons only SYS has initial execute privileges on the

DBMS_AQ package; however, it is a simple grant of the AQ_USER_ROLE to grant execute to other users as required.

ENQUEUE

The procedure enqueue has the following input and output parameters:

Input:

q_schema	varchar2 with a default of null
q_name	varchar2
corrid	varchar2 with a default of null
transactional	boolean with a default of TRUE
priority	positive integer with a default value of 1
delay	date with a default of null
expiration	natural number with a default of 0 (zero)
relative_msgid	number with a default of null
seq_deviation	char with a default of 'A'
exception_queue_schema	varchar 2 with a default of null
exception_queue	varchar2 with a default of null
reply_queue_schema	varchar2 with a default of null
reply_queue	varchar2 with a default of null
user_data	raw/any object type

Output:

msgid	raw

The purpose of the enqueue procedure is to load a message into a queue specified by the user. The parameters for enqueue have the following definitions:

q_schema—This is the name of the schema containing the queue table object. In 8.0.2 the schema must be specified; in later releases it will default to the user's queue if not specified.

q_name—This is the name of the queue table.

corrid—This is the correlation identifier. This is optional but can be used to tell an application how to correlate this message with other messages.

transactional—This indicates whether or not the message being enqueued is part of the current transaction. TRUE means the operation is complete when the transaction commits; this is the default. FALSE means the enqueue is not part of the current transaction and it is to be considered as a separate transaction. This transaction (the enqueue) must complete before the outer transaction (which placed the enqueue) can complete.

priority—Priorities range from 1 to 100 with 100 being the highest priority. Messages with a higher priority are dequeued first regardless of the order in which they were received in relation to lower priority messages.

delay—This specifies a date calculation to be performed against the enqueue time of the message before it is processed.

expiration—This specifies the expiration time in seconds for a message. If the message is not dequeued before this time limit expires, as measured from enqueue time, then the message is placed in the exception queue and will be removed from the active queue.

relative_msgid—This specifies the message id of the message which must be processed before this message. This field is required if the seq_deviation is set to "B" for before.

seq_deviation—This is normally set to "A" for after, or normal processing. If set to "B" then some value must be entered into the relative_msgid parameter to tell what message should be "before" this one. If this is set to "T" (top) then this message is placed on top of the dequeue list ahead of any other message in this queue.

exception_queue_schema—This is the name of the schema where the exception queue table is stored. Each queue table has a default exception queue table (aq$_<queuetable_name>$_E). If this is left to null the user's default schema is used.

exception_queue—This is the name of the exception queue table where excepted queue entries are placed for resolution. This defaults to aq$_<queuetable_name>$_E if not specified to some other value.

reply_queue_schema—This is the name of the schema where the reply queue table resides. If not specified it defaults to the user's default schema.

reply_queue—This is the name of the reply queue table.

user_data—This is used for user data and is a straight pass through by the AQ processes. If nonnull, the application must specify an in parameter with the same type as the one defined for the queue, otherwise an ORA_25221 error will be returned.

msgid—This is a globally unique identifier for this message. The msgid serves as a handle for subsequent operations against this message.

The purpose of the enqueue procedure is to place messages into the queue table.

DEQUEUE

The dequeue procedure has the following input and output parameters:

Input:

q_schema	varchar2 with a default of null
q_name	varchar2
corrid	varchar2 with a default of null
deq_mode	char with a default of 'D'
wait_time	natural number with a default of 0 (zero)
transactional	boolean with a default of TRUE

Output:

out_msgid	number
out_corrid	varchar2
priority	positive integer with a default value of 1
delay	date with a default of null
retry	natural number
exception_queue_schema	varchar2
exception_queue	varchar2
reply_queue_schema	varchar2 with a default of null
reply_queue	varchar2 with a default of null
user_data	raw/any object type

The purpose of the dequeue procedure is to unload a message from a queue specified by the user. The parameters for dequeue have the following definitions:

q_schema—This is the name of the schema containing the queue table object. In 8.0.2 the schema must be specified; in later releases it will default to the user's queue if not specified.

q_name—This is the name of the queue table from which the message should be dequeued. Unless a specific msgid or corrid is specified only messages ready to be dequeued will dequeue.

msgid—This is the message id of the specific message (if any) to dequeue.

corrid—This is the user-supplied correlation identifier. AQ will retrieve the first available message with this corrid.

deq_mode—This specifies execution of request and disposition of the message:

   D—dequeue and destroy

B—Browse this message using consistent read, dequeue, but don't destroy.

L—Browse this message and lock it. This is nondestructive dequeue and lock. To unlock do a normal DEQUEUE against message.

wait_time—This specifies the number of seconds a dequeue should wait if it finds no messages.

transactional—This indicates whether or not the message being dequeued is part of the current transaction. TRUE means the operation is complete when the transaction commits; this is the default. FALSE means the dequeue is not part of the current transaction and it is to be considered as a separate transaction. This transaction (the enqueue) must complete before the outer transaction (which placed the enqueue) can complete.

out_msgid—This returns the system supplied identifier of the message that has been dequeued.

out_corrid—This returns the application-supplied correlation identifier of the message.

priority—This returns the priority of the message; all messages must have priority.

delay—This returns the requested time delay of the dequeued message.

expiration—This returns the expiration time in seconds of a message.

retry—This returns the number of dequeue operations performed on this message before it was successfully dequeued.

exception_queue_schema—This returns the name of the schema where the exception queue table is stored. Each queue table has a default exception queue table (aq$_<queuetable_name>$_E). If this is left to null, the user's default schema is used.

exception_queue—This returns the name of the exception queue table where excepted queue entries are placed for resolution. This defaults to aq$_<queuetable_name>$_E if not specified to some other value.

reply_queue_schema—This returns the name of the schema where the reply queue table resides. If not specified, it defaults to the user's default schema.

reply_queue—This returns the name of the reply queue table.

user_data—This returns user data and is a straight pass through by the AQ processes. If nonnull, the application must specify an in parameter with the same type as the one defined for the queue; otherwise an ORA_25221 error will be returned.

The purpose of the dequeue procedure is to remove messages from the queue table for processing.

Required init<SID>.ora Parameters

In order to work, the advanced queuing feature must have one queue process started. This is accomplished via the initialization parameter AQ_TM_PROCESSES. This parameter must be set to 1 (one) and only 1 in 8.0.2. It is promised that in later releases multiple queue processes will be allowed, but for initial releases this must be set to 1 and the database shut down and restarted to turn advanced queuing on.

11.4 DBMS_AQADM

The dbms_aqadm package provides the administrative support packages for the advanced queueing option. Administrative support includes the building and dropping of queue tables and queues as well as the stopping, starting, and altering of queues. The advanced queuing feature of Oracle is new in Oracle8.

CREATE_QTABLE

The procedure create_qtable accepts the following input parameters:

q_schema	VARCHAR2
q_table	VARCHAR2
q_object_type_schema	VARCHAR2 with a default of NULL
q_object_type	VARCHAR2 with a default of NULL
object_type_format	VARCHAR2 with a default of 'U'
storage_space	VARCHAR2 with a default of NULL
sort_list	VARCHAR2 with a default of NULL
user_comment	VARCHAR2 with a default of NULL
lob_storage	VARCHAR2 with a default of NULL
lob_tspace	VARCHAR2 with a default of NULL

The purpose of the procedure is to build a queue table and supporting query view for use by the advanced queuing option. Before a queue can be started it must have a supporting queue table built by this procedure. The table will have a value of "aq$ as a prefix. A default ordering of the queue can be enforced by specifying a value for sort_list which is a comma-separated list of sort_column/sort_order pairs. The procedure's input parameters are defined as follows:

q_schema—This is the name of the schema in which the queue table is to be built.

q_table—This is the name of the queue table to be built. Since this is used for default naming of other objects where prefixes and suffixes will be added to it, keep it to 25 characters as a maximum.

q_object_type_schema—This is the name of the schema to which the q_object_type belongs; it will default to the value of q_schema if not specified.

q_object_type—This specifies the object type of the user data stored (if any). If specified the object type must exist when the table is created.

object_type_format—This specifies whether the object type should be created "P"—(packed) or "U"—(unpacked). Unpacked is the default.

storage_space—This is used to specify the storage parameters when the table is created. This parameter can be made up of any combinations of PCTFREE, PCTUSED, INITRANS, MAXTRANS, and a STORAGE clause.

sort_list—This is a comma-separated list of column names and sort orders. This is used to specify the ordering of the queue. Currently the allowed column names are msgid, priority, and enq_time. Use A for ascending order and D for descending order. If not specified, the queue will be FIFO (first in first out, except for priority-coded messages).

user_comment—This is a description of the table which will be added to the queue catalog.

lob_storage—This is a list of storage parameters for the lob column of the queue table.

lob_tspace—Tablespace name for the lob column of the queue table.

There are no documented exceptions generated by this procedure.

CREATE_Q

The procedure create_q has the following input parameters:

q_schema	VARCHAR2
q_name	VARCHAR2
q_table	VARCHAR2
q_type	VARCHAR2 with a default of 'N'
max_retries	NUMBER with a default of 0
retry_delay	NUMBER with a default of 0
misc_tracking	BOOLEAN with a default of false
retention	BOOLEAN with a default of false
ret_time	NATURAL number with a default of NULL
comment	VARCHAR2 with a default of NULL

The purpose of this procedure is to add the configuration information of a new queue into the catalog table sys.aq$queues. Once a queue is created, the start_q, stop_q and alter_q procedures can be used to control it. The q_type parameter is used to control whether a queue is a normal or an exception queue. Only dequeue operations are allowed on an exception queue.

The procedure's input parameters have the following definitions:

q_schema—This specifies the name of the schema to which the queue belongs.

q_name—This specifies the name of the queue that is to be created.

q_table—This specifies the name of the queue table which the queue is to use.

q_type—This specifies the type of queue:

"**N**"—The queue is "normal"; this is the default.

"**E**"—This is an exception queue.

max_retries—Ranges from 1 to 20 and is the number of times processing is retried after a failure. The default of 0 (zero) means no retries and the parameter is ignored.

retry_delay—This specifies the time in seconds to wait to retry this message execution after a transaction rollback. This defaults to 0 (zero), which means that the message should be retried as soon as possible. This parameter has no meaning if the value of max_retries is 0 (zero).

retention—If this is set to TRUE all messages are retained in the queue. The default is FALSE, which tells AQ to destroy a message after a successful dequeue.

ret_time—If specified this is the number of days messages should be retained in the queue after successful execution. If retention is set to TRUE then this value should be nonzero.

user_comment—This is a user-entered comment that is stored in the queue catalog.

There are no documented exceptions for this procedure.

DROP_Q

The procedure drop_q has two input parameters: q_schema (VARCHAR2) and q_name (VARCHAR2). The purpose of this procedure is to drop an existing queue. A queue must be stopped with the stop_q procedure before it can be dropped. If the queue has been stopped when drop_q is executed against it, it cleans up all queue entries and returns. If the queue hasn't been stopped, then a message giving a resource busy error is returned.

The procedure's input parameters are defined as follows:

q_schema—This specifies the name of the schema to which the queue belongs.

q_name—This specifies the name of the queue that should be dropped.

DROP_QTABLE

The procedure drop_qtable has three input parameters: q_schema (VARCHAR2), q_table (VARCHAR2), and force (VARCHAR2 with a default value of 'N'). The purpose of this procedure is to drop an existing queue table.

The procedure's input parameters are defined as follows:

q_schema—The name of the schema to which the queue table to be dropped belongs.

q_table—The name of the queue table to be dropped. A table of the same name is created as a repository for the queue messages.

force—If the parameter is set to "N" then the DBA has to explicitly stop and drop all the queues that use the table before it can be dropped. If set to "Y" then all queues are stopped and dropped internally.

There are no documented exceptions for this procedure.

START_Q

The procedure start_q has three input parameters: q_name (VARCHAR2), enqueue (BOOLEAN with a default of TRUE), and dequeue (BOOLEAN with a default of TRUE). The purpose of the procedure is to start a queue that has just been created or has been stopped via the stop_q command. Queues have to be started before they can be used. The parameters enqueue and dequeue enable and disable queueing of messages. By default both enqueue and dequeue of messages are allowed.

The procedure's input parameters are defined as follows:

q_schema—This is the name of the schema to which the queue belongs.

q_name—This is the name of the queue to start.

enqueue—If TRUE (the default), allows queueing of messages to the queue. FALSE means no messages can be enqueued to the queue.

dequeue—If TRUE (the default), allows de-queueing of messages from the queue. FALSE means no messages can be dequeued from the queue.

There are no documented exceptions on this procedure.

STOP_Q

The procedure stop_q has the following input parameters:

q_schema   VARCHAR2
q_name   VARCHAR2

enqueue	BOOLEAN with a default of TRUE
dequeue	BOOLEAN with a default of TRUE
wait	BOOLEAN with a default of TRUE

The purpose of the procedure is to stop processing on the specified queue. The procedure can selectively stop enqueues, dequeues, or both.

The procedure's input parameters are defined as follows:

q_schema—This is the name of the schema to which the queue belongs.

q_name—This is the name of the schema to operate against.

enqueue—TRUE stops enqueue processing (default). FALSE allows enqueues to continue.

dequeue—TRUE stops dequeue processing (default). FALSE allows dequeues to continue.

wait—TRUE allows transactions currently using the queue to complete before the specified action(s) are taken. FALSE attempts to stop the queue. If no transactions are using the queue it returns immediately; if transactions are using the queue then a resource busy error is returned.

There are no documented exceptions for this procedure.

ALTER_Q

The procedure alter_q accepts the following input arguments:

q_schema	VARCHAR2
q_name	VARCHAR2
max_retries	NUMBER
retry_delay	NUMBER
retention	BOOLEAN

The purpose of the procedure is to alter the specified queue's characteristics. The procedure's input parameters have the same definitions as in the CREATE_Q procedure.

This procedure has no documented exceptions.

11.5   UTL_RAW

This package provides SQL functions for raws that concat, substr, and so on to and from raws. This package is necessary because normal SQL functions do not operate on raws and PL/SQL does not allow overloading between a raw and a char datatype. Also included are routines which convert various COBOL number formats to and from raws.

UTL_RAW is not specific to the database environment and may actually be used in other environments as it exists here. For this reason, the prefix UTL has been given to the package instead of DBMS.

There are many possible uses for the raw functions. The functionality allows a raw "record" to be composed of many elements. By using the raw datatype, character set conversion will not be performed, keeping the raw in its original format when being transferred via rpc. The raw functions also give the ability to manipulate binary data, which was previously limited to the hextoraw and rawtohex functions.

CONCAT

The function concat accepts up to 12 RAW data variables, concatenates them into one larger RAW, and returns the large RAW. Each of the fragments defaults to NULL if not explicitly set to an existing RAW fragment. The function asserts purity so it can be used external to the parent package in other packages. If the concatenated size exceeds 32 K, an error is returned.

The function raises the following exception:

VALUE_ERROR

This exception is raised if the sum of the lengths of the inputs exceeds the maximum allowable length for a RAW (to be revised in a future release).

CAST_TO_RAW

The function cast_to_raw accepts a single input parameter: c (VARCHAR2) and returns a RAW with the equivalent values. The function asserts purity so that it can be used in packages other than the parent package. The purpose of the package as indicated above is to convert a varchar2 represented using N data bytes into a raw with N data bytes. The data is not modified in any way; only its datatype is recast to a RAW datatype.

CAST_TO_VARCHAR2

The function cast_to_varchar2 accepts a single input parameter: r (RAW) and returns a VARCHAR2. The function asserts purity and so may be used in packages other than its parent package. The function's purpose is to cast a raw to a varchar2. This function converts a raw represented using N data bytes into varchar2 with N data bytes.

TIP   When casting to a varchar2, the current NLS character set is used for the characters within that varchar2. Remember that a RAW may be up to 32 K in length while a VARCHAR2 is limited to 2000 in Oracle7 and 4000 in Oracle8.

LENGTH

The function length accepts a single input parameter: r (RAW) and returns a number value. The function asserts purity so it may be used in packages outside of the parent package. The purpose of the function is to return the length in bytes of a RAW. Remember that due to size limits this function should be run before using the cast_to_varchar2 function to prevent data truncation from casting a 32-K RAW into a 4000-byte Oracle8 VARCHAR2.

SUBSTR

The function substr accepts three input parameters: r (RAW), pos (BINARY_ INTEGER), and len (BINARY_INTEGER that defaults to NULL). The function returns a RAW value. The function asserts purity so it may be used in packages outside of the parent package. The purpose of substr is to return a substring portion of raw r beginning at pos for len bytes. If pos is positive, substr counts from the beginning of r to find the first byte. If pos is negative, substr counts backwards from the end of the r. The value pos cannot be 0. If len is omitted, substr returns all bytes to the end of r. The value len cannot be less than 1.

When casting a RAW to a VARCHAR2 it is important to remember that a RAW can be up to 32 K in size while an Oracle8 VARCHAR2 is only 4000 bytes; therefore, the length function should always be used before a casting operation from RAW to VARCHAR2 and if required this function (substr) should be used to parse the RAW into a more manageable size.

The function raises the following exception:

VALUE_ERROR, (to be revised in a future release):
    When pos = 0
    When len < 0

TRANSLATE

The function translate accepts three input parameters: r (RAW), from_set (RAW), and to_set (RAW) and returns a RAW. The function asserts purity so it can be used in packages other than its parent package. The purpose of the function is to translate the bytes in the input r raw according to the bytes in the translation raws, from_set and to_set. If a byte in r has a matching byte in from_set, then it is replaced by the byte in the corresponding position in to_set, or deleted. Bytes in r but undefined in from_set are copied to the result. Only the first (leftmost) occurrence of a byte in from_set is used; subsequent duplicates are not scanned and are ignored. If to_set is shorter than from_set, the extra from_set bytes have no translation correspondence and any bytes in r matching such uncorresponded bytes are deleted from the result raw.

Note these differences from TRANSLITERATE:

- Translation raws have no defaults.
- r bytes undefined in the to_set translation raw are deleted.
- The result raw may be shorter than input r raw.

The function's input parameters are defined as follows:

r—This is the raw source byte-string to be translated.

from_set—These are the raw byte-codes to be translated, if present in r.

to_set—These are the raw byte-codes to which corresponding from_str bytes are translated.

The function raises the following exception:

VALUE_ERROR, (to be revised in a future release):

When r is null and/or has 0 length

When from_set is null and/or has 0 length

When to_set is null and/or has 0 length

TRANSLITERATE

The function transliterate has four input parameters: r (RAW), to_set (RAW with a default value of NULL), from_set (RAW with a default value of NULL), and pad (RAW with a default value of NULL) RETURN RAW. The function asserts purity so it can be used in a package outside of its parent package. The purpose of the function is to transliterate the bytes in the input r raw according to the bytes in the transliteration raws, from_set and to_set. Successive bytes in r are looked-up in the from_set and, if not found, copied unaltered to the result raw, or if found, replaced in the result raw by either corresponding bytes in the to_set or the pad byte when no correspondence exists. Bytes in r but undefined in from_set are copied to the result. Only the first (left-most) occurrence of a byte in from_set is used; subsequent duplicates are not scanned and are ignored.

The result raw is always the same length as r. The from_set and to_set may be of any length. If the to_set is shorter than the from_set, then the pad byte is placed in the result raw when a selected from_set byte has no corresponding to_set byte (as if the to_set were extended to the same length as the from_set with pad bytes).

Note the differences from TRANSLATE:

- r bytes undefined in to_set are padded.
- The result raw is always the same length as input r raw.

The function's input parameters are defined as follows:

r—This is the raw input byte-string to be transliterated.

from_set—These are the raw byte-codes to be translated, if present in r.

to_set—These are the raw byte-codes to which corresponding from_set bytes are translated.

pad—One byte is used when to-set is shorter than the from_set.

The function has the following defaults and optional parameters:

- from_set—x'00 through x'ff

  to_set—to the null string and effectively extended with pad to the length of from_set as necessary
- pad—x'00'

The function returns a raw-transliterated byte-string.

The function raises the following exception:

VALUE_ERROR

This exception is raised when r is null and/or has 0 length (to be revised in a future release).

OVERLAY

The function overlay has these input parameters: overlay_str (RAW), target (RAW), pos (BINARY_INTEGER with a default of 1), len (BINARY_INTEGER with a default of NULL, and pad (RAW with a default of NULL). The function returns a RAW. The function asserts purity so it can be used in packages outside of the parent packages. As its name implies, the purpose of the function is to overlay the specified portion of target raw with overlay raw, starting from byte position pos of target and proceeding for len bytes. If the specified overlay has less than len bytes, it is extended to len bytes using the pad byte. If the specified overlay exceeds len bytes, the extra bytes in the overlay are ignored. If len bytes beginning at position pos of target exceeds the length of target, target will be extended to contain the entire length of overlay (up to 32 K). The data values have the following limitations:

- len, if specified, must be => 0.
- pos, if specified, must be => 1.

If pos exceeds the length of target, target will be padded with pad bytes to position pos, and then target is further extended with overlay bytes.

The function's input parameters are defined as follows:

overlay_str—This is the byte-string used to overlay target.

target—This is the byte-string which is to be overlaid.

pos—This is the position in target (numbered from 1) to start overlay.

len—This is the number of target bytes to overlay.

pad—This is the pad byte used when overlay len exceeds overlay length or pos exceeds target length.

The function raises the following exception:

VALUE_ERROR, (to be revised in a future release):

> When overlay is null and/or has 0 length
>
> When target is missing or undefined
>
> When length of target exceeds maximum length of a raw
>
> When len < 0
>
> When pos < 1

COPIES

The function copies accepts two input parameters, r (RAW) and n (NUMBER), and returns a RAW. The function asserts purity so it can be used in packages outside of its parent package. The purpose of copies is to return n copies of r concatenated together.

The function's input parameters are defined as follows:

r—This is the raw to be copied.

n—This is the number of times to copy the raw (must be positive).

The function returns a single RAW that contains the raw copied n times. The function raises the following exception:

VALUE_ERROR, (to be revised in a future release):

> When r is missing, null and/or 0 length
>
> When n < 1
>
> When length of result exceeds maximum length of a raw

XRANGE

The function xrange accepts two input parameters: start_byte (RAW with a default of NULL) and end_byte (RAW with a default of NULL). The function returns a RAW. The function asserts purity so it can be used in packages outside of its parent package. The purpose of the function is to return a raw containing all valid 1-byte encodings in succession beginning with the value start_byte and ending with the value end_byte. If start_byte is greater than end_byte, the succession of result bytes begins with start_byte, wraps through 'FF'x to '00'x, and ends at end_byte. If specified, start_byte and end_byte must be single-byte raws.

The function has the following input parameters:

start_byte—This is the beginning byte-code value of resulting sequence (defaults to x'00').

end_byte—This is the ending byte-code value of resulting sequence (defaults to x'FF').

The function returns a raw containing a succession of 1-byte hexadecimal encodings.

REVERSE

The function reverse accepts one input parameter, r (RAW), and returns a RAW. The function asserts purity so it may be used in packages outside of its parent package. The purpose of reverse is to reverse a byte sequence in raw r from end to end. For example, x'0102F3' would be reversed into x'F30201' and 'xyz' would be reversed into 'zyx'. The result length is the same as the input raw length.

The function raises the following exception:

VALUE_ERROR

This exception is raised when r is null and/or has 0 length (to be revised in a future release).

COMPARE

The function compare accepts three input parameters: r1 (RAW), r2 (RAW), and pad (RAW with a default of NULL). The function returns a NUMBER. The function asserts purity so it can be used in packages outside of its parent package. The function compares raw r1 against raw r2 and returns 0 if r1 and r2 are identical; otherwise, it returns the position of the first byte from r1 that does not match r2. If r1 and r2 differ in length, the shorter raw is extended on the right with pad if necessary. The default pad byte is x'00'.

The function's input parameters are defined as follows:

r1—This is the first raw to be compared; may be null and/or 0 length.

r2—This is the second raw to be compared; may be null and/or 0 length.

pad—This is the byte to extend whichever of r1 or r2 is shorter.

CONVERT

The function convert accepts three input parameters: r (RAW), to_charset (VARCHAR2), and from_charset (VARCHAR2). The function returns a RAW. The function asserts purity so it may be used in packages outside of the parent package. The purpose of the function is to convert raw r from character set from_charset to character set to_charset and return the resulting raw. Both from_charset and to_charset must be supported character sets defined to the Oracle server.

The function's input parameters are defined as follows:

r—This is the raw byte-string to be converted.

to_charset—This is the name of the NLS character set to which r is converted.

from_charset—This is the name of the NLS character set in which r is supplied.

The function raises the following exception:

VALUE_ERROR, (to be revised in a future release):

When r missing, null and/or 0 length

When from_charset or to_charset are missing, null, and/or 0 length

When from_charset or to_charset names are invalid or unsupported

BIT_AND

The function bit_and accepts two input parameters: r1 (RAW) and r2 (RAW). The function returns a RAW. The function asserts purity so it can be used in packages other than the parent package. The purpose of the bit_and function is to perform bitwise logical "and" of the values in raw r1 with raw r2 and return the "anded" result raw. If r1 and r2 differ in length, the "and" operation is terminated after the last byte of the shorter of the two raws, and the unprocessed portion of the longer raw is appended to the partial result. The result length equals the longer of the two input raws.

The function's input parameters are defined as follows:

r1—This is the raw to "and" with r2.

r2—This is the raw to "and" with r1.

The function returns a raw containing the "and" of r1 and r2 or a null if either the r1 or r2 input parameter was null.

BIT_OR

The function bit_or accepts two input parameters: r1 (RAW) and r2 (RAW). The function returns a RAW. The function asserts purity so it can be used in packages outside of the parent package. The purpose of the function is to perform bitwise logical "or" of the values in raw r1 with raw r2 and return the "or'd" result raw. If r1 and r2 differ in length, the "or" operation is terminated after the last byte of the shorter of the two raws, and the unprocessed portion of the longer raw is appended to the partial result. The result length equals the longer of the two input raws.

The function has the following input parameters:

r1—This is the raw to "or" with r2.

r2—This is the raw to "or" with r1.

The function returns raw containing the "or" of r1 and r2 or a null if either the r1 or r2 input parameter was null.

BIT_XOR

The function bit_xor accepts two input parameters: r1 (RAW) and r2 (RAW). The function returns a RAW. The function asserts purity so it can be used in packages external to the parent function. The function performs a bitwise logical "exclusive or" of the values in raw r with raw r2 and returns the "xor'd" result raw. If r1 and r2 differ in length, the "xor" operation is terminated after the last byte of the shorter of the two raws, and the unprocessed portion of the longer raw is appended to the partial result. The result length equals the longer of the two input raws.

The function's input parameters are defined as follows:

r1—This is the raw to "xor" with r2.

r2—This is the raw to "xor" with r1.

The function returns a raw containing the "xor" of r1 and r2 or a null if either the r1 or r2 input parameter was null.

BIT_COMPLEMENT

The function bit_complement accepts a single parameter: r (RAW). The function returns a RAW. The function asserts purity so it can be used in packages other than its parent package. The purpose of the bit_complement function is to perform bitwise logical "complement" of the values in the provided raw variable and return the "complemented" result raw. The result length equals the input raw r length.

The function's input parameter is defined as follows:

r—This is the raw to perform the "complement" operation.

The function's return value is raw, which is the "complement" of r1, or null if the r input parameter was null.

11.6   OTHER SQL SCRIPTS PROVIDED BY ORACLE

In addition to the Oracle Provided Packages and Procedures, Oracle Corporation also has provided several utility SQL scripts for use by DBAs. These scripts help with dependency mapping, index verification, and many other very useful tasks.

The UTL Series of Scripts

Generally speaking, the scripts with a prefix of "UTL" are used for tuning and troubleshooting. The exceptions are the utlfile.sql and utlraw.sql scripts that build the utl_file and utl_raw packages, which were covered in previous sections.

utlbstat.sql and utlestat.sql The utlbstat (begin statistics) and utlestat (end statistics) are two companion scripts. They are used to take a start and end snapshot of vital system statistics for tuning purposes. The utlbstat script creates a table and selects tuning-specific statistics (see Chapter 15), placing them into the table as a start snapshot. The utlestat reselects the statistics and does a delta comparison, then generates a set of reports that the DBA can use to help diagnose tuning problems.

utlchain.sql The utilchain.sql script creates the table for use with the ANALYZE TABLE LIST CHAINED ROWS command. It creates a table of the form:

```
create table CHAINED_ROWS (
    owner_name          varchar2(30),
    table_name          varchar2(30),
    cluster_name        varchar2(30),
    partition_name      varchar2(30),
    head_rowid          rowid,
    analyze_timestamp   date
);
```

in the current schema.

utldidxs.sql, utloidxs.sql and utlsidxs.sql Very often, when an application is running slowly, the reason will be the presence of an unneeded index or the absence of a needed one. These scripts help in pinpointing those situations.

These three scripts allow analysis of a user's indexes, or indexed columns:

UTLSIDXS.SQL	The main script
UTLOIDXS.SQL	Run for ONE index
UTLDIDXS.SQL	Display statistics

UTLSIDXS.SQL—This script runs UTLOIDXS.SQL on multiple tables and columns. It takes two parameters: the table name and the column name to run it on. It will not accept a column that is not part of a nonunique index.

UTLOIDXS.SQL—This script takes two parameters: the table name and the column name to do the analysis on. It will accept any column of any table. It should be used to analyze possible new candidates for indexes.

UTLDIDXS.SQL—This script reports the index statistics generated by the previous two scripts. It takes the same two parameters, either of which may be wildcarded in standard SQL fashion (%, for example).

In order to use the scripts, normally, users should run UTLSIDXS.SQL on their current application, then run UTLDIDXS.SQL, looking for tables with a large amount of BADNESS or very nondistinct keys.

Then, if users wish to check on new index columns, they use UTLOIDXS.SQL on those columns.

Since the scripts create two tables (see below), users should remember to drop them when the analysis is finished.

> **T**IP   Two tables are created by the scripts—INDEX$INDEX_STATS, which holds global statistics for each table, and INDEX$BADNESS_STATS, which holds the badness tables for each table.

> **T**IP   The code currently does not understand concatenated indexes. However, a technique for fooling the script is shown in Chapter 14.

utldtree.sql This procedure, view, and temp table will allow you to see all objects that are (recursively) dependent on the given object. The script creates the procedure dep_tree owned by the current schema.

> **T**IP   You will only see objects for which you have permission.

Here are some examples:

- For a procedure:

```
SQL>execute deptree_fill('procedure', 'accts_dba', 'billing');
SQL>select * from deptree order by seq#;
```

- For a table:

```
SQL>execute deptree_fill('table', 'accts_dba', 'emp');
SQL>select * from deptree order by seq#;
```

- For a package body:

```
SQL>execute deptree_fill('package body', 'accts_dba', 'accts_payable');
SQL>select * from deptree order by seq#;
```

   A prettier way to display this information than:

```
select * from deptree order by seq#;
```

is:

```
select * from ideptree;
```

This view, ideptree (indented dependency tree), shows the dependency relationship via indenting. Notice that no order by clause is needed with ideptree as is needed with the deptree table select.

utlexcpt.sql This script is used to create the exceptions table used with the ALTER TABLE command to enable constraints using the EXCEPTIONS INTO clause. This is the table to put exceptions into. The table has the following structure:

```
create table exceptions(
       row_id          rowid,
       owner           varchar2(30),
       table_name      varchar2(30),
       constraint      varchar2(30));
```

utlexp6.sql This script is used to create a list of objects from an Oracle7 or Oracle8 database that will not be exported using the Oracle version 6 export. The script is a series of selects against various data dictionary tables.

utllockt.sql This script is used to print out the lock wait-for graph in tree-structured fashion. This is useful for diagnosing systems that are hung on locks.

The script prints the sessions in the system that are waiting for locks, and the locks that they are waiting for. The printout is tree structured. If a session id is printed immediately below and to the right of another session, then it is waiting for that session. The session ids printed at the left-hand side of the page are the ones that processes are waiting for.

For example, in Listing 11.1, session 9 is waiting for session 8, 7 is waiting for 9, and 10 is waiting for 9.

LISTING 11.1 Lock wait tree example.

WAITING_SESSION	TYPE	MODE REQUESTED	MODE HELD	LOCK ID1	LOCK ID2
8	NONE	None	None	0	0
9	TX	Share (S)	Exclusive (X)	55547	16
7	RW	Exclusive (X)	S/Row-X (SSX)	33554440	2
10	RW	Exclusive (X)	S/Row-X (SSX)	33554440	2

The lock information to the right of the session id describes the lock that the session is waiting for (not the lock it is holding).

Note that this is a script and not a set of view definitions because connect-by is used in the implementation and therefore a temporary table is created and dropped since you cannot do a join in a connect-by.

The script has two small disadvantages. First, a table is created when this script is run. To create a table, a number of locks must be acquired. This might cause the session running the script to get caught in the lock problem it is trying to diagnose. Second, if a session waits on a lock held by more than one session (share lock) then the wait-for graph is no longer a tree and the connect-by will show the session (and any sessions waiting on it) several times.

The script creates the table lock_holders:

```
create table LOCK_HOLDERS      / temporary table /
(
  waiting_session              number
  holding_session              number,
  lock_type                    varchar2(26),
  mode_held                    varchar2(14),
  mode_requested               varchar2(14),
  lock_id1                     varchar2(22),
  lock_id2                     varchar2(22)
);
```

And the table dba_locks_temp which is a simple "CREATE TABLE dba_locks_temp AS SELECT * FROM DBA_LOCKS". This is essentially a copy of the dba_waiters view but runs faster since it caches the result of selecting from dba_locks.

utlmail.sql   The utlmail.sql script is used to upgrade the mail database for access from rpc. The script will upgrade the mail database with the appropriate user, views, and privileges so that the dbms_mail pl/sql package can be used to send email.

TIP   Run the utlmail.sql script as user "email."

The password of the email account of this database need not be divulged.

There needs to be a user in this database (e.g., rmail/rmail) so that the package "dbms_mail" can be created. This account should only have "connect" privilege. This account name and password will need to be given to the installer of the "dbms_mail" package so that he or she can create appropriate database links. This user also needs to be a valid Oracle*Mail user. For example, create user rmail as follows:

```
SQL> create user rmail identified by rmail;
SQL> grant connect to rmail;
<now add rmail as a valid Oracle*Mail user>
```

T IP   If you run this script multiple times, you will get an error regarding the creation of the sequence "m_id_seq" since it already exists. This error message is *OK*. Do not drop this sequence once created. If you do, and recreate it, you will then get DUPLICATE mail ids.

utlsampl.sql This is the birthplace (actually one of many) for scott/tiger and its associated tables, indexes. and what-have-you.

utltkprf.sql This script creates the role tkprofer which facilitates the running of the tkprof utility in later versions of Oracle7 and in Oracle8.

utlxplan.sql This script creates the explain_plan table used by the explain plan facility (covered in Chapter 14). The table doesn't have to be named plan_table but it does have to have the same structure:

This is the format for the table that is used by the EXPLAIN PLAN statement. The explain statement requires the presence of this table in order to store the descriptions of the row sources. This is the Oracle8 format:

```
create table PLAN_TABLE (
    statement_id           varchar2(30),
    timestamp              date,
    remarks                varchar2(80),
    operation              varchar2(30),
    options                varchar2(30),
    object_node            varchar2(128),
    object_owner           varchar2(30),
    object_name            varchar2(30),
    object_instance        numeric,
    object_type            varchar2(30),
    optimizer              varchar2(255),
    search_columns         number,
    id                     numeric,
    parent_id              numeric,
    position               numeric,
    cost                   numeric,
    cardinality            numeric,
    bytes                  numeric,
    other_tag              varchar2(255),
    partition_start        varchar2(255),
    partition_stop         varchar2(255),
    partition_id           numeric,
    other                  long);
```

This is the Oracle7 format (7.3.2):

```
create table PLAN_TABLE (
    statement_id           varchar2(30),
```

```
timestamp               date,
remarks                 varchar2(80),
operation               varchar2(30),
options                 varchar2(30),
object_node             varchar2(128),
object_owner            varchar2(30),
object_name             varchar2(30),
object_instance         numeric,
object_type             varchar2(30),
optimizer               varchar2(255),
search_columns          numeric,
id                      numeric,
parent_id               numeric,
position                numeric,
cost                    numeric,
cardinality             numeric,
bytes                   numeric,
other_tag               varchar2(255),
other                   long);
```

The Scripts Run by catproc.sql

All of these scripts are located in the $ORACLE_HOME/rdbms/admin directory or its equivalent on your platform. These scripts build virtually the entire set of Oracle utilities including PL/SQL.

Basic Procedural Views

catprc.sql This creates data dictionary views for types, stored procedures, and triggers. This script must be run while connected to sys or internal.

catjobq This script creates the catalog views for the job queue. This script must be run while connected as SYS or INTERNAL.

Remote Views

catrpc This script creates internal views for RPC (Remote Procedural Calls). These views are needed only for databases with the procedural option that are accessed by remote databases. This script must be run as SYS.

Setup for pl/sql

dbmsstdx.sql This package provides kernel extensions to package standard. Routines in this package do not need to be qualified by the owner or package name, similar to the behavior of package 'standard'. This package mostly contains utility routines for triggers.

pipidl.sql This creates the package Portable IDL.

pidian.sql This creates the infamous package Diana.

diutil.sql This creates Diana application routines.

pistub.sql This script generates the subprogram stub generator.

plitblm.sql This is PL/sql Index-TaBLe Methods Package for index-table operations. This package must be loaded by catproc.sql script. This file needs to be kept in sync with its .pls version (icd/plitblm.pls) currently. We hope to soon eliminate this dependency once we automate the generation of .pls version.

Packages Implementing PL/SQL File Data Type
utlfile.sql and prvtfile.plb This creates the utl_file package.

PL/SQL Packages Used for RDBMS Functionality
prvtssql.plb This creates the DBMS_SYS_SQL package (similar to the DBMS_SQL package).

dbmsutil.sql and prvtutil.plb This creates numerous utility packages including DBMS_UTILITY, DBMS_DDL, DBMS_SESSION, and so on.

dbmsapin.sql and prvtapin.plb This creates the DBMS_APPLICATION_INFO package.

dbmssyer.sql and prvtsyer.plb This creates the DBMS_SYS_ERROR-pl/sql routines for system error messages for DBMS* routines.

dbmslock.sql and prvtlock.plb This creates the DBMS_LOCK package.

dbmspipe.sql and prvtpipe.plb This creates the DBMS_PIPE package.

dbmsalrt.sql and prvtalrt.plb This creates the DBMS_ALERT package.

dbmsotpt.sql and prvtotpt.plb This creates the DBMS_OUTPUT package.

dbmsdesc.sql and prvtdesc.plb This creates the DBMS_DESCRIBE package.

dbmssql.sql and prvtsql.plb This creates the DBMS_SQL package.

dbmspexp and prvtpexp.plb This creates the DBMS_EXPORT_EXTENSIONS package.

dbmsjob.sql and prvtjob.plb This creates the DBMS_JOB package.

Tables, Views, and Packages for AQ
catqueue.sql This file contains the queue dictionary information which is created in the SYSTEM schema. There are three main tables:

- aq$_queue_tables—stores information about all the queue tables
- aq$_queue_table_sort—stores information about the queue sort columns
- aq$_queues—stores information about all the queues

This script also calls the following:

dbmsaq.plb and prvtaq.plb This creates the DBMS_AQ package.

dbmsaqad.sql and prvtaqad.plb This creates the DBMS_AQADM package.

Views and Tables for Deferred RPC

catdefer.sql This script creates the catalog of deferred rpc queues. This file contains sql which creates the base tables used to store deferred remote procedure calls for use in transaction replication. Here is a list of the tables:

    defTran
    defTranDest
    defError
    defCallDest
    defDefaultDest
    defCall
    defSchedule

Tables created in this file are owned by user system, not sys. Views owned by sys, and a synonym owned by sys are created to preserve code compatibility. The defcalldest view defined in this file is replaced with a different view by the catrepc.sql script. If the repcat tables are installed, the catrepc.sql script should always be run after this script is run. Tables are created in catdefrt.sql. All other objects are created here.

catdefrt.sql This creates the catalog for deferred rpc tables. This is called from catdefer.sql and must be called after the DBMS_AQADM package is built.

catsnap This script creates data dictionary views for snapshots and must be run while connected to SYS or INTERNAL.

TIP   dbmsdfrd is replaced by dbmsdefr for the replication option.

---

dbmsdfrd.sql and prvtdfrd.plb These create the packages that enable replicated deferred remote procedure calls. The external interfaces and bodies of two replication packages are also included, as are some sequences used by the packages. All objects are created in the schema 'SYS'.

Packages created by these scripts are as follows:

dbms_defer

dbms_defer_query

dbms_defer_sys

The algorithms used here were originally conceived by Sandeep Jain, and are described in an internal Oracle Corporation memo by Sandeep Jain and Dean Daniels, titled "A Method for Deferring Remote Procedure Calls Utilizing a Relational Database System."

These packages use calls from the DBMS_SQL, DBMS_ASYNCRPC, and DBMS_DEFER_PACK packages. This script is to be run by users connected as SYS or INTERNAL.

Tables and sequences created by this script are kept private. The dbms_defer package is granted to public, but it is reasonable to restrict access to users creating replicated applications. The dbms_defer_query package can be executed by users who need to monitor deferred rpc queues, for example, a DBA correcting conflicts. The dbms_defer_sys package is granted to DBAs (by default). The dbms_defer_internal_sys packages is kept private. The dbms_defer_pack package is kept private, as is dbms_asyncrpc.

dbmsitrg.sql and prvtitrg.plb These are internalized triggers package specs.

dbmssnap.sql and prvtsnap.plb These create the DBMS_SNAPSHOT utilities for snapshots.

prvtxpsw.plb This creates the package dbms_pswmg_import used by the password management utilities.

Probe Packages

dbmspb.sql and prvtpb.plb This creates the ProBe (PL/SQL debugger) server-side packages, server-side packages that implement server-side Probe support. This package must be installed as SYS. This package is not intended to be used directly by the ordinary user: it is a low-level interface to Probe services.

Views for Tablespace Point-in-Time Recovery

catpitr.sql This script creates the tablespace point-in-time specific views. This script must be run while connected as SYS or INTERNAL.

dbmspitr and prvtpitr.plb These create tablespace point-in-time recovery functions. This package contains a set of procedures used during a tablespace point-in-time recovery. This package uses dynamic SQL to execute DDL statements. CATPROC. SQL script should be run. The script creates the package DBMS_PITR.

This package contains procedures which get called during the import phase and export phase of point-in-time recovery (PITR). During the export phase, EXP calls this package to obtain the text of two anonymous PL/SQL blocks. The first block goes at the front of the .dmp file, and the second block goes at the end. In between the two blocks are the DDL commands created by EXP to reconstruct the dictionary for the tablespaces being PITR'd.

The emitted PL/SQL code contains calls to other procedures in this package. IMP must read each anonymous PL/SQL block from the .dmp file, collect it into a single contiguous memory buffer, and then parse and execute the PL/SQL block. The parsed SQL statement (the plsql anonymous block) must be the precise lines of text that were returned to EXP from this package, with no characters added or deleted. If things are changed you will get an error and won't be able to recover.

The "emit" procedures are intended to be called in the following sequence:

```
dbms_pitr.beginExport;
dbms_pitr.selectTablespace('tsname_1'); \
     :                      > called once per tablespace
dbms_pitr.selectTablespace('tsname_N'); /
dbms_pitr.selectBlock(dbms_pitr.ts_pitr_begin);
dbms_pitr.getLine;  > called until it returns NULL
dbms_pitr.selectBlock(dbms_pitr.ts_pitr_end);
dbms_pitr.getLine;  > called until it returns NULL
```

In the exp.dmp file, it would look like this:

```
dbms_pitr.beginImport;
dbms_pitr.adjustCompatibility(...);
     :
dbms_pitr.beginTablespace(tsname);
dbms_pitr.doFileVerify(...);
     :
dbms_pitr.endTablespace;
dbms_pitr.commitPitr
dbms_pitr.endImport;
```

TIP   This data is for information only. Do *not* try tablespace point-in-time recovery without the assistance of Oracle Technical Support.

PL/SQL Packages for LOB (Large Objects)

dbmslob.sql and prvtlob.plb These create the DBMS_LOB package, the DBMS package specification for Oracle8 large objects. This package provides routines for operations on BLOB and CLOB datatypes.

The procedural option is needed to use this package. This package must be created under SYS (connect internal). Operations provided by this package are performed under the current calling user, not under the package owner SYS.

11.7   SCRIPTS NOT RUN BY CATPROC.SQL

There are numerous useful routines not included in the standard Oracle PL/SQL build routine catproc.sql. I have attempted to list as many as I can here in this section. Depending on the version of Oracle you have, you may or may not have all of these.

Scripts Run by catalog.sql

catadt.sql This SQL script creates data dictionary views for showing metadata information for types and other object features in the RDBMS. This script must be run while connected as SYS or INTERNAL.

cataudit.sql This script creates data dictionary views for auditing. Must be run while connected to SYS or INTERNAL.

catexp.sql This script creates the data dictionary views for export and import. If the proper version isn't run during upgrades you may not be able to import or export properly.

catldr.sql This script creates the views for direct loading of data into the database.

catsvrmg.sql This script creates the views for the server manager.

catpart.sql This script creates the data dictionary views for partitioned objects such as tables and indexes.

11.8   INDEPENDENT SCRIPTS

There are several independent scripts that aren't run by any major package. A couple of them are pretty useful, such as catblock.sql and dbmspool.sql, and why they aren't run as a matter of course, I don't know. Anyway, here are most of the major ones; run them if you need or want to.

catblock.sql

I always run this script when I build a database. The script creates views of Oracle locks. DBA_LOCKS, WAITERS, and BLOCKERS views are created by this script.

catdbsyn.sql—Catalog DBA Synonyms

This script creates private synonyms for DBA-only dictionary views. This file is made obsolete as DBA is now a role. All DBA_% catalog views have a corresponding public synonym, and are accessible to any user with SELECT ANY TABLE privilege.

catexp6.sql and catexp7.sql

These are catexp6.sql or catexp7.sql—CATalog EXPort views for v6 or v7 SQL scripts. The scripts create v6 or v7 style export/import views against the v8 RDBMS or v7 RDBMS (for v6) so that EXP/IMP v7 or v6 can be used to read out data in a v8 RDBMS or v7 RDBMS (for v6).

The v7 file is organized into 3 sections:

Section 1: Views needed *both* by export and import

Section 2: Views required *only* by import

Section 3: Views required *only* by export

catio.sql—I/O-per-Table Statistics

This script allows the kernel to collect I/O-per-table (actually object) statistics by statistical sampling. This works by sampling the buffer at the end of the buffer cache LRU list. The theory is that this buffer was read in at some point and therefore counts as an IO. All buffers that are read in will eventually find themselves at the end of the LRU list. There is a stored procedure that periodically samples the buffer at the end of the lru list and a view that generates a database object name given the block number of the buffer.

Note that this file will tell you the distribution of IOs between tables, but it will not tell you the exact number of IOs.

catparr.sql

This script creates the parallel-server specific views for performance queries, and so on. (also some useful views for other queries such as the v$bh and ping tables). This script must be run while connected as SYS or INTERNAL. I suggest running this script even though you may not be running parallel (shared) server. The tables the script creates keep track of the status of all SGA blocks.

catsnmp.sql

This script creates an SNMPAgent role to access the v$ tables.

cattrust.sql

This script creates the views for Trusted ORACLE. This script must be run at DBLOW while connected as SYS or INTERNAL.

dbmspool.sql and prvtpool.plb

These scripts create the DBMS_SHARED_POOL package. I always run this package when the database is created along with catblock.sql and catparr.sql.

pupbld.sql

This script is generally located in the dbs subdirectory or under the plus/demo or plus/admin subdirectory. This script is the one responsible for those annoying errors about the "product_user_profile table" that you can get when you build your own database. This script should be run from SYSTEM, not SYS or INTERNAL. This script is used by the DBA to create the product_profile and user_profile tables in the SYSTEM account. There are two views, product_privs and user_privs, which are what users will see as product_profile and user_profile. They allow users to see (and in the case of user_profile, modify) only their own privileges or profiles.

These tables are actually pretty useless in most cases although they can still be used to restrict access via SQL*Plus to various SQL commands. The entire mess will probably be done away with in later releases.

11.9   VERSION 7 SPECIFIC SCRIPT RUN BY CATPROC.SQL UNDER VERSION 7

standard.sql—Standard Types and Functions

This is generated in a PLSQL dve from stdspc.pls and stdbdy.pls using a PLSQL tool (ps2s.pls). This has been internalized in Oracle8 and thus is no longer run by catproc.sql, although several scripts make reference to it.

CHAPTER 12

Monitoring Database Tables, Clusters, Snapshots, Types, and Indexes

Since the days of SQLDBA or nothing, Oracle has come a long way with its database monitoring tools. Server Manager (SVRMGR), Enterprise Manager, and the numerous other monitoring tools that Oracle has provided have made the monitoring of databases easier. However, many of these still only look at the very top level of the data dictionary, answering questions such as how many users, how many tables, and how many indexes but doing little in the way of deep monitoring (What is user X doing? When will table y extend next?) There are several companies which offer excellent monitoring tools: Savant, with its Q package (demo included on CD), Patrol from BMC, ECO Tools, and the many offerings from Platinum Technologies spring to mind.

All of these tools, while freeing some DBAs, end up crippling others because they never learn the underlying structures of the data dictionary. I am a firm believer in not providing complex, feature-rich tools to beginning DBAs, until they understand the data dictionary. The tools still only go so far and a DBA has to be able to dig into the data dictionary to find and correct problems. If you believe great tools make great works, try giving the best materials and the best tools to poor workers; the result may be better than with poor materials and tools, but it will still probably be unsatisfactory. As with all things, in Oracle knowledge means power: the power to solve problems and to prevent them from happening in the first place.

In the last few years since my first book, I have had to interview dozens of candidates for DBA and developer positions. Some had great resumes but when you began asking about the data dictionary and V$ tables, really getting under the hood of Oracle, they were clueless. I don't want anyone to say that about you. Appendices D and E should become your map, guide, and bible to the Oracle data dictionary and support tables. Refer to Appendices D and E (on the CD-ROM) throughout this chapter for definitions of the various views and tables used by the monitoring scripts. I have attempted to provide a "roadmap" of the views that relate to a specific topic (such as table or indexes). Use this map and Appendices D and E on the CD-ROM to see how the data dictionary views are laid out.

The data dictionary tables (which are usually suffixed with a dollar ($) sign but there are exceptions) are owned by the SYS user and normally shouldn't be accessed except when the supporting views don't have the required data. These are documented in Appendix D on the CD-ROM. Instead, Oracle has provided DBA_, USER_, and ALL_ views into these tables, which should be used whenever possible; the DBA_ views are documented in Appendix E on the CD-ROM. In addition, Oracle has provided the dynamic performance tables (DPTs) that provide running statistics and internals information. These DPTs all begin with V$ or, in their pristine form, V_$. The DPTs are also documented in Appendix D.

The data dictionary views are created by the catalog.sql script located in the $ORACLE_HOME/rdbms/admin directory. The catalog.sql script is a required readme file. The script has numerous remarks and comments that will improve your understanding of the data dictionary views severalfold. I warn you though, the catalog.sql script is over two hundred pages long.

12.1   USING THE ORACLE7 AND ORACLE8 DATA DICTIONARY

These tables, views, and DPTs provide detailed information about the system, the data dictionary, and the processes for the Oracle database. Reports can access the data dictionary objects to give the DBA just about any cut on the data he or she desires. Many if not all of the reports in the following sections utilize these objects either directly or indirectly via the $tables, V$ DPTs, or DBA_ views.

The data dictionary objects can also be queried interactively during a DBA user session to find the current status of virtually any system parameter. Use of dynamic SQL against the DBA_ views can shorten a DBA task, such as switching users from one temporary tablespace to another or dropping a set of tables, by a factor of 10 or more.

In the days of SQLDBA it was often easier to monitor with scripts than with the Oracle-provided monitor screens. The SVRMGR product, with its GUI interface, is an improvement as is the Enterprise Manager. However, these still don't provide the flexibility available from user-generated scripts. The Performance Pack can be customized to add user-generated monitoring queries. However, the Performance Pack is a cost add-on to the system DBA tools.

However, all of the above lack adequate report capabilities. To remedy this shortfall, DBAs must be prepared to create SQL, SQL*Plus, and PL/SQL reports that provide just the cut of information they require. The next sections discuss these reports and show example scripts used to generate them. It is suggested that the DBA review the contents of the V$ and DBA_ views as listed in either the *Oracle8* or *Oracle7 Server Administrator's Guide*. Additional information is contained in the *Oracle8* or *Oracle7 Server Reference Guide*.

12.2 USING THE VIEWS AND DYNAMIC PERFORMANCE TABLES TO MONITOR TABLES, CLUSTERS, SNAPSHOTS, TYPES, AND INDEXES

Now that we know all about the views and DPTs, let's look at how they are used to monitor various database-table-related constructs.

Monitoring Tables with the V$ and DBA_ Views

It used to be that for tables, the DBA had four major concerns. Who owns them, where are they created, are they clustered, and what is their space utilization? Now, with Oracle8 the DBA also has to be concerned with issues such as: Is the table an object or relational table? Does the table contain REFs, VARRAYS, or NESTED TABLES? Is the table (if relational) partitioned? The scripts and techniques in this section will answer these types of questions about tables. The Oracle Administrator toolbar provides the schema manager, which allows GUI-based management of database schema objects. The screen for Oracle version 7.3 of this product is shown in Figure 12.1. The Oracle Administrator product is great for on-screen viewing of database objects, but lacks suitable report capabilities, so the ability to monitor database

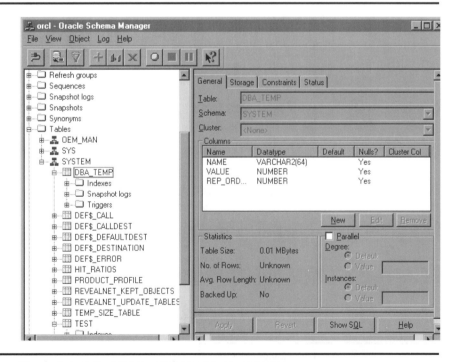

FIGURE 12.1   Oracle Enterprise Manager Schema Manager screen.

objects via scripts is still critical. To this end, we will examine a few simple reports, and look at Figure 12.2, which shows the cluster of DBA_ views used to monitor tables.

Monitoring Ownership, Placement, and Clustering The first three items on this list can be determined with a single report. This report for tables is shown in

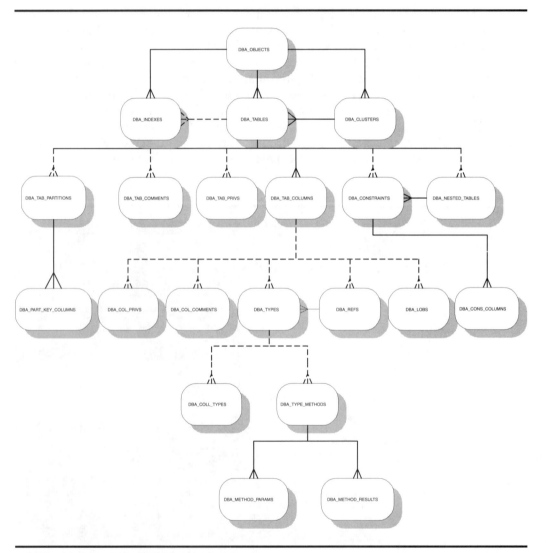

FIGURE 12.2   DBA_TABLES view cluster.

Source 12.1. It is also important to monitor tables right after they have been created for proper sizing and storage parameters. This can be accomplished through use of the script in Source 12.1, which documents how a table was created. The Enterprise Manager application provides this data in a very user-friendly format.

SOURCE 12.1   Table report script.

```
REM
REM NAME          : TABLE.SQL
REM FUNCTION      : GENERATE TABLE REPORT
REM Limitations : None
REM MRA 6/12/97 Updated to ORACLE8
REM
CLEAR COLUMNs
COLUMN owner              FORMAT a15    HEADING 'Table|Owner'
COLUMN table_name                       HEADING Table
COLUMN tablespace_name    FORMAT A15    HEADING Tablespace
COLUMN pct_increase                     HEADING 'Pct|Increase'
COLUMN init                             HEADING 'Initial|Extent'
COLUMN next                             HEADING 'Next|Extent'
COLUMN partitioned        FORMAT a15    HEADING 'Partitioned?'
BREAK ON owner ON tablespace_name
SET PAGES 48 LINES 132
START title132 "ORACLE TABLE REPORT"
SPOOL rep_out\&db\tab_rep
SELECT
     owner,
     tablespace_name,
     table_name,
     initial_extent Init,
     next_extent Next,
     pct_increase,
     partitioned
FROM
     sys.dba_tables
WHERE
     owner NOT IN ('SYSTEM', 'SYS')
ORDER BY
     owner,
     tablespace_name,
     table_name;
SPOOL OFF
CLEAR COLUMNS
PAUSE Press enter to continue
SET PAGES 22 LINES 80
TTITLE OFF
CLEAR COLUMNS
CLEAR BREAKS
```

LISTING 12.1   Example of the table report script output.

```
Date: 06/13/97                                                    Page:    1
Time: 09:13 PM                    ORACLE TABLE REPORT                 SYSTEM
                                 ORTEST1 database


Table                                       Initial    Next     Pct
Owner      Tablespace   Table                Extent    Extent   Increase Partitioned?
--------   -----------  -----------------   ---------  -------- -------- ------------
TELE_DBA   RAW_DATA     LOAD_TEST           420474880  104857600       0 NO
           SCOPUS_DATA  ACCOUNT_EXECS           12288      12288       0 NO
                        ADDRESSES           209715200  104857600       0 NO
                        ADDRESSESV8             20480      20480      50 NO
                        ADDRESS_TEST            20480      20480      50 NO
                        AUDIT_RECORDS           12288      12288       0 NO
                        BATCH_CONTROL           20480   14729216      50 NO
                        BATCH_CONTROL2       20971520    5242880       0 NO
                        CIRCUITSV8              20480      20480      50 NO
                        CIRCUIT_ID_INFO     209715200  104857600       0 NO
                        CLIENTPROFILES          53248      53248       0 NO
                        CLIENTS             209715200  104857600       0 NO
                        CLIENTSV8            20971520   10485760       0 NO
                        COMPANY                 20480      20480      50 NO
                        CONTRACTS               12288      12288       0 NO
                        CONTRACTSV8             20480      20480      50 NO
                        DUNS_TRACKING_RECORDS   12288      12288       0 NO
                        EARNINGS_INFO_NMBRS 209715200  104857600       0 NO
                        EARNINGS_INFO_NUMBERSV8 20971520 10485760      0 NO
                        EMPLOYEES               20480      20480       0 NO
                        FRANCHISE_CODES      78643200   10485760       0 NO
                        INTERACTION_LOG         32768      32768       0 NO
                        INTERACTION_LOG_ACTIVITY 12288    12288       0 NO
                        LOOKUPS                 12288      12288       0 NO
                        SIC_CODES           104857600  104857600       0 NO
                        SYSTEM_USER_PROFILES    12288      12288       0 NO

26 rows selected.
```

One thing to notice about the script in Source 12.1 is that it excludes the tables owned by SYSTEM and SYS. Since a good DBA never uses these users unless absolutely required, no extraneous tables should be created after product loads; therefore the data won't change. We are more concerned with new tables for the purposes of this report. The items the DBA should watch for in the output of this report script shown in Listing 12.1 follow.

1. Tables that should belong to a specific application belonging to a specific user rather than the assigned application owner.
2. Excessive use of clusters.
3. Tables showing up in the SYSTEM tablespace, or in tablespaces other than where they belong.

You will also note this report gives no sizing information. This is covered next. The determination whether the sizing of tables is correct is one of the important tasks of the DBA.

Monitoring Size of Tables One method to determine if your default storage sizing is correct for a tablespace is to monitor the extents for each of the tables that reside in the tablespace. Another method is to monitor the used space against the available space for each table. Scripts to perform these functions are shown in Sources 12.2 and 12.3.

SOURCE 12.2   SQL*Plus report to show extents for each table in each tablespace.

```
REM
REM NAME              : EXTENTS.SQL
REM FUNCTION          : GENERATE EXTENTS REPORT
REM USE               : FROM SQLPLUS OR OTHER FRONT END
REM LIMITATIONS       : NONE
REM
CLEAR COLUMNS
COLUMN segment_name     HEADING 'Segment'       FORMAT A15
COLUMN tablespace_name  HEADING 'Tablespace'    FORMAT A10
COLUMN owner            HEADING 'Owner'         FORMAT A10
COLUMN segment_type     HEADING 'Type'          FORMAT A10
COLUMN size             HEADING 'Size'             FORMAT 999,999,999
COLUMN extents          HEADING 'Current|Extents'
COLUMN max_extents      HEADING 'Max|Extents'
COLUMN bytes            HEADING 'Size|(Bytes)'
SET PAGESIZE 58 NEWPAGE 0 LINESIZE 130 FEEDBACK OFF
SET ECHO OFF VERIFY OFF
ACCEPT extents PROMPT 'Enter max number of extents: '
BREAK ON tablespace_name SKIP PAGE ON owner
START TITLE132 "Extents Report"
DEFINE output = rep_out\&db\extent
SPOOL &output
SELECT  tablespace_name,
        segment_name,
        extents,
        max_extents,
        bytes,
        owner "owner",
        segment_type
FROM    dba_segments
WHERE extents >= &extents AND owner LIKE UPPER('%&owner%')
ORDER BY tablespace_name,owner,segment_type,segment_name;
SPOOL OFF
CLEAR COLUMNS
CLEAR BREAKS
SET TERMOUT ON FEEDBACK ON VERIFY ON
UNDEF extents
UNDEF owner
TTITLE OFF
UNDEF OUTPUT
PAUSE Press enter to continue
```

LISTING 12.2   Example output of the extents script.

```
Date: 06/12/97                                              Page:    1
Time: 09:55 PM               Extents Report                SYSTEM
                             ORTEST1 database


                     Current   Max    Size
Tablespace Segment   Extents Extents (Bytes) Owner         Type
---------- ---------------- ------- ------- ------- ---------- --------
SYSTEM     C_OBJ#              10     249 1323008 SYS         CLUSTER
           C_TOID_VERSION#      7     249  352256             CLUSTER
           I_ARGUMENT1          6     249  229376             INDEX
           I_COL1               8     249  565248             INDEX
           I_COL2               6     249  258048             INDEX
           I_COL3               5     249  176128             INDEX
           I_DEPENDENCY1        5     249  147456             INDEX
           I_DEPENDENCY2        5     249  147456             INDEX
           I_OBJ2               5     249  147456             INDEX
           I_SOURCE1           11     249 1765376             INDEX
           SYSTEM              16     249  983040             ROLLBACK
           ACCESS$              6     249  229376             TABLE
           ARGUMENT$            6     249  229376             TABLE
           COM$                 5     249  147456             TABLE
           DEPENDENCY$          5     249  147456             TABLE
           IDL_CHAR$            5     249  147456             TABLE
           IDL_SB4$             6     249  229376             TABLE
           IDL_UB1$             9     249  802816             TABLE
           IDL_UB2$            10     249 1191936             TABLE
           OBJ$                 6     249  229376             TABLE
           SOURCE$             13     249 3915776             TABLE
           VIEW$                9     249  802816             TABLE
```

SOURCE 12.3   Actual size report.

```
rem     ****************************************************************
rem
rem     NAME: ACT_SIZE.sql
rem
rem     HISTORY:
rem     Date           Who                 What
rem     --------   ------------------   -------------------------------
rem     09/??/90  Maurice C. Manton    Creation for IOUG
rem     12/23/92  Michael Brouillette  Assume TEMP_SIZE_TABLE exists.Use
rem     DBA info.
rem     Prompt for user name. Spool file = owner.
rem      07/15/96  Mike Ault Updated for Oracle 7.x, added indexes
rem      06/12/97  Mike Ault Updated for Oracle 8.x (use DBMS_ROWID)
rem     FUNCTION:  Will show actual blocks used vs allocated for all tables
rem     for a user.
rem     INPUTS: owner = Table owner name.
rem     ****************************************************************
```

```
ACCEPT owner PROMPT 'Enter table owner name: '
SET HEADING OFF FEEDBACK OFF VERIFY OFF ECHO OFF RECSEP OFF PAGES 0
COLUMN db_block_size NEW_VALUE blocksize NOPRINT
TTITLE OFF
DEFINE cr='chr(10)'
DEFINE qt='chr(39)'
TRUNCATE TABLE temp_size_table;
SELECT value db_block_size FROM v$parameter WHERE name='db_block_size';
SPOOL fill_sz.sql
SELECT
 'INSERT INTO temp_size_table'||&&cr||
 'SELECT '||&&qt||segment_name||&&qt||&&cr||
 ',COUNT(DISTINCT(dbms_rowid.rowid_block_number(rowid))) blocks'||&&cr||
 'FROM &&owner..'||segment_name, ';'
FROM
  dba_segments
WHERE
  segment_type ='TABLE'
  AND owner = UPPER('&owner');
SPOOL OFF
SPOOL index_sz.sql
SELECT
    'CREATE TABLE stat_temp AS SELECT * FROM index_stats;'||&&cr||
    'TRUNCATE TABLE stat_temp;'
FROM
    dual;
SELECT
'ANALYZE INDEX '||owner||'.'||index_name||' VALIDATE STRUCTURE;'||&&cr||
'INSERT INTO stat_temp SELECT * FROM index_stats;'||&&cr||
'COMMIT;'
FROM
    dba_indexes
WHERE
    owner=UPPER('&owner');
SPOOL OFF
SET FEEDBACK ON TERMOUT ON LINES 132
START index_sz.sql
INSERT INTO temp_size_table SELECT name,trunc(used_space/&&blocksize)
FROM stat_temp;
DROP TABLE stat_temp;
DEFINE temp_var = &&qt;
START fill_sz
HOST rm fill_size_table.sql
DEFINE bs = '&&blocksize K'
COLUMN t_date         NOPRINT NEW_VALUE t_date
COLUMN user_id        NOPRINT NEW_VALUE user_id
COLUMN segment_name      FORMAT A25          HEADING "SEGMENT|NAME"
COLUMN segment_type      FORMAT A7           HEADING "SEGMENT|TYPE"
COLUMN extents           FORMAT 999          HEADING "EXTENTS"
COLUMN kbytes            FORMAT 999,999,999 HEADING "KILOBYTES"
COLUMN blocks            FORMAT 9,999,999   HEADING "ALLOC.|&&bs|BLOCKS"
COLUMN act_blocks        FORMAT 9,999,990   HEADING "USED|&&bs|BLOCKS"
```

```
COLUMN pct_block          FORMAT 999.99      HEADING "PCT|BLOCKS|USED"
START title132 "Actual Size Report for &owner"
SET PAGES 55
BREAK ON REPORT ON segment_type SKIP 1
COMPUTE SUM OF kbytes ON segment_type REPORT
SPOOL rep_out\&db\&owner
SELECT
    segment_name,
    segment_type,
    SUM(extents) extents,
    SUM(bytes)/1024 kbytes,
    SUM(a.blocks) blocks,
    NVL(MAX(b.blocks),0) act_blocks,
    (MAX(b.blocks)/SUM(a.blocks))*100 pct_block
 FROM
    sys.dba_segments a,
    temp_size_table b
 WHERE
    segment_name = UPPER( b.table_name )
 GROUP BY
    segment_name,
    segment_type
 ORDER BY
    segment_type,
    segment_name;
SPOOL OFF
TRUNCATE TABLE temp_size_table;
SET TERMOUT ON FEEDBACK 15 VERIFY ON PAGESIZE 20 LINESIZE 80 SPACE 1
UNDEF qt
UNDEF cr
TTITLE OFF
CLEAR COLUMNS
CLEAR COMPUTES
PAUSE press enter to continue
```

The script to calculate the actual size of a table or index (shown in Source 12.3) uses the TEMP_SIZE_TABLE, which is created with the script shown in Source 12.4. As shown, the act_size script will only work with Oracle8. To use act_size with Oracle7 replace the call to the dbms_rowid.rowid_block_number procedure with SUBSTR(ROWID,1,8).

SOURCE 12.4   Script to create TEMP_SIZE_TABLE.

```
rem
rem Create temp_size_table for use by actsize.sql
rem
CREATE TABLE temp_size_table (
    table_name VARCHAR2(64),
    blocks NUMBER);
```

LISTING 12.3   Example output of actual size report.

```
Date: 06/12/97                                                    Page:   1
Time: 11:28 PM                   Actual Size Report for tele_dba         SYSTEM
                                 ORTEST1 database

                                                     ALLOC.      USED      PCT
SEGMENT               SEGMENT                        4096 K     4096 K   BLOCKS
NAME                  TYPE     EXTENTS   KILOBYTES   BLOCKS     BLOCKS     USED
--------------------  -------  -------   ---------   ------     ------   ------
FK_ACCOUNT_EXECS_1    INDEX        1            12        3          0      .00
FK_ADDRESSES_1                     1        10,240    2,560          0      .00
FK_ADDRESSES_2                     1        51,200   12,800      2,480    19.38
FK_ADDRESSES_3                     1        51,200   12,800      2,967    23.18
FK_FRANCHISE_CODES_1               1        10,240    2,560        461    18.01
FK_SIC_CODES_1                     1        51,200   12,800      3,893    30.41
FK_USERS_1                         1       102,400   25,600          0      .00
LI_LOAD_TEST                       1        40,960   10,240      5,536    54.06
OID_CLIENTSV8                      1            20        5          0      .00
OID_EARNINGS_INFO_NMBRS            1            20        5          0      .00
...
PK_ADDRESSES                       1       102,400   25,600      5,203    20.32
PK_CLIENTS                         1       102,400   25,600      3,212    12.55
PK_EARNINGS_INFO_NMBRS             1       102,400   25,600      2,780    10.86
PK_FRANCHISE_CODES                 1        51,200   12,800        573     4.48
PK_SIC_CODES                       1        51,200   12,800      4,863    37.99
UI_EARNINGS_INFO_NMBRS_ID          1        51,200   12,800      4,466    34.89
UK_CLIENTS                         1        51,200   12,800      4,292    33.53
UK_LOAD_TEST                       1        51,200   12,800      4,650    36.33
                      *******              ---------
                      sum                  1,116,564

ACCOUNT_EXECS         TABLE        1            12        3          0      .00
ADDRESSES                          1       204,800   51,200     32,827    64.12
ADDRESS_TEST                       1            20        5          1    20.00
CLIENTS                            2       307,200   76,800     61,587    80.19
....
EARNINGS_INFO_NMBRS                1       204,800   51,200     28,485    55.63
EARNINGS_INFO_NUMBERSV8            1        20,480    5,120          0      .00
EMPLOYEES                          1            20        5          0      .00
FRANCHISE_CODES                    1        76,800   19,200        803     4.18
INTERACTION_LOG_ACTIVITY           1            12        3          0      .00
LOAD_TEST                          3       615,420  153,855    140,441    91.28
LOOKUPS                            1            12        3          0      .00
SIC_CODES                          1       102,400   25,600     16,765    65.49
USERS                              1       204,800   51,200          1      .00
                      *******              ---------
                      sum                  2,036,056

                                           ---------
sum                                        3,152,620
```

Each of the above reports gives specific information. In the report from Source 12.2, if a table shows greater than five to ten extents, the DBA should review its size usage via the report in Source 12.3 and rebuild the table with better storage parameters. In the report in Listing 12.3, if a table shows that it is using far less space than it has been allocated, and history has shown it won't grow into the space, it should be recreated accordingly.

Monitoring Table Statistics Under Oracle7 and Oracle8 the DBA_TABLES view has several additional columns that are populated once a table has been analyzed using the ANALYZE TABLE command. The columns document table-specific data such as number of rows, number of allocated blocks, number of empty blocks, average percent of free space in a table, number of chained rows, and average row length. This provides the DBA with a more detailed view of the tables in the database than ever before. This shows the need for a new report to document this data in hardcopy format so a DBA can easily track a table's growth, space usage, and chaining. The example script in Source 12.5 shows such a report.

SOURCE 12.5   Script to report additional table statistics.

```
rem
rem  NAME: tab_stat.sql
rem  HISTORY:
rem  Date       Who                   What
rem  --------   --------------------  ----------------
rem  5/27/93    Mike Ault             Initial creation
rem
rem  FUNCTION:  Will show table statistics for a user's
rem  FUNCTION:  tables or all tables.
rem
SET PAGES 56 LINES 132 NEWPAGE 0 VERIFY OFF ECHO OFF
SET FEEDBACK OFF
rem
COLUMN owner                FORMAT a12           HEADING "Table Owner"
COLUMN table_name           FORMAT a20           HEADING "Table"
COLUMN tablespace_name      FORMAT a20           HEADING "Tablespace"
COLUMN num_rows             FORMAT 999,999,999   HEADING "Rows"
COLUMN blocks               FORMAT 999,999       HEADING "Blocks"
COLUMN empty_blocks         FORMAT 999,999       HEADING "Empties"
COLUMN space_full           FORMAT 999.99        HEADING "Percent|Full"
COLUMN chain_cnt            FORMAT 999,999       HEADING "Chains"
COLUMN avg_row_len          FORMAT 999,999       HEADING "Avg|Length (Bytes)"
rem
START title132 "Table Statistics Report"
SPOOL report_output/&&db/tab_stat
rem
SELECT
     owner,
     table_name,
     tablespace_name,
     num_rows,
     blocks,
```

```
      empty_blocks,
      1-((blocks * avg_space)/(blocks * 2048)) space_full,
      chain_cnt,
      avg_row_len
FROM
      dba_tables
WHERE
      owner = UPPER('&owner')
      AND tablespace_name = UPPER('&tablespace')
ORDER BY
      owner,
      tablespace_name;
SPOOL OFF
```

LISTING 12.5   Example output of report in Source 12.5.

```
Date: 06/10/93                      "Your Company Name"                Page:  1  Time: 01:14 PM
Table Statistics Report                  SYSTEM
                                     "Your Database"

                                                                                     Average
Table                                                            Percent             Length
Owner    Table            Tablespace    Rows    Blocks  Empties    Full    Chains    (Bytes)
------   ---------------  ----------    ----    ------  -------   -------  --------   -------
SYSTEM   MENU_B_APPL      ORA_TOOLS       6       1      22.56                77        216
         MENU_B_CIRCLE                            1        .00
         MENU_B_GROUP                     1       1        .98                20         57
         MENU_B_GRP_PRIV                164       3      61.39                23         63
         MENU_B_OBJ_TEXT                142       5      72.11                52         15
         MENU_B_OPTION                  141       8      80.90                94         27
         MENU_B_PARAM                             1        .00
         MENU_B_PARM_XREF                         1        .00
         MENU_B_PRIV                    141       3      75.73                33        110
         MENU_B_PROCEDURE                         1        .00
         MENU_B_REF                               1        .00
         MENU_B_USER                      2       1       1.95                20         33
         PRODUCT_ACCESS                           1        .00
         PRODUCT_PROFILE                  1       1       2.00                41        107
         SRW_CMD_NAMES                   77       1      67.68                18         27
17 rows selected.
```

If indicated by the actual space report, or if the report shown in Source 12.9 shows improper space utilization or excessive chaining, the table(s) involved should be rebuilt.

One method of rebuilding a table is:

1. Using a SQL script, unload the table into a flat file.
2. Drop the table and recreate it with a more representative storage clause.
3. Use SQLLOADER to reload the table data.

A second method would be:

1. Using the CREATE TABLE ... AS SELECT ..... FROM command build a second table that is an image of the first table (SELECT * FROM first table) with a storage clause that specifies a larger initial extent.
2. Delete the first table.
3. Use the RENAME command to rename the second table with the first table's name.

Monitoring Table Types (Partition, Nested, IOT) With Oracle8 the new type of tables caused numerous new columns to be added to the DBA_TABLES view. These rows tell a DBA if a table is nested, if a table is partitioned, whether or not a table is an index only or overflow table, as well as its logging status. A simple report like that shown in Source 12.6 provides a convenient report that pulls this data into a manageable format.

SOURCE 12.6   Example script to document extended table parameters.

```
REM
REM     Name:       tab_rep.sql
REM     FUNCTION:   Document table extended parameters
REM     Use:        From SQLPLUS
REM     MRA 6/13/97 Created for ORACLE8
REM
COLUMN owner             FORMAT a10 HEADING 'Owner'
COLUMN table_name        FORMAT a15 HEADING 'Table'
COLUMN tablespace_name   FORMAT a12 HEADING 'Tablespace'
COLUMN table_type_owner  FORMAT a10 HEADING 'Type|Owner'
COLUMN table_type        FORMAT a13 HEADING 'Type'
COLUMN iot_name          FORMAT a10 HEADING 'IOT|of'
COLUMN iot_type          FORMAT a12 HEADING 'IOT or|of'
COLUMN nested            FORMAT a6  HEADING 'Nested'
SET LINES 130 VERIFY OFF FEEDBACK OFF PAGES 58
START title132 'Extended Table Report'
SPOOL rep_out\&&db\ext_tab.lis
SELECT
     owner,
     table_name,
     tablespace_name,
     iot_name,
     logging,
     partitioned,
     iot_type,
     table_type_owner,
     table_type,
     packed,
     temporary,
     nested
```

```
FROM
     dba_tables
WHERE
     owner LIKE UPPER('%&owner%');
SPOOL OFF
SET VERIFY ON LINES 80 PAGES 22 FEEDBACK ON
```

The output from the report on extended table parameters is shown in Listing 12.6. This is about the only spot you will find documentation on index-only tables, unless you go back to the XX$ table level.

LISTING 12.6   Example output from the extended table parameters report.

```
Date: 06/13/97                                                      Page:   1
Time: 08:45 PM                      Extended Table Report              SYSTEM
                                      ORTEST1 database

                                  IOT          IOT  Type
Owner     Table           Tablespace  OF  LOG PAR  or  OF  Owner     Type          P T Nest
--------  --------------  ----------  ---  ------- -------  --------  ------------  - - ----
TELE_DBA  SIC_CODES       APPL_DATA        YES NO                                   N NO
TELE_DBA  AUDIT_RECORDS   APPL_DATA        YES NO                                   N NO
TELE_DBA  TEST_IOT        APPL_DATA        YES NO   IOT                             N NO
TELE_DBA  ADDRESS_TEST    APPL_DATA        YES NO            TELE_DBA  ADDRESS_TYPE N N NO
TELE_DBA  EARNINGS_INFO   APPL_DATA        YES NO            TELE_DBA  EARNING_T    N N NO
TELE_DBA  CLIENTSV8       APPL_DATA        YES NO            TELE_DBA  CLIENT_T     N N NO
TELE_DBA  ADDRESSSESV8    APPL_DATA        YES NO                                   N YES
TELE_DBA  CONTRACTSV8     APPL_DATA        YES NO                                   N YES
TELE_DBA  CIRCUITSV8      APPL_DATA        YES NO                                   N YES
```

The report output in Listing 12.6 shows the following information for Oracle8 tables:

Owner—The owner of the table.

Table—The table name.

Tablespace—The tablespace name.

IOT Overflow—Gives the name of the IOT tables overflow table.

LOG—Does this table use redo logging?

PAR—Is this table partitioned?

IOT or **Overflow**—Is this table an IOT or overflow table?

Type Owner—The owner of the type used to build this table.

Type—The main type used to build this table.

P—Is this table stored in packed format (applicable to typed tables only)?

T—Is this a temporary table?

Nested—Is this a nested table store table?

Monitoring Table Columns To round out the general table reports we need a report on the columns within a table. The script in Source 12.7 fulfills this need.

SOURCE 12.7   Script to report table columns by owner and table.

```
rem
rem tab_col.sql
rem
rem FUNCTION: Report on Table and View Column Definitions
rem
rem MRA 9/18/96
rem MRA 6/14/97 Added table level selectivity
rem
COLUMN owner          FORMAT a10      HEADING Owner
COLUMN table_name     FORMAT a30      HEADING "Table or View Name"
COLUMN COLUMN_name    FORMAT a32      HEADING "Table or View Column"
COLUMN data_type      FORMAT a15      HEADING "Data|Type"
COLUMN data_length                    HEADING Length
COLUMN nullable       FORMAT a5       HEADING Null?
BREAK ON owner ON table_name SKIP 1
SET LINES 132 PAGES 48 FEEDBACK OFF VERIFY OFF
START title132 "Table Columns Report"
SPOOL rep_out/&db/tab_col
SELECT
     a.owner,
     table_name||' '||object_type table_name,
     column_name,
     data_type,
     data_length,
     DECODE(nullable,'N','NO','YES') nullable
FROM
     dba_tab_columns a, dba_objects b
WHERE
     a.owner NOT IN ('SYS','SYSTEM') AND
     a.owner=UPPER('&owner') AND
     a.owner=b.owner AND
     a.table_name LIKE UPPER('%&table%') AND
     a.table_name=b.object_name AND
     object_type IN ('TABLE','VIEW','CLUSTER')
ORDER BY
     owner,
     object_type,
     table_name,
     column_id
/
SPOOL OFF
TTITLE OFF
SET LINES 80 PAGES 22 FEEDBACK ON VERIFY ON
```

The script in Source 12.7 allows you to specify for a specific owner the table for which you want to see the columns. If a naming convention that includes prefix or suffix designations is used when naming tables then the prefix or suffix can be specified to pull the values for a specific type of table. The output from the script is shown in Listing 12.7.

LISTING 12.7   Example of the output from the table column report.

```
Date: 06/14/97                                                        Page:   1
Time: 10:50 AM                      Table Columns Report                 SYSTEM
                                    ORTEST1 database


                                                     Data
Owner    Table or View Name         Table or View Column  Type       Length Null?
-------- ------------------------   --------------------  ----------- ------ -----
TELE_DBA CLIENTSV8 TABLE            CLIENTS_ID            NUMBER          22 NO
                                    ADDRESSES             ADDRESS_LIST    16 YES
                                    CUSTOMER_NAME         VARCHAR2        35 YES
                                    ACCOUNT_AE            NUMBER          22 YES
                                    ACTIVE_FLAG           VARCHAR2         1 YES
                                    FAX                   VARCHAR2        20 YES
                                    LOOKUPS               LOOKUP_T         9 YES
                                    PHONE                 VARCHAR2        20 YES
                                    CORPORATE_NAME        VARCHAR2        30 YES
                                    CREATION_TS           DATE             7 YES
                                    CREATION_SY_USER      NUMBER          22 YES
                                    SPP_RATING            CHAR             2 YES
                                    RATING_DATE           DATE             7 YES
                                    COMPETITOR_LOSS       NUMBER          22 YES
                                    NOTE                  VARCHAR2       250 YES
                                    LAST_CONTACT_TS       DATE             7 YES
                                    DELETE_STATUS         CHAR             1 YES
                                    NAME_SOUNDEX          CHAR             4 YES
                                    SALES_VOLUME          VARCHAR2        15 YES
                                    SALES_VOLUME_CODE     CHAR             1 YES
                                    TOTAL_EMPLOYEES       VARCHAR2         9 YES
                                    LINE_OF_BUS           VARCHAR2        19 YES
                                    PCT_GROWTH_SALES      VARCHAR2         4 YES
                                    TERRITORY_COVERED     CHAR             1 YES
                                    MRC                   VARCHAR2         4 YES
                                    CEO                   CEO_T            8 YES
                                    FRANCHISE_INDCTR      CHAR             1 YES
                                    SIC_CODES             SIC_V          668 YES
                                    FRANCHISE_CODES       FRANCHISE_V    550 YES

         EARNINGS_INFO_NUMBERSV8 TABLE EARNINGS_INFO_ID   NUMBER          22 NO
                                    CLIENTS_ID_R          CLIENT_T        50 YES
                                    LISTED_NAME           VARCHAR2       100 YES
                                    EARNING_NUMBER        CHAR            13 YES
                                    SERVICE_CLASS         VARCHAR2         5 YES
                                    CPNI                  CPNI_T           8 YES
                                    NO_OF_LINES           NUMBER          22 YES
                                    DISCONNECT_DATE       DATE             7 YES
                                    DISCONNECT_REASON     CHAR             2 YES
```

BILLING_NAME	VARCHAR2	40	YES
PHONE	VARCHAR2	10	YES
BTN	CHAR	13	YES
OLD_EARNINGS_NUMBER	CHAR	13	YES
SERVICE_ADDRESS	VARCHAR2	100	YES
CENT	CHAR	3	YES
CON_CTRL_NUMBER	CHAR	15	YES
TERM_AGREEMENT	CHAR	13	YES
SHARED_TENANT_SVCS	VARCHAR2	10	YES
INSTALLATION_DATE	DATE	7	YES
CONTRACTS	CONTRACT_LIST	16	YES
CIRCUITS	CIRCUIT_LIST	16	YES

Monitoring Table Keys As per the requirements of third normal form, each table is required to have a unique identifier that consists of one or more of the table's columns. As an alternative, a derived key can be used that consists of a number pulled from an Oracle sequence. This alternative method of using sequence number for a key should only be used if the key would be excessively long (over three columns). This is called the primary key of the table. This primary key should be identified using a constraint clause when the table is created. A second type of key, called a foreign key, is also present in most tables. The foreign key is used to enforce relationships between two or more tables. The foreign key consists of the primary key from the related table. Again, this foreign key should be identified by a constraint clause when the table is created.

If the two types of keys have been identified via the constraint clause during table creation, they can be readily monitored via an SQL script report (see Sources 12.8 and Listing 12.8).

SOURCE 12.8   PL/SQL script to list primary and foreign keys in tables for an owner.

```
REM FUNCTION: SCRIPT FOR DOCUMENTING DATABASE CONSTRAINTS
REM
REM FUNCTION: This script must be run by the constraint owner.
REM
REM FUNCTION: This script is intended to run with Oracle7 or Oracle8.
REM
REM FUNCTION: Running this script will document the
REM FUNCTION: primary key - foreign key
REM FUNCTION: constraints in the database
REM
REM
REM Only preliminary testing of this script was performed.
REM Be sure to test
REM it completely before relying on it.
REM
REM MRA 6/14/97 Verified for Oracle8
REM
```

```
SET ARRAYSIZE 1 VERIFY OFF  FEEDBACK OFF TERMOUT OFF ECHO OFF PAGESIZE 0
SET LONG 4000
SET TERMOUT ON
SELECT 'Creating constraint documentation script...' FROM dual;
SET TERMOUT OFF

CREATE TABLE cons_temp (owner VARCHAR2(30),
          constraint_name VARCHAR2(30),
          constraint_type VARCHAR2(11),
          search_condition VARCHAR2(2000),
          table_name VARCHAR2(30),
          referenced_owner VARCHAR2(30),
          referenced_constraint VARCHAR2(30),
          delete_rule VARCHAR2(9),
          constraint_columns VARCHAR2(2000),
          con_number NUMBER);
TRUNCATE TABLE cons_temp;

DECLARE

   CURSOR cons_cursor IS
     SELECT
     owner,
        constraint_name,
        DECODE(constraint_type,'P','Primary Key',
              'R','Foreign Key',
              'U','Unique',
              'C','Check',
              'D','Default'),
        search_condition,
        table_name,
        r_owner,
        r_constraint_name,
        delete_rule
       FROM
        user_constraints
       WHERE
        owner NOT IN ('SYS','SYSTEM')
       ORDER BY
        owner;

   CURSOR cons_col (cons_name in VARCHAR2) IS
     SELECT
        owner,
        constraint_name,
        column_name
       FROM
        user_cons_columns
       WHERE
        owner NOT IN ('SYS','SYSTEM') AND
        constraint_name = UPPER(cons_name)
```

```
      ORDER BY
        owner,
        constraint_name,
        position;

    CURSOR get_cons (tab_nam in VARCHAR2) IS
      SELECT DISTINCT
        owner,
        table_name,
        constraint_name,
        constraint_type
      FROM
        cons_temp
      WHERE
        table_name=tab_nam
        AND constraint_type='Foreign Key'
      ORDER BY
        owner,
        table_name,
        constraint_name;

    CURSOR get_tab_nam is
      SELECT
       DISTINCT table_name
      FROM
       cons_temp
      WHERE
       constraint_type='Foreign Key'
      ORDER BY
       table_name;

      tab_nam        user_constraints.table_name%TYPE;
      cons_owner     user_constraints.owner%TYPE;
      cons_name      user_constraints.constraint_name%TYPE;
      cons_type      VARCHAR2(11);
      cons_sc        user_constraints.search_condition%TYPE;
      cons_tname     user_constraints.table_name%TYPE;
      cons_rowner     user_constraints.r_owner%TYPE;
      cons_rcons     user_constraints.r_constraint_name%TYPE;
      cons_dr        user_constraints.delete_rule%TYPE;
      cons_col_own   user_cons_columns.owner%TYPE;
      cons_col_nam   user_cons_columns.constraint_name%TYPE;
      cons_column    user_cons_columns.column_name%TYPE;
      cons_tcol_name user_cons_columns.table_name%TYPE;
      all_columns    VARCHAR2(2000);
      counter        INTEGER:=0;
      cons_nbr       INTEGER;

BEGIN
   OPEN cons_cursor;
```

```
   LOOP
      FETCH cons_cursor INTO cons_owner,
                cons_name,
                cons_type,
                cons_sc,
                cons_tname,
                cons_rowner,
                cons_rcons,
                cons_dr;
      EXIT WHEN cons_cursor%NOTFOUND;
      all_columns :='';
      counter := 0;
      OPEN cons_col (cons_name);
      LOOP
      FETCH cons_col  INTO
            cons_col_own,
            cons_col_nam,
            cons_column;
      EXIT WHEN cons_col%NOTFOUND;
      IF cons_owner = cons_col_own AND cons_name=cons_col_nam
      THEN
        counter := counter+1;
        IF counter = 1 THEN
          all_columns := all_columns||cons_column;
        ELSE
          all_columns := all_columns||', '||cons_column;
        END IF;
      END IF;
      END LOOP;
      CLOSE cons_col;
      INSERT INTO cons_temp VALUES (cons_owner,
                      cons_name,
                      cons_type,
                      cons_sc,
                      cons_tname,
                      cons_rowner,
                      cons_rcons,
                      cons_dr,
                      all_columns,
                      0);
   COMMIT;
   END LOOP;
   CLOSE cons_cursor;
   COMMIT;
BEGIN
 OPEN get_tab_nam;
LOOP
  FETCH get_tab_nam INTO tab_nam;
  EXIT WHEN get_tab_nam%NOTFOUND;
/*sys.dbms_output.put_line(tab_nam);*/
```

```
  OPEN get_cons (tab_nam);
  cons_nbr:=0;
  LOOP
    FETCH get_cons INTO cons_owner,
              cons_tname,
              cons_name,
              cons_type;
    EXIT WHEN get_cons%NOTFOUND;
    cons_nbr:=cons_nbr+1;
/*    sys.dbms_output.put_line('cons_nbr='||cons_nbr);*/
/*sys.dbms_output.put_line(cons_owner||'.'||cons_name||'
'||cons_type);*/
    UPDATE cons_temp SET con_number=cons_nbr
    WHERE
      constraint_name=cons_name AND
      constraint_type=cons_type AND
      owner=cons_owner;
  END LOOP;
  CLOSE get_cons;
  COMMIT;
END LOOP;
CLOSE get_tab_nam;
COMMIT;
END;
END;
/
CREATE INDEX pk_cons_temp ON cons_temp(constraint_name);
CREATE INDEX lk_cons_temp2 ON cons_temp(referenced_constraint);
SET FEEDBACK OFF TERMOUT OFF ECHO OFF
SET VERIFY OFF
SET PAGES 48 LINES 132
COLUMN pri_own FORMAT a10 HEADING 'Pri Table|Owner'
COLUMN for_own FORMAT a10 HEADING 'For Table|Owner'
COLUMN pri_tab FORMAT a25 HEADING 'Pri Table|Name'
COLUMN for_tab FORMAT a25 HEADING 'For Table|Name'
COLUMN pri_col FORMAT a25 HEADING 'Pri Key|COLUMNs' word_wrapped
COLUMN for_col FORMAT a25 HEADING 'For Key|COLUMNs' word_wrapped
START title132 'Primary Key - Foreign Key Report'
SPOOL rep_out\&db\pk_fk
BREAK ON pri_own ON pri_tab ON for_own ON for_tab
SELECT
    b.owner pri_own,
    b.table_name pri_tab,
    RTRIM(b.constraint_columns) pri_col,
    a.owner for_own,
    a.table_name for_tab,
    RTRIM(a.constraint_columns) for_col
FROM
    cons_temp a,
    cons_temp b
```

```
WHERE
     a.referenced_constraint=b.constraint_name
ORDER BY
     b.owner,b.table_name,a.owner,a.table_name;
SPOOL OFF
DROP TABLE cons_temp;
SET VERIFY ON FEEDBACK ON TERMOUT ON PAGESIZE 22 LINES 80
CLEAR COLUMNS
CLEAR BREAKS
TTITLE OFF
```

LISTING 12.8   Example output of the primary/foreign key report.

```
Date: 06/14/97                                                    Page:   1
Time: 11:31 AM               Primary Key - Foreign Key Report        TELE_DBA
                                ORTEST1 database

Pri Table  Pri Table         Pri Key            For Table  For Table           For Key
Owner      Name              Columns            Owner      Name                Columns
---------- ----------------- ------------------ ---------- ------------------- ---------
TELE_DBA   CLIENTS           CLIENTS_ID         TELE_DBA   ACCOUNT_EXECS
CLIENTS_ID
                             CLIENTS_ID                    ADDRESSES
CLIENTS_ID
                             CLIENTS_ID                    CLIENTPROFILES
CLIENTS_ID
                             CLIENTS_ID                    EARNINGS_INFO_NMBRS
CLIENTS_ID
                             CLIENTS_ID                    FRANCHISE_CODES
CLIENTS_ID
                             CLIENTS_ID                    INTERACTION_LOG
CLIENTS_ID
                             CLIENTS_ID                    SIC_CODES
CLIENTS_ID
                             CLIENTS_ID                    USERS
CLIENTS_ID
           EARNINGS_INFO     EARNINGS_INFO_ID   TELE_DBA   ADDRESSES           E_I_ID
                             EARNINGS_INFO_ID              AUDIT_RECORDS       E_I_ID
                             EARNINGS_INFO_ID              CIRCUIT_ID_INFO     E_I_ID
                             EARNINGS_INFO_ID              CONTRACTS           E_I_ID
                             EARNINGS_INFO_ID              DUNS_TRACK_RECORDS  E_I_ID
           INTERACTION_LOG   INTER_LOG_ID       TELE_DBA   INTERACT_LOG_ACTVTY
INTR_LOG_ID
           USERS             USERID             TELE_DBA   ACCOUNT_EXECS       AE_USERID
                             USERID                        ADDRESSES           USERID
                             USERID                        EARNINGS_INFO       USERID
                             USERID                        EMPLOYEES           USERID
                             USERID                        INTERACTION_LOG     USERID
                             USERID                        SYS_USER_PROFILES   USERID
                             USERID                        USERPROFILES        USERID
```

Monitoring Tables for Chained Rows Chaining occurs as data is added to an existing record. When there is insufficient room for the addition, the row is chained to another block and added there. This can lead to significant performance degradation if chaining is occurring regularly. This degradation is caused by the requirements to read multiple blocks to retrieve a single record. An example script to monitor a single table for chained rows is shown in Source 12.9. This script is limited in that the table must have a primary or unique key defined in order for it to work. With a companion script all tables in an application can be checked with this script.

The Analyze Command The ANALYZE command can also be used to generate chained row information into the DBA_TABLES view. Actual chained-row rowids can be listed into a separate table if desired. The general format of this command follows.

```
ANALYZE TABLE-or-CLUSTER [schema.]table-or-cluster
LIST CHAINED ROWS INTO [schema.]table;
```

Under Oracle7 and Oracle8 there is a script called utlchain.sql that will build the chained row table for you. An example script to perform a chain analysis of a table for an owner is shown in Source 12.9. Source 12.10 shows a second script which, with the script in Source 12.9 altered as annotated, will analyze all tables for a specified owner for chains. Listing 12.10 shows the results of this automated chain analysis for an owner's tables.

SOURCE 12.9   Interactive SQL script to determine chained rows in a table.

```
rem    ********************************************************************
rem
rem    NAME:     CHAINING.sql
rem
rem    FUNCTION: Report on the number of CHAINED rows within a named table
rem
rem    NOTES:  Requires DBA priviledges.
rem        The target table must have a column that is the leading portion
rem          of an index and is defined as not null.
rem          Uses the V$SESSTAT table where USERNAME is the current user.
rem          A problem if > 1 session active with that USERID.
rem          The statistics in V$SESSTAT may change between releases and
rem          platforms.  Make sure that 'table fetch continued row' is
rem          a valid statistic.
rem          This routine can be run by AUTO_CHN.sql by remarking the two
rem          accepts and un-remarking the two defines.
rem
rem    INPUTS: obj_own = the owner of the table.
rem            obj_nam = the name of the table.
rem
rem    ********************************************************************
```

```
ACCEPT obj_own PROMPT 'Enter the table owner''s name: '
ACCEPT obj_nam PROMPT 'Enter the name of the table: '

rem DEFINE obj_own = &1   <- Remove comment to use with auto_chain
rem DEFINE obj_nam = &2   <- Remove comment to use with auto_chain

SET TERMOUT OFF FEEDBACK OFF VERIFY OFF ECHO OFF HEADING OFF EMBEDDED ON
COLUMN statistic# NEW_VALUE stat_no NOPRINT
SELECT
    statistic#
FROM
    v$statname

WHERE
    n.name = 'table fetch continued row'
/
rem  Find out who we are in terms of sid
COLUMN sid NEW_VALUE user_sid
SELECT
    distinct sid
FROM
    v$session
WHERE
    audsid = USERENV('SESSIONID')
/

rem  Find the last col of the table and a not null indexed column
COLUMN column_name      NEW_VALUE last_col
COLUMN name         NEW_VALUE indexed_column
COLUMN value        NEW_VALUE before_count
SELECT
    column_name
  FROM
    dba_tab_columns
 WHERE
    table_name = upper('&&obj_nam')
        and owner = upper('&&obj_own')
 ORDER BY
    column_id
/
SELECT
    c.name
  FROM
    sys.col$ c,
    sys.obj$ idx,
    sys.obj$ base,
    sys.icol$ ic
 WHERE
    base.obj#       = c.obj#
        and ic.bo#      = base.obj#
```

```
        and ic.col#     = c.col#
        and base.owner# = (SELECT user# FROM sys.user$
                WHERE name = UPPER('&&obj_own'))
        and ic.obj#     = idx.obj#
        and base.name   = UPPER('&&obj_nam')
        and ic.pos#     = 1
        and c.null$     > 0
/
SELECT value
  FROM v$sesstat
 WHERE v$sesstat.sid = &user_sid
   AND v$sesstat.statistic# = &stat_no
/
rem  Select every row from the target table
SELECT &last_col xx
  FROM &obj_own..&obj_nam
 WHERE &indexed_column <= (SELECT MAX(&indexed_column)
                FROM &obj_own..&obj_nam)
/
COLUMN value NEW_VALUE after_count
SELECT value
  FROM v$sesstat
 WHERE v$sesstat.sid = &user_sid
   AND v$sesstat.statistic# = &stat_no
/
SET TERMOUT ON

SELECT
'Table '||UPPER('&obj_own')||'.'||UPPER('&obj_nam')||' contains '||
       (TO_NUMBER(&after_count) - TO_NUMBER(&before_count))||
       ' chained row'||
       DECODE(to_NUMBER(&after_count) -
TO_NUMBER(&before_count),1,'.','s.')
  FROM dual
 WHERE RTRIM('&indexed_column') IS NOT NULL
/

rem If we don't have an indexed column this won't work so say so
SELECT 'Table '||
       UPPER('&obj_own')||'.'||UPPER('&obj_nam')||
      ' has no indexed, not null columns.'
  FROM dual
 WHERE RTRIM('&indexed_column') IS NULL
/

SET TERMOUT ON FEEDBACK 15 VERIFY ON PAGESIZE 20 LINESIZE 80 SPACE 1
SET HEADING ON
UNDEF obj_nam
UNDEF obj_own
UNDEF before_count
```

```
UNDEF after_count
UNDEF indexed_column
UNDEF last_col
UNDEF stat_no
UNDEF user_sid
CLEAR COLUMNS
CLEAR COMPUTES
```

SOURCE 12.10   The AUTO_CHN.SQL script to automate chaining determination.

```
rem    **********************************************************
rem
rem    NAME: AUTO_CHN.sql
rem
rem    FUNCTION: Run CHAINING.sql for all of a users tables.
rem
rem    NOTES:Requires mod to CHAINING.sql. See CHAINING.sql header
rem
rem    INPUTS:
rem            tabown = Name of owner.
rem
rem    **********************************************************
rem
ACCEPT tabown PROMPT 'Enter table owner: '
rem
SET TERMOUT OFF FEEDBACK OFF VERIFY OFF ECHO OFF HEADING OFF PAGES 999
SET EMBEDDED ON
COLUMN name NEW_VALUE db NOPRINT
SELECT name FROM v$database;
SPOOL rep_out\auto_chn.gql
rem
SELECT 'start chaining &tabown '||table_name
  FROM dba_tables
 WHERE owner = UPPER('&tabown')
/

SPOOL OFF
SPOOL rep_out\&db\chaining
START rep_out\auto_chn.gql
SPOOL OFF
UNDEF tabown
SET TERMOUT ON FEEDBACK 15 VERIFY ON PAGESIZE 20 LINESIZE 80 SPACE 1
SET EMBEDDED OFF
HO del rep_out\auto_chn.gql
PAUSE Press enter to continue
```

LISTING 12.10   Example output when AUTO_CHN.SQL is run against a user's tables.

```
Table SYSTEM.CGS_REFLINE contains 0 chained rows.
Table SYSTEM.CGS_WKSTATION contains 0 chained rows.
Table SYSTEM.CGS_WSATTRIBUTES contains 0 chained rows.
Table SYSTEM.CGS_WSCOLORS contains 0 chained rows.
Table SYSTEM.CGS_WSFONTS contains 0 chained rows.
Table SYSTEM.CGS_WSLNSTYLES contains 0 chained rows.
Table SYSTEM.CGS_WSPATTERNS contains 0 chained rows.
Table SYSTEM.DBA_TEMP has no indexed, not null columns.
Table SYSTEM.DEF$_CALL contains 0 chained rows.
Table SYSTEM.DEF$_CALLDEST contains 0 chained rows.
Table SYSTEM.DEF$_DEFAULTDEST contains 0 chained rows.
```

Also provided is a column showing chained rows for a specific table in the DBA_ TABLES view. If you don't particularly care what rows are chained, just whether you have chaining, a simple query against this view will tell you, if you have analyzed the table.

Monitoring Grants on a Table The DBA also needs to monitor grants on tables. It is good to know who is granting what privileges to whom. The script to determine this is shown in Source 12.11. Listing 12.11 shows the listing generated from Source 12.11.

SOURCE 12.11   SQL script to show object level grants.

```
rem*********************************************************************
rem   NAME: db_tgnts.sql
rem
rem   FUNCTION: Produce report of table or procedure grants showing
rem   GRANTOR, GRANTEE or ROLE and specific GRANTS.
rem
rem   INPUTS: Owner name
rem   *******************************************************************
rem
COLUMN grantee          FORMAT A18      HEADING "Grantee|or Role"
COLUMN owner            FORMAT A18      HEADING "Owner"
COLUMN table_name       FORMAT A30      HEADING "Table|or Proc"
COLUMN grantor          FORMAT A18      HEADING "Grantor"
COLUMN privilege        FORMAT A10      HEADING "Privilege"
COLUMN grantable        FORMAT A19      HEADING "Grant|Option?"
rem
BREAK ON owner SKIP 4 ON table_name SKIP 1 ON grantee ON grantor ON
REPORT
rem
SET LINESIZE 130 PAGES 56 VERIFY OFF FEEDBACK OFF
START title132 "TABLE GRANTS BY OWNER AND TABLE"
```

```
DEFINE OUTPUT = report_output/&&db/db_tgnts
SPOOL &output
REM
SELECT
    owner,
    table_name,
    grantee,
    grantor,
    privilege,
    grantable
FROM
    dba_tab_privs
WHERE
    owner NOT IN ('SYS','SYSTEM')
ORDER BY
    owner,
    table_name,
    grantor,
    grantee;
REM
SPOOL OFF
PAUSE Press enter to continue
```

LISTING 12.11   Example of report from grant script.

```
Date: 05/22/96                                                    Page:1
Time: 01:49 PM            TABLE GRANTS BY OWNER AND TABLE          SYSTEM
                             ORDSPTD6 database

         Table     Grantee                                    Grant
Owner    or Proc   or Role      Grantor     Privilege         Option?
-------- --------- ------------ ----------- ------------------ -------
DSPTDBA  ACCCAR    DSPT_DEV     DSPTDBA     DELETE             NO
                                            INSERT             NO
                                            SELECT             NO
                                            UPDATE             NO
                                            ALTER              NO
                   DSPT_USER    DSPTDBA     DELETE             NO
                                            UPDATE             NO
                                            SELECT             NO
                                            INSERT             NO
         ACT       DSPT_DEV     DSPTDBA     DELETE             NO
                                            SELECT             NO
                                            UPDATE             NO
                                            ALTER              NO
                                            INSERT             NO
                   DSPT_USER    DSPTDBA     DELETE             NO
                                            UPDATE             NO
                                            SELECT             NO
                                            INSERT             NO
         ADD_REC   DSPT_USER    DSPTDBA     EXECUTE            NO
```

Using the above report it is easy to monitor the grants on specific objects. A close look at the generation script shows that this report is very selective, down to the individual object level, or as general as the entire database. Using this script the DBA can find out the level of protection for any and all database objects.

Monitoring Partitioned Tables Partitioned tables and indexes are new with Oracle8. The DBA will be tasked with monitoring these new types of tables. Essentially the DBA will want to know what tables are partitioned, the ranges for each partition, and the table fraction locations for each partition. Let's examine a couple of reports that provide this level of information. The first report script provides information on partition names, partitioning value, partition tablespace location, and whether the partition is logging or not. The script is shown in Source 12.12.

SOURCE 12.12   Script to report on partitioned table structure.

```
rem
rem Name: tab_part.sql
rem Function : Report on partitioned table structure
rem History: MRA 6/13/97 Created
rem
COLUMN table_owner     FORMAT a10 HEADING 'Owner'
COLUMN table_name      FORMAT a15 HEADING 'Table'
COLUMN partition_name  FORMAT a15 HEADING 'Partition'
COLUMN tablespace_name FORMAT a15 HEADING 'Tablespace'
COLUMN high_value      FORMAT a10 HEADING 'Partition|Value'
SET LINES 78
START title80 'Table Partition Files'
BREAK ON table_owner ON table_name
SPOOL rep_out/&&db/tab_part.lis
SELECT
     table_owner,
     table_name,
     partition_name,
     high_value,
     tablespace_name,
     logging
FROM sys.dba_tab_partitions
ORDER BY table_owner,table_name
/
SPOOL OFF
```

The output from the script in Source 12.12 is shown in Listing 12.12. One thing to remember when looking at the report in Source 12.12 is that the PARTITION VALUE column contains the value that the partition values will be LESS THAN but won't include.

LISTING 12.12 Example output of the partitioned table structures report.

```
Date: 06/14/97                                                      Page:  1
Time: 12:49 PM                            Table Partition Files      SYSTEM
                                          ORTEST1 database

                                                        Partition
Owner    Table            Partition              Value  Tablespace  LOG
------   --------------   ----------------------  --------  ----------  ---
SYSTEM   PARTITION_TEST   TEST_P1                10     RAW_DATA    YES
                          TEST_P2                20     RAW_DATA    YES
                          TEST_P3                30     RAW_DATA    YES
```

The second set of data a DBA will want to know about a partition structure is the storage characteristics. The report in Source 12.13 shows an example report with this type of information.

SOURCE 12.13 Example script to report on partition storage characteristics.

```
rem
rem NAME:    Tab_pstor.sql
rem FUNCTION: Provide data on part. table stor. charcacteristics
rem HISTORY: MRA 6/13/97 Created
rem
COLUMN table_owner         FORMAT a6        HEADING 'Owner'
COLUMN table_name          FORMAT a14       HEADING 'Table'
COLUMN partition_name      FORMAT a9        HEADING 'Partition'
COLUMN tablespace_name     FORMAT a11       HEADING 'Tablespace'
COLUMN pct_free            FORMAT 9999      HEADING '%|Free'
COLUMN pct_used            FORMAT 999       HEADING '%|Use'
COLUMN ini_trans           FORMAT 9999     HEADING 'Init|Tran'
COLUMN max_trans           FORMAT 9999     HEADING 'Max|Tran'
COLUMN initial_extent      FORMAT 9999999  HEADING 'Init|Extent'
COLUMN next_extent         FORMAT 9999999  HEADING 'Next|Extent'
COLUMN max_extent                          HEADING 'Max|Extents'
COLUMN pct_increase        FORMAT 999       HEADING '%|Inc'
COLUMN partition_position  FORMAT 9999      HEADING 'Part|Nmbr'
SET LINES 130
START title132 'Table Partition File Storage'
BREAK ON table_owner on table_name
SPOOL rep_out/&&db/tab_pstor.lis
SELECT
     table_owner,
     table_name,
     tablespace_name,
     partition_name,
     partition_position,
```

```
     pct_free,
     pct_used,
     ini_trans,
     max_trans,
     initial_extent,
     next_extent,
     max_extent,
     pct_increase
FROM sys.dba_tab_partitions
ORDER BY table_owner,table_name
/
SPOOL OFF
```

Example output from the script in Source 12.14 is shown in Listing 12.14.

SOURCE 12.14   Example partition storage report output.

```
Date: 06/14/97                                                           Page:   1
Time: 01:16 PM                    Table Partition File Storage              SYSTEM
                                     ORTEST1 database

                                        Part  %    %  Init Max Init    Next     Max    %
Owner  Table      Tablespace Partition  Nmbr Free Use Tran Tran Extent  Extent   Extents Inc
------ ---------  ---------- ---------- ---- ---- --- ---- ---- ------  ------   ------- ---
SYSTEM PART_TEST  RAW_DATA   TEST_P1      1   10   90  1    255 1048576 1048576  249     0
                  RAW_DATA   TEST_P2      2   10   90  1    255 1048576 1048576  249     0
                  RAW_DATA   TEST_P3      3   10   90  1    255 1048576 1048576  249     0
```

Generally speaking, the storage characteristics for your partitions should be similar if not identical for a given table. However, having said that let me say that only you know your data and if, say, you are partitioning a sales table by month and your particular industry always has a slump in the summer (like you sell skis), then your summer months partitions would be different from those for the peak months.

Monitoring Nested Tables   Another new type of table for Oracle8 is the nested table. A nested table is a table called by reference in another table where the reference value appears as a column . In a previous section in the table columns report, the columns where the name is "xxxx_list", by my self-imposed naming conventions, is a nested table reference column. I suggest that for ease in recognizing a nested table column you do something similar. Each of these "xxx_list" columns contains a pointer value that points to a nested table. The DBA_NESTED_TABLES view provides a convenient place to monitor nested tables. An example report against the DBA_NESTED_ TABLES view is shown in Source 12.15.

SOURCE 12.15 Example script to monitor nested tables.

```
rem
rem NAME: tab_nest.sql
rem PURPOSE: Report on Nested Tables
rem HISTORY: MRA 6/14/97 Created
rem
COLUMN owner              FORMAT a10 HEADING 'Owner'
COLUMN table_name         FORMAT a20 HEADING 'Store Table'
COLUMN table_type_owner   FORMAT a10 HEADING 'Type|Owner'
COLUMN table_type_name    FORMAT a15 HEADING 'Type|Name'
COLUMN parent_table_name  FORMAT a25 HEADING 'Parent|Table'
COLUMN parent_table_column FORMAT a15 HEADING 'Parent|Column'
SET PAGES 58 LINES 132 VERIFY OFF FEEDBACK OFF
START title132 'Nested Tables'
BREAK ON owner
SPOOL rep_out\&db\tab_nest.lis
SELECT
     owner,
     table_name,
     table_type_owner,
     table_type_name,
     parent_table_name,
     parent_table_column
FROM sys.dba_nested_tables
ORDER BY owner;
SPOOL OFF
```

The output from the script in Source 12.15 is shown in Listing 12.15. Again, and I can't stress this enough, a good naming convention is essential with the new table types, object types, and various new structures in Oracle8. If you don't maintain proper naming discipline with developers and with yourself under Oracle8, you will quickly become lost when trying to track down various components.

LISTING 12.15 Example output from nested table script.

```
Date: 06/14/97                                                  Page:   1
Time: 02:07 PM                    Nested Tables                 SYSTEM
                               ORTEST1 database

                      Type        Type           Parent            Parent
Owner      Store Table Owner       Name           Table             Column
--------   ----------- --------    -------------  ----------------  ---------
TELE_DBA   CONTRACTSLV8 TELE_DBA   CONTRACT_LIST  EARNINGS_INFO_V8  CONTRACTS
           CIRCUITSLV8  TELE_DBA   CIRCUIT_LIST   EARNINGS_INFO_V8  CIRCUITS
           ADDRESSESLV8 TELE_DBA   ADDRESS_LIST   CLIENTSV8         ADDRESSES
```

I have included several other table-monitoring scripts in the appendices on the CD-ROM to monitor bound tables and tables that can't get their next extent.

Using the V$ and DB_ Views for Monitoring Indexes

Oracle8 has expanded indexes to include the concept of partitions, in addition to the old monitoring requirements. In Oracle7 (7.3.2) an additional type of index, bitmapped, was added. As with prior versions the DBA will also have to monitor table indexes to verify uniqueness, determine if the appropriate columns are indexed, and to determine if ownership of indexes for a given application is proper. In addition, the DBA needs a convenient reference to show what tables have indexes and what is indexed in case of loss of a table, or for use during table maintenance. The diagram in Figure 12.3 shows the cluster of DBA_ views that a DBA needs to use for monitoring indexes.

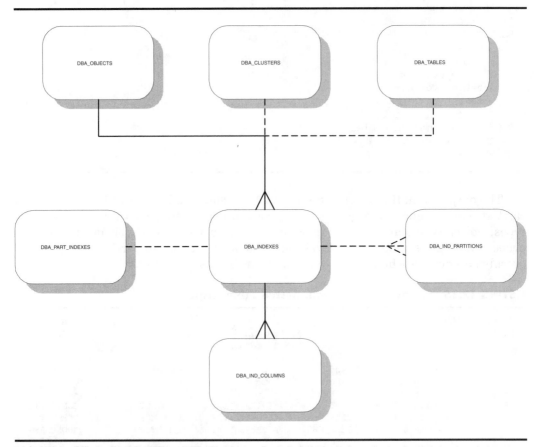

FIGURE 12.3   DBA_INDEXES view cluster.

The report in Source 12.16 provides a convenient format for the DBA to review indexed tables and columns, and is selective down to the single table, single owner level. The report should be run after database maintenance involving table rebuilds, exports and imports, or database rebuilds. Listing 12.16 is an example of the output from Source 12.16.

SOURCE 12.16   SQL script to generate index report.

```
rem
rem NAME: ind_rep.sql
rem FUNCTION: Report on indexes
rem HISTORY: MRA 6/14/97 Creation
rem
COLUMN owner                    FORMAT a8        HEADING 'Index|Owner'
COLUMN index_name               FORMAT a27       HEADING 'Index'
COLUMN index_type               FORMAT a6        HEADING 'Type|Index'
COLUMN table_owner              FORMAT a8        HEADING 'Table|Owner'
COLUMN table_name               FORMAT a24       HEADING 'Table Name'
COLUMN table_type               FORMAT a10       HEADING 'Table|Type'
COLUMN uniqueness               FORMAT a1        HEADING 'U|n|i|q|u|e'
COLUMN tablespace_name          FORMAT a13       HEADING 'Tablespace'
COLUMN column_name              FORMAT a25       HEADING 'Col. Name'
SET PAGES 58 LINES 130 FEEDBACK OFF VERIFY OFF
BREAK ON owner
START title132 'Expandeded Index Report'
SPOOL rep_out\&db\ind_exp.lis
SELECT
     a.owner,
     a.index_name,
     a.index_type,
     a.table_owner,
     a.table_name,
     a.table_type,
     DECODE
     (a.uniqueness, 'UNIQUE', 'U','NONUNIQUE','N') uniqueness,
      a.tablespace_name,
      b.column_name
FROM
     dba_indexes a, dba_ind_columns b
WHERE
     owner LIKE UPPER('%&owner%')
     AND a.owner=b.index_owner(+)
     AND a.index_name=b.index_name(+)
ORDER BY
     owner, index_type;
SPOOL OFF
```

LISTING 12.16   Example output from index report.

```
Date: 06/14/97                                                        Page:   1
Time: 04:35 PM                      Expandeded Index Report           SYSTEM
                                        ORTEST1 database


                                                         U
                                                         n
                                                         i
                                                         q
  Index                        Type  Table          Table u
  Owner  Index                 Index Owner Table Name Type  e Tablespace Col. Name
  ------ --------------------- ----- ------ ------------- ------ - ---------- ---------
  SYSTEM PK_TEST_IOT           IOT - SYSTEM TEST_IOT     TABLE  U RAW_DATA   TEST1
                               TOP

         SYS_IL0000001562C00035$ LOB   SYSTEM DEF$_AQCALL   TABLE  U SYSTEM
         SYS_IL0000001571C00035$ LOB   SYSTEM DEF$_AQERROR  TABLE  U SYSTEM
         SYS_IL0000001588C00005$ LOB   SYSTEM DEF$_LOB      TABLE  U SYSTEM
         SYS_IL0000001597C00002$ LOB   SYSTEM DEF$_TEMP$LOB TABLE  U SYSTEM
         SYS_IL0000001597C00001$ LOB   SYSTEM DEF$_TEMP$LOB TABLE  U SYSTEM
         SYS_IL0000001588C00006$ LOB   SYSTEM DEF$_LOB      TABLE  U SYSTEM
         SYS_IL0000001588C00004$ LOB   SYSTEM DEF$_LOB      TABLE  U SYSTEM
         SYS_IL0000001597C00003$ LOB   SYSTEM DEF$_TEMP$LOB TABLE  U SYSTEM
         AQ$_QUEUES_CHECK       NORMAL SYSTEM AQ$_QUEUES   TABLE  U SYSTEM    NAME
         AQ$_QUEUES_PRIMARY     NORMAL SYSTEM AQ$_QUEUES   TABLE  U SYSTEM    OID
         BM_TEST_BITMAP         BITMAP SYSTEM TEST_BITMAP  TABLE  N SYSTEM    TEST_COL1
```

Monitoring Index Statistics   Under Oracle7 the DBA_INDEXES view was extended
to include B-tree level, number of leaf blocks, number of distinct keys, average number
of leaf blocks per key, average number of data blocks per key, and the index clustering
factor. In addition, a column to show the index status, either DIRECT LOAD or
VALID, has been added. The TYPE column shows if the index is NORMAL, an IOT, a
LOB, or a BITMAP index. This is about the only indicator for BITMAP type indexes.

Index statistics generated from the ANALYZE command are stored in the
INDEX_STATS view. The major limitation of the index_stats view is that it only
shows the most currently analyzed index. The script in Source 12.17 should be run if
you wish to get results from all of the indexes in a particular schema.

**SOURCE 12.17   Script to produce index statistics reports from ANALYZE INDEX
command.**

```
rem
rem NAME: brown.sql
rem FUNCTION: Analyze indexes and produce stat report
rem FUNCTION: Including browning indicator
rem
rem HISTORY: MRA 6/15/97 Created
rem
```

```
COL del_lf_rows_len FORMAT 999,999,999 HEADING 'Deleted Bytes'
COL lf_rows_len     FORMAT 999,999,999 HEADING 'Filled Bytes'
COL browning        FORMAT 999.90      HEADING 'Percent|Browned'
COL height          FORMAT 999,999     HEADING 'Height'
COL blocks          FORMAT 999,999     HEADING 'Blocks'
COL distinct_keys   FORMAT 999,999,999 HEADING '#|Keys'
COL most_repeated_key FORMAT 999999999 HEADING 'Most|Repeated|Key'
COL used_space      FORMAT 999999999   HEADING 'Used|Space'
COL rows_per_key    FORMAT 999999      HEADING 'Rows|Per|Key'
ACCEPT owner PROMPT 'Enter table owner name: '
SET HEADING OFF FEEDBACK OFF VERIFY OFF ECHO OFF RECSEP OFF
SET PAGES 0
TTITLE OFF
DEFINE cr='CHR(10)'
SPOOL index_sz.sql
SELECT
   'CREATE TABLE stat_temp AS SELECT * FROM index_stats;'||&&cr||
   'TRUNCATE TABLE stat_temp;'
FROM dual;
SELECT
'ANALYZE INDEX '||owner||'.'||index_name||
' VALIDATE STRUCTURE;'||&&cr||
     'INSERT INTO stat_temp SELECT * FROM index_stats;'||&&cr||
     'COMMIT;'
FROM
     dba_indexes
WHERE
     owner=UPPER('&owner');
SPOOL OFF
PROMPT 'Analyzing Indexes'
SET FEEDBACK OFF TERMOUT OFF LINES 132 VERIFY OFF
START index_sz.sql
SET TERMOUT ON FEEDBACK ON VERIFY ON LINES 132 PAGES 58
START title132 "Index Statistics Report"
SPOOL rep_out/&db/browning.lst
SELECT
     name,
     del_lf_rows_len,
     lf_rows_len,
(del_lf_rows_len/
DECODE((lf_rows_len+del_lf_rows_len),0,1,lf_rows_len+
del_lf_rows_len))*100 browning,
     height,
     blocks,
     distinct_keys,
     most_repeated_key,
     used_space,
     rows_per_key
FROM
     stat_temp
```

```
WHERE rows_per_key>0;
SPOOL OFF
SET FEEDBACK ON TERMOUT ON LINES 80 VERIFY ON
HOST del stat_temp
```

An example report from the script in Source 12.17 is shown in Listing 12.17.

LISTING 12.17   Example output from index statistics from ANALYZE command report.

```
Date: 06/15/97                                                    Page:   1
Time: 10:31 AM                   Index Statistics Report          SYSTEM
                                   ORTEST1 database

                                                          Most              Rows
                                  Percent            #  Repeat    Used      Per
NAME              Deleted  Filled Browned Height Blocks Keys    Key   Space  Key
----------------- ------- ---------- ------- ------ ------ ------- ------ -------- -----
FK_ADDRESSES_2         0  10,126,346    .00      3  12800  583996      2 10159315    1
FK_ADDRESSES_3         0  12,115,956    .00      3  12800  758357      1 12153926    1
FK_FRANC_CDS_1         0   1,880,298    .00      3   2560   19619      6  1888613    6
FK_SIC_CODES_1         0  15,896,017    .00      3  12800  875966      3 15948812    1
LI_LOAD_TEST           0  22,568,301    .00      3  10240  875966   8461 22676759    1
PK_ADDRESSES           0  21,249,760    .00      3  25600 1392036      1 21312498    1
PK_CLIENTS             0  13,121,655    .00      3  25600  875966      1 13159342    1
PK_EARNINGS            0  11,357,779    .00      3  25600  758369      1 11390423    1
PK_FRANC_CDS           0   2,340,249    .00      3  12800  117714      1  2349540    1
PK_SIC_CODES           0  19,856,433    .00      3  12800  994826      1 19921338    1
PK_USERS               0          13    .00      1  25600       1      1       13    1
SYS_C00800             0          27    .00      1      5       1      1       27    1
TEST_INDEX             0          17    .00      1      5       1      1       17    1
UI_EARNINGS_1          0  18,200,856    .00      3  12800  758369      1 18295755    1
UK_CLIENTS             0  17,519,320    .00      3  12800  875966      1 17584123    1
16 rows selected
```

If the rows/key column in the report in Listing 12.17 exceeds 100 then consider making the index a bitmap index (post-7.3.2).

The new column clustering factor shows how well the table being indexed is ordered. If the value for clustering factor is near the number of table blocks, the table is well ordered. If instead it is near the number of rows in the table, the table is not well ordered (unless the row size is close to block size).

A script for reporting some of the statistics stored in the DBA_INDEXES view is shown in Source 12.18. These statistics are not dynamic; they are only 100% valid at the time the ANALYZE command is run. This is why I am pleased that Oracle has included the last date analyzed field in Oracle8.

SOURCE 12.18   Example statistics report for Oracle8 indexes.

```
rem   NAME: IN_STAT.sql
rem
rem   FUNCTION: Report on index statistics
rem   INPUTS:    1 = Index owner    2 = Index name
rem
DEF iowner = '&OWNER'
DEF iname  = '&INDEX'
SET PAGES 56 LINES 130 VERIFY OFF FEEDBACK OFF
COLUMN owner                     FORMAT a8          HEADING "Owner"
COLUMN index_name                FORMAT a25         HEADING "Index"
COLUMN status                    FORMAT a7          HEADING "Status"
COLUMN blevel                    FORMAT 9,999       HEADING "Tree|Level"
COLUMN leaf_blocks               FORMAT 999,999,999 HEADING "Leaf Blk"
COLUMN distinct_keys             FORMAT 999,999,999 HEADING "# Keys"
COLUMN avg_leaf_blocks_per_key   FORMAT 9,999       HEADING "Avg.|LB/Key"
COLUMN avg_data_blocks_per_key   FORMAT 9,999       HEADING "Avg.|DB/Key"
COLUMN clustering_factor         FORMAT 999,999     HEADING "Clstr|Factor"
COLUMN num_rows                  FORMAT 999,999,999 HEADING "Number|Rows"
COLUMN sample_size               FORMAT 99,999      HEADING "Sample|Size"
COLUMN last_analyzed             HEADING 'Analysis|Date'
rem
BREAK ON owner
START title132 "Index Statistics Report"
SPOOL rep_out\&db\ind_stat
rem
SELECT
     owner, index_name, status, blevel, leaf_blocks,
     distinct_keys, avg_leaf_blocks_per_key,
     avg_data_blocks_per_key, clustering_factor,
     num_rows, sample_size, last_analyzed
FROM
     dba_indexes
WHERE
     owner LIKE UPPER('&&iowner')
     AND index_name LIKE UPPER('&&iname')
     AND num_rows>0
ORDER BY
     1,2;
rem
SPOOL OFF
SET PAGES 22 LINES 80 VERIFY ON FEEDBACK ON
CLEAR COLUMNS
UNDEF iowner
UNDEF iname
UNDEF owner
UNDEF name
TTITLE OFF
```

LISTING 12.18 Example report output from the script in Source 12.18.

```
Date: 06/14/97                                                      Page:    1
Time: 08:22 PM                    Index Statistics Report                SYSTEM
                                    ORTEST1 database

                        Tr. Lf.              Avg.  Avg.  Clstr  Number  Sam. Anl.
Owner     Index         Status Lev Blk   # Keys LB/Key DB/Key Factor   Rows   Size Date

TELE_DBA FK_ADDRESS_2   VALID   2 2650   583996    1     1    14191   633679    0 14-JUN-97
TELE_DBA FK_ADDRESS_3   VALID   2 3171   758357    1     1    18637   758357    0 14-JUN-97
TELE_DBA FK_FRAN_CD_1   VALID   2  492    19619    1     1      803   117714    0 14-JUN-97
TELE_DBA FK_SIC_CDS_1   VALID   2 4160   875966    1     1    16765   994826    0 14-JUN-97
TELE_DBA LI_LOAD_TEST   VALID   2 6474   875966    1     1   140442  1074681    0 14-JUN-97
TELE_DBA PK_ADDRESSES   VALID   2 5560  1392036    1     1    32827  1392036    0 14-JUN-97
TELE_DBA PK_CLIENTS     VALID   2 3433   875966    1     1    61587   875966    0 14-JUN-97
TELE_DBA PK_EARNINGS    VALID   2 2972   758369    1     1    28485   758369    0 14-JUN-97
TELE_DBA PK_FRAN_CDS    VALID   2  613   117714    1     1      803   117714    0 14-JUN-97
TELE_DBA PK_SIC_CODES   VALID   2 5204   994826    1     1    16765   994826    0 14-JUN-97
TELE_DBA PK_USERS       VALID   0    1        1    1     1        1        1    0 14-JUN-97
TELE_DBA SYS_C00800     VALID   0    1        1    1     1        1        1    0 14-JUN-97
TELE_DBA TEST_INDEX     VALID   0    1        1    1     1        1        1    0 14-JUN-97
TELE_DBA UI_EARNINGs_1  VALID   2 6738   758369    1     1   727251   758369    0 14-JUN-97
TELE_DBA UK_CLIENTS     VALID   2 4493   875966    1     1    61587   875966    0 14-JUN-97
TELE_DBA UK_LOAD_TEST   VALID   2 5456   758369    1     1   733393   758369    0 14-JUN-97
```

The various values in the report in Listing 12.18 are interpreted as follows:

BLEVEL—This is the depth, or number of levels, from the root block of the index to its leaf blocks. A depth of 1 will indicate that they are all on the same level.

LEAF_BLOCKS—This is the number of leaf blocks in the index.

AVG_LEAF_—This indicates a nonunique index if its value is greater than 1.

BLOCKS_PER_KEY—If greater than 1, it indicates the key has duplicate values.

AVG_DATA_—This indicates the average number of data blocks in the **BLOCKS_PER_KEY** indexed table that are pointed to by a distinct value in the index.

CLUSTERING_FACTOR—This value indicates the orderliness of the table being indexed. If it is near the number of blocks in table, it indicates a well-ordered table. If it is near the number of rows, it indicates a disordered table.

SAM. SIZE—If the index was analyzed using the estimate clause, this tells the sample size specified.

ANALYSIS DATE—This is the last date the index was analyzed.

Monitoring Partitioned Indexes Partitioned indexes in Oracle8 also will require monitoring by the DBA. The DBA_IND_PARTITIONS view is almost identical to the DBA_TAB_PARTITIONS view with the exception of the index/table specific statistics. The scripts shown here are just examples which should be modified to your own needs.

The first script shows partition file parameters. The script, ind_part.sql, is listed in Source 12.19.

SOURCE 12.19   Example script to monitor index partition files.

```
rem
rem Name: ind_part.sql
rem Function : Report on partitioned index structure
rem History: MRA 6/14/97 Created
rem
COLUMN index_owner          FORMAT a10 HEADING 'Owner'
COLUMN index_name           FORMAT a15 HEADING 'Index'
COLUMN partition_name       FORMAT a15 HEADING 'Partition'
COLUMN tablespace_name      FORMAT a15 HEADING 'Tablespace'
COLUMN high_value           FORMAT a10 HEADING 'Partition|Value'
SET LINES 78
START title80 'Index Partition Files'
BREAK ON index_owner ON index_name
SPOOL rep_out/&&db/ind_part.lis
SELECT
    index_owner,
    index_name,
    partition_name,
    high_value,
    tablespace_name,
    logging
FROM sys.dba_ind_partitions
ORDER BY index_owner,index_name
/
SPOOL OFF
```

The output from the script in Source 12.19 is shown in Listing 12.19.

LISTING 12.19   Example output from the index partition file script.

```
Date: 06/14/97                                         Page:  1
Time: 08:51 PM              Index Partition Files       SYSTEM
                              ORTEST1 database


                                    Partition
Owner    Index           Partition  Value    Tablespace        LOG
------   -------------   ---------  ---------  ---------------  ---
SYSTEM   PART_IND_TEST   TEST_P1     10        RAW_DATA         YES
                         TEST_P2     20        RAW_DATA         YES
                         TEST_P3     30        RAW_DATA         YES

3 rows selected.
```

The DBA_IND_PARTITIONS view also provides the statistics and storage characteristics for partitioned indexes. Source 12.20 is an example script to use for monitoring some of these statistics.

SOURCE 12.20   Example script to report on partitioned index storage and statistics.

```
rem
rem NAME:        ind_pstor.sql
rem FUNCTION: Provide data on partitioned index storage charcacteristics
rem HISTORY: MRA 6/13/97 Created
rem
COLUMN owner              FORMAT a6         HEADING 'Owner'
COLUMN index_name         FORMAT a14        HEADING 'Table'
COLUMN partition_name     FORMAT a9         HEADING 'Partition'
COLUMN tablespace_name    FORMAT a11        HEADING 'Tablespace'
COLUMN pct_free           FORMAT 9999       HEADING '%|Free'
COLUMN ini_trans          FORMAT 9999       HEADING 'Init|Tran'
COLUMN max_trans          FORMAT 9999       HEADING 'Max|Tran'
COLUMN initial_extent     FORMAT 9999999    HEADING 'Init|Extent'
COLUMN next_extent        FORMAT 9999999    HEADING 'Next|Extent'
COLUMN max_extent                           HEADING 'Max|Extents'
COLUMN pct_increase       FORMAT 999        HEADING '%|Inc'
COLUMN distinct_keys      FORMAT 9999999    HEADING '#Keys'
COLUMN clustering_factor  FORMAT 999999     HEADING 'Clus|Fact'
SET LINES 130
START title132 'Index Partition File Storage'
BREAK ON index_owner on index_name
SPOOL rep_out/&&db/ind_pstor.lis
SELECT
     index_owner,
     index_name,
     tablespace_name,
     partition_name,
     pct_free,
     ini_trans,
     max_trans,
     initial_extent,
     next_extent,
     max_extent,
     pct_increase,
     distinct_keys,
     clustering_factor
FROM sys.dba_ind_partitions
ORDER BY index_owner,index_name
/
SPOOL OFF
```

The output from the script in Source 12.20 resembles the report in Listing 12.20.

LISTING 12.20   Example output from the partitioned index storage script.

```
Date: 06/14/97                                                           Page:   1
Time: 09:25 PM                    Index Partition File Storage                SYSTEM
                                      ORTEST1 database

                                    % Init  Max  Init   Next   Max   %       Clus
Owner   Index       Tablespace Partition Free Tran Tran Extent Extent Extents Inc #Keys Fac
------  ----------  ---------- --------- ---- ---- ---- ------ ------ ------- --- ----- ----
SYSTEM P_IND_TEST   RAW_DATA   TEST_P1    10    2  255 20480  20480     249  50     0    0
                    RAW_DATA   TEST_P2    10    2  255 20480  20480     249  50     0    0
                    RAW_DATA   TEST_P3    10    2  255 20480  20480     249  50     0    0

3 rows selected.
```

Monitoring Clusters Using DBA_ and V_$ Views

Clusters can be indexed or hashed in Oracle7. Using the various views and tables available to the DBA they can be readily monitored. The DBA_CLUSTERS, DBA_CLU_COLUMNS, DBA_CLUSTER_HASH_FUNCTIONS, and DBA_TABLES views are utilized to monitor clusters. Figure 12.4 shows the relationships between the views used to monitor clusters. A script for generating a cluster report is shown in Source 12.21 and the example report is shown in Listing 12.21.

SOURCE 12.21   Example script to produce a cluster report.

```
rem
rem File:      CLU_REP.SQL
rem Purpose:      Document Cluster Data
rem Use:       From user with access to DBA_ views
rem
rem When         Who          What
rem -------      ---------    -------------------------
rem 5/27/93      Mike Ault     Initial Creation
rem 6/15/97      Mike Ault     Verified against Oracle8
rem
COLUMN owner               FORMAT a10
COLUMN cluster_name        FORMAT a15 HEADING "Cluster"
COLUMN tablespace_name     FORMAT a20 HEADING "Tablespace"
COLUMN table_name          FORMAT a20 HEADING "Table"
COLUMN tab_column_name     FORMAT a20 HEADING "Table Column"
COLUMN clu_column_name     FORMAT a20 HEADING "Cluster Column"
SET PAGES 56 LINES 130 FEEDBACK OFF
START title132 "Cluster Report"
```

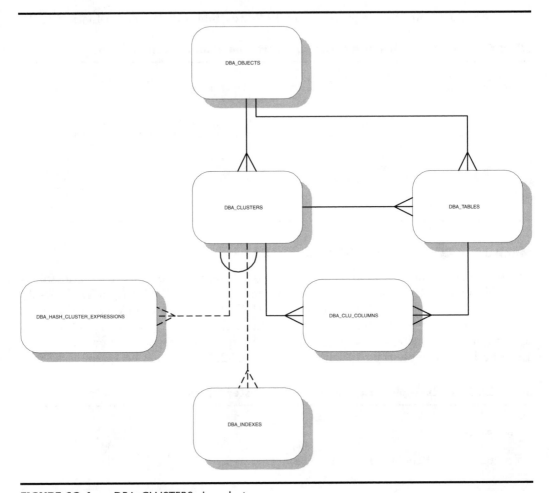

FIGURE 12.4 DBA_CLUSTERS view cluster.

```
BREAK ON owner SKIP 1 ON cluster ON tablespace
SPOOL rep_out\&db\cluster
SELECT
     a.owner,a.cluster_name,tablespace_name,
     table_name,tab_column_name,clu_column_name
FROM
     dba_clusters a,dba_clu_columns b
WHERE
     a.owner = b.owner and
     a.cluster_name=b.cluster_name
ORDER BY 1,2,3,4
/
SPOOL OFF
```

LISTING 12.21   Example output from cluster report.

```
Date: 06/15/97                                                    Page:   1
Time: 04:51 PM                    Cluster Report                  SYSTEM
                                 ORTEST1 database


OWNER   Tablespace    Cluster         Table          Table Column   Cluster Column
-----   ----------    --------------  ---------      ------------   --------------
SYS     SYSTEM        C_COBJ#         CCOL$          OBJ#           OBJ#
                                      CDEF$          OBJ#           OBJ#
                      C_FILE#_BLOCK#  SEG$           FILE#          SEGFILE#
                                                     BLOCK#         SEGBLOCK#
                                                     TS#            TS#
                                      UET$           TS#            TS#
                                                     SEGBLOCK#      SEGBLOCK#
                                                     SEGFILE#       SEGFILE#
                      C_MLOG#         MLOG$          MOWNER         MOWNER
                                                     MASTER         MASTER
                                      SLOG$          MASTER         MASTER
                                                     MOWNER         MOWNER
                      C_OBJ#          ATTRCOL$       OBJ#           OBJ#
                                      CLU$           OBJ#           OBJ#
                                      COL$           OBJ#           OBJ#
```

Monitoring Cluster Storage Statistics As a DBA you may be interested in the storage statistics used to create each cluster. This data is found in the DBA_ CLUSTERS view. The script in Source 12.22 is an example of this type of report. An example of the script's output is shown in Listing 12.22.

SOURCE 12.22   Example script to produce a cluster sizing report.

```
rem Name: clus_siz.sql
rem
rem FUNCTION: Generate a cluster sizing report
rem
COLUMN owner                 FORMAT a10
COLUMN cluster_name          FORMAT a15            HEADING "Cluster"
COLUMN tablespace_name       FORMAT a15            HEADING
"Tablespace"
COLUMN pct_free              FORMAT 999            HEADING "%|Fre"
COLUMN pct_used              FORMAT 999            HEADING "%|Use"
COLUMN key_size              FORMAT 999999         HEADING "Key Size"
COLUMN ini_trans             FORMAT 999            HEADING "Ini|Trn"
COLUMN max_trans             FORMAT 999            HEADING "Max|Trn"
COLUMN initial_extent        FORMAT 999999999      HEADING "Init Ext"
COLUMN next_extent           FORMAT 999999999      HEADING "Next Ext"
COLUMN min_extents           FORMAT 999            HEADING "Min|Ext"
COLUMN max_extents           FORMAT 999            HEADING "Max|Ext"
COLUMN pct_increase          FORMAT 999            HEADING "%|Inc"
SET PAGES 56 LINES 130 FEEDBACK OFF
```

```
START title132 "Cluster Sizing Report"
BREAK ON owner ON tablespace_name
SPOOL rep_out\&db\cls_sze
SELECT
     owner,
     tablespace_name,
     cluster_name,
     pct_free,
     pct_used,
     key_size,
     ini_trans,
     max_trans,
     initial_extent,
     next_extent,
     min_extents,
     max_extents,
     pct_increase
FROM
     dba_clusters
ORDER BY
     1,2,3
/
SPOOL OFF
CLEAR COLUMNS
CLEAR BREAKS
SET PAGES 22 LINES 80 FEEDBACK ON
PAUSE Press enter to continue
```

LISTING 12.22   Example output of the cluster sizing report.

```
Date: 05/17/96                                                        Page:   1
Time: 04:06 PM                     Cluster Sizing Report                    SYS
                     ORDSPTD6 database


Schema                      %   %         Int Max                    Min Max %
Owner   Tablespace Cluster  Fre Use Key Size Trn Trn Init Ext Next Ext Ext Ext Inc
-----   ---------- --------------- --- --- --- ---- --- --- -------- ---------- --- --- ---
SYS     SYSTEM     C_COBJ#       10  50     300   2 255    51200      83968   1 121  50
                   C_FILE#_BLOCK# 10  40     225   2 255    20480     190464   1 121  50
                   C_MLOG#       10  40         2 255    10240      10240   1 121  50
                   C_OBJ#         5  40     800   2 255   122880     430080   1 121  50
                   C_RG#         10  40         2 255    10240      10240   1 121  50
                   C_TS#         10  40         2 255    10240      16384   1 121  50
                   C_USER#       10  40     315   2 255    10240      10240   1 121  50
                   HIST$          5  40     200   2 255    10240      10240   1 121  50
```

The reports in Sources 12.19 and 12.20 give the DBA information on cluster keys, cluster columns, cluster tables, and columns and cluster sizing. Combined with the actual size and extent reports previously shown. the DBA can have a complete picture of clusters in his or her database.

Monitoring Cluster Statistics The DBA_CLUSTERS view has several additional columns. These additional columns provide a more detailed glimpse of cluster status. The additional columns in the DBA_CLUSTERS view are: AVG_BLOCKS_PER_KEY, CLUSTER_TYPE, FUNCTION, and HASHKEYS. The above report script can either be modified to include these columns (since 132 is about the widest you can go, not a good choice) or a new report can be created. An example of this report is shown in Source 12.23. An example of Source 12.23 output is shown in Listing 12.23.

SOURCE 12.23 Report script for new Oracle7 DBA_CLUSTERS columns.

```
rem Name          : clu_stat.sql
rem Purpose       : Report on new DBA_CLUSTER columns
rem Use           : From an account that accesses DBA_ views
rem
COLUMN owner               FORMAT a10      HEADING "Owner"
COLUMN cluster_name        FORMAT a15      HEADING "Cluster"
COLUMN tablespace_name     FORMAT a10      HEADING "Tablespace"
COLUMN avg_blocks_per_key  FORMAT 999999   HEADING "Blocks per Key"
COLUMN cluster_type        FORMAT a8       HEADING "Type"
COLUMN function            FORMAT 999999   HEADING "Function"
COLUMN hashkeys            FORMAT 99999    HEADING "# of Keys"
SET PAGES 56 LINES 79 FEEDBACK OFF
START title80 "Cluster Statistics Report"
SPOOL report_output/&db/clu_type
SELECT
    owner,
    cluster_name,
    tablespace_name,
    avg_blocks_per_key,
    cluster_type,
    function,
    hashkeys
FROM
    dba_clusters
ORDER BY 2
GROUP BY  owner, tablespace, type
/
SPOOL OFF
SET PAGES 22 LINES 80 FEEDBACK ON
CLEAR COLUMNS
TTITLE OFF
```

LISTING 12.23   Example output from cluster statistics report script.

```
Date: 05/22/96                                              Page:   1
Time: 12:54 PM                  Cluster Type Report         SYSTEM
                                ORDSPTD6 database

                                Blocks
                                per                         # of
Owner   Cluster         Tablespace Key      Type    Function    Keys
-----   --------------- ---------- ------   -----   --------    ----
SYS     C_COBJ#         SYSTEM              INDEX
        C_FILE#_BLOCK#
        C_MLOG#
        C_OBJ#
        C_RG#
        C_TS#
        C_USER#
        HIST$
        C_RG#
```

Monitoring Cluster Hash Expressions As of later versions of Oracle7 the capability to specify your own hash expressions for a hash cluster has been provided. These hash expressions can be viewed for a specific cluster by querying the DBA_CLUSTER_HASH_EXPRESSION view. The DBA_CLUSTER_HASH_EXPRESSION view has three columns, OWNER, CLUSTER_NAME, and HASH_EXPRESSION. HASH_EXPRESSION is a LONG, so be sure to allow for extra length character strings by using the WORD_WRAPPED parameter on a COLUMN command when querying this value.

Monitoring of Snapshots and Snapshot Logs Using DBA_ and V Type Views

Snapshots and snapshot logs are Oracle7 and Oracle8 features. These allow read-only copies of a table or columns from multiple tables to be maintained in several locations. The refresh rate of the snapshots can be varied and accomplished automatically. The DBA needs tools to monitor snapshots and snapshot logs. The SQLDBA program in Oracle7 and SVRMGR/OEM in Oracle8 provide screens to allow the DBA to see the status of the database's snapshots. However, it is more convenient at times to have a hardcopy listing documenting snapshots and snapshot logs. The script in Source 12.24 and report in Listing 12.24 and Source 12.25 document a database's snapshots and snapshot logs.

SOURCE 12.24   Example script to document snapshots.

```
rem
rem Name:       snap_rep.sql
rem Purpose:Report on database Snapshots
rem Use:        From an account that accesses DBA_ views
rem
rem   When       Who         What
rem   -------    ---------   ----------------
rem   5/27/93    Mike Ault   Initial Creation
rem
SET PAGES 56 LINES 130 FEEDBACK OFF VERIFY OFF
rem
COLUMN snapshot        FORMAT a30       HEADING "Snapshot"
COLUMN source          FORMAT a30       HEADING "Source Table"
COLUMN link            FORMAT a20       HEADING "Link"
COLUMN log                              HEADING "Use|Log?"
COLUMN refreshed                        HEADING "Refreshed?"
COLUMN type            FORMAT a10       HEADING "Ref|Type"
COLUMN refreshed                        HEADING "Last Refresh"
COLUMN start           FORMAT a13       HEADING "Start Refresh"
COLUMN error                            HEADING "Error"
COLUMN next            FORMAT a13       HEADING "Next Refresh"
rem
PROMPT Percent signs are wild card
ACCEPT snap_owner PROMPT Enter the snapshot owner
START title132 "Snapshot Report for &snap_owner"
SPOOL snap_rep&db
rem
SELECT
    name||'.'||table_name Snapshot, master_view,
    master_owner||'.'||master Source,
    master_link Link,
    can_use_log Log, last_refresh Refreshed,
    start_with start,
    DECODE(type,'FAST','F','COMPLETE','C'),
    next,
    start_with Started, query
FROM dba_snapshots
WHERE owner LIKE UPPER('%&snap_owner%')
ORDER BY owner,3,5;
rem
SPOOL OFF
```

Under Oracle8 there are several new columns that should also be monitored, perhaps in a second script to avoid data clutter. These columns are:

UPDATABLE

REFRESH_METHOD

FR_OPERATIONS

CR_OPERATIONS

REFRESH_GROUP

UPDATE_TRIG

UPDATE_LOG

MASTER_ROLLBACK_SEGMENT

LISTING 12.24   **Example output of the script in Source 12.24.**

```
Date: 06/10/93                  "Your  Company Name "                      Page:   1
Time: 04:28 PM              Snapshot Report for DEV7_DBA                       DEV7_DBA
                               "Your Database"
                            Use            Ref
Snapshot           View     Source   Log Last Ref  Typ Next Ref  Started   Query
---------------- -------- -------- --- --------- --- --------- --------- ------------------
TEST.SNAP$_TEST  MVIEW$_  DEV7_DBA. YES 10-JUN-93 F   SYSDATE+7 10-JUN-93 SELECT CHECK_DATE
     TEST        HIT_RATIO                                                 FROM  HIT_RATIOS
```

SOURCE 12.25   **Example script to generate snapshot log report.**

```
rem
rem Name:   snap_log_rep.sql
rem Purpose:      Report on database Snapshot Logs
rem Use:      From an account that accesses DBA_ views
rem
rem    When       Who         What
rem    -------    ---------   -----------------
rem    5/27/93    Mike Ault   Initial Creation
rem
SET PAGES 56 LINES 130 FEEDBACK OFF
START title132 "Snapshot Log Report"
SPOOL snap_log_rep&db
rem
COLUMN log_owner      FORMAT a10 HEADING "Owner"
COLUMN master         FORMAT a20 HEADING "Master"
COLUMN log_table      FORMAT a20 HEADING "Snapshot"
COLUMN trigger        FORMAT a20 HEADING "Trigger Text"
COLUMN current                   HEADING "Last Refresh"
rem
```

```
SELECT
     log_owner, master, log_table table,
     log_trigger trigger, rowids, filter_columns filtered,
      current_snapshots current, snapshot_id id
FROM
     dba_snapshot_logs
ORDER BY 1;
rem
SPOOL OFF
```

The reports from Sources 12.24 and 12.25 will provide the DBA with hardcopy documentation of all snapshots and snapshot logs in the database. With use of "where" clauses each can be made more restrictive by selecting on a specific set of values such as owner or log_owner, type, or date since last refresh (last_refresh > &date or current_snapshots > &date).

Monitoring Oracle8 Types, Collections, and Methods

Under Oracle8 Oracle has added an entire new set of objects to monitor. These new objects have been called collections, types, user-defined types, ADTs, and so on. I prefer the all-inclusive terms types, collections, and methods. Types allow grouping of related data and then use of these grouped data sets to form more complex objects. For example, a table object may consist of standard columns, a user-defined type, a nested table (built from a type), and a collection (called a VARRAY), which is in itself a type. In order to declare a table to be an object and have it have OIDs implicitly defined, it must be created as an object type from a defined type.

As was said in previous sections there can be types that, while being named, have no other attributes. These are called incomplete types and are used where circular references may need to be defined. Of course, these incomplete types must be completed before an object is built from them.

The major view for types is the DBA_TYPES view. The cluster of views associated with types is shown in Figure 12.5.

Monitoring Types A simple report to tell us some basic information about the types stored in our database is shown in Source 12.26. The report uses the DBA_TYPES view. To get detailed information on the attributes for each type, join to the DBA_TYPE_ATTRS view.

SOURCE 12.26 Example types report.

```
rem
rem NAME: types.sql
rem FUNCTION: Provide basic report of all database types
rem HISTORY : MRA 6/15/97 Created
rem
```

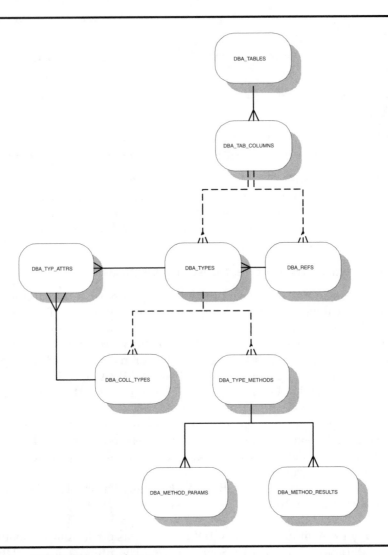

FIGURE 12.5 DBA_TYPES view cluster.

```
COLUMN owner       FORMAT a10        HEADING 'Type|Owner'
COLUMN type_name   FORMAT a30        HEADING 'Type|Name'
COLUMN typecode    FORMAT a27        HEADING 'Type|Code'
COLUMN predefined  FORMAT a3         HEADING Pre?
COLUMN incomplete  FORMAT a3         HEADING Inc?
COLUMN methods     FORMAT 9999999    HEADING '#|Methods'
COLUMN attributes  FORMAT 999999     HEADING '#|Attrib'
SET LINES 130 PAGES 58 VERIFY OFF FEEDBACK OFF
```

```
BREAK ON owner
START title132 'Database Types Report'
SPOOL rep_out\&db\types.lis
SELECT
     DECODE(owner, null,'SYS-GEN',owner) owner,
     type_name,
     typecode,
     attributes,
     methods,
     predefined,
     incomplete
FROM dba_types
ORDER BY owner, type_name;
SPOOL OFF
```

The script in Source 12.24 produces a report similar to the one shown in Listing 12.24. The only column not reported is the TYPE_OID RAW column.

LISTING 12.26   Example output from types basic report.

```
Date: 06/15/97                                            Page:   1
Time: 11:35 PM          Database Types Report               SYSTEM
                        ORTEST1 database

Type         Type              Type               #      #
Owner        Name              Code          Attrib Methods Pre? Inc?
--------     ----------------  ---------------- ------ ------- --- ---
SYS          KOKED             OBJECT             2       0  YES  NO
             KOTAD             OBJECT            15       0  YES  NO
             KOTMD             OBJECT             7       0  YES  NO
             KOTMI             OBJECT             1       0  YES  NO
             KOTTB             OBJECT            10       0  YES  NO
             KOTTD             OBJECT            10       0  YES  NO
SYS-GEN      BFILE             BFILE              0       0  YES  NO
             BINARY ROWID      BINARY ROWID       0       0  YES  NO
             BLOB              BLOB               0       0  YES  NO
             CANONICAL         CANONICAL          0       0  YES  NO
             CFILE             CFILE              0       0  YES  NO
             CHAR              CHAR               0       0  YES  NO
             CLOB              CLOB               0       0  YES  NO
             CONTIGUOUS ARRAY  CONTIGUOUS ARRAY   0       0  YES  NO
SYSTEM       TEST_INCOMPLETE   OBJECT             0       0  NO  YES
TELE_DBA     ADDRESS_LIST      COLLECTION         0       0  NO   NO
             ADDRESS_T         OBJECT            16       0  NO   NO
             ADDRESS_TYPE      OBJECT             8       0  NO   NO
             CEO_T             OBJECT             6       0  NO   NO
             CIRCUIT_LIST      COLLECTION         0       0  NO   NO
             CIRCUIT_T         OBJECT             2       0  NO   NO
```

CLIENT_T	OBJECT	29	1	NO	NO
CONTRACT_LIST	COLLECTION	0	0	NO	NO
CONTRACT_T	OBJECT	1	0	NO	NO
CONTRACT_V	COLLECTION	0	0	NO	NO
CPNI_T	OBJECT	5	0	NO	NO
EARNING_T	OBJECT	21	1	NO	NO
FRANCHISE_T	OBJECT	1	0	NO	NO
FRANCHISE_V	COLLECTION	0	0	NO	NO
LOOKUP_T	OBJECT	9	0	NO	NO
SIC_T	OBJECT	3	0	NO	NO
SIC_V	COLLECTION	0	0	NO	NO

Notice that there are many kinds of types. Many of these (the ones labeled SYSGEN) are system generated at system build; others such as OBJECT and COLLECTION are user defined. The collection types are further documented in the DBA_COLL_TYPES view.

Monitoring Type Collections Another kind of type is a collection (such as a VARRAY). The script in Source 12.25 generates a simple report that documents the important columns from DBA_COLL_TYPES. If you find you need the other data (for simple scalar collections) then by all means add them to the script. To determine the attributes that map into each collection, join to the DBA_TYPE_ATTRS view.

SOURCE 12.27   This script produces a report similar to that in Listing 12.27.

```
rem
rem NAME: col_type.sql
rem FUNCTION: Document the collection types in the database
rem HISTORY: MRA 6/15/97 Created
rem
COL owner           FORMAT a10 HEADING 'Collec.|Owner'
COL type_name       FORMAT a16 HEADING 'Type|Name'
COL coll_type       FORMAT a15 HEADING 'Collec.|Type'
COL upper_bound                HEADING 'VARRAY|Limit'
COL elem_type_owner FORMAT a10 HEADING 'Elementary|Type|Owner'
COL elem_type_name  FORMAT a11 HEADING 'Elementary|Type|Name'
SET PAGES 58 LINES 78 VERIFY OFF FEEDBACK OFF
START title80 'Collection Type Report'
SPOOL rep_out\&db\col_type.lis
select
     owner,
     type_name,
     coll_type,
     upper_bound,
     elem_type_owner,
     elem_type_name
FROM dba_coll_types
WHERE owner LIKE '%&owner%'
/
SPOOL OFF
```

LISTING 12.27   Example output from the collection type report.

```
Date: 06/16/97                                        Page:   1
Time: 12:17 AM              Collection Type Report         SYSTEM
                              ORTEST1 database

                                          Elem.  Elem.
Collec.  Type            Collec.    VARRAY Type   Type
Owner    Name            Type       Limit  Owner  Name
-------- --------------- ---------------- ------ ------ -----------
TELE_DBA ADDRESS_LIST    TABLE             TELE_DBA ADDRESS_T
         CIRCUIT_LIST    TABLE             TELE_DBA CIRCUIT_T
         CONTRACT_LIST   TABLE             TELE_DBA CONTRACT_T
         FRANCHISE_V     VARYING ARRAY  10 TELE_DBA FRANCHISE_T
         SIC_V           VARYING ARRAY   6 TELE_DBA SIC_T
```

Monitoring Type Methods Types can also have methods associated with them. A type is a procedure or function that is intrinsic to (an integral part of) the type and is defined (generally speaking) at the time the type is created. If you will take a close look at Listing 12.28, it only shows two types with defined methods. The methods are documented in the DBA_TYPE_METHODS view and additional drilldown information is located in the DBA_METHOD_PARAMS and DBA_METHOD_RESULTS views. A simple report to show the types with methods in the database is shown in Source 12.28. The report that results from running this source is shown in Listing 12.28.

SOURCE 12.28   Example script to generate type methods report.

```
rem
rem NAME typ_meth.sql
rem FUNCTION : Create a report of type methods
rem HISTORY: MRA 6/16/97 Created
rem
COLUMN owner           FORMAT a10      HEADING 'Owner'
COLUMN type_name       FORMAT a13      HEADING 'Type|Name'
COLUMN method_name     FORMAT a17      HEADING 'Method|Name'
COLUMN method_type                     HEADING 'Method|Type'
COLUMN parameters      FORMAT 99999    HEADING '#|Param'
COLUMN results         FORMAT 99999    HEADING '#|Results'
COLUMN method_no       FORMAT 999999   HEADING 'Meth.|Number'
BREAK ON owner ON type_name
SET LINES 80 PAGES 58 VERIFY OFF FEEDBACK OFF
START title80 'Type Methods Report'
SPOOL rep_out\&db\typ_meth.lis
SELECT
    owner,
```

```
    type_name,
    method_name,
    method_no,
    method_type,
    parameters,
    results
FROM dba_type_methods
ORDER BY owner, type_name;
SPOOL OFF
```

LISTING 12.28   Example output from the type methods report.

```
Date: 06/16/97                                          Page:  1
Time: 12:43 AM              Type Methods Report          SYSTEM
                             ORTEST1 database


        Type      Method              Meth.  Method   #      #
Owner   Name      Name                Number Type   Param  Results
------- --------- ------------------- ------ ------ ----- -------
TELE_DBA CLIENT_T DO_SOUNDEX              1  PUBLIC    3      0
         EARNING_T GET_CLIENT_ID_REF      1  PUBLIC    3      0
```

Monitoring Type REFs   The only object-oriented method of relating two object tables
in Oracle8 is via a REF. A REF internalizes the foreign key relationship between a
child and parent table. A REF always goes between child and parent since a REF can
only reference one column. The DBA_REFS view documents existing REFs in the
database. The script in Source 12.29 shows how a report can be generated to show
the REFs in the database.

SOURCE 12.29   Example REF column report.

```
rem
rem NAME: tab_ref.sql
rem FUNCTION: Generate a lit of all REF columns in the database
rem HISTORY: MRA 6/16/97 Created
rem
COLUMN owner             FORMAT a8   HEADING 'Owner'
COLUMN table_name        FORMAT a23  HEADING 'Table|Name'
COLUMN column_name       FORMAT a15  HEADING 'Column|Name'
COLUMN with_rowid        FORMAT a5   HEADING 'With|Rowid'
COLUMN is_scoped         FORMAT a6   HEADING 'Scoped'
COLUMN scope_table_owner FORMAT a8   HEADING 'Scope|Table|Owner'
```

```
COLUMN scope_table_name  FORMAT a15 HEADING 'Scope|Table|Name'
BREAK ON owner
SET PAGES 58 LINES 130 FEEDBACK OFF VERIFY OFF
START title132 'Database REF Report'
SPOOL rep_out\&db\tab_ref.lis
SELECT
    owner,
    table_name,
    column_name,
    with_rowid,
    is_scoped,
    scope_table_owner,
    scope_table_name
FROM
    dba_refs
ORDER BY
    owner;
SPOOL OFF
```

Listing 12.29 shows an example report from the script in Source 12.29.

LISTING 12.29   Example output from the database REF report.

```
Date: 06/16/97
Page:   1
Time: 01:03 AM                   Database REF Report
SYSTEM
                                  ORTEST1 database


                                                    Scope     Scope
            Table              Column       With     Table     Table
Owner       Name               Name         Rowid  Scoped Owner     Name
--------  --------------------  ------------  -----  ------  --------  -----
TELE_DBA EARNINGS_INFO_NUMBERSV8 CLIENTS_ID_R  YES    YES    TELE_DBA
CLIENTSV8
```

12.3   FURTHER DBA READING

The DBA may find these references of interest when planning to do monitoring activities:

Corey, M.J., M. Abbey, D.J. Dechichio, Jr., *Tuning Oracle,* Oracle Press, 1995.
Loney, Kevin. *Oracle DBA Handbook*, Oracle Press, 7.3 Edition, 1994. *Oracle7 Server Administrator's Guide*, Release 7.3, PART# A32535-1 Feb. 1995, Oracle Corp.

Oracle7 Server Administrator's Guide, Release 7.3, PART# 6694-70-1292, Dec. 1992, Oracle Corp.

Oracle7 Server Reference, Release 7.3, PART# A32589-1, Jan. 1996, Oracle Corp.

Oracle7 Server Tuning , Release 7.3, PART# A32537-1, June 1996, Oracle Corp.

Oracle8 Server Administrator's Guide, Release 8.0, Beta-2, PART# A50648-1, Feb. 1997, Oracle Corp.

Oracle8 Server Reference, Release 8.0-Beta2, PART# A50665-1, Jan. 1997, Oracle Corp.

Oracle8 Server SQL Reference, Release 8.0-Beta2, PART #A50605-1, Feb. 1997, Oracle Corp.

Trezzo. Joseph C., *Oracle7.3/8: A New Expanding Frontier and As Always a New Expanding Data Dictionary*, TUSC, IOUG-A Alive!, 1997

CHAPTER 13

Monitoring Users and Other Database Objects

In Chapter 12 we covered the monitoring of Oracle table-related objects. In this chapter we will discuss the monitoring of virtually every other database object. Since information about users is stored in the database and, indeed, a DBA creates users, I am lumping users in with the "other" database objects.

As with tables, clusters, snapshots, types, and indexes, all other database objects are monitored using the data dictionary tables and views. Again, I refer users to the Dictionary Lite application on the accompanying CD-ROM for lookups as they review the scripts provided. The data dictionary is a powerful tool in the hands of someone who knows how to use it.

13.1 USING THE V$ AND DBA_ VIEWS FOR MONITORING USERS

What do DBAs need to know about the users of their databases? There are many important facts about each user the DBA needs to keep track of, for instance, privileges, quotas, tables owned, file space used, and database default locations, just to name a few. The Oracle Administrator toolbar (part of the Oracle Enterprise Manager tool set) has a nice GUI in its Security Manager section but has no report capability. Figure 13.1 shows the GUI for the Security Manager.

The DBA_USERS view is only the root of a tree of related DBA_ views that give a full picture of the privileges, resources, and roles granted to users. Use Figure 13.2 to see how all of these views in the DBA_ user view cluster relate to each other.

How can the DBA keep track of this information for hundreds or thousands of possible users? Scribble it down as it displays on the SVRMGR or OEM screen? Use some sort of screen capture or screen print facility? Hardly. To keep track of this information the DBA needs reports. Whether DBAs store the reports on-line or use

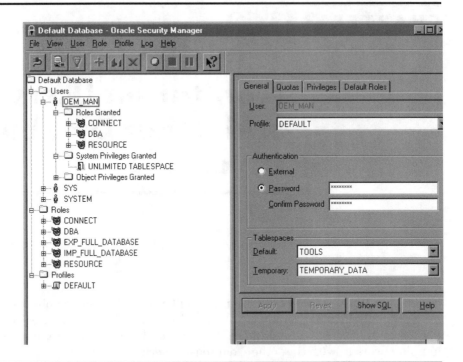

FIGURE 13.1   Oracle Enterprise Manager Security Manager screen.

a three-ring binder, good reports tell them exactly what they need to know. Let's address the relevant topics.

Monitoring User Setup

The first report we will look at uses the DBA_USERS view to provide information on users, user default and temporary tablespace assignments, and user database-level privileges. The script for this report is shown in Source 13.1.

SOURCE 13.1   Example of user report listing.

```
REM
REM NAME        : DB_USER.SQL
REM
REM FUNCTION    : GENERATE USER_REPORT
REM Limitations : None
REM
REM Updates     : MRA 6/10/97 added Oracle8 account status
REM
```

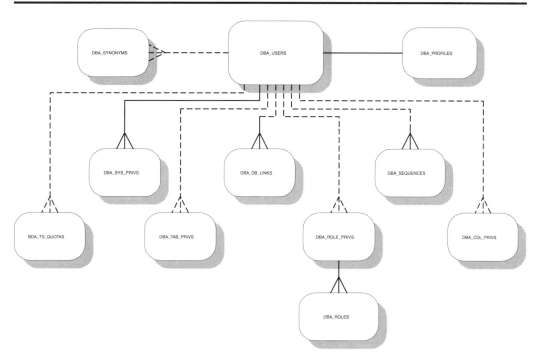

NOTE: Users, which equate to schemas, own all database objects and
thus also have links to all DBA_ views related to objects such as tables,
indexes, clusters, views, etc. However I have chosen for clarity's sake not
to include all of these links on this diagram, please remember them as
implicit.

FIGURE 13.2   DBA_USERS view cluster.

```
SET PAGESIZE 58   LINESIZE 131 FEEDBACK OFF
rem
COLUMN username                 FORMAT a10 HEADING User
COLUMN account_status           FORMAT a10 HEADING Status
COLUMN default_tablespace       FORMAT a15 HEADING Default
COLUMN temporary_tablespace     FORMAT a15 HEADING Temporary
COLUMN granted_role             FORMAT a21 HEADING Roles
COLUMN default_role             FORMAT a9  HEADING Default?
COLUMN admin_option             FORMAT a7  HEADING Admin?
COLUMN profile                  FORMAT a15 HEADING Profile
rem
START title132 'ORACLE USER REPORT'
DEFINE output = rep_out\&db\db_user
BREAK ON username SKIP 1 ON account_status ON default_tablespace
ON temporary_tablespace ON profile
```

```
SPOOL &output
rem
SELECT username,
       account_status,
       default_tablespace,
       temporary_tablespace,
       profile,
       granted_role,
       admin_option,
       default_role
FROM sys.dba_users a,
     sys.dba_role_privs b
WHERE a.username = b.grantee
ORDER BY username,
         default_tablespace,
         temporary_tablespace,
         profile,
         granted_role;
rem
SPOOL OFF
SET TERMOUT ON FLUSH ON FEEDBACK ON VERIFY ON
CLEAR COLUMNS
CLEAR BREAKS
PAUSE Press Enter to continue
```

Several items about this report script bear mentioning. First, notice the header format. Each report should contain a header section similar to this one. It tells what the report script does, who wrote it, and, most important, what changes have been made to it. Next, notice the START command. This command is calling a script that generates a standard 132-column header for use in reports. This script is shown in Appendix B on the CD-ROM. The report header programs also return the database name so that it may be included in the file name. This report was written for use on the UNIX platform. To use it on other platforms, the file specification format will have to be modified; no other changes need to be made. You may wish to add the LOCK_DATE and EXPIRY_DATE from the DBA_USERS view if you use the password control options available in Oracle8. The output from this report is shown in Listing 13.1.

LISTING 13.1   Example of user report format.

```
Date: 06/11/96                                                        Page:    1
Time: 10:08 PM                       ORACLE USER REPORT                  SYSTEM
                                     ORTEST1 database


User      Status    Default  Temporary       Profile Roles                    Admin?  Default?
----      ------    -------  --------------   ------- --------------------     ------  --------
SYS       OPEN      SYSTEM   TEMPORARY_DATA   DEFAULT AQ_ADMINISTRATOR_ROLE YES        YES
                                                      AQ_USER_ROLE           YES        YES
                                                      CONNECT                YES        YES
```

```
                                                 DBA                  YES    YES
                                                 DELETE_CATALOG_ROLE  YES    YES
                                                 EXECUTE_CATALOG_ROLE YES    YES
                                                 EXP_FULL_DATABASE    YES    YES
                                                 IMP_FULL_DATABASE    YES    YES
                                                 RESOURCE             YES    YES
                                                 SELECT_CATALOG_ROLE  YES    YES

SYSTEM   OPEN    USER_DATA TEMPORARY_DATA DEFAULT DBA                  YES    YES

TELE_DBA OPEN    APPL_DATA TEMPORARY_DATA DEFAULT CONNECT              NO     YES
                                                 RESOURCE             NO     YES
```

As you can see, this report takes care of several of our requirements: user names, default tablespace assignments, temporary tablespace assignments, and database roles. The report is currently sorted, using the "ORDER BY" command by username. If you want, it could be sorted by default or temporary tablespace or by individual role. In this script there will be one row for each role granted to the user.

Monitoring User Roles

Monitoring user setup is important, but it is only the beginning. A companion script to show roles and administration options is also required. This is shown in Source 13.2. As you can see, it is very important under Oracle7 and Oracle8 to assign roles to users. If you assign each privilege to each user as it is required it will soon be impossible to manage your user base. Start by only assigning the default roles and then expanding those roles as required. For example, for a user who needs to create tables and indexes, a role called CREATOR could be constructed that has the role CONNECT plus the CREATE_TABLE and CREATE_INDEX privileges. It should also be obvious that the DBA will need to track the roles and have them available at a moment's notice in hard copy to refer to as users are assigned to the system. See Listing 13.2 for an Oracle Roles Report.

SOURCE 13.2   Example of role report listing for Oracle7 and Oracle8.

```
REM
REM NAME        : sys_role.SQL
REM PURPOSE: GENERATE SYSTEM GRANTS and ROLES REPORT
REM USE     : CALLED BY SQLPLUS
REM Limitations    : None
REM Revisions:
REM Date            Modified by   Reason for change
REM 08-Apr-1993     MIKE AULT      INITIAL CREATE
REM 10-Jun-1997     Mike Ault      Update to Oracle8
REM
SET FLUSH OFF TERM OFF PAGESIZE 58  LINESIZE 78
```

```
COLUMN grantee          HEADING 'User or Role'
COLUMN admin_option     HEADING Admin?
START title80 'SYSTEM GRANTS AND ROLES REPORT'
DEFINE output = rep_out\&&db\role_report
SPOOL &output
SELECT
    grantee,
    privilege,
    admin_option
FROM
    sys.dba_sys_privs
GROUP BY
    grantee;
SPOOL OFF
```

LISTING 13.2   Example of output from script in Source 13.2.

```
Date: 06/09/93              "Your Company Name"                Page:   1
Time: 03:12 PM              ORACLE ROLES REPORT                   SYSTEM
                              "Your Database"


User or Role                PRIVILEGE                         Adm
--------------------        ----------------------------------  ---
CONNECT                     ALTER SESSION                     NO
                            CREATE CLUSTER                    NO
                            CREATE DATABASE LINK              NO
                            CREATE SEQUENCE                   NO
                            CREATE SESSION                    NO
                            CREATE SYNONYM                    NO
                            CREATE TABLE                      NO
                            CREATE VIEW                       NO


DBA                         ALTER ANY CLUSTER                 YES
                            ALTER ANY INDEX                   YES
                            ALTER ANY PROCEDURE               YES
                            ALTER ANY ROLE                    YES
                            CREATE SEQUENCE                   YES
                            CREATE SESSION                    YES
                            CREATE SNAPSHOT                   YES
                                     .
                                     .
                                     .
DEV7_DBA                    UNLIMITED TABLESPACE              NO
```

Monitoring User Profiles

In addition to roles, each user is also assigned profiles. Each user gets the default profile if he or she is not explicitly assigned to a profile. Profiles control resource usage and, with Oracle8, password security. Another script, to show the different user profiles, is shown in Source 13.3.

**SOURCE 13.3   Script to generate a report on Oracle7 and Oracle8
user resource profiles.**

```
REM NAME          : PROFILE_REPORT.SQL
REM PURPOSE       : GENERATE USER PROFILES REPORT
REM Revisions:
REM Date           Modified by      Reason for change
REM 08-Apr-1993    MIKE AULT        INITIAL CREATE
SET FLUSH OFF TERM OFF PAGESIZE 58 LINESIZE 78
COLUMN profile             HEADING Profile
COLUMN resource_name       HEADING 'Resource:'
COLUMN limit               HEADING Limit
START title80 'ORACLE PROFILES REPORT'
DEFINE output = rep_out/&&db/prof_rep
SPOOL &output
SELECT
     profile,
     resource_name,
     limit
FROM
     sys.dba_profiles
GROUP BY
     profile;
SPOOL OFF
```

LISTING 13.3   Example of output from the report in Source 13.3.

```
Date: 06/13/97                                       Page:   1
Time: 06:55 PM          ORACLE PROFILES REPORT        SYSTEM
                         ORTEST1 database

Profile              Resource:                        Limit
------------------   ------------------------------   ---------
DEFAULT              COMPOSITE_LIMIT                  UNLIMITED
                     FAILED_LOGIN_ATTEMPTS            UNLIMITED
                     SESSIONS_PER_USER                UNLIMITED
                     PASSWORD_LIFE_TIME               UNLIMITED
                     CPU_PER_SESSION                  UNLIMITED
                     PASSWORD_REUSE_TIME              UNLIMITED
```

```
            CPU_PER_CALL                      UNLIMITED
            PASSWORD_REUSE_MAX                UNLIMITED
            LOGICAL_READS_PER_SESSION         UNLIMITED
            PASSWORD_VERIFY_FUNCTION          UNLIMITED
            LOGICAL_READS_PER_CALL            UNLIMITED
            PASSWORD_LOCK_TIME                UNLIMITED
            IDLE_TIME                         UNLIMITED
            PASSWORD_GRACE_TIME               UNLIMITED
            CONNECT_TIME                      UNLIMITED
            PRIVATE_SGA                       UNLIMITED

16 rows selected.
```

One thing to notice about the report in Listing 13.3 is that it displays the values for the DEFAULT profile. As you can see, the default profile has unlimited resources. This is fine if you are a DBA type of account, but for the majority of general users, you will probably want to restrict some of the quotas and define a new profile for them. Remember to set the RESOURCE_LIMIT parameter in the initialization file to TRUE in order to enable resource quota usage.

Monitoring User Table and Column Grants

Keeping track of what users and roles have access to what objects in the database is a vital part of the process of monitoring users. Two reports, one on table-level grants and one on column-level grants, are required to monitor the users' permissions and grants profile. Source 13.4 shows a script to generate information on a users' table-level grants. For the output, see Listing 13.4.

SOURCE 13.4   Example of script to generate a table grants report for Oracle7 and Oracle8.

```
rem   PURPOSE: Produce report of table grants showing
rem                 GRANTOR, GRANTEE and
rem                   specific GRANTS.
rem   LIMITATIONS: User must have access to DBA_TAB_PRIVS
rem   INPUTS: Owner name
rem   OUTPUTS: Report of table grants
rem
rem   HISTORY:
rem Who:           What:                Date:
rem Mike Ault      Initial creation     3/2/95
rem Mike Ault      Oracle8 verified 6/10/97
rem
rem NOTES: Will not report grants to SYS or SYSTEM
rem
```

```
COLUMN GRANTEE          FORMAT A18    HEADING "Grantee"
COLUMN OWNER            FORMAT A18    HEADING "Owner"
COLUMN TABLE_NAME       FORMAT A30    HEADING "Table"
COLUMN GRANTOR          FORMAT A18    HEADING "Grantor"
COLUMN PRIVILEGE        FORMAT A10    HEADING "Privilege"
COLUMN GRANTABLE        FORMAT A19    HEADING "With Grant Option?"
REM
BREAK ON owner SKIP 4 ON table_name SKIP 1 ON grantee ON grantor ON REPORT
REM
SET LINESIZE 130 PAGES 56 VERIFY OFF FEEDBACK OFF
START title132 "TABLE GRANTS BY OWNER AND TABLE"
SPOOL rep_out\&db\grants
REM
SELECT
     owner,
     table_name,
     grantee,
     grantor,
     privilege,
     grantable
  FROM
     dba_tab_privs
  WHERE
     owner NOT IN ('SYS','SYSTEM')
  ORDER BY
     owner,
     table_name,
     grantor,
     grantee;
REM
SPOOL OFF
PAUSE Press Enter to continue
SET LINESIZE 80 PAGES 22 VERIFY ON FEEDBACK ON
CLEAR BREAKS
CLEAR COLUMNS
TTITLE OFF
```

LISTING 13.4   Example of output from table grant script.

```
Date: 06/11/96                                           Page:   1
Time: 10:54 PM        TABLE GRANTS BY OWNER AND TABLE        SYSTEM
                          ORTEST1 database

Owner        Table         Grantee Grantor   Privilege  Grant Opt?
--------     ------------  ------- --------   ---------  ----- ----
TELE_DBA     ADDRESS_TEST  SYSTEM  TELE_DBA   ALTER      NO
                                              DELETE     NO
                                              INDEX      NO
```

```
                                        INSERT      NO
                                        REFERENCES  NO
                                        UPDATE      NO
                                        SELECT      NO

           CLIENTS      SYSTEM  TELE_DBA SELECT      NO

           USERS        SYSTEM  TELE_DBA ALTER       NO
                                        DELETE      NO
                                        INDEX       NO
                                        INSERT      NO
                                        SELECT      NO
                                        UPDATE      NO
                                        REFERENCES  NO
```

The last bit of data to be gathered on user (or role) table grants is whether they have column-level grants. Column-level grants don't seem to be used much in Oracle. Perhaps this is because SELECT and DELETE privileges cannot be granted in this manner (they are considered table-level grants). A script to re-create table column-level grants is shown in Source 13.5.

SOURCE 13.5   Example of script to capture table column grants.

```
REM FUNCTION:   SCRIPT FOR CAPTURING TABLE COLUMN GRANTS
REM
REM
REM This script is intended to run with Oracle7 or Oracle8.
REM
REM Running this script will create a script of all the grants
REM on columns
REM
REM Grants must be made by the original grantor so the script
REM connects as that user using the username as the password
REM edit the proper password in at time of running
REM
REM NOTE:  Grants made to 'SYS','CONNECT','RESOURCE','DBA',
REM     'EXP_FULL_DATABASE','IMP_FULL_DATABASE' are not captured.
REM
REM     Only preliminary testing of this script was performed.
REM     Be sure to test it completely before relying on it.
REM
SET VERIFY OFF FEEDBACK OFF TERMOUT OFF ECHO OFF PAGESIZE 0
SET EMBEDDED ON HEADING OFF
SET TERMOUT ON
PROMPT Creating table grant script...
SET TERMOUT OFF
DEFINE cr=CHR(10);
```

```
BREAK ON line1
COLUMN dbname NEW_VALUE db NOPRINT
SELECT name dbname FROM v$database;
SPOOL rep_out\&db\grt_cols.sql
rem
SELECT
  'CONNECT '||grantor||'/'||grantor line1,'GRANT '||&&cr||
  lower(privilege)||'('||column_name||') ON
 '||owner||'.'||table_name||&&cr||
 ' TO '|| lower(grantee) ||&&cr||
 decode(grantable,'YES',' WITH ADMIN OPTION;',';')
FROM
  sys.dba_col_privs
WHERE
  grantee NOT IN ('SYS','CONNECT','RESOURCE','DBA',
'EXP_FULL_DATABASE','IMP_FULL_DATABASE')
ORDER BY grantor, grantee
/
SPOOL OFF
SET VERIFY ON FEEDBACK ON TERMOUT ON PAGESIZE 22 EMBEDDED OFF
CLEAR COLUMNS
CLEAR COMPUTES
CLEAR BREAKS
```

The output from the table column grant capture script is shown in Listing 13.5.

LISTING 13.5   Example of output from table column grant capture script.

```
CONNECT TELE_DBA/TELE_DBA
GRANT
insert(DELETE_STATUS) ON TELE_DBA.CLIENTS
 TO system
 ;


GRANT
update(DELETE_STATUS) ON TELE_DBA.CLIENTS
 TO system
 ;
```

In most environments, weekly monitoring of users is sufficient. In some high-use, rapidly changing environments where several DBAs or other types of administrative personnel are adding users, the reports may have to be run more frequently.

Monitoring Currently Logged-In User Processes

A final report that I have found useful lists currently logged-in processes, their user ids and operating system ids as well as any programs they are currently running. Of course, the Q product on the accompanying CD does a better job, but I don't always have time to start it up just to check on users. The script, called pid.sql, is shown in Source 13.6, and an example of its output is shown in Listing 13.6.

SOURCE 13.6   Example of script to show active users.

```
rem
rem  Name:     pid.sql
rem
rem  FUNCTION: Generate a list of current Oracle sids/pids
rem
COLUMN program        FORMAT a25
COLUMN pid            FORMAT 9999
COLUMN sid            FORMAT 9999
COLUMN osuser                         HEADING Oper|System|User
SET LINES 132 PAGES 58
BREAK ON username
COMPUTE COUNT OF pid ON username
START title132 "Oracle Processes"
SPOOL rep_out\&db\cur_proc
SELECT
    NVL(a.username,'Null') username,
    b.pid,
    a.sid,
    DECODE(a.terminal,'?','Detached',a.terminal) terminal,
    b.program,
    b.spid,
    a.osuser,
    a.serial# ser#
 FROM
    v$session a,
    v$process b
WHERE
    a.paddr=b.paddr          -- note: alta script on disk
ORDER BY
    a.username,
    b.pid
/
SPOOL OFF
CLEAR BREAKS
CLEAR COLUMNS
SET PAGES 22 LINES 80
TTITLE OFF
PAUSE Press Enter to continue
```

LISTING 13.6   Example of output of the current users report (pid.sql).

```
Date: 05/21/97                                        Page:    1
Time: 02:42 PM              Oracle Processes              SYS
                           ORCNETT3 database


                                                Oper
                                                system
USERNAME PID SID TERMINAL PROGRAM            SPID  User    SER#
-------- --- --- -------- ------------------ ----- ------- ----
DBO        9   9 pts/4    oracle@a124 (SNP0) 17581 nltptck 1085
******** ---
count      1
QDBA      13  13          oracle@a124 (D001) 15638         2956
******** ---
count      1
Null       1   1 Detached PSEUDO                  oracle    1
           2   2 Detached oracle@a124 (PMON) 15627 oracle    1
           3   3 Detached oracle@a124 (DBWR) 15628 oracle    1
           4   4 Detached oracle@a124 (ARCH) 15629 oracle    1
           5   5 Detached oracle@a124 (LGWR) 15630 oracle    1
           6   6 Detached oracle@a124 (CKPT) 15631 oracle    1
           7   7 Detached oracle@a124 (SMON) 15632 oracle    1
           8   8          oracle@a124 (RECO) 15633         3655
******** ---
count      8

10 rows selected.
```

13.2   USING THE V$ AND DB_ VIEWS TO MONITOR TABLESPACES

The DBA needs to monitor more than just users. Tablespaces also require watching. Tablespaces are not unchanging objects. They are subject to becoming filled and becoming fragmented. The Oracle Administrator toolbar provides for a GUI-based monitoring of tablespaces via the Storage Manager (Figure 13.3); unfortunately, it provides no report output. Luckily, it is a fairly easy thing to monitor tablespaces using the V$ and DB_ views. Look at Figure 13.4, which shows the DBA_ views that relate to tablespaces, as we examine a script or two that provide us with information we can put our hands on.

Monitoring Tablespace Free Space and Fragmentation

Let's examine a report that covers two critical parameters, available space and fragmentation (not covered in the GUI). See Source 13.7.

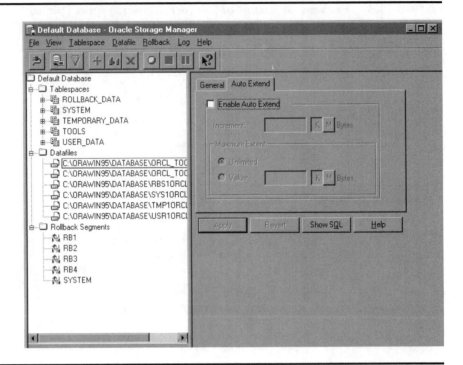

FIGURE 13.3 Oracle Enterprise Manager Storage Manager screen.

SOURCE 13.7 A report on tablespace space usage and fragmentation.

```
rem
rem Name:      free_spc2.sql
rem
rem FUNCTION: Provide data on tablespace extent status
rem FUNCTION: this report uses the free_space2 view
rem FUNCTION: includes fsfi from DBA Handbook
rem
SET FEED OFF
SET FLUSH OFF
SET VERIFY OFF
set pages 58 LINES 132
COLUMN tablespace        HEADING Name              FORMAT a30
COLUMN files             HEADING '#Files'          FORMAT 9,999
COLUMN pieces            HEADING Frag              FORMAT 9,999
COLUMN free_bytes        HEADING 'Free|Byte'       FORMAT 9,999,999,999
COLUMN free_blocks       HEADING 'Free|Blk'        FORMAT 999,999
COLUMN largest_bytes     HEADING 'Biggest|Bytes'   FORMAT 9,999,999,999
COLUMN largest_blks      HEADING 'Biggest|Blks'    FORMAT 999,999
COLUMN ratio             HEADING 'Percent'         FORMAT 999.999
```

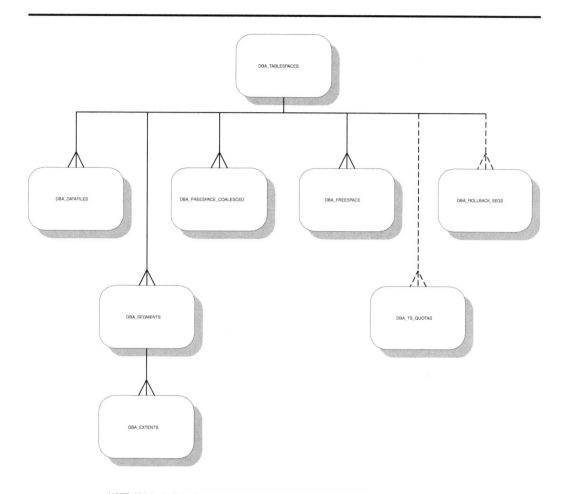

NOTE: All "physical" database objects such as tables, clusters, indexes, and partitions also have links back to tablespaces. For the purposes of clarity I have not included these on this diagram but it should be understood they are implicit.

FIGURE 13.4   DBA_TABLESPACES view cluster.

```
COLUMN average_fsfi    HEADING 'Average|FSFI'    FORMAT 999.999
START title132 "FREE SPACE REPORT"
DEFINE 1 = report_output/&&db/free_spc
SPOOL &1
SELECT
      tablespace,
      COUNT(*) files,
```

```
        SUM(pieces) pieces,
        SUM(free_bytes) free_bytes,
        SUM(free_blocks) free_blocks,
        SUM(largest_bytes) largest_bytes,
        SUM(largest_blks) largest_blks,
        SUM(largest_bytes)/sum(free_bytes)*100 ratio,
        SUM(fsfi)/COUNT(*) average_fsfi
FROM
        free_space
GROUP BY
        tablespace;
SPOOL OFF
CLEAR COLUMNS
TTITLE OFF
SET FEED ON
SET FLUSH ON
SET VERIFY ON
SET PAGES 22 LINES 80
PAUSE Press Enter to continue
```

The report in Source 13.7 uses the view FREE_SPACE, which is based on the DBA_ view DBA_FREE_SPACE. This view is shown in Source 13.8. The free space report is shown in Listing 13.7.

SOURCE 13.8   Free space view listing.

```
rem
rem Name:     free_space_view.sql
rem
rem FUNCTION: Create free_space view for use by freespc reports
rem
CREATE VIEW free_space
    (tablespace, file_id, pieces, free_bytes, free_blocks,
     largest_bytes,largest_blks, fsfi) AS
SELECT tablespace_name, file_id, COUNT(*),
    SUM(bytes), SUM(blocks),
    MAX(bytes), MAX(blocks),
    SQRT(MAX(blocks)/SUM(blocks))*(100/SQRT(SQRT(COUNT(blocks))))
FROM sys.dba_free_space
GROUP BY tablespace_name, file_id;
```

LISTING 13.7   Example of report from free space report script.

```
Date: 07/19/96                                                    Page:   1
Time: 08:24 AM                      FREE SPACE REPORT             SYSTEM
                                    ORTDMS database

                         Free      Free     Biggest  Biggest          Average
Name         #Files Frag Byte      Blk      Bytes    Blks    Percent   FSFI
----------   ------ ---- --------- ------   --------- ------- -------  -------
RBS              1    3   54,228,992  26,479   24,258,560  11,845   44.734   50.820
SYSTEM           1    1   20,133,888   9,831   20,133,888   9,831  100.000  100.000
TDMS_DATA        1    2  181,204,992  88,479  113,047,552  55,199   62.387   66.418
TDMS_INDEX       1    2  153,987,072  75,189  136,857,600  66,825   88.876   79.275
TEMP             2    2   94,367,744  46,078   94,367,744  46,078  100.000  100.000
TOOLS            1    1    6,223,872   3,039    6,223,872   3,039  100.000  100.000
USERS            1    1   10,483,712   5,119   10,483,712   5,119  100.000  100.000
```

In an ideal situation, the tablespace data file(s) (there will be one line in the report for each tablespace data file) will show one extent, and the biggest area will match the free area. In most cases, if the tablespace has been used for any length of time there will be several extents, and the free area (which corresponds to total free space in the tablespace) and the biggest area (which corresponds to the biggest area of contiguous free space) will not be equal. If the number of extents isn't large, say, less than twenty, and the mismatch between the two sizes is small, say, less than 10 percent difference between biggest and free, then there is probably nothing to worry about. If either of these values are exceeded, the DBA should consider using the defragmentation methods described earlier.

Under Oracle7 and Oracle8 the tablespaces are automatically defragmented by the SMON process if the value for the default storage parameter PCTINCREASE is set to greater than zero. The FSFI (Free Space Fragmentation Index) tells how much the free space in a tablespace is fragmented and comes to us by way of the *DBA Handbook* by Kevin Loney (Publisher: Oracle Press 1994). A high value is good (with 100 the best) and a low value is bad.

If you find yourself adding several data files to a single tablespace in a relatively short period of time, it may be wise to extrapolate the growth and then export, drop, and re-create the tablespace to the size required to prevent excessive addition of data files.

Spreading data files for large databases across several drives may be desirable for equalizing disk IO. This is a database-specific question and needs to be answered on a case-by-case basis. If you have several large tables that would benefit from being spread across several disks, you might consider placing them in their own tablespaces, then sizing the data files for the tablespaces such that the data contained in the tables is spread. For instance, if you have a single table that contains a gigabyte of data, it may be advisable to spread this file across several platters. To do this in Oracle7, create a table-specific tablespace on each of the platters that will hold the file, with each tablespace a fraction of the total size of the table; that is, if you want to spread the file across four drives, each data file would be 250 megabytes in size. Then, when you import the table, it will be spread across the four drives. The database will see the table as one contiguous entity, but you will gain IO speed by having spread the table across the available drives. Under Oracle8, this can be accomplished with table partitioning, which allows a single table to be spread, by value range, across several files.

You should create each tablespace with a default storage parameter that takes into account the performance-critical tables in the application that resides in it. You should also do the best job you can estimating the size requirements for the tables as they are created and only default to the default storage for minor tables. Ideally, this size estimation should be pushed down to the developers of the applications.

Monitoring Tablespace Autoextend Settings

In addition to space usage and fragmentation monitoring you need to monitor database autoextend status and data file locations. Source 13.9 shows the SQL to create a view that monitors autoextend data for pre-Oracle8. In pre-Oracle8 versions the only way to get this information was to query the SYS table FILEXT$. Unfortunately, this table looks like this:

Name	Null?	Type
FILE#	NOT NULL	NUMBER
MAXEXTEND	NOT NULL	NUMBER
INC	NOT NULL	NUMBER

This structure means that in order to get back to the actual file name and tablespace you need to join to several other tables, namely, FILE$, TS$, and V$DBFILE. A script to create a data file view is shown in Source 13.9.

SOURCE 13.9   **Script to create a data file view.**

```
CREATE VIEW dba_file_data AS
SELECT
  a.name tablespace,a.dflminext min_extents,
  a.dflmaxext max_extents,
  a.dflinit init,a.dflincr next,
  a.dflextpct pct_increase, d.name datafile,
  b.blocks datafile_size, c.maxextend max_extend,
  c.inc ext_incr
FROM ts$ a, file$ b, filext$ c, v$dbfile d
WHERE
  a.ts#=b.ts# and b.file#=c.file# and b.file#=d.file#
/
```

This script creates the view DBA_FILE_DATA, which will look like this when queried:

```
Name                            Null?       Type
----------------------------    --------    ------------
TABLESPACE                      NOT NULL    VARCHAR2(30)
MIN_EXTENTS                     NOT NULL    NUMBER
MAX_EXTENTS                     NOT NULL    NUMBER
INIT                            NOT NULL    NUMBER
NEXT                            NOT NULL    NUMBER
PCT_INCREASE                    NOT NULL    NUMBER
DATAFILE                                    VARCHAR2(257)
DATAFILE_SIZE                   NOT NULL    NUMBER
MAX_EXTEND                      NOT NULL    NUMBER
EXT_INCR                        NOT NULL    NUMBER
```

Using this view it is now easy to create a simple select that gets autoextend and data file location information from a single view, along with all of the pertinent sizing information. The Oracle Administrator Storage Manager does show this information under the data files section.

Monitoring Tablespace Data Files

As the DBA you should also monitor the size and location of the data files associated with the tablespaces under your control—if for no other reason than to prevent yourself from placing index tablespace data files alongside those that deal with table data you need to have an accurate map of data files. The script in Source 13.10 creates the report in Listing 13.10 that provides this data file map. A script to document tablespace data files is shown in Source 13.10.

SOURCE 13.10   Script to document tablespace data files.

```
REM
REM     Name:       datafile.sql
REM     FUNCTION:   Document  file sizes and locations
REM     Use:        From SQLPLUS
REM
CLEAR COMPUTES
COLUMN file_name                FORMAT A50
COLUMN tablespace_name          FORMAT A15
COLUMN meg                      FORMAT 99,999.90
START title80 'DATABASE DATA FILES'
SPOOL rep_out\&db\datafile
BREAK ON tablespace_name SKIP 1 ON REPORT
COMPUTE SUM OF meg ON tablespace_name
COMPUTE SUM OF meg ON REPORT
```

```
SELECT
     tablespace_name,
     file_name,
     bytes/1048576 meg
FROM
     dba_data_files
ORDER BY
     tablespace_name
/
SPOOL OFF
CLEAR COLUMNS
CLEAR COMPUTES
PAUSE Press Enter to continue
```

LISTING 13.10   Example of output from data file report.

```
Date: 05/22/96                                          Page:    1
Time: 11:06 PM               DATABASE DATA FILES         SYSTEM
                              ORTEST1 database

TABLESPACE_NAME FILE_NAME                                MEG
--------------- ---------------------------------------  --------
RAW_DATA        E:\ORACLE3\ORTEST1\DATA\RAW01_TEST.DBF    700.00
***************                                          --------
sum                                                       700.00


RAW_INDEX       C:\ORACLE1\ORTEST1\DATA\RAW_INDEX.DBF     500.00
***************                                          --------
sum                                                       500.00


ROLLBACK_DATA   C:\ORACLE1\ORTEST1\DATA\RBS1ORTEST1.DBF   500.00
***************                                          --------
sum                                                       500.00


APPL_DATA       D:\ORACLE2\ORTEST1\DATA\APLDAT1ORTEST1.DBF  500.00
                D:\ORACLE2\ORTEST1\DATA\APLDAT2ORTEST1.DBF  500.00
                D:\ORACLE2\ORTEST1\DATA\APLDAT3ORTEST1.DBF  500.00
                E:\ORACLE3\ORTEST1\DATA\APLDAT4ORTEST1.DBF  500.00
***************                                          --------
sum                                                      2,000.00


APPL_INDEX      F:\ORACLE4\ORTEST1\DATA\APLIDX1ORTEST1.DBF  500.00
                E:\ORACLE3\ORTEST1\DATA\APLIDX2ORTEST1.DBF  500.00
***************                                          --------
sum                                                      1,000.00


SYSTEM          C:\ORACLE1\ORTEST1\DATA\SYSTEST.ORA         50.00
***************                                          --------
```

```
sum                                                        50.00

TEMPORARY_DATA   F:\ORACLE4\ORTEST1\DATA\TMP1ORTEST1.DBF   600.00
***************                                          --------
sum                                                       600.00

USER_DATA        C:\ORACLE1\ORTEST1\DATA\USR1ORTEST1.DBF    10.00
***************                                          --------
sum                                                        10.00


                                                        --------
sum                                                     5,360.00

12 rows selected.
```

Monitoring Tablespace Extent Mapping

A final set of information that is handy to have around and that the Oracle tools don't provide (many third-party tools will provide a GUI-based map) is the location of the free space in a tablespace and the sizes of the fragments themselves. The script in Source 13.11 provides this data.

SOURCE 13.11 Script to document free space extents inside a tablespace.

```
rem
rem Name: mapper.sql
rem Function: create an extent map for a specific tablespace
rem   Based on a technique from DBA Handbook
rem Mike Ault 7/19/96 Trecom/RevealNet
rem
SET PAGES 47 LINES 132 VERIFY OFF FEEDBACK OFF
COLUMN file_id        HEADING 'File|id'
COLUMN value          NEW_VALUE dbblksiz NOPRINT
COLUMN meg            FORMAT 9,999.99
SELECT value FROM v$parameter WHERE name='db_block_size';
START title132 '&&ts Mapping Report'
SPOOL rep_out/&db/ts_map
SELECT
     'free space' owner, '        ' object,
     file_id, block_id, blocks,
     (blocks*&dbblksiz)/(1024*1024) meg
FROM
     dba_free_space
WHERE
     tablespace_name=UPPER('&&ts')
UNION
```

```
SELECT
     SUBSTR(owner,1,20), SUBSTR(segment_name, 1,32),
     file_id, block_id, blocks,
     (blocks*&dbblksiz)/(1024*1024) meg
FROM
     dba_extents
WHERE
     tablespace_name = UPPER('&&ts')
ORDER BY 3,4;
SPOOL OFF
UNDEF ts
SET PAGES 22 LINES 80 VERIFY ON FEEDBACK ON
CLEAR COLUMNS
TTITLE OFF
```

The output from the script in Source 13.11 is shown in Listing 13.11.

LISTING 13.11 Example of output of the mapper script.

```
Date: 06/13/97                                           Page:    1
Time: 07:29 PM         raw_data Mapping Report            SYSTEM
                       ORTEST1 database


                            File
OWNER        OBJECT          id   BLOCK_ID    BLOCKS      MEG
----------   ------------   ----  --------    ------    ------
TELE_DBA     LOAD_TEST       11          2    102655    401.00
TELE_DBA     LOAD_TEST       11     102657     25600    100.00
TELE_DBA     LOAD_TEST       11     128257     25600    100.00
SYSTEM       PARTITION_TEST  11     153857       260      1.02
SYSTEM       PARTITION_TEST  11     154117       260      1.02
SYSTEM       PARTITION_TEST  11     154377       260      1.02
free space                   11     154637     24564     95.95
```

13.3   USING THE V$ AND DB_ VIEWS FOR MONITORING SEQUENCES

Sequences are used to generate integer numbers for use in keys or in any other column that requires either repeating or nonrepeating numbers. There were no changes made to sequences under Oracle8. Essentially, the only monitoring that the DBA can do is to identify the sequences, their owners, and so on. The DBA can query the sequence's values, but then those values are lost. The view used in the SQL script in Source 13.12 holds the last value written to disk; this is all the data on the actual sequence value that the DBA can get nondestructively.

TIP: One technique I have found useful is to use a select against the DBA_SEQUENCES table LAST_NUMBER column when I use a sequence for the primary key of a table I am loading, instead of using a COUNT(*) to determine the progress of the load. This technique provides a virtually instantaneous return of the value and doesn't contend with the load process. Of course, this only applies if the sequence is used as a part of a SQLLOADER load or a SQL load, and is reset to start at 1 at the beginning of the load.

The DBA should monitor the last value written against the maximum value for ascending and the minimum value for descending sequences. If the sequence is near its limit and is not a cycled sequence, the DBA will have to alter the minimum or maximum values using the ALTER SEQUENCE command if the sequence value is approaching the minimum or maximum value. If this isn't done, the tables depending on the sequence will fail any selects to retrieve sequence values.

As with other objects, if sequences are used in applications, they should be owned by a central DBA account for the application. This report, if used with the wild card (%) option, will report on all sequences, thus showing privately owned sequences. To alter the ownership of a sequence, it must either be dropped and re-created, with possible loss of continuity in sequence numbers, or it can be exported and then imported into the new owner with no loss of values.

In addition, the DBA should monitor the number of values being cached. If this value is excessive, large numbers of cached sequence values are lost during shutdown. If the value is too small, performance can suffer if the sequence is accessed frequently. The default value for cache is ten (10).

A heads up is also required for the following scenario. If someone adds a value or values to the DUAL table (this is a SYS-owned table with a single column, DUMMY, and a single value, X), then any selects in PL/SQL against DUAL to fetch a NEXTVAL or CURVAL will error out with the error: "ORA-01422: exact fetch returns more than the requested number of rows." In addition, several of the DBMS_ packages depend on this table, so if they start giving ORA-01422 errors, check this table immediately. Source 13.12 shows a report format from a sequence report.

SOURCE 13.12 SQL script to generate a sequence report.

```
rem   NAME: Sequence.sql
rem
rem   HISTORY:
rem   Date            Who                      What
rem   --------        ----------------------   ---------------
rem   5/10/93       Mike Ault                  Creation
rem   FUNCTION: Generate report on Sequences
```

```
rem   INPUTS:
rem
rem      1 - Sequence Owner or Wild Card
rem      2 - Sequence Name or Wild Card
rem
rem   ********************************************************************
SET HEADING OFF VERIFY OFF PAUSE OFF
PROMPT ** Sequence Report **
PROMPT
PROMPT Percent signs are wild
ACCEPT sequence_owner char  'Enter account to report on (or pct
sign):';
ACCEPT sequence_name char  'Enter sequence to report on (or pct
sign):';
PROMPT
PROMPT Report file name is SEQUENCE.LIS
SET HEADING ON
SET LINESIZE 130 PAGESIZE 56 NEWPAGE 0 TAB OFF SPACE 1
SET TERMOUT OFF
BREAK ON sequence_owner SKIP 2
COLUMN sequence_owner       FORMAT A30      HEADING 'Sequence Owner'
COLUMN sequence_name        FORMAT A30      HEADING 'Sequence Name'
COLUMN min_value                            HEADING 'Minimum'
COLUMN max_value                            HEADING 'Maximum'
COLUMN increment_by         FORMAT 9999     HEADING 'Incr.'
COLUMN cycle_flag                           HEADING 'Cycle'
COLUMN order_flag                           HEADING 'Order'
COLUMN cache_size           FORMAT 99999    HEADING 'Cache'
COLUMN last_number                          HEADING 'Last Value'
START title132 "SEQUENCE REPORT"
SPOOL report_output/&&db/sequence
SELECT
     sequence_owner,
     sequence_name,
     min_value,
     max_value,
     increment_by,
     DECODE(cycle_flag,'Y','YES','N','NO') cycle_flag,
     DECODE(order_flag,'Y','YES','N','NO') order_flag,
     cache_size,
     last_number
FROM
     dba_sequences
WHERE
     sequence_owner LIKE UPPER('&sequence_owner') AND
     sequence_name LIKE UPPER('&sequence_name')
ORDER BY
     1,2;
SPOOL OFF
```

LISTING 13.12   Example of report format from sequence script.

```
Date: 05/11/93              "Your Company Name"              Page:   1
Time: 11:03 AM              SEQUENCE REPORT                  SYSTEM
                           "Your" Database

Sequence  Sequence   Min    Max         Incr.
Owner     Name       Value  Value       Value  Cyc  Ord  Cache  Last Value
--------- ---------- -----  ----------  -----  ---  ---  -----  ----------
ADHOC_DBA MTD_EXPENSE  1    1.0000E+27    1     NO   NO   20        1
          WORK_EFFRT   1    1.0000E+27    1     NO   NO   20        1
CT_DBA    AUDITOR      1    1.0000E+27    1     NO   NO   20        21
3 Rows Selected
```

13.4   MONITORING SYNONYMS USING THE V$ AND DBA_ VIEWS

For Oracle7 and Oracle8 synonyms remain the same. The major changes that have affected synonyms are the changes to the structure of the connection strings from SQLNET V1 to V2 to NET8. In all the reports reviewed for this book, not one seemed to cover synonyms. Yet synonyms are the key to providing cross-database access for queries and a means of implementing distributed data across nodes, systems, and databases. Recall that a synonym allows a shorthand version of an object name to be specified. The parts of a synonym are the object name (which usually includes an owner) and, possibly, a database link that will also provide an Oracle user name and password to a remote system. A complete report will show all of these items.

Why is it important to monitor synonyms? Synonyms can be used to access data, sometimes data that shouldn't be accessed if object grants have been too widely granted. In addition, they are the means for reaching other nodes and databases. If a connect string becomes invalid, a user name is disconnected or its password changes, or a node name changes, it is good to be able to see what object synonyms will be affected. Source 13.13 shows a script for a synonym report, and Listing 13.13 shows an example of output from a synonym script.

SOURCE 13.13   Script for synonym report.

```
REM
REM NAME    : SYNONYM.SQL
REM PURPOSE    : GENERATE REPORT OF A USERS SYNONYMS
REM USE    : FROM SQLPLUS
REM Limitations    : None
REM Revisions:
REM Date                Modified by Reason for change
REM 12/MAY/93    Mike Ault    Initial Creation
REM 15/Jun/97    Mike Ault    Verified for Oracle8
```

```
REM
PROMPT Percent signs are Wild Cards
PROMPT
ACCEPT own PROMPT 'Enter the user who owns synonym: '
SET PAGES 56 LINES 130 VERIFY OFF FEEDBACK OFF TERM OFF
START title132 "Synonym Report"
SPOOL rep_out/&&db/synonym
COLUMN host            FORMAT a24 HEADING "Connect String"
COLUMN owner           FORMAT a15
COLUMN table           FORMAT a35
COLUMN db_link         FORMAT a6  HEADING Link
COLUMN username        FORMAT a15
SELECT
     a.owner,
     synonym_name ,
     table_owner ||'.'|| table_name "Table" ,
     b.db_link,
     username,
     host
FROM
     dba_synonyms a,
     dba_db_links b
WHERE
     a.db_link = b.db_link(+) AND
     a.owner LIKE UPPER('&own');
SPOOL OFF
```

LISTING 13.13   Example of output from synonym script.

```
Date: 05/12/93              "Your Company Name"              Page:   1
Time: 05:35 PM                Synonym Report              OPS$NM91263
                             "Your" Database


Owner          Synonym         Table             Link User          Conn
Name           Name            Name              Name Name          String
-----------    --------------  ------------------ ---- -----------   -------
OPS$NM91263    DEV_INSTANCE    DEV_DBA.INSTANCE   DEV  OPS$NM91263   ORADEV
OPS$NM91263    DEV_HIT_RATIO   DEV_DBA.HIT_RATIO  DEV  OPS$NM91263   ORADEV
OPS$NM91263    KCGC_INSTANCE   KCG_DBA.INSTANCE   KCG  OPS$NM91263   ORACASE
OPS$NM91263    KCGC_HIT_RATIO  KCG_DBA.HIT_RATIO  KCG  OPS$NM91263   ORACASE

  .              .               .                 .    .             .
  .              .               .                 .    .             .

OPS$NM91263    CDI_MCUI        CASE.CDI_MCUI
OPS$NM91263    ENTITIES          CASE.ENTITIES
OPS$NM91263    CDI_MTUI          CASE.CDI_MTUI
OPS$NM91263    SDD_COLUMNS     CASE.SDD_COLUMNS
```

13.5 MONITORING DATABASE LINKS USING V$ AND DBA_ VIEWS

Database links provide connection paths to external databases. They specify user name, password, and connection string data. In earlier versions a protocol had to be specified; now protocol-specific data is placed in the TNSNAMES.ORA file and is hidden from the user. Database links can be either private, used by a single user, or public and accessible by all users. Database links can be used on the fly in queries or can be made invisible to the common user by using synonyms. The DBA_DB_LINKS view is used to monitor them. Source 13.14 shows an example of a database link report, and Listing 13.14 shows an example of a listing from a DB Link report script.

SOURCE 13.14   Example of database link report.

```
REM
REM NAME          : DBLINK.SQL
REM FUNCTION      : GENERATE REPORT OF DATABASE LINKS
REM USE           : FROM SQLPLUS
REM Limitations   : None
REM
SET PAGES 58 LINES 130 VERIFY OFF TERM OFF
START title132 "Db Links Report"
SPOOL report_output/&db/dblinks
COLUMN host              FORMAT a60      HEADING "Connect|String"
COLUMN owner             FORMAT a15      HEADING "Creator"
COLUMN db_link           FORMAT a10      HEADING " DB Link|Name"
COLUMN username          FORMAT a15      HEADING "Connecting|User"
COLUMN create                            HEADING "Date|Created"
SELECT
     host,
     owner,
     db_link,
     username,
     created
FROM
     dba_db_links
ORDER BY
     owner,
     host;
SPOOL OFF
PAUSE Press Enter to continue
```

LISTING 13.14   Example of listing from DB Link report script.

```
Date: 05/16/97                      "Your Company Name"                    Page:   1
Time: 05:35 PM                     Database Links Report                  OPS$NM91263
                                     "Your" Database

Connect                          DB                   Connecting  Date
String                           Link       Creator   User        Created
------------------------------   ---------------  ----------  -----------  ------------
ORACASE.WORLD                    ORACASE    KC_DBA    CASE_DB     15-MAY-1997
ORADEV.WORLD                     ORADEV     KC_DBA    CASE_DB     10-APR-1997
ORADLBP1.WORLD                   ORADLBP1   KC_DBA    CASE_DB     10-MAY-1997
ORADLBD1.WORLD                   ORADLBD1   KC_DBA    CASE_DB     10-MAY-1997
ORALIMP1.WORLD                   ORALIMP1   KC_DBA    CASE_DB     12-MAY-1997
ORALIMD1.WORLD                   ORALIMD1   KC_DBA    CASE_DB     12-MAY-1997
```

13.6   MONITORING DATABASE ROLLBACK SEGMENTS USING V$ AND DBA_ VIEWS

Rollback segments must be monitored. Their tablespace area is monitored through the free space and extents reports shown in previous sections. It would be good to have a report just for rollback segments to present rollback-related data in one convenient location.

Monitoring Rollback Usage and Statistics

Unfortunately, the DBA_ROLLBACK_SEGS view is just too large to allow a single report to cover all of the parameters it shows; therefore, two views and two reports are required to adequately cover the DBA_ROLLBACK_SEGS view and the monitoring of rollback segments. The scripts in Source 13.15 create two views, ROLLBACK1 and ROLLBACK2, both based on the V$ROLLSTAT and V$ROLLNAME views, which are very important for monitoring rollback activity. The DBA_ view, DBA_ROLLBACK_SEGS, is based on these two tables.

SOURCE 13.15   SQL scripts to generate ROLLBACK1 and ROLLBACK2 views.

```
REM
REM FUNCTION: create views required for rbk1 and rbk2 reports.
REM
REM
CREATE OR REPLACE VIEW rollback1 AS
SELECT
      d.segment_name,
      extents,
      optsize,
      shrinks,
```

```
        aveshrink,
        aveactive,
        d.status
FROM
        v$rollname n,
        v$rollstat s,
        dba_rollback_segs d
WHERE
        d.segment_id=n.usn(+)
        AND d.segment_id=s.usn(+)
;

CREATE OR REPLACE VIEW rollback2 AS
SELECT
        d.segment_name,
        extents,
        xacts,
        hwmsize,
        rssize,
        waits,
        wraps,
        extends,
        d.status
FROM
        v$rollname n,
        v$rollstat s,
        dba_rollback_segs d
WHERE
        d.segment_id=n.usn(+)
        AND d.segment_id=s.usn(+);
```

Once the ROLLBACK1 and ROLLBACK2 views have been created, two simple SQL scripts are used to monitor rollback segments. These scripts are shown in Source 13.16, and their output is shown in Listing 13.16.

SOURCE 13.16 Example of rollback report scripts.

```
REM
REM NAME              : RBK1.SQL
REM FUNCTION          : REPORT ON ROLLBACK SEGMENT STORAGE
REM FUNCTION     : USES THE ROLLBACK1 VIEW
REM USE               : FROM SQLPLUS
REM Limitations       : None
REM
COLUMN tablespace_name   FORMAT a10        HEADING 'TABLESPACE'
COLUMN segment_name      FORMAT A10        HEADING 'ROLLBACK'
```

```
COLUMN extents          FORMAT 9,999      HEADING 'CUR EXTENTS'
COLUMN optsize          FORMAT 99,999,999 HEADING 'OPTL SIZE'
COLUMN shrinks          FORMAT 9,999      HEADING 'SHRINKS'
COLUMN aveshrink        FORMAT 99,999,999 HEADING 'AVE SHRINK'
COLUMN aveactive        FORMAT 99,999,999 HEADING 'AVE TRANS'
COLUMN status           FORMAT A8         HEADING 'STATUS'
REM
SET FEEDBACK OFF VERIFY OFF LINES 80 PAGES 58
@title80 "ROLLBACK SEGMENT STORAGE"
SPOOL rep_out\&db\rollbck1
rem
SELECT * FROM rollback1 ORDER BY segment_NAME;
SPOOL OFF
PAUSE Press Enter to continue
CLEAR COLUMNS
TTITLE OFF
SET FEEDBACK ON VERIFY ON LINES 80 PAGES 22


REM
REM NAME        : RBK2.SQL
REM FUNCTION    : REPORT ON ROLLBACK SEGMENT STATISTICS
REM FUNCTION    : USES THE ROLLBACK2 VIEW
REM USE         : FROM SQLPLUS
REM Limitations : None
REM
COLUMN SEGMENT_NAME    FORMAT A10     HEADING 'ROLLBACK'
COLUMN EXTENTS  FORMAT 9,999          HEADING 'EXTENTS'
COLUMN XACTS    FORMAT 9,999          HEADING 'TRANS'
COLUMN HWMSIZE  FORMAT 99,999,999     HEADING 'LARGEST|TRANS'
COLUMN RSSIZE   FORMAT 99,999,999     HEADING 'CUR SIZE'
COLUMN WAITS    FORMAT 9,999          HEADING 'WAITS'
COLUMN WRAPS    FORMAT 9,999          HEADING 'WRAPS'
COLUMN EXTENDS  FORMAT 9,999          HEADING 'EXTENDS'
COLUMN STATUS   FORMAT A7             HEADING 'STATUS'
REM
SET FEEDBACK OFF VERIFY OFF lines 80 pages 58
REM
@title80 "ROLLBACK SEGMENT STATISTICS"
SPOOL rep_out\&db\rollbck2
rem
SELECT * FROM rollback2 ORDER BY segment_name;
SPOOL OFF
SET LINES 80 PAGES 20 FEEDBACK ON VERIFY ON
TTITLE OFF
CLEAR COLUMNS
PAUSE Press Enter to continue
```

LISTING 13.16   Example of rollback segment reports output.

```
Date: 06/17/97                                              Page:   1
Time: 02:04 AM              ROLLBACK SEGMENT STORAGE          SYSTEM
                              oracle database


ROLLBACK CUR EXTENTS OPTL SIZE SHRINKS AVE SHRINK AVE TRANS STATUS
-------- --- ------- ---- ---- ------- --- ------ --- ----- ------
RB1           2                   0          0         0 ONLINE
RB2           2                   0          0         0 ONLINE
RB3           2                   0          0         0 ONLINE
RB4           2                   0          0         0 ONLINE
SYSTEM        15                  0          0         0 ONLINE

Date: 06/17/97                                        Page:   1
Time: 02:10 AM          ROLLBACK SEGMENT STATISTICS        SYSTEM
                          oracle database


                     LARGEST
ROLLBACK EXTENTS TRANS   TRANS CUR SIZE WAITS WRAPS EXTENDS STATUS
-------- ------- -----  ------- -------- ----- ----- ------- ------
RB1         2      0    100,352 100,352    0     0       0 ONLINE
RB2         2      0    100,352 100,352    0     0       0 ONLINE
RB3         2      0    100,352 100,352    0     1       0 ONLINE
RB4         2      0    100,352 100,352    0     1       0 ONLINE
SYSTEM      15     0    765,952 765,952    0     0       0 ONLINE
```

The parameters of concern to the DBA in the reports shown in Listing 13.16 are location, status, and sizing data. The DBA needs to verify that no rollback segments have been created outside of the prescribed tablespaces for rollback segments. In addition, the DBA should verify that all rollback segments that are supposed to be on-line are in fact on-line and that those that are supposed to be off-line, such as the second SYSTEM rollback segment used for maintenance, are off-line. Excessive waits indicate the need for more rollback segments. Excessive extends indicate you may need larger extent sizes. If optimal is set and you get excessive shrinks, this indicates you need larger rollback segment extents.

Monitoring Rollback Current Usage

To identify which users are using which rollback segments, the script in Source 13.17 should be run. The report generated shows the Oracle Process ID, the System Process ID, and the rollback segment in use. Listing 13.17 shows an example of output from an active rollback report.

SOURCE 13.17   Example of SQL script to generate active rollback report.

```
rem    Name     : TX_RBS.SQL
rem    Purpose: Generate a report of active rollbacks
rem    Use      : From SQL*Plus
rem    History:
rem    Date       Who              What
rem    Sept 91    Lan Nguyen       Presented in paper at IOUG
rem               Walter Lindsey
rem    5/15/93    Mike Ault        Added Title80, sets and output
rem    1/4/97     Mike Ault        Verified against 7.3
rem************************************************************
COLUMN   name FORMAT a21          HEADING "Rollback Segment Name"
COLUMN   pid  FORMAT 9999999999   HEADING "Oracle PID"
COLUMN   spid FORMAT 9999999999   HEADING "Sys PID"
SET PAGES 56  LINES 130 VERIFY OFF FEEDBACK OFF
START title132 "Rollback Segments in Use"
SPOOL report_output/&db/tx_rbs
SELECT
     r.name, l.Sid, p.spid,
     NVL(p.username, 'no transaction') "Transaction",
     p.terminal "Terminal"
FROM
     v$lock l,
     v$process p,
     v$rollname r
WHERE
     l.Sid = p.pid (+)
     and TRUNC(l.id1(+) / 65536) = r.usn
     and l.type(+) = 'TX'
     and l.lmode(+) = 6
ORDER BY r.name;
SPOOL OFF
SET PAGES 22  LINES 80 VERIFY ON FEEDBACK ON
CLEAR COLUMNS
TTITLE OFF
```

LISTING 13.17   Example of output from active rollback report.

```
Date: 05/24/96                                        Page:   1
Time: 09:41 AM          Rollback Segments in Use         SYSTEM
                           ORDSPTD6 database

Rollback Segment Name      SID Sys PID  Transaction     Terminal
---------------------      -------- -------  --------------  --------
R01                                           no transaction
R02                          21               no transaction
R03                                           no transaction
R04                                           no transaction
SYSTEM                                        no transaction
```

Monitoring Rollback Transaction Size

To determine if your rollback segments are properly sized, you can run some example transactions through the script in Source 13.18. To run a transaction through the script in Source 13.18 simply place the SQL from the transaction or the call to the transaction into the script where indicated and execute the script. Your transaction should be the only one running when you do the test, or the results will be invalid.

SOURCE 13.18   Script to generate total rollback bytes used in a transaction.

```
rem*************************************************************
rem  Name    : UNDO.SQL
rem  Purpose: Document rollback usage for a single
rem    transaction
rem  Use  : Note: You must alter the UNDO script and add a
rem    call to the transaction at the indicated line
rem  Restrictions:    : The database should be placed in DBA mode and
rem    this transaction should be the only one running.
rem  History:
rem   Date             Who         What
rem   Sept 91      Lan Nguyen        Presented in paper at IOUG
rem                   Walter Lindsey
rem   5/15/93      Mike Ault Changed to use one table
rem
SET FEEDBACK OFF  TERMOUT OFF
COLUMN name FORMAT a40
DEFINE undo_overhead=54
DROP TABLE undo_data;
CREATE TABLE undo_data
    (
    tran_no number, start_writes number, end_writes number
    );
INSERT INTO undo_data
SELECT 1, SUM(writes),0 from v$rollstat;
SET FEEDBACK ON  TERMOUT ON
rem
rem    INSERT TRANSACTION HERE
rem
SET FEEDBACK OFF  TERMOUT OFF
UPDATE undo_data SET end_writes = SUM(writes) FROM v$rollstat;
 WHERE tran_no=1;
SET FEEDBACK ON  TERMOUT ON
SELECT  ((end-writes - start_writes) - &undo_overhead)
"Number of Rollback Bytes Generated"
FROM undo_data;
SET TERMOUT OFF FEEDBACK OFF
DROP TABLE undo_data;
```

If the DBA has one transaction whose rollback usage he or she is concerned about, the script in Source 13.18 can be run with the transaction in question executed in the indicated spot in the script. The data generated will tell the DBA the exact amount of rollback usage for the transaction. This data can then be used to create a custom rollback segment that can be brought on-line and used during that transaction. The script and test run of the transaction must be the only active transactions in the database when the test is run.

Monitoring Deferred Rollback Segments

If a rollback segment is taken off-line, its transactions may be placed in a temporary segment in the rollback segment's tablespace. These temporary segments are referred to as deferred rollback segments. The following SQL code will list any deferred rollbacks in your 7.x or 8.x database:

```
SELECT segment_name, segment_type, tablespace_name
FROM sys.dba_segments
WHERE segment_type = 'DEFERRED ROLLBACK';

Example output from the precedingselect statement:

SEGMENT_NAME    SEGMENT_TYPE        TABLESPACE_NAME
------------    ----------------    ---------------
RBK1            DEFERRED ROLLBACK   USERS
```

Under Oracle7, if a rollback segment is taken off-line, its status is changed to PENDING OFFLINE and it is taken off-line as soon as its pending transactions are complete. The preceding select statement could be used to determine if any of these active transactions are in a deferred state. To determine if a rollback segment under Oracle7 has outstanding transactions, the following select statement is used.

```
SELECT name, xacts 'ACTIVE TRANSACTIONS'
FROM     v$rollname, v$rollstat
WHERE status = 'PENDING OFFLINE'
AND          v$rollname.usn = v$rollstat.usn;
```

TIP: Be sure your database has a sufficient number of on-line rollback segments. If the ratio TRANSACTIONS/TRANSACTIONS_PER_ROLL-BACK is exceeded, the system automatically brings on-line any available public rollback segments. If the only available public rollback happens to be the maintenance segment in the system space, it is brought on-line and could cause havoc in the system tablespace as it extends to accommodate transactions.

There are hints in the new structures added to, but not documented in, the DBA_ and V$ views that Oracle may be coming out with grouped rollback segments (rather like redo log grouping). This would allow implicit assignment of rollback segments to a specific parallel server instance (like threads in redo logs). However, none of the documentation discusses this feature (yet).

Monitoring Redo Activity with V$ and DBA_ views

The redo logs provide the information required to redo transactions performed on the database. For an Oracle7 or Oracle8 database, redo logs are placed in log groups that have members that consist of individual log files. For Oracle7 or Oracle8, there should be at least two mirrored groups of log files on separate drives to start up; three are highly recommended. In high-activity environments, the use of five mirrored groups of five megabytes each will ensure that there is no log contention. Sizing or redo logs and number required are not exact sciences; they must be done by trial and error. Monitor the alert log for waits on log switches or checkpoints to see if your logs are large enough or if you have enough of them.

Monitoring Redo Log Status

Redo log status should be monitored to tell the DBA what logs are in use and if there are any odd status codes such as stale log indications or indications of corrupt redo logs. The log files can have the following status values:

USED—Status of a log that has just been added (never used) or that a resetlogs command has been issued.

CURRENT—Indicates a valid log that is in use.

ACTIVE—Indicates a valid log file that is not currently in use.

CLEARING—Log is being re-created as an empty log due to DBA action.

CLEARING CURRENT—Current log is being cleared of a closed thread. If a log stays in this status, it could indicate there is some failure in the log switch.

INACTIVE—Log is no longer needed for instance recovery but may be needed for media recovery.

The v$logfile table has a status indicator that also gives these additional codes:

INVALID—File is inaccessible.

STALE—File contents are incomplete (such as when an instance is shutdown with SHUTDOWN ABORT or due to a system crash).

DELETED—File is no longer used.

The script in Source 13.19 provides some basic information on log status. Listing 13.19 shows an example of output from LOG_STAT.SQL script.

SOURCE 13.19   Example of script to monitor redo log status.

```
Date: 06/15/97                                              Page:    1
Time: 01:39 PM              Current Redo Log Status         SYSTEM
                              ORTEST1 database

Th# Grp#  Seq#      BYTES Mem Arc? STATUS     Change# Switch Time
--- ----  -----   ------- ---- ---- --------   ------- ------------------
  1    1 4,489   1048576    2 NO   INACTIVE    719114 15-JUN-97 16:54:23
       2 4,490   1048576    2 NO   INACTIVE    719117 15-JUN-97 16:56:10
       3 4,491   1048576    2 NO   CURRENT     719120 15-JUN-97 17:02:22
```

LISTING 13.19   Example of output from LOG_STAT.SQL script.

```
rem
rem Name:     log_stat.sql
rem
rem FUNCTION: Provide a current status for redo logs
rem
rem
COLUMN first_change# FORMAT 99999999   HEADING Change#
COLUMN group#        FORMAT 9,999       HEADING Grp#
COLUMN thread#       FORMAT 999         HEADING Th#
COLUMN sequence#     FORMAT 999,999     HEADING Seq#
COLUMN members       FORMAT 999         HEADING Mem
COLUMN archived      FORMAT a4          HEADING Arc?
COLUMN first_time    FORMAT a21         HEADING 'Switch Time'
BREAK ON thread#
SET PAGES 60 LINES 131 FEEDBACK OFF
START title132 'Current Redo Log Status'
SPOOL rep_out\&db\log_stat
SELECT thread#,
       group#,
       sequence#,
       bytes,
       members,
       archived,
       status,
       first_change#,
       TO_CHAR(first_time, 'DD-MM-YYYY HH24:MI:SS') first_time
   FROM
       sys.v_$log
   ORDER BY
       thread#,
       group#;
SPOOL OFF
PAUSE Press Enter to continue
SET PAGES 22 LINES 80 FEEDBACK ON
CLEAR BREAKS
CLEAR COLUMNS
TTILE OFF
```

Monitoring Redo Log Switches

In addition to the alert logs, the frequency of log switches can also be monitored via the v$log_history and v$archived_log DPTs. A script that uses these DPTs for this purpose is shown in Source 13.20. Listing 13.20 shows an example of output from an archive log switch script.

SOURCE 13.20   Script to monitor archive log switches.

```
REM
REM NAME    :log_hist.sql
REM PURPOSE:Provide info on logs for last 24 hours since last REM PURPOSE:log
switch
REM USE     : From SQLPLUS
REM Limitations     : None
REM
COLUMN thread#              FORMAT 999       HEADING 'Thrd#'
COLUMN sequence#            FORMAT 99999     HEADING 'Seq#'
COLUMN first_change#                         HEADING 'SCN Low#'
COLUMN next_change#                          HEADING 'SCN High#'
COLUMN archive_name         FORMAT a50       HEADING 'Log File'
COLUMN first_time           FORMAT a20       HEADING 'Switch Time'
COLUMN name                 FORMAT a30       HEADING 'Archive Log'
SET LINES 132
@title132 "Log History Report"
SPOOL rep_out\&db\log_hist
REM
SELECT
    a.recid,
    a.thread#,
    a.sequence#,
    a.first_change#,
    a.next_change#,
    TO_CHAR(a.first_time,'DD-MON-YYYY HH24:MI:SS') first_time,
    x.name
FROM
 v$log_history a, v$archived_log x
WHERE
  a.first_time>
   (SELECT b.first_time-1
   FROM v$log_history b WHERE b.next_change# =
    (SELECT MAX(c.next_change#) FROM v$log_history c)) AND
    a.recid=x.sequence#(+);
SPOOL OFF
SET LINES 80
CLEAR COLUMNS
TTITLE OFF
PAUSE Press Enter to continue
```

LISTING 13.20   Example of output from archive log switch script.

```
Date: 06/15/97                                                    Page:   1
Time: 04:15 PM                      Log History Report              SYSTEM
                                    ORTEST1 database

RECID Thrd# Seq#    SCN Low# SCN High# Switch Time         Archive Log
----- ----- -----  -------- --------- -------------------  --------------------------------
4492    1   4492    739132    739211  15-JUN-1997 15:54:45 D:\ORANT8\RDBMS80\ARC04492.001
4493    1   4493    739211    739213  15-JUN-1997 16:12:41 D:\ORANT8\RDBMS80\ARC04493.001
4494    1   4494    739213    739215  15-JUN-1997 16:12:43 D:\ORANT8\RDBMS80\ARC04494.001
4495    1   4495    739215    739217  15-JUN-1997 16:12:44 D:\ORANT8\RDBMS80\ARC04495.001
4496    1   4496    739217    739219  15-JUN-1997 16:12:48 D:\ORANT8\RDBMS80\ARC04496.001
```

Monitoring Redo Statistics

In Oracle there are no views that will allow the user to look at a log file's statistical data directly. Instead of direct views, we must look at statistics based on redo log and log writer process statistics. These statistics are in the views V$STATNAME, V$SESSION, V$PROCESS, V$SESSTAT, V$LATCH, and V$LATCHNAME. An example report that uses these views is shown in Source 13.21; an example of the scripts output is shown in Listing 13.21.

SOURCE 13.21   Script to generate reports on redo statistics.

```
REM
REM NAME          : rdo_stat.sql
REM PURPOSE       : Show REDO latch statistics
REM USE           : from SQLPlus
REM Limitations   : Must have access to v$_ views
REM
SET PAGES 56 LINES 78 VERIFY OFF FEEDBACK OFF
START title80 "Redo Latch Statistics"
SPOOL rep_out/&&db/rdo_stat
rem
COLUMN name       FORMAT a30        HEADING Name
COLUMN percent    FORMAT 999.999    HEADING Percent
COLUMN total                        HEADING Total
rem
SELECT
    l2.name,
    immediate_gets+gets Total,
    immediate_gets "Immediates",
    misses+immediate_misses "Total Misses",
    DECODE (100.*(GREATEST(misses+immediate_misses,1)/
    GREATEST(immediate_gets+gets,1)),100,0) Percent
FROM
    v$latch l1,
    v$latchname l2
```

```
WHERE
    l2.name like '%redo%'
    and l1.latch#=l2.latch# ;
rem
PAUSE Press Enter to continue
rem
rem Name: Redo_stat.sql
rem
rem Function: Select redo statistics from v$sysstat
rem History:
rem Who             What               Date
rem ---------       ----------------   -------
rem Mike Ault       Revised from V6    1/04/97
rem Mike Ault       Verified Oracle8   6/15/97
rem
COLUMN name      FORMAT a30            HEADING 'Redo|Statistic|Name'
COLUMN value     FORMAT 999,999,999 HEADING 'Redo|Statistic|Value'
SET PAGES 80 LINES 60 FEEDBACK OFF VERIFY OFF
START title80 'Redo Log Statistics'
SPOOL rep_out/&&db/redo_stat
SELECT
    name,
    value
FROM
    v$sysstat
WHERE
    name LIKE '%redo%'
ORDER BY statistic#;
SPOOL OFF
SET LINES 24 FEEDBACK ON VERIFY ON
```

LISTING 13.21 Example of output from redo report scripts.

```
Date: 06/15/97                                      Page:  1
Time: 04:42 PM        Redo Latch Statistics         SYSTEM
                         ORTEST1 database

Name                    Total    Immediates Total Misses Percent
--------------------- --------- ---------- ------------ -------
redo allocation           831          0            0
redo copy                  50         50            0

Press Enter to continue

Date: 06/15/97                                  Page:  1
Time: 04:42 PM        Redo Log Statistics       SYSTEM
                         ORTEST1 database

Redo                                     Redo
```

```
Statistic                         Statistic
Name                                  Value
--------------------------------  ---------
redo synch writes                         2
redo synch time                           0
redo entries                             44
redo size                             9,192
redo entries linearized                   0
redo buffer allocation retries            0
redo small copies                        28
redo wastage                          5,064
redo writer latching time                 0
redo writes                              17
redo blocks written                      30
redo write time                           0
redo log space requests                   0
redo log space wait time                  0
redo log switch interrupts                0
redo ordering marks                       0
```

Of course, right about now you are probably asking what good all these numbers do you. Let's look at what they mean and how you can use them. Actually, the first section of the report in Source 13.21 is self-explanatory. There are two latches that the redo logs use, the REDO ALLOCATION latch and the REDO COPY latch.

In general, if the PERCENT statistic (actually, the ratio of total misses to total gets) is greater than 10 percent, contention is occurring and the DBA needs to examine the way he or she is doing redo logs (more about this in a second). The initial latch granted for redo is the REDO_ALLOCATION latch. The REDO_COPY latch is granted to a user when the size of his or her entry is greater than the _LOG_ SMALL_ENTRY_MAX_SIZE parameter in the initialization file. If you see REDO_ ALLOCATION latch contention, decrease the value of _LOG_SMALL_ENTRY_MAX_ SIZE. If there is more than one user that requires the REDO_COPY latch, you get contention on single CPU systems. The number of REDO_COPY latches is limited to twice the number of CPUs on the system. If you have a single CPU, only one is allowed. It is normal to see high contention for this latch on single CPU systems, and there is nothing the DBA can do to increase the number of REDO_COPY latches. However, even on single CPU systems you can force Oracle to prebuild redo entries, reducing the number of latches required. This is accomplished by setting the _LOG_ ENTRY_PREBUILD_THRESHOLD entry in the initialization file higher. On multiple CPU systems, increase the number of REDO_COPY latches to twice the number of CPUs.

In the second half of the report, statistics from the caches are shown that affect redo operations. Let's look at what these numbers are telling us. The most important of the listed statistics are "redo blocks written," "redo entries linearized," "redo small copies," and "redo writes."

- "redo blocks written" is useful when two entries are compared for a specified time period. This will indicate how much redo is generated for the period between the two checks.
- "redo small copies" tells how many times the entry was effectively written on a "redo allocation" latch. This indicates a "redo copy" latch was not required for this entry. This statistic should be compared with the "redo entries" parameter. If there is close to a one-to-one relationship, then your system is making effective use of the "redo allocation" latch. If there is a large difference, then the LOG_SMALL_ENTRY_MAX_SIZE INIT.ORA parameter should be increased. If the LOG_SIMULTANEOUS_COPIES parameter is zero, this value is ignored.
- "redo writes" is the total number of redo writes to the redo buffer. If this value is too large compared to the "redo entries" parameter value, then the DBA should tune the INIT.ORA parameters mentioned in the previous sections to force prebuilding of the entries. If the entries are not prebuilt, the entry may require several writes to the buffer before it is fully entered; if it is prebuilt, it only requires one.
- "redo log space wait" is the statistic that tells you if users are having to wait for space in the redo buffer. If this value is nonzero, increase the size of the LOG_BUFFER in the initialization file.
- "redo buffer allocation retries" is the statistic that tells the DBA the number of repeated attempts to allocate space in the redo buffer. If this value is high in comparison to redo entries, it indicates that the redo logs may be too small and should be increased in size. Normally, this value should be much less than the redo entries statistic. In the example, it has a value of five compared to the entries value of 1044; this is satisfactory.
- "redo size" tells the total number of redo bytes generated since the database was started. Comparison of two readings will give the amount generated over time. This value can then be used to determine if the log switch interval is proper. Too many log switches over a small amount of time can impair performance. Use the following formula to look at log switches over time:

```
(X / (dN / dt)) / interval of concern
```

Where

X is the value of LOG_CHECKPOINT_INTERVAL or size of the redo log in system blocks.

dN is the change in the "redo size" over the time interval

dt is the time differential for the period (usually minutes)

Once the number of log switches is known, the DBA can use this value to determine the size of redo logs based on system IO requirements. If you need to reduce the number of log switches, increase the redo log size; of course, this may impact system availability since it takes longer to write out a large redo log buffer than a small one to disk. A balance must be struck between undersizing the redo logs and taking a database performance hit, on the one hand, and making the logs too large and taking an IO hit, on the other.

Monitoring Directories and Libraries

Directories and libraries are new Oracle8 internal database structures. Libraries are pointers to external shareable libraries of 3GL routines that can be called via the external procedures call option, new with Oracle8. Directories, as their name implies, are pointers to external directories where BFILE and other LOB data objects can be stored outside the database.

Monitoring Directories

Directory information is available from the DBA_DIRECTORIES view. This view has three columns. A simple report to show everything the database knows about directories is shown in Source 13.22.

SOURCE 13.22   Example of script to report on database directories.

```
rem NAME: dir_rep.sql
rem FUNCTION: Report on directories known by the database
rem HISTORY: MRA 6/16/97 Created
rem
COLUMN owner              FORMAT a10 HEADING 'Owner'
COLUMN directory_name     FORMAT a10 HEADING 'Directory'
COLUMN directory_path     FORMAT a40 HEADING 'Full Path'
SET VERIFY OFF PAGES 58 LINES 78 FEEDBACK OFF
START title80 'Database Directories Report'
SPOOL rep_out\&db\dir_rep.lis
SELECT
     owner,
     directory_name,
     directory_path
FROM
     dba_directories
ORDER BY
     owner;
SPOOL OFF
```

Listing 13.22 shows an example of output from the directories report script in Source 13.22. Remember, directories aren't verified for existence until access is attempted.

LISTING 13.22 Example of output from the directories report.

```
Date: 06/16/97                                          Page:   1
Time: 01:58 AM        Database Directories Report       SYSTEM
                           ORTEST1 database


Owner       Directory  Full Path
---------   ---------  ----------------------------------------
SYS         TEST_DIR   c:\oracle1\ortest1\admin\bfile
```

Monitoring Libraries

Libraries are monitored through the DBA_LIBRARIES view. The DBA_LIBRARIES view contains five fields. An example report for monitoring libraries is shown in Source 13.23.

SOURCE 13.23 Example of script to document external library specifications.

```
rem
rem NAME: lib_rep.sql
rem FUNCTION: Document External Library Entries in Database
rem HISTORY: MRA 6/16/97 Created
rem
COLUMN owner          FORMAT a8     HEADING 'Library|Owner'
COLUMN library_name   FORMAT a15    HEADING 'Library|Name'
COLUMN file_spec      FORMAT a30    HEADING 'File|Specification'
COLUMN dynamic        FORMAT a7     HEADING 'Dynamic'
COLUMN stauts         FORMAT a10    HEADING 'Status'
BREAK ON owner
SET FEEDBACK OFF VERIFY OFF LINES 78 PAGES 58
START title80 'Database External Libraries Report'
SPOOL rep_out\&db\lib_rep.lis
SELECT
     owner,
     library_name,
     file_spec,
     dynamic,
     status
FROM
     dba_libraries
ORDER BY
     owner;
SPOOL OFF
```

The output from the library report script is shown in Listing 13.23.

LISTING 13.23   Example of output from the library report.

```
Date: 06/16/97                                            Page:   1
Time: 02:11 AM    Database External Libraries Report    SYSTEM
                          ORTEST1 database


Library  Library          File
Owner    Name             Specification              Dynamic STATUS
-------  ---------------  -----------------------    ------- -------
SYS      DBMS_AQ_LIB      e:\lib\aqlib.dll              N      VALID
         DBMS_REPAPI_LIB  e:\lib\replib.dll             N      VALID
```

Remember, as with directories, the existence of the actual libraries isn't tested until they are called by an external procedure.

13.7   MONITORING CONTROL FILES AND INITIALIZATION PARAMETERS

The control files have traditionally been a "don't ask, don't tell" item with Oracle. Everyone knew they were there but not exactly what they were for or how they could be monitored. Although initialization parameters were easy to monitor, no one did so. Now with Oracle7 and Oracle8 monitoring both of these items, which are critical to database health and well-being, is much easier.

Monitoring Control Files

Oracle7 (from release 7.3 on) and Oracle8 provide the V$CONTROLFILE view to help keep track of the control files. Oracle8 provides the V$CONTROLFILE_RECORD view that is used with Recovery Manager. Let's look at a quick script in Source 13.24 to monitor control file status.

SOURCE 13.24   Script to monitor control file location and status.

```
rem
rem NAME : con_file.sql
rem FUNCTION: Document control file location and status
rem HISTORY: MRA 6/16/97 Creation
rem
COLUMN name   FORMAT a60 HEADING 'Con|File|Location' WORD_WRAPPED
COLUMN status FORMAT a7 HEADING 'Con|File|Status'
SET LINES 78 FEEDBACK OFF VERIFY OFF
START title80 'Control File Status'
SPOOL rep_out\&db\con_file.lis
```

```
SELECT
     name,
     status
FROM
     v$controlfile;
SPOOL OFF
```

The output from the script in Source 13.24 is documented in Listing 13.24.

LISTING 13.24 Example of output of control file script.

```
Date: 06/16/97                                           Page:  1
Time: 06:56 PM           Control File Status                SYSTEM
                         ORTEST1 database

Control
File
Location                                                 Status
-------------------------------------------------------- ----------
C:\ORACLE1\ORTEST1\CONTROL\CTL1ORTEST1.ORA
D:\ORACLE2\ORTEST1\CONTROL\CTL2ORTEST1.ORA
```

The Control File Status should always be blank. If it shows a status this means the control file is corrupt, which, since the database can't start up if the file is corrupt, is an unlikely occurrence. You should look to see that the files are on separate disks or disk arrays.

> TIP: In previous versions of Oracle (prior to 8) the control files were usually less than one megabyte in size. With Oracle8 they can be tens of megabytes in size due to the extra material monitored. Be careful to allow for this in your file systems.

The v$controlfile_record_section gives statistics on each type of record contained in the control file. A script to monitor this table is shown in Source 13.25.

SOURCE 13.25 Script to monitor the control file record sections.

```
rem
rem NAME: con_rec.sql
rem FUNCTION: Provide documentation of control file record stats
rem HISTORY: MRA 6/16/97 Creation
rem
```

```
COLUMN type          FORMAT a17       HEADING 'Record Type'
COLUMN record_size   FORMAT 999999    HEADING 'Record|Size'
COLUMN records_used  FORMAT 999999    HEADING 'Records|Used'
COLUMN first_index   FORMAT 9999999   HEADING 'First|Index'
COLUMN last_index    FORMAT 9999999   HEADING 'Last|Index'
COLUMN last_recid    FORMAT 999999    HEADING 'Last|Record|ID'
SET LINES 80 PAGES 58 FEEDBACK OFF VERIFY OFF
START title80 'Control File Records'
SPOOL rep_out\&db\con_rec.lis
SELECT
    type,
    record_size,
    records_total,
    records_used,
    first_index,
    last_index,
    last_recid
FROM
    v$controlfile_record_section;
SPOOL OFF
```

The output from the script in Source 13.25 is shown in Listing 13.25.

LISTING 13.25   Results from the control file records report.

```
Date: 06/16/97                                    Page:   1
Time: 07:11 PM        Control File Records          SYSTEM
                        ORTEST1 database


                                                      Last
                     Record           Record First  Last Record
Record Type            Size RECORDS_TOTAL  Used Index Index    ID
-----------------    ------ ------------- ------ ----- ----- ------
DATABASE                192             1      1     0     0      0
CKPT PROGRESS             1             1      0     0     0      0
REDO THREAD             104             1      1     0     0      0
REDO LOG                 72            32      3     0     0      6
DATAFILE                180           200     12     0     0     14
FILENAME                524           265     18     0     0      0
TABLESPACE               68           200      8     0     0     10
RESERVED1                 1             1      0     0     0      0
RESERVED2                 1             1      0     0     0      0
LOG HISTORY              36          7239   4496     1  4496   4496
OFFLINE RANGE            56           218      0     0     0      0
ARCHIVED LOG            584           104      5     1     5      5
BACKUP SET               40           203      0     0     0      0
BACKUP PIECE            736           403      0     0     0      0
BACKUP DATAFILE         116           421      0     0     0      0
```

BACKUP REDOLOG	76	107	0	0	0	0
DATAFILE COPY	660	401	0	0	0	0
BACKUP CORRUPTION	44	277	0	0	0	0
COPY CORRUPTION	40	203	0	0	0	0
DELETED OBJECT	20	203	0	0	0	0
RESERVED3	1	4072	0	0	0	0
RESERVED4	1	4072	0	0	0	0

The control file records report can tell you the number of data files, redo logs, archived logs, and a plethora of other information about your database. The Records Used column indicates how many of a particular type has been assigned for your database.

Monitoring Database Initialization Parameters

The database initialization parameters are critical parts of the database. I have seen many installations where they were very diligent about database backups but neglected to document the settings of their initialization parameters. Sometimes DBAs—or should I say DBBSs (Database Baby-Sitters)—didn't even know the location of the init<SID>.ora file. We have covered the documentation of the parameters in earlier sections; the v$parameter file provides the source for discovering the value and status of any documented initialization file parameter. A simple script to generate a nearly ready-for-prime-time init<SID>.ora file is listed in Source 13.26.

SOURCE 13.26   Script to re-create the init<SID>.ora file.

```
REM
REM NAME        : init_ora_rct.sql
REM FUNCTION    : Re-create the instance init.ora file
REM USE         : GENERAL
REM Limitations : None
REM
SET NEWPAGE 0 VERIFY OFF
SET ECHO OFF FEEDBACK OFF TERMOUT OFF PAGES 300 LINES 80 HEADING OFF
COLUMN name   FORMAT a80 WORD_WRAPPED
COLUMN dbname NEW_VALUE db NOPRINT
SELECT name dbname FROM v$database;
DEFINE OUTPUT = 'rep_out\&db\init.ora'
SPOOL &OUTPUT
SELECT '# Init.ora file FROM v$parameter' name FROM dual
UNION
SELECT '# generated on:'||sysdate name FROM dual
UNION
SELECT '# script by MRA 11/7/95 REVEALNET' name FROM dual
UNION
```

```
SELECT '#' name FROM dual
UNION
SELECT name||' = '||value name   FROM v$parameter
WHERE value IS NOT NULL;
SPOOL OFF
CLEAR COLUMNS
SET NEWPAGE 0 VERIFY OFF
SET TERMOUT ON PAGES 22 LINES 80 HEADING ON
SET TERMOUT ON
UNDEF OUTPUT
PAUSE Press Enter to continue
```

An example of output from the script in Source 13.26 is shown in Listing 13.26.

LISTING 13.26   Example of output from the INIT.ORA re-creation script.

```
#
# Init.ora file from v$parameter
# generated on:16-JUN-97
# script by MRA 11/7/95 REVEALNET
background_dump_dest = c:\oracle1\ortest1\admin\bdump
checkpoint_process = TRUE
control_files = C:\ORACLE1\ORTEST1\CONTROL\ctl1ORTEST1.ora,
D:\ORACLE2\ORTEST1\CONTROL\ctl2ORTEST1.ora

db_block_size = 4096
db_files = 100
db_name = ORTEST1
dml_locks = 200
ifile = c:\oracle1\ortest1\admin\pfile\initortest1.ora
log_archive_start = TRUE
log_buffer = 1048576
log_checkpoint_interval = 100000
max_dump_file_size = 102400
processes = 100
remote_login_passwordfile = SHARED
rollback_segments = rb1, rb2, rb3, rb4, rb5
sequence_cache_entries = 100
sequence_cache_hash_buckets = 89
shared_pool_size = 10000000
sort_area_retained_size = 2097152
sort_area_size = 8388608
text_enable = TRUE
user_dump_dest = c:\oracle1\ortest1\admin\udump
```

Notice that the WHERE clause in the query for the init.ora re-creation script restricts the return values to only those that have been changed from their default settings. If you do not restrict the return from the query you get all hundred-plus parameters.

Monitoring Undocumented Initialization Parameters

There are also undocumented initialization parameters. The undocumented parameters are those that are (a) undergoing testing or (b) were too good to get rid of completely. Unfortunately, the undocumented values are a wee bit more difficult to get at. For Oracle7.2 and earlier, the following script

```
COLUMN parameter FORMAT a40
COLUMN value FORMAT a30
COLUMN ksppidf HEADING 'Is|Default'
SET FEEDBACK OFF VERIFY OFF PAGES 55
START title80 'Undocumented Init.ora Parameters'
SPOOL rep_out/&db/undoc
SELECT
     ksppinm "Parameter",
        ksppivl "Value",
        ksppidf
FROM
     x$ksppi
WHERE
     ksppinm like '/_%' escape '/'
/
SPOOL OFF
TTITLE OFF
```

would return the values. But since Oracle sees fit to monkey with the structure of the k and x$ tables frequently you have to use the following script for Oracle7.3 and above:

```
REM Script for getting undocumented init.ora
REM parameters from a 7.3 or 8.0.2 instance
REM MRA - Revealnet 4/23/97
REM
COLUMN parameter              FORMAT a37
COLUMN description       FORMAT a30 WORD_WRAPPED
COLUMN "Session VALUE"       FORMAT a10
COLUMN "Instance VALUE" FORMAT a10
SET LINES 100 PAGES 0
SPOOL undoc.lis
SELECT
     a.ksppinm  "Parameter",
     a.ksppdesc "Description",
     b.ksppstvl "Session Value",
     c.ksppstvl "Instance Value"
FROM
     x$ksppi a,
     x$ksppcv b,
     x$ksppsv c
```

```
WHERE
     a.indx = b.indx
     AND a.indx = c.indx
     AND a.ksppinm LIKE '/_%' escape '/'
/
SPOOL OFF
```

The actual parameters are listed in Chapter 2 if you would like to review them. The preceding scripts have been tested up to Oracle8.0.2 but aren't guaranteed above that.

13.8   MONITORING LOCKS AND LATCHES

Monitoring latches and locks can be a challenge with Oracle. With the V$LOCK DPT alone, multiple joins are usually required to get to the information you desire. I suggest running the CATBLOCK.SQL script in that it creates several useful views for locks. The CATBLOCK.SQL script is located in the /oracle/rdbms/admin directory on UNIX, c:\orant\rdbmsxx\admin on NT. The script creates DBA_KGLLOCK, DBA_LOCK, DBA_LOCK_INTERNAL, DBA_DML_LOCKS, DBA_DDL_LOCKS, DBA_WAITERS, and DBA_BLOCKERS. I suggest executing this script with echo set to ON since in many releases it contains errors that you must correct before it will run properly. On early Oracle7 releases there were also problems with permissions on some of the lock views, which required that they be queried from SYS or INTERNAL only.

Monitoring Sessions Waiting for Locks

If you run the catblock.sql script you will have access to the dba_waiters view. The dba_waiters view gives information on sessions waiting for locks held by other sessions. By joining v$session with dba_waiters you can obtain detailed information about the locks and sessions that are waiting. A report on this information is shown in Source 13.27.

SOURCE 13.27   Script to report sessions waiting for locks.

```
rem NAME: waiters.sql
rem FUNCTION: Report on sessions waiting for locks
rem HISTORY: MRA 1/12/96 Creation
rem
COLUMN busername        FORMAT a10      HEADING 'Holding|User'
COLUMN wusername        FORMAT a10      HEADING 'Waiting|User'
COLUMN bsession_id                      HEADING 'Holding|SID'
COLUMN wsession_id                      HEADING 'Waiting|SID'
COLUMN mode_held        FORMAT a20      HEADING 'Mode|Held'
COLUMN mode_requested   FORMAT a20      HEADING 'Mode|Requested'
COLUMN lock_id1         FORMAT a20      HEADING 'Lock|ID1'
```

```
COLUMN lock_id2          FORMAT a20      HEADING 'Lock|ID2'
COLUMN type                              HEADING 'Lock|Type'
SET LINES 132 PAGES 59 FEEDBACK OFF ECHO OFF
START title132 'Processes Waiting on Locks Report'
SPOOL rep_out/&db/waiters
SELECT
     holding_session bsession_id,
     waiting_session wsession_id,
     b.username busername,
     a.username wusername,
     c.lock_type type,
     mode_held, mode_requested,
     lock_id1, lock_id2
FROM
     sys.v_$session b,
     sys.dba_waiters c,
     sys.v_$session a
WHERE
     c.holding_session=b.sid and
     c.waiting_session=a.sid
/
SPOOL OFF
PAUSE press Enter to continue
CLEAR COLUMNS
SET LINES 80 PAGES 22 FEEDBACK ON
TTITLE OFF
```

In the script in Source 13.27 the lock_id1 and lock_id2 columns map into the object that the lock is being held upon.

Monitoring Sessions Causing Blocked Locks

Again, the catblock.sql script must be run in order to create the dba_blockers view. The dba_blockers view indicates all sessions that are currently causing blocks that aren't blocked themselves. Source 13.28 looks at the other side of the coin; it reports on the sessions that are causing blocks by joining against v$session and dba_locks.

SOURCE 13.28   Example of script to generate a report of sessions causing blocks.

```
rem NAME: blockers.sql
rem FUNCTION: Show all processes causing a dead lock
rem HISTORY: MRA 1/15/96 Created
rem
COLUMN username          FORMAT a10      HEADING 'Holding|User'
COLUMN session_id                        HEADING 'SID'
COLUMN mode_held         FORMAT a20      HEADING 'Mode|Held'
COLUMN mode_requested    FORMAT a20      HEADING 'Mode|Requested'
```

```
COLUMN lock_id1          FORMAT a20     HEADING 'Lock|ID1'
COLUMN lock_id2          FORMAT a20     HEADING 'Lock|ID2'
COLUMN type                             HEADING 'Lock|Type'
SET LINES 132 PAGES 59 FEEDBACK OFF ECHO OFF
START title132 'Sessions Blocking Other Sessions Report'
SPOOL rep_out\&db\blockers
SELECT
    a.session_id,
    username,
    type,
    mode_held,
    mode_requested,
    lock_id1,
    lock_id2
FROM
    sys.v_$session b,
    sys.dba_blockers c,
    sys.dba_locks a
WHERE
    c.holding_session=a.session_id AND
    c.holding_session=b.sid
/
SPOOL OFF
PAUSE press Enter to continue
CLEAR COLUMNS
SET LINES 80 PAGES 22 FEEDBACK ON
```

Monitoring DDL and DML Locks

The other aspects of locks are the DDL (Data Definition) and DML (Data Manipulation) locks. The views DBA_DML_LOCKS and DBA_DDL_LOCKS are both created by the catblock.sql script and are used to monitor DML and DDL locks. Let's look at two scripts (Source 13.29 and 13.30) that report on these items.

SOURCE 13.29   Example of script to report on DDL (Data Definition) locks.

```
rem Name: ddl_lock.sql
rem Function: Document DDL Locks currently in use
rem History: MRA 1/15/97 Creation
rem
COLUMN owner           FORMAT a15   HEADING 'User'
COLUMN session_id                   HEADING 'SID'
COLUMN mode_held       FORMAT a20   HEADING 'Lock|Mode|Held'
COLUMN mode_requested  FORMAT a20   HEADING 'Lock|Mode|Requested'
COLUMN type                         HEADING 'Type|Object'
COLUMN name                         HEADING 'Object|Name'
```

```
SET FEEDBACK OFF ECHO OFF PAGES 59 LINES 131
START title132 'Report on All DDL Locks Held'
SPOOL rep_out\&db\ddl_lock
SELECT
      NVL(owner,'SYS') owner,
      session_id,
      name,type,
      mode_held,
      mode_requested
FROM
      sys.dba_ddl_locks
ORDER BY 2
/
SPOOL OFF
PAUSE press Enter to continue
CLEAR COLUMNS
SET FEEDBACK ON ECHO ON PAGES 22 LINES 80
TTITLE OFF
```

Some example output from the script in Source 13.29 is shown in Listing 13.29.

LISTING 13.29   Example of output from the DDL_LOCK report.

```
Date: 06/16/97                                         Page:   1
Time: 09:30 PM          Report on All DDL Locks Held       SYSTEM
                             ORTEST1 database

                                             Lock  Lock
             Object                    Type   Mode  Mode
User  SID Name                         Object Held  Requested
----  --- -------------------- ------------------- ---- ---------
SYS    8 DBMS_APPLICATION_INFO Body                Null None
SYS    8 DBMS_APPLICATION_INFO Table/Procedure Null None
SYS    8 X$KQP326              Body                Null None
SYS    8 X$KQP326              Table/Procedure Null None
SYS    8 DBMS_OUTPUT           Table/Procedure Null None
SYS    8 DBMS_OUTPUT           Body                Null None
```

The next script (Source 13.30) documents any DML locks.

SOURCE 13.30   Script to report DML locks.

```
rem NAME: dml_lock.sql
rem FUNCTION: Document DML locks currently in use
rem HISTORY: MRA 1/15/96 Creation
rem
COLUMN owner               FORMAT a15      HEADING 'User'
```

```
COLUMN session_id                         HEADING 'SID'
COLUMN mode_held        FORMAT a20        HEADING 'Mode|Held'
COLUMN mode_requested   FORMAT a20        HEADING 'Mode|Requested'
SET FEEDBACK OFF ECHO OFF PAGES 59 LINES 131
START title132 'Report on All DML Locks Held'
SPOOL rep_out\&db\dml_lock
SELECT
     NVL(owner,'SYS') owner,
     session_id,
     name,
     mode_held,
     mode_requested
FROM
     sys.dba_dml_locks
ORDER BY 2
/
SPOOL OFF
PAUSE press Enter to continue
CLEAR COLUMNS
SET FEEDBACK ON ECHO ON PAGES 22 LINES 80
TTITLE OFF
```

When contention is suspected, a quick look at these DDL and DML reports can tell the DBA if a session is holding a lock on the table or object involved. Since these reports contain volatile information they are only useful for pinpoint monitoring (i.e., when there is a problem).

Monitoring Internal Locks

The last type of lock we will look at is the "internal" lock (see Source 13.31). Internal locks are generated by the database internal processes. The dba_internal_locks view is created by the catblock.sql script.

SOURCE 13.31   Example of script to document internal locks currently held.

```
rem NAME: int_lock.sql
rem FUNCTION: Document current internal locks
rem HISTORY: MRA 1/15/96 Creation
rem
COLUMN username        FORMAT a10      HEADING 'Lock|Holder'
COLUMN session_id                      HEADING 'User|SID'
COLUMN lock_type       FORMAT a27      HEADING 'Lock Type'
COLUMN mode_held       FORMAT a10      HEADING 'Mode|Held'
COLUMN mode_requested  FORMAT a10      HEADING 'Mode|Requested'
COLUMN lock_id1        FORMAT a30      HEADING 'Lock/Cursor|ID1'
COLUMN lock_id2        FORMAT a10      HEADING 'Lock|ID2'
```

```
PROMPT 'ALL is all types or modes'
ACCEPT lock PROMPT 'Enter Desired Lock Type: '
ACCEPT mode PROMPT 'Enter Lock Mode: '
SET LINES 132 PAGES 59 FEEDBACK OFF ECHO OFF VERIFY OFF
BREAK ON username
START title132 'Report on Internal Locks Mode: &mode Type: &lock'
SPOOL rep_out\&db\int_locks
SELECT
    NVL(b.username,'SYS') username,
    session_id,lock_type,mode_held,
    mode_requested,lock_id1,lock_id2
FROM
    sys.dba_lock_internal a, sys.v_$session b
WHERE
    UPPER(mode_held) like UPPER('%&mode%') OR
    UPPER('&mode')='ALL' AND
    UPPER(lock_type) like UPPER('%&lock%') OR
    UPPER(mode_held) like UPPER('%&mode%') OR
    UPPER('&mode')='ALL' AND
    UPPER('&lock')='ALL' AND
    a.session_id=b.sid
ORDER BY 1,2
/
SPOOL OFF
PAUSE press Enter to continue
SET LINES 80 PAGES 22 FEEDBACK ON VERIFY ON
CLEAR COLUMNS
CLEAR BREAKS
UNDEF LOCK
UNDEF MODE
```

13.9   MONITORING EVENTS

Oracle is an event-driven system. Sessions wait for calls, locks and latches spin, processes wake up and go back to sleep—all based on events. The V$SESSION_ EVENT DPT tracks all current events by session. The report in Source 13.32 will generate a report on current events (Oracle-wise anyway).

SOURCE 13.32   Script to generate an event report.

```
rem
rem FUNCTION: Generate a report on session events by user
rem
rem NAME:events.sql
rem HISTORY: MRA 6/15/97 Created
rem
```

```
COLUMN sid               HEADING Sid
COLUMN event             HEADING Event               FORMAT a40
COLUMN total_waits       HEADING Total|Waits
COLUMN total_timeouts    HEADING Total|Timeouts
COLUMN time_waited       HEADING Time|Waited
COLUMN average_wait      HEADING Average|Wait
COLUMN username          HEADING User
BREAK ON username
START title132 "Session Events By User"
SPOOL rep_out\&db\events
SET LINES 132 PAGES 59
SELECT
     username,
     event,
     total_waits,
     total_timeouts,
     time_waited,
     average_wait
FROM
     sys.v_$session_event a,
     sys.v_$session b
WHERE
     a.sid= b.sid
ORDER BY 1;
SPOOL OFF
PAUSE Press Enter to continue
CLEAR COLUMNS
CLEAR BREAKS
SET LINES 80 PAGES 22
TTITLE OFF
```

An example of the event report is shown in Listing 13.32.

LISTING 13.32   Example of output from the session events report.

```
Date: 06/16/97                                            Page:   1
Time: 10:17 PM              Session Events by User         SYSTEM
                              ORTEST1 database

                              Total    Total    Time      Average
User          Event           Waits    Timeouts Waited    Wait
------------- -------------------------- -------- -------- -------- --------
SYSTEM        db file sequential read        1        0        0        0
              file open                      1        0        0        0
              SQL*Net message to client     89        0        0        0
              SQL*Net message from client   88        0        0        0
              SQL*Net more data to client    7        0        0        0
              pmon timer                 36198    36197        0        0
              rdbms ipc message          36206    36196        0        0
```

rdbms ipc message	36261	36195	0	0
rdbms ipc message	36206	36197	0	0
rdbms ipc message	62	62	0	0
rdbms ipc message	367	361	0	0
enqueue	2	0	0	0
enqueue	1	0	0	0
enqueue	1	0	0	0
control file sequential read	60	0	0	0
control file sequential read	80	0	0	0

13.10 MONITORING OTHER DATABASE OBJECTS

Generally speaking, the other database objects consist of stored objects such as packages, procedures, and functions. About the only thing these stored objects can be monitored for (other than tuning stats, which we cover in the next chapter) is status, that is, either valid or invalid.

Monitoring for Invalid Objects

The script in Source 13.33 generates a listing of invalid database objects. If the object is valid you don't need to monitor it!

SOURCE 13.33 Example of script to report object status.

```
rem Name: inv_obj.sql
rem Purpose: Show all invalid objects in database
rem Mike Ault 7/2/96 TreCom/RevealNet
rem
COLUMN object_name      FORMAT A30      HEADING 'Object|Name'
COLUMN owner            FORMAT a10      HEADING 'Object|Owner'
COLUMN last_time        FORMAT a20      HEADING 'Last Change|Date'
SET LINES 80 FEEDBACK OFF PAGES 0 VERIFY OFF
START title80 'Invalid Database Objects'
SPOOL rep_out/&db/inv_obj
SELECT
    owner,
    object_name,
    object_type,
    TO_CHAR(last_ddl_time,'DD-MON-YY hh:mi:ss') Last_time
FROM
    dba_objects
WHERE
    status='INVALID'
/
PAUSE Press Enter to continue
SET LINES 80 FEEDBACK ON PAGES 22 VERIFY ON
CLEAR COLUMNS
TTITLE OFF
```

Example of output from the object monitoring script is shown in Listing 13.33.

LISTING 13.33   Example of output from invalid objects script.

```
Date: 06/16/97                                      Page:    1
Time: 10:46 PM          Invalid Database Objects        SYSTEM
                          ORTEST1 database


Object      Object                          Last Change
Owner       Name                OBJECT_TYPE Date
----------  ------------------- ----------- ------------------
SYS         DBMS_ALERT          PACKAGE BODY 16-APR-96 11:22:12
SYS         DBMS_AQADM          PACKAGE BODY 16-APR-96 11:22:43
SYS         DBMS_AQ_IMP_INTERNAL PACKAGE BODY 16-APR-96 11:22:54
SYS         DBMS_DEBUG          PACKAGE BODY 16-APR-96 11:24:12
SYS         DBMS_IREFRESH       PACKAGE      16-APR-96 11:23:27
SYS         DBMS_IREFRESH       PACKAGE BODY 16-APR-96 11:23:50
SYS         DBMS_ISNAPSHOT      PACKAGE BODY 16-APR-96 11:23:46
SYS         DBMS_PIPE           PACKAGE BODY 16-APR-96 11:22:10
SYS         DBMS_REFRESH        PACKAGE      16-APR-96 11:23:24
SYS         DBMS_REFRESH        PACKAGE BODY 16-APR-96 11:23:48
SYS         DBMS_SHARED_POOL    PACKAGE BODY 17-APR-96 01:25:55
SYS         DBMS_SNAPSHOT       PACKAGE      16-APR-96 11:23:24
SYS         DBMS_SNAPSHOT       PACKAGE BODY 16-APR-96 11:23:58
SYS         DBMS_SNAPSHOT_UTL   PACKAGE BODY 16-APR-96 11:23:35
SYS         DBMS_SNAP_INTERNAL  PACKAGE BODY 16-APR-96 11:23:56
SYS         DBMS_UTILITY        PACKAGE BODY 09-MAY-96 08:31:06
TELE_DBA    CONTRACT_V          TYPE         19-MAY-96 03:30:52
TELE_DBA    LOAD_CLIENTS        PROCEDURE    18-APR-96 10:06:13
TELE_DBA    LOAD_EI             PROCEDURE    19-APR-96 07:32:15
```

If your search reveals that you have invalid objects, then a script similar to that in Source 13.34 can be executed to recompile the objects.

SOURCE 13.34   Example of Dynamic SQL script to recompile invalid objects.

```
rem Name: com_proc.sql
rem Function: Create a compile list for invalid procedures
rem
rem MRA 5/1/96
rem
DEFINE cr='chr(10)'
SET HEADING OFF PAGES 0 ECHO OFF TERMOUT OFF FEEDBACK OFF VERIFY OFF
SPOOL recompile.sql
SELECT 'ALTER '||object_type||' '||object_name||' COMPILE;'||&&cr||
'SHOW ERROR'
FROM dba_objects WHERE status='INVALID'
/
SPOOL OFF
SET HEADING ON TERMOUT ON FEEDBACK ON VERIFY ON
UNDEF cr
```

13.11 MONITORING MULTIPLE DATABASES

More and more DBAs are called upon to manage multiple instances. In this era of corporate downsizing, what was a manageable job a few years ago has rapidly descended into the chaos of a *Doom* episode gone wrong as more and more responsibility is being placed on fewer and fewer people. Today, it's imperative for DBAs to automate the management of multiple databases, especially if the databases are physically remote.

For multiple databases a DBA has several options. If your budget can afford it (the tools seem to get more expensive as the hardware decreases in cost) purchase a good monitoring tool such as Patrol by BMC or Eco-Tools as well as a "point-and-shoot" monitor such as Q by Savant Corporation, Platinum Technologies' offerings, or any of the plethora of new tools that seem to spring up each year. If the budget is not there for purchasing tools or, like me, you are a bit of a masochist, you may want to develop your own tools based on the scripts in this book.

To develop your own tools you must first decide what you want to monitor. Once you have, in a central monitoring database, design and install a small set of database tables to store the data with an identifier and date stamp for each entry. On each of the remote databases, establish a monitoring user that has select privileges against all required tables. Next, establish a database link from the remote databases to the central monitoring instance. On the central monitoring instance, establish a set of monitoring users with a set of synonyms that point to the remote database tables. Finally, set up a group of monitoring jobs that execute the monitoring scripts via the database links and synonyms against the remote databases and store the results in the results tables. Once the tables are loaded, you can report against them.

The Oracle Enterprise Manager provides for remote monitoring for multiple instances but not remote reporting.

Tuning Oracle Applications

Oracle7 and Oracle8 have come a long way since I wrote my first book on Oracle versions 6 and 7 in 1994. Since then, there has been a great explosion in the number and complexity of databases and in the tools for monitoring and tuning databases. When I wrote the first book, a database of several hundred megabytes was considered large, and a database in the gigabyte range was considered the purview of legacy mainframes. This is not the case anymore. With Oracle8, the size a database can reach is virtually unlimited—in the petabyte range (more than a single human mind could store if that person lived well into old age). Obviously, this explosion in the number and size of Oracle databases (a size of hundreds of gigabytes is now common) has led to differences in tuning methodology.

In addition to purely size-related issues, Oracle has added advanced replication, queuing, the multithreaded server, the parallel query, the parallel server, and, indeed, parallel everything. How is the poor DBA supposed to keep up? Although we look at a majority of these issues, this is not a database tuning book. Unfortunately, back around Oracle 7.1.16 or so that topic became far too complex for a single chapter in a single book to cover. Now, books of over 800 pages on tuning Oracle alone are the norm. I will, however, attempt to cover the major aspects of tuning. For more complete coverage, see the suggested DBA readings at the end of this chapter.

The Oracle Object-Relational Database Management System (ORDBMS) has been compared to an operating system that overlays a system's existing operating system. This is still true today. The Oracle ORDBMS handles its own buffering, caching, and file management within pseudodisks known as tablespaces. All of these internal Oracle functions can enhance or detract from performance. Oracle provides numerous tuning options to optimize these functions under both Oracle7 and Oracle8.

For version 7, the manual *Oracle7 Server Tuning*, Release 7.3, provides guidelines for tuning Oracle's various functions. For Oracle8, the manual *Oracle8 Server Tuning*, Release 8.0, Beta 2, February 1997 (or most current), provides insight into tuning both Oracle7 and Oracle8 databases. In most cases, the tuning that applies to version 7 will also apply to Oracle8. Where differences exist, this book will try to point them out.

Tuning Oracle is a three-part process. Throughout the process, the old 80/20 rule applies: 80 percent of the gains will be accomplished through 20 percent of the work. With Oracle, this 20 percent corresponds to the first part of the process, that is, application design. Figure 14.1 shows the relationship between the cost of work to tune a database verses the gains from that tuning as a project moves from development to maturity.

Some 80 percent of your performance gains will be accomplished through proper application design. By simply using appropriate relational concepts and then properly denormalizing a table layout, you can realize immense performance gains. The proper design of any system starts with appropriate business, or system, rules. The designers of your system have to be familiar with Oracle; they can't design in a vacuum. If the designers aren't aware of Oracle's features and strengths, how can they take advantage of them? In one project I worked on, for example, the designers used no functions, packages, or procedures because they weren't aware of them. In another, all of the referential integrity (RI) was done through triggers; again, the designers weren't aware how Oracle performed RI.

Once the Oracle system is designed on sound business rules and sound Oracle-based design practice, phase two begins. This is when the application developers take the Oracle-based design and implement it using sound, Oracle-based development practices. Spend the time to find, and the cash to hire, experienced Oracle developers. The time you save in redoing code, correcting mistakes, and teaching Oracle to off-the-shelf developers will more than compensate for the dollars you could have spent on qualified people in the first place. Experience with the "S" or the "I" database doesn't

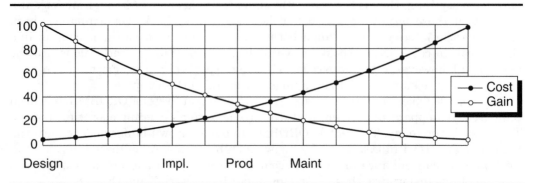

FIGURE 14.1   Generalized cost-benefit graph for tuning.

qualify a developer to develop in Oracle. While the concepts are similar, the execution in many cases is far different. Again, do you want to pay for learning-curve time?

Proper specification of business rules, application of the rules to a design, and implementation of the design using Oracle-savvy developers will give you 80 percent of your database performance. Developers must be familiar with Oracle application statement tuning. Statement tuning is not a DBA responsibility; it should be the responsibility of the developers. All of your developers should be familiar with EXPLAIN PLAN, TKPROF, and the strengths and weaknesses of the cost- and rule-based optimizers. Provide good tools to good people and you will be amazed at the results. There are numerous tools available now that automatically analyze code, and some, such as those offered by Precise, Inc., will even suggest alternative, better-performing ways to do a particular piece of code.

In some cases, merely adding a hint, analyzing a table, or changing the structure of a query will improve a statement's performance by an order of magnitude. Imagine what performance gains can be made over an entire application. In one case, adding a simple index reduced a four-hour process into a job of less than 10 seconds. The mere act of analyzing a recently loaded table may translate into hours of saved processing time.

The remaining 20 percent of your performance gains can be realized by tuning the structures and processes that make up the Oracle system. This kind of tuning is the DBA's job. Reducing disk, memory, and IO contention and improving sort and checkpoint speed will all improve performance. Of course, if all of these functions are really out of tune, database performance may show more than a 20 percent gain. In general, though, a 20 percent gain is a good rule of thumb. Unfortunately, DBAs are usually not hired until the programmer who got to be DBA because no one else wanted the job has made a complete mess of things. Indeed, by the time a true DBA is hired a project is usually only weeks from production, and then Oracle, and the DBA, are blamed for poor performance.

14.1 APPLICATION TUNING

Application tuning is a multifaceted concept. It involves both the design (logical as well as physical) and execution of an application. Depending on how your company's organization is laid out, you may or may not have any control over application development. If you have no control, try to show management the value you can add by providing application tuning skills to the developers. Each developer should attend the application tuning class provided by Oracle Corporation for the release of Oracle he or she is using. If developers cannot be sent to training, see if you can sponsor a workshop where the application tuning concepts can be presented to them.

Application tuning involves several steps.

1. Proper specification of system or business rules.
2. Proper logical design.
   a. Normalization of data
   b. Denormalization of selected tables for performance

3. Proper physical layout of application areas.
   a. Placement of tables in multiple tablespaces
   b. Placement of indexes away from tables
   c. Placement of other database objects
4. Tuning of application statements.
   a. Determination of index requirements
   b. Proper use, and nonuse, of indexes
   c. Query tuning—the use of TKPROF and EXPLAIN PLAN
5. Tuning of Oracle internals and processes.
   a. SGA
   b. Shared pool and large pool
   c. Parallel query
   d. MTS
   e. Archive logging
   f. Latches and locks
6. Application processing scheduling.
   a. Concurrent processes
   b. Batch jobs

Let's examine each of these areas.

Proper Specification of System or Business Rules

Unfortunately, you will probably be hired well after the system and business rules have been specified. If not, try to have as much input as possible into the process. You need to ensure that the rules make sense from a database point of view. If a rule can't be clearly understood, it can't be clearly programmed into a database.

You have to ensure that a proper balance is struck between too amorphous a set of rules, where anything that can store data (up to and including a leaky bucket) will meet them, and rules that are so specific they tell you what color shoes to wear when tuning the database. A rule should give the requirement, not the solution.

If possible, the DBA should have the right to inspect the rules and ask for clarifications where needed. After all, the database will probably outlast the managers and designers that build it.

Proper Logical Design

Normalization. Take a minute and review the section "A Brief Overview of Relational Jargon" in the introduction to this book. Pay attention specifically to the normalization rules. Following these rules will lead to a proper *logical* design. Simply stated, a fully normalized design is one in which all attributes for a specific entity relate to the entity's unique identifier and only to the entity's unique identifier. To say this in laymen's terms, they relate to the whole key and nothing but the key.

Denormalization. Sometimes, for performance of special reports or important, frequently run queries, it may be desirable to denormalize a table or tables in your design. Denormalization is the process by which columns from multiple tables are combined into a single table to speed queries on the data contained in those columns. In cases where the data from two or more tables is accessed repeatedly for reports or special queries, denormalization will speed access. It may be better to cluster the tables rather than denormalize. This will depend on how often the tables will have update or insert activity.

Denormalization will involve redundant storage of database information. If denormalization is used, be sure that your application performs updates for all of the data storage locations. The major problems with denormalized data are update, delete, and insert anomalies. In Oracle7, the use of database-stored triggers is suggested to handle the possible storage problems brought on by denormalization. Build stored triggers for each redundant field so that an update, delete, or insert activity must affect all values in the database.

One very powerful tool that can assist developers and DBAs in checking logical design is a good CASE (Computer-Aided Software Engineering) tool. Since we are dealing with Oracle, it is suggested that the Oracle Designer/Developer2000 tool set be used. The Oracle CASE system has tools for both the design—DEV2000 and DES2000—and implementation—generators for FORMS, MENUS, and REPORTS—of database applications. The dictionary and design tools provide numerous reports that allow the cross-checking of designs for possible problems.

Proper Physical Design

Physical design involves the physical design of the tables themselves. In this area, you as the DBA are concerned with the table, index, and cluster sizing and storage parameters. Let's look at these issues and attempt to give you some guidelines for using them properly.

Sizing. Use of the sizing formulas provided in the various subsections of Chapter 2 should provide you with detailed sizing data for the database objects. Be sure you have sized the tables for at least a year's worth of activity (unless, of course, the application's expected lifetime is less than a year). If the amount of storage used is not the prime consideration, oversizing is better than undersizing. Whenever possible, you don't want dynamic space extension in database objects. In fact, there may be benefits to sizing rows to take up equal fractions of an Oracle block.

Dynamic space extension is the process by which a database object grows past its initial settings. If the database objects have been created too small, this can result in the Swiss-cheese type of tablespace fragmentation that is very detrimental to performance. Generally speaking, you want as few extensions per table as possible. This is where a test database can be helpful.

Use of a test database. A small test database should be created and loaded with test data that is representative of what you expect the data in the real database to look like.

In order to get good sizing estimates, you should load at least 10 percent of the data (or a representative sample if the database is so large that 10 percent would qualify as a VLDB in its own right) you expect in the final database into the test database. Run the various sizing reports and check the database objects for dynamic extension. Once you are satisfied that the best sizing parameters have been used, ratio up the sizing parameters for your production installation. This involves deriving the ratio of how much data is expected in the actual table against how much was loaded into the test database table. This number is then applied to the sizing numbers from the test database.

Key sizing parameters. The initial, next, and, pctincrease values are the key sizing parameters. If you are dealing with legacy systems where a great deal of existing data is to be loaded, make the initial extent large enough to handle this existing data *plus a year's worth* of additional data. Make the next parameter big enough to deal with an additional year's worth of expected entries for the table. If you aren't sure how much the data entry requirements will be that far in the future, perform a SWAG (Scientific Wild-Assed Guess) and use the pctincrease parameter to take up the slack. Remember, the pctincrease is an incrementally applied value. The first extent added after the extent that uses the next parameter will be (1 + pctincrease/100) times larger than the next parameter, the next extent after that one will be another (1 + pctincrease/100) times larger, and so on. This factor is only applied to the size of the previous extent generated. In previous versions of Oracle, the factor was applied via formula so a seemingly minor increase in the factor could result in a catastrophically large next extent.

The actual value for the initial and next extent values should be carefully calculated to allow as close as possible to an even number of entries per extent for the table. For some fixed length entries this is easy; for entries that vary in length, it will require a careful determination of the average row length. Again, the scripts in Sources 5.28 and 5.31 can be of help if there is an existing database; if not, the calculations in Chapter 3 will be helpful. To facilitate the DBWR and other processes, and make extent reuse easier, some experts say to make table extents a standard size. Most, however, feel this wastes more space than it saves.

Table placement. Read the section in Chapter 1 concerning the Optimal Flexible Architecture (OFA). If these principles are applied, file placement can be easily accomplished. Generally speaking, you want to distribute an Oracle database across as many drives as possible. Ideally, one table per tablespace and one tablespace per drive would give the ultimate in performance. Of course, few, if any of us, can afford such an extensive disk array as would be required in this scenario, nor would any of us wish to manage this complex an environment. The next best thing is to spread the disk IO across available platters as evenly as possible. With the widespread acceptance of RAID technologies of various denominations (0, 1, 0+1, 0+1+5), this concept tends to blur as the concept of "disk" morphs into "disk array." Most RAID implementations will balance IO across the platters, especially if RAID 1 (striping) is used. However, it is still wise to place indexes on one disk array and tables on another. The file spreading rules now are applied over disk arrays or controllers instead of just disks.

High-volume, high-activity files should be placed in their own tablespaces on their own platters if possible. Low-volume, low-activity tables, such as static lookup tables, can be placed together in a single tablespace, preferably away from the high-volume tables. Other database tables such as redo logs, rollback segments, and system tablespaces should be placed to reduce disk contention and maximize dependability and recoverability. A few general rules are as follows:

1. Place redo logs and archive files on separate platters or arrays.
   Since one is a backup for the other this only makes sense.

2. Place redo logs and rollback segments on different platters or arrays.
   Both of these tend to be high-activity; separation reduces disk contention.

3. Separate the system tablespace from other application tablespaces if possible.
   The system tablespace is called by all others; separation reduces contention.

4. Run exports to a separate drive or array from archive logs.
   These provide two of the three legs of recovery: archives, exports, and system backups. Separation of each from the other improves recoverability.

5. Place archive logs away from active disks or arrays, preferably on their own platter.
   These files can be large and numerous. If there isn't adequate space to store these archive files, the database will stop.

Table striping. As DBA, you will also make decisions regarding striping of tables. Large tables may exceed the storage capacity of a single disk. In other cases, it may be desirable to place a table across several disks to optimize performance. Under Oracle7, this can be accomplished in the following manner:

1. Determine the size of each table fragment. It is suggested that each be the same size.

2. Create a tablespace that has data files spread across the platters; the data files should each be sized to hold one table fragment.

```
    CREATE TABLESPACE ACCOUNT_SPREAD
    DATAFILE ('/oracle01/ORTEST1/data/account_file1.dbf'
SIZE 500M REUSE,
    '/oracle02/ORTEST1/data/account_file2.dbf'
SIZE 500M REUSE,
    '/oracle03/ORTEST1/data/account_file3.dbf'
SIZE 500M REUSE)
    ONLINE;
```

3. Create the table in the tablespace from step 2 with X initial extents, each the same size as the data files from step 2.

```
CREATE TABLE accounts(acct_no number
   CONSTRAINT pk_acct PRIMARY KEY,
                       acct_name varchar2(32)
   CONSTRAINT nn_act_name NOT NULL,
                       acct_size number,
                       acct_desc  varchar2(64))
PCTFREE 5  PCTUSED 90
TABLESPACE ACCOUNT_SPREAD
STORAGE (INITIAL 495M   NEXT 495M
         MINEXTENTS 3   MAXEXTENTS 3
         PCTINCREASE 0)
```

4. Load the data into the table, either using SQL loader or IMPORT.

If you choose to spread a table in this manner, attempt to sort the data before it is loaded. If the data is already loaded into existing tables, use a query to load the data that presorts the records. If the data is in flat files or in another database, attempt to use operating system utilities or existing database reporting capabilities to sort the data. This will improve the accessibility of the data to your users once it is loaded into the spread data table. Data partitioning under Oracle7 is virtually impossible unless individual tables are created for each partition. However, later versions of Oracle7 allow for a partitioned view where, if proper criteria are met, a set of related partitioned tables can look like one table.

With Oracle8, data partitioning can easily be accomplished with the PARTITION clause of the CREATE TABLE command. The major advantage of the new partitioning in Oracle8 is that it is by ranges of data instead of a hit-or-miss separation. In addition to the CREATE TABLE command PARTITION clause the INDEX CREATE command also has a PARTITION clause. The partitions can be placed on individual disks to enhance performance. Data can simply be spread in multiple, equal-sized extents, or you can specify data ranges for each partition. Both indexes and tables can be partitioned if desired. By default, a partitioned table will have indexes that are partitioned the same, up to and including the tablespace locations. If you are using partitioned tables, be sure to specify the locations for your index partitions. Only standard relational style tables can be partitioned in version 8.0.2 of Oracle; they cannot include collections, nested tables, or varrays.

Tuning Application Query Statements

Tuning application queries is a complex topic. Such factors as index use, index nonuse, order of query where clauses, and Oracle optimizer settings can all affect query performance. In addition, the number of data dictionary caches and database buffers also affects query performance, as does the sort area size.

Use of TKPROF to Tune Statements Oracle provides two tools to tune SQL statements, TKPROF and EXPLAIN PLAN. TKPROF uses the Oracle trace facility to give statistics and query plans on all statements executed while the session is in trace mode. EXPLAIN PLAN is used on any query at any time. First, let's examine the use of TKPROF. As an example, look at the two queries in Source 14.1.

SOURCE 14.1   Example queries.

```
Query 1:
SELECT C.OWNER, C.TABLE_NAME, C.CONSTRAINT_NAME,
CC.COLUMN_NAME, R.TABLE_NAME REF_TABLE,
RC.COLUMN_NAME REF_COLUMN
FROM DBA_CONSTRAINTS C, DBA_CONSTRAINTS R, DBA_CONS_COLUMNS CC,
DBA_CONS_COLUMNS RC
WHERE C.R_CONSTRAINT_NAME = R.CONSTRAINT_NAME
AND C.R_OWNER = R.OWNER AND C.CONSTRAINT_NAME = CC.CONSTRAINT_NAME
AND C.OWNER = CC.OWNER AND R.CONSTRAINT_NAME = RC.CONSTRAINT_NAME
AND R.OWNER = RC.OWNER AND CC.POSITION = RC.POSITION
AND C.CONSTRAINT_TYPE = 'R' AND C.OWNER <> 'SYS'
AND C.OWNER <> 'SYSTEM'
ORDER BY C.OWNER, C.TABLE_NAME, C.CONSTRAINT_NAME, CC.POSITION

Query 2:
SELECT C.OWNER, C.TABLE_NAME, C.CONSTRAINT_NAME,
CC.COLUMN_NAME, R.TABLE_NAME REF_TABLE,
RC.COLUMN_NAME REF_COLUMN
FROM DBA_CONSTRAINTS C, DBA_CONSTRAINTS R,
DBA_CONS_COLUMNS CC, DBA_CONS_COLUMNS RC
WHERE C.CONSTRAINT_TYPE = 'R'
AND C.OWNER NOT IN ('SYS','SYSTEM')
AND C.R_OWNER = R.OWNER
and C.R_CONSTRAINT_NAME = R.CONSTRAINT_NAME
AND C.CONSTRAINT_NAME = CC.CONSTRAINT_NAME
AND C.OWNER = CC.OWNER
AND R.CONSTRAINT_NAME = RC.CONSTRAINT_NAME
AND R.OWNER = RC.OWNER
AND CC.POSITION = RC.POSITION
ORDER BY C.OWNER, C.TABLE_NAME, C.CONSTRAINT_NAME, CC.POSITION
```

TKPROF is executed by either moving to the directory where the trace files are located (the value of the initialization parameter "user_dump_destination" gives this information) or by moving the trace file to a work directory and executing the TKPROF command against it:

```
tkprof input output explain=user/password sort=(sort options)
```

Both of the queries are complex queries against views. Both of the queries retrieve the same information from the database. Close examination reveals that the only difference between them is the order of the where clause columns. Listing 14.1 shows the results of analyzing the preceding queries with the TKPROF tool. As you can see, the second query performs better. This is due to the placement of the most restrictive columns first, thus reducing the volume of subsequent merges and sorts. As you can see, the explain plan generated is huge since this is a multitable and multiview join. Unfortunately, a query against views that are not owned by the user running TKPROF cannot be run through the EXPLAIN PLAN option, so if the queries you analyze involve views from multiple owners an explain plan output will not be available.

LISTING 14.1   TKPROF results from queries in Source 14.1.

```
*****************************************************************

select c.owner,c.table_name,c.constraint_name,
cc.column_name,r.table_name ref_table,
rc.column_name ref_column
from dba_constraints c, dba_constraints r, dba_cons_columns cc,
dba_cons_columns rc
where c.r_constraint_name=r.constraint_name
and c.r_owner=r.owner and c.constraint_name=cc.constraint_name
and c.owner=cc.owner and r.constraint_name=rc.constraint_name
and r.owner=rc.owner and cc.position=rc.position
and c.constraint_type='R' and c.owner<>'SYS'
and c.owner<>'SYSTEM'
order by c.owner, c.table_name, c.constraint_name,cc.position

call     count   cpu elapsed    disk  query current       rows
-------  -----  ---- -------    ----  ----- -------  -----------
Parse        1  2.67    2.67       0      0       0          0
Execute      1  0.00    0.00       0      0       0          0
Fetch        3  0.52    0.52       0   6737       2         21
-------  -----  ---- -------    ----  ----- -------  -----------
total        5  3.19    3.19       0   6737       2         21

Misses in library cache during parse: 0
Optimizer goal: CHOOSE
Parsing user id: SYS

Rows     Execution Plan
-------  -------------------------------------------------------
      0  SELECT STATEMENT   GOAL: CHOOSE
      0   SORT (ORDER BY)
      0    NESTED LOOPS (OUTER)
      0     NESTED LOOPS
      0      NESTED LOOPS
      0       NESTED LOOPS
      0        NESTED LOOPS (OUTER)
      0         NESTED LOOPS (OUTER)
      0          NESTED LOOPS
      0           NESTED LOOPS
```

```
0              NESTED LOOPS
0               NESTED LOOPS
0                NESTED LOOPS
0                 NESTED LOOPS
0                  NESTED LOOPS
0                   NESTED LOOPS (OUTER)
0                    NESTED LOOPS (OUTER)
0                   NESTED LOOPS
0                    NESTED LOOPS
0                     NESTED LOOPS
0                      NESTED LOOPS
0                       NESTED LOOPS
0                        NESTED LOOPS
0                         NESTED LOOPS (OUTER)
0                          NESTED LOOPS
0                           NESTED LOOPS
0                            NESTED LOOPS
0                             TABLE ACCESS
                                  (FULL) OF 'OBJ$'
0                             TABLE ACCESS
                                  (CLUSTER) OF 'CCOL$'
0                              INDEX
                                  (UNIQUE SCAN) OF
                                  'I_COBJ#' (CLUSTER)
0                             INDEX (UNIQUE
                                  SCAN) OF 'I_CDEF1'
                                  (UNIQUE)
0                            TABLE ACCESS (BY
                                  INDEX ROWID) OF 'COL$'
0                             INDEX (UNIQUE
                                  SCAN) OF 'I_COL3'
                                  (UNIQUE)
0                           TABLE ACCESS
                                  (CLUSTER) OF 'ATTRCOL$'
0                          TABLE ACCESS (BY
                                  INDEX ROWID) OF 'CON$'
0                           INDEX (UNIQUE SCAN)
                                  OF 'I_CON2' (UNIQUE)
0                         TABLE ACCESS (CLUSTER)
                                  OF 'USER$'
0                          INDEX (UNIQUE SCAN)
                                  OF 'I_USER#' (CLUSTER)
0                        TABLE ACCESS (BY INDEX
                                  ROWID) OF 'USER$'
0                         INDEX (UNIQUE SCAN) OF
                                  'I_USER1' (UNIQUE)
0                       TABLE ACCESS (BY INDEX
                                  ROWID) OF 'CON$'
0                        INDEX (UNIQUE SCAN) OF
                                  'I_CON1' (UNIQUE)
```

```
   0                        TABLE ACCESS (BY INDEX ROWID)
                               OF 'CDEF$'
   0                      INDEX (UNIQUE SCAN) OF
                             'I_CDEF1' (UNIQUE)
   0                    TABLE ACCESS (BY INDEX ROWID)
                           OF 'OBJ$'
   0                      INDEX (UNIQUE SCAN) OF
                             'I_OBJ1' (UNIQUE)
   0                    TABLE ACCESS (BY INDEX ROWID) OF
                           'CON$'
   0                      INDEX (UNIQUE SCAN) OF
                             'I_CON2' (UNIQUE)
   0                  TABLE ACCESS (CLUSTER) OF 'USER$'
   0                    INDEX (UNIQUE SCAN) OF 'I_USER#'
                           (CLUSTER)
   0                  TABLE ACCESS (BY INDEX ROWID) OF
                         'USER$'
   0                    INDEX (UNIQUE SCAN) OF 'I_USER1'
                           (UNIQUE)
   0                  TABLE ACCESS (BY INDEX ROWID) OF
                         'USER$'
   0                    INDEX (UNIQUE SCAN) OF 'I_USER1'
                           (UNIQUE)
   0                TABLE ACCESS (BY INDEX ROWID) OF 'CON$'
   0                  INDEX (UNIQUE SCAN) OF 'I_CON1'
                         (UNIQUE)
   0                TABLE ACCESS (BY INDEX ROWID) OF 'CON$'
   0                  INDEX (UNIQUE SCAN) OF 'I_CON1' (UNIQUE)
   0              INDEX (UNIQUE SCAN) OF 'I_CDEF1' (UNIQUE)
   0              TABLE ACCESS (BY INDEX ROWID) OF 'CDEF$'
   0              INDEX (UNIQUE SCAN) OF 'I_CDEF1' (UNIQUE)
   0              TABLE ACCESS (BY INDEX ROWID) OF 'OBJ$'
   0              INDEX (UNIQUE SCAN) OF 'I_OBJ1' (UNIQUE)
   0              TABLE ACCESS (BY INDEX ROWID) OF 'CON$'
   0              INDEX (UNIQUE SCAN) OF 'I_CON2' (UNIQUE)
   0              TABLE ACCESS (CLUSTER) OF 'USER$'
   0                INDEX (UNIQUE SCAN) OF 'I_USER#' (CLUSTER)
   0              TABLE ACCESS (BY INDEX ROWID) OF 'CCOL$'
   0                INDEX (RANGE SCAN) OF 'I_CCOL2' (UNIQUE)
   0            INDEX (UNIQUE SCAN) OF 'I_OBJ1' (UNIQUE)
   0            TABLE ACCESS (BY INDEX ROWID) OF 'COL$'
   0              INDEX (UNIQUE SCAN) OF 'I_COL3' (UNIQUE)
   0          TABLE ACCESS (CLUSTER) OF 'ATTRCOL$'


*****************************************************************

select c.owner,c.table_name,c.constraint_name,
cc.column_name,r.table_name ref_table,
rc.column_name ref_column
from dba_constraints c, dba_constraints r, dba_cons_columns cc,
```

```
dba_cons_columns rc
where c.constraint_type='R'
and c.owner not in ('SYS','SYSTEM')
and c.r_owner=r.owner
and c.r_constraint_name=r.constraint_name
and c.constraint_name = cc.constraint_name
and c.owner=cc.owner
and r.constraint_name=rc.constraint_name
and r.owner=rc.owner
and cc.position=rc.position
order by c.owner, c.table_name, c.constraint_name,cc.position
```

call	count	cpu	elapsed	disk	query	current	rows
Parse	1	0.02	0.01	0	0	0	0
Execute	1	0.00	0.00	0	0	0	0
Fetch	3	0.51	0.52	0	6737	2	21
total	5	0.53	0.53	0	6737	2	21

```
Misses in library cache during parse: 1
Optimizer goal: CHOOSE
Parsing user id: SYS
```

```
Rows      Execution Plan
-------   --------------------------------------------------------
      0   SELECT STATEMENT   GOAL: CHOOSE
      0    SORT (ORDER BY)
      0     NESTED LOOPS (OUTER)
      0      NESTED LOOPS
      0       NESTED LOOPS
      0        NESTED LOOPS
      0         NESTED LOOPS (OUTER)
      0          NESTED LOOPS (OUTER)
      0           NESTED LOOPS
      0            NESTED LOOPS
      0             NESTED LOOPS
      0              NESTED LOOPS
      0               NESTED LOOPS
      0                NESTED LOOPS
      0                 NESTED LOOPS
      0                  NESTED LOOPS (OUTER)
      0                   NESTED LOOPS (OUTER)
      0                    NESTED LOOPS
      0                     NESTED LOOPS
      0                      NESTED LOOPS
      0                       NESTED LOOPS
      0                        NESTED LOOPS
      0                         NESTED LOOPS
      0                          NESTED LOOPS
      0                           NESTED LOOPS (OUTER)
```

```
0                      NESTED LOOPS
0                      NESTED LOOPS
0                      NESTED LOOPS
0                      TABLE ACCESS
                          (FULL) OF 'OBJ$'
0                      TABLE ACCESS
                          (CLUSTER) OF 'CCOL$'
0                        INDEX
                          (UNIQUE SCAN) OF
                          'I_COBJ#' (CLUSTER)
0                        INDEX (UNIQUE
                          SCAN) OF 'I_CDEF1'
                          (UNIQUE)
0                      TABLE ACCESS (BY
                          INDEX ROWID) OF 'COL$'
0                      INDEX (UNIQUE
                          SCAN) OF 'I_COL3'
                          (UNIQUE)
0                      TABLE ACCESS
                          (CLUSTER) OF 'ATTRCOL$'
0                      TABLE ACCESS (BY
                          INDEX ROWID) OF 'CON$'
0                      INDEX (UNIQUE SCAN)
                          OF 'I_CON2' (UNIQUE)
0                      TABLE ACCESS (CLUSTER)
                          OF 'USER$'
0                      INDEX (UNIQUE SCAN)
                          OF 'I_USER#' (CLUSTER)
0                      TABLE ACCESS (BY INDEX
                          ROWID) OF 'USER$'
0                      INDEX (UNIQUE SCAN) OF
                          'I_USER1' (UNIQUE)
0                      TABLE ACCESS (BY INDEX
                          ROWID) OF 'CON$'
0                      INDEX (UNIQUE SCAN) OF
                          'I_CON1' (UNIQUE)
0                      TABLE ACCESS (BY INDEX ROWID)
                          OF 'CDEF$'
0                      INDEX (UNIQUE SCAN) OF
                          'I_CDEF1' (UNIQUE)
0                      TABLE ACCESS (BY INDEX ROWID)
                          OF 'OBJ$'
0                      INDEX (UNIQUE SCAN) OF
                          'I_OBJ1' (UNIQUE)
0                      TABLE ACCESS (BY INDEX ROWID) OF
                          'CON$'
0                      INDEX (UNIQUE SCAN) OF
                          'I_CON2' (UNIQUE)
0                      TABLE ACCESS (CLUSTER) OF 'USER$'
```

```
0                       INDEX (UNIQUE SCAN) OF 'I_USER#'
                          (CLUSTER)
0                   TABLE ACCESS (BY INDEX ROWID) OF
                          'USER$'
0                     INDEX (UNIQUE SCAN) OF 'I_USER1'
                          (UNIQUE)
0                   TABLE ACCESS (BY INDEX ROWID) OF
                          'USER$'
0                     INDEX (UNIQUE SCAN) OF 'I_USER1'
                          (UNIQUE)
0                 TABLE ACCESS (BY INDEX ROWID) OF 'CON$'
0                   INDEX (UNIQUE SCAN) OF 'I_CON1'
                          (UNIQUE)
0               TABLE ACCESS (BY INDEX ROWID) OF 'CON$'
0                 INDEX (UNIQUE SCAN) OF 'I_CON1' (UNIQUE)
0               INDEX (UNIQUE SCAN) OF 'I_CDEF1' (UNIQUE)
0             TABLE ACCESS (BY INDEX ROWID) OF 'CDEF$'
0               INDEX (UNIQUE SCAN) OF 'I_CDEF1' (UNIQUE)
0             TABLE ACCESS (BY INDEX ROWID) OF 'OBJ$'
0               INDEX (UNIQUE SCAN) OF 'I_OBJ1' (UNIQUE)
0             TABLE ACCESS (BY INDEX ROWID) OF 'CON$'
0               INDEX (UNIQUE SCAN) OF 'I_CON2' (UNIQUE)
0           TABLE ACCESS (CLUSTER) OF 'USER$'
0             INDEX (UNIQUE SCAN) OF 'I_USER#' (CLUSTER)
0           TABLE ACCESS (BY INDEX ROWID) OF 'CCOL$'
0             INDEX (RANGE SCAN) OF 'I_CCOL2' (UNIQUE)
0           INDEX (UNIQUE SCAN) OF 'I_OBJ1' (UNIQUE)
0         TABLE ACCESS (BY INDEX ROWID) OF 'COL$'
0           INDEX (UNIQUE SCAN) OF 'I_COL3' (UNIQUE)
0       TABLE ACCESS (CLUSTER) OF 'ATTRCOL$'

*******************************************************************
```

As you can see, the rearrangement of the where clause has reduced the CPU and elapsed statistics for the parse phase of the query processing. You may find it difficult to get truly valid results unless your data sets are large or your processor is slow.

To use the TKPROF tool and get timing results, the TIMED_STATISTICS parameter in the INIT.ORA file must be set to TRUE. To limit the size of the generated trace file set the INIT.ORA parameter MAX_DUMP_FILE_SIZE to the desired file size limit. If you want the files to be created in locations other than the ORA_INSTANCE, the ORA_TRACE, or the $ORACLE_HOME directory, set the USER_DUMP_DEST to the desired file location. In order for these parameters to take effect, the instance has to be shut down and restarted. Once testing is finished, reset the TIMED_STATISTIC parameter to FALSE or there will be a performance hit due to continuous statistics collection.

Setting TIMED_STATISTICS to TRUE will allow individual users to set the SQL_TRACE value for their process to TRUE, which will then generate a trace file in the ORA_TRACE or selected directory. Users should then execute the statements from within SQLPLUS. To use the trace facility in SQL*Plus, use the ALTER SESSION command. For example,

```
ALTER SESSION SET SQL_TRACE TRUE;
```

Use of TKPROF. Once the SQL statements or forms have been run, exit SQLPLUS or the forms-based application and look for the proper trace file that corresponds to the PID of the process that generated it. For example, if the database is testb, the PID in Oracle is 5, and the program being run is SQLPLUS the trace file will be SQLPLUS_F30_TESTB_005.TRC. On your system the file naming may be different. Usually, the name will contain the PID. If you try to look at this file without processing through TKPROF, you will receive little benefit. TKPROF formats the trace files into a user-readable form. The format of the TKPROF command follows.

Invoke TKPROF using this syntax:

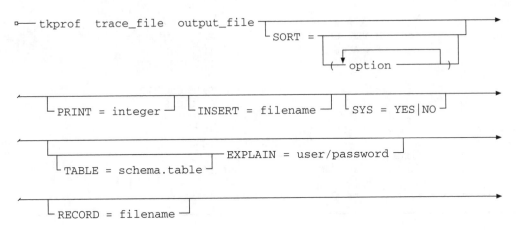

If you invoke TKPROF with no arguments, online help is displayed.

Use the following arguments with TKPROF:

trace file	Specifies the input file, that is, a trace file containing statistics produced by the SQL trace facility. This file can be either a trace file produced for a single session or a file produced by concatenating individual trace files from multiple sessions.
output file	Specifies the file to which TKPROF writes its formatted output.
AGGREGATE	If you specify AGGREGATE = NO, then TKPROF does not aggregate multiple users of the same SQL text.
EXPLAIN	Determines the execution plan for each SQL statement in the trace file and writes these execution plans to the output file. TKPROF determines execution plans by issuing the EXPLAIN

PLAN command after connecting to Oracle, with the user and password specified in this parameter. The specified user must have CREATE SESSION system privileges. TKPROF will take longer to process a large trace file if the EXPLAIN option is used.

TABLE   Specifies the schema and name of the table into which TKPROF temporarily places execution plans before writing them to the output file. If the specified table already exists, TKPROF deletes all rows in the table, uses it for the EXPLAIN PLAN command (which writes more rows into the table), and then deletes those rows. If this table does not exist, TKPROF creates it, uses it, and then drops it.

The specified user must be able to issue INSERT, SELECT, and DELETE statements against the table. If the table does not already exist, the user must also be able to issue CREATE TABLE and DROP TABLE statements. For the privileges to issue these statements, see the *Oracle8 Server SQL Reference*.

This option allows multiple individuals to run TKPROF concurrently with the same user in the EXPLAIN value. These individuals can specify different TABLE values and avoid destructively interfering with each other's processing on the temporary plan table. If you use the EXPLAIN parameter without the TABLE parameter, TKPROF uses the table PROF$PLAN_TABLE in the schema of the user specified by the EXPLAIN parameter. If you use the TABLE parameter without the EXPLAIN parameter, TKPROF ignores the TABLE parameter.

INSERT   Creates a SQL script that stores the trace file statistics in the database. TKPROF creates this script with the name filename3. This script creates a table and inserts a row of statistics for each traced SQL statement into the table.

SYS   Enables and disables the listing of SQL statements issued by the user SYS, or recursive SQL statements into the output file. The default value of YES causes TKPROF to list these statements. The value of NO causes TKPROF to omit them. Note that this parameter does not affect the optional SQL script. The SQL script always inserts statistics for all traced SQL statements, including recursive SQL statements.

SORT   Sorts the traced SQL statements in descending order of the specified sort option before listing them into the output file. If more than one option is specified, the output is sorted in descending order by the sum of the values specified in the sort options. If you omit this parameter, TKPROF lists statements into the output file in order of first use.

The sort options are as follows:

PRSCNT — number of times parsed

PRSCPU — CPU time spent parsing

PRSELA — elapsed time spent parsing

PRSDSK — number of physical reads from disk during parse

PRSMIS — number of consistent mode block reads during parse

PRSCU — number of current mode block reads during parse

PRSMIS — number of library cache misses during parse

EXECNT — number of executes

EXECPU — CPU time spent executing

EXEELA — elapsed time spent executing

EXEDSK — number of physical reads from disk during execute

EXEQRY — number of consistent mode block reads during execute

EXECU — number of current mode block reads during execute

EXEROW — number of rows processed during execute

EXEMIS — number of library cache misses during execute

FCHCNT — number of fetches

FCHCPU — CPU time spent fetching

FCHELA — elapsed time spent fetching

FCHDSK — number of physical reads from disk during fetch

FCHQRY — number of consistent mode block reads during fetch

FCHCU — number of current mode block reads during fetch

FCHROW — number of rows fetched

PRINT — Lists only the first integer-sorted SQL statements into the output file. If you omit this parameter, TKPROF lists all traced SQL statements. Note that this parameter does not affect the optional SQL script. The SQL script always inserts statistics for all traced SQL statements.

RECORD — Creates a SQL script with the specified file name with all of the nonrecursive SQLs in the trace file. This can be used to replay the user events from the trace file.

The EXPLAIN option of TKPROF. To use the EXPLAIN option, a user must have resource privileges on a tablespace so the required tables can be created. The command is issued at the operating system level. To split the command on multiple lines in VMS, place a dash at the end of each line. For UNIX, you simply place a "/" (backslash) character at the end of the line to be continued.

The preceding command will generate a file named to whatever you specified the output file to be. If you include the SORT qualifier, the output will be sorted accordingly. If you include the EXPLAIN qualifier, a temporary table will be created in the user's default tablespace, and the various SQL statements will be "explained" in accordance with the formats of the EXPLAIN PLAN command.

TKPROF statistics. Each line of the statistics will correspond to either the parse, execute, or fetch part of the query operation. These parts of a query are defined as follows:

Parse	The query is translated into an execution plan. If the user doesn't have the proper security or table authorization or the objects in the query don't exist, this step will catch it as well.
Execute	The execution plan is executed against the ORDBMS.
Fetch	In this final step, all rows that satisfy the query are retrieved from the database.

For each step the following parameters are traced:

count	This is the number of times this step was repeated.
cpu	This is the total CPU time for the step in hundredths of a second.
elapsed	This is the total elapsed time for the step in hundredths of a second.
disk	This is the total number of database blocks read from disk for the step.

In Oracle7 this column is called Disk.

query	This is the number of buffers retrieved in a consistent read mode.
current	This is the number of buffers retrieved in current mode.
rows	This is the number of rows processed during the SQL statement execution step.

TKPROF Example Tuning Session Let's look at some example outputs from the TKPROF using EXPLAIN. We will run through some tuning scenarios on an example query. The descriptions for tables being used for these examples are shown in Source 14.2.

SOURCE 14.2   Structures of tables used in TKPROF examples.

```
DESC TKP_EXAMPLE
Name                                  Null?     Type
------------------------------------- --------- -------------
USERNAME                              NOT NULL  VARCHAR2(30)
USER_ID                               NOT NULL  NUMBER
```

```
PASSWORD                                 VARCHAR2(30)
ACCOUNT_STATUS                 NOT NULL  VARCHAR2(32)
LOCK_DATE                                DATE
EXPIRY_DATE                              DATE
DEFAULT_TABLESPACE             NOT NULL  VARCHAR2(30)
TEMPORARY_TABLESPACE           NOT NULL  VARCHAR2(30)
CREATED                        NOT NULL  DATE
PROFILE                        NOT NULL  VARCHAR2(30)
EXTERNAL_NAME                            VARCHAR2(4000)

Record count for TKP_EXAMPLE: 21



     DESC TKP_EXAMPLE2
Name                             Null?     Type
-------------------------------- --------  ------------
OWNER                                      VARCHAR2(30)
OBJECT_NAME                                VARCHAR2(128)
OBJECT_TYPE                                VARCHAR2(15)
TABLESPACE_NAME                            VARCHAR2(30)

Record count for TKP_EXAMPLE2: 5113
```

In the first examples, let's look at the TKPROF output from some queries using these tables without indexes (Listing 14.2). Of course, what we expect is that the ORDBMS will do full table scans no matter how complex the query. Remember, it isn't always bad to use a full table scan; it depends entirely upon the selectivity of your query. If you are only returning a few rows, it is advisable to use an index. The old rule of thumb is if your query returns less than 10 to 15 percent of rows in the table, use an index. However, with the new parallel capabilities in Oracle7 and Oracle8, full table scans may actually be the fastest method for returning data for a broader range of queries. To quote Michael Abby in his opening statements at the Oracle's of Oracle presentation at IOUGA-Dallas, 1997, "Table Scan is no longer a four-letter word." The select statement in Listing 14.2 is a two-table join, stripping out system tables, of the two tables in Source 14.2. Experienced system managers will recognize these tables as a copy of portions of the DBA_USERS, DBA_OBJECTS, and the DBA_TABLES views. They were created using the CREATE TABLE command with the AS clause.

LISTING 14.2   Query against example tables with no indexes.

```
select
     username,
     default_tablespace,
     tablespace_name,
     object_name
```

```
from
    tkp_example, tkp_example2
where
    username != 'SYS' and
    username != 'SYSTEM' and
    default_tablespace=tablespace_name and
    owner=username
```

call	count	cpu	elapsed	disk	query	current	rows
Parse	1	0.01	0.01	0	0	0	0
Execute	1	0.00	0.00	0	0	0	0
Fetch	57	0.22	0.22	0	28	6	849
total	59	0.23	0.23	0	28	6	849

```
Misses in library cache during parse: 1
Optimizer goal: CHOOSE
Parsing user id: 5  (SYSTEM)

Rows     Execution Plan
-------  --------------------------------------------------------
      0  SELECT STATEMENT    GOAL: CHOOSE
    849    MERGE JOIN
   5113      SORT (JOIN)
   5113        TABLE ACCESS (FULL) OF 'TKP_EXAMPLE2'
     19      SORT (JOIN)
     21        TABLE ACCESS (FULL) OF 'TKP_EXAMPLE'
```

As you can see, the performance isn't as bad as expected. Even after stripping out the system tables and other objects 849 rows were still returned. As we expected, the query performed two full table scans. But what are MERGE JOIN, SORT(JOIN), and so on? These are part of the execution plan that the parse step generated. In addition to the information presented in Listing 14.2, Oracle7's TKPROF also provides the number of misses in the library cache during the parse step and adds a ROWS column to the query plan. Let's look at the possible outputs from the EXPLAIN portion of the TKPROF output.

Action:	*What It Means:*
AND-EQUAL	If the where clause contains references to unique indexed columns only, the system will choose to use the ROWIDs from the indexes to perform the table intersections. This is faster than a full table scan type of intersection.

CONNECT BY

This only shows up in queries that use a connect clause. When a CONNECT BY is executed it forces a tree-walk of the table structure to perform the operation.

CONCATENATION

This is a full union of two or more tables. For small tables it won't hurt; for large tables it can kill you.

COUNT

This action happens if the query uses the COUNT aggregate to return the number of rows. The STOP-KEY value, if returned, shows that a ROWNUM was used to limit the number of returns.

FILTER

This is a process by which rows not meeting the selection criteria are removed from the returned set of values.

FIRST ROW

This shows that only the first row of a query was returned; this shows activity with a cursor.

FOR UPDATE

This shows that the query operation involved a possible update situation (such as in a form or SELECT. . . . FOR UPDATE). This indicates that the rows involved were write-locked during the operation.

INDEX (UNIQUE, or RANGE, SCAN)

This action shows that a query used an index to resolve the needed values. The UNIQUE qualifier shows that the index was scanned for specific unique values. The RANGE qualifier shows that a specific range of values was searched, such as that specified in a BETWEEN or less-than—greater-than construct. The RANGE SCAN may also have the DESCENDING qualifier.

INTERSECTION

This shows that the query retrieved the rows from the tables in the query that were common to each of the tables based on the conditions in the where clause. The rows are sorted.

MERGE JOIN (OUTER)

This shows that two sorted sets of operations were joined to resolve the query. The OUTER qualifier shows that an outer join was performed.

MINUS

This shows that an INTERSECTION-type operation was performed, but instead of similar rows being returned only rows that didn't match the specified criteria were returned.

NESTED LOOPS (OUTER)

This shows that for each of the first-child operations, one or more of the other-child operations that follow it were performed. If the OUTER qualifier is present, it signifies that an outer join was performed between the results.

PROJECTION	This shows that a subset of a tables columns was returned.
REMOTE	This shows that a retrieval from other than the current database was performed to resolve the query.
SEQUENCE	This shows that a sequence was accessed during a query.
SORT (UNIQUE GROUP BY JOIN ORDER BY AGGREGATE)	This shows that a query used one of the ordering clauses; the type of clause will be listed as a qualifier.
TABLE ACCESS (BY ROWID FULL CLUSTER HASH)	This shows that a table access was performed. Some queries can be resolved by an INDEX scan only. The type of access performed is shown by the included qualifier. ROWID is generally the fastest form of table access and shows that an index scan was also used.
UNION	This shows that a retrieval of unique rows from each table was performed with the duplicates removed from the output.
VIEW	This shows the query accessed a view to resolve the query.

Let's look at this first query's EXPLAIN output in light of the preceding definitions.

Execution plan:

MERGE JOIN	This shows that the results from the following operations are merged.
SORT (JOIN)	This shows that the results are sorted before being passed to the MERGE.
TABLE ACCESS (FULL) OF 'TKP_EXAMPLE'	This indicates that the full table was scanned.
SORT (JOIN)	This shows that the results are sorted before being passed to the MERGE.

TABLE ACCESS   This indicates that the full table was scanned.
(FULL) OF
'TKP_EXAMPLE'

What does this tell us? First, both tables were fully scanned to retrieve the rows that met the where clause's criteria. Next, the results from each were sorted. Finally, the results were merged based on the selection criteria. Can these results be improved upon for this type of query? Let's add some indexes (listed in Source 14.3) and find out.

The attempt has been made to ensure that the indexes have high selectivity and that the columns most accessed in the tables are the leading portion of one or more indexes. Let's reissue the select in Source 14.2 and see what happens.

SOURCE 14.3   Indexes added to tables from Source 14.2.

```
SQL> CREATE  UNIQUE INDEX TKP_EXP_INDEX
      2  ON TKP_EXAMPLE(
    USERNAME,
    DEFAULT_TABLESPACE,
    TEMPORARY_TABLESPACE);

SQL> CREATE  UNIQUE INDEX TKP_EXP_INDEX2
      2  ON TKP_EXAMPLE(
    TEMPORARY_TABLESPACE,
    USERNAME,
    DEFAULT_TABLESPACE);

SQL> CREATE  UNIQUE INDEX TKP_EXP_INDEX3
      2  ON TKP_EXAMPLE(
    DEFAULT_TABLESPACE,
    TEMPORARY_TABLESPACE,
    USERNAME);

SQL> CREATE UNIQUE INDEX TKP_EXP2_INDEX ON
 2 TKP_EXAMPLE2(
    OWNER,
    OBJECT_NAME
    OBJECT_TYPE);

SQL> CREATE UNIQUE INDEX TKP_EXP2_INDEX2 ON
 2 TKP_EXAMPLE2(
    OWNER,
    TABLESPACE_NAME,
    OBJECT_NAME,
    OBJECT_TYPE);

SQL> CREATE UNIQUE INDEX TKP_EXP2_INDEX3 ON
 2 TKP_EXAMPLE2(
    TABLESPACE_NAME,
    OWNER,
    OBJECT_NAME,
    OBJECT_TYPE);
```

LISTING 14.3   The results on the query from Source 14.2 of indexes.

```
call     count     cpu elapsed     disk      query     current
rows
-------  -----   ------- -------  --------  ----------  ----------
Parse      1     0.00    0.00        0         0           0
0
Execute    1     0.00    0.00        0         0           0
0
Fetch     57     0.38    0.38        0        6932         3
849
-------  -----   ------- -------  --------  ----------  ----------
total     59     0.38    0.38        0        6932         3
849

Misses in library cache during parse: 0
Optimizer goal: CHOOSE
Parsing user id: 5   (SYSTEM)

Rows       Execution Plan
-------    -------------------------------------------------
     0     SELECT STATEMENT    GOAL: CHOOSE
   849     NESTED LOOPS
  5113      TABLE ACCESS (FULL) OF 'TKP_EXAMPLE2'
  2738      INDEX (RANGE SCAN) OF 'TMP_EXP_INDEX' (UNIQUE)
```

As you can see in Listing 14.3, the indexes didn't improve performance; in fact, they made performance worse. A key indicator that something is wrong is that the current parameter jumped by several orders of magnitude. This is an example of a query that returns more than 15 percent of a table. How can we restore performance? If we use the NOT or LIKE clause instead of the comparison operators ("!=", "=") are indexes used? Let's look at the same query with the NOT clause replacing the "!=" in the select statement. Listing 14.4 shows the TKPROF results from this query. Did performance improve? No, in fact the results are almost identical even down to the execution plan. NOT and "!=" are treated identically.

LISTING 14.4   Results of replacing the != with a NOT IN.

```
select
        username,
        default_tablespace,
        tablespace_name,
        object_name
from
        tkp_example, tkp_example2
where
        username not in ('SYS','SYSTEM') and
```

```
       default_tablespace=tablespace_name and
       owner=username

call      count  cpu  elapsed disk    query    current        rows
-------   -----  ----- ------- ----  --------  ----------  -----------
Parse         1  0.01    0.01     0         0           0            0
Execute       1  0.00    0.00     0         0           0            0
Fetch        57  0.33    0.33     0      6932           3          849
-------   -----  ----- ------- ----  --------  ----------  -----------
total        59  0.34    0.34     0      6932           3          849

Misses in library cache during parse: 1
Optimizer goal: CHOOSE
Parsing user id: 5  (SYSTEM)


Rows      Execution Plan
-------   -----------------------------------------------------
      0   SELECT STATEMENT    GOAL: CHOOSE
    849     NESTED LOOPS
   5113       TABLE ACCESS (FULL) OF 'TKP_EXAMPLE2'
   2738       INDEX (RANGE SCAN) OF 'TMP_EXP_INDEX' (UNIQUE)
```

LISTING 14.5   Results of replacing the = with LIKE.

```
select
       username,
       default_tablespace,
       tablespace_name,
       object_name
from
       tkp_example, tkp_example2
where
       username not in ('SYS','SYSTEM') and
       default_tablespace like tablespace_name and
       owner like username

call      count    cpu  elapsed disk   query    current        rows
-------   -----  ------- ------- ----- ------  ----------  -----------
Parse         1   0.00    0.00     0        0           0            0
Execute       1   0.00    0.00     0        0           0            0
Fetch        57   0.56    0.56     1     6932           3          849
-------   -----  ------- ------- ----- ------  ----------  -----------
total        59   0.56    0.56     1     6932           3          849

Misses in library cache during parse: 1
Optimizer goal: CHOOSE
Parsing user id: 5  (SYSTEM)
```

```
Rows      Execution Plan
-------   ----------------------------------------------------------------
      0   SELECT STATEMENT    GOAL: CHOOSE
    849   NESTED LOOPS
   5113      TABLE ACCESS (FULL) OF 'TKP_EXAMPLE2'
  19866      INDEX (RANGE SCAN) OF 'TMP_EXP_INDEX3' (UNIQUE)
```

Why are the results the same for the queries in Listings 14.3 and 14.4? In the query in Listing 14.5 the controlling table will be TKP_EXAMPLE2;, the NOT doesn't affect the TKP_EXAMPLE2 table, which was already using a full table scan. Let's replace the "=" operator with a LIKE statement and see what happens; see Listing 14.6.

Even by replacing the "=" with LIKE we have not forced full table scans; performance still isn't as good as with the original nonindexed tables. The index scanned was changed from TKP_EXP_INDEX to TKP_EXP_INDEX3. The performance is still poor because for each row of the TKP_EXAMPLE2 table, there is a scan of the TKP_EXP_INDEX3 index with the scans rejecting tables owned by SYS and SYSTEM. Notice that cpu and elapsed increased. This increase was due to the increased number of index scans.

To achieve the results from the first query, we should be able to defeat the use of indexes by adding a zero to a number column or concatenating a null to a character column. Let's look at this and see if we can get back to the performance we want to achieve.

LISTING 14.6   Use of null concatenation to defeat indexes.

```
select
        username,
        default_tablespace,
        tablespace_name,
        object_name
from
        tkp_example, tkp_example2
where
        username not in ('SYS','SYSTEM') and
        default_tablespace||''=tablespace_name and
        owner||''=username

call     count   cpu  elapsed   disk   query    current       rows
------   -----   ----  -------  ------  -------  ----------  -----------
Parse        1   0.00    0.00       0        0           0            0
Execute      1   0.00    0.00       0        0           0            0
Fetch       54   0.51    0.51       0    10101           3          849
------   -----   ----  -------  ------  -------  ----------  -----------
total       56   0.51    0.51       0    10101           3          849
```

```
Misses in library cache during parse: 0
Optimizer goal: CHOOSE
Parsing user id: 5  (SYSTEM)

Rows       Execution Plan
-------    ----------------------------------------------------------------
      0    SELECT STATEMENT    GOAL: CHOOSE
    849    NESTED LOOPS
   5113      TABLE ACCESS (FULL) OF 'TKP_EXAMPLE2'
   8531      INDEX (RANGE SCAN) OF 'TMP_EXP_INDEX' (UNIQUE)
```

As Listing 14.6 shows, the index was still used. Look at the last section of the where clause. The order compares OWNER to USERNAME; this causes the TKP_EXAMPLE2 table to drive the query. If we switch the order of this comparison, we can use the shorter table TKP_EXAMPLE instead of TKP_EXAMPLE2. The index is still used, but the shorter table significantly reduces the query execution time.

LISTING 14.7   Results of switching the where order.

```
select
        username,
        default_tablespace,
        tablespace_name,
        object_name
from
        tkp_example, tkp_example2
where
        username not in ('SYS','SYSTEM') and
        default_tablespace||''=tablespace_name and
        username||''=owner
```

call	count	cpu	elapsed	disk	query	current	rows
Parse	1	0.00	0.00	0	0	0	0
Execute	1	0.00	0.00	0	0	0	0
Fetch	54	0.03	0.14	9	101	3	810
total	56	0.03	0.14	9	101	3	810

As you can see in Listing 14.7, performance is back to the levels we had before we created the indexes. Did the use of null concatenation really affect performance for this query? Leaving the where clause the same, let's go back to the standard comparison and see if the results change.

LISTING 14.8   Effects of the switched where clause and no null concatenation.

```
select
        username,
        default_tablespace,
        tablespace_name,
        object_name
from
        tkp_example, tkp_example2
where
        username not in ('SYS','SYSTEM') and
        default_tablespace=tablespace_name and
        username=owner

call     count    cpu  elapsed   disk   query   current        rows
------   -----  -----  -------  ------  ------- ----------  -----------
Parse        1   0.01     0.01       0        0          0            0
Execute      1   0.00     0.00       0        0          0            0
Fetch       57   0.35     0.35       0     6932          3          849
------   -----  -----  -------  ------  ------- ----------  -----------
total       59   0.36     0.36       0     6932          3          849

Misses in library cache during parse: 1
Optimizer goal: CHOOSE
Parsing user id: 5  (SYSTEM)

Rows      Execution Plan
-------   ------------------------------------------------------------
      0   SELECT STATEMENT    GOAL: CHOOSE
    849   NESTED LOOPS
   5113    TABLE ACCESS (FULL) OF 'TKP_EXAMPLE2'
   2738    INDEX (RANGE SCAN) OF 'TMP_EXP_INDEX' (UNIQUE)
```

As can be seen in Listing 14.8, the results look virtually identical to those we had before we switched the where clause. So for this type of statement it would be best to defeat as many indexes as possible and force execution driven by the shortest table.

In Oracle7 and Oracle8 the cost-based optimizer is also available. In order to use the cost-based optimizer all tables in the application that contain data should be analyzed. For larger tables, consider sampling only about 20 percent of the rows. For small tables, analyze the entire table. For our example, we will analyze all of the tables rows in each table. We will use our worst-performing query, from Listing 14.3, and see what results we get with the optimizer using cost- instead of rule-based optimization (see Listing 14.9).

LISTING 14.9   Example using cost-based optimizer.

```
select
        username,
        default_tablespace,
```

```
        tablespace_name,
        object_name
from
        tkp_example, tkp_example2
where
        username not in ('SYS','SYSTEM') and
        default_tablespace like tablespace_name and
        owner like username

call     count   cpu elapsed  disk    query    current        rows
------  -----  ----- -------  -----  --------  ----------  -----------
Parse       1   0.01   0.01      0         0           0            0
Execute     1   0.00   0.00      0         0           0            0
Fetch      57   0.55   0.55      0       588          57          849
------  -----  ----- -------  -----  --------  ----------  -----------
total      59   0.56   0.56      0       588          57          849

Misses in library cache during parse: 1
Optimizer goal: CHOOSE
Parsing user id: 5  (SYSTEM)


Rows        Execution Plan
-------     ------------------------------------------------------------
      0     SELECT STATEMENT    GOAL: CHOOSE
    849      NESTED LOOPS
     22       INDEX GOAL: ANALYZED (RANGE SCAN) OF 'TMP_EXP_INDEX'
              (UNIQUE)
  97147       TABLE ACCESS    GOAL: ANALYZED (FULL) OF
              'TKP_EXAMPLE2'
```

As you can see, the cost-based optimizer does a good job of performing optimization if its statistics are good. The performance here is similar to our midrange performance, however, notice that the table scans of TKP_EXAMPLE2 were excessive.

Again, this underscores the need to understand the application, the size and use of its tables, and how its indexes are constructed. If the DBA doesn't understand the application, the developer should tune the application with the DBA assisting.

When do indexes do us any good? If the query returns a small percentage of the table values an index will improve performance. An example of a restricted query with no index is shown in Listing 14.10, and with indexes in Listing 14.11.

LISTING 14.10 Restricted query with full table scans (no indexes).

```
select
        username,
        default_tablespace,
        tablespace_name,
        object_name
```

```
from
        tkp_example,
        tkp_example2
where
        username='SYSTEM' and
        default_tablespace=tablespace_name and
        owner=username

call     count   cpu elapsed   disk     query     current        rows
------   -----  ----- -------  -----  --------  ----------  -----------
Parse        1  0.00    0.00      0         0           0            0
Execute      1  0.00    0.00      0         0           0            0
Fetch        2  0.16    0.16      0        28           6           25
------   -----  ----- -------  -----  --------  ----------  -----------
total        4  0.16    0.16      0        28           6           25


Misses in library cache during parse: 1
Optimizer goal: CHOOSE
Parsing user id: 5  (SYSTEM)

Rows      Execution Plan
-------   -----------------------------------------------------------
      0   SELECT STATEMENT    GOAL: CHOOSE
     25    MERGE JOIN
   5113     SORT (JOIN)
   5113      TABLE ACCESS (FULL) OF 'TKP_EXAMPLE2'
      1     SORT (JOIN)
     21      TABLE ACCESS (FULL) OF 'TKP_EXAMPLE'
```

LISTING 14.11 Same query as in Listing 14.10 but using indexes.

```
select
        username,
        default_tablespace,
        tablespace_name,
        object_name
from
        tkp_example,
        tkp_example2
where
        username='SYSTEM' and
        default_tablespace=tablespace_name and
        owner=username

call     count   cpu elapsed   disk     query     current        rows
-----    -----  ----- -------  -----  --------  ----------  -----------
Parse        1  0.00    0.00      0         0           0            0
```

```
Execute   1  0.00    0.00     0        0          0          0
Fetch     2  0.00    0.00     0        5          0         25
-------  ---- ----  ------   ----   -------   ---------  ----------
total     4  0.00    0.00     0        5          0         25

Misses in library cache during parse: 0
Optimizer goal: CHOOSE
Parsing user id: 5  (SYSTEM)

Rows      Execution Plan
-------   --------------------------------------------------------
      0   SELECT STATEMENT    GOAL: CHOOSE
     25   NESTED LOOPS
      2    INDEX (RANGE SCAN) OF 'TKP_EXP_INDEX' (UNIQUE)
     26    INDEX (RANGE SCAN) OF 'TKP_EXP2_INDEX3' (UNIQUE)
```

As you can see, the performance gains, even for these small tables, is rather large, especially in regard to the number of rows processed per step.

An additional indicator of problems with a query is a high current-to-rows ratio. If this value exceeds 15, the query needs tuning.

So, what have we learned? First, statement tuning is complex. The optimizer built into the SQL processor makes choices based on built-in optimization rules that are based on statement rank in the rule-based optimizer, or on cost under the cost-based optimizer. At times, this optimizer doesn't always use the right index or truly optimize the statement.

For unrestricted queries that return most if not all of the values in a table or group of tables, use methods to restrict the use of indexes as much as possible. With unrestricted queries, start the where clause by restricting the values to be retrieved as much as possible as rapidly as possible. Try to get full table scans on small tables first and use their results to search other tables.

There is some debate whether placing the small table as the controlling table really improves performance. If the small table can be completely cached in memory, it may make more sense to drive from the larger table since multiblock reads can then be used rather than random reads, which may reread the same block several times. This would have the effect of reducing time-consuming physical block reads for the query. Since this will be application- and index-controlled, in situations where this happens use TKPROF to determine the facts before simply following a possibly outmoded rule.

Indexing guidelines. For restricted queries that retrieve a small percentage of the tables' entries, create indexes that will assist the query. The guidelines for indexing columns follow.

Index columns that are used frequently in where clauses, are used frequently in MIN or MAX selects, are used to join tables, or have high selectivity.

TIP   Remember, you can concatenate two low-selectivity columns to form a higher selectivity index than either column has singly.

Don't index columns in small tables (less than 5 blocks) or columns that don't have high selectivity or are frequently modified.

TIP   You never get something for nothing. The more indexes you have, the longer inserts, updates, and deletes will take. Optimizing queries doesn't gain you much if you pay a stiff penalty for update activity.

Concatenated indexes are only used when the predicate value is equality (i.e., e.jobname = f.jobname). The full key is only used if all the concatenated values are referenced in the where clause. If the concatenated key is used, only the leading edge of the columns is used. The new index type, bitmapped, should be used on low cardinality data where possible if that data is frequently accessed.

It would be wonderful if the rules for optimizing your tables, indexes, and queries could be simply stated and listed and you could be guaranteed that if they were followed your application would run as you hope. Unfortunately, this is not the case. Just when we think we have the proper cast on optimization Oracle will release a new version that throws a monkey wrench into our logic and makes us start again. As a DBA, you will have to keep abreast of changes to Oracle and filter the new ways of optimization down to the developers.

Query paths and ranks. The paths a query can take are ranked according to speed; the lower the rank, the higher the speed. The paths for the rule-based optimizer follow.

Rank	*Path*
1	Single row by ROWID
2	Single row by cluster join
3	Single row by hash cluster key with unique or primary key
4	Single row by unique or primary key
5	Cluster join
6	Hash cluster key
7	Indexed cluster key
8	Composite index
9	Single column index

10	Bounded range search on indexed columns
11	Unbounded range search on indexed columns
12	Sort-merge join
13	MAX or MIN on indexed column
14	ORDER BY indexed columns
15	Full table scan

Oracle7 and Oracle8 Optimizers and ANALYZE Under Oracle7 the optimizer uses cost-based optimization and can be forced to use rules-based optimization. Cost-based optimization assigns a cost to each possible execution path based on data distribution statistics for the objects used in the SQL statement being optimized. These statistics are loaded into the various object tables and views using the ANALYZE command.

Use of ANALYZE. For various applications, the ANALYZE command must be run on periodically, perhaps based on table growth. In systems using similar schemes, the analyzer had to be run for each 30 percent change in a table's contents. Note that this is for a change in contents, not just size. If a table has a fairly constant size but its contained data is being altered frequently, thus affecting the row size and index structure, then ANALYZE needs to be run on it as well. A simple script can be built using dynamic SQL that will analyze all the tables for a specific user. The script will resemble one of the scripts in Source 14.4.

SOURCE 14.4   Scripts to analyze tables and schemas.

```
Script to create a procedure for single table analysis:

CREATE OR REPLACE PROCEDURE analyze_table(table_name in VARCHAR2) AS
CURSOR get_index(tab_name varchar2) IS
   SELECT index_name FROM user_indexes
   WHERE table_name=tab_name;
i_name      index_stats.name%TYPE;
i_stats     .....index_stats%ROWTYPE;
cur1  INTEGER;
cur2  INTEGER;
processed    INTEGER;
com_strng    VARCHAR2(90);
BEGIN
   com_strng:='ANALYZE TABLE '||table_name||
             ' ESTIMATE STATISTICS SAMPLE 15 PERCENT';
   cur1:=dbms_sql.open_cursor;
   dbms_sql.parse(cur1,com_strng,dbms_sql.v7);
   processed:=dbms_sql.execute(cur1);
   dbms_sql.close_cursor(cur1);
   OPEN get_index(table_name);
```

```
      FETCH get_index INTO i_name;
      LOOP
   .        EXIT WHEN get_index%NOTFOUND;
            cur2:=dbms_sql.open_cursor;
            com_strng:='ANALYZE INDEX '||i_name||
                    ' VALIDATE STRUCTURE';
            dbms_sql.parse(cur2,com_strng,dbms_sql.v7);
            processed:=dbms_sql.execute(cur2);
            dbms_sql.close_cursor(cur2);
            INSERT INTO ind_stat_tab SELECT * FROM index_stats;
      END LOOP;
END;
/
```

Script to use DBMS_UTILITY package to analyze all schema in the database:

```
SET HEADING OFF VERIFY OFF PAGES 0 FEEDBACK OFF
TTITLE OFF
SPOOL analz_sch.sql
SELECT DISTINCT 'EXECUTE dbms_utility.analyze_schema(
'||chr(39)||owner||chr(39)||','||chr(39)||'&METHOD'||chr(39)||
','||&NUM_OF_ROWS||',
&PERCENT_TO_USE);'
FROM dba_tables WHERE owner NOT IN ('SYS','SYSTEM')
/
SPOOL OFF
SPOOL analz_sch.log
SET ECHO ON
START analz_sch.sql
SET ECHO OFF
SPOOL OFF
```

Procedure to analyze tables when contents increase/decrease >30percent:

```
CREATE OR REPLACE PROCEDURE check_tables (owner_name in varchar2) AS

CURSOR get_tab_count (own varchar2) IS
        SELECT table_name, nvl(num_rows,1)
        FROM dba_tables
        WHERE owner = upper(own);

tab_name        VARCHAR2(32);
rows            INTEGER;
string          VARCHAR2(255);
cur             INTEGER;
ret             INTEGER;
row_count       INTEGER;
com_string      VARCHAR2(255);

BEGIN
OPEN get_tab_count (owner_name);
```

```
LOOP
        FETCH get_tab_count INTO tab_name, rows;
        IF rows=0 THEN
          rows:=1;
        END IF;
EXIT WHEN get_tab_count%NOTFOUND;
dbms_output.put_line('Table name: '||tab_name||' rows: '||to_char(rows));
com_string :=
        'SELECT COUNT(*) from '||tab_name;
   cur := dbms_sql.open_cursor;
   dbms_sql.parse(cur,com_string,dbms_sql.v7);
   dbms_sql.define_column(cur,1,row_count);
   ret := dbms_sql.execute(cur);
   IF dbms_sql.fetch_rows(cur)>0 THEN
    dbms_sql.column_value(cur,1,row_count);
   END IF;
   dbms_sql.close_cursor(cur);
   IF row_count=0 THEN
        row_count:=1;
   END IF;
dbms_output.put_line('Row count for '||tab_name||': '||TO_CHAR(row_count));
dbms_output.put_line('Ratio: '||to_char(row_count/rows));
        IF ABS((row_count/rows))>1.42 THEN
           string :=
     'ANALYZE TABLE '||tab_name||' ESTIMATE STATISTICS SAMPLE 20 PERCENT';
           cur := dbms_sql.open_cursor;
           dbms_sql.parse(cur,string,dbms_sql.v7);
           ret := dbms_sql.execute(cur)   ;
           dbms_sql.close_cursor(cur);
           dbms_output.put_line(' Table: '||tab_name||' had to be
analyzed.');
        END IF;
END LOOP;
CLOSE get_tab_count;

EXCEPTION
   WHEN OTHERS THEN
      raise_application_error(-20002,'Error in analyze:
'||to_char(sqlcode)||' on '||tab_name,TRUE);
      IF dbms_sql.is_open(cur) THEN
        dbms_sql.close_cursor(cur);
      END IF;
END;
/
```

The DBA needs to watch the growth of the main tables in an application; the reports shown in Chapter 12 should provide the needed data. If the DBA isn't using an automated script like the one in Source 14.4, once the required threshold for percentage change is reached, the ANALYZE command should be run. The ANALYZE command format follows.

ANALYZE TABLE [schema.]table COMPUTE—or—ESTIMATE

   —or—INDEX [schema.]index

   —or—CLUSTER [schema.]schema

(for estimate) SAMPLE n ROWS—or—PERCENT

STATISTICS;

Where

COMPUTE	Calculates statistics on all rows; this may take a long time.
ESTIMATE	Calculates statistics based on the SAMPLE clause; if you don't specify the number of ROWS or a value for PERCENT, 1064 rows are sampled. If over 50 percent of the table is specified the entire table is computed.

The results are loaded into the SYS tables and can be examined via the DBA_, USER_ or ALL_ views. For an excellent discussion of how Oracle7 uses cost-based optimization, see Chapter 13 of the *Oracle7 Server Concepts Manual*.

T IP   There are other methods an application tuner can use to boost performance. The best tips follow.
   ▪ Use PL/SQL to speed processing. A PL/SQL statement is parsed once and allows loop processing. This reduces reparsing. The statements in a PL/SQL block are passed at the same time, reducing the number of ORDBMS calls.
   ▪ Use sequence generators. Sequence numbers are cached, speeding access to numbers used for keys or in applications for tracking entries. This eliminates the SQL calls used in a trigger that calls up the current MAX value and then increments it by 1.
   ▪ Use clusters for frequently joined tables. However, if the tables are frequently updated, clustering can have a negative effect on performance. Use the TKPROF tool to check a test database that is clustered versus one that is not clustered.
   ▪ Use array processing in applications where multiple values are required. This will reduce ORDBMS calls.

Use of Standalone EXPLAIN PLAN   The EXPLAIN PLAN program can be used in standalone fashion without the TKPROF application. In order to use EXPLAIN PLAN in this way, the user must create a "PLAN" table in his or her tablespace. This can either be done with the supplied SQL script UTLXPLAN.SQL, which is located in the directory pointed at by the ORA_RDBMS logical in VMS or in the oracle/rdbms/admin directory on most UNIX systems.

The UTLXPLAN.SQL procedure creates the PLAN_TABLE. As an alternative, the user can create a table with any name he or she chooses, but the table must have the columns and data types shown in Source 14.5.

SOURCE 14.5   Contents of the Explain Plan table.

```
        Characteristics of file to hold EXPLAIN PLAN output:
CREATE TABLE plan_table
        (statement_id      VARCHAR2(30),
        timestamp          DATE,
        remarks            VARCHAR2(80),
        operation          VARCHAR2(30),
        options            VARCHAR2(30),
        object_node        VARCHAR2(128),
        object_owner       VARCHAR2(30),
        object_name        VARCHAR2(30),
        object_instance    NUMERIC,
        object_type        VARCHAR2(30),
        optimizer          VARCHAR2(255),
        search_columns     NUMERIC,
        id                 NUMERIC,
        parent_id          NUMERIC,
        position           NUMERIC,
        cost               NUMERIC,
        cardinality        NUMERIC,
        bytes              NUMERIC,
        other_tag          VARCHAR2(255)
         other             LONG);
```

The PLAN_TABLE used by the EXPLAIN PLAN command contains the following columns:

STATEMENT_ID	The value of the option STATEMENT_ID parameter specified in the EXPLAIN PLAN statement.
TIMESTAMP	The date and time when the EXPLAIN PLAN statement was issued.
REMARKS	Any comment (of up to 80 bytes) you wish to associate with each step of the explained plan. If you need to add or change a remark on any row of the PLAN_TABLE, use the UPDATE statement to modify the rows of the PLAN_TABLE.
OPERATION	The name of the internal operation performed in this step. In the first row generated for a statement, the column contains one of the following values:

'DELETE STATEMENT'

'INSERT STATEMENT'

'SELECT STATEMENT'

'UPDATE STATEMENT'

OPTIONS	A variation on the operation described in the OPERA-TION column.
OBJECT_NODE	The name of the database link used to reference the object (a table name or view name). For local queries using the parallel query option, this column describes the order in which output from operations is consumed.
OBJECT_OWNER	The name of the user who owns the schema containing the table or index.
OBJECT_NAME	The name of the table or index.
OBJECT_INSTANCE	A number corresponding to the ordinal position of the object as it appears in the original statement. The numbering proceeds from left to right, outer to inner with respect to the original statement text. Note that view expansion will result in unpredictable numbers.
OBJECT_TYPE	A modifier that provides descriptive information about the object; for example, NONUNIQUE for indexes.
OPTIMIZER	The current mode of the optimizer.
SEARCH_COLUMNS	Not currently used.
ID	A number assigned to each step in the execution plan.
PARENT_ID	The ID of the next execution step that operates on the output of the ID step.
POSITION	The order of processing for steps that all have the PARENT_ID.
OTHER	Other information that is specific to the execution step, which a user may find useful.
OTHER_TAG	Describes the contents of the OTHER column. More information on the possible values for this column is given later.
PARTITION_START	The start partition of a range of accessed partitions.
PARTITION_STOP	The stop partition of a range of accessed partitions.
PARTITION_ID	The step that has computed the pair of values of the PARTITION_START and PARTITION_STOP columns.
COST	The cost of the operation as estimated by the optimizer's cost-based approach. For statements that use the rule-based approach, this column is null. Cost is not determined for table access operations. The value of this column does not have any particular unit of measurement; it is merely a weighted value used to compare costs of execution plans.

CARDINALITY   The estimate by the cost-based approach of the number of rows accessed by the operation.

BYTES   The estimate by the cost-based approach of the number of bytes accessed by the operation.

The next section describes the values that may appear in the OTHER_TAG column.

OTHER_TAG Text	Interpretation
(blank)	serial execution
serial_from_remote	serial execution at a remote site
serial_to_parallel	serial execution; output of step is partitioned or broadcast to parallel query servers
parallel_to_parallel	parallel execution; output of step is repartitioned to second set of parallel query servers
parallel_to_serial	parallel execution; output of step is returned to serial "query coordinator" process
parallel_combined_with_parent	parallel execution; output of step goes to next step in same parallel process. No interprocess communication to parent
parallel_combined_with_child	parallel execution; input of step comes from prior step in same parallel process. No interprocess communication from child

The TKPROF section lists each combination of OPERATION and OPTION values produced by the EXPLAIN PLAN command as well as its meaning within an execution plan.

When TKPROF is run using the EXPLAIN option, the table is created and dropped automatically. If it is created for use in EXPLAIN PLAN, it is permanent. The table should have the DELETE command issued against it between runs of EXPLAIN PLAN or duplicate rows will be inserted into the table and into any output generated based on the table.

Once this table is generated, the user issues the EXPLAIN PLAN command from within SQLPLUS to generate output to the table. The EXPLAIN PLAN command format follows.

EXPLAIN PLAN [SET STATEMENT_ID = 'descriptor']
    [INTO table]
FOR SQL statement;

Where

descriptor table   This is a short name to identify the SQL statement by. If not specified, the entire statement will be used as the identifier. If other than the PLAN_TABLE is used, this is where it is named.

SQL statement   This is the SQL statement to analyze.

An example of the use of the EXPLAIN PLAN command is shown in Source 14.6.

SOURCE 14.6   Example use of the EXPLAIN PLAN command.

```
SQL> explain plan
   2  set statement_id='EXP PLAN EXAMPLE'
   3  for
   4  select t.owner,t.table_name,t.tablespace_name,
   5  i.index_name,i.tablespace_name
   6  from tkp_example t, tkp_example2 i
   7  where
   8  t.table_name=i.table_name and
   9  t.owner not in ('SYS','SYSTEM')
  10*

Explained.
```

To get the results of the EXPLAIN PLAN command, the table PLAN_TABLE, or whatever table was specified in the EXPLAIN PLAN command, must be queried. Let's look at a simple query of this table for the preceding SQL statement. The query and output from the query are shown in Source 14.7. While this type of query will provide useful information, it leaves the logical arrangement of the information retrieved to the user. By using the padding options and connect features available in SQL the user can generate a pseudoexecution plan comparable to the one generated in the TKPROF command. The query used for this and the output generated in place of the tabular information in Source 14.7 are shown in Source 14.8.

This new format, shown in Source 14.8, is easier to understand. The TKPROF output for each statement also needs to be reviewed, as was shown in the first part of this chapter. Just because index rather than table scans are used doesn't mean the query executed faster. If the index is not a bitmapped index and is not selective, using index can actually slow a query rather than speed it up.

SOURCE 14.7   Example query of the PLAN_TABLE.

```
SQL> column position format 99999999
SQL> column object_name format a12
SQL> column options format a7
SQL> column operation format a15
```

```
SQL> select operation, options, object_name, id,  parent_id,
  2  position
  3  from plan_table
  4  where statement_id='EXP PLAN EXAMPLE'
  5* order by id

OPERATION        OPTIONS OBJECT_NAME        ID PARENT_ID  POSITION
---------------- ------- ----------------- -- ---------  --------
SELECT STATEMENT                            0
MERGE JOIN                                  1         0         1
SORT             JOIN                       2         1         1
TABLE ACCESS     FULL    TKP_EXAMPLE2       3         2         1
SORT             JOIN                       4         1         2
TABLE ACCESS     FULL    TKP_EXAMPLE        5         4         1

6 rows selected
```

SOURCE 14.8   SQL statement to generate an execution plan from the PLAN_TABLE.

```
SQL> column query_plan format a60
SQL> select lpad(' ',2*level)||operation||' '||object_name query_plan
  2  from plan_table where statement_id is not null
  3  connect by prior id=parent_id
  4  start with id=0;

QUERY_PLAN
-----------------------------------------------------------
  SELECT STATEMENT
    MERGE JOIN
      SORT
        TABLE ACCESS TKP_EXAMPLE2
      SORT
        TABLE ACCESS TKP_EXAMPLE

6 rows selected.
```

One thing to remember is that these plans need to be read from the bottom up; for example, in the plan in Source 14.8, the TKP_EXAMPLE table is accessed and all rows that don't have the OWNER SYS or SYSTEM are retrieved. Then, the TKP_EXAMPLE2 table is accessed for each row in the TKP_EXAMPLE table; all rows that have matches in the TABLE_NAME column are selected. The results for both accesses are then sorted and merged to form the final output.

The Oracle8 table also has columns to document if partitions are being used, and this data can be added to the select statement if desired as well as a number of other columns that you may find useful.

Use of the UTLSIDXS Utility Another tuning tool provided with Oracle is the UTLSIDXS utility. This utility consists of three scripts, UTLSIDXS.SQL, UTLOIDXS.SQL, and UTLDIDXS.SQL, under Oracle7 and Oracle8. These scripts are located in the directory specified in the ORA_RDBMS logical under VMS, in the oracle/rdbms/admin directory on most UNIX systems, and in the x:\orant\ rdbms80\admin directory on NT4.0 (replace the X with the drive letter where you installed Oracle). These scripts provide detailed statistics on indexes used for a specific table.

The scripts provide the following functionality:

UTLSIDX.SQL	This script starts the UTLOIDXS.SQL script on multiple tables and columns. It requires the input of the table name and the column name. Its main use is to provide the selectivity information on key candidates.
UTLOIDXS.SQL	This script is called by UTLSIDXS.SQL.
UTLDIDXS.SQL	This script is run after UTLOIDXS.SQL is run. It takes the same arguments as UTLSIDX.SQL and can take "%" as a wild card value. UTLDIDXS.SQL generates a report based on the statistics. The report is only shown on screen; to have hard-copy output you must modify the script to add SPOOL and SPOOL OFF statements.

To use the scripts, the tables and columns must exist. The scripts are used on single-column indexes, generally speaking. To run the scripts on a concatenated index, create a test table that consists of a single column that simulates the concatenated index as a single column. For example, if your index is on po_num, po_date create a test table that concatenates these into a single column:

```
CREATE TABLE test_index AS SELECT po_num||po_date  po_ind FROM
purchase_order;
```

Once the test table is created, the script is run the same as if the user were analyzing a normal single-column index candidate. This is essentially a three-step process:

1. Choose the candidate columns from the table.
2. Log on to SQLPLUS and run UTLSIDXS.SQL for entire applications and UTLOIDXS.SQL for single tables, giving UTLOIDXS.SQL the table and column name.
3. Use UTLDIDXS.SQL to generate a report on the index candidate(s).

An example run of UTLSIDXS, including an example UTLDIDXS report, is shown in Source 14.9.

SOURCE 14.9   Example use of UTLSIDXS, UTLOIDXS, and UTLDIDXS.

```
SQL> @c:\orawin95\rdbms73\admin\utloidxs tkp_example owner

TKP_EXAMPLE OWNER

SQL> @c:\orawin95\rdbms73\admin\utldidxs tkp_example owner

TAB_NAME                              COL_NAME
------------------------------        -------------------------------
TKP_EXAMPLE                           OWNER

TABLE_NAME       COLUMN_NAME      STAT_NAME                  STAT_VALUE
-----------      ---------------  ----------------------     ----------
TKP_EXAMPLE      OWNER            Rows - Null                      0.00
TKP_EXAMPLE      OWNER            Rows - Total                1,366.00
TKP_EXAMPLE      OWNER            Rows per key - avg            341.50
TKP_EXAMPLE      OWNER            Rows per key - dev            251.68
TKP_EXAMPLE      OWNER            Rows per key - max            658.00
TKP_EXAMPLE      OWNER            Rows per key - min             42.00
TKP_EXAMPLE      OWNER            Total Distinct Keys             4.00
TKP_EXAMPLE      OWNER            db_gets_per_key_hit           240.55
TKP_EXAMPLE      OWNER            db_gets_per_key_miss          480.61

TABLE_NAME   COLUMN_NAME BADNESS KEYS_COUNT ROW_PERCENT KEY_PRCNT
-----------  ----------- ------- ---------- ----------- ----------
TKP_EXAMPLE  OWNER           658          1       48.17      25.00
TKP_EXAMPLE  OWNER           335          1       24.52      25.00
TKP_EXAMPLE  OWNER           331          1       24.23      25.00
TKP_EXAMPLE  OWNER            42          1        3.08      25.00

SQL> @c:\orawin95\rdbms73\admin\utloidxs tkp_example object_name

TKP_EXAMPLE     OBJECT_NAME

SQL> @c:\orawin95\rdbms73\admin\utldidxs tkp_example object_name

TAB_NAME                              COL_NAME
------------------------------        -------------------------------
TKP_EXAMPLE                           OBJECT_NAME

TABLE_NAME    COLUMN_NAME STAT_NAME                          STAT_VALUE
------------  ----------- ---------------------              ----------
TKP_EXAMPLE   OBJECT_NAME Rows - Null                              0.00
TKP_EXAMPLE   OBJECT_NAME Rows - Total                         1,366.00
TKP_EXAMPLE   OBJECT_NAME Rows per key - avg                        1.24
TKP_EXAMPLE   OBJECT_NAME Rows per key - dev                        0.47
TKP_EXAMPLE   OBJECT_NAME Rows per key - max                        3.00
TKP_EXAMPLE   OBJECT_NAME Rows per key - min                        1.00
TKP_EXAMPLE   OBJECT_NAME Total Distinct Keys                   1,102.00
TKP_EXAMPLE   OBJECT_NAME db_gets_per_key_hit                       1.04
```

```
TKP_EXAMPLE   OBJECT_NAME db_gets_per_key_miss                    1.41

TABLE_NAME    COLUMN_NAME BADNESS KEYS_COUNT ROW_PERCENT KEY_PRCNT
-----------   ----------- ------- ---------- ----------- ---------
TKP_EXAMPLE OBJECT_NAME         3         19        4.17      1.72
TKP_EXAMPLE OBJECT_NAME         2        226       33.09     20.51
TKP_EXAMPLE OBJECT_NAME         1        857       62.74     77.77
```

As you can see by examining the preceding UTLDIDXS reports, OWNER would not make a very good index. It has a low selectivity, and its db_gets_per_key_hits is 50 percent lower than its db_gets_per_key_misses, which means it misses a row twice as much as it finds it. This is further witnessed by its high badness of 143 and low keys_count, where the badness is low (badness ratings are summarized by the number of keys that exhibit that amount of badness). On the other hand, TABLE_NAME makes a good index because of its high selectivity, its nearly unity hit/miss ratio, and its low badness ratings. But how often will we look for a table strictly by its name? What would the performance be if we made a concatenated index of both OWNER and TABLE_NAME? Let's find out in Source 14.10.

SOURCE 14.10 Example test of a pseudoconcatenated index.

```
SQL> REM CONCAT_INDEX is a table made by selecting
SQL> REM "owner||object_name||object_type" into
SQL> REM column ONE_COL. The column values are selected from SQL> REM
TKP_EXAMPLE. It shows the performance of a concatenated SQL> REM index on
these three columns.
SQL>
SQL> create table concat_index as
  2  select owner||object_name||object_type one_col
  3* from tkp_example

SQL> @c:\orawin95\rdbms73\admin\utloidxs concat_index one_col

CONCAT_INDEX    ONE_COL

SQL> @c:\orawin95\rdbms73\admin\utldidxs concat_index one_col

TAB_NAME                         COL_NAME
------------------------------   ------------------------------
CONCAT_INDEX                     ONE_COL

TABLE_NAME  COLUMN_NAME STAT_NAME                   STAT_VALUE
----------- ----------- --------------------------- ----------
CONCAT_INDEX ONE_COL    Rows - Null                       0.00
CONCAT_INDEX ONE_COL    Rows - Total                  1,366.00
CONCAT_INDEX ONE_COL    Rows per key - avg                1.00
CONCAT_INDEX ONE_COL    Rows per key - dev                0.00
```

```
CONCAT_INDEX ONE_COL     Rows per key - max              1.00
CONCAT_INDEX ONE_COL     Rows per key - min              1.00
CONCAT_INDEX ONE_COL     Total Distinct Keys         1,366.00
CONCAT_INDEX ONE_COL     db_gets_per_key_hit            1.00
CONCAT_INDEX ONE_COL     db_gets_per_key_miss           1.00

TABLE_NAME    COLUMN_NAME BADNESS KEYS_COUNT ROW_PRCNT KEY_PRCNT
------------  ----------- ------- ---------- --------- ---------
CONCAT_INDEX ONE_COL            1      1,366    100.00    100.00
```

As can be seen by making the same comparisons as with either OWNER or OBJECT_NAME, this new concatenated index would perform better than either of the previous single-column indexes. It has the added benefit of allowing us to search on OWNER with no performance penalties. In fact, in a simple query looking for OWNER's and OBJECT_NAME's performance should be much better since it can be resolved completely in the index.

Using Hints in Oracle7 to Force Behavior   One important feature of Oracle is the ability to issue hints to the optimizer. In Oracle7 and Oracle8 you can tell the optimizer directly to use a specific type of action for your queries. This gives the DBA or application developer more control than was ever possible in earlier versions. Let's look at how this feature is used.

Hints are enclosed within comments to the SQL commands DELETE, SELECT, or UPDATE or are designated by two dashes and a plus sign. To show the format only the SELECT statement will be used, but the format is identical for all three commands.

```
SELECT      /*+ hint -or- text */
[statement body]
```

or

```
SELECT      -+ hint -or- text
[statement body]
```

Where

/*   This is the comment delimiter.

+   This tells Oracle a hint follows; it must come immediately after the /*.

hint   This is one of the allowed hints.

text   This is the comment text.

Hint: Meaning:

+   Must be immediately after the comment indicator; tells Oracle this is a list of hints.

ALL_ROWS	Use the cost-based approach for best throughput.
CHOOSE	Default; if statistics are available will use cost; if not, rule.
FIRST_ROWS	Use the cost-based approach for best response time.
RULE	Use rules-based approach; this cancels any other hints specified for this statement. This will not be available after Oracle7.

Access method hints:

CLUSTER(table)	This tells Oracle to explicitly do a cluster scan to access the table.
FULL(table)	This tells the optimizer to do a full scan of the specified table.
HASH(table)	Tells Oracle to explicitly choose the hash access method for the table.
HASH_AJ(table)	Transforms a NOT IN subquery to a hash anti-join.
ROWID(table)	Forces a ROWID scan of the specified table.
INDEX(table [index])	Forces an index scan of the specified table using the specified index(s). If a list of indexes is specified, the optimizer chooses the one with the lowest cost. If no index is specified, then the optimizer chooses the available index for the table with the lowest cost.
INDEX_ASC (table [index])	Same as INDEX, only it performs an ascending search of the index chosen; this is functionally identical to the INDEX statement.
INDEX_DESC(table [index])	Same as INDEX except it performs a descending search. If more than one table is accessed, this is ignored.
INDEX_COMBINE(table index)	Combines the bitmapped indexes on the table if the cost shows that to do so would give better performance.
INDEX_FFS(table index)	Performs a fast full index scan rather than a table scan.
MERGE_AJ (table)	Transforms a NOT IN subquery into a merge antijoin.

USE_CONCAT	Forces combined OR conditions in the where-clause to be transformed into a compound query using the UNION ALL set operator.
AND_EQUAL(table index index [index index index])	
	This hint causes a merge on several single-column indexes. Two must be specified; five can be.

Hints for join orders:

ORDERED	This hint forces tables to be joined in the order specified. If you know table X has fewer rows, then ordering it first may speed execution in a join.
STAR	Forces the largest table to be joined last using a nested_loops join on the index.

Hints for join operations:

NO_MERGE (table)	This causes Oracle to join each specified table with another row source without a sort-merge join.
USE_HASH (table)	This causes Oracle to join each specified table with another row source with a hash join.
USE_NL(table)	This operation forces a nested loop using the specified table as the controlling table.
USE_MERGE(table,[table, . . .])	This operation forces a sort-merge-join operation of the specified tables.

Hints for parallel operations:

APPEND NOAPPEND	This specifies that data is to be appended or not appended to the end of a file rather than into existing free space. Use only with INSERT commands.
NOPARALLEL (table)	This specifies the operation is not to be done in parallel.
PARALLEL(table, instances)	This specifies the operation is to be done in parallel.
PARALLEL_INDEX	Allows parallelization of a fast full index scan on any index.

Other hints:

CACHE	Specifies that the blocks retrieved for the table in the hint are placed at the most recently used end of the LRU list when the table is full table scanned.
NOCACHE	Specifies that the blocks retrieved for the table in the hint are placed at the least recently used end of the LRU list when the table is full table scanned.
PUSH_SUBQ	This causes nonmerged subqueries to be evaluated at the earliest possible point in the execution plan.

As you can see, our dilemma in the first part of this chapter with the stubborn index usage could have been easily solved using hints. You must know the application to be tuned. The DBA can provide guidance to developers, but in all but the smallest development projects it will be nearly impossible for a DBA to know everything about each application. It is clear that responsibility for application tuning rests solely on the developer's shoulders with help and guidance from the DBA.

14.2 SUGGESTED ADDITIONAL READING

If you want more detailed information about using TKPROF, EXPLAIN PLAN, Rule- and Cost-based optimization, the following references are suggested:

Developer Tuning: Now You Are the Expert!, Richard J. Niemiec, TUSC, IOUG-A Alive!, Dallas, Texas, 1997, Paper No. 136.

Explain Plan: An Aid to Query Optimization, H. Sankar and M. Fardoost, Oracle Corporation, IOUG Proceedings, 1992 IOUG Symposium, Los Angeles, California.

Explain Plan: Everything You Wanted to Know and Had No One to Ask, Eyal Aronoff, Kevin Loney, and Noorali Sonawalla, ECO 97, Boston, Massachusetts, Paper No. 147.

How to Translate TKPROFS and IDXSTAT into Meaningful Applications Changes, M. C. Manton, III, TESTMARK, IOUG Proceedings, 1991 IOUG Symposium, Miami, Florida.

Identifying and Improving Expensive SQL Statements, J. J. Ecker and Michael Speights, Practical Database Solutions, Database Solutions, IOUG-A Alive! Dallas, Texas, 1997, Paper No. 89.

Optimizing Distributed Queries, A. Bakker, Oracle Netherlands, IOUG Proceedings, 1992 IOUG Symposium, Los Angeles, California.

Optimizing Query Performance in Oracle7, E. Peeler, Oracle Corporation, IOUG Proceedings, 1992 IOUG Symposium, Los Angeles, California.

Oracle for UNIX Performance Tuning Tips, C. Boeheim, Oracle Corporation, part number 53134-0293, February 1993.

Oracle7 Server Concepts Manual, Chapter 13, Oracle Corporation, part number A20321-2, March 1995.

Oracle7 Server Tuning, part number A25421-1, Oracle Corporation, April 1995.

Oracle8 Server Concepts, Release 8.0, Beta2, part number A50654-1, Oracle Corporation, February 1997.

Oracle8 Server SQL Reference, Release 8.0, Beta2, part number A50605-1, Oracle Corporation, February 1997.

Oracle8 Server Tuning, Release 8.0, Beta2, part number A50660-1, Oracle Corporation, February 1997.

Performance Comparisons Using Bitmap Indexes, Hash Clusters, and Histograms, Pete W. Cassidy, Database Consulting, Inc., IOUG-A Alive! Dallas, Texas, 1997, Paper No. 23.

Performance Optimization through SQL Query Decomposition Testing, R. J. Rausch, Pacific Bell Directory, IOUG Proceedings, 1991 IOUG Symposium, Miami, Florida.

Performance Optimization: The Next Step, R. J. Rausch, Pacific Bell Directory, IOUG Proceedings, 1992 IOUG Symposium, Los Angeles, California.

Put the Smallest Table Last and Other Tuning Myths, M. Gardner, Oracle Corporation, IOUG Proceedings, 1991 IOUG Symposium, Miami, Florida.

Query and Application Tuning Using EXPLAIN and TKPROF Utility, D. L. Presley, Oracle Corporation, IOUG Proceedings, 1991 IOUG Symposium, Miami, Florida.

CHAPTER 15

Database Internals Tuning

Database internals tuning is a complex topic. Every time you think you have Oracle internals figured out Oracle slips in some new features, takes old ones away, or, from some perverse sense of fun, changes the structures of tried-and-true tables and views. Actually, it's all a secret plot between senior Oracle DBAs and Oracle to maintain job security.

This chapter will cover one of the more challenging and critical aspects of the DBA's job, analyzing, diagnosing, and fixing database internals performance problems. Chapter 14 discussed application tuning. You will get a majority of the performance gains in an application from proper database configuration and application tuning. However, where you will be most exposed is in the area of internals tuning. Squeezing that last bit of performance from the database seems to be the one area managers like to focus on when there are problems (they forgot the bit about application tuning and now expect you to work miracles).

As mentioned at the end of the last chapter, once the application is tuned, the DBA's job really begins. Now you can begin tuning the Oracle system itself to take advantage of the tuned application discussed in Chapter 14. This step of the tuning process is typically a five-part process:

1. Reviewing and setting all initialization parameters for your application and operating system.
2. Tuning memory allocation.
3. Eliminating IO bottlenecks.
4. Tuning resource contention.
5. Tuning sorts, free lists, and checkpoints.

The first step involves reading the operating system-specific release manual and database readme files for any new, changed, or improved initialization parameters. Using your knowledge of the number of users, the size of the system memory, the number and configuration of disks, the sizing of tables, and other system and application parameters, you must do your best to set all of the initialization parameters that will help your system perform better.

The second step requires an up-and-operating database against which you run various performance monitoring scripts and tools and then readjust the initialization parameters.

The third step requires monitoring your disk assets and their performance. Your system administrator will be critical to assuring the success of this step. Hopefully, if you were able to have a hand in designing the system layout you won't have much IO-related tuning. An inherited database (especially those from aftermarket products) usually requires extensive file movements and optimizations so this step could actually give the most performance gains.

In one system I inherited, a well-meaning DBA had rebuilt the application indexes by disabling and then reenabling the primary keys, without specifying the location for the indexes. Of course, you will remember what this causes—all of the indexes were in the same tablespace as the data tables. Simply moving the indexes to their (empty) tablespace resulted in an over 300 percent performance gain (one 30-minute query dropped to less than a minute). I was an instant hero. What this anecdote should tell you is that you should carefully examine any inherited database for badly placed indexes, tablespaces, rollback segments, and redo logs. Just putting everything where it should be can provide dramatic improvements in performance for badly laid-out systems.

Step four involves more monitoring with tools or scripts. Contention for system resources (latches, rollbacks, logs, memory, etc.) can be a real performance drain. Always review the alert log for all databases you inherit; they will tell you if there are some forms of contention such as for redo logs. The scripts that follow will help determine if there are other types of contention.

Step five will involve monitoring system statistics on a running application. There are numerous tools as well as the scripts included with this section that will tell you if you have problems with sorts, free lists, and checkpoints. Tuning sorts is especially important in DSS and reporting databases. In one case, a 10-minute sort dropped to less than a minute by bumping up the SORT_AREA_SIZE parameter from two to three megabytes, thus preventing disk sorts.

The following sections each discuss a specific area with reports and scripts to help you monitor your database.

15.1　THE UTLBSTAT AND UTLESTAT SCRIPTS AND THEIR USE

Oracle provides the UTLBSTAT.SQL and UTLESTAT.SQL scripts to assist the DBA in tuning the database internals. These scripts take a beginning snapshot (BSTAT) and an ending snapshot (ESTAT) of database statistics and generate a set of difference reports.

Use of UTLESTAT/UTLBSTAT

After shutting down the database, setting the TIMED_STATISTICS parameter of the initialization file to TRUE, and then restarting the database, the script UTLBSTAT is run from the SQLDBA, SVRMGR, or the SQL Worksheet under the SYS user after the database has reached equilibrium (i.e., after the database has been started and the buffers and caches have stabilized). If you don't wait until the database has reached a steady-state condition, the statistics will reflect "startup noise" from the various process startups and will not give a true baseline. Once UTLBSTAT has been run, the application you wish to test is then run through its paces. When you are satisfied that the application has been fully wrung out under as close to actual running conditions as possible (a one-user test of a 20-user application isn't going to tell you much), run the UTLESTAT script, again from SQLDBA, SVRMGR, or the SQL Worksheet from the SYS user. The UTLESTAT script calculates various statistics for the database and generates several reports that can then be used for tuning. Let's look at these reports and see how they can help with the various aspects of tuning.

The UTLBSTAT/UTLESTAT script reports. Listing 15.1 shows the first of the UTLBSTAT/UTLESTAT reports. These reports cover virtually every aspect of internals and general database tuning.

TIP   The first line of both reports is a connect internal. If you are using password files (such as on NT) then you must either edit the file to include the password or remove this line and just log in before you run it. Sometimes in trying to "help," Oracle makes our jobs harder.

UTLESTAT Cache Report   The first report is the library caches report. The DBA should pay attention to the hit ratios and the reloads and invalidations. Essentially, the hit ratios should be as close as possible to 1; values less than .80 are too low(assuming the GETS and PINS values have significantly high values). The RELOADS should be as close to zero as possible, as should the INVALIDATIONS. If the caches aren't big enough then when a statement needs to be parsed and Oracle can't find room an old statement is aged out. If the statement that was aged from the cache is then needed again, it has to be reloaded, which is not good. INVALIDATIONS happen when a table, index, procedure, or other object becomes invalid. Usually, invalidations don't happen in a production environment, but they can be significant in a development arena.

As far as tuning for latches, it is actually very simple; increase the size of the initialization parameter SHARED_POOL_SIZE, which on the next startup of the database will automatically increase the sizes of the cache regions.

LISTING 15.1   Library cache report from UTLESTAT.SQL.

```
LIBRARY GETS     GETHITRATIO  PINS   PINHITRATIO  RELOADS   INVALIDATES
-------  ------   -----------  -----  -----------  -------   -----------
BODY         8              1      8            1        0             0
CLUSTER      7              1     11            1        0             0
INDEX        0              1      0            1        0             0
OBJECT       0              1      0            1        0             0
PIPE         0              1      0            1        0             0
SQL AREA   434           .963   1432         .977        0             9
TABLE/PROC  42           .905    104         .942        0             0
TRIGGER      0              1      0            1        0             0
8 rows selected.
```

UTLESTAT Session Statistics Report   The next report is session-based statistics. An example of this report is shown in Listing 15.2. The important statistics are as follows:

- **consistent changes**   This is the number of times a block was changed and/or rollback had to be read for a transaction to have consistent reads. If this figure is high this could indicate there were long-running updates during prime usage times.
- **consistent gets**   If a block is acquired in a consistent mode, this increments. The statistic is incremented for each block read in a full table scan and by the height of any indexes that are scanned. The statistic increments for each block read in an index-only read as well.
- **db block changes**   This is the total number of used or dirty blocks in the buffer cache. The term dirty means the block has been changed. Even if multiple rows in a block are changed this counts only as one block change. This statistic will also give an indication of the amount of redo used for the BSTAT/ESTAT period.
- **db block gets**   This indicates the number of blocks read for update, such as updates to temporary segment headers, rollback segments, index segments as well as extent allocation or high- water-mark update.
- **DBWR checkpoints**   If this number gets to be excessive then you should consider starting up a checkpoint process using the CHECKPOINT_PROCESSES initialization parameter to relieve the DBWR process of the checkpoint duties. If for some reason you don't want another process, adjust the LOG_CHECKPOINT_INTERVAL and LOG_CHECKPOPINT_TIMEOUT initialization parameter to reduce the number of checkpoints. The size of your redo logs also has an effect on the checkpoint frequency. Generally speaking, you only want a checkpoint at log

switch time; therefore set LOG_CHECKPOINT_TIMEOUT to zero (0), which actually means infinite, and LOG_CHECKPOINT_INTERVAL to a size larger than your redo log size in blocks.

- **DBWR timeouts**   Every three seconds the DBWR scans the buffer cache looking for dirty buffers to write (not really important for database tuning).
- **DBWR make free requests**   This statistic can be used to determine if DB_BLOCK_BUFFERS is tuned correctly. If you increase DB_BLOCK_BUFFERS and this statistic decreases substantially then it shows you needed more buffers. It increments each time a request is made to the buffer cache to clean up so more data can be loaded (i.e., there wasn't enough free space available without removing items from the least-used side of the LRU list).
- **DBWR free buffers found**   This statistic shows the number of times that DBWR found free buffers on the LRU list. Free buffers can either be clean—they don't have to be written to disk—or dirty—they do have to be written before they can be used again. To find the percentage of buffers that were clean calculate

```
(DBWR free buffers found / DBWR make free requests) * 100
```

- **free buffer waits**   This statistic shows the number of times a free buffer was requested and none were available. If this statistic shows excessive values (i.e., continues to increase after startup and during application activity) then you need to increase DB_BLOCK_BUFFERS.
- **physical reads and physical writes**   These tell how many times the database reads from or writes to the disks. Each is incremented only once for each read or write regardless of the number of blocks read or written in the read or write operation (one increment for each DB_FILE_MULTIBLOCK_READ_COUNT).
- **recursive calls**   This statistic tells you the number of times the database had to use dynamic extension and make recursive calls to the library caches. If this parameter seems excessive, check your object sizing and increase SHARED_POOL_SIZE.
- **redo log space requests**   This statistic tells you that a session or process had to wait for a redo log. It can indicate that you have redo logs that are too small or that you don't have enough redo log groups. Usually this is caused by the logs filling faster than the log writer can write them to disk. Ideally, this statistic should be as close to zero as possible (on many of the systems I manage it is at zero, so it can be done).
- **sorts(disk)**   This indicates that the size of a sort exceeded SORT_AREA_SIZE and the sort had to be completed using the temporary tablespace for the user. Ideally, this should be zero. If you see a ratio of (sorts(disk) / (sorts(memory) + sorts(disk)) that is greater than 0.01, increase your SORT_AREA_SIZE. However, having said this, let me also tell you that the SORT_AREA_SIZE for non-MTS systems is assigned to each user when they log in to Oracle so a tradeoff between disk sorts and SORT_AREA_SIZE may have to be made on memory-poor systems. In MTS systems, the SORT_AREA_SIZE comes out of the SHARED POOL on

Oracle7 systems and, if it is configured, the LARGE POOL on Oracle8 systems, so be sure to size these areas for the number of users you expect.

- **table fetch continued row** This indicates row chaining if it is greater than zero. If it is small in comparison to "table fetch by ROWID" then don't worry. But if it exceeds 1 to 2 percent you should consider evaluating all tables with VARCHAR2 variables for row chaining. Also, adjust PCTFREE to a higher value for affected tables. If you use LONG values, you may want to increase the size of your database blocks (DB_BLOCK_SIZE); but, remember, to do this you must rebuild the entire database.

- **table scans (short tables)** This tells the number of rows read from the table whose size was smaller than _SMALL_TABLE_THRESHOLD. Yes, the leading underscore is part of the parameter. In earlier versions this was a documented parameter; in Oracle7 (later versions) and Oracle8 it is now undocumented This defaults to 10 percent of the allocated DB_BLOCK_BUFFERS, so if you have set DB_BLOCK_BUFFERS at 20,000, any table less than 2000 blocks in size would count as a small table. I would suggest setting it to the size of your most-used index if you explicitly size it.

- **table scans (long tables)** This tells the number of rows read from the table whose size was larger than _SMALL_TABLE_THRESHOLD. Yes, the leading underscore is part of the parameter. In earlier versions, this was a documented parameter, in Oracle7 (later versions) and Oracle8 it is now undocumented. This size defaults to 10 percent of the allocated size of the DB_BLOCK_BUFFERS size in blocks. So if you specify 20,000 DB_BLOCK_BUFFERS, scans of any table less than 2000 blocks will be treated as a small table scan. I would suggest setting it to the size of your most-used index, if you explicitly size it. This allows you to do a Q&D (quick and dirty) calculation of the ratio of index scans to full table scans to determine index efficiency.

- **hit ratio** This is not a reported calculation but is a calculable one from statistics in the ESTAT/BSTAT statistics report. Essentially, the hit ratio we will calculate tells how efficiently you are using your database buffers. A high hit ratio (near one [1]) is what you desire, and any hit ratio less than 95 percent for an OLTP environment or 85 percent for batch applications should be investigated. The calculation is

```
hit ratio = ((consistent gets+db block gets) - physical reads)/consistent
gets+db block gets
```

So, from the example report in Listing 15.2

```
consistent gets = 124351
db block gets = 10806
physical reads = 117581

hit ratio = ((124351 + 10806) - 117581)/(124351 + 10806)

hit ratio =  0.13
```

So the instance that this report was run on probably needs more DB_BLOCK_ BUFFERS.

Appendix C of the *Oracle8 Server Reference Manual*, Release 8.0, part number A50665-1, January 23,1987, has detailed descriptions of all of the other statistics in Listing 15.2.

LISTING 15.2   Session statistics report from UTLESTAT.SQL.

Statistic	Total	Per Trans	Per Logon	Per Sec
CPU used by this session	19092	19092	4773	12.81
CPU used when call started	5694	5694	1423.5	3.82
DBWR buffers scanned	145100	145100	36275	97.38
DBWR free buffers found	144985	144985	36246.25	97.31
DBWR lru scans	2902	2902	725.5	1.95
DBWR make free requests	2900	2900	725	1.95
DBWR summed scan depth	145100	145100	36275	97.38
DBWR timeouts	486	486	121.5	.33
SQL*Net roundtrips to/from	129	129	32.25	.09
background timeouts	1493	1493	373.2	1
buffer is not pinned count	968	968	242	.65
buffer is pinned count	123553	123553	30888.25	82.92
bytes received via SQL*Net	10389	10389	2597.25	6.97
bytes sent via SQL*Net to c	5700	5700	1425	3.83
calls to get snapshot scn:	576	576	144	.39
calls to kcmgas	44	44	11	.03
calls to kcmgcs	8	8	2	.01
calls to kcmgrs	835	835	208.75	.56
change write time	4	4	1	0
cleanouts only - consistent	71	71	17.75	.05
cluster key scan block gets	544	544	136	.37
cluster key scans	288	288	72	.19
commit cleanout failures: b	72	72	18	.05
commit cleanouts	102	102	25.5	.07
commit cleanouts successful	30	30	7.5	.02
consistent gets	124351	124351	31087.75	83.46
cursor authentications	8	8	2	.01
db block changes	1197	1197	299.25	.8
db block gets	10806	10806	2701.5	7.25
deferred (CURRENT) block cl	9	9	2.25	.01
enqueue releases	356	356	89	.24
enqueue requests	350	350	87.5	.23
execute count	576	576	144	.39
free buffer requested	108001	108001	27000.25	72.48
immediate (CR) block cleano	71	71	17.75	.05
immediate (CURRENT) block c	5	5	1.25	0
logons cumulative	4	4	1	0
logons current	1	1	.25	0
messages received	2977	2977	744.25	2

```
messages sent                     2977       2977     744.25        2
no work - consistent read g     123549     123549   30887.25    82.92
opened cursors cumulative          422        422     105.5        .28
opened cursors current               2          2        .5         0
parse count (hard)                  16         16        4         .01
parse count (total)                433        433     108.25       .29
parse time cpu                      21         21       5.25       .01
parse time elapsed                  27         27       6.75       .02
physical reads                  117581     117581   29395.25    78.91
physical writes                   9845       9845    2461.25      6.61
process last nonidle time    912827947  912827947  206986.75  2636.21
recursive calls                   6931       6931    1732.75      4.65
recursive cpu usage                147        147      36.75        .1
redo blocks written                334        334      83.5        .22
redo entries                       689        689     172.25       .46
redo size                       144528     144528    36132        97
redo small copies                  229        229      57.25       .15
redo synch time                      4          4        1          0
redo synch writes                    3          3        .75        0
redo wastage                     11864      11864     2966        7.96
redo write time                    326        326      81.5        .22
redo writes                         45         45      11.2        .03
session connect time           2827947    2827947    6986.75    636.21
session logical reads           125436     125436    31359       84.19
session pga memory             5725488    5725488  1431372     3842.61
session pga memory max        13293956   13293956  3323489     8922.12
session uga memory               54552      54552    13638       36.61
session uga memory max          163460     163460    40865      109.7
sorts (disk)                         2          2        .5         0
sorts (memory)                      14         14       3.5        .01
sorts (rows)                   6723541    6723541  1680885.25  4512.44
table fetch by rowid                43         43      10.75       .03
table scan blocks gotten            80         80      20          .05
table scan rows gotten              53         53      13.25       .04
table scans (short tables)          14         14       3.5        .01
total file opens                    14         14       3.5        .01
user calls                         125        125      31.25       .08
user commits                         1          1        .25        0
write requests                      47         47      11.75       .03

78 rows selected.
```

UTLESTAT Average Dirty Buffer Write Queue Report The next report shows the average length of the dirty buffer write queue. The report output is shown in Listing 15.3. If this is larger than the value of

1. (db_files * db_file_simultaneous_writes)/2
   or (whichever is smaller)
2. 1/4 of db_block_buffers

and there is a platform-specific limit on the write batch size (normally 1024 or 2048 buffers), increase db_file_simultaneous_writes or db_files. Also check for disks that are doing many more IOs than other disks and look at spreading their database files over more drives.

LISTING 15.3   Average Write Queue Length report from UTLESTTAT.SQL.

```
Average Write Queue Length
--------------------------
                         0
1 row selected.
```

UTLESTAT Systemwide Wait Events (Nonbackground) Report The next report shows systemwide wait events for nonbackground processes (PMON, SMON, etc.). Times are in hundredths of a second. Each one of these is a context switch that costs CPU time. By looking at the total time you can often determine what the bottleneck is that processes are waiting for. This shows the total time spent waiting for a specific event and the average time per wait on that event. The example reports show that the SQL*Net wait was the most significant; however, the SQL*Net event waits will probably always be the largest so you should probably disregard this event and look at the next largest. In this case that is the "db file scattered read," which could indicate that disk contention or excessive full table scans are occurring. The output from this report is shown in Listing 15.4.

LISTING 15.4   Wait Event Reports for Non-SYS-owned processes from UTLESTAT.SQL.

```
Event Name                      Count   Total Time   Avg Time
-----------------------------   -----   ----------   --------
SQL*Net message from client       157       257932    1642.88
db file scattered read           5629        23374       4.15
db file sequential read         18505        17284        .93
rdbms ipc reply                    33           61       1.85
direct path write                  16           28       1.75
control file sequential read       11           13       1.18
log file sync                       3            4       1.33
file identify                       3            2        .67
SQL*Net break/reset to client       6            0          0
file open                          28            0          0
SQL*Net message to client         158            0          0
11 rows selected.
```

UTLESTAT Systemwide Wait Events (Background) Report The next report shows systemwide wait events for background processes (PMON, SMON, etc.). If excessive waits are shown in these processes then the process should be tuned. The "rdbms ipc message" event waits are an indication that this system was mostly idle; the timer waits show that the processes were idle as well. Generally, timer waits and message waits of this type are normal and can be disregarded. Some amount of read/write waits can be expected as well. For a detailed discussion of all wait events, see the *Oracle8 Server Reference Manual,* Release 8.0. The output from this report is shown in Listing 15.5.

LISTING 15.5   Wait event report for SYS-owned processes.

Event Name	Count	Total Time	Avg Time
rdbms ipc message	4460	775075	173.78
pmon timer	496	148800	300
smon timer	4	120000	30000
log file parallel write	45	326	7.24
db file parallel write	47	45	.96
db file sequential read	15	21	1.4
db file scattered read	5	14	2.8
log file sync	1	0	0
8 rows selected.			

UTLESTAT Latch Statistics   The next report (see Listing 15.6) deals with latch statistics. Latch contention will show up as a large value for the "latch-free" event in the preceding wait events. Sleeps should be low. The hit_ratio should be high (near or equal to 1). Most latch contention problems (depending on the latch) are resolved by increasing the SHARED_POOL_SIZE initialization parameter.

LISTING 15.6   Latch report from UTLESTAT.SQL.

LATCH_NAME	GETS	MISSES	HIT_RATIO	SLEEPS	SLEEPS/MISS
Active checkpoint	495	0	1	0	0
Checkpoint queue l	108448	0	1	0	0
Token Manager	653	0	1	0	0
cache buffer handl	51	0	1	0	0
cache buffers chai	492336	0	1	0	0
cache buffers lru	111063	0	1	0	0
dml lock allocatio	253	0	1	0	0
enqueue hash chain	692	0	1	0	0
enqueues	1001	0	1	0	0
ktm global data	4	0	1	0	0
library cache	5974	0	1	0	0
library cache load	12	0	1	0	0
list of block allo	87	0	1	0	0
loader state objec	4	0	1	0	0
messages	12006	3	1	0	0

```
modify parameter v        4        0        1        0        0
multiblock read ob    11272        0        1        0        0
ncodef allocation        23        0        1        0        0
process allocation        4        0        1        0        0
redo allocation        1325        0        1        0        0
row cache objects      3472        0        1        0        0
sequence cache            9        0        1        0        0
session allocation       55        0        1        0        0
session idle bit        258        0        1        0        0
session switching        23        0        1        0        0
shared pool             895        0        1        0        0
sort extent pool          8        0        1        0        0
system commit numb      923        0        1        0        0
transaction alloca      139        0        1        0        0
undo global data        283        0        1        0        0
user lock                10        0        1        0        0
31 rows selected.
```

UTLESTAT No Wait Gets Latch Report The next report (see Listing 15.7) shows statistics on no_wait gets of latches. A no_wait get does not wait for the latch to become free; it immediately times out. As long as the hit ratio is near one there is no problem. If the hit ratio drops beneath 0.9 (indicating processes are missing gets) increase the SHARED_POOL_SIZE parameter.

LISTING 15.7   Latches no_waits Report from UTLESTAT.SQL.

```
LATCH_NAME           NOWAIT_GETS  NOWAIT_MISSES  NOWAIT_HIT_RATIO
------------------   -----------  -------------  ----------------
cache buffers chai      384761              0                  1
cache buffers lru        18031              0                  1
process allocation           4              0                  1
redo copy                  538              0                  1
4 rows selected.
```

UTLESTAT Buffer Busy Waits Report The next report (see Listing 15.8) is on buffer busy wait statistics. If the value for "buffer busy wait" in the wait event statistics is high, then this table will identify which class of blocks is having high contention. If there are high "undo header" waits then add more rollback segments. If there are high "segment header" waits then adding free lists might help. Check v$session_wait to get the addresses of the actual blocks having contention. The report only shows classes with counts greater than zero. The possible classes are as follows:

bitmap block

bitmap index block

data block

extent map

free list

save undo block

save undo header

segment header

sort block

system undo block

system undo header

undo block

undo header

unused

LISTING 15.8   Latch contention report from UTLESTAT.SQL.

```
CLASS                COUNT               TIME
-----------------    ----------------    ----------------
0 rows selected.
```

UTLESTAT Rollback Segment Statistics Report The next report (see Listing 15.9) deals with rollback segment statistics (UNDO_SEGMENTS). High Waits_for_trans_tbl implies you should add rollback segments. Excessive shrinks may indicate that your rollback extent sizes are too small and the rollbacks should be rebuilt.

LISTING 15.9   Rollback segment statistics report from UTLESTAT.SQL.

UNDO SEGMENT	TRANS_TBL GETS	TRANS_TBL WAITS	UNDO_BYTES WRITTEN	SEGMENT SIZE_BYTES	XACTS	SHRINKS	WRAPS
0	5	0	0	978944	0	0	0
2	161	0	44780	3190784	0	0	0
3	5	0	0	2125824	0	0	0
4	5	0	0	2125824	0	0	0
5	5	0	0	2125824	0	0	0
6	5	0	0	2125824	0	0	0

6 rows selected.

UTLESTAT Initialization Parameter Report The next report (see Listing 15.10) is informational and is not used for tuning purposes. The next report shows the initialization parameters currently in effect that are set other than to their default value.

LISTING 15.10   Initialization parameter report from UTLESTAT.SQL.

```
NAME                        VALUE
--------------------------  ------------------------------------
background_dump_dest        c:\oracle1\ortest1\admin\bdump
checkpoint_process          TRUE
control_files               C:\ORACLE1\ORTEST1\CONTROL\ctlORTST.
db_block_size               4096
db_files                    100
db_name                     ORTEST1
dml_locks                   200
ifile                       c:\oracle1\ortest1\admin\pfile\inito
log_archive_start           TRUE
log_buffer                  1048576
log_checkpoint_interval     100000
max_dump_file_size          102400
processes                   100
remote_login_passwordfile   SHARED
rollback_segments           rb1, rb2, rb3, rb4, rb5
sequence_cache_entries      100
sequence_cache_hash_buckets 89
shared_pool_size            10000000
sort_area_retained_size     2097152
sort_area_size              8388608
text_enable                 TRUE
timed_statistics            TRUE
user_dump_dest              c:\oracle1\ortest1\admin\udump
23 rows selected.
```

UTLESTAT Data Dictionary Cache Report The next report (see Listing 15.11)
shows the DC cache statistics (a part of the shared pool). The get_miss and scan_miss
statistics should be very low compared to the requests. The cur_usage statistic is the
number of entries in the cache that are being used. If the get_miss and scan_miss statistics are high compared to requests, increase the SHARED_POOL_SIZE parameter.
The get_reqs and get_miss columns should be summed and then ratioed. If the overall
ratio of get_misses to get_reqs is greater than 10 percent, increase the SHARED_
POOL_SIZE parameter. For a quick look at this, use the following query of the
V$ROWCACHE table:

LISTING 15.11   Data dictionary cache report from UTLESTAT.SQL.

```
SELECT (SUM(getmisses) / SUM(gets)) 'DD CACHE MISS RATIO'
FROM V$ROWCACHE;
NAME             GET_REQS GET_MISS SCAN_REQ SCAN_MIS MOD_REQS COUNT    CUR_USAG
---------------  -------- -------- -------- -------- -------- -------- --------
dc_tablespaces         72        1        0        0        0        8        4
dc_free_extents       310       67       33        0      165       63       34
```

```
dc_segments          43      4      0      0     35     53     41
dc_rollback_seg      56      0      0      0      0     10      8
dc_used_extents      66     33      0      0     66     50     32
dc_users             31      0      0      0      0     21     14
dc_user_grants       20      0      0      0      0     21     14
dc_objects           33      3      0      0      0    222    214
dc_usernames          9      1      0      0      0     20      4
dc_object_ids        14      1      0      0      0    132    130
dc_profiles           3      0      0      0      0      3      1
dc_histogram_de      73     73      0      0     73     77     73
12 rows selected.
```

UTLESTAT Tablespace IO Summary Report The next report (see Listing 15.12) shows sum of IO operations over tablespaces. If your application is spread over several tablespaces, this report can help show "hot" tablespaces that should perhaps have tables moved out into other tablespaces on separate disks or arrays. In this case, the index tablespaces were hit the hardest. So if we were approaching a read/write limit on the disks where the index tablespaces were located I would consider moving some of the indexes or perhaps partitioning them.

LISTING 15.12   Tablespace IO Report from UTLESTAT.SQL.

```
TABLE_SPACE      READS  BLKS_READ READ_TIME WRITES  BLKS_WRT WRITE_TIME MEGABYTES
--------------- ------  --------- --------- ------- -------- ---------- ----------
RAW_DATA             0          0         0       0        0          0        734
RAW_INDEX         6774       6774     11394       0        0          0        524
ROLLBACK_DATA       20         20        31      29       29         29        524
SCOPUS_DATA       5632      90016     23400       0        0          0       2096
SCOPUS_INDEX     10944      10944      3828       0        0          0       1048
SYSTEM             107        119       259      83       83         85         52
TEMPORARY_DATA     670       9718      1816     621     9733         28        629
USER_DATA            0          0         0       0        0          0         10
8 rows selected.
```

UTLESTAT Disk IO Spread Report The next report (see Listing 15.13) shows the spread of IO across the disk drive setup. IO should be spread evenly across drives. A big difference between phys_reads and phys_blks_rd implies that table scans are taking place. If the IO is concentrated into specific data files, consider spreading the data file contents by physically moving the contents or partitioning tables or indexes. Use of index-only tables and bitmapped indexes can also reduce IO loads on a system. In this case, we again see the most IO in our index data files.

LISTING 15.13 Data file/disk IO report from UTLESTAT.SQL.

TABLESPACE	FILE_NAME	PHYS READS	PHYS BLKS READ	READ TIME	PHYS WRITES	PHYS BLKS_WRT	WRITE_TIME	MEGABYTES
RAW_DATA	E:\ORTEST1\RAW01.DBF	0	0	0	0	0	0	734
RAW_INX	C:\ORTEST1\RAW_I1.DBF	6774	6774	11394	0	0	0	524
RBK_DATA	C:\ORTEST1\RBS1.DBF	20	20	31	29	29	29	524
APPL_DATA	D:\ORTEST1\APLDAT1.DBF	0	0	0	0	0	0	524
APPL_DATA	D:\ORTEST1\APLDAT2.DBF	3197	51111	13483	0	0	0	524
APPL_DATA	D:\ORTEST1\APLDAT3.DBF	1786	28531	7369	0	0	0	524
APPL_DATA	E:\ORTEST1\APLDAT4.DBF	649	10374	2548	0	0	0	524
APPL_INX	E:\ORTEST1\APLIDX2.DBF	6430	6430	2212	0	0	0	524
APPL_INX	F:\ORTEST1\APLIDX1.DBF	4514	4514	1616	0	0	0	524
SYSTEM	C:\ORTEST1\SYSTEST.ORA	107	119	259	83	83	85	52
TEMP	F:\ORTEST1\TMP1.DBF	670	9718	1816	621	9733	28	629
USER	C:\ORTEST1\USR1.DBF	0	0	0	0	0	0	10

12 rows selected.

UTLESTAT Time and Version Reports The final two reports (see Listings 15.14 and 15.15) are informational and tell you the times that BSTAT and ESTAT were run and the version information for the instance.

LISTING 15.14 UTLBSTAT/UTLESTAT start and stop times report.

```
START_TIME              END_TIME
------------------      ------------------
19-jun-97 17:00:25      19-jun-97 17:25:15
1 row selected.
```

LISTING 15.15 Instance version data report from UTLESTAT.SQL.

```
BANNER
--------------------------------------------------------------
Oracle8 Server Release 8.0.2.0.1 - Beta
PL/SQL Release 3.0.2.0.1 - Beta
CORE Version 4.0.2.0.1 - Production
TNS for 32-bit Windows: Version 3.0.2.0.0 - Beta
NLSRTL Version 3.3.0.0.1 - Beta
5 rows selected.
```

Further reading. For more information on tuning using BSTAT/ESTAT and on tuning in general, the following extra reading is suggested:

Oracle7 Server Administrator's Guide, Release 7.3, Chapter 21, Oracle Corporation, Part No. A32535-1, February 1995.

Oracle7 Server Application Developer's Guide, Appendix B, Oracle Corporation, Part No. 6695-70-1292, December 1992.

Oracle7 Server Tuning, Release 7.3, Part No. A32537-1, June 1996, Oracle Corporation.

Performance Tuning with BSTAT/ESTAT, K. Powell, Oracle Corporation, 1991 IOUG Proceedings, Miami, Florida.

Tuning Oracle, Michael J. Corey, Michael Abbey, and Daniel J. Dechichio Jr., Oracle Press—Osborne McGraw-Hill, 1995.

15.2   OTHER TOOLS FOR INTERNALS TUNING

The UTLBSTAT/UTLESTAT series of reports are a great source of information for tuning your database. However, using them on a day-to-day basis would be a bit much for most DBAs to handle. This section will give the DBA several additional tuning and reporting tools to add to their tuning toolbox.

The tuning guides for Oracle list several areas where tuning is required; they are as follows:

Tuning Memory Allocation

SQL and PL/SQL areas
Shared pool in Oracle7
Database buffer cache

Tuning Input and Output

Disk IO
Space allocation
Dynamic extension

Tuning Contention

Rollback segments
Redo logs
Oracle7—multithread server

Other Tuning Topics

Sorts
Free lists
Checkpoints

Tools for Tuning Memory Contention

Memory contention will make the best-tuned application perform poorly. If the application constantly has to go to disk to get the data dictionary and actual data then performance will suffer. Remember that the SGA is divided into three major areas: the shared pool under Oracle7, the redo log buffer, and the database buffers. Under Oracle8 there is an additional area in the SGA—the large pool—for databases using the multithreaded server and NET8.

Tuning the Shared Pool Missing a get on the data dictionary or shared pool area of the SGA is more costly than missing a get on a data buffer or waiting for a redo buffer. Therefore, we will look at a SQL script that allows the DBA to look at the current status of the data dictionary or shared pool area. This SQL script is shown in Source 15.1.

Something to notice about the script in Source 15.1 is that the script only selects statistics that have been used more than 100 times and have had getmisses occur. Obviously, if the parameter has had no getmisses, it should be satisfactory. The factor of 100 gets was selected to ensure that the parameter has had enough activity to generate valid statistics. You might also notice that the percentage of misses is automatically calculated and reported for each parameter. If the DBA desires, the percentage value could be used to generate a decoded value of "RAISE" if the percentage is greater than 10 or "LOWER" if the value is less than a predetermined value. An example of this script output is shown in Listing 15.16.

SOURCE 15.1   Script to generate data dictionary cache statistics report.

```
REM
REM NAME     : DD_CACHE.SQL
REM FUNCTION: GENERATE REPORT ON DATA DICTIONARY CACHE CONDITION
REM USE      : FROM SQLPLUS
REM Limitations    : None
REM Revisions:
REM Date             Modified by      Reason for change
REM 21-AUG-1991      MIKE AULT        INITIAL CREATE
REM 27-NOV-1991      MIKE AULT        ADD % CALCULATION TO REPORT
REM 28-OCT-1992      MIKE AULT        ADD CALL TO TITLE PROCEDURE
REM 21-Jun-1997      MIKE AULT        Updated to ORACLE8REM SET FLUSH OFF
REM SET TERM OFF
SET PAGESIZE 59
SET LINESIZE 79
COLUMN parameter   FORMAT A20
COLUMN type        FORMAT a10
COLUMN percent     FORMAT 999.99 HEADING "%";
START title80 "DATA DICTIONARY CACHE STATISTICS"
SPOOL rep_out/&db/ddcache.lis
```

```
SELECT
    parameter,
    type,
    gets,
    getmisses,
    ( getmisses / gets * 100) percent,
    count,
    usage
FROM
    v$rowcache
WHERE
    gets > 100 AND
    getmisses > 0
ORDER BY parameter;
SPOOL OFF
```

LISTING 15.16   Example data dictionary cache report.

```
Date: 06/21/97                                      Page:   1
Time: 05:04 PM      DATA DICTIONARY CACHE STATISTICS    SYSTEM
                        ORTEST1 database


PARAMETER              TYPE     GETS GETMISSES    % COUNT USAGE
-------------------- ------- ----- --------- ----- ----- -------
dc_free_extents        PARENT  8845        29  .33    44      29
dc_object_ids          PARENT   193        22 11.40   72      71
dc_objects             PARENT   407        64 15.72  121     113
dc_rollback_segments PARENT    4386         7  .16     9       8
```

In reviewing this report, the following things should be checked:

1. Review Count and Usage columns. If Usage is equal to Count the cache area is being fully utilized. If Usage is consistently low compared to Counts, consider reducing the INIT.ORA parameter that controls the caches (SHARED_POOL).

2. If Counts and Usage are equal and Percents are greater than 10 percent, consider increasing the INIT.ORA parameter that controls the caches (SHARED_POOL_SIZE).

Since we are actually only concerned with an aggregate look at the cache area performance, the following query can be substituted into the report to give you an overall health indicator:

```
SELECT (SUM(getmisses) / SUM(gets)) 'DD CACHE MISS RATIO'
FROM V$ROWCACHE;
```

This substitution simplifies the report into the following:

```
Date: 06/21/97                                          Page:   1
Time: 04:39 PM           DD Cache Hit Ratio             SYSTEM
                         ORTEST1 database


     RATIO
   ---------
   .01141403


1 row selected.
```

Tuning the Library Cache An additional area of the shared pool deals with the tuning of the library cache. The library cache is used to store information concerning the shared objects. These consist mainly of the SQL AREA, TABLE/PROCEDURE, BODY, and TRIGGER type objects. These areas are monitored via the V$LIBRARYCACHE table. This table has the columns NAMESPACE, GETS, GETHITRATIO, PINS, PINHITRATIO, RELOADS, and INVALIDATIONS.

NAMESPACE refers to the type of object (listed in the preceding paragraph). PINS refers to the number of times the object was executed. RELOADS shows the number of library cache misses on execution steps. If the ratio of reloads to pins exceeds 1 percent the SHARED_POOL_SIZE parameter should be increased. This can be determined by a simple query:

```
SELECT (SUM(reloads)/SUM(pins)) * 100 'Miss %'
FROM v$librarycache;
```

To fully utilize the higher value for SHARED_POOL_SIZE, you may also want to increase the number of cursors available to each user. This is accomplished via the OPEN_CURSORS INIT.ORA parameter.

Additional gains can be realized by making your SQL statements identical, not just in content, but in form as well, right down to the spaces, capitalization, and punctuation. This will allow the SQL statements to share the shared SQL area. Standardization of queries can be accomplished by using views to replace queries and encapsulating standard reports into PL/SQL. I suggest using the new UTLFILE package to generate output directly to files from PL/SQL. The report in Source 15.2 reports on the library caches.

SOURCE 15.2   Script to report on library cache health.

```
rem Title: libcache.sql
rem FUNCTION: Generate a library cache report
COLUMN namespace                      HEADING "Library Object"
COLUMN gets                           HEADING "Gets"
COLUMN gethitratio      FORMAT 999.99 HEADING "Get Hit%"
COLUMN pins                           HEADING "Pins"
COLUMN pinhitratio      FORMAT 999.99 HEADING "Pin Hit%"
COLUMN reloads                        HEADING "Reloads"
```

```
COLUMN invalidations                      HEADING  "Invalidations"
COLUMN db                 FORMAT a10
SET PAGES 58 LINES 80
START title80 "Library Caches Report"
DEFINE output = rep_out\&db\lib_cache
SPOOL &output
SELECT
     namespace,gets,
     gethitratio*100 gethitratio,
     pins,
     pinhitratio*100 pinhitratio,
     reloads,invalidations
FROM
     v$librarycache
/
SPOOL OFF
PAUSE Press Enter to continue
SET PAGES 22 LINES 80
TTITLE OFF
UNDEF output
```

Listing 15.17 shows what the output for the script in Source 15.2 should look like.

LISTING 15.17   Library cache report.

```
Date: 06/21/97                                      Page:   1
Time: 05:24 PM          Library Caches Report       SYSTEM
                          ORTEST1 database

Library Object  Gets Get Hit%  Pins Pin Hit% Reloads Invalidates
--------------- ---- --------- ---- -------- ------- -----------
SQL AREA         890    90.34  2466    93.03       0           0
TABLE/PROCEDURE  557    80.79   905    80.99       0           0
BODY              12    75.00    12    75.00       0           0
TRIGGER            0   100.00     0   100.00       0           0
INDEX             27      .00    27      .00       0           0
CLUSTER          114    95.61   156    96.79       0           0
OBJECT             0   100.00     0   100.00       0           0
PIPE               0   100.00     0   100.00       0           0
```

If your gethitratio (Get Hit%) or pinhitratio (Pin Hit%) fall below 70 to 80 percent for objects with high values for Gets and Pins then you should increase your SHARED_POOL parameter. If you see excessive reloads then you will also want to increase the SHARED_POOL. Invalidations should not occur in a production environment but are probably going to be seen frequently under development.

Monitoring and Tuning the Shared SQL Area The shared SQL area contains the Pcode versions of all of the current SQL commands that haven't been aged out of the shared pool. There are numerous statistics available via the v$sqlarea DPT. The test of SQL statements in the shared pool can be retrieved (at least the first tens of bytes) from the v$sqltext DPT. Let's look at a report (Source 15.3) that displays the SQL statements in the SQL area with the greatest amount of disk reads (these will probably be the ones you will want to review and tune).

SOURCE 15.3   Script to monitor SQL area disk reads by script.

```
rem Name: sqldrd.sql
rem Function: return the sql statements from the shared area with
rem Function: highest disk reads
rem History: Presented in paper 35 at IOUG-A 1997, converted for
rem use 6/24/97 MRA
rem
DEFINE access_level = 1000 (NUMBER)
COLUMN parsing_user_id FORMAT 9999999     HEADING 'User Id'
COLUMN executions       FORMAT 9999       HEADING 'Exec'
COLUMN sorts            FORMAT 99999      HEADING 'Sorts'
COLUMN command_type     FORMAT 99999      HEADING 'CmdT'
COLUMN disk_reads        FORMAT 999,999,999 HEADING 'Block Reads'
COLUMN sql_text         FORMAT a40 HEADING 'Statement' WORD_WRAPPED
SET LINES 130 VERIFY OFF FEEDBACK OFF
START title132 'SQL Statements With High Reads'
SPOOL rep_out/&db/sqldrd.lis
SELECT
     parsing_user_id, executions,
     sorts,command_type,
     disk_reads,sql_text
FROM
     v$sqlarea
WHERE
     disk_reads > &&access_level
ORDER BY
     disk_reads;
SPOOL OFF
SET LINES 80 VERIFY ON FEEDBACK ON
```

LISTING 15.18   Example of output from SQL disk read script.

```
Date: 06/24/97                                    Page:   1
Time: 11:35 PM        SQL Statements with High Reads    SYSTEM
                         ORTEST1 database
User
Id   Exec Sorts CmdT Block Reads Statement
---- ---- ----- ---- ----- ----- --------------------------------
   0  403     0    3          11 select f.file#, f.block#,f.ts#,
                                 f.length from fet$ f, ts$ t
                                 where
                                 t.ts#=f.ts# and t.dflextpct!=0
```

```
0   11   0   3        11 select order#,columns,types
                         from
                         access$ where d_obj#=:1

0   12   0   3        12 select /*+ index(idl_ub1$
                         i_idl_ub11)
                         +*/ piece#,length,piece from
                         idl_ub1$
                         where obj#=:1 and part=:2 and
                         version=:3 order by piece#

5   34   0   3        13 SELECT NAME,VALUE   FROM
                         V$SYSSTAT
                             WHERE NAME = 'db block gets'

0   12   0   3        14 select /*+ index(idl_ub2$
                         i_idl_ub21)
                         +*/ piece#,length,piece from
                         idl_ub2$
                         where obj#=:1 and part=:2 and
                         version=:3 order by piece#

0   17   0   3        27 select file#, block#, ts# from
                         seg$
                         where type# = 3

0   1    1   3        79 select distinct
                         d.p_obj#,d.p_timestamp
                         from sys.dependency$ d, obj$ o
                         where
                         d.p_obj#>=:1 and
                         d.d_obj#=o.obj# and
                         o.status!=5

5   34   0   47       90 DECLARE job BINARY_INTEGER :=
                         :job;
                         next_date DATE := :mydate;
                         broken
                         BOOLEAN := FALSE; BEGIN
                         hitratio;
                         :mydate := next_date; IF broken
                         THEN :b
                         := 1; ELSE :b := 0; END IF;
                         END;
```

The example report in Listing 15.18 was taken using a size of 10 for reads limit. Usually, disk reads will be in the range specified by the define statement.

You might also be interested in the amount of memory used by a single user. This could point to a user who is using too much ad hoc query type SQL and not enough packages, procedures, and functions. The script in Source 15.4 gives this information.

SOURCE 15.4   SQL area memory summary report and supporting view.

```
rem
rem FUNCTION: Generate a summary of SQL Area Memory Usage
rem FUNCTION: uses the sqlsummary view.
rem            showing user SQL memory usage
rem
rem sqlsum.sql
rem
COLUMN areas                                HEADING Used|Areas
COLUMN sharable      FORMAT 999,999,999  HEADING Shared|Bytes
COLUMN persistent    FORMAT 999,999,999  HEADING Persistent|Bytes
COLUMN runtime       FORMAT 999,999,999  HEADING Runtime|Bytes
COLUMN username      FORMAT A15          HEADING "User"
START TITLE80 "USERS SQL AREA MEMORY USE"
SPOOL rep_out\&db\sqlsum
SET PAGES 59 LINES 80
BREAK ON REPORT
COMPUTE SUM OF sharable ON REPORT
COMPUTE SUM OF persistent ON REPORT
COMPUTE SUM OF runtime ON REPORT
SELECT
     username,
     SUM(sharable_mem) Sharable,
     SUM( persistent_mem) Persistent,
     SUM( runtime_mem) Runtime,
     COUNT(*) Areas
FROM
     sql_summary
GROUP BY
     username
ORDER BY
     2;
SPOOL OFF
PAUSE Press Enter to continue
CLEAR COLUMNS
CLEAR BREAKS
SET PAGES 22 LINES 80
TTITLE OFF

The report uses the following view:

CREATE OR REPLACE VIEW sql_summary AS
SELECT username, sharable_mem, persistent_mem, runtime_mem
FROM sys.v_$sqlarea a, dba_users b
WHERE a.parsing_user_id = b.user_id;
```

The output from the SQL summary report is shown in Listing 15.19.

LISTING 15.19   Example of output from the SQL summary report.

```
Date: 06/25/97                                            Page:   1
Time: 12:10 AM          Users SQL Area Memory Use         SYSTEM
                            ORTEST1 database

                     Shared    Persistent      Runtime       Used
User                  Bytes         Bytes        Bytes      Areas
-----------------   ---------   -----------   -----------   --------
SYS                   546,933        42,196       140,108         63
SYSTEM                580,693        13,172        83,180         24
-----------------   ---------   -----------   -----------   --------
sum                 1,127,626        55,368       223,288

2 rows selected.
```

From the looks of the report in Listing 15.19 there aren't really any problems in ORTEST1 since the shared pool is 12 megabytes and in total I am using less than 2 megabytes.

If you detect a user that seems to be using more than his or her share of the shared pool, the script in Source 15.5 can be run to see exactly what he or she has been executing. From the results of the script (Listing 15.20), you might be able to help the user optimize his or her processing (or want to take a two-by-four to their backside).

SOURCE 15.5   Script to show shared memory usage for a user (or users).

```
rem
rem FUNCTION: Generate a report of SQL Area Memory Usage
rem           showing SQL Text and memory catagories
rem
rem sqlmem.sql
rem
COLUMN sql_text       FORMAT a40   HEADING Text word_wrapped
COLUMN sharable_mem                HEADING Shared|Bytes
COLUMN persistent_mem              HEADING Persistent|Bytes
COLUMN parse_calls                 HEADING Parses
COLUMN users          FORMAT a15   HEADING "User"
COLUMN executions                  HEADING "Executions"
START title132 "Users SQL Area Memory Use"
SPOOL rep_out\&db\sqlmem
SET LONG 1000 PAGES 59 LINES 132
BREAK ON users
COMPUTE SUM OF sharable_mem ON users
COMPUTE SUM OF persistent_mem ON users
COMPUTE SUM OF runtime_mem ON users
SELECT username users, sql_text, Executions, parse_calls, sharable_mem,
persistent_mem
```

```
FROM sys.v_$sqlarea a, dba_users b
WHERE a.parsing_user_id = b.user_id
AND b.username LIKE UPPER('%&user_name%')
ORDER BY 1;
SPOOL OFF
PAUSE Press Enter to continue
CLEAR COLUMNS
CLEAR COMPUTES
CLEAR BREAKS
SET PAGES 22 LINES 80
```

LISTING 15.20   Example of output from the SQL memory usage for a user report.

```
Date: 06/25/97                                                    Page:  1
Time: 12:21 AM                 Users SQL Area Memory Use                SYSTEM
                                 ORTEST1 database


                                                         Shared   Persist
User            Text                        Exec   Parses Bytes    Bytes
-------------   --------------------------- ------- ------ -------- --------
SYSTEM          DECLARE job BINARY_INTEGER := :job;   34    34   10207     460
                next_date DATE := :mydate;  broken
                BOOLEAN := FALSE; BEGIN hitratio;
                :mydate := next_date; IF broken THEN :b
                := 1; ELSE :b := 0; END IF; END;

                INSERT INTO HIT_RATIOS VALUES (        34    34    8931     552
                :b1,:b2,:b3,:b4,:b5,:b6,0,0,:b7  )

                SELECT        parsing_user_id,          1     1   50861     744
                executions,         sorts,command_type,
                disk_reads,sql_text FROM
                v$sqlarea WHERE         disk_reads >10

                SELECT        parsing_user_id,          1     1   51150     744
                executions,         sorts,command_type,
                disk_reads,sql_text FROM
                v$sqlarea WHERE         disk_reads >100

                SELECT  parsing_user_id, executions,    2     2   52384     748
                sorts,command_type,  disk_reads,sql_text
                FROM  v$sqlarea WHERE  disk_reads > 10
                ORDER BY  disk_reads

                SELECT  parsing_user_id, executions,    3     3   52234     748
                sorts,command_type,  disk_reads,sql_text
                FROM  v$sqlarea WHERE  disk_reads > 1000
                ORDER BY  disk_reads

                SELECT COUNT(*)  FROM V$SESSION  WHERE  34    34   51205     476
                USERNAME IS NOT NULL

                SELECT DECODE('A','A','1','2') FROM DUAL 3     3    7485     460
                SELECT NAME,VALUE   FROM V$SYSSTAT      34    34   13099     524
                WHERE NAME = 'consistent gets'
```

SELECT NAME,VALUE FROM V$SYSSTAT WHERE NAME = 'db block gets'	34	34	13713	524
SELECT NAME,VALUE FROM V$SYSSTAT WHERE NAME = 'physical reads'	34	34	13666	524
SELECT TO_CHAR(SYSDATE,'DD-MON-YY') FROM DUAL	34	34	5656	460
SELECT TO_CHAR(SYSDATE,'HH24') FROM DUAL	34	34	4935	460
SELECT TO_CHAR(SYSDATE,'MM/DD/YY') TODAY, TO_CHAR(SYSDATE,'HH:MI AM') TIME, name||' database' DATABASE, rtrim(name) passout, user passout2 FROM	1	1	32736	680

```
***************                                          ------- -------
sum                                                       663349   14044

25 rows selected.
```

(Before you e-mail me, yes, I am aware the preceding total is incorrect and so is the count of rows; I truncated this report so it would fit nicely here—the original is three pages long.)

The final step to tuning the shared pool is to determine if some objects should be pinned. Pinning is the process of telling the Oracle LRU algorithm that certain objects in the shared pool are hands-off. Pinning is accomplished using the DBMS_SHARED_POOL.KEEP procedure. I have heard several questions about how to determine the size of objects in the shared pool, and how to keep the LRU algorithm from forcing objects out of the shared pool. The DBMS_SHARED_POOL package provides procedures to facilitate these actions.

The DBMS_SHARED_POOL.SIZES procedure searches the shared pool for any objects larger than the size (in kilobytes) of the argument it is passed. Generally, the larger the size, the greater the likelihood that the object is a package and you will want to keep it in the pool. Smaller objects tend to be individual queries and can be aged out of the pool. The use of DBMS_SHARED_POOL.SIZES is shown in Source 15.6.

SOURCE 15.6   Example of the use of the DBMS_SHARED_POOL.SIZES procedure.

```
SQL> set serveroutput on size 4000;
SQL> execute sys.dbms_shared_pool.sizes(10);
SIZE(K) KEPT    NAME
------- -----   ------------------------------------------------------------
139             SYS.STANDARD                 (PACKAGE)
56              SYS.DBMS_SHARED_POOL           (PACKAGE BODY)
31              SELECT TO_CHAR(SHARABLE_MEM / 1000 ,'999999')
                SZ,DECODE(KEPT_VE
```

```
                      RSIONS,0,'        ',RPAD('YES(' ||
                      TO_CHAR(KEPT_VERSIONS)    |
                      | ')' ,6)) KEEPED,RAWTOHEX(ADDRESS) || ',' ||
                      TO_CHAR(HASH
                      _VALUE)  NAME,SUBSTR(SQL_TEXT,1,354) EXTRA    FROM
                      V$SQLAREA
                      WHERE SHARABLE_MEM > :b1 * 1000    UNION SELECT
                      TO_CHAR(SH
                      ARABLE_MEM / 1000 ,'999999')
                      SZ,DECODE(KEPT,'YES','YES
                      (004D7F84,2008220828)         (CURSOR)
  30                  SYS.STANDARD                   (PACKAGE BODY)
  27                  SYS.DBMS_SHARED_POOL             (PACKAGE)
  17                  SYS.V$SQLAREA             (VIEW)
  16                  SYS.V$DB_OBJECT_CACHE       (VIEW)
  15                  insert into
                      idl_ub2$(obj#,part,version,piece#,length,piece)
                      values(:1,:2,:3,:4,:5,:6)
                      (0027BA44,-512326869)         (CURSOR)
PL/SQL procedure successfully completed.
```

The "set serveroutput on size 4000" command in Source 15.6 limits the size of the output buffer to 4000 bytes. The "set serveroutput" command is required. Perhaps in the future if we all bug Oracle for an enhancement they will incorporate the use of UTIL_FILE and just generate a report listing for us so we can peruse as we desire. As you can see from Source 15.6, there is one large package in shared memory. Let's issue a keep against this package to retain it. Source 15.7 shows the results of this action.

SOURCE 15.7   Example of the use of DBMS_SHARED_POOL.KEEP packaged procedure.

```
SQL> execute dbms_shared_pool.keep('sys.standard');
PL/SQL procedure successfully completed.
SQL> execute dbms_shared_pool.sizes(130);
SIZE(K) KEPT    NAME
------- ----    ------------------------------------------------------------
139     YES     SYS.STANDARD  (PACKAGE)
PL/SQL procedure successfully completed.
```

By issuing keeps against large packages to hold them in memory you can mitigate the shared pool fragmentation results in the ORA-04031 error. By pinning the packages so they don't age out this prevents smaller queries, cursors, and procedures from taking their areas. Then, when the packages are reloaded, voila!, an ORA-04031 error as the package seeks a large enough group of areas in which to install itself. Under Oracle8, this is supposed to be eliminated because of the way the shared memory area is now used. For those of you still on previous Oracle7 versions, I have included some scripts on the CD-ROM that accompanies the text that check for a set of packages you specify and, if they aren't pinned, load and pin them. This set of scripts is in the dbms_revealnet.sql package.

Tuning the BUFFER CACHE   The buffer cache is the area in memory where data is stored from data tables, indexes, rollback segments, clusters, and sequences. By ensuring that enough buffers are available for storage of these data items, you can speed execution by reducing required disk reads.

The statistics "db block gets," "consistent gets" (their sum is logical reads), and "physical reads" from the V$SYSSTAT table show the relationship between "logical," or cache, hits and "physical," or disk hits, while retrieving the type of data just described. The statistic called "hit ratio" is determined by the simple formula:

```
logical reads = db_block_gets+consistent_gets
hit ratio(%) = ((logical reads - physical reads) / logical reads) * 100 .
```

If hit ratio is less than 80 to 90 percent in a loaded and running database, there may be insufficient buffers allocated. If the hit ratio is less than 80 to 90 percent, increase the INIT.ORA parameter DB_BLOCK_BUFFERS.

Monitoring hit ratio. A PL/SQL procedure that can be used to periodically load hit ratio, usage, and number of users into a table for later review is shown in Source 15.8. The script in Source 15.8 can be run hourly, every half hour, every four hours—in short, at what ever periodicity the DBA decides to monitor for, with minor changes. This can provide valuable information about peak usage times and hit ratio at those peak times. By adding columns, other statistics can be measured if desired. A script more suited for this is shown later in this section.

A common mistake many DBAs make is to monitor only the cumulative hit ratio. Remember, all the statistics are cumulative; therefore, any ratios or calculated values will be cumulative in nature unless you do as the UTLBSTAT/UTLESTAT reports do and use a holding table for the statistics and then monitor over discrete time periods calculating deltas and the application of the ratios to the deltas.

For instantaneous or period hit ratio, a table to store this information must be created; its structure is as follows:

```
create table hit_ratios (
      CHECK_DATE              DATE,
      CHECK_HOUR              NUMBER,
      DB_BLOCK_GETS           NUMBER,
      CONSISTENT              NUMBER,
      PHY_READS               NUMBER,
      HITRATIO                NUMBER,
      PERIOD_HIT_RATIO        NUMBER,
      PERIOD_USAGE            NUMBER,
      USERS                   NUMBER)
storage (initial 10k next 10k pctincrease 0);
```

In addition, a unique index on CHECK_DATE, CHECK_HOUR should be created to prevent duplicate entries.Since the script in Source 15.7 creates a stored procedure you must call manually, call from a SQL script or schedule using the DBMS_JOB package. The script in Source 15.8 demonstrates the use of a SQL script to call the hitratio stored procedure.

SOURCE 15.8   SQL script used to run hit ratio PL/SQL procedure.

```
REM
REM NAME       :RUN_B_HRATIO.SQL
REM PURPOSE    :RUN PROCEDURE TO LOAD HIT RATIO AND USAGE DATA
REM USE        :FROM RUN_B_HRATIO.COM
REM Limitations       : None
REM Revisions:
REM     Date            Modified by Reason for change
REM     10-JUL-1992     M. AULT     INITIAL CREATE
REM     22-Jun-1997     M. Ault     Modified to call proc
EXECUTE hitratio;
EXIT
```

If manual scheduling or cron isn't for you then the stored procedure in Source 15.9 can then be scheduled using the Oracle job queues to run hourly. If you want it to run with greater or lesser periodicity, the PL/SQL procedure will have to be modified. If you decide just to run the script as needed on a manual basis, the command to run this script is executed in the SQLPLUS environment so a small file consisting of an EXECUTE command needs to be built (such as in Source 15.8), and this file is what is actually run by the batch scheduling program.

SOURCE 15.9   PL/SQL procedure to monitor period hit ratio.

```
CREATE OR REPLACE PROCEDURE hitratio IS
    c_date      DATE;
    c_hour      NUMBER;
    h_ratio     NUMBER;
    con_gets    NUMBER;
    db_gets     NUMBER;
    p_reads     NUMBER;
    stat_name CHAR(64);
    temp_name CHAR(64);
    stat_val    NUMBER;
    users       NUMBER;
BEGIN
  SELECT TO_CHAR(sysdate,'DD-MON-YY') INTO c_date FROM DUAL;
  SELECT TO_CHAR(sysdate,'HH24') INTO c_hour FROM DUAL;
  SELECT
    name, value
```

```
INTO
   temp_name, stat_val
FROM
   v$sysstat
WHERE
   NAME = 'db block gets';
db_gets:=stat_val;
dbms_output.put_line(temp_name||'='||to_char(db_gets));
SELECT
   name, value
INTO
   temp_name, stat_val
FROM
   v$sysstat
WHERE
   name = 'consistent gets';
con_gets:=stat_val;
dbms_output.put_line(temp_name||'='||to_char(con_gets));
SELECT
   name, value
INTO
   temp_name, stat_val
FROM
   v$sysstat
WHERE
   name = 'physical reads';
p_reads:=stat_val;
dbms_output.put_line(temp_name||'='||to_char(p_reads));
SELECT COUNT(*)
INTO users
FROM v$session
WHERE username IS NOT NULL;
dbms_output.put_line('Users='||to_char(users));
   H_RATIO := (
   ((DB_GETS+CON_GETS-p_reads)/(DB_GETS+CON_GETS))*100);
dbms_output.put_line('h_ratio='||to_char(h_ratio));
   INSERT INTO  hit_ratios
     VALUES
     (c_date,c_hour,db_gets,con_gets,p_reads,h_ratio,0,0,users);
COMMIT;
UPDATE hit_ratios SET period_hit_ratio =
   (SELECT ROUND(
    (((h2.consistent-h1.consistent)+
     (h2.db_block_gets-h1.db_block_gets)-
      (h2.phy_reads-h1.phy_reads))/
      ((h2.consistent-h1.consistent)+
       (h2.db_block_gets-h1.db_block_gets)))*100,2)
    FROM hit_ratios h1, hit_ratios h2
    WHERE h2.check_date = hit_ratios.check_date
     AND h2.check_hour = hit_ratios.check_hour
```

```
      AND (
      (h1.check_date = h2.check_date
      AND h1.check_hour+1 = h2.check_hour)
      OR (h1.check_date+1 = h2.check_date
          AND h1.check_hour = '23' AND h2.check_hour='0')))
  WHERE period_hit_ratio = 0;
  COMMIT;
  UPDATE hit_ratios SET period_usage =
    (SELECT (
      (h2.consistent-h1.consistent)+
      (h2.db_block_gets-h1.db_block_gets))
    FROM hit_ratios h1,
         hit_ratios h2
    WHERE h2.check_date = hit_ratios.check_date
      AND h2.check_hour = hit_ratios.check_hour
      AND ((h1.check_date = h2.check_date
            AND h1.check_hour+1 = h2.check_hour)
           OR (h1.check_date+1 = h2.check_date
           AND h1.check_hour = '23' and h2.check_hour='0')))
  WHERE period_USAGE = 0;
  COMMIT;
  EXCEPTION
    WHEN ZERO_DIVIDE THEN
    INSERT INTO  hit_ratios  VALUES
    (c_date,c_hour,db_gets,con_gets,p_reads,0,0,0,users);
    COMMIT;
END;
/
```

The procedure in Source 15.9 is designed for hourly monitoring of hit ratio. The script can be called from a standard SQL script similar to Source 15.8. Once the script completes it is rescheduled to run the next hour. Of course, it is easier to use the DBMS_JOB package to allow Oracle to execute the procedure automatically. The script in Source 15.10 demonstrates how this is done. To use a job queue, the initialization parameters JOB_QUEUE_PROCESSES and JOB_QUEUE_INTERVAL have to be set and the instance restarted. The hit ratio for the previous hour is calculated as is the cumulative hit ratio and usage as a function of read/write activity. Some example results from this script, generated by the script in Source 15.10 are shown in Listings 15.21 and 15.22. Using the decode and pad statements, the hit ratio data can be plotted on any printer as a graph. This program is shown in Source 15.11.

SOURCE 15.10 Example PL/SQL script to submit hit ratio procedure to job queue.

```
DECLARE
jobno NUMBER;
BEGIN
dbms_job.submit (jobno, 'HITRATIO;',sysdate,'sysdate+1');
```

```
dbms_output.put_line(TO_CHAR(jobno));
END;

Note: You must put a semicolon at the end of the "HITRATIO" statement.
```

SOURCE 15.11   Script to generate hit ratio and usage report.

```
REM
REM NAME     :HRSUMM.SQL
REM FUNCTION:GENERATE REPORT OF PERIOD HIT RATIOS AND USAGE
REM FUNCTION:BETWEEN TWO DATES
REM USE      :FROM SQLPlus
REM Limitations      : None
REM Revisions:
REM     Date          Modified by    Reason for change
REM     10-JUL-1992   M. AULT        INITIAL CREATE
REM     23-Jun-1997   M. AULT        Verify against 8
REM
SET VERIFY OFF PAGES 58 NEWPAGE 0
START title80 "HIT RATIO AND USAGE FOR &&CHECK_DATE1 TO &&CHECK_DATE2"
DEFINE output = rep_out/&db/hrsumm.lis
SPOOL &output
SELECT
     check_date,
     check_hour,
     period_hit_ratio,
     period_usage,
     users
FROM
     hit_ratios
WHERE
     check_date BETWEEN '&&check_date1' AND '&&check_date2'
ORDER BY
     check_date,check_hour;
SPOOL OFF
PAUSE Press Enter to continue
```

LISTING 15.21   Example of output of periodic hit ratio report.

```
Date: 06/23/97                                          Page:   1
Time: 05:59 HIT RATIO AND USAGE FOR 22-jun-97 TO 23-jun-97 SYS
                      ORTEST1 database

CHECK_DAT CHECK_HOUR PERIOD_HIT_RATIO PERIOD_USAGE     USERS
--------- ---------- ---------------- ------------ ---------
22-JUN-97         13                                       1
22-JUN-97         15                                       2
22-JUN-97         16            97.76         2098          2
```

```
22-JUN-97        17              100            1066          2
22-JUN-97        18              100            1098          2
22-JUN-97        19              100            1067          2
22-JUN-97        20              100            1096          2
22-JUN-97        21              100            1066          2
22-JUN-97        22              100            1096          2
22-JUN-97        23              100            1067          2
23-JUN-97         0              100            1096          2
23-JUN-97         1              100            1073          2
23-JUN-97         2              100            1096          2
23-JUN-97         3              100            1067          2
23-JUN-97         4              100            1324          2
23-JUN-97         5              100            1067          2

16 rows selected.

Note: The 100 hit ratios shown here are not a result of the fact that I am
the perfect DBA; they are a result of the way the system treats purely
internal (V$) requests and an artifact of the calculation process.
```

The problem with sporadic monitoring of hit ratios is that the DBA may catch the system at a low point or just when the database usage has switched from one user to another on a different application. All of this can contribute to incorrect hit ratio results. The use of a periodic script to monitor hit ratio tends to even these fluctuations out and provide a better look at the statistic.

Another problem with looking at hit ratio as it is described in the Oracle manuals is that you are looking at a running average, a cumulative value. This will result in low readings when the database is started and high readings after it has been running. Graphs showing actual periodic hit ratio and cumulative hit ratio are shown in Listings 15.22 and 15.23.

LISTING 15.22   Periodic hit ratio for 18 May 1993.

```
Date: 06/05/93                  "Your Company Name"      Page:   1
Time: 03:52 PM                Period HR by hour for 18-may-93             DEV_DBA
                                  "Your" Database


  HRZCCCCCCCCCCCCCCCCCCCCCCCCCCCCCCCCCCCCCCCCCCCCCCCCMCCCCCCCCCCCCCCCCCCCCCCCCCCCCCCCECCCCCCCCC
  --------------------------------------------------------------------------------
                      o
      1                         o
      2                         o
      3                         o
      4                         o
      5                         o
      6                         o
      7                         o
```

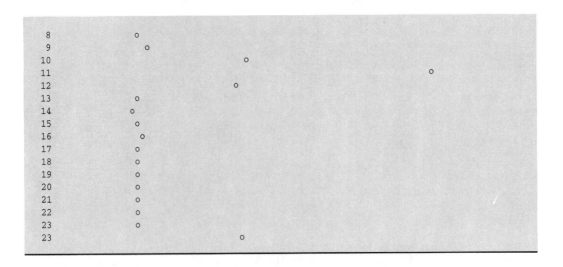

```
     8                    o
     9                      o
    10                                o
    11                                                              o
    12                               o
    13               o
    14              o
    15               o
    16                o
    17               o
    18               o
    19               o
    20               o
    21               o
    22               o
    23               o
    23                               o
```

LISTING 15.23   Graph of cumulative hit ratio for 18 May 1993.

```
Date: 06/05/93              "Your Company Name"              Page:   1
Time: 03:52 PM          HR on the hour by hour on 18-may-93         DEV_DBA
                        "Your" Database


  HRZCCCCCCCCCCCCCCCCCCCCCCCCCCCCCCCCCCCCCCCCCCCCCCMCCCCCCCCCCCCCCCCCCCCCCCCCCCCCCCCCCCCCNCC
  ----------------------------------------------------------------------------------------
                                o
     1                           o
     2                           o
     3                           o
     4                           o
     5                           o
     6                          o
     7                          o
     8                          o
     9                           o
    10                           o
    11                             o
    12                             o
    13                            o
    14                            o
    15                           o
    16                           o
    17                           o
    18                           o
    19                           o
    20                           o
    21                          o
    22                          o
```

The preceding graphs were generated by a script similar to the script in Source 15.12. For the cumulative graph, hit_ratio instead of period_hit_ratio is fed into the decode statements. This technique can be used to plot just about any data set if you normalize the numbers to between zero and one hundred. As you can see, the cumulative hit ratio graph stayed fairly constant for the period, while the actual or period hit ratio varied between 18.78 and 92.95 percent. In fact, the cumulative hit ratio will reach a steady, slowly increasing value, shortly after startup.

SOURCE 15.12   SQL script to generate a 132-column hit ratio graph.

```
REM
REM NAME     :HRATIO_REPORT.SQL
REM PURPOSE:CREATE PLOT OF PERIOD HIT RATIO FOR 1 DAY
REM USE         :FROM STATUS_REPORTS.COM
REM Limitations : None
REM Revisions:
REM   Date   Modified by    Reason for change
REM   10-JUL-1992   M. AULT INITIAL CREATE
REM          23-Jun-1997 M. Ault      Verify for 8
REM
REM host SET TERM/WID=132 REM: For VMS , won't work under UNIX
SET LINES 131 NEWPAGE 0 VERIFY OFF PAGES 180 SPACE 0
SET FEEDBACK OFF COLUMN HR FORMAT 99
START title132 "Period HR for &&check_date1 TO &&check_date2"
DEFINE OUTPUT = 'rep_out/&db/phrgrph.lis'
SPOOL &output
SELECT
    check_hour hr,
    DECODE(ROUND(period_hit_ratio),0,'o',NULL) zchk0,
    DECODE(ROUND(period_hit_ratio),1,'o',NULL) chk1,
    DECODE(ROUND(period_hit_ratio),2,'o',NULL) chk2,
    DECODE(ROUND(period_hit_ratio),3,'o',NULL) chk3,
    DECODE(ROUND(period_hit_ratio),4,'o',NULL) chk4,
    DECODE(ROUND(period_hit_ratio),5,'o',NULL) chk5,

      .
      .
      .

    DECODE(ROUND(period_hit_ratio),94,'o',NULL) chk94,
    DECODE(ROUND(period_hit_ratio),95,'o',NULL) chk95,
    DECODE(ROUND(period_hit_ratio),96,'o',NULL) chk96,
    DECODE(ROUND(period_hit_ratio),97,'o',NULL) chk97,
    DECODE(ROUND(period_hit_ratio),98,'o',NULL) chk98,
    DECODE(ROUND(period_hit_ratio),99,'o',NULL) chk99,
    DECODE(ROUND(period_hit_ratio),100,'o',NULL) chk100
FROM hit_ratios
WHERE CHECK_DATE BETWEEN '&&CHECK_DATE1' AND '&&CHECK_DATE2'
ORDER BY CHECK_DATE,check_hour;
SPOOL OFF
PAUSE 'PRESS ENTER TO CONTINUE'
REM host SET TERM/WID=80  rem: for VMS, will not work on UNIX
```

If your hit ratio for periods of high usage is below 70 to 90 percent, increase the DB_BLOCK_BUFFERS INIT.ORA parameter. As you can see from the listing in Listing 15.22, when database usage was minimal, the hit ratio hovered at 18 to 20 percent; once usage increased above 10,000 to 20,000, hit ratio leapt to greater than 90 percent, as would be expected.

If DB_BLOCK_BUFFERS is set too high, you may run out of PAD area under VMS or exceed shared memory size on UNIX for your instance. Another possible result is that the entire Oracle process could be swapped out due to memory contention with other processes. In either case, it is not a desirable condition. To avoid exceeding your PAD or shared memory areas, be sure you set these values high when the instance is created. To avoid swapping, know how much memory you are able to access; check with your system administrator to find this out.

Use of X$CBRBH and X$CBCBH tables. Oracle provides a virtual table owned by the SYS user to provide information on the effects of adding buffers to the buffer cache. This is the X$CBRBH table. This table has two columns, INDX and COUNT. The table is activated by setting the value of the initialization parameter DB_BLOCK_LRU_EXTENDED_STATISTICS to a nonzero value indicating the number of buffers you wish to add. The value you set for this parameter will determine the number of rows in the X$CBRBH table. There is one row for each additional buffer.

Once DB_BLOCK_LRU_EXTENDED_STATISTICS is set, the database will have to be shut down and restarted. This parameter should not be left enabled as it will cause a performance hit. The magnitude of the performance hit is directly proportional to the number of additional buffers about which data is collected.

There are two methods for reviewing the statistics collected in V$CBRBH; the first is to select the sum of the values of COUNT over a specific interval:

```
SELECT SUM(count) "interval total"
     FROM v$kcbrbh
     WHERE indx BETWEEN ( interval start, interval end);
```

The second gives more detailed information and is the suggested method. It provides summation over several intervals and gives the DBA more detail upon which to base his or her choice of the number of buffers to add:

```
SELECT
     50 * TRUNC(indx/50)+1||' to '||
     50 * (TRUNC(indx/50)+1) "interval",
     SUM(count) "Buffer Cache Hits"
FROM   sys.x$kcbrbh
GROUP BY TRUNC(indx/50);
```

The output from the preceding select looks like the following:

```
Interval            Buffer Cache Hits
1 to 50                 17350
51 to 100                9345
101 to 150                404
151 to 200              19568
```

The value 50 can be changed to any appropriate value. The output of this report shows the interval and the expected increase in buffer cache hits that could be expected from adding that many buffers to the cache. The preceding examples show that adding 50, 100, or 200 buffers would add significantly to the number of hits. Adding 150 buffers would add very few hits. Therefore, add 50, 100, or 200 additional buffers, but not 150.

A more detailed report is demonstrated in Source 15.13. This report prompts for the value to increment the summation by and then generates a report that also lists the percentage gain for each increment.

SOURCE 15.13 More detailed report of DD cache increment results.

```
rem   ************************************************************
rem
rem   NAME: SGA_INC.sql
rem
rem   HISTORY:
rem   Date        Who                 What
rem   --------    ------------------  ----------------------------
rem   10/25/92  Cary Millsap          Creation
rem   01/07/93  Michael Brouillette   Switched to title80
rem   06/05/93  Mike Ault             Added capability to use interval
rem
rem   FUNCTION: Examine the statistice in X$KCBRBH table with the
rem   intent to increase the size of the SGA.
rem
rem   ************************************************************
COLUMN bufval   NEW_VALUE nbuf        NOPRINT
COLUMN thits    NEW_VALUE tot_hits    NOPRINT
SELECT  value  bufval
FROM   v$parameter
WHERE
   LOWER(name) = 'db_block_lru_extended_statistics';
SELECT SUM(count)   thits FROM v$kcbrbh;
@title80 "Prospective Hits if &nbuf Cache Buffers were Added"
COLUMN interval    FORMAT           a20 JUSTIFY c HEADING 'Buffers'
COLUMN cache_hits FORMAT 999,999,990 JUSTIFY c HEADING -
   'Cache Hits that would have been|gained by adding Buffers'
COLUMN cum        FORMAT 99.99 HEADING 'Percent of Gain'
SET TERMOUT OFF FEEDBACK OFF VERIFY OFF ECHO OFF
SPOOL rep_out/&db/sga_inc.lis
SELECT
    LPAD(TO_CHAR((&nbuf/&incr)*TRUNC(
    indx/(&nbuf/&&incr))+1,'999,990'),8)||' to '||
    LPAD(TO_CHAR((&nbuf/&&incr)*(TRUNC(
    indx/(&nbuf/&&incr))+1),'999,990'),8)      interval,
```

```
     SUM(count) cache_hits, SUM(count)/&tot_hits * 100 cum
FROM v$kcbrbh
GROUP BY
  TRUNC(indx/(&nbuf/&&incr));
SPOOL OFF
SET TERMOUT ON FEEDBACK 15 VERIFY ON
UNDEF NBUF
```

Of course, the analysis of the buffer cache may indicate that the buffers have been overallocated. The X$KCBCBH table will provide data on the result of removing buffers from the buffer cache. There is a row for each buffer in the current buffer cache in the table. The collection of statistics is enabled by setting the DB_BLOCK_LRU_STATISTICS to TRUE then shutting down and restarting the database. This data collection will cause a performance hit; the severity is proportional to the number of current buffers in the buffer cache. Once data collection is complete, the DB_BLOCK_LRU_STATISTICS parameter should be set to FALSE.

To review data in the X$KCBCBH table, the methods are similar to those used for the X$KCBCBH table. You can select for a specific interval or gather summation for ranges of buffers.

To determine the results from having, say, only 100 buffers in the cache, perform the following select:

```
SELECT SUM(count) "Hit Misses"
     FROM x$kcbcbh
     WHERE indx >= 100;
```

To summarize data over intervals of buffers, a select similar to the following could be used:

```
SELECT 10*TRUNC(indx/10)+1||' to '||
       10*(TRUNC(indx/10)+1) "Interval",
SUM(copunt) 'Buffer Hits'
FROM x$kcbcbh
WHERE indx > 0
GROUP BY TRUNC(indx/10);
```

The results will look like the following:

```
Interval          Buffer Hits
1 to 10           2500
11 to 20          1345
21 to 30          1097
31 to 40           896
41 to 50           110
```

In this case, if the number of buffers was reduced by 10 there would be few hits lost. If anything greater than 10 is dropped, significant losses in hits would occur. Therefore, drop only 10 buffers in this situation.

A more detailed report can be generated with the script in Source 15.14.

Once the buffer cache is tuned, you have completed the tuning of memory. The next step is to tune IO contention.

SOURCE 15.14 Example of buffer cache decrement detailed report script.

```
rem   ************************************************************
rem   NAME: SGA_DEC.sql
rem
rem   HISTORY:
rem   Date            Who                 What
rem   --------        --------------------    ---------------------------------
rem   10/25/92  Cary Millsap          Creation
rem   01/07/93  Michael Brouillette   Switched to title80
rem   06/05/93  Mike Ault             Added selectable ranges
rem   FUNCTION: Examine statistics in the X$KCBCBH table with intent to
rem             shrink the SGA.
rem   ************************************************************
COLUMN bufval   NEW_VALUE nbuf NOPRINT
COLUMN thits    NEW_VALUE tot_hits NOPRINT
SELECT value  bufval
FROM v$parameter
WHERE
  LOWER(name) = 'db_block_buffers';
SELECT SUM(count) thits
FROM x$kcbhcbh;
START title80 "Lost Hits if &nbuf Cache Buffers were Removed"
COLUMN interval    FORMAT         a20 JUSTIFY c HEADING 'Buffers'
COLUMN cache_hits FORMAT 999,999,990 JUSTIFY c HEADING -
  'Hits that would have been lost|had Cache Buffers been removed'
COLUMN cum FORMAT 99.99 'Percent of loss'
SET TERMOUT OFF FEEDBACK OFF VERIFY OFF ECHO OFF
SPOOL rep_out/&db/sga_dec.lis
SELECT
  LPAD(to_char(&&incr*(trunc(
    indx/&&incr)+1),'999,990'),8)||
..' to '||
  LPAD(to_char(&&incr*(trunc(
    indx/&&incr)+1),'999,990'),8) interval,
  SUM(count)  cache_hits,
  SUM(count)/&tot_hits * 100 cum
FROM x$kcbcbh
WHERE indx > 0
GROUP BY
  TRUNC(indx/&&incr) ;
SPOOL OFF
SET TERMOUT ON FEEDBACK 15 VERIFY ON
```

Tools for Tuning IO Contention

Once the shared SQL areas and buffer caches have been tuned, the DBA must turn his or her eyes to the IO performance of the disks and files associated with the Oracle system to realize further performance gains.

Tuning IO to avoid bottlenecks. Once the application and memory areas have been tuned, the next performance bottleneck can be the disk subsystem. This system is tuned by tuning the input and output processes that Oracle uses, reducing contention for disk resources, and reducing or eliminating dynamic space allocation within database data files.

Tuning the DBWR Process The DBWR process manages the buffer cache. In this capacity, it writes filled buffers from the buffer cache in the SGA to the disks. Obviously, a properly tuned DBWR process will be the first step in tuning IO for the Oracle system. The DBWR process, as described in the section on UTLBSTAT and UTLESTAT, uses the hidden INIT.ORA parameters _DB_BLOCK_WRITE_BATCH and _DB_BLOCK_MAX_SCAN_CNT to determine when it should write used, or dirty, buffers to the disk, thus freeing them for further use. DBWR triggers on the following conditions:

1. A user process writes a used buffer to the dirty buffer list and finds it is _DB_BLOCK_WRITE_BATCH / 2 long.
2. A user process searches _DB_BLOCK_MAX_SCAN_CNT buffers without finding a clean one.
3. If DBWR has been inactive for three seconds.
4. When a checkpoint occurs LGWR signals DBWR, triggering it to write.

The DBWR writes out _DB_BLOCK_WRITE_BATCH buffers each time it is triggered. If there aren't that many buffers in the dirty buffer list, the buffers on the LRU list are written until _DB_BLOCK_WRITE_BATCH buffers are written.

DBWR is monitored using the statistic free buffer waits. The free buffer waits statistic (available from the V$SYSSTAT table) should be as low as possible and should remain at a slowly increasing value. What this means for your system you will have to decide. I suggest using a method similar to that shown in the previous section to follow the delta values for this statistic; if you see spikes when database activity is high, consider using either more DB writers by setting the initialization parameter DB_WRITERS equal to the number of disks used by Oracle (if your system doesn't support asynchronous IO) or by setting the ASYNC_IO initialization parameter to TRUE if your system supports asynchronous IO. If setting either DB_WRITERS or ASYNC_IO doesn't help reduce the spikes on free buffer waits, verify that _DB_BLOCK_MAX_SCAN_CNT is set at 30 or greater. Normally, the default value of 30 is fine for this parameter. If you are dissatisfied with the performance of DBWR, try increasing the INIT.ORA parameter _DB_BLOCK_WRITE_BATCH first. Increasing this parameter improves DBWR's ability to use operating system facilities to write to multiple disks and write adjacent blocks in a single IO operation. Increasing the number of db block buffers may also be in order if DBWR performance is poor.

Disk Contention Once DBWR is tuned, the DBA needs to look at disk contention. Disk contention happens when one or more users attempt to read the same disk at the same time or, in some cases, access a different disk through the same controller path at the same time. This is prevented by spreading Oracle-related files across several platters or sets of platters—the more the better. The new RAID options don't relieve the DBA of file placement concerns. You should be sure that the RAID volumes are properly set. I had one system in which a system administrator set up multiple RAID 5 volumes using two disks for each volume (a hint: the 5 is a meaningful number for RAID 5).

The DBA can monitor disk activity by looking at the statistics for disk IO stored in the database virtual tables. Using the hit ratio scripts from the previous section as a model, the DBA should be able to devise a periodic monitoring script that calculates periodic disk usage as well as the cumulative figures already stored in the virtual tables. The script in Source 15.15 shows how to access the SYS tables for this cumulative information.

To perform periodic measurements simply perform the select shown in Source 15.15 as part of an update to a DBA-created table. In addition to the disk information, append a date and time stamp and then the table can be used to perform periodic disk IO calculations just like the HIT_RATIOS table in the previous pages. Instead of indexing by only date and hour, index by date, hour, and file name.

SOURCE 15.15   SQL script for report on disk activity.

```
REM
REM NAME    :FILE_EFF.SQL
REM PURPOSE :GENERATE FILE IO EFFICIENCIES REPORT
REM USE     :FROM STATUS_REPORTS.COM
REM Limitations :MUST BE RUN FROM ORACLE DBA ACCOUNT
REM Revisions:
REM Date           Modified by       Reason for change
REM 10-JUL-1992    M. AULT             INITIAL CREATE
REM 07-JUN-1993    M.AULT            Added reads to writes, reformatted
REM 23-Jun-1997    M.Ault            kcffio went away, rewrote to use
REM                                  existing views/tables
SET PAGES 58 NEWPAGE 0
SET LINES 131
COLUMN eff    FORMAT A6            HEADING '% Eff'
COLUMN rw     FORMAT 9,999,999     HEADING 'Phys Block|read/writes'
COLUMN ts     FORMAT A22           HEADING 'Tablespace Name'
COLUMN name FORMAT A40             HEADING 'File Name'
start title132 "FILE IO EFFICIENCY"
BREAK ON ts
DEFINE OUTPUT = 'rep_out/&db/file_io.lis'
spool &OUTPUT
```

```
SELECT
    f.tablespace_name ts,
    f.file_name name,
    v.phyreads+v.phywrts rw,
    TO_CHAR(DECODE(v.phyblkrd,0,null,
    ROUND(100*(v.phyrds+v.phywrts)/
            (v.phyblkrd+v.phyblkwrt),2))) eff
FROM dba_data_files f, v$filestat v
WHERE f.file_id=v.file#
ORDER BY 1,file#;
SPOOL OFF
PAUSE Press Enter to continue
```

This report is a cumulative report that gives information based on IO since the Oracle Instance was started. The report generated will list physical block reads and efficiency (the efficiency number measures the percentage of time Oracle asked for and got the right block the first time; this is a function of the type of table scan and indexing). An example of Source 15.15 output is shown in Listing 15.24.

LISTING 15.24   Example of the output of file IO efficiency report.

```
Date: 06/23/97                                                      Page:   1
Time: 11:30 AM                      FILE IO EFFICIENCY                    SYS
                                    ORCNETT3 database

                                                        Phys Block
Tablespace name File Name                               read/writes  % Eff
--------------- ------------------------------------    -----------  -------
RBS             /oracle04/ORCNETT3/data/rbs01.dbf             3,728    100
APPL_DATA       /oracle05/ORCNETT3/data/APLDAT01_ORCNETT3.dbf    10    100
                /oracle05/ORCNETT3/data/APLDAT02_ORCNETT3.dbf   427    100
                /oracle05/ORCNETT3/data/APLDAT03_ORCNETT3.dbf    10    100
                /oracle05/ORCNETT3/data/APLDAT04_ORCNETT3.dbf     1    100
                /oracle05/ORCNETT3/data/APLDAT05_ORCNETT3.dbf     4    100
                /oracle05/ORCNETT3/data/APLDAT06_ORCNETT3.dbf   223    100
APPL_INDEX      /oracle06/ORCNETT3/data/APLIND01_ORCNETT3.dbf    15    100
                /oracle06/ORCNETT3/data/APLIND02_ORCNETT3.dbf   494    100
                /oracle06/ORCNETT3/data/APLIND03_ORCNETT3.dbf   166    100
                /oracle06/ORCNETT3/data/APLIND04_ORCNETT3.dbf    51    100
SYSTEM          /oracle00/ORCNETT3/data/system01.dbf          2,552  65.71
TEMP            /oracle01/ORCNETT3/data/temp01.dbf                0
                /oracle01/ORCNETT3/data/temp02.dbf                0
TOOLS           /oracle02/ORCNETT3/data/tools01.dbf           2,710  88.28
USERS           /oracle03/ORCNETT3/data/user01.dbf               23    100

16 rows selected.
```

Some things to notice about the example report in Listing 15.24 are the following:

- The relatively low efficiency of the SYSTEM areas in general. This is due to indexes and tables being mixed together in the SYSTEM area. A classic case on Oracle's part of "Do what we say, not what we do."
- If your temporary tablespace (TEMP in the example) shows an efficiency number, someone is using it for real instead of temporary tables.
- Rollback efficiency should always be 100 percent; if not, someone is using the rollback area for tables.
- Index tablespace should always show high efficiencies; if they don't, then either the indexes are bad or someone is using the index areas for normal tables.
- An attempt should be made to even out IO. In the preceding example too much IO is being done on Oracle04; some of these data files should be spread to other disks.
- This report shows total IO for the time frame beginning with the Oracle system startup.
- The results could be stored for two or more dates and times and then subtracted to show the disk IO for a selected period of time. UTLBSTAT/UTLESTAT should be used for this type of measurement.

With a copy of this report run before an application test run and a copy run after the test run, an idea of the disk IO profile for the application can be developed. This profile combined with information concerning the maximum IO supported by each disk, or each controller, will enable the DBA to determine how best to split out the application's files between disks.

Further reading. For more detailed information and further reading, take a look at the following:

The Key 20 Scripts for the DBA to Ensure Sleep Is Not Just a Dream, Joseph C. Trezzo, TUSC, IOUG-A Alive! Dallas, Texas, 1997, Paper No. 35.

Oracle Performance Tuning, Mark Gurry, Peter Corrigan, and O'Reilly and Associates, Inc., 2d ed., November 1996.

Oracle7 Server Administrator's Guide, Release 7.3, Part No. A32535-1, Oracle Corporation.

Oracle7 Server Tuning, Release 7.3, Part No. A32537-1, June 1996, Oracle Corporation.

Oracle8 Server Tuning, Release 8.0, Beta2, February 1997, Part No. A50660-1, Oracle Corporation.

Quick Impact Tuning for the DBA and Developer, Richard J. Niemiec, TUSC, IOUG-A Alive! Dallas, Texas, Paper No. 136.

Tuning an Oracle RDBMS, One View, Paul Osborn, Menlo Software, IOUG-A Alive! Dallas, Texas, 1997, Paper No. 15.

Tuning Oracle, Michael J. Corey, Michael Abbey, and Daniel J. Dechichio Jr., Oracle Press—Osborne-McGraw-Hill, 1995.

Tuning to Prevent Contention Contention occurs when a number of users attempt to access the same resource at the same time. This can occur for any database object but is most noticeable when the contention is for rollback segments, redo logs, latches, or locks. Under Oracle7 you can also experience contention with the processes involved with the multithreaded server.

To correct contention you must first realize that it is occurring. The script shown in Source 15.16 can be used to monitor for contention. The report generated by this script is shown in Listing 15.25.

SOURCE 15.16   SQL and PL/SQL scripts to generate contention statistics.

```
REM
REM NAME     : DO_CALSTAT.SQL
REM FUNCTION :Generate calculated statisitics report using
REM FUNCTION :just_statistics procedure
REM USE      :FROM STATUS.SQL or SQLPLUS
REM Limitations    :
REM Revisions:
REM Date          Modified By      Reason For change
REM 05-MAY-1992    Mike Ault       Initial Creation
REM 23-JUN-1997    Mike Ault       Updated to V8
REM
SET PAGES 58  NEWPAGE 0
EXECUTE just_statistics
START title80 "CALCULATED STATISTICS REPORT"
DEFINE output = rep_out\&db\cal_stat.lis
SPOOL &output
SELECT * FROM dba_temp;
SPOOL OFF


Listing of just_statistics - The called PL/SQL procedure

CREATE OR REPLACE PROCEDURE just_statistics AS
     start_date      DATE;
     dd_ratio        NUMBER := 0;
     r_calls         NUMBER := 0;
     h_ratio         NUMBER := 0;
     suhw_cont       NUMBER := 0;
     subw_cont       NUMBER := 0;
     uhw_cont        NUMBER := 0;
     ubw_cont        NUMBER := 0;
     db_gets         NUMBER := 0;
     con_gets        NUMBER := 0;
     p_reads         NUMBER := 0;
     suh_waits       NUMBER := 0;
     sub_waits       NUMBER := 0;
     uh_waits        NUMBER := 0;
     ub_waits        NUMBER := 0;
     u_calls         NUMBER := 0;
     calls_u         NUMBER := 0;
     rlog_wait       NUMBER := 0;
     stat_name       VARCHAR2(64);
```

```
    temp_name          VARCHAR2(64);
    stat_val           NUMBER := 0;
    temp_value         NUMBER := 0;
    version            VARCHAR2(9);
CURSOR get_latch IS
  SELECT a.name,100.*b.sleeps/b.gets
  FROM v$latchname a, v$latch b
  WHERE a.latch# = b.latch# AND b.sleeps > 0;
CURSOR get_totals IS
  SELECT object_type,COUNT(*)
  FROM dba_objects
  WHERE owner NOT IN ('SYS','SYSTEM')
  GROUP BY object_type
  ORDER BY object_type;
CURSOR get_stat(stat IN VARCHAR2) IS
  SELECT name,value
  FROM  v$sysstat
  WHERE name = stat;
CURSOR get_count(stat IN VARCHAR2) IS
  SELECT class,"COUNT"
  FROM v$waitstat
  WHERE class = stat_name;
BEGIN
  DELETE dba_temp;
BEGIN
DBMS_REVEALNET.STARTUP_DATE(start_date);
  IF start_date IS NOT NULL THEN
   INSERT INTO dba_temp VALUES
   'Startup Date:'||TO_CHAR(start_date,'dd-mon-yy hh24:mi:ss'),0,1);
  ELSE
   INSERT INTO dba_temp values ('Startup Date: unknown',0,1);
  END IF;
END;
BEGIN
  stat_name := 'recursive calls';
    OPEN get_stat(stat_name);
    FETCH get_stat INTO temp_name, r_calls;
    CLOSE get_stat;
EXCEPTION
   WHEN NO_DATA_FOUND THEN
CLOSE get_stat;
END;
BEGIN
  stat_name := 'DATA DICTIONARY MISS %';
  SELECT
    stat_name,(SUM(getmisses)/SUM(gets))*100 INTO temp_name,dd_ratio
  FROM v$rowcache;
  INSERT INTO dba_temp VALUES (stat_name, dd_ratio,17);
EXCEPTION
   WHEN NO_DATA_FOUND THEN
```

```
        INSERT INTO dba_temp VALUES (stat_name,0,17);
     COMMIT;
END;
BEGIN
  stat_name := 'user calls';
     OPEN  get_stat(stat_name);
     FETCH get_stat INTO temp_name, u_calls;
     CLOSE get_stat;
EXCEPTION
   WHEN NO_DATA_FOUND THEN
CLOSE get_stat;
END;
BEGIN
  stat_name := 'db block gets';
     OPEN get_stat(stat_name);
     FETCH get_stat INTO temp_name, db_gets;
     CLOSE get_stat;
EXCEPTION
   WHEN NO_DATA_FOUND THEN
CLOSE get_stat;
END;
BEGIN
  stat_name := 'consistent gets';
     OPEN get_stat(stat_name);
     FETCH get_stat INTO temp_name, con_gets;
     CLOSE get_stat;
EXCEPTION
   WHEN NO_DATA_FOUND THEN
CLOSE get_stat;
END;
BEGIN
  stat_name := 'physical reads';
     OPEN get_stat(stat_name);
     FETCH get_stat INTO temp_name, p_reads;
     CLOSE get_stat;
EXCEPTION
   WHEN NO_DATA_FOUND THEN
CLOSE get_stat;
END;
BEGIN
  stat_name := 'system undo header';
     OPEN get_count(stat_name);
     FETCH get_count INTO temp_name, suh_waits;
     CLOSE get_count;
EXCEPTION
   WHEN NO_DATA_FOUND THEN
CLOSE get_count;
END;
BEGIN
  stat_name := 'system undo block';
```

```
      OPEN get_count(stat_name);
      FETCH get_count INTO temp_name, sub_waits;
      CLOSE get_count;
EXCEPTION
    WHEN NO_DATA_FOUND THEN
CLOSE get_count;
END;
BEGIN
  stat_name := 'undo header';
      OPEN get_count(stat_name);
      FETCH get_count INTO temp_name, uh_waits;
      CLOSE get_count;
EXCEPTION
    WHEN NO_DATA_FOUND THEN
CLOSE get_count;
END;
BEGIN
  stat_name := 'undo block';
      OPEN get_count(stat_name);
      FETCH get_count INTO temp_name, ub_waits;
      CLOSE get_count;
EXCEPTION
    WHEN NO_DATA_FOUND THEN
CLOSE get_count;
END;
BEGIN
    calls_u   := (r_calls/u_calls);
    h_ratio   := ((db_gets+con_gets)/(db_gets+con_gets+p_reads));
    suhw_cont := (suh_waits/(db_gets+con_gets)*100);
    subw_cont := (sub_waits/(db_gets+con_gets)*100);
    uhw_cont  := (uh_waits/(db_gets+con_gets)*100);
    ubw_cont  := (ub_waits/(db_gets+con_gets)*100);
    stat_name := 'RECURSIVE CALLS PER USER';
  INSERT INTO dba_temp VALUES (stat_name, calls_u,18);
    stat_name := 'CUMMULATIVE HIT RATIO';
  INSERT INTO dba_temp VALUES (stat_name, H_RATIO,2);
    stat_name := 'SYS UNDO HDR WAIT CONTENTION %';
  INSERT INTO dba_temp VALUES (stat_name, suhw_cont,3);
    stat_name := 'SYS UNDO BLK WAIT CONTENTION %';
  INSERT INTO dba_temp VALUES (stat_name, subw_cont,3);
    stat_name := 'UNDO HDR WAIT CONTENTION %';
  INSERT INTO dba_temp VALUES (stat_name, uhw_cont,3);
    stat_name := 'UNDO BLK WAIT CONTENTION %';
  INSERT INTO dba_temp VALUES (stat_name, ubw_cont,3);
    stat_name := 'freelist';
    OPEN get_count(stat_name);
    FETCH get_count INTO temp_name, stat_val;
    CLOSE get_count;
  stat_name := 'FREE LIST CONTENTION RATIO';
    INSERT INTO dba_temp VALUES (stat_name,
```

```
stat_val/(db_gets+con_gets),18);
EXCEPTION
    WHEN ZERO_DIVIDE THEN
      INSERT INTO dba_temp VALUES (stat_name,0,32);
      CLOSE get_count;
    COMMIT;
    WHEN NO_DATA_FOUND THEN
      INSERT INTO dba_temp VALUES (stat_name,0,32);
      CLOSE get_count;
    COMMIT;
END;
BEGIN
version:=DBMS_REVEALNET.RETURN_VERSION;
IF substr(version,1,5) in
('7.2.3','7.3.0','7.3.1','7.3.2','7.3.3','8.0.0',
 '8.0.0','8.0.1','8.0.2', '8.0.3') THEN
  stat_name := 'LATCH MISS %';
     SELECT (1-((SUM(sleeps)+SUM(immediate_misses))/(
     SUM(gets)+SUM(immediate_misses)+SUM(immediate_gets)))*100)
     INTO stat_val
     FROM v$latch;
     INSERT INTO dba_temp VALUES (stat_name, stat_val,4);
END IF;
EXCEPTION
    WHEN NO_DATA_FOUND THEN
      INSERT INTO dba_temp VALUES (stat_name,0,4);
    COMMIT;
END;
BEGIN
  stat_name := 'ROLLBACK WAIT %';
     SELECT (SUM(waits)/SUM(gets))*100 INTO stat_val
     FROM v$rollstat;
     INSERT INTO dba_temp VALUES (stat_name, stat_val,5);
EXCEPTION
    WHEN NO_DATA_FOUND THEN
      INSERT INTO dba_temp VALUES (stat_name,0,5);
    COMMIT;
END;
BEGIN
  stat_name := 'LIBRARY RELOAD %';
     SELECT SUM(reloads)/SUM(pins)*100  INTO stat_val
     FROM v$librarycache;
     INSERT INTO dba_temp VALUES (stat_name, stat_val,5);
EXCEPTION
    WHEN NO_DATA_FOUND THEN
      INSERT INTO dba_temp VALUES (stat_name,0,5);
    COMMIT;
END;
BEGIN
```

```
    stat_name := 'table fetch by rowid';
      OPEN get_stat(stat_name);
      FETCH get_stat INTO temp_name, stat_val;
      CLOSE get_stat;
      INSERT INTO dba_temp VALUES (stat_name, stat_val,9);
EXCEPTION
    WHEN NO_DATA_FOUND THEN
      INSERT INTO dba_temp VALUES (stat_name,0,9);
CLOSE get_stat;
    COMMIT;
END;
BEGIN
  stat_name:='NON-INDEX LOOKUP RATIO';
  SELECT a.value/(a.value+b.value) INTO stat_val
  FROM v$sysstat a, v$sysstat b
  WHERE a.name='table scans (long tables)'
  AND b.name='table scans (short tables)';
  INSERT INTO dba_temp VALUES (stat_name, stat_val,8);
EXCEPTION
    WHEN NO_DATA_FOUND THEN
      INSERT INTO dba_temp VALUES (stat_name,0,8);
      CLOSE get_stat;
    COMMIT;
END;
BEGIN
  stat_name := 'table fetch continued row';
      OPEN get_stat(stat_name);
      FETCH get_stat INTO temp_name, stat_val;
      CLOSE get_stat;
      INSERT INTO dba_temp VALUES (stat_name, stat_val,14);
EXCEPTION
    WHEN NO_DATA_FOUND THEN
      INSERT INTO dba_temp VALUES (stat_name,0,14);
      CLOSE get_stat;
      COMMIT;
END;
BEGIN
  stat_name := 'sorts (memory)';
      OPEN get_stat(stat_name);
      FETCH get_stat INTO temp_name, stat_val;
      CLOSE get_stat;
      INSERT INTO dba_temp VALUES (stat_name, stat_val,15);
EXCEPTION
    WHEN NO_DATA_FOUND THEN
      INSERT INTO dba_temp VALUES (stat_name,0,15);
      CLOSE get_stat;
      COMMIT;
END;
BEGIN
```

```
   stat_name := 'sorts (disk)';
      OPEN get_stat(stat_name);
      FETCH get_stat INTO temp_name, stat_val;
      CLOSE get_stat;
   INSERT INTO dba_temp VALUES (stat_name, stat_val,16);
EXCEPTION
      WHEN NO_DATA_FOUND THEN
       INSERT INTO dba_temp VALUES (stat_name,0,16);
       CLOSE get_stat;
       COMMIT;
END;
BEGIN
   stat_name := 'redo log space requests';
      OPEN get_stat(stat_name);
      FETCH get_stat INTO temp_name, stat_val;
      CLOSE get_stat;
   INSERT INTO dba_temp VALUES (stat_name, stat_val,6);
EXCEPTION
      WHEN NO_DATA_FOUND THEN
       INSERT INTO dba_temp VALUES (stat_name,0,6);
       CLOSE get_stat;
       COMMIT;
END;
BEGIN
   stat_name := 'redo log space wait time';
      OPEN get_stat(stat_name);
      FETCH get_stat INTO temp_name, stat_val;
      CLOSE get_stat;
   INSERT INTO dba_temp VALUES (stat_name, stat_val, 6);
EXCEPTION
      WHEN NO_DATA_FOUND THEN
       INSERT INTO dba_temp VALUES (stat_name,0,6);
       CLOSE get_stat;
       COMMIT;
END;
BEGIN
   stat_name := 'TOTAL ALLOCATED MEG';
      SELECT SUM(BYTES)/1048576 INTO stat_val
      FROM dba_data_files WHERE
      STATUS = 'AVAILABLE';
   INSERT INTO dba_temp VALUES (stat_name, stat_val,25);
EXCEPTION
      WHEN NO_DATA_FOUND THEN
       INSERT INTO dba_temp VALUES (stat_name,0,25);
       COMMIT;
END;
BEGIN
   stat_name := 'TOTAL USED MEG';
      SELECT SUM(BYTES)/1048576 INTO stat_val
      FROM dba_extents;
```

```
    INSERT INTO dba_temp VALUES (stat_name, stat_val,26);
EXCEPTION
    WHEN NO_DATA_FOUND THEN
      INSERT INTO dba_temp VALUES (stat_name,0,26);
    COMMIT;
END;
BEGIN
  stat_name := 'TOTAL SGA SIZE';
      SELECT stat_name, SUM(b.value) INTO temp_name, stat_val
      FROM v$sga b;
  INSERT INTO dba_temp VALUES (stat_name, stat_val,31);
EXCEPTION
    WHEN NO_DATA_FOUND THEN
      INSERT INTO dba_temp VALUES (stat_name,0,31);
    COMMIT;
END;
BEGIN
OPEN get_latch;
LOOP
    FETCH get_latch INTO stat_name,stat_val;
    EXIT WHEN get_latch%NOTFOUND;
      INSERT INTO dba_temp VALUES (stat_name, stat_val,33);
END LOOP;
    CLOSE get_latch;
    COMMIT;
END;
BEGIN
OPEN get_totals;
LOOP
    FETCH get_totals INTO stat_name,stat_val;
    EXIT WHEN get_totals%NOTFOUND;
      INSERT INTO dba_temp VALUES (stat_name, stat_val,34);
END LOOP;
    CLOSE get_totals;
    COMMIT;
END;
  COMMIT;
END;
```

The first section of Source 15.16 shows the SQL script used to call and run the PL/SQL script located in the second section of Source 15.16. This script retrieves contention and database health-related statistics and calculates other statistics based upon those it retrieves. An example of the report generated by these two scripts is shown in Listing 15.25. The calls to the dbms_revealnet package shouldn't worry you; this package is included on the CD-ROM with this book and is listed in the appendices, also on the CD-ROM.

LISTING 15.25   Example of calculated statistics report.

```
Date: 06/23/97                                        Page:   1
Time: 01:46 PM          CALCULATED STATISTICS REPORT    SYSTEM
                            ORCNETD1 database


NAME                                                 VALUE
-------------------------------------------------    ---------
Startup Date: 22-jun-97 19:09:38                             0
CUMMULATIVE HIT RATIO                                .94986157
SYS UNDO HDR WAIT CONTENTION %                               0
UNDO BLK WAIT CONTENTION %                                   0
UNDO HDR WAIT CONTENTION %                                   0
SYS UNDO BLK WAIT CONTENTION %                               0
LATCH MISS %                                         .99029399
ROLLBACK WAIT %                                              0
LIBRARY RELOAD %                                     .09405527
redo log space requests                                     1
redo log space wait time                                   79
NONINDEX LOOKUPS RATIO                               .00130208
table fetch by rowid                                  1756693
table fetch continued row                                6311
sorts (memory)                                           6307
sorts (disk)                                               12
DATA DICTIONARY MISS %                               .45421233
RECURSIVE CALLS PER USER                             1.4314641
FREE LIST CONTENTION RATIO                                   0
TOTAL ALLOCATED MEG                                      19228
TOTAL USED MEG                                       7303.5547
TOTAL SGA SIZE                                       251581848
cache buffers chains                                 1.469E-05
library cache                                        .02203606
virtual circuit queues                               .00136422
virtual circuit buffers                              .00383542
shared pool                                          .08755574
cache buffers lru chain                              .00758422
row cache objects                                    .00045992
DATABASE LINK                                               1
FUNCTION                                                   46
INDEX                                                     804
PACKAGE                                                    11
CLUSTER                                                     1
PACKAGE BODY                                               11
PROCEDURE                                                 317
SEQUENCE                                                  190
SYNONYM                                                  1697
TABLE                                                     781
TRIGGER                                                   272
VIEW                                                     249

41 rows selected.
```

The statistics that are calculated in Listing 15.25 are shown in capital letters. The "raw" values are reported in lowercase letters. What is this report telling us? Let's look at each of the statistics and see.

Startup Date: 22-jun-97 19:09:38   This is self-explanatory; it is the startup time for this instance. The reason I report it is that because the statistics are cumulative, if you run the report immediately upon startup the results will be skewed; this is a quick check that the numbers will be valid.

CUMMULATIVE HIT RATIO   As the name implies, this is the total cumulative hit ratio since the instance was started. Normally, it should rise to a maximum value and stay near there. If the max is much less than 0.90, you should look at increasing DB_BLOCK_BUFFERS.

SYS UNDO HDR WAIT CONTENTION %   This is the contention for the system rollback segment. This is basically for information purposes only. If you are seeing contention for the system rollback segment, too many people have access to SYS, SYSTEM, and INTERNAL since these are the only users that should be using the system rollback segment.

UNDO BLK WAIT CONTENTION %   This statistic shows contention for rollback segment blocks. If it reaches whole numbers you should look at increasing the number of rollback segments.

UNDO HDR WAIT CONTENTION %   This statistic shows contention for rollback segments. If you are getting rollback segment wait activity then you need either more rollback segments or more extents in the existing rollbacks.

SYS UNDO BLK WAIT CONTENTION %   See the previous entry for the system rollback segment.

LATCH MISS %   This statistic indicates if you are experiencing latch contention. If it reaches 5 to 10 percent, look into the CONTEND.SQL report to see what latches are causing the contention. Usually, this will be fixed by increasing the SHARED_POOL_SIZE initialization parameter.

ROLLBACK WAIT %   This statistic is related to the preceding UNDO statistics. If it gets into the whole percentages, look at increasing rollback segments or the number of extents.

LIBRARY RELOAD %   This statistic shows how much the library cache is having to reload. This indicates the SHARED_POOL_SIZE parameter needs to be increased to prevent premature aging of objects.

redo log space requests   This statistic shows that contention for redo logs is happening. If you get values for this parameter you may need to increase the number of redo log groups.

redo log space wait time   This statistic goes hand in hand with redo log space requests. You must have the TIMED_STATISTICS initialization parameter set to TRUE to get meaningful values for this statistic.

NONINDEX LOOKUPS RATIO   This calculated statistic gives the ratio of table scans (long tables) to the sum of table scans (long tables) plus table scans (short tables), based on the assumption that indexes will be much smaller than the tables they serve and more indexes will represent short tables. The ratio is a quick means to tell if you have enough (and proper) indexes.

table fetch by ROWID   This tells the number of times a value was retrieved using the fetch by ROWID access path.

table fetch continued row   This statistic indicates that chained rows exist in the database. If it is greater than 10 percent of the table fetches total (table fetch by ROWID + table fetch continued row) then you need to look at your high update tables where you have VARCHAR2 values and analyze these tables for chained rows.

sorts (memory)   This statistic tells you how many memory sorts are being done. Memory sorts are good.

sorts (disk)   This tells you how many disk sorts are being done; generally speaking, disk sorts are bad and should be avoided. If you get sorts(disk), increase your SORT_AREA_SIZE initialization parameter.

DATA DICTIONARY MISS %   This statistic tells you the health of the data dictionary caches. If this value should increase to more than 10 percent, increase the SHARED_POOL_SIZE initialization parameter.

RECURSIVE CALLS PER USER   This is a calculated ratio of total recursive calls against total cumulative users. This statistic tells you on average the number of times the database is having to search outside of the data dictionary and buffers for data and if dynamic space management is occurring. If this statistic stays above 10 then look at increasing your DB_BLOCK_BUFFERS and adjusting your table storage parameters.

FREE LIST CONTENTION RATIO   This statistic shows that contention for table or index free lists is occurring. If this statistic reaches 0.1, look at rebuilding tables and indexes with more free lists.

TOTAL ALLOCATED MEG   This calculated statistic tells how much physical disk area has been allocated to Oracle.

TOTAL USED MEG   This statistic tells how much of the allocated space is being used by object extents. This doesn't mean the space is filled with data; it just means the space has been grabbed by an object.

TOTAL SGA SIZE   This is a summation of the V$SGA DPT.

The following parameters are latches that are showing contention. If the contention is higher than 0.1, consider increasing the SHARED_POOL_SIZE initialization parameter.

- cache buffers chains
- library cache
- virtual circuit queues
- virtual circuit buffers
- shared pool
- cache buffers lru chain
- row cache objects

The following statistics show the total number of the particular type of object in the database.

- DATABASE LINK
- FUNCTION
- INDEX
- PACKAGE
- CLUSTER
- PACKAGE BODY
- PROCEDURE
- SEQUENCE
- SYNONYM
- TABLE
- TRIGGER
- VIEW

Buffer contention. If you think there may be contention for buffers as shown by the buffer busy waits statistic mentioned in previous sections, the report in Source 15.17 can be run to show possible areas of contention.

SOURCE 15.17   SQL script for report to show possible contention areas.

```
REM
REM NAME: CONTEND.SQL
REM FUNCTION: Shows where possible contention for resources
REM            in buffer busy waits use to pinpoint additional
REM            tuning areas.
REM
REM USE: Called from status
REM
SET VERIFY OFF FEEDBACK OFF
SET PAGES 58
SET LINES 79
START title80 "AREA OF CONTENTION REPORT"
DEFINE output = 'rep_out\&db\contend'
SPOOL &output
SELECT
    class,
    SUM(count) total_waits,
    SUM(time) total_time
FROM
    v$waitstat
GROUP BY
    class;
SPOOL OFF
PAUSE Press Enter to continue
SET VERIFY ON FEEDBACK ON PAGES 22 LINES 80
```

LISTING 15.26   Example of output from CONTEND.SQL script.

```
TTITLE OFF
Date: 06/13/97                                          Page:   1
Time: 08:05 AM        AREA OF CONTENTION REPORT         SYSTEM
                         ORCNETP1 database

CLASS               TOTAL_WAITS  TOTAL_TIME
------------------- -----------  ----------
data block                  27          23
free list                    0           0
save undo block              0           0
save undo header             0           0
segment header               0           0
sort block                   0           0
system undo block            0           0
system undo header           0           0
undo block                   0           0
undo header                  4           1
```

The report in Listing 15.26 covers the following types of blocks in the buffer cache:

data block   This statistic shows waits for blocks in the data buffer cache.

free list   This statistic shows waits for free lists (free list contention).

system undo header   This statistic shows waits for header blocks of the system rollback segment.

system undo block   This statistic shows waits for buffers containing other than header blocks for the system rollback segment.

undo header   This statistic shows waits for buffers containing nonsystem rollback segment header blocks.

undo blocks   This statistic shows waits for buffers containing other than header blocks for the nonsystem rollback segments.

segment header, save undo header, save undo block and **sort block** are not used by DBAs for tuning.

The statistic with the highest value shows the area where DBAs should concentrate their tuning efforts. From the example report (no statistic is actually high enough to warrant action), the initialization parameter DB_BLOCK_BUFFERS could be increased to reduce data block buffer contention.

If rollback contention is indicated ("undo" statistics), increase the number of rollback segments. Contention is indicated when any one area shows greater than a 1 percent value for the calculation

```
parameter / (db block gets + consistent gets)
```

Latch contention. The next type of contention deals with latches. Look at the script in Source 15.18. This script generates a report shown in Listing 15.27, of latch contention. The script restricts output to only those latches that exhibit a greater than zero timeout value. Obviously, if a latch shows zero timeouts, there is no contention for that latch. This restriction greatly reduces the amount of information the DBA has to review.

SOURCE 15.18   SQL script to generate latch contention report.

```
REM
REM NAME         : LTCH7_CO.SQL
REM FUNCTION     : Genereate latch contention report
REM USE          : From SQLPlus or other front end
REM Limitations  : None
REM
COLUMN name    FORMAT A30
COLUMN ratio1  FORMAT 999.999
COLUMN ratio2  FORMAT 999.999
SET PAGES 58 NEWPAGE 0
START title80 "LATCH CONTENTION REPORT"
SPOOL rep_out\&db\latchs
SELECT
  a.name,
  100.*b.misses/b.gets ratio1
  100.*b.immediate_misses/
  (b.immediate_gets+b.immediate_misses) ratio2
FROM
  v$latchname a, v$latch b
WHERE
    a.latch# = b.latch# AND b.misses > 0;
SPOOL OFF
PAUSE PRESS ENTER TO CONTINUE
CLEAR COLUMNS
TTITLE OFF
SET PAGES 22
```

LISTING 15.27   Example report generated by LATCH_CO.SQL.

```
Date: 06/23/97                                      Page:   1
Time: 03:40 PM        LATCH CONTENTION REPORT         SYSTEM
                       ORCNETD1 database

NAME                             RATIO1    RATIO2
-------------------------------- ------   --------
session allocation                .0034     .0000
messages                          .0005     .0000
cache buffers chains              .0000
```

```
cache buffers lru chain          .0082
row cache objects                .0006
shared pool                      .0740    .0000
library cache                    .0107
virtual circuit buffers          .0021    .0000
virtual circuit queues           .0007    .0000
virtual circuits                 .0003    .0000

10 rows selected.
```

As you can see, this report is much easier to look at than the many tool's monitor screens. The suggested calculations are done behind the scenes, and the DBA can tell at a glance if any latches are suffering contention. One interesting thing to notice is that all of these values are fractional percentages. If these values get up into whole percentages, reduce contention by increasing the SHARED_POOL_SIZE parameter under Oracle7 or Oracle8.

Some latches may not have exact correspondences (i.e., redo_copy, redo_allocation, etc.). These have been discussed in the section on UTLBSTAT and UTLESTAT. The material from that section is recapped next, so if you've already read that section, you can skip over this to the next section.

The following latches are the major ones the DBA needs to be concerned about; the others shouldn't require tuning.

Cache Buffers Chain This latch indicates user processes are waiting to scan the SGA for block access. To tune this latch, adjust DB_BLOCK_BUFFERS.

Cache Buffers LRU Chains This latch indicates waits when the user attempts to scan the LRU (Least Recently Used) chain that contains all the used blocks in the database buffers. To reduce waits on this latch increase the INIT.ORA parameter DB_BLOCK_BUFFERS or the INIT.ORA parameter _DB_BLOCK_WRITE_BATCH.

Enqueues This latch is controlled by the INIT.ORA parameter ENQUEUE_RESOURCES. If the ratio of timeouts to total exceeds 1 percent in Oracle7 increase ENQUEUE_RESOURCES.

Redo Allocation This latch controls the allocation of space in the redo buffer. There is only one allocation latch per instance in Oracle7. To reduce contention for this latch reduce the value of the INIT.ORA parameter LOG_SMALL_ENTRY_MAX_SIZE on multi-CPU systems to force use of a redo copy latch. On single CPU systems the value of CPU_COUNT in the INIT.ORA file is set to zero; this indicates no redo copy latches are allowed. Setting the CPU_COUNT to 1 and LOG_SIMULTANEOUS_COPIES to 2 is not recommended by Oracle for single CPU machines even though two redo copy latches are allowed per CPU. In the example report, 90 uses of the redo copy latch are shown even though the CPU count for the computer was set to zero; this indicates there are redo copy latches even on single CPU machines.

Redo copy This latch is used when an entry's size exceeds LOG_SMALL_ENTRY_SIZE and use of a redo copy latch is forced. This happens on both single and multi-CPU computers. On multi-CPU computers you can reduce redo copy latch contention by increasing LOG_SIMULTANEOUS_COPIES to twice the value of CPU_COUNT. The LOG_SMALL_ENTRY_MAX_SIZE parameter is used to specify the maximum size of a redo entry that can be copied on the redo allocation latch.

On single CPU systems, changing LOG_SIMULTANEOUS_COPIES and LOG_SMALL_ENTRY_MAX_SIZE has no effect.

row cache objects This latch shows waits for the user processes attempting to access the cached data dictionary values. To reduce contention for this latch, the shared SQL area is tuned. This will be covered in a later section.

Other than those listed previously, the rest of the latches shouldn't require tuning. If excessive contention is shown for them, contact the Oracle Support Group.

Tools for Additional Tuning Concerns

Once the DBA has tuned memory, tuned IO, and tuned contention, there are still a couple of minor items that he or she needs to consider. These items will improve performance, but any improvement would be masked by the other tuning areas if they are not taken care of first. This is why these are addressed last. The final tuning areas concern sorts, free lists, and checkpoints.

Sorts, Free Lists, and Checkpoints The final section in this chapter is on sorts, free lists, and checkpoints. Improvement of sort speed provides obvious benefits. Free lists provide information on the free blocks inside database tables. If there aren't enough free lists, this can have an impact on performance. Checkpoints are writes from buffers to disk. Checkpoints, if excessive, can adversely affect performance as well; if there aren't enough checkpoints, recovery from disasters can be impeded.

The DBA needs to monitor these items on a regular basis and tune them as needed to get peak performance from the database.

Tuning Oracle sorts. Sorts are done when Oracle performs operations that retrieve information and require the information retrieved to be an ordered set, in other words, sorted. Sorts are done when the following operations are performed:

- Index creation
- Group by or Order by statements
- Use of the distinct operator
- Join operations
- Union, Intersect, and Minus set operators

Each of these operations requires a sort. There is one main indicator that your sorts are going to disk and therefore your sort area in memory is too small. This area is defined by the initialization parameter SORT_AREA_SIZE in both Oracle7 and Oracle8.

The primary indicator is the sorts (disk) statistic shown in Listing 15.25. If this parameter exceeds 10 percent of the sum of sorts(memory) and sorts(disk), increase the SORT_AREA_SIZE parameter. Large values for this parameter can induce paging and swapping, so be careful you don't overallocate. In Oracle7 this area is allocated either directly from memory to each user or, if the multithreaded server (MTS) is used, a section of the shared pool is allocated to each user. In Oracle8 an extra shared area called the LARGE POOL is used (if it has been initialized).

Under Oracle7 the SORT_AREA_SIZE parameter controls the maximum sort area. The sort area will be dynamically reallocated down to the size specified by the initialization parameter SORT_AREA_RETAINED_SIZE.

In Oracle7.2 and later, the initialization parameters SORT_DIRECT_WRITES, SORT_WRITE_BUFFER_SIZE and SORT_WRITE_BUFFERS control how needed disk sorts are optimized. By specifying SORT_DIRECT_WRITES to TRUE you can improve your sort times severalfold because this forces writes direct to disk rather than using the buffers. The SORT_WRITE_BUFFER_SIZE parameter should be set such that SORT_WRITE_BUFFERS * SORT_WRITE_BUFFER_SIZE is as large as you dare have it be on your system and still not get swapping. The SORT_ WRITE_BUFFERS is a value from 2 to 8 and the SORT_WRITE_BUFFER_SIZE is set between 32 and 64K bytes. Therefore, the maximum size this can be will be 8*64k = 512k or half a megabyte.

Some additional sort parameters are SORT_READ_FAC and SORT_SPACEMAP_ SIZE. The SORT_READ_FAC parameter assists with sort merges. Set this to between 25 and 100 percent of the value of the DB_BLOCK_MULTIBLOCK_READ_COUNT parameter. The SORT_SPACEMAP_SIZE parameter if set correctly helps with actions such as index builds. The suggested setting is

```
((total sort bytes/(SORT_AREA_SIZE)) + 64
```

where total sort bytes = (number of records in sort) * (average row length + (2 * No_of_ columns)). However, setting it higher temporarily isn't harmful and can speed the index build appreciably.

For standard sorts you should set the SORT_AREA_SIZE to the average sort size for your database. The temporary tablespaces initial and next default storage parameter should be set to the value of SORT_AREA_SIZE. For use with parallel query sorts a temporary tablespace should be spread (striped) across as many disks as the degree of parallelism.

Reducing free list contention. As was stated earlier a free list is a list of data blocks that contain free lists. Every table has one or more free lists. This is determined by the storage clause parameter FREE_LISTS and FREE_LIST_GROUPS, FREE_LISTS has its default value set to one (1). The maximum value of FREE_LISTS is block-size dependent and should be set to the number of simultaneous update processes that will be inserted into or updating the table. The setting of this parameter at the time the table is created determines the number of free lists for the table. The FREE_LIST_GROUPS parameter is only used in parallel server (not parallel query!) installations and should be set equal to the number of instances accessing the table. Both parameters apply to tables; only FREE_LISTS applies to indexes.

Under Oracle7 each table specifies its own number of free lists by use of the FREELISTS parameter of the CREATE TABLE command; this parameter will default to 1 if not specified explicitly.

Free list contention is shown by contention for data blocks in the buffer cache. If you get contention as shown in the report in Listing 15.26 under the data block area this can also indicate there aren't enough free lists.

Tuning checkpoints. Checkpoints provide for rolling forward after a system crash. Data is applied from the time of the last checkpoint forward from the redo entries. Checkpoints also provide for reuse of redo logs. When a redo log is filled, the LGWR process automatically switches to the next available log. All data in the now inactive log is written to disk by an automatic checkpoint. This frees the log for reuse or for archiving.

Checkpoints occur when a redo log is filled, when the INIT.ORA parameter LOG_CHECKPOINT_INTERVAL ORACLE7 is reached (total bytes written to a redo log), or the elapsed time has reached the INIT.ORA parameter LOG_-CHECKPOINT_TIMEOUT expressed in seconds or every three seconds, or when an ALTER SYSTEM command is issued with the CHECKPOINT option specified under Oracle7.

While frequent checkpoints will reduce recovery time, they will also decrease performance. Infrequent checkpoints will increase performance but increase required recovery times. To reduce checkpoints to only happen on log switches, set LOG_CHECKPOINT_INTERVAL to larger than your redo log size, and set LOG_CHECK-POINT_TIMEOUT to zero.

If checkpoints still cause performance problems, set the INIT.ORA parameter CHECKPOINT_PROCESS to TRUE to start the CKPT process running. This will free the LGWR from checkpoint and increase performance. The INIT.ORA parameter PROCESSES may also have to be increased.

15.3   NEW ORACLE TUNING OPTIONS

Under later versions of Oracle7 and Oracle8 there are numerous new tuning areas and capabilities. Use of histograms, anti-joins, hash-joins—all of these can be used to increase the performance of Oracle, not to mention using bitmapped indexes and partitioned tables and indexes.

Use of Histograms

Histograms help optimize queries and other actions against data that is nonuniformly distributed about a mean. The common term for poorly distributed data is *skewed data*. In particular, especially in earlier versions of Oracle7, the cost-based optimizer would go out to lunch if you handed it skewed data. There is a cost associated with histograms so they should only be used for badly skewed data. Histograms are static and must be periodically renewed just like table statistics.

Histograms should not be used if

- all predicates on the column use bind variables.
- the column data is uniformly distributed.
- the column is not used in where clauses of queries.
- the column is unique and is only used equality predicates.

Histograms are created in "bands" of value ranges. For example, if the data in your test_result tables measurement column is skewed into six general ranges then you would want to create six bands of history:

```
ANALYZE TABLE test_result
COMPUTE STATISTICS FOR COLUMNS measurement SIZE 6;
```

Histogram statistics are stored in the DBA_, USER_ and ALL_ HISTOGRAMS views. Additional row statistics appear in the USER_TAB_COLUMNS, ALL_TAB_COLUMNS, and DBA_TAB_COLUMNS views.

New Types of Joins

There are two new types of joins that became available in late Oracle7 and Oracle8; these are the ANTI-JOIN and HASH-JOIN joins.

Hash joins. The hash join has nothing to do with hash clusters or TABLE ACCESS HASH method. A hash join compares two tables in memory. The first table is full table scanned and a hashing function is applied to the data in memory. Then, the second table is full table scanned and the hashing function used to compare the values. Matching values are returned to the user. The user usually has nothing to do with this process and it is completely optimizer- controlled. However, it can only be used by the cost-based optimizer. Generally, hash joins will only gain something for you if you are using parallel query. Generally, the optimizer will use hash joins for small tables that can be scanned quickly. To use hash joins the HASH_JOIN_ENABLED initialization parameter must be set to TRUE.

There are several HASH parameters that affect how hash joins are used:

HASH_JOIN_ENABLED Set to true to use hash joins.

HASH_AREA_SIZE Large value reduces cost of hash joins so they are used more frequently (set to half the square root of the size of the smaller of the two objects but not less than 1 megabyte). Suggested range is between 8 and 32 megabytes.

HASH_MULTIBLOCK_IO_COUNT Large value reduces cost of hash joins so they are used more frequently. Suggested size is 4.

Anti-Joins. To use anti-joins you must set the initialization parameter ALWAYS_ANTI_JOIN to HASH or MERGE. This causes the NOT IN clause in queries to always be resolved using a parallel-hash or parallel-merge anti-join. If the ALWAYS_ANTI_JOIN parameter is set to anything other than HASH or MERGE the NOT IN will be evaluated as a correlated subquery. You can force Oracle to perform a specific query as an ANTI-JOIN by using the MERGE_AJ or HASH_AJ hints.

Multitier Statement Tuning

Oracle is more and more being used in multitier client/server applications. If you don't take care when designing the queries used in these client/server applications your performance will be terrible. You want the server to still do the processing of the result set and just pass the result set back to the client. An improperly worded query can return the entire contents of the source tables to your PC and expect the PC to process the data, something you don't want in most situations. The bane of many networks is excessive packet traffic soaking up bandwidth. To prevent bandwidth absorption you want to encapsulate SQL statements as much as possible. There are some general rules to follow when designing applications for client/server:

1. Push processing to the server; pull results back.
2. Use views to prebuild queries.
3. Use MTS only when your number of connections exceeds 50 to 100 users.
4. Use PL/SQL blocks, stored procedures, and functions on both client and server.

How we accomplish the preceding is generally easy although for specific applications it can be complex and in an ad hoc environment impossible. Let's examine some general techniques.

1. Push processing to the server; pull results back.

This is accomplished by using views and using PL/SQL encapsulation.

Using views. If you issue

```
SELECT * FROM EMP WHERE DEPTNO=10;
```

in an ad hoc query chances are the contents of EMP may get passed back to you to be processed. However, if a server view is created

```
CREATE VIEW EMP10 AS
  SELECT * FROM EMP
  WHERE DPTNO=10;
```

and then you issue

```
SELECT * FROM EMP10;
```

you get the same result set, but it is processed on the server and passed back to you.

Using PL/SQL encapsulation. If you have several related commands it will be best to encapsulate them in a PL/SQL block rather than issue each individual command. A PL/SQL block is treated as a single statement by NET8, so a single packet set is used to transfer it to the server, greatly reducing network travel. Let's look at an example.

We have a status report that selects several statistics into a temporary table and then a report is generated. Right now the script to run this report looks like this:

```
INSERT INTO dba_temp
  SELECT name, value, 1
  FROM v$sysstat
  WHERE name='consistent gets';
INSERT INTO dba_temp
  SELECT name, value, 2
  FROM v$sysstat
  WHERE name='physical reads';
INSERT INTO dba_temp
  SELECT name, value, 3
  FROM v$sysstat
  WHERE name='db block gets';
INSERT INTO dba_temp
  SELECT 'Hit Ratio',
      (a.value+b.value)-c.value/(a.value+b.value)
  FROM v$sysstat a, v$sysstat b, v$sysstat c
  WHERE a.name='consistent gets' and
  b.name='db block gets' and
  c.name='physical reads';
SELECT * FROM DBA_TEMP;
```

So we have five calls to the database, five parses, and five statements stored in the Shared pool. This is not very efficient, and the network round trips can get significant. Let's see if a PL/SQL routine to perform this (at least the initial processing) can be written:

```
CREATE OR REPLACE PROCEDURE hitratio
p_reads number;
db_gets number;
con_gets number;
h_ratio number;
param varchar2(32);
CURSOR get_param (stat_name varchar2) IS
SELECT value FROM v$sysstat WHERE name=stat_name;
PROCEDURE write_it (stat_name VARCHAR2,p_value NUMBER,
  reporder INTEGER) IS
    BEGIN
```

```
          INSERT INTO dba_temp
          VALUES (stat_name, p_value, reporder);
          END;
  BEGIN
    param:='consistent gets';
    OPEN get_param(param);
    FETCH get_param INTO con_gets;
    CLOSE get_param;
    write_it(param, con_gets, 1);
    param:='db block gets';
    OPEN get_param(param);
    FETCH get_param INTO db_gets;
    write_it(param, db_gets, 2);
    param:='physical reads';
    OPEN get_param(param);
    FETCH get_param INTO p_reads;
    write_it(param, p_reads, 3);
    h_ratio:=(
      (con_gets+db_gets)-p_reads)/(con_gets+db_reads);
    param:='Hit Ratio';
    write_it(param, h_ratio, 4);
    COMMIT:
  END;
```

Once the preceding procedure is compiled on the server, the preceding SQL script becomes

```
EXECUTE hitratio;
SELECT * FROM dba_temp;
```

Now we have reduced the round trips to two, and since the stored procedure is on the server we may not even have to parse the statement. All of the actions between the BEGIN and END are treated as a single transaction. If we make the call to dba_temp a call to a view we can be sure that any processing is done for that table on the server. There is also a method to use the UTLFILE package to output directly to a file on a client, but it would result in more net round trips in this situation.

More complex processing using variables could be done using the DBMS_SQL package and dynamic SQL.

Using views to prebuild queries. We have already discussed this trick. Essentially, if you have a standard data set that is selected against repeatedly then create a view to preprocess this data set and select against the view. This ensures that processing is pushed to the server and not to the client.

Use of MTS. The Multithreaded Server (MTS) allows for large numbers of users to connect through a limited number of database connections. This is great for large environments where it would be impossible for everyone to connect if they had to use individual connect processes. However, unless you normally run with at least 50 to 100 concurrent processes, accessing Oracle at the same time as MTS can hurt your performance. Use of parallel query will just about guarantee that you should use MTS.

In a test using a multigig database and 10 users, a standard set of queries generated over 200 separate processes using dedicated connections. Some queries required over 30 minutes to complete. We switched on MTS and ran the same queries. No queries took over five minutes using MTS, the SGA utilization (it had been running 100 percent for DB block buffers) dropped to 75 percent (as shown by the Q monitor system from Savant) and login times dropped to zero (under a dedicated server we saw up to five-minute delays logging in to the machine). The machine was an E6000 from Sun with nine CPUs, 3 gigabytes of memory, and a 600-gig disk farm using RAID0-1 and RAW disks. Access was over a normal Ethernet type network from PC clients using TCP/IP protocols.

MTS is a queuing system for database connections; it allows multiple users to share the same single connection to the database by a time-sharing mechanism. If only 5 to 10 users are connecting, they may actually see delays in statement execution and processing due to this queuing mechanism.

Use PL/SQL blocks, procedures, and functions on both the server and client. Always look at multistep SQL scripts, whether they are standalone or embedded in an application and ask yourself if they could be changed into either a stored procedure, function, or anonymous PL/SQL block. Even with 3GL programs running from a client to a database server if you encapsulate the SQL with BEGIN-END block construction (assuming this can be done; some statements can't be done this way) then they will be passed as a single network transaction to the server.

As was demonstrated earlier, a complex set of SQL statements can be converted into a PL/SQL procedure or function and the procedure or function can be stored on the server, allowing a simple EXECUTE or direct function call. For example, about the only way from SQL to get the bytes of a tables records is to issue a SUM(bytes) type statement against the tables entry in DBA_EXTENTS. If you want to include a count of the rows in a report you either have to ANALYZE the table and pull the count from out of DBA_TABLES as a join or use a local variable and do the SELECT COUNT into the local variable. This results in more network round trips and server work. However, if you create a function that does this type of operation for you then you can issue the call to the function directly from a BEGIN-END block or even from the SELECT itself. For example:

```
CREATE OR REPLACE FUNCTION get_sum(table_name VARCHAR2)
RETURN NUMBER AS
sum_bytes NUMBER;
BEGIN
  SELECT SUM(bytes) INTO sum_bytes FROM dba_extents
  WHERE segment_name=UPPER(table_name) AND
    segment_type='TABLE';
  RETURN sum_bytes;
END;
```

Using the preceding function (compiled and stored on the server) we can now select the sum of bytes used by any table just like a regular column:

```
SELECT table_name, get_sum(table_name) tab_size
 FROM dba_tables;
```

Techniques like this can reduce network traffic substantially. Use of functions and procedures force processing to the server and return only results to the client. Your goal as a DBA tuning in a multitier environment is to pack as much content into each piece of network traffic as is possible. To do this you have to move more into the Object Paradigm by passing messages (such as just a procedure or function call) rather than an entire procedural structure such as a SQL routine. This also ensures proper use of the shared pool and SGA resources since multiple "almost virtually" identical statements won't end up being stuffed into your SGA.

CHAPTER 16

Managing in a Distributed Environment

The Oracle database in either Oracle7 or Oracle8 can be operated in one of several types of object/relational environments. These types are:

- Exclusive, nonshared database
- Parallel server database
- Distributed database
- Client/server database
- Multithreaded server database
- Combinations of these five

For the most part, we have been discussing the database as if it were an exclusive type database. The characteristics of this type of database are as follows:

- Standalone operation; the database doesn't require other databases to be available in order to function.
- Single location with either single or multiple CPU; the database resides in one physical location and uses one or more CPUs.
- Database administration is independent of other sites and little, if any, intersite cooperation is required.

If you feel your applications will never operate outside of these parameters, then you can skip this chapter. If your applications will require a more complex environment involving multiple CPUs, sites, and databases, then read on.

16.1   MANAGEMENT IN A "SHARED" ENVIRONMENT

In a shared database, the CPUs involved are loosely coupled, such as in a VAX cluster, and they share disk resources. In UNIX you will have to (usually) use RAW disk resources since most UNIX platforms at the time this book was written couldn't share other than RAW disks in a manner Oracle can use. The database is called shared because the database files themselves are shared between several instance process sets on several CPUs or nodes.

The benefits of this type of installation are severalfold.

- The data is maintained on one disk farm, allowing ease of backup and management.
- The user processing load is spread across several CPUs thus allowing more users and faster access to data.
- Different types of users can be placed on different machines to allow distribution of types of processing. For example, users who require large sorts and intense CPU activity can be placed on a cluster node with faster or multiple CPUs and larger internal RAM (for a larger sort area), while users who only query limited sets of data can be placed on a smaller CPU.
- This type of configuration is good for databases without a lot of update activity or where the types of update activity can be distributed between the nodes in the cluster. For example, the group that uses node A only deals with tables A, B, and C on drive A, while the group that uses node B only deals with tables D, E, and F on drive B.

Figure 16.1 shows an example of a shared or parallel system. The major disadvantage to this configuration is that a single point of failure can result in loss of all database file access. For example, if the disk farm is hung off of a single disk controller on one VAX in the cluster and either the disk controller or VAX itself fails, access to the database is lost. The possibility of this happening can be reduced by using mirrored disk configurations.

The disadvantages to this type of configuration are as follows:

- Each instance must have its own SGA, which will have to be maintained in parallel with the main SGA.
- Additional overhead due to the parallel lock manager.

Initialization Parameters for a Shared Database

Most of the INIT.ORA parameters that control a parallel instance are prefixed with "GC_". These parameters are listed in the next sections. These parameters are subject to change and this list is only a general guideline; you should use the most current version of the *Oracle7 Parallel Server Administrator's Guide* or *Oracle8 Parallel Server*

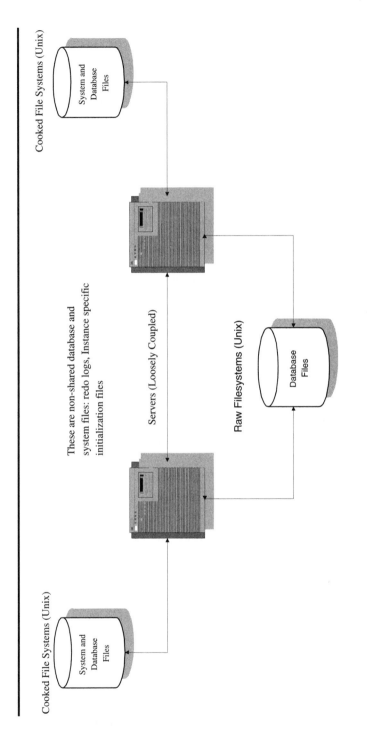

Cooked File Systems (Unix)

System and
Database
Files

These are non-shared database and
system files: redo logs, Instance specific
initialization files

Servers (Loosely Coupled)

Raw Filesystems (Unix)

Database
Files

Shared Database Files: Rollback Segments, Data and
Index Datafiles, Shared Initialization File

Cooked File Systems (Unix)

System and
Database
Files

FIGURE 16.1   Example of a shared database configuration.

Guide for your database for the most current list. Another good reference will be the README files that come with the most current release CD or tape.

Initialization Parameters That Must Match in All Shared Instances

CACHE_SIZE_THRESHOLD (New in 7.1) This parameter defaults to (0.1*db_block_buffers). The parameter specifies the maximum size of a cached table partition that is spread among the caches of a parallel server instance set. If the partition is larger than this, it isn't cached.

CONTROL_FILES This parameter gives the location for all control files for the database.

DB_FILES This specifies the soft limit for the number of database files; the hard limit is set by the CREATE DATABASE - MAX_DATAFILES parameter.

DB_NAME If set, it must be the same for all instances of shared database. If the value is not explicitly set in the initialization file it must be explicitly used in all database-related commands from the instance.

DB_BLOCK_SIZE Is set at database creation, and the database must be rebuilt to change it. Since all instances share the same database, it must be the same for all instances.

DML_LOCKS If nonzero, individual instances can have different values. If set to zero on one instance all instances must be set to zero.

GC_DB_LOCKS (Obsolete in Oracle8) Specifies the total number of PCM locks covering data blocks cached in the multiple SGAs of a parallel server. Must be set to at least one plus the sum of locks specified in the parameter GC_FILES_TO_LOCKS. If this is zero, enables fine-grain locking. This is always rounded up to the next prime number. If this value is specified in a nonshared database, it will consume SGA resources and produce no return benefit.

GC_FILES_TO_LOCKS (Changed in Oracle8) This parameter controls the mapping of PCM locks to data files. The format for this parameter is

```
GC_FILES_TO_LOCKS = "{file_list=lock_count[!blocks][EACH]} [:] . . ."
```

File_list is a list of one or more data files listed *by their file numbers* or *ranges of file numbers*. The lock_count is the number of locks to assign to the files listed; a zero enables fine-grain locking. The !blocks tells how many blocks to assign to each lock if it covers multiple locks; this defaults to one if not specified. The EACH key word specifies that each file in the file list receives lock_count number of locks. So, if you wanted to give files one to three 1000 locks, each covering 100 blocks per lock, the command would be

```
GC_FILES_TO_LOCKS="1-3=1000!100EACH"
```

Note that there are no spaces allowed inside the quotation marks. If the ratio of file_blocks/locks exceeds the !value specified, then each lock will cover the ratio file_blocks/locks number of locks (rounded up).

GC_FREELIST_GROUPS (New in 7.3) (Obsolete in Oracle8) This parameter defaults to five times the value of the GC_SEGMENTS parameter. The parameter determines the number of locks to specify for freelist group blocks for an instance.

GC_LCK_PROCS This parameter sets the number of background lock processes (LCK0 through LCK9) for an instance in the parallel server. This defaults to one, which is usually sufficient. If the instance lock request rate saturates the lock process, increase this parameter.

GC_ROLLBACK_LOCKS (Changed in Oracle8) For each rollback segment, this sets the number of instance locks available for simultaneously modified rollback segment blocks. This defaults to twenty, which is usually sufficient. Don't specify this parameter in a nonshared instance or it will allocate SGA resources with no benefit.

GC_ROLLBACK_SEGMENTS (Obsolete for Oracle8) This sets the maximum number of rollback segments including the system rollback segment. This parameter is for all instances in the shared environment that share the same database.

GC_SAVE_ROLLBACK_LOCKS (Obsolete for Oracle8) This parameter reserves instance locks for deferred rollback segments. The deferred rollback segments contain rollback entries for tablespaces that were taken off-line. Set this to ten per each instance in the shared environment that shares the same database.

GC_SEGMENTS (Obsolete for Oracle8) This parameter governs how many simultaneous segment extensions can occur over the entire set of shared instances. If you have sized properly, the default is fine; if you get frequent extensions it may have to be increased. Do not specify this parameter in exclusive mode, or SGA resources will be allocated with no benefits returned.

GC_TABLESPACES (Obsolete for Oracle8) This is the maximum number of table-spaces that can be brought from off-line to on-line or on-line to off-line concurrently. Do not specify this parameter in exclusive mode, or SGA resources will be allocated with no benefits returned.

LOG_FILES This must be set to a minimum of MAXLOGFILES*MAXLOGMEM-BERS. If it defaults to its maximum of 255, don't fool with it.

MAX_COMMIT_PROPAGATION_DELAY This parameter controls how quickly the SCN (System Change Number) is refreshed by LGWR. Units are in hundredths of a second. The default of 90,000 (15 minutes) allows the existing high-performance mechanism to remain in place. Only change it to a lower value if the environment has numerous changes to the same data from multiple instances simultaneously. A setting of zero causes the SCN to be refreshed immediately after a commit.

PARALLEL_DEFAULT_MAX_INSTANCES (New in 7.1) This parameter is set to the maximum number of instances that can simultaneously cache a table's values for shared operations. Specifies the default number of instances to split a table across for parallel query processing. The value of this parameter is used if the INSTANCES DEFAULT is specified in the PARALLEL clause of a table's definition.

PARALLEL_DEFAULT_MAX_SCANS (New in 7.1) The maximum number of query servers that can be used by default for a query. This parameter is only used if there is no numeric value specified in a PARALLEL hint or in the PARALLEL clause of the table's definition. This limits the number of query servers that are selected by default when the value of the PARALLEL_DEFAULT_SCANSIZE parameter is used by a query coordinator.

REMOTE_LOGIN_PASSWORDFILE (New in 7.1) Specifies whether Oracle checks for a password file and how many databases can use the password file. Setting the parameter to NONE signifies that Oracle should ignore any password file (and therefore privileged users must be authenticated by the operating system). Setting the parameter to EXCLUSIVE signifies that the password file can only be used by one database and the password file can contain names other than SYS and INTERNAL. Setting the parameter to SHARED allows more than one database to use a password file; however, the only users recognized by the password file are SYS and INTERNAL.

ROW_LOCKING Specifies if row locking should be used. It is set to ALWAYS by default and should not be changed.

SERIALIZABLE If TRUE, then queries acquire table-level read locks, preventing any update of objects read until the transaction containing the query is committed. This mode of operation provides repeatable reads and ensures that two queries for the same data within the same transaction see the same values.

Setting SERIALIZABLE to TRUE provides ANSI degree three consistency at a considerable cost in concurrency.

SINGLE_PROCESS Must be *false* for *all* instances!

Initialization Parameters That Must Be Different

THREAD This parameter sets the redo log thread that will be used by the instance.

ROLLBACK_SEGMENTS This parameter sets the rollback segments that will be used by the instance.

INSTANCE_NUMBER This sets the instance identifying number.

Initialization Parameters That Can Be the Same or Different

CHECKPOINT_PROCESS If set to TRUE, sets up a checkpoint process for the instance to perform checkpoints independent of the LGWR process.

CPU_COUNT Normally won't be explicitly set; this is set by Oracle to the number of CPUs on the system.

INIT_SQL_FILES (Obsolete in 7.3) This becomes an undocumented parameter for releases after 7.3.

LOG_ARCHIVE_DEST This parameter specifies the destination for archive logging. It cannot be a raw device.

LOG_ARCHIVE_FORMAT Normally, this should be the same for all instances in a shared set of instances, but it doesn't have to be. This parameter specifies the format for the log files.

LOG_ARCHIVE_START This parameter is used to start archive logging on an instance. In a shared environment only one instance has to archive log to ensure the database is recoverable.

LOG_CHECKPOINT_INTERVAL This specifies the interval in blocks between log checkpoints. Setting it to larger than the size of your redo logs allows checkpoints only when logs fill.

LOG_CHECKPOINT_TIMEOUT This parameter specifies the time interval between log checkpoints. Setting this to zero forces checkpoints only when logs fill.

LOG_ENTRY_PREBUILD_THRESHOLD This parameter tells the instance how big a redo entry must be before it is prebuilt.

PARALLEL_MIN_PERCENT (New in 7.3) This parameter specifies the minimum percentage of threads required for parallel query. This prevents a parallel query from being done sequentially if resources aren't available. If the parameter is set to zero then the query will use as many slaves as are available. If the percentage of parallel query slaves available is less than the specified value then the query will terminate with an error.

PARALLEL_MAX_SERVERS (New in 7.1) This parameter sets the maximum number of query servers that Oracle can start on demand.

PARALLEL_MIN_SERVERS (New in 7.1) This parameter sets the number of query servers that Oracle starts on startup and the number that the instance will always have as a minimum number running.

PROCESSES This parameter sets the maximum number of simultaneous processes that Oracle will allow to connect to the instance.

RECOVERY_PARALLELISM (New in 7.1) This parameter sets the number of processes that will be used to recover an instance. A setting of zero will force serial recovery.

ROW_LOCKING This parameter sets the value for row locking and should always be set to ALWAYS. A setting of DEFAULT is identical to ALWAYS. A setting of INTENT means row locks are used on a SELECT FOR UPDATE but at update time table locks are acquired.

SEQUENCE_CACHE_ENTRIES This parameter sets the number of sequence caches that will be used if the CACHE value isn't specified in a CREATE SEQUENCE command.

TRANSACTIONS_PER_ROLLBACK_SEGMENT This parameter determines how Oracle acquires public rollback segments. If the ratio transactions/transactions_per_rollback_segment exceeds the number of available on-line rollback segments, any off-line public rollback segments are brought on-line.

New Oracle8 Parameters

FREEZE_DB_FOR_FAST_INSTANCE_RECOVERY This parameter is a parallel server parameter. If an instance in a parallel server environment requires recovery if this parameter is set to TRUE then the entire database is frozen until the instance completes recovery. This allows faster instance recovery, but the database is unavailable to other instances.

LM_LOCKS This parameter is the number of lock manager locks. Where R is the number of resources, N is the total number of instances (nodes), and L is total number of locks, the calculation is

```
L = R + ( R * ( N - 1 )) / N
```

LM_PROCS This parameter sets the number of total processes; this should be set to the number of processes times the number of instances.

LM_RESS This parameter controls the number of resources that can be locked by the lock manager. It should be set to much less than 2 * DML_LOCKS + 20. This is roughly equivalent to the sum of DML_LOCKS, DDL locks, cache locks, and file and log management locks.

INSTANCE_GROUPS This parameter controls the groups that the instance belongs to. These values can be different for all instances. This parameter is not dynamic and is set only at startup.

PARALLEL_INSTANCE_GROUP This specifies which group to use for parallel operations. This parameter can be altered using the ALTER SESSION or ALTER SYSTEM command.

TIP   Use a central initialzation file for shared parameters and refer to it using the "IFILE=" parameter from the individual instances initialization files.

16.2   USE OF SQLDBA OR SVRMGR

There are two types of instance in a parallel environment, the DEFAULT and the CURRENT instance. The DEFAULT instance is the instance that is resident on the node where the SQLDBA or SVRMGR program is invoked; the CURRENT instance is the instance where you have used the CONNECT command to attach to using a connect string. The CURRENT and DEFAULT instances will be the same if you don't specify a connect string in the connect command. You can change the instance by using the SET INSTANCE command

The following commands apply under SQLDBA or SVRMGR when you are connected to an instance:

ARCHIVE LOG	Current instance only.
CONNECT	Uses default instance if no connect string is specified.
CONNECT INTERNAL	Always applies to the current instance.
HOST	Applies to the node you are on regardless of the setting of the instance.

MONITOR	Applies to the current instance.
RECOVER	Applies to the database, not the instance.
SHOW INSTANCE	Always applies to the default instance, not the current instance.
SHOW PARAMETERS	Applies to the current instance.
SHOW SGA	Applies to current instance only.
SHUTDOWN	This is a privileged SVRMGR command, applies to current instance.
STARTUP	Always applies to the current instance; it is a privileged SVRMGR command.

You change the DEFAULT instance by disconnecting from the CURRENT installation and issuing the "SET INSTANCE con string" command. Note there is no username or password.

16.3   BASIC PROCEDURE FOR CREATING A SHARED ORACLE DATABASE

Everything must start somewhere. A parallel database starts with a single instance. This instance is created exactly like an exclusive instance. Once the instance is up and operating, the additional instances that will share the database are defined. The final step is to bring the INIT.ORA files into sync and start all the instances in shared mode.

There are several parts of the database that need to be considered when designing and starting up a parallel instance, these are:

- File structures
- Data dictionary
- Sequence number generators
- Rollback segments
- Redo log files
- Database creation

By properly designing these six items, resource contention can be avoided, thus optimizing performance.

All instances in a parallel database use the same control files and data files. Each instance has its own SGA and redo logs. Each instance can have differing numbers of redo logs and different degrees of mirroring. Each instance must have its own dedicated rollback segment(s).

TIP   For UNIX, use 100-megabyte cooked file systems arranged in an OFA configuration on each server to act as locations for the soft links to the raw devices. This allows "human" understandable file names to be used.

What does all this mean? First, before we can start up a parallel instance, there must be sufficient redo log threads and private rollback segments available to split up among the instances. Next, there must be sufficient memory available on each node to handle the SGA requirements for each instance.

The rollback segments can be either public or private. It is suggested that they be made as private rollback segments so that they can be positioned on the disk farm for each instance and made exclusive to that instance. Additional rollback segments can be specified from any active instance. Each instance acquires its private rollback segments by specifying their name in the INIT.ORA parameter ROLLBACK_SEGMENTS. At least one rollback segment must be available for each instance. This can be guaranteed via use of the private rollback segments.

Let's look at a more detailed procedure.

1. Using either the OEM or commands, create the initial instance. Verify that the parameters MAXINSTANCES, MAXLOGFILES, ARCHIVELOG, and MAXLOG-HISTORY are set in accordance with the values you require. You should alter the INIT.ORA parameter DB_BLOCK_SIZE to ensure the database can provide the number of freelists and extents you require. You should also set the DB_NAME parameter.

2. Add a second rollback segment to this new instance and then bring it on-line; add the second name to the INIT.ORA file via the ROLLBACK_SEGMENTS parameter, so that when you start up the instance again it will acquire the rollback segment. Under Oracle7, there is no need to shut down; once the rollback segment is created it can be brought on-line with the ALTER ROLLBACK SEGMENT command.

3. Add required tablespaces to the instance. As a minimum, add the following additional tablespaces:

   TOOLS—For forms, reports, and menu files owned by SYSTEM.
   USERS—To use for the DEFAULT tablespace for users.
   TEMP—To use as the TEMPORARY tablespace for users.
   ROLLBACKSn—To use for rollbacks for this instance. If there are different disk strings attached to other nodes, you may want to add additional rollback segment tablespaces for each set of disks that will be used by the parallel instance. n is an integer that specifies an arbitrary number assigned to each instance in the database.

4. Create additional rollback segments. There should be one rollback segment for every four to ten users you expect for each instance. If you expect 50 users on instance 1, 24 users on instance 2, and 50 users on instance 3, assign 32 rollback segments total, spread over the three ROLLBACKn tablespaces (one tablespace for each instance), assuming the lower value of four users per rollback is used.

5. Create enough redo log threads for all of the expected instances. Each thread must have at least two groups of one redo log each; three groups per instance thread are suggested.

6. Shutdown the instance; deassign the rollback segment assigned in step 2 by removing it from the ROLLBACK_SEGMENTS parameter. Assign the rollback segments for this instance only by placing their names in the ROLLBACK_SEGMENTS parameter. Alter the GC_ROLLBACK_SEGMENTS parameter (or add it) to the total number of rollback segments expected to ever be created by all instances in the parallel database. For Oracle7 and Oracle8, you can take the additional system rollback segment off-line with the ALTER ROLLBACK SEGMENT command and bring on this instance's rollback segments with the same command without shutting down the instance.

7. Add the THREAD parameter to the INIT.ORA file and set the THREAD value for this instance.

8. Set the ARCHIVE_LOG_DEST and the ARCHIVE_LOG_FORMAT parameters.

9. Set all INIT.ORA GC_ parameters.

10. Set the INIT.ORA parameter INSTANCE_NUMBER for the initial instance to 1. For additional instances, increment this number so each instance has a unique value. This value determines the freelist used by the instance. If one instance uses this parameter, they all should. If it is not used, each instance acquires the lowest available instance number and the DBA has no control over it.

11. Be sure the SINGLE_PROCESS value is set to FALSE in the INIT.ORA file for this and all other instances in the parallel instance.

12. If not already shut down, shut down and then restart the instance in parallel mode.

13. Create the additional instances, edit their INIT.ORA files in accordance with the parameters shown in previous sections, and specify, for each instance, the appropriate rollback segments and the redo thread.

14. Create a common INITS.ORA file in which the common initialization files are placed. For a parallel database, all instances must have the same value for the following parameters:

CONTROL_FILES	GC_SEGMENTS
DB_BLOCK_SIZE	GC_TABLESPACES
DB_FILES	LOG_FILES
DB_NAME	LICENSE_MAX_SESSIONS
GC_DB_LOCKS	LICENSE_MAX_USERS
GC_FILES_TO_LOCKS	LICENSE_SESSIONS_WARNING
GC_LCK_PROCS	ROW_LOCKING
GC_ROLLBACK_LOCKS	SERIALIZABLE
GC_ROLLBACK_SEGMENTS	SINGLE_PROCESS
GC_SAVE_ROLLBACK_LOCKS	LM_LOCKS
IFILE	LM_PROCS
LM_RESS	

The IFILE parameter should be specified in each of the instance's INIT.ORA file to point to the location of the INITSHARE.ORA file that contains the rest of the parameters.

15. Start the additional instances in parallel.

Archive logging—Archive logging is controlled independently for each instance; however, if one archives it is suggested that all archive.

Backup—Backup can be either on-line or off-line. Any instance can issue the ALTER TABLESPACE name BEGIN | END command. For ease of management, it is suggested that the first instance created be used as the management instance and all backup and export actions be initiated there if possible.

Recovery—Recovery of a single failed node is accomplished by the SMON process of one of the other nodes when the failed node comes back on-line. Recovery of data, redo, or rollback files can be accomplished from any instance in the database, but it is suggested that recovery be done with the other instances shut down and that the instance used for recovery be in EXCLUSIVE mode. See Chapter 17 for database recovery instructions.

16.4 DISTRIBUTED DATABASE MANAGEMENT

The next form of database we will look at is the distributed database. The distributed database exists at numerous locations, perhaps even on different types of computers. The distributed database is linked via a network, be it LAN (Local Area Network), WAN (Wide Area Network), or a combination of both. Figure 16.2 shows how these relate to each other.

As its name implies, in the database itself, the files that make up the database are spread across the various nodes of the system. This could lead to duplication of data, bad updates due to network problems, indeed, a whole plethora of problems. In Oracle7, Oracle solved many of these possible problems through several methods. These methods are the two-phase commit, table replication through database replication servers, and table snapshots. In Oracle8, with the addition of advanced queuing, distributed databases have been made easier to control and operate.

Essentially, you as DBA are responsible for seeing that the data someone needs is available when they need it, whether the data is on the VAX in the next room or on the HP9000 UNIX platform in Ankara, Turkey. This can be a bit of a challenge. Let's examine the tools and techniques used to implement a distributed database.

First, the communication between the platforms will most likely be DECNET, NOVELL, TCP/IP or one of the other major protocols. For the purposes of this book, we will limit ourselves to DECNET, the major DEC/VAX protocol, and TCP/IP, the major UNIX protocol.

No matter what protocol you use, you will have to have the Oracle SQL*NET or NET8 package that is compatible. Under Oracle7 and Oracle8, you have a core module known as the TNS (Transparent Network Substrate) and the drivers for the protocol you need. You can have as many drivers as you have supported protocols; normally for VMS, for instance, you will need both DECNET for your LAN and TCP/IP for communication with a WAN. For NT, you may need named pipes, IPX, SPX, or TCP/IP. Usually for UNIX, TCP/IP is sufficient.

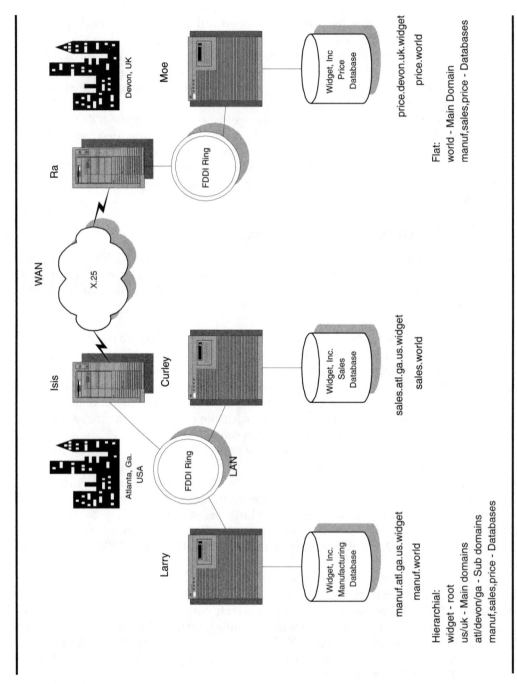

FIGURE 16.2 Example of a distributed database setup.

Use of SQL*NET and NET8

In its most basic form, a distributed database would consist of a link that allows update and query between two databases.

Under version 7 and Oracle8, the DBA should supply a DATABASE LINK to the database users. For example, if we have a database in Devonshire, England, and one in Dallas, Texas, and we want to be able to query the database in Devonshire for the local price of fish and chips (which is, of course, stored in the LUNCH table of the PRICE database) we must specify an internal database link specification.

The TNSNAMES.ORA file is used to store protocol-specific connection information that previously had to be specified in an external connection string. Each database we want to connect to via SQL*NET or NET8 must have a valid entry showing its address and protocol information in the TNSNAMES.ORA file. For an excellent coverage of SQL*NET and NETWORK issues, I suggest either the book *Oracle Networking*, Hugo Toledo (Oracle Press, 1996) or the *Oracle Administrator*, On-line Oracle Reference, RevealNet, Inc., Version 97-2, 1997, or most current available from www.revealnet .com/, coauthored by Hugo (for networking) and myself (for most of the other content).

Source 16.1 is an example entry from a TNSNAMES file.

SOURCE 16.1   Example of TNSNAMES.ORA file entry.

```
price.devon.uk.widget =
  (DESCRIPTION =
    (ADDRESS_LIST =
       (ADDRESS =
         (COMMUNITY = devon.uk.widget)
         (PROTOCOL = TCP)
         (Host = moe)
         (Port = 1521)
       )
    )
    (CONNECT_DATA = (SID = PRICE)
    )
  )
```

Once the TNSNAMES file is properly set up, it becomes easy to define our internal link:

```
SQLPLUS  JOHN/HUNGRY
SQL> CREATE DATABASE LINK price
    2: CONNECT TO DEVON_USER IDENTIFED BY LOW_PRIVS
    3: USING "price.devon.uk.widget"
    4:/
```

The first line names the database link. If we wanted to share and were using an account with the CREATE PUBLIC DATABASE LINK privilege, we could have specified CREATE PUBLIC DATABASE LINK price instead. The next line of the command tells Oracle what user and password to connect to at the remote database. If this isn't specified, it will try to use your current database username and password. The next to last line tells Oracle to use the previously established tnsnames connection information. Once defined, the link is resident in the database until it is dropped.

Finally, we should tie a synonym to the table name-link name combination to make it easier to use.

```
CREATE SYNONYM LUNCH FOR LUNCH@PRICE;
```

Now, if DEVON_USER owns LUNCH or, has a synonym LUNCH pointing to the LUNCH table, all that we need to do is query LUNCH to determine the data we wanted.

```
SQL>SELECT COST , FOOD_TYPE
    2: FROM LUNCH
    3: WHERE FOOD_TYPE='FISH AND CHIPS' AND
    4: DATE_OF _PRICE = (SELECT SYSDATE FROM DUAL);
COST              FOOD_TYPE
----              ---------
1.50              "FISH AND CHIPS"
```

Of course, we'll have to convert it from pounds sterling to dollars. . . .

If you need to query more than a few remote databases, the OPEN_LINKS parameter of the INIT.ORA file needs to be bumped up. This parameter specifies the maximum number of open links any one user can have in one transaction. The OPEN_LINKS parameter defaults to four under Oracle7 and Oracle8.

Once we establish the synonyms for all the tables of interest, we can then query at will as long as the other database is up and running. At one installation, a DBA used this technique to monitor ten different instances from a central database. As long as you don't have to update, this works fine. The only method to update a table from one database to another is to select into the desired table from the remote table. This is limited to nonlong data fields. Long data fields can be copied using the COPY command.

Use of the COPY Command

The format of the COPY command follows.

```
COPY {FROM username [/password]@db_spec |
TO username[/password]@db_spec |
FROM username [/password]@db_spec TO
username[/password]@db_spec}
{APPEND|CREATE|INSERT|REPLACE| dest_table [(column list)]
USING query
```

The COPY command can be used to copy entire tables, subsections based on the query used, or to append data into an existing table. For the append and replace options, if the destination table doesn't exist, the command creates it. The db_spec variable is the connect string. If you don't specify a password, the command prompts for it without echoing it, so security is maintained.

Use of SQL*NET/TCP/IP

SQL*NET has come a long way since late version 6 and early Oracle7 implementations. SQL*NET, version 2, did away with the multiplicity of connect strings and connect string formats, allowing us (as was shown earlier) to specify a simple connection alias for any type of SQL*NETNET connection by placing the specification in a central TNSNAMES file. In addition, the concept of a multifunctional listener that listens on ports for a set of different protocols helped simplify the management of distributed databases. The listener process is defined by the LISTENER.ORA file.

The database specification now consists of a domain name and a database base name. You can use either a hierarchical network structure or a flat structure. The hierarchical structure uses a root such as MIL, COM, EDU and then builds up from there, using company, country, location, and finally instance name. You can have as many or as few levels of hierarchy as you desire. The flat network has the root *world* and all systems hang off of the root. For a small set of databases, I suggest the flat structure. Source 16.2 shows how both of these hierarchies would look for our mythical world-spanning distributed database.

These names look very similar to the internet address format. For example, if you had a database that was in the U.S. branch of the company, located in Nebraska, on the UOB campus, the domain name might be "UOB.NEBR.USA.EDU." If the database name is STUDENTS, the full specification for a database name in a connect string would be STUDENTS.UOB.NEBR.USA.EDU. Of course, this can be synonymed. Then, to specify a table you would add the table specification to the database identifier:

```
STUD_DBA.GRADES@STUDENTS.UOB.NEBR.USA.EDU
```

For this example, the database is STUDENTS, the domain is UOB.NEBR.USA .EDU, and the table is GRADES in the schema STUD_DBA (short for STUDENTS DBA, of course).

In general, the link will follow the Internet protocol. This protocol uses a general identifier, for educational institutions, EDU; for commercial companies, COM; and for military, MIL. There are other identifiers, but these are the main ones, and their use in your SQL*NET or NET8 hierarchy is purely voluntary; in fact, most don't use them. This is followed by an identifier for your activity; for example, Oracle uses Oracle (ORACLE.COM). Then, you can add further identifiers to give greater restriction, such as country, state, and branch of company or user identification. The strings are read from right to left. However, you don't have to use these and can make your own standard.

If the INIT.ORA parameter GLOBAL_NAME is set to TRUE, the link name is checked against the remote database name and the domain. The database domain is specified by using the DB_DOMAIN INIT.ORA parameter, and the database name must be specified by the DB_NAME parameter. If the GLOBAL_NAME parameter is set to FALSE (the default value), no checking is performed.

The logical connection string now specifies a port number and a protocol. This allows the TNS to connect the user with the appropriate dispatcher process (Dnnn). Generally speaking, there will be at least one dispatcher per protocol used in your network. For a database needing both DECNET and TCP/IP, there would be two dispatchers. These are specified in the listener file.

SOURCE 16.2   Example of the LISTENER.ORA file from a UNIX installation.

```
listener =
  (ADDRESS_LIST =
    (ADDRESS =
        (PROTOCOL = TCP)
        (HOST = larry)
        (PORT = 1521)
    )
    (ADDRESS =
        (PROTOCOL = IPC)
        (KEY = MANUF)
    )
)
sid_list_listener =
  (SID_LIST =
    (SID_DESC =
      (SID_NAME = MANUF)
      (ORACLE_HOME=/bto/sys/oracle/product/7.2.3)
    )
)
STARTUP_WAIT_TIME_LISTENER = 1
CONNECT_TIMEOUT_LISTENER = 10
TRACE_LEVEL_LISTENER = OFF
```

There are two additional files that you will maintain under SQL*NET, version 2. These are the TNSNAMES.ORA and LISTENER.ORA files. These files define the number and type of listeners and the database logical connections.

Oracle8 with its NET8 replacement for SQL*NET enhances performance by allowing multiplexing of connections to the database and greater ease of setup and management with enhanced capabilities to seek out and self-define databases within the local area network.

16.5   DISTRIBUTED DATABASE INITIALIZATION PARAMETERS

There are several new INIT.ORA parameters for use with a distributed environment. These are shown in Table 16.1.

TABLE 16.1   Initialization Parameters for Use with Distributed Database Transactions

Parameter:	Purpose:
COMMIT_POINT_STRENGTH	Specifies the numeric value to determine the commit point for a transaction; the highest value for an instance in a distributed transaction wins.
DB_DOMAIN	Specifies the domain to which this database belongs. This defaults to WORLD.
DB_NAME	Should be set for all databases in a distributed network.
DISTRIBUTED_LOCK_TIMEOUT	This parameter specifies the time that must expire before a distributed transaction waiting on a resource will expire. The default for this parameter is 60 seconds.
DISTRIBUTED_RECOVERY_CONNECTION_HOLD_TIME	This parameter specifies how long a transaction that loses communication with a remote database should hold the link to that database open in the hopes that it will reconnect.
DISTRIBUTED_TRANSACTIONS	This parameter specifies the number of distributed transactions this database can participate in. This parameter cannot exceed the value of TRANSACTIONS. If set to zero, no distributed transactions are allowed and RECO doesn't start up (the distributed transaction recovery process).
GLOBAL_NAMES	This forces database links to use the same name as the database to which it connects.
MAX_TRANSACTION_BRANCHES	This parameter controls the number of branches in a distributed transaction.
OPEN_LINKS	The maximum number of database links any single process can have open. This is set to 4 as a default.
REMOTE_DEPENDENCIES_MODE	This sets how dependencies upon remote stored procedures are handled. It defaults to TIMESTAMP and the other allowed value is SIGNATURE. If the timestamps match then a procedure is allowed to execute in TIMESTAMP mode; if the signature (name) is present then the procedure is allowed to execute without recompilation in SIGNATURE mode.

16.6   ORACLE DATA REPLICATION FEATURES

Under Oracle7 and Oracle8, the DBA has a much wider selection of data replication options. For tables in a distributed environment that have dependent values, such as sales, inventory, and required purchases tables, the two-phase commit will be employed.

For maintaining duplicate copies of tables or for copying subsets of tables, database table replication triggers are available under Oracle7. The use of triggers and procedures are automatically built via a set of stored packages and procedures. These triggers fire whenever rows are updated, inserted, or deleted and replicate the changes throughout the distributed environment. Unlike a simple update using the two-phase commit process, if a database level trigger fails you can build automated recovery procedures using Oracle-provided resolution scripts that wait for the condition to clear and resend the data from a journal. For high-use tables, this can seriously degrade database performance. However, if it is important that all sites maintain up-to-the-minute data at all times, this may be the option of choice.

The other mechanism that can be used for table duplication under Oracle7 and Oracle8 is the snapshot method. This method is periodic in nature and only happens as specified by the snapshot parameters. This allows a frequently updated table to be replicated at low-use times. If it isn't critical that all sites have up-to-the-minute data, this method works well.

The snapshot method can also be used to provide read-only copies of subsets of data for either a single table or several tables. Values can also be calculated for a snapshot. Snapshots can also support what is known as N-way replication where master and slave sites are designated and you can control how updates are promulgated back and forth between sites.

The full use of these objects, besides two-phase commit, was covered in Chapter 2. The two-phase commit will be covered in the next section.

The DBA will have to coordinate the best method of data replication between the sites in a distributed database. The two-phase commit, table replication triggers, and snapshotting provide a true distributed database environment.

It should be noted that anytime more than one node is involved in a transaction involving updates, inserts, or deletes, the two-phase commit is used. If the DBA wishes to avoid the use of the two-phase commit, he or she should use single-point transaction logic. That is, only update the data on a single node at a time followed by a commit.

The Use of Two-Phase Commit

What exactly is a two-phase commit and how is it used? As more and more databases are distributed across multiple systems as companies grow, this question will have to be addressed by most DBAs. Let's examine these questions and hopefully give some concrete answers.

What Is a Two-Phase Commit?

Under Oracle7 and Oracle8, the programmer or application developer doesn't have to do anything special for the two-phase commit (TPC) to be used. The DBA has several initialization parameters to specify, but other than that little or no action is required on their part either. Anytime a transaction updates data (insert, update, or delete functions) across multiple nodes with a single set of commands with no intervening commits, a TPC will be used.

The actual mechanism of a TPC is easily stated: each transaction shall be committed, or rolled back, as a unit. How this is actually accomplished is another thing altogether.

As was stated before, the TPC should only be used when there are data dependencies between two or more tables in a distributed environment. In most cases, it shouldn't be used for simple data replication. The TPC, as its name implies, depends on two phases of activity to work. These are as follows:

The prepare phase—In this phase, the initiating node (called the "global coordinator") asks the nodes participating in the TPC to prepare. This consists of being ready to commit or roll back the transaction even in the event of a network or node failure.

The commit phase—In this phase, all participants in the TPC commit; if they can't all commit, the coordinator tells all the nodes to roll back.

Under a TPC, each transaction has a session tree. This is a structure that shows each site involved and its role in the TPC. These roles can be any one of the following:

- Client
- Database server
- Global coordinator
- Local coordinator
- Commit point site

The role for each node is determined by where the transaction originates, the commit point strength as set in the INIT.ORA file, whether or not the data that is available at the node or other nodes need to be referenced, and whether or not the node is read-only (if the data to be updated on the node is in a read-only snapshot, the node will not participate). What do the various roles do in a TPC? Let's look and see.

Clients—Clients are nodes that request data from other nodes in a distributed transaction.

Database Servers—Database servers are nodes that are directly referenced or are requested to participate by a referenced node in a distributed transaction.

The Global Coordinator—This is the node that has requested the distributed transaction. This is the parent or root of the session tree. The global coordinator performs the following:

- Sends all SQL statements used by the distributed transaction.
- Communicates with all directly referenced nodes other than the commit point sites.
- Once all nodes are prepared, asks the commit point site to initiate the commit of the transaction across all nodes.

Local Coordinator—This is a node that references other nodes to complete a request. The local coordinator is responsible for coordination of the request activities among the nodes it references through the following activities:

- Relay of information to the referenced nodes.
- Collection of information from the referenced nodes.
- Return of collected data to the node that called it.

Commit Point Site—The commit point site is the node or nodes that have the highest value of the COMMIT_POINT_STRENGTH parameter in their INIT.ORA file. There can be more than one commit point site for a given transaction. Generally speaking, if a session tree has several branches, there will be several commit point sites. The commit point site fulfills the following functions:

- This should be the site that is most reliable and thus holds the most critical data. Critical data is data that is never in doubt, even in a failure situation.
- The commit point site, as its name implies, determines if the data is committed or if it is rolled back. If the update fails at the commit point site, it is rolled back for all sites; if the data is successfully updated at the commit point site, it is updated at all sites. The global coordinator ensures all sites treat the data the same as the commit point site.

Commit Point Strength—As was stated earlier, the COMMIT_POINT_STRENGTH INIT.ORA parameter, set by the DBA, determines if a site is a commit point site. The global coordinator site determines the commit point site from within its branch of the session tree. If the commit point site sees another site within its own branch of the session tree with a greater value of commit point strength, it will not commit or roll back unless that site commits or rolls back, and so on down the branches of the session tree.

Examples of a Distributed Transaction

As was stated earlier, a distributed transaction is one with multiple updates to tables spread across multiple nodes with no intervening commits. For example, the transaction

```
insert into grades@uob (student, class, grade) values ('9999','1072','3.8');
commit;
insert into grades@sui (student, class, grade) values ('9999','1072','3.8');
commit;
```

wouldn't be a distributed transaction since there are intervening commits between the actions on different nodes ("uob" and "sui"). However, the following transaction,

```
insert into grades@uob (student, class, grade) values ('9999','1072','3.8');
insert into grades@sui (student, class, grade) values ('9999','1072','3.8');
commit;
```

TIP   If you need to defeat 2PC processing, simply add commits at each transaction branch.

---

would be a distributed transaction since the commit follows both insert statements. In the first transaction, a TPC wouldn't be used, while for the second transaction a TPC would occur. Let's look at the second transaction in more detail.

For the purpose of this discussion, the transaction was started at node "central." The following are the commit point strengths for the nodes:

```
central - 80
uob - 255
sui - 150
```

From this data you can see that the node "uob" would be the commit point, the node "central" would be the global coordinator, and the node "sui" is a client. Both "uob" and "sui" are database servers. The nodes are in a simple triangle connection with "central" at the apex and "uob" and "sui" at the legs.

What would the process look like for the TPC for this transaction? Let's look.

The SQL statements are sent out to each site and the needed locks are established. The global coordinator issues a commit, initiating the TPC.

First, the global coordinator, "central," determines who is the commit point site by looking at the directly connected node's commit point strengths. The global coordinator would compare its value of commit point strength to the other nodes and determine the commit point for the transaction. In this case, "uob" would be the commit point. The global coordinator would then send out a call for the clients involved to prepare.

Next, the clients report they are prepared; for this transaction only "sui" is a client. Once "sui" reports that it is prepared, the global coordinator sends out a commit order to the commit point site, "uob". If the commit point site can commit, all other sites commit, if the commit point site cannot commit, the transaction is rolled back.

If the transaction is not completed—say, the commit point site committed and then the database link failed due to a network error—there are two database views that will show the problem. These are the DBA_2PC_PENDING and DBA_2PC_NEIGHBORS views. If this situation occurs, the DBA has three possible actions:

1. Manually complete the transaction by having the remote site DBAs either roll back or commit the transaction number specified by the global transaction number.

2. Wait for the database link to be reestablished and allow RECO to recover the transaction.
3. Respecify a different link by use of a synonym pointing to a link that is still active and allow RECO to recover the transaction.

If the same recovery option isn't performed on all nodes, the databases will be left in an inconsistent state. It is always the best option to allow RECO to recover the transaction. To this end, it is suggested that all database links be specified via synonyms so that if an alternate connection is required a simple drop and redefine of the synonym is all that is needed to recover the transaction (assuming multiple paths are available).

For a detailed discussion of the two-phase commit mechanism and other two-phase commit topics, read most current version of the *Oracle7 (Or Oracle8) Server Concepts Manual* (Oracle Corp., 1997).

16.7   CLIENT/SERVER RELATIONAL DATABASES

Client/server databases are databases where a central node acts as database server and connecting nodes do all or a part of the execution of tools and programs. An example of this configuration would be a CPU with a large disk farm that holds the database, which is connected to by several other CPUs, each running their own version of the tools, such as ORA*FORMS or ORA*REPORT with the two-task link option.

The basic method for setting up a client/server database is as follows.

1. Set up the main database server, link all tools two-task (usually the "T" option) . The main server will run the RDBMS and all SQL*NET protocols. The database files will be created on the server and will be owned by the server.
2. Set up the client machines with the tools and whatever SQL*NET protocol they require; again, be sure the tools are linked two-task.
3. Configure SQL*NET protocols on each of the clients so that they reference the server.

Note that there are no database data files on any of the clients. All data files, control files, redo logs, rollbacks, and the like, are located on the server. As the clients need data, they connect via a SQL*NET link over their own protocols (DECNET, TCP/IP, ASYNC, etc.) and use the data on the server.

Benefits of Client/Server

The benefits of a client/server configuration are severalfold.

- The database can be placed on a machine optimized for speed of access.
- The tools processing overhead is offloaded to other CPUs; for example, the GUI generation work load could be offloaded to workstations.

- Processing can be compartmentalized to optimize the type of CPU required. CASE could be placed on high-speed workstations, forms applications on slower CPUs, and so on.

Client/server requires SQL*NET and the protocol drivers you will be using. Installation of ODBC drivers on a PC client, for instance, requires the installation of not only an Oracle-compatible ODBC protocol (a noncompatible or almost compatible will probably show up as space leak errors in your SGA) driver set but also the applicable SQL*NET or NET8 driver and the network (such as TCP/IP or IPX) drivers for SQL*NET or NET8. This is on top of the system drivers for the communication protocol.

Replication and Advanced Replication

Basic replication consists of either simple or complex snapshots. Basic replication is fairly easy to set up using database links and the CREATE SNAPSHOT and CREATE SNAPSHOT log commands we have already discussed.

Advanced replication is another thing altogether from snapshots and snapshot logs. Advanced replication involves the creation of special procedures, triggers, and tables on both the master site and replication site. Advanced replication also involves setting up rules within the database to handle conflict resolution. Finally, advanced replication also supports the concept of updateable snapshots and multiple updateable snapshot sites (N-way replication).

Advance replication is controlled via the concept of replication objects and replication groups. Replication groups are the basic unit for managing advanced replication. Replication groups are created by the replication manager for all objects associated with a single application and are to be replicated to a series of sites.

In advanced replication, DML (data manipulation language) and DDL (data definition language) changes are sent out to each site involved in the replicant. Advanced replication allows the database to replicate tables, views, indexes, sequences, and synonyms.

Advanced replication involves snapshot master sites and snapshot sites. Each master site receives a full copy of the replication group of objects, while each snapshot site may only receive a partial set.

Advanced replication is too complex a topic to even attempt to cover in a single chapter. I suggest you review the references at the end of this chapter before taking on advanced replication.

16.8   USE OF THE MULTITHREADED SERVER

The multithreaded server under Oracle7 allows multiple-user processes to share the same Oracle server process. This reduces the number of Oracle-related processes required to support multiple users under operating systems that require dedicated servers (UNIX). In other environments that may use two-task linked Oracle, such as in the client/server configuration, the multithreaded server is also useful. The

INIT.ORA parameters shown in Source 16.3 control the multithreaded server; this should be obvious since their names begin with MTS.

The multithreaded server uses the listener process to assign users to specific types of servers. The listener is configured via the MTS parameters and controlled with the LSNRCTL program. The SQL*NET LSNRCTL options are as follows.

start	Will start the listener on the node.
stop	Will stop the listener on the node.
status	Will report the status for the node.
reload	Will reload parameters from the LISTENER.ORA file.
trace	Will request the listener process to start or stop tracing.
version	Will provide the version number of the TNS listener process being used.

The command format is LSNRCTL "command" "node." If no node is specified, the command operates on the current node. A general procedure to start the multi-threaded server process follows.

1. Edit the INIT.ORA file in accordance with your system's requirements. Source 16.3 can be used as a template.
2. Create the LISTENER.ORA and TNSNAMES.ORA (if required) files to configure the listener process. The format for the LISTENER.ORA file is shown in Source 16.3.
3. Shut down and restart the instance(s) to reconfigure the INIT.ORA parameters.
4. Start the listener process using the appropriate LSNRCTL command.

MTS_SERVICE	Specifies the database name; should usually be set to the SID for the database.
MTS_SERVERS	Specifies the number of server (S00n) processes to be brought on-line at startup.
MTS_MAX_SERVERS	Specifies the maximum number of server processes.
MTS_DISPATCHERS	Specifies the type and number of dispatcher processes for the type of protocol specified. ("tcp, 1," "decnet, 3") Only one protocol specification for each MTS_DISPATCHERS parameter; parameter can be specified multiple times.
MTS_LISTENER_ADDRESS	The address that the listener process should use to listen for the specified protocol. There should be one MTS_LISTENER_ADDRESS for each protocol; the address must also be listed in the LISTENER.ORA file. Not every address in the LISTENER.ORA needs to be in the INIT.ORA.

An example of a section of an INIT.ORA file using these parameters is shown in Source 16.3.

SOURCE 16.3   Multithreaded server INIT.ORA parameters.

```
#  Example MTS parameters
#
mts_dispatchers = tcp,5, ipc,5
mts_listener_address = (ADDRESS=
(PROTOCOL=TCP)(HOST=larry)(PORT=1521)),
(ADDRESS=(PROTOCOL=IPC)(KEY=MANUF))
mts_max_dispatchers = 10
mts_max_servers = 10
mts_servers = 5
mts_service = MANUF
mts_multiple_listeners = FALSE
#
```

Connecting to the Multithreaded Server—The users can connect to the multithreaded server by the same commands as were used before in version 2 of SQL*NET. The multithreaded server requires a two-task type of connection; so the users will generally specify a connect string. The listener will automatically assign them to a server process based on the type of protocol specified for the connect alias listed in the tnsnames.ora file.

The DBA needs to monitor the dispatcher processes and if they exceed 50% busy as indicated by the BUSY column of the V$DISPATCHER table, he or she should start another dispatcher process by use of the ALTER SYSTEM SET MTS_DISPATCHERS (protocol., integer) command. The DBA can also increase the number of database servers by use of the "ALTER SYSTEM SET MTS_SERVERS integer" command. An example script to monitor dispatcher processes is shown in Source 16.4.

SOURCE 16.4   Example of script to monitor dispatcher processes.

```
rem Name: mts_disp.sql
rem Function: Generate percent busy report for dispatchers
rem History: MRA Revealnet script
COLUMN protocol FORMAT A9 HEADING 'Dispatcher|Protocol'
COLUMN busy FORMAT 999.99 HEADING 'Percent|Busy'
SET FEEDBACK OFF VERIFY OFF LINES 78 PAGES 58
START title80 'Dispatcher Status'
SPOOL rep_out\&&db\mts_disp.lis
SELECT network protocol,
    ((SUM(busy]/(SUM(busy)+SUM(idle))*100) busy
FROM v$dispatcher
GROUP BY network;
SPOOL OFF
SET FEEDBACK ON VERIFY ON
TTITLE OFF
```

Monitoring Average Wait Time—If wait time gets to be excessive, then more dispatchers need to be activated. If the value increases as the number of concurrent users increases, increase the number of dispatchers. An example script to determine this is shown in Source 16.5. The report in Source 16.5 should be run multiple times daily during both light and heavy usage. For convenience, I suggest a good monitor tool like the Q product from Savant. It not only tells you how many dispatchers, servers, and processes are currently active (at least within the last ten-second interval) but also all of the wait statistics mentioned here.

SOURCE 16.5   Script to report on dispatcher wait time statistic.

```
rem Name: mts_wait.sql
rem Function: Generate wait time report for dispatchers
rem History: MRA Revealnet script
COLUMN network FORMAT A9 HEADING 'Protocol'
COLUMN aw FORMAT A30 HEADING 'Average Wait Time %'
SET FEEDBACK OFF VERIFY OFF LINES 78 PAGES 58
START title80 'Dispatcher Wait Times'
SPOOL rep_out\&&db\mts_wait.lis
SELECT
    NETWORK,
    DECODE (SUM(totalq),0,'No responses',
    SUM(wait)/SUM(totalq)*100||'Seconds Wait Per response') aw
FROM v$queue q, v$dispatcher d
WHERE q.type = 'DISPATCHER' AND
      q.paddr = d.paddr
GROUP BY network;
SPOOL OFF
SET FEEDBACK ON VERIFY ON
TTITLE OFF
```

Monitoring for server process contention—Server process contention is shown by excessive wait times in the request queues. If this value becomes excessive or is slowly increasing as user load increases, consider increasing the number of servers. A script to report on this is shown in Source 16.6.

SOURCE 16.6   Script to report on average wait time per request.

```
rem Name: mts_awt.sql
rem Function: Generate Average wait time report for dispatchers
rem History: MRA Revealnet script
COLUMN awt FORMAT A30 HEADING 'Average Wait Time per Request'
SET FEEDBACK OFF VERIFY OFF LINES 78 PAGES 58
START title80 'Dispatcher Average Wait Time'
SPOOL rep_out\&&db\mts_awt.lis
```

```
SELECT
     DECODE (TOTALQ,0, 'No Requests',
     (wait/totalq)*100||'Seconds Request Wait') awt
FROM
     v$queue
WHERE
     type = 'COMMON';
SPOOL OFF
SET FEEDBACK ON VERIFY ON LINES 80 PAGES 22
PAUSE Press Enter to continue
```

Increasing the Number of Servers/Dispatchers—The ALTER SYSTEM command can be used to increase the number of MTS_SERVERS or the number of MTS_DISPATCHERS up to the maximums set in the initialization parameters. If you know the load isn't transitory and will remain at the level that required the increase, increase the initialization parameters accordingly.

16.9 ADDITIONAL DBA READING

For additional reading on distributed databases, multithreaded servers, and client/server type topics, the DBA should consult the following references:

Oracle Administrator, On-line Oracle Reference, RevealNet, Inc., Version 97-2, 1997, or most current available from www.revealnet.com/.

Oracle8 Parallel Server Concepts & Administration, Release 8.0, Beta2 (or most current release), January 23, 1997, Oracle Corporation.

Oracle8 Server Distributed Systems, Release 8.0, Beta2, Part No. A50664-1, February 1997 (or most recent).

Backup and Recovery Procedures for Oracle

As should be obvious from the previous chapters, Oracle is a complex, interrelated set of files and executables. With Oracle8 it hasn't gotten any simpler. The database files include data segments, redo logs, rollback segments, control files, bfiles, libraries, and system areas. Each of these files is not a separate entity but is tightly linked to the others. For instance, the data files are repositories for all table data; the data file structure is controlled by the control file, implemented by the system areas, and maintained by a combination of the executables, redo, and rollback segments. Data files reference bfiles that are tied to external procedures stored in libraries that are referenced in procedures stored in data files. This complexity leads to the requirement of a threefold backup recovery methodology to ensure that data recovery can be made.

The threefold recovery methodology consists of

1. Normal backups using system backups, Oracle Backup Manager, Recovery Manager or a third party, tested against Oracle tool.
2. Exports and imports.
3. Archive logging of redo logs.

Let's look at each of these and how they are used.

17.1 BACKUPS

Normal system backups, referred to as either hot or cold backups, are used to protect the system from media failure. Each can and should be used when required.

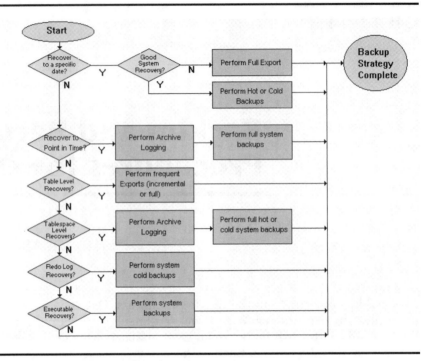

FIGURE 17.1   Backup recovery strategy flowchart.

Cold VMS Backups

A cold backup, that is, one done with the database in a shutdown state, provides a complete copy of the database that can be restored exactly. The procedure for using a cold backup is as follows:

1. Using the shutdown script(s) provided, shutdown the Oracle instance(s) to be backed up.
2. Ensure that there is enough backup media to back up the entire database.
3. Mount the first volume of the backup media (9 track, WORM, TK50, TK70, etc.) using the VMS mount command:

```
$ mount/foreign dev: volume_name
```

4. Issue the VMS backup command to initiate the backup.

```
$ backup/log=ora_<date>.log -
$ ora_diskx:[oracle...]*.*,-
$ ora_diskx+1:[oracle...]*.*
$ ora_diskx+2:[oracle...]*.*
```

.
.
.

```
$ ora_diskx+n:oracle...] dev:ora_<date>.sav/save
```

Where

ora_diskx. . . . ora_diskn represents the system logicals in accordance with OFA rules, with n being the highest numbered disk and x being the lowest.

<date> represents the date for the backup.

dev: represents the backup media device name such as mua0:
/log=log_<date>.log names a file to log the results from the backup.

/save this tells BACKUP to archive the files in save set format; this requires less room than an image backup.

5. Once the backup is complete, be sure all backup volumes are properly labeled and stored, *away from the computer*. The final volume is dismounted from the tape drive using the VMS DISMOUNT command:

```
$ DISMOUNT dev:
```

6. Restart the Oracle instances using the appropriate startup script(s).

Note in step 5 the italicized phrase *away from the computer*. In a number of computer facilities backups are kept close at hand, sometimes in the same room as the computer. What would happen if a site disaster destroyed the computer room? Not only the hardware, but all of the system backups and your data could be lost. Store backups in another building or even totally off-site somewhere. This assures that come fire, flood, or typhoon, you should be able to get backup one way or another.

VMS Hot Backups

A hot backup, or one taken while the database is active, can only give a read-consistent copy but doesn't handle active transactions. You must ensure that all redo logs archived during the backup process are also backed up. The hot backup differs from the cold backup in that only sections of the database are backed up at one time. This is accomplished by using the ALTER command to modify a tablespace's status to backup. Be sure that you restore the status to normal once the database is backed up or else redo log mismatch and improper archiving/rollbacks can occur.

While it is quite simple (generally speaking) to do a cold backup by hand, a hot backup can be quite complex and should be automated. The automated procedure should then be thoroughly tested on a dummy database for both proper operation and ability to restore prior to its use on the production database(s).

Limitations on hot or on-line backups:

1. The database must be operating in ARCHIVELOG mode for hot backups to work.
2. Hot backups should only be done during off or low-use periods.
3. During the hot backups the entire block containing a changed record, not just the changed record, is written to the archive log, requiring more archive space for this period.

The hot backup consists of three processes:

1. The tablespace data files are backed up.
2. The archived redo logs are backed up.
3. The control file is backed up.

These three parts have to be repeated for each tablespace in the database. For small databases, this is relatively easy. For large, complex databases with files spread across several drives, this can become a nightmare if not properly automated in VMS DCL command scripts. An example of this type of a backup DCL script is shown in Source 17.1.

SOURCE 17.1   Example of script to perform on-line "hot" backup.

```
$!*****************************************************************
$! Name      : Hot_backup.com
$! Purpose     : Perform a hot backup of an Oracle Database
$! Use     : @Hot_backup.com
$! Limitations    : Creates a read-consistent image but doesn't back up in-
process transactions
$!
$! Revision History:
$! Date      Who        What
$! ---------  ------------  -------------------------------
$! June 1993 K. Loney     Featured in Oracle Mag. Article
$! 29-Jun-93 M. Ault      Modified, commented
$!*************************************************************
$!
$! Define symbol for backup command so don't have to fully
$!b specify it each time
$ dup_it = "backup/ignore=(noback,interlock,label) /log"
$ !
$ svrmgrl
    connect internal
    alter tablespace system begin backup;
    exit
$ dup_it m_ora_disk2:[m_oracle.oracle6.db_example]ora_system_1.dbs
  mua0:ora_system.bck/save
$!
 svrmgrl
    connect internal
```

```
   alter tablespace system end backup;
   alter tablespace tools begin backup;
   exit
$ dup_it m_ora_disk3:[m_oracle.oracle6.db_example]ora_tools_1.dbs
  mua0:ts_tools.bck/save
$!
svrmgrl
   connect internal
   alter tablespace tools end backup;
   alter tablespace user_tables begin backup;
   exit
$ dup_it m_ora_disk3:[m_oracle.oracle6.db_example]ora_user_tables_1.dbs
  mua0:ts_tools.bck/save
$!
   svrmgrl
   alter tablespace user_tables end backup;
   exit
$! force write of all archive logs
$!
$ svrmgrl
   connect internal
   alter system switch logfile;
   archive log all;
   exit
$!
$ rename m_ora_disk5:[m_oracle.oracle6.db_example.archives]*.arc *.oldarc
$! Now backup a control file
$!
$ svrmgrl
   connect internal
   alter database example
   backup controlfile to
   'm_ora_disk1:[m_oracle.oracle6.db_example]ora_control.bac
   reuse;
   exit
$ dup_it m_ora_disk1:[m_oracle.oracle6.db_example]ora_control1.con
mua0:ora_control.bac/save
$! now backup all archive logs
$!
$! you don't want to delete logs if an error causes them not to
$! be backed up
$ on error goto end_it
$!
$ dup_it m_ora_disk5:[m_oracle.oracle6.db_example.archives]*.oldarc
mua0:ora_archives.bck/save
$! Now delete logs
$!
$ delete/log m_ora_disk5:[m_oracle.oracle6.db_examples.archives]*.oldarc;*
$ end_it:
$ exit
```

As you can see, this is a bit more complex than a full cold backup and requires more monitoring than a cold backup. Recovery from this type of backup consists of restoring all tablespaces and logs and then recovering. You only use the backup of the control file if the current control file was also lost in the disaster; otherwise, be sure to use the most current copy of the control file for recovery operations.

UNIX Backups

The type of backup you perform in UNIX is dependent upon whether you use RAW devices or not. RAW devices will require backup of the entire device, while use of the mounted file systems will allow partial backups.

Cold UNIX Backup

1. Using the shutdown script(s) provided, shutdown the Oracle instance(s) to be backed up.
2. Ensure that there is enough backup media to back up the entire database.
3. Mount the tape using the appropriate UNIX command.
4. Using the dump, tar, or cpio commands make a backup of the Oracle subdirectories. Usually the tar command is used for cooked filesystems; however, RAW filesystems will have to be backed up either to another disk (use "dd") or directly to tape. If you use links, be sure you copy the raw partition and not just the link.
5. Once the backup is complete, dismount the final media volume using the umount command. Be sure the backups are stored in a safe place, *preferably away from the system.*
6. Restart the Oracle instance(s) using the appropriate startup script(s).

TIP   In a number of computer facilities backups are kept close at hand, sometimes in the same room as the computer. What would happen if a site disaster destroyed the computer room? Not only the hardware, but all of the system backups and your data could be lost. Store backups in another building or even totally off-site somewhere. This assures that come fire, flood, or typhoon, you should be able to get backup one way or another.

UNIX Hot Backups

A hot backup, or one taken while the database is active, can only give a read-consistent copy but doesn't handle active transactions. The hot backup differs from the cold backup in that only sections of the database are backed up at one time. Under UNIX, this will require the use of normal mounted file systems and not RAW devices.

A hot backup is accomplished by using the ALTER command to modify tablespace status to begin backup. Be sure that you restore the status of the tablespace to normal once the tablespace is backed up or else redo log mismatch and improper archiving/ rollbacks can occur. This will cause the database to assume that a full recovery of the affected tablespace is required upon the next startup of the database.

While it is quite simple (generally speaking) to do a cold backup by hand, a hot backup can be quite complex and should be automated. The automated procedure should then be thoroughly tested on a dummy database for both proper operation and ability to restore prior to its use on the production database(s).

Limitations on hot or on-line backups:

1. The database must be operating in ARCHIVELOG mode for hot backups to work.
2. Hot backups should only be done during off or low-use periods.
3. During the hot backups the entire block containing a changed record, not just the changed record, is written to the archive log, requiring more archive space for this period.

The UNIX hot backup consists of three parts identical to the VMS hot backup:

1. The tablespace data files are backed up.
2. The archived redo logs are backed up.
3. The control file is backed up.

These three parts have to be repeated for each tablespace in the database. For small databases, this is relatively easy. For large complex databases with files spread across several drives, this can become a nightmare if not properly automated in VMS DCL command scripts. An example of this type of a backup KORNE shell script is shown in Source 17.2.

SOURCE 17.2   Example of hot backup script for UNIX KORNE shell.

```
#*******************************************************************
# Name     : hot_backup
# Purpose     : Perform a hot backup of an Oracle Database
# Use     : sh hot_backup
# Limitations     : Creates a read-consistent image, but doesn't back up in-process
transactions
#
# Revision History:
# Date          Who          What
# ---------     ----------     -------------------------------------------------
# June 1993     K. Loney       Featured in Oracle Mag. Article
# 29-Jun-93     M. Ault        Modified, commented
# 02-Aug-93     M. Ault        Converted to UNIX script
# 03-Aug-93     M. Phillips    Added error detection
#**********************************************************************************
#
```

```
ERROR="FALSE"
LOGFILE="$ORACLE_HOME/adhoc/scripts/hot_back_log"
while [ "$error"=FALSE ]
do
svrmgrl << ending1
     connect internal
     alter tablespace system begin backup;
     exit
ending1
     if ( tar cfv /oracle/backup /data/ORA_SYSTEM_1.DBF )
     then
          :
     else
         ERROR="TRUE";
             echo "Tar backup failed for ora_system1.dbf" >$LOGFILE
     fi
svrmgrl << ending2
connect internal
     alter tablespace system end backup;
     exit
ending2

dup_it="tar rv /oracle/backup"
svrmgrl << ending3
     connect internal
     alter tablespace user_tables begin backup;
     exit
ending3
if ( $dup_it /data/ora_user_tables_1.dbf )
then
     :
else
    ERROR="TRUE";echo "Tar backup failed for ora_user_tables_1.dbf">>$LOGFILE
fi #we must still end backup for tablespaces
svrmgrl << ending4
     connect internal
     alter tablespace user_tables end backup;
     exit
ending4
# force write of all archive logs
svrmgrl << ending5
     connect internal
     alter system switch logfile;
     archive log all;
     exit
ending5
if ( cp /usr/oracle/oracle7/db_example.archives/*.arc *.oldarc )
then
     :
else
    ERROR="TRUE";echo "Copy of archive logs failed">>$LOGFILE
fi
# Now backup a control file
svrmgrl << ending6
```

```
        connect internal
        alter database example
        backup controlfile to
        '/usr/oracle/oracle7/db_example/ora_control.bac
        reuse;
        exit
ending6
if ( $dup_it /usr/oracle/oracle7/db_example/ora_control.bac )
then
        :
else
    ERROR="TRUE";echo "Tar backup failed for control file">>$LOGFILE
fi
# now backup all archive logs
if ( $dup_it /usr/oracle/oracle7/db_example.archives/*.oldarc )
then
        :
else
    ERROR="TRUE";echo "Tar backup failed for archive files">>$LOGFILE
fi
# Now delete logs
if ( rm /usr/m_oracle/oracle7/db_examples.archives/*.oldarc;* )
then
    ERROR="TRUE"
else
    ERROR="TRUE";echo "Delete of archive files failed">>$LOGFILE
fi
done
exit
done
```

One problem with a canned script of the types shown for VMS and UNIX hot backup is that they don't automatically reconfigure themselves to include new tablespaces. The script in Source 17.3 is an example of how to let Oracle build its own hot backup script using dynamic SQL and the data dictionary. This script is excerpted from *Oracle Administrator* from RevealNet, Inc. Version 97.2 (an online reference product).

SOURCE 17.3   Example of script to generate a hot backup script on UNIX.

```
rem******* RevealNet Oracle Administration*********************
rem
rem   File: oline_bu.sql
rem
rem   This is a part of the RevealNet Oracle Administration library.
rem   Copyright (C) 1996-97 RevealNet, Inc.
rem   All rights reserved.
rem
rem   For more information, call RevealNet at 1-800-REVEAL4
```

```
rem  or check out our Web page: www.revealnet.com
rem
rem  Modifications (Date, Who, Description)
rem
rem FUNCTION: Perform Hot Unix backup
rem
rem ************************************************************
rem
CREATE TABLE bu_temp (line_no NUMBER,line_txt VARCHAR2(2000));
SET VERIFY OFF
DEFINE dest_dir=&1;
DECLARE
CURSOR get_tbsp IS
     SELECT
          tablespace_name
     FROM
          dba_tablespaces;
CURSOR bbu_com (tbsp VARCHAR2) IS
     SELECT
          'ALTER TABLESPACE '||tablespace_name||' BEGIN BACKUP;'
     from
          dba_tablespaces
     WHERE
          tablespace_name=tbsp;
cursor tar_com (tbsp varchar2) is
     SELECT
          '!/bin/tar cvf - '||file_name||'|compress>&&dest_dir/'||
          SUBSTR(file_name,INSTR(file_name,'/',-1,1)+1,
          LENGTH(file_name))||'.Z'
     FROM
          dba_data_files
     WHERE
          tablespace_name=tbsp;
CURSOR ebu_com (tbsp varchar2) IS
     SELECT
          'ALTER TABLESPACE '||tablespace_name||' END BACKUP;'
     FROM
          dba_tablespaces
     WHERE
          tablespace_name=tbsp;
tbsp_name VARCHAR2(64);
line_num NUMBER:=0;
line_text VARCHAR2(2000);
BEGIN
line_num := line_num+1;
OPEN get_tbsp;
LOOP
     FETCH get_tbsp INTO tbsp_name;
     EXIT WHEN get_tbsp%NOTFOUND;
       OPEN bbu_com (tbsp_name);
```

```
          FETCH bbu_com INTO line_text;
          INSERT INTO bu_temp VALUES (line_num,line_text);
          CLOSE bbu_com;
          OPEN tar_com (tbsp_name);
          LOOP
              FETCH tar_com INTO line_text;
              EXIT WHEN tar_com%NOTFOUND;
            line_num:=line_num+1;
              INSERT INTO bu_temp VALUES (line_num,line_text);
          END LOOP;
      CLOSE tar_com;
      OPEN ebu_com(tbsp_name);
      FETCH ebu_com INTO line_text;
      line_num:=line_num+1;
      INSERT INTO bu_temp VALUES (line_num,line_text);
      CLOSE ebu_com;
END LOOP;
      CLOSE get_tbsp;
      SELECT
          'alter system switch logfile;'
      INTO
          line_text
      FROM
          dual;
      line_num:=line_num+1;
      INSERT INTO bu_temp VALUES (line_num,line_text);
      SELECT '!compress '||SUBSTR (value,1,INSTR(value,'/',-1,1))||'*'
      INTO line_text FROM v$parameter WHERE name='log_archive_dest';
      line_num:=line_num+1;
      INSERT INTO bu_temp VALUES (line_num,line_text);
      SELECT '!tar cvf - '||SUBSTR (value,1,INSTR(value,'/',-1,1))||'*.Z'||
      '|compress>&&dest_dir/'||
      SUBSTR(value,instr(value,'/',-1,1)+1,LENGTH(value))||'.Z'
      INTO line_text FROM v$parameter WHERE name='log_archive_dest';
      line_num:=line_num+1;
      INSERT INTO bu_temp VALUES (line_num,line_text);
END;
/
SET VERIFY OFF FEEDBACK OFF HEADING OFF TERMOUT OFF PAGES 0
SET EMBEDDED ON LINES 132
COLUMN line_no NOPRINT
COLUMN dbname NEW_VALUE db NOPRINT
SELECT name dbname FROM v$database;
SPOOL rep_out\&db\thot_bu.sql
SELECT * FROM bu_temp ORDER BY line_no;
SPOOL OFF
rem uncomment this next line and change
rem directory syntax for UNIX
rem
! sed '1,$ s/ *$//g' rep_out\&db\thot_bu.sql>rep_out\&db\hot_bu.sql
```

```
rem
DROP TABLE bu_temp;
SET VERIFY ON FEEDBACK ON HEADING ON TERMOUT ON PAGES 22
SET EMBEDDED OFF LINES 80
CLEAR COLUMNS
undef dest_dir
```

The output from the script for my test database is shown in Source 17.4.

SOURCE 17.4   Example of output from the hot backup script generator.

```
alter tablespace SYSTEM begin backup;
!/bin/tar cvf -
/oracle0/ORTEST1/data/system01.dbf|compress>\
/oracle16/ORTEST1/backups/system01.dbf.Z
alter tablespace SYSTEM end backup;

alter tablespace RBS begin backup;
!/bin/tar cvf -
/oracle2/ORTEST1/data/rbs01.dbf|compress>\
/oracle16/ORTEST1/backups/rbs01.dbf.Z
alter tablespace RBS end backup;

alter tablespace TEMP begin backup;
!/bin/tar cvf -
/oracle3/ORTEST1/data/temp01.dbf|compress>\
/oracle16/ORTEST1/backups/temp01.dbf.Z
alter tablespace TEMP end backup;

alter tablespace TOOLS begin backup;
!/bin/tar cvf -
/oracle3/ORTEST1/data/tools01.dbf|compress>\
/oracle16/ORTEST1/backups/tools01.dbf.Z
alter tablespace TOOLS end backup;

alter tablespace APPL_INDEX begin backup;
!/bin/tar cvf -
/oracle5/ORTEST1/data/ORTEST1_APPL_index01.dbf|compress>\
/oracle16/ORTEST1/backups/ORTEST1_APPL_index01.dbf.Z
alter tablespace APPL_INDEX end backup;

alter tablespace APPL_DATA begin backup;
!/bin/tar cvf -
/oracle0/ORTEST1/data/ORTEST1_APPL_data01.dbf|compress>\
/oracle16/ORTEST1/backups/ORTEST1_APPL_data01.dbf.Z
alter tablespace APPL_DATA end backup;

alter system switch logfile;
!/bin/tar cvf -
```

```
/oracle0/ORTEST1/redo/log1a.dbf|compress>\
/oracle16/ORTEST1/backups/log1a.dbf.Z

!/bin/tar cvf -
/oracle1/ORTEST1/redo/log2a.dbf|compress>\
/oracle16/ORTEST1/backups/log2a.dbf.Z

!/bin/tar cvf -
/oracle2/ORTEST1/redo/log3a.dbf|compress>\
/oracle16/ORTEST1/backups/log3a.dbf.Z

!compress /oracle4/ORTEST1/admin/arch/*
!tar cvf -
/oracle4/ORTEST1/admin/arch/*.Z|compress>\
/oracle16/ORTEST1/backups/arch.log.Z
```

17.2 IMPORTS/EXPORTS

Imports and exports extract or insert an Oracle-readable copy of the actual data and structures in the database. The exports can be used to recover single data structures to the date and time the export was taken. Exports come in three types: full, cumulative, and incremental. Full, as its name implies, provides a full logical copy of the database and its structures. A cumulative provides a complete copy of altered structures since the last full or the last cumulative export. Incremental exports provide a complete copy of altered structures since the last incremental, cumulative, or full export.

Limitations on export/import:

1. A database must be running to perform either an export or import.
2. Export files shouldn't be edited and can only be used by import.
3. (Import only) imports full tables; it can't be used to do a conditional load.
4. Exported data is only a logical copy of the data. An export can only allow recovery to the date and time the export was taken.

Imports and exports are accomplished using the Oracle IMPORT and EXPORT utilities. For exports, the EXPORT utility is used. The format for using this command follows.

```
Format:  EXP KEYWORD=value —or— KEYWORD=(list of values)
Example: EXP AULT/AUTHOR GRANTS=N TABLES=(CHAPTERS, EDITORS,ADVANCES)
```

Keyword	*Description (Default)*
USERID	username/password
BUFFER	size of data buffer

FILE	output file (EXPDAT.DMP)
COMPRESS	import into one extent (Y)
GRANTS	export grants (Y)
INDEXES	export indexes (Y)
ROWS	export data rows (Y)
CONSTRAINTS	export table constraints (Y)
CONSISTENT	cross-table consistency (N)
LOG	log file of screen output (None)
STATISTICS	analyze objects (ESTIMATE)
DIRECT	Bypass the SQL command processing layer (N) (new in Oracle8)
FEEDBACK	Show a process meter (a dot) every X rows exported (0 – X value)
HELP	
MLS, MLS_LABEL_FORMAT	Used with secure Oracle; we won't cover these.
FULL	export entire file (N)
OWNER	list of owner usernames
TABLES	list of table names
RECORDLENGTH	length of IO record
INCTYPE	incremental export type
RECORD	track incr. export (Y)
PARFILE	parameter file name

Exports should be automated and scheduled to run automatically. An export methodology should be worked out such that the DBA is reasonably certain a deleted file can be recovered.

The format of the IMPORT command follows.

```
Format:  IMP KEYWORD=value —or— KEYWORD=(list of values)
Example: IMP AULT/AUTHOR IGNORE=Y TABLES=(EXPENSES, ADVANCES) FULL=N
```

Keyword	*Description (Default)*
USERID	username/password
BUFFER	size of data buffer
FILE	output file (EXPDAT.DMP)
SHOW	just list file contents (N)
IGNORE	ignore create errors (N)

RECORDLENGTH	length of IO record
GRANTS	import grants (Y)
INDEXES	import indexes (Y)
ROWS	import data rows (Y)
LOG	log file of screen output
INDEXFILE	write table/index info to specified file
FULL	import entire file (N)
FROMUSER	list of owner usernames
TOUSER	list of usernames
TABLES	list of table names
FEEDBACK	Provide dot status graph (0)
INCTYPE	incremental import type
COMMIT	commit array insert (N)
PARFILE	parameter file name
DESTROY	overwrite tablespace data (N)
CHARSET	char. set of export file (NLS_LANG)

Under Oracle7, the user must be granted the EXP_FULL_DATABASE role in order to do full exports. In order to perform a full import, the user must have the IMP_FULL_DATABASE role. The users with the DBA role are granted these implicitly.

An example of when the DBA would want to grant these roles to a user would be a user whose password is specified in the command script used for doing the automatic exports. If the only role granted to the user is CREATE_SESSION and EXP_FULL_DATABASE even if the user's password is compromised, they won't be able to do much damage.

17.3 ARCHIVE LOGS

The redo logs store all transactions that alter the database, all committed updates, adds, or deletes of tables, structures, or data. If archiving is disabled, only data in the current off-line and on-line redo logs can be recovered. If the system recycles through all redo logs, the old ones are reused, destroying their contents. If archive logging is enabled, the redo logs are written out to storage before reuse. Archive logging allows recovery to a specific point in time since the last full cold backup or complete off-line backup.

Under Oracle7 and Oracle8 redo logs are specified in groups; each group forms a shadow set and is archived together. Under Oracle7 archive logs can also be assigned to threads for use in parallel or shared instances. Individual logs are called members. Threads hold groups that hold members. Each member of a redo log group is the same size and should be on separate physical platters. Oracle automatically synchronizes members of a group into a shadow set.

Redo logs cannot be used to recover a database brought back from a full export.

A proper use of these backup/recovery tools allows the DBA to recover from any possible failure.

17.4   BACKUP METHODOLOGIES

VMS or UNIX System Backup

1. VMS (BACKUP) or UNIX system backups (such as TAR or DUMP) should be taken on at least a weekly basis. The Oracle database(s) should be shut down and a full cold backup taken if possible since this is the most easily recovered backup. If this isn't possible, consider developing a hot backup procedure.

2. Once the full cold backup or full hot backup is taken, archive logs and exports from the time period prior to the backup can be copied to tape and removed from the system; assuming the backup is good, they are no longer needed.

3. Hot backups, where Oracle is not shut down, can be taken periodically; however, the DBA is cautioned that full recovery may not be possible if this is the sole backup method used. Great care must be taken to ensure all redo logs and a good copy of the control file are taken along with the hot backups of the data files.

4. It should be remembered that recovery is only to the time the backup was taken. All control, data, and archive logs must be backed up at the same time. The data from the backup forward is recovered from the archive and on-line redo logs. Therefore, even though redo logs are backed up, they should not be restored unless the on-line redo logs have been lost. Always recover using an on-line redo log and the most current control file if possible.

Import/Export

1. As a minimum, the following export schedule should be used:

   Daily: Incremental export during off-peak time
   Weekly: Full export during off-peak time

2. Once the full export is taken, the DBA can remove previous full and incremental backups. This schedule should be implemented using batch queues and DCL or CRON and shell scripts.

3. A more aggressive export schedule could be as follows:

   - Daily: Incremental export
   - Weekly: Cumulative export
   - Monthly: Full export

4. The expired exports would be deleted as before. This would also be implemented using automated procedures.

5. All export procedures should be logged so that they can be reviewed. Some data corruption problems, such as unreadable characters in a record, will only be caught by the export process.

Archive Logging

1. Archive logging is strongly suggested for all Oracle databases.
2. Archive logging is automatic; it may consume disk resources in a highly active environment. If recovery is required, the system will ask for the archive logs it needs and perform recovery from them. Archive logs allow point-in-time recovery. To use hot backup, archive logging is required. Some sites switch on archive logging during a hot backup and then switch it off; however, this means they can only recover to the time of the last archive log.
3. Using Oracle INIT.ORA parameters, the destination and frequency of the archive logging can be controlled, although the size of the redo log plays more of a role in the frequency of archive logging than any initialization parameter.

Recovery Types

Recovery depends entirely upon how the backup methodology was employed. It also depends upon what the DBA has to recover.

Recoveries can consist of

- REDO Log Recovery—Off-line or On-line log
- ROLLBACK Segment Recovery
- Tablespace Recovery
- Table Recovery
- Recovery of the entire database
- Recovery of executables
- Recovery of control files

Each recovery may consist of one or a combination of these, depending on file placement.

Recovery generally is required only after a physical insult to the database file system. Most internal errors are corrected automatically by Oracle using the REDO and rollback logs and data buffers.

Since each site will have differing file placement and each recovery will most likely be unique, it is suggested that the *Oracle7* or *Oracle8 Server Recovery Manual* (Oracle, Corporation, 1997) be consulted for the appropriate recovery methodology that applies to the situation(s) in which the DBA may find him- or herself. Another good resource is *Oracle Backup and Recovery* by Rama Velpuri (Oracle Press, 1996).

17.5 AN EXAMPLE SET OF RECOVERY PROCEDURES

Understanding how various system failures will affect the Oracle database system requires an understanding of how the system is physically located on the disk farm. The purpose of this set of procedures is to provide a single source for database recovery options. The procedures that follow will have to be run depending on the type of failure that occurs. Where important, the file names for the instance are referred to. As DBA, you should use these procedures to model your own set of backup and recovery procedures.

Disk Setup Information

We assume in these procedures that the DBA has spread the Oracle files across several platters to reduce disk contention and speed access. The current configuration is as follows:

DISK	LOGICAL	CONTENTS
1	/oracle0	EXECUTABLES, FORMS, REPORTS, MENUS, COM FILES, ONE CONTROL FILE, TRACE FILES, LOGS, SOME REDO LOGS
2	/oracle1	THE DATA FILES INCLUDING SYSTEM, COPY OF THE CONTROL FILE, TEMPORARY TABLESPACE, SOME REDO LOGS
3	/oracle2	COPY OF THE CONTROL FILE, INDEXES, SOME REDO LOGS
4	/oracle3	ROLLBACK SEGMENTS, EXPORTS
5	/oracle4	ALL ARCHIVE LOGS

Recovery from loss of one of these disks would depend on what files were contained on the disk. Detailed Oracle recovery procedures are contained in *Oracle8 Server Backup and Recovery Guide*, Release 8.0, Beta2, Part No. A50610-1 (Oracle Corporation, February 1997, or most current). Although the *Backup and Recovery Guide* shows an ideal for a small-sized database, the Oracle system is flexible enough to be installed on as few as two disks or may be installed across a massive disk farm. The DBA should ensure that proper separation of high-use files, redo logs, archives, and exports is accomplished should fewer than five disks be used.

General Discussion

1. Loss of /oracle0:

    The loss of /oracle0 would require a backup restore operation (performed by the SYSTEM MANAGER from UNIX backup tapes) to recover the system's executables, com (command), forms, reports, menus, log, trace, and the most recent control file—all should be recovered from an unaffected disk. The control file would have to be copied from a nonaffected disk before starting the instance if changes to database structure had occurred since the last backup. This is required because the control file contains the latest data on archive log usage and data file locations. The CONTROL file on the backup contains out-of-date information. The REDO log loss would require a recovery to the most current archive log file. If the redo log was the on-line redo log and no mirroring was used, then some data loss will occur.

2. Loss of /oracle1:

The loss of /oracle1 would be the most serious loss because it contains the majority of data files. Recovery would consist of restoration of the most current backup then application of all archive logs from the last backup to the current date. A second method of recovery would be to re-create the database and then import the most recent full export and apply all cumulative and incremental exports. However, this restore (using exports) would only be current to the date and time of the last export file applied, and no further recovery would be possible. The redo log recovery would be automatic once a copy of the redo log was replaced from backup. If the affected redo log was on-line at the time of loss, and no mirroring is used, then some data loss will occur.

3. Loss of /oracle2:

The loss of /oracle2 would slow data access but would not necessarily require immediate recovery. If the index tablespaces are taken off-line using the SVRMGRL utility, users could still access the data for query-only operations in the database since indexes are not required. However, you will probably have to shut down since updates involving keyed or indexed files would not be possible. The index tablespaces would then be recovered using the archive logs and the tablespace recovery procedure. If the redo logs lost were on-line and no mirroring was being used, some data loss will occur.

4. Loss of /oracle3:

The loss of /oracle3 would require a complete restore of the database, similar to the loss of /oracle1. Any transactions currently in process would not be able to be rolled back. It is suggested that multiple rollback segment files be used if possible to prevent the total loss of all rollback segments from a single failure.

5. Loss of /oracle4:

The loss of /oracle4 would require an immediate Oracle shutdown and full backup or a full export followed by shutdown. This is to ensure data recoverability should recovery of the lost archives and exports be impossible. The DBA would then reset the archive log destination and restart Oracle. If immediate shutdown is not possible, the DBA can reset the archive log destination and continue operation; this is not a safe condition for full recovery but will allow continued use until a full backup can be taken.

TIP Since the backup of the archive disk would be one week old, it would be useless. Only those archive logs since the last backup are needed for a recovery. By shutting down and backing up the database, the lost archive logs become irrelevant.

---

6. Loss of a single file:

In the event that a user lost data due to inadvertent table deletion, the table would be recovered from the last full export or the last incremental export that contains the table up to the day prior to the loss. If exports are not taken, recovery of a single table would require the restoration of the entire tablespace and the application of archive logs up to the time just prior to the table loss (this requires the tablespace to be off-line). There are various data dictionary views that tell you when a table was last exported.

7. Partial disk loss:

In the event that only a small section of a disk is lost, recovery would depend on the type of Oracle file that occupied that area of the disk.

8. Nonphysical data problems:

Other than physical data loss, such as disk crash, all other recovery scenarios are handled automatically by the Oracle kernel. These include program failure, CPU failure, instance failure due to bug, and system failure due to power loss or forced crash.

17.6   DETAILED PROCEDURES

Recovery of the Full Database Using Export Files

1. Create a new version of the affected database using a script similar to that shown in Source 17.5. The script for your database should be located in the appropriate ORA_INSTANCE or $ORACLE_HOME for the instance of concern. This logical or environmental variable is set automatically. If you don't have a script, use the provided scripts to create SQL to rebuild the database and tablespaces immediately. The script to rebuild the database itself is shown in Source 17.5.

SOURCE 17.5   DB_RCT.SQL script to build database rebuild script.

```
REM FUNCTION: SCRIPT FOR CREATING DB
REM       This script must be run by a user with the DBA role.
REM       This script is intended to run with Oracle7.
REM       Running this script will in turn create a script to
REM       rebuild the database.  This created
```

```
REM       script, crt_db.sql,  is run by SQLDBA
REM       Only preliminary testing of this script was performed.
REM       Be sure to test it completely before relying on it.
REM M. Ault 3/29/96 TRECOM, REVEALNET
REM
SET VERIFY OFF FEEDBACK OFF ECHO OFF PAGES 0
SET TERMOUT ON
prompt Creating db build script...
SET TERMOUT OFF
CREATE TABLE db_temp
    (lineno NUMBER,  text VARCHAR2(255))
/
DECLARE
   CURSOR dbf_cursor IS
     SELECT  file_name,bytes
     FROM  dba_data_files
     WHERE tablespace_name='SYSTEM';
   CURSOR grp_cursor IS
     SELECT group# FROM v$log;
   CURSOR mem_cursor (grp_num number) IS
     SELECT   a.member, b.bytes
     FROM v$logfile a, v$log b
     WHERE a.group#=grp_num
     AND a.group#=b.group#
     ORDER BY member;
   grp_member            v$logfile.member%TYPE;
   bytes                 v$log.bytes%TYPE;
   db_name               VARCHAR2(8);
   db_string             VARCHAR2(255);
   db_lineno             NUMBER := 0;
   thrd                  NUMBER;
   grp                   NUMBER;
   fname                 dba_data_files.file_name%TYPE;
   sz                    NUMBER;
   begin_count           NUMBER;
   max_group             NUMBER;
   PROCEDURE write_out(p_line INTEGER,
                p_string VARCHAR2) IS
       BEGIN
          INSERT INTO db_temp (lineno,text)
             VALUES (db_lineno,db_string);
     END;
BEGIN
    SELECT MAX(group#) INTO max_group FROM v$log;
    db_lineno:=db_lineno+1;
   SELECT 'CREATE DATABASE '||name INTO db_string
     FROM v$database;
     write_out(db_lineno,db_string);
     db_lineno:=db_lineno+1;
   SELECT 'CONTROLFILE REUSE' INTO db_string
```

```
        FROM dual;
        write_out(db_lineno,db_string);
        db_lineno:=db_lineno+1;
    SELECT 'LOGFILE ' INTO db_string
        FROM dual;
        write_out(db_lineno,db_string);
COMMIT;
IF grp_cursor%ISOPEN
THEN
        CLOSE grp_cursor;
        OPEN grp_cursor;
ELSE
        OPEN grp_cursor;
END IF;
LOOP
        FETCH grp_cursor INTO grp;
        EXIT WHEN grp_cursor%NOTFOUND;
        db_lineno:=db_lineno+1;
        db_string:= ' GROUP '||grp||' (';
        write_out(db_lineno,db_string);
        IF mem_cursor%ISOPEN THEN
            CLOSE mem_cursor;
            OPEN mem_cursor(grp);
        ELSE
                OPEN mem_cursor(grp);
        END IF;
        db_lineno:=db_lineno+1;
        BEGIN_count:=db_lineno;
        LOOP
            FETCH mem_cursor INTO grp_member, bytes;
            EXIT when mem_cursor%NOTFOUND;
            IF begin_count=db_lineno THEN
                db_string:=CHR(39)||grp_member||CHR(39);
                write_out(db_lineno,db_string);
                db_lineno:=db_lineno+1;
            ELSE
                db_string:=','||CHR(39)||grp_member||CHR(39);
                write_out(db_lineno,db_string);
                db_lineno:=db_lineno+1;
            END IF;
        END LOOP;
        db_lineno:=db_lineno+1;
        IF grp=max_group
        THEN
            db_string:=' ) SIZE '||bytes;
            write_out(db_lineno,db_string);
        ELSE
            db_string:=' ) SIZE '||bytes||',';
            write_out(db_lineno,db_string);
```

```
        END IF;
END LOOP;
IF dbf_cursor%ISOPEN THEN
     CLOSE dbf_cursor;
     OPEN dbf_cursor;
ELSE
     OPEN dbf_cursor;
END IF;
begin_count:=db_lineno;
LOOP
     FETCH dbf_cursor INTO fname, sz;
     EXIT WHEN dbf_cursor%NOTFOUND;
     IF begin_count=db_lineno THEN
db_string:='DATAFILE '||chr(39)||fname||chr(39)||
          ' SIZE '||sz||' REUSE';
     ELSE
db_string:=','||chr(39)||fname||chr(39)||' SIZE '||sz||' REUSE';
     END IF;
     db_lineno:=db_lineno+1;
     write_out(db_lineno,db_string);
END LOOP;
COMMIT;
SELECT DECODE(value,'TRUE','ARCHIVELOG','FALSE','NOARCHIVELOG')
     INTO db_string FROM v$parameter WHERE name='log_archive_start';
     db_lineno:=db_lineno+1;
     write_out(db_lineno,db_string);
SELECT ';' INTO db_string FROM  dual;
     db_lineno:=db_lineno+1;
     write_out(db_lineno,db_string);
CLOSE dbf_cursor;
CLOSE mem_cursor;
CLOSE grp_cursor;
COMMIT;
END;
/
COLUMN dbname NEW_VALUE db NOPRINT
SELECT name dbname FROM v$database;
SET HEADING OFF PAGES 0 VERIFY OFF RECSEP OFF
SPOOL rep_out\&db\crt_db.sql
COLUMN text FORMAT a80 WORD_WRAP
SELECT text FROM db_temp ORDER BY  lineno;
SPOOL OFF
SET FEEDBACK ON VERIFY ON TERMOUT ON
DROP table db_temp;
PROMPT Press Enter to continue
SET VERIFY ON FEEDBACK ON PAGES 22 TERMOUT ON
CLEAR COLUMNS
```

The reason this script is so long is that there may be multiple data files for the SYSTEM tablespace and there most certainly will be multiple redo logs, redo log groups, and possibly redo log threads. This multiplicity of files results in the need for a cursor for each of the possible recursions and a loop-end loop construct to support the selection of the data from the database.

It is ironic that all of the preceding code is used to produce the output in Listing 17.5.

LISTING 17.5   Example of output from the DB_RCT.SQL script.

```
CREATE DATABASE ORTEST1
CONTROLFILE REUSE
LOGFILE
GROUP 1 (
'C:\ORACLE1\ORTEST1\REDO\LOG11ORTEST1.DBF'
,'E:\ORACLE3\ORTEST1\REDO\LOG12ORTEST1.DBF'
) SIZE 1048576,
GROUP 2 (
'D:\ORACLE2\ORTEST1\REDO\LOG21ORTEST1.DBF'
,'F:\ORACLE4\ORTEST1\REDO\LOG22ORTEST1.DBF'
) SIZE 1048576,
GROUP 3 (
'D:\ORACLE2\ORTEST1\REDO\LOG32ORTEST1.DBF'
,'E:\ORACLE3\ORTEST1\REDO\LOG31ORTEST1.DBF'          1
) SIZE 1048576
DATAFILE 'C:\ORACLE1\ORTEST1\DATA\SYSTEST.DBF'
  SIZE 52428800 REUSE
ARCHIVELOG
;
```

However, the script in Source 17.5 is not complete. You must use the

```
ALTER DATABASE BACKUP CONTROLFILE TO TRACE;
```

command to get the MAX set of parameters to edit into the script or you will be stuck with the Oracle defaults.

Of course, you must also rebuild the tablespaces. The script in Source 17.6 will do this for you. The output from this script is shown in Listing 17.6.

SOURCE 17.6   Script to create a tablespace re-create script.

```
REM TBSP_RCT.SQL
REM
REM FUNCTION: SCRIPT FOR CREATING TABLESPACES
REM
REM FUNCTION: This script must be run by a user with select on
REM the DBA views.
```

```
REM
REM This script is intended to run with Oracle7 or Oracle8
REM
REM FUNCTION: Running this script will create a script to build
REM   all the tablespaces in the database.  This created script,
REM   crt_tbls.sql, can be run by any user with the DBA role
REM   or with the 'CREATE TABLESPACE' system privilege.
REM
REM Only preliminary testing of this script was done. Be sure to
REM test it completely before relying on it.
REM
DEFINE cr='CHR(10)'
SET VERIFY OFF TERMOUT OFF FEEDBACK OFF ECHO OFF PAGES 0;
SET TERMOUT ON
SELECT 'Creating tablespace build script...' from dual;
SET TERMOUT OFF
CREATE table ts_temp (lineno NUMBER, ts_name VARCHAR2(30),
                      text VARCHAR2(800))
/
DECLARE
   CURSOR ts_cursor IS SELECT    tablespace_name,
                                 initial_extent,
                                 next_extent,
                                 min_extents,
                                 max_extents,
                                 pct_increase,
                                 status
                       FROM      sys.dba_tablespaces
                       WHERE tablespace_name != 'SYSTEM'
                       AND status != 'INVALID'
                       ORDER BY tablespace_name;
   CURSOR df_cursor (c_ts VARCHAR2) IS
.....SELECT    file_name,
               bytes
      FROM     sys.dba_data_files
      WHERE    tablespace_name = c_ts
               AND tablespace_name != 'SYSTEM'
      ORDER BY file_name;
   lv_tablespace_name     sys.dba_tablespaces.tablespace_name%TYPE;
   lv_initial_extent      sys.dba_tablespaces.initial_extent%TYPE;
   lv_next_extent         sys.dba_tablespaces.next_extent%TYPE;
   lv_min_extents         sys.dba_tablespaces.min_extents%TYPE;
   lv_max_extents         sys.dba_tablespaces.max_extents%TYPE;
   lv_pct_increase        sys.dba_tablespaces.pct_increase%TYPE;
   lv_status              sys.dba_tablespaces.status%TYPE;
   lv_file_name           sys.dba_data_files.file_name%TYPE;
   lv_bytes               sys.dba_data_files.bytes%TYPE;
   lv_first_rec           BOOLEAN;
   lv_string              VARCHAR2(800);
   lv_lineno              NUMBER := 0;
```

```
   PROCEDURE write_out(p_line INTEGER, p_name VARCHAR2,
           p_string VARCHAR2) is
   BEGIN
     INSERT INTO ts_temp (lineno, ts_name, text)
     VALUES(p_line, p_name, p_string);
   END;

BEGIN
   OPEN ts_cursor;
   LOOP
      FETCH ts_cursor INTO lv_tablespace_name,
                           lv_initial_extent,
                           lv_next_extent,
                           lv_min_extents,
                           lv_max_extents,
                           lv_pct_increase,
                           lv_status;
     EXIT WHEN ts_cursor%NOTFOUND;
     lv_lineno := 1;
     lv_string := ('CREATE TABLESPACE '||lower(lv_tablespace_name));
     lv_first_rec := TRUE;
     write_out(lv_lineno, lv_tablespace_name, lv_string);
     OPEN df_cursor(lv_tablespace_name);
     LOOP
        FETCH df_cursor INTO lv_file_name,
                             lv_bytes;
        EXIT WHEN df_cursor%NOTFOUND;
        IF (lv_first_rec) THEN
           lv_first_rec := FALSE;
           lv_string := 'DATAFILE '||&&cr;
        ELSE
           lv_string := lv_string || ',';
        end if;
        lv_string:=lv_string||''''||lv_file_name||''''||
                   ' SIZE '||to_char(lv_bytes) ||' REUSE';
     END LOOP;
     CLOSE df_cursor;
        lv_lineno := lv_lineno + 1;
        write_out(lv_lineno, lv_tablespace_name, lv_string);
        lv_lineno := lv_lineno + 1;
        lv_string := (' DEFAULT STORAGE (INITIAL ' ||
                   TO_CHAR(lv_initial_extent) ||
                   ' NEXT ' || lv_next_extent);
        write_out(lv_lineno, lv_tablespace_name, lv_string);
        lv_lineno := lv_lineno + 1;
        lv_string := (' MINEXTENTS ' ||
                   lv_min_extents ||
                   ' MAXEXTENTS ' || lv_max_extents);
        write_out(lv_lineno, lv_tablespace_name, lv_string);
```

```
            lv_lineno := lv_lineno + 1;
            lv_string := (' PCTINCREASE ' ||
                          lv_pct_increase || ')');
         write_out(lv_lineno, lv_tablespace_name, lv_string);
            lv_string := ('    '||lv_status);
         write_out(lv_lineno, lv_tablespace_name, lv_string);
            lv_lineno := lv_lineno + 1;
            lv_string:='/';
         write_out(lv_lineno, lv_tablespace_name, lv_string);
            lv_lineno := lv_lineno + 1;
            lv_string:='                                        ';
         write_out(lv_lineno, lv_tablespace_name, lv_string);
      END LOOP;
      CLOSE ts_cursor;
END;
/
COLUMN dbname NEW_VALUE db NOPRINT
SELECT name dbname FROM v$database;
SPOOL rep_out\&db\crt_tbsp.sql
SET HEADING OFF RECSEP OFF
COLUMN text FORMAT a80 WORD_WRAP
SELECT    text
FROM      ts_temp
ORDER BY ts_name, lineno;
SPOOL OFF;
DROP table ts_temp;
SET VERIFY ON RECSEP ON TERMOUT ON HEADING ON FEEDBACK ON
SET PAGESIZE 22 LINES 80
CLEAR COLUMNS
```

LISTING 17.6   Example of output from the TBSP_RCT.SQL script.

```
CREATE TABLESPACE raw_data
DATAFILE
'E:\ORACLE3\ORTEST1\DATA\RAW01_TEST.DBF' SIZE 734003200 REUSE
DEFAULT STORAGE (INITIAL 20480 NEXT 20480
MINEXTENTS 1 MAXEXTENTS 249
PCTINCREASE 50)
ONLINE
/

CREATE TABLESPACE raw_index
DATAFILE
'C:\ORACLE1\ORTEST1\DATA\RAW01_INDEX.DBF' SIZE 524288000 REUSE
DEFAULT STORAGE (INITIAL 20480 NEXT 20480
MINEXTENTS 1 MAXEXTENTS 249
PCTINCREASE 50)
ONLINE
```

```
/
CREATE TABLESPACE rollback
DATAFILE
'C:\ORACLE1\ORTEST1\DATA\RBS1ORTEST1.DBF' SIZE 524288000 REUSE
DEFAULT STORAGE (INITIAL 20480 NEXT 20480
MINEXTENTS 1 MAXEXTENTS 249
PCTINCREASE 50)
ONLINE
/

CREATE TABLESPACE appl_data
DATAFILE
'D:\ORACLE2\ORTEST1\DATA\APLDAT1ORTEST1.DBF' SIZE 524288000
REUSE, 'D:\ORACLE2\ORTEST1\DATA\APLDAT2ORTEST1.DBF' SIZE
524288000 REUSE, 'D:\ORACLE2\ORTEST1\DATA\APLDAT3ORTEST1.DBF'
SIZE 524288000 REUSE,
'E:\ORACLE3\ORTEST1\DATA\APLDAT4ORTEST1.DBF' SIZE 524288000
REUSE
DEFAULT STORAGE (INITIAL 20480 NEXT 20480
MINEXTENTS 1 MAXEXTENTS 249
PCTINCREASE 50)
ONLINE
/

CREATE TABLESPACE appl_index
DATAFILE
'E:\ORACLE3\ORTEST1\DATA\APLIDX1ORTEST1.DBF' SIZE 524288000
REUSE, 'F:\ORACLE4\ORTEST1\DATA\APLIDX2ORTEST1.DBF' SIZE
 524288000 REUSE
DEFAULT STORAGE (INITIAL 20480 NEXT 20480
MINEXTENTS 1 MAXEXTENTS 249
PCTINCREASE 50)
ONLINE
/

CREATE TABLESPACE temp
DATAFILE
'F:\ORACLE4\ORTEST1\DATA\TMP1ORTEST1.DBF' SIZE 629145600 REUSE
DEFAULT STORAGE (INITIAL 20480 NEXT 20480
MINEXTENTS 1 MAXEXTENTS 249
PCTINCREASE 50)
ONLINE
/

CREATE TABLESPACE user_data
DATAFILE
'C:\ORACLE1\ORTEST1\DATA\USR1ORTEST1.DBF' SIZE 10485760 REUSE
DEFAULT STORAGE (INITIAL 20480 NEXT 20480
MINEXTENTS 1 MAXEXTENTS 249
PCTINCREASE 50)
ONLINE
/

NOTE: The preceding paths are NT4.0 syntax.
```

2. Add new rollback segments; use the script in Source 17.7 to create a script such as Listing 17.7 from your existing database to rebuild your rollbacks as required.

SOURCE 17.7   Example of script to build a rollback segment create script.

```
REM rbk_rct.sql
REM
REM FUNCTION: SCRIPT FOR CREATING ROLLBACK SEGMENTS
REM
REM This script USED  by a user with select on the DBA views.
REM
REM This script is intended to run with Oracle7 or Oracle8.
REM
REM Running this script will in turn create a script to rebuild
REM the database rollback segments. The created script is called
REM crt_rbks.sql and can be run by any user with the DBA
REM role or with the 'CREATE ROLLBACK SEGMENT' system privilege.
REM
REM NOTE:  This script will NOT capture the optimal storage for
REM        a rollback segment that is off-line.
REM
REM  The rollback segments must be manually brought back on-line
REM        after running the crt_rbks.sql script.
REM
REM   Only preliminary testing of this script was performed.  Be
REM   sure to test it completely before relying on it.
REM
SET VERIFY OFF FEEDBACK OFF TERMOUT OFF ECHO OFF PAGES 0
SET TERMOUT ON
SELECT 'Creating rollback segment build script...' from dual;
SET TERMOUT OFF
DEFINE cr='CHR(10)'
CREATE table rb_temp (lineno NUMBER, rb_name VARCHAR2(30),
          text VARCHAR2(800))
/

DECLARE
   CURSOR rb_cursor IS
             SELECT segment_name,
               tablespace_name,
               decode (owner, 'PUBLIC', 'PUBLIC ', NULL),
               segment_id,
               initial_extent,
               next_extent,
               min_extents,
               max_extents,
               status
             FROM sys.dba_rollback_segs
            WHERE segment_name <> 'SYSTEM';
```

```
        CURSOR rb_optimal (r_no number) IS
                    SELECT usn,
                        DECODE(optsize, null, 'NULL', TO_CHAR(optsize))
                FROM sys.v_$rollstat
                WHERE usn=r_no;
    lv_seg_name                 sys.dba_rollback_segs.segment_name%TYPE;
    lv_tablespace_name          sys.dba_rollback_segs.tablespace_name%TYPE;
    lv_owner                    VARCHAR2(10);
    lv_segment_id               sys.dba_rollback_segs.segment_id%TYPE;
    lv_initial_extent           sys.dba_rollback_segs.initial_extent%TYPE;
    lv_next_extent              sys.dba_rollback_segs.next_extent%TYPE;
    lv_min_extents              sys.dba_rollback_segs.min_extents%TYPE;
    lv_max_extents              sys.dba_rollback_segs.max_extents%TYPE;
    lv_status                   sys.dba_rollback_segs.status%TYPE;
    lv_usn                      sys.v_$rollstat.usn%TYPE;
    lv_optsize                  VARCHAR2(40);
    lv_string                   VARCHAR2(800);
    lv_lineno                   NUMBER := 0;

    PROCEDURE write_out(
       p_line INTEGER, p_name VARCHAR2, p_string VARCHAR2) IS
    BEGIN
        INSERT INTO rb_temp (lineno, rb_name, text)
        VALUES(p_line, p_name, p_string);
    END;

BEGIN
  OPEN rb_cursor;
  LOOP
     FETCH rb_cursor INTO lv_seg_name,
                 lv_tablespace_name,
                 lv_owner,
                 lv_segment_id,
                 lv_initial_extent,
                 lv_next_extent,
                 lv_min_extents,
                 lv_max_extents,
                 lv_status;
     EXIT WHEN rb_cursor%NOTFOUND;
      lv_lineno := 1;
  OPEN rb_optimal(lv_segment_id);
  LOOP
     FETCH rb_optimal INTO lv_usn,
                 lv_optsize;
     EXIT WHEN rb_optimal%NOTFOUND;
  END LOOP;
  CLOSE rb_optimal;
IF lv_status = 'ONLINE' THEN
lv_string:='CREATE ' || lv_owner || 'ROLLBACK SEGMENT ' ||
```

```
            LOWER(lv_seg_name);
write_out(lv_lineno, lv_seg_name, lv_string);
lv_lineno := lv_lineno + 1;
lv_string:='TABLESPACE ' || LOWER(lv_tablespace_name);
write_out(lv_lineno, lv_seg_name, lv_string);
lv_lineno := lv_lineno + 1;
lv_string:='STORAGE ' || '(INITIAL '||lv_initial_extent||' NEXT '||
        lv_next_extent||&&cr||' MINEXTENTS '||lv_min_extents||
        ' MAXEXTENTS '|| lv_max_extents||&&cr||
        ' OPTIMAL ' || lv_optsize || ')' ;
write_out(lv_lineno, lv_seg_name, lv_string);
lv_lineno := lv_lineno + 1;
lv_string:=
'/'||&&cr||'ALTER ROLLBACK SEGMENT '||lv_seg_name||' ONLINE;'||&&cr;
write_out(lv_lineno, lv_seg_name, lv_string);
ELSE
lv_string:='CREATE ' || lv_owner || 'ROLLBACK SEGMENT ' ||
        LOWER(lv_seg_name);
write_out(lv_lineno, lv_seg_name, lv_string);
lv_lineno := lv_lineno + 1;
lv_string:='TABLESPACE ' || LOWER(lv_tablespace_name);
write_out(lv_lineno, lv_seg_name, lv_string);
lv_lineno := lv_lineno + 1;
lv_string:='STORAGE ' || '(INITIAL '||lv_initial_extent||' NEXT '||
        lv_next_extent||&&cr||' MINEXTENTS '||lv_min_extents||
        ' MAXEXTENTS '|| lv_max_extents||')';
write_out(lv_lineno, lv_seg_name, lv_string);
lv_lineno := lv_lineno + 1;
lv_string:=
'/'||&&cr||'ALTER ROLLBACK SEGMENT '||lv_seg_name||' ONLINE;'||&&cr;
write_out(lv_lineno, lv_seg_name, lv_string);
END IF;
END LOOP;
  CLOSE rb_cursor;
END;
/
COLUMN dbname NEW_VALUE db NOPRINT
SELECT name dbname FROM v$database;
SPOOL rep_out\&db\crt_rbks.sql
SET HEADING OFF
COLUMN text FORMAT a80 WORD_WRAP
SELECT text FROM  rb_temp ORDER BY rb_name, lineno;
SPOOL OFF;
DROP TABLE rb_temp;
SET VERIFY ON FEEDBACK ON TERMOUT ON PAGESIZE 22 LINES 80 HEADING ON
CLEAR COLUMNS
```

LISTING 17.7   Example of output from RBKS_RCT.SQL.

```
CREATE ROLLBACK SEGMENT rb1
TABLESPACE rollback_data
STORAGE (INITIAL 1048576 NEXT 1048576
MINEXTENTS 2 MAXEXTENTS 249
OPTIMAL 3145728)

/
ALTER ROLLBACK SEGMENT RB1 ONLINE;

CREATE ROLLBACK SEGMENT rb2
TABLESPACE rollback_data
STORAGE (INITIAL 1048576 NEXT 1048576
MINEXTENTS 2 MAXEXTENTS 249
OPTIMAL 3145728)

/
ALTER ROLLBACK SEGMENT RB2 ONLINE;

CREATE ROLLBACK SEGMENT rb3
TABLESPACE rollback_data
STORAGE (INITIAL 1048576 NEXT 1048576
MINEXTENTS 2 MAXEXTENTS 249
OPTIMAL 3145728)

/
ALTER ROLLBACK SEGMENT RB3 ONLINE;

CREATE ROLLBACK SEGMENT rb4
TABLESPACE rollback_data
STORAGE (INITIAL 1048576 NEXT 1048576
MINEXTENTS 2 MAXEXTENTS 249
OPTIMAL 3145728)

/
ALTER ROLLBACK SEGMENT RB4 ONLINE;

CREATE ROLLBACK SEGMENT rb5
TABLESPACE rollback_data
STORAGE (INITIAL 1048576 NEXT 1048576
MINEXTENTS 2 MAXEXTENTS 249
OPTIMAL 3145728)

/
ALTER ROLLBACK SEGMENT RB5 ONLINE;
```

3. If not done in step 1, create the required tablespaces in the new database using script similar to Listing 17.5. This script is created and maintained by the DBA.

4. Re-create all users. The users should be documented using scripts from section 17.4, "Backup Methodologies." A script similar to Source 17.8, or one from Chapter 3, should be run periodically to keep an up-to-date user re-creation script handy. Other than quotas and such, the import process will reissue all grants.

SOURCE 17.8   Script to build a re-create user's script for Oracle7 or Oracle8.

```
SET HEADING OFF VERIFY OFF TERMOUT OFF FEEDBACK OFF ECHO OFF
SET PAGES 0 LINES 132
SPOOL recreate_users.sql

SELECT 'CREATE USER '||username|| 'IDENTIFIED BY VALUES '||CHR(39)||PASSWORD||CHR(39)
'DEFAULT TABLESPACE '||default_tablespace||
'TEMPORARY TABLESPACE '||temporary_tablespace||
'PROFILE '||profile||';'
/

SPOOL OFF
EXIT
```

5. Get a list of the full (or complete), cumulative, and incremental exports on-line. Use the most current full or complete and subsequent cumulative and/or incremental exports. The commands are executed after setting the default directory to the location of your exports (in this example /oracle4/ORTEST1/admin/exports) using the command

```
$cd /oracle4/ORTEST1/admin/exports
```

6. Import the most recent incremental export file (or cumulative export file if no incrementals have been taken) using the INCTYPE=SYSTEM option.

```
$imp SYSTEM/[PASSWORD] INCTYPE=SYSTEM FULL=Y FILE=last_incr
```

7. Import the most recent complete (FULL) export file using the INCTYPE = RESTORE option

```
$imp SYSTEM/[PASSWORD] INCTYPE=RESTORE FULL=Y FILE=last_full
```

8. Import all CUMULATIVE and INCREMENTAL exports using the INCTYPE = RESTORE option.

```
$imp SYSTEM/[PASSWORD] INCTYPE=RESTORE FULL=Y FILE=first_cum
$imp SYSTEM/[PASSWORD] INCTYPE=RESTORE FULL=Y FILE=next_cum
$imp SYSTEM/[PASSWORD] INCTYPE=RESTORE FULL=Y FILE=last_cum
$imp SYSTEM/[PASSWORD] INCTYPE=RESTORE FULL=Y FILE=first_incr
$imp SYSTEM/[PASSWORD] INCTYPE=RESTORE FULL=Y FILE=next_incr
$imp SYSTEM/[PASSWORD] INCTYPE=RESTORE FULL=Y FILE=last_incr
```

Note that the last incremental export is applied twice, once in step 5 and once here. This will recover to the time of the last incremental export. Also, the options can be lowercase if desired; Oracle doesn't care.

Procedures for Recovery from Individual Disk Lost

1. Recovery from loss of /oracle0:

TIP   Since /oracle0 contains all the executable files and system tablespace data files, database activity will cease upon loss of /oracle0.

---

   a. Have the System Manager restore the /oracle0/ORTEST1/* directory structures from the latest backup.
   b. Overwrite the /oracle0/ORTEST1/control/ora_control1.con file using the OS copy command from either the /oracle1/ORTEST1/control/ora_control3.con or /oracle2/ORTEST1/control/ora_control2.con control file copies.
   c. Use the procedure for total database recovery to restore the SYSTEM tablespace (the system tablespace requires a full database restore to recover)
   d. Log in to the Oracle system user and from svrmgrl shut down and restart the database.

2. Recovery from loss of /oracle1 or /oracle2

   Loss of /oracle1 would mean loss of all data files for the database system. Loss of /oracle2 would mean loss of all indexes. The loss of /oracle1 would result in the halting of all database activity. Loss of /oracle2 would result in the slowing of all index-based queries and loss of update capability to indexed fields unless the indexes are explicitly dropped. Recovery of /oracle1 would also result in recovery of /oracle2 since tales and indexes are tightly coupled.

   a. Have the System Manager recover both the /oracle1/ORTEST1/data/* and the /oracle2/ORTEST1/data/* directory structures from the latest Oracle backup.
   b. If the instance is still operating,
      i. Log in to the Oracle system user.
      ii. Start the svrmgrl program and connect internal.
      iii. Issue the SHUTDOWN ABORT <DATABASE> command.
   c. Issue the following svrmgrl command to restart the instance:

   ```
   STARTUP RESTRICTED MOUNT <DATABASE>
   ```

   d. If the failure resulted in relocation of the affected files, you must re-name the files using the following svrmgrl command:

   ```
   ALTER DATABASE RENAME FILE 'OLD' TO 'NEW'
   ```

   where "Old" and "New" are full path file names for each of the affected files.

e. To ensure all database files are on-line, issue the following svrmgrl command for each of the affected database files; if the database is recovered with the data file off-line, all of its data will be lost.

```
ALTER  DATABASE DATAFILE ['name'] ONLINE
```

Where " 'name' " is the full path file name enclosed by single quotation marks.

f. Once all of the data files are on-line, issue the svrmgrl RECOVER command with no parameters:

```
RECOVER DATABASE
```

g. Oracle will prompt for the names of the ARCHIVE files required, beginning with the oldest file. The archive files are stored in: /oracle4/ORTEST1/admin/ arch. All required logs should be on-line. Each file begins with a DBA-specified string followed by filler zeros, then the log number, usually followed by ".arc."

h. After each log is applied, the system will prompt for the next one it requires. After the last one has been applied, the system will respond

```
Media recovery complete.
```

i. This concludes the recovery. The database can now be brought on-line by issuing the svrmgrl command:

```
ALTER DATABASE [name] OPEN
```

TIP   In some cases, specifiying the database name is not required.

---

3. Recovery from the loss of a single tablespace's data file(s) from /oracle1 or /oracle2.
   a. Log in to the Oracle user.
   b. If the tablespace that uses the data file is on-line, take it off-line with the following svrmgrl commands:

```
CONNECT INTERNAL
ALTER TABLESPACE [name] OFFLINE
```

where [name] is the tablespace name, such as DEV or PROD.
   c. Correct the problem, or find a new location for the file(s).
   d. Have the System Manager recover the latest copy of the data file from the latest Oracle backup tape into the selected location.
   e. If the file had to be relocated, alter the name in the database with the following svrmgrl command to reflect the change:

```
ALTER DATABASE RENAME FILE 'old' TO 'new'
```

Where " 'old' " and " 'new' " are full path file names enclosed in single quotation marks.

f. Execute the svrmgrl RECOVER command using the TABLESPACE option as follows:

```
RECOVER TABLESPACE [name]
```

where [name] is the tablespace name such as DMS or AEONIC.

g. Oracle will prompt for the names of the ARCHIVE files required, beginning with the oldest file. The archive files are stored in /oracle4/ORTEST1/admin/ arch. All required logs should be on-line. Each file begins with a DBA-specified string followed by filler zeros, then the log number, usually followed by ".arc."

h. Once all logs have been applied to the affected tablespace, the system will respond

```
Media recovery complete.
```

i. Bring the tablespace back on-line with the svrmgrl command:

```
ALTER TABLESPACE [name] ONLINE
```

where [name] is the tablespace name such as DEV or PROD.

This completes the recovery of the data file.

4. Recovery from loss of /oracle3.

TIP Loss of /oracle3 would result in loss of all rollback segments and exports.

---

a. Recovery from loss of all of the rollback segments.
  i. Log in as the Oracle user.
  ii. Use the editor of your choice to alter the instance initialization file in the /oracle0/ORTEST1/admin/pfile directory in this example, to comment out the ROLLBACK_SEGMENTS entry. This prevents the system from trying to acquire anything but the rollback segment contained in the SYSTEM tablespace on restart.
  iii. Shut down and restart the instance using svrmgrl.
  iv. Create a second rollback segment using the svrmgrl command

```
CREATE ROLLBACK SEGMENT [segment name]
TABLESPACE [tablespace name]
```

where

[segment name] is the name of the rollback segment such as ROLLBACK_1.

[tablespace name] is the tablespace for the rollback segments or SYSTEM.

Since this segment will be dropped later, use the default storage parameters.

v. Alter the instance initialization file in the /oracle0/ORTEST1/admin/pfile directory in this example to edit the ROLLBACK_SEGMENTS entry to list only the name of the segment created in step iv.

vi. Shut down and start up the instance using svrmgrl.

vii. Drop the old rollback segment tablespace

```
DROP TABLESPACE ROLLBACK_SEGS INCLUDING CONTENTS
```

viii. Use the svrmgrl command to create a new rollback segment tablespace:

```
CREATE TABLESPACE ROLLBACK_SEGS
DATAFILE 'FILE SPEC'
DEFAULT STORAGE (
INITIAL 500K NEXT 500K
MAXEXTENTS 99)
ONLINE
```

If the location is the same, use the REUSE option on the file spec. The size should be the same as before.

You can use the script creates in the import/export scenario to generate a rebuild script for your rollback segments to use in this type of situation; of course, it has to be run against your instance before your rollback segments have problems.

ix. Use the DBA-created procedure to rebuild rollback segments to create the new rollback segments.

x. Shut down the database, then edit the initialization file to return it to the condition it was in before the loss of the rollback segments (the ROLL-BACK SEGMENTS statement listing all the rollback segments and not listing the second segment in the SYSTEM tablespace). Restart the database.

xi. Using svrmgrl, drop the rollback segment you created in the SYSTEM tablespace. This completes the recovery from the loss of the ROLLBACK SEGMENTS.

xii. Since the export files have been lost, perform a full export.

b. Recovery from loss of the active rollback segment.

T IP: If you notice ORA-600 series errors in the ALERT.LOG in reference to the rollback segment, this indicates that the rollback segment in use has become corrupted.

To recover from a loss of in-use or online rollback segment, perform the following steps:

  i. Log in as the Oracle operating system user.
  ii. Edit the initialization file, adding the following line:

```
_OFFLINE_ROLLBACK_SEGMENTS = ([name])
```

  iii. While still in the editor, remove reference to the problem rollback segment from the ROLLBACK SEGMENTS entry. Exit the editor.
  iv. Shut down and restart the database using svrmgrl.

TIP   You can attempt to take the rollback segment off-line with the command, `ALTER TABLESPACE [name] OFFLINE;` but this may not always work.

---

  v. Using svrmgrl drop the corrupted rollback segment using the svrmgrl commands:

```
CONNECT INTERNAL
DROP ROLLBACK SEGMENT [name]
```

  vi. Re-create the rollback segment using the svrmgrl command:

```
CREATE ROLLBACK SEGMENT [name]
TABLESPACE ROLLBACK_SEGS
 STORAGE (INITIAL 500K NEXT 500K
MAXEXTENTS 99);
```

  vii. Edit the initialization file to remove the _OFFLINE_ROLLBACK_ SEGMENTS line and add back the name of the rollback segment to the ROLLBACK_SEGMENTS line. Exit the editor.
  viii. Shut down and restart the database using svrmgrl. Actually, you can bring the rollback segment on-line using the

```
ALTER ROLLBACK SEGMENT [name] ONLINE;
```

  command, but I like to verify that the initialization file changes are made properly by a shutdown/restart cycle. Call me old-fashioned.
  ix. The integrity of the database should be checked after this procedure using the following steps:
a. Set the default to the export directory:

```
$cd /oracle3/ORTEST1/admin/exports
```

b. Issue the following command:

```
$exp SYSTEM/[password] FULL=YES INDEXES=YES ROWS=NO
```

If no errors are returned, the database is consistent; if the database is not consistent, use the svrmgrl command RECOVER DATABASE to recover the database. Usually, the startup/shutdown cycle will catch and correct any problems.

c. Recovery from loss of an Inactive REDO log with no mirroring.

1. Log in as Oracle. Start svrmgrl and issue the following commands:

```
CONNECT INTERNAL
SHUTDOWN ABORT
```

2. Exit out to the operating system and copy an archived or backup copy of the damaged file to the damaged files location.

3. Use svrmgrl to issue the following commands:

```
CONNECT INTERNAL
STARTUP MOUNT
```

4. If the failure was a result of media damage, which required moving the REDO log to a different disk, rename the log using the following svrmgrl command:

```
ALTER DATABASE RENAME FILE 'old' TO 'new'
```

Where "old" and "new" are the full path file names enclosed in single quotation marks.

5. Issue the svrmgrl command:

```
ALTER DATABASE OPEN
```

If no error occurs, recovery is complete.

6. If step 5 resulted in an error, the wrong archival copy may have been used; check the file and, if needed, repeat steps 1 to 5. If you are certain that the file is correct and you still receive an error, go on to step 7.

7. Using svrmgrl, shut down the Oracle database and then have the System Manager perform a full backup of the Oracle system.

8. Using svrmgrl, restart the database following the backup and using svrmgrl stop archiving with these commands:

```
CONNECT INTERNAL
ALTER DATABASE NOARCHIVELOG
```

9. Using svrmgrl, replace the lost redo file with a new one using the following commands:

```
ALTER DATABASE ADD LOGFILE 'new file'
```

Where "'new file'" is the full path file name enclosed in single quotation marks.

10. Still using svrmgrl, drop the damaged file using the command

```
ALTER DATABASE DROP LOGFILE MEMBER 'old name'
```

Where 'old name' is the full path file name enclosed in single quotation marks.

If this results in an error, go to the procedure for recovering from loss of an active redo log.

11. Exit from svrmgrl and have the System Manager back up all the redo logs including the one created in step 9.

12. Back up the current control file using the svrmgrl commands

```
CONNECT INTERNAL
ALTER DATABASE BACKUP CONTROL FILE TO 'backup file'
```

Where " 'backup file' " is the full path file name enclosed in single quotation marks.

13. Using svrmgrl, shut down the database and have the System Manager back up the database files.

14. Restart the database using svrmgrl; issue the following commands:

```
CONNECT INTERNAL
STARTUP
ALTER DATABASE ARCHIVELOG
```

15. Issue the following svrmgrl commands to shut down and restart the database:

```
SHUTDOWN
STARTUP OPEN
```

If this results in an error, go to the procedure for recovering an active redo log.

d. Recovery from loss of an active REDO log file with no mirroring.

1. Log in as Oracle. Using svrmgrl, shut down the database using the following commands:

```
CONNECT INTERNAL
SHUTDOWN ABORT
```

2. Exit svrmgrl and have the System Manager back up all database files. This provides you with a restart point should the rest of the recovery fail.

3. Correct the problem that caused the failure or find a new location for the redo logs.

4. Have the System Manager restore all database files using the latest backup; not the backup from step 2.

5. Start the database and mount it using the svrmgrl commands

```
CONNECT INTERNAL
STARTUP MOUNT
```

6. Make sure all database files are on-line by executing the following command for each file:

```
ALTER DATABASE DATAFILE 'filename' ONLINE
```

Where " 'filename' " is the full path file name enclosed in single quotation marks.

If a database is recovered with a data file off-line, that data file's data is lost.

7. If the original location of the redo logs has become invalid, rename the files with the svrmgrl command

```
ALTER DATABASE RENAME FILE 'old' TO 'new'
```

Where " 'old' " and " 'new' " are full path file names enclosed in single quotation marks.

Each file must be renamed if its location has changed.

8. Recover the database in manual mode using the command

```
RECOVER DATABASE MANUAL
```

9. Oracle will prompt for the names of the ARCHIVE files required, beginning with the oldest file. The archive files are stored in /oracle4/ORTEST1/admin/arch in this example scenario.

All required logs should be on-line. Each file begins with a DBA-specified string followed by filler zeros, then the log number, usually followed by ".arc."

10. After each log is applied, the system will request the next one in sequence, when the log just prior to the damaged log is applied, issue the command

```
CANCEL
```

to abort the restore operation. Recovery is complete at this point. All data in the damaged redo log is lost and must be reentered.

11. Restart the database with the svrmgrl command

```
ALTER DATABASE OPEN RESETLOGS
```

12. Once the database is open, immediately shut down with the svrmgrl command

```
SHUTDOWN NORMAL
```

13. Exit svrmgrl and have the System Manager make a complete backup of the Oracle system. All previous archive logs are now invalid and may be disposed of.

14. Using svrmgrl, restart the Oracle system.

e. Recovery from loss of /oracle4 (the archive log disk)

1. If the System Manager can fix the problem, shut down the system. Have the System Manager perform a full backup and then restart the Oracle system.

2. If the system operator cannot fix the problem and a new archive log location is set up, perform the following steps:

a. Using svrmgrl, issue the commands

```
CONNECT INTERNAL
ARCHIVE LOG 'DEST'
```

Where DEST is the new location; for example, if the new location is disk /oracle5/ORTEST1/admin/arch, DEST would be

```
/oracle5/ORTEST1/admin/arch
```

  b. Exit svrmgrl and edit the initialization file to reflect the new archive log location.
  c. Using svrmgrl shut down the Oracle system.
  d. Have the System Manager perform a full backup of the Oracle system, then use svrmgrl to restart the system.
  f. Recovery of a deleted table from a tablespace

1. Determine from the user when the table was deleted and when the last entry, modification, or deletion was made to the table.
2. Log in as Oracle and get a list of the full export files and the incremental export files on the system. If a full export has been done since the last update, but before the file was deleted, use this file in step 4.
3. From the list of incremental exports, determine the export that is just after the date the file was last modified but before the date the file was deleted. If the date of modification and deletion are the same, select the last incremental after a file modification. If there is no file on the system, have the System Manager restore the /oracle3/ORTEST1/admin/exports directory contents from the last backup and recheck. If the file still is not available, repeat the restore request with the backup previous to that. If the file needed is not on the available backups, the table is not recoverable. If the file was not modified, it will not be in the incremental export and must be recovered from a full export.
4. Once the export is located, spawn out to the operating system and set the default directory to the export file location using the command

```
cd /oracle3/ORTEST1/admin/exports
```

5. Use the following import command from the system, prompt to restore the table:

```
$imp SYSTEM/[password] FROMUSER=[user] TOUSER=[user] -
TABLES=([table_name]) FILE=[export file name]
```

Where

```
[password] is the DBA user - SYSTEM's password
[user] is the owner's user name
[table_name] is the name of the table to be recovered
[export file name] is the name of the export file
```

This recovers the table to the date of the export. If data was added or removed from the table since this export the data must be reentered. This may result in loss of referential integrity so any referential integrity constraints may have to be disabled until data is fully restored.

g. Recovery from loss of all control files.

If for some unimaginable reason you lose all copies of your control file (if you follow OFA guidelines about the only way would be deliberate sabotage) there is a command available to rebuild them. You must know the following information in order to rebuild the control files:

1. All redo log file names and locations.
2. All database file data files and locations.
3. The values for MAXLOGFILES, MAXDATAFILES, and MAXINSTANCES.
4. The status of archive logging.

Items 1, 3, and 4 should be available via the original CREATE_<db_name> script. Item 2 should be documented, before it is needed, with a script similar to the one shown in Source 17.9. The output is shown in Listing 17.9.

SOURCE 17.9   Example of script to document file sizes and locations.

```
REM
REM     Name:      datafile.sql
REM     FUNCTION:  Document  file sizes and locations
REM     Use:       From SQLPLUS
REM
CLEAR COMPUTES
COLUMN file_name                FORMAT A50
COLUMN tablespace_name          FORMAT A15
COLUMN meg                      FORMAT 99,999.90
START title80 'DATABASE DATAFILES'
SPOOL rep_out\&db\datafile
BREAK ON tablespace_name SKIP 1 ON REPORT
COMPUTE SUM OF meg ON tablespace_name
COMPUTE SUM OF meg ON REPORT
SELECT
     tablespace_name, file_name, bytes/1048576 meg
FROM
     dba_data_files
ORDER BY
     tablespace_name
/

SPOOL OFF
CLEAR COLUMNS
CLEAR COMPUTES
PAUSE Press Enter to continue
```

LISTING 17.9   Example of output from script in Source 17.9.

```
Date: 05/22/96                                          Page:   1
Time: 11:06 PM              DATABASE DATAFILES          SYSTEM
                            ORTEST1 database


TABLESPACE_NAME FILE_NAME                                   MEG
--------------- ---------------------------------------- --------
RAW_DATA        E:\ORACLE3\ORTEST1\DATA\RAW01_TEST.DBF    700.00
***************                                          --------
sum                                                       700.00


RAW_INDEX       C:\ORACLE1\ORTEST1\DATA\RAW_INDEX.DBF     500.00
***************                                          --------
sum                                                       500.00


ROLLBACK_DATA   C:\ORACLE1\ORTEST1\DATA\RBS1ORTEST1.DBF   500.00
***************                                          --------
sum                                                       500.00


APPL_DATA       D:\ORACLE2\ORTEST1\DATA\APLDAT1OTST.DBF   500.00
                D:\ORACLE2\ORTEST1\DATA\APLDAT2OTST.DBF   500.00
                D:\ORACLE2\ORTEST1\DATA\APLDAT3OTST.DBF   500.00
                E:\ORACLE3\ORTEST1\DATA\APLDAT4OTST.DBF   500.00
***************                                          --------
sum                                                     2,000.00


APPL_INDEX      F:\ORACLE4\ORTEST1\DATA\APLIDX1OTST.DBF   500.00
                E:\ORACLE3\ORTEST1\DATA\APLIDX2OTST.DBF   500.00
***************                                          --------
sum                                                     1,000.00


SYSTEM          C:\ORACLE1\ORTEST1\DATA\SYSTEST.ORA        50.00
***************                                          --------
sum                                                        50.00


TEMPORARY_DATA  F:\ORACLE4\ORTEST1\DATA\TMP1OTST.DBF      600.00
***************                                          --------
sum                                                       600.00


USER_DATA       C:\ORACLE1\ORTEST1\DATA\USR1OTST.DBF       10.00
***************                                          --------
sum                                                        10.00


                                                        --------
sum                                                     5,360.00
```

The data files can either be the current files or can be files needing recovery. Any data file containing a rollback segment must be available or recovery will fail. The CREATE CONTROLFILE command is used to rebuild a destroyed control file. The syntax of the CREATE CONTROLFILE command follows.

```
CREATE CONTROLFILE [REUSE]
     DATABASE name
     [LOGFILE  filespec, filespec,... filespec]
     RESETLOGS | NORESETLOGS
     [MAXLOGFILES n]
     [DATAFILE    filespec, filespec,...filespec]
     [MAXDATAFILES n]
     [MAXINSTANCES n]
     [MAXLOGFILES n]
     [MAXLOGHISTORY n]
     [ARCHIVELOG | NOARCHIVELOG]
     [SHARED | EXCLUSIVE]
```

Where

REUSE	If this is specified, the control files may already exist. For example, if an improperly specified backup didn't allow recovery of the most current control files, you could use the REUSE option to overwrite the old version. If this option is not specified, the control files must not currently exist. If specified, the file locations from the INIT.ORA file will be used.
[SET] DATABASE	The name specified here must match the database names in the data and log files. The SET option allows changing the database name under Oracle7.
LOGFILE [GROUP n]	This clause lists all on-line logs used for the database. If not specified, the platform-specific defaults for either VMS or UNIX will be used.
RESETLOGS	This is the option of choice for this command. It will force the use of ALTER DATABASE OPEN RESETLOGS when starting the database. Media recovery is allowed before issuing this command. This should always be used unless the logs on-line are the current logs. If the logs were restored from backup and all logs are listed, NORESETLOGS may be used, but it is not recommended.
MAXLOGFILES	This may be larger than the value used in the original CREATE DATABASE command but cannot be smaller than the number that the database ever contained, including dropped log files.

DATAFILES	All data files must be listed. All data files must be accessible since they are assumed to be on-line. The files may be backup copies needing recovery.
MAXDATAFILES	May be different than in the original CREATE DATABASE but cannot be smaller than the maximum number of data files ever used by the database.
MAXINSTANCES	May be different than in the original control file.
[NO] ARCHIVELOG	NOARCHIVELOG is the default if not specified. If you intend to use archived logs, use ARCHIVELOG even though ALTER DATABASE can be used to reset the option at a later time.
SHARED—or—EXCLUSIVE	Same use as in a CREATE DATABASE command.
MAXLOGMEMBERS	This specifies the maximum number of members for a redo log group under Oracle7. Defaults to 1.
MAXLOGHISTORY	This specifies the maximum number of archived redo logs that can be applied for recovery of an Oracle parallel server. This is only used for parallel server-based databases.

To use the CREATE CONTROLFILE command, use the following procedure:

1. Back up all existing files.
2. Log in to svrmgrl.
3. Issue the STARTUP NOMOUNT command.
4. Issue the CREATE CONTROLFILE command.
5. Issue the ALTER DATABASE MOUNT command.
6. Apply required recovery to the database files.
7. Shut down cleanly (SHUTDOWN with no options) and back up the recovered database.
8. Restart the database.

To be proactive, every time you make a change to your control file, issue the following command:

```
ALTER DATABASE BACKUP CONTROLFILE TO TRACE;
```

This command will generate a script that with minimal editing will allow re-creation of your control file. As with the other re-creation scripts, this must be done *before* there is a problem. The output from the command will be placed in a trace file located in the background_dump_destination directory specified in the initialization file for the instance. The output will resemble Listing 17.10.

LISTING 17.10 Example of the output generated by the control file trace.

```
Dump file c:\oracle1\ortest1\admin\udump\ORA00283.TRC
Tue Jul 01 00:07:01 1997
ORACLE V8.0.2.0.1 - Beta vsnsta=1
vsnsql=c vsnxtr=3
Windows NT V4.0, OS V5.101, CPU type 586
Oracle8 Server Release 8.0.2.0.1 - Beta
With the distributed, heterogeneous, replication, objects
and parallel query options
PL/SQL Release 3.0.2.0.1 - Beta
Windows NT V4.0, OS V5.101, CPU type 586
Instance name: test

Redo thread mounted by this instance: 1

Oracle process number: 13

pid: 11b


Tue Jul 01 00:07:01 1997
Tue Jul 01 00:07:01 1997

*** SESSION ID:(10.377) 1997.07.01.00.07.01.093
# The following commands will create a new control file and use it
# to open the database.
# Data used by the recovery manager will be lost. Additional logs may
# be required for media recovery of off-line data files. Use this
# only if the current version of all on-line logs are available.
STARTUP NOMOUNT
CREATE CONTROLFILE REUSE DATABASE "ORTEST1" NORESETLOGS ARCHIVELOG
    MAXLOGFILES 32
    MAXLOGMEMBERS 2
    MAXDATAFILES 200
    MAXINSTANCES 1
    MAXLOGHISTORY 7239
LOGFILE
  GROUP 1 (
    'C:\ORACLE1\ORTEST1\REDO\LOG11ORTEST1.ORA',
    'E:\ORACLE3\ORTEST1\REDO\LOG12ORTEST1.DBF'
  ) SIZE 1M,
  GROUP 2 (
    'D:\ORACLE2\ORTEST1\REDO\LOG21ORTEST1.ORA',
    'F:\ORACLE4\ORTEST1\REDO\LOG22ORTEST1.DBF'
  ) SIZE 1M,
  GROUP 3 (
    'E:\ORACLE3\ORTEST1\REDO\LOG31ORTEST1.ORA',
    'D:\ORACLE2\ORTEST1\REDO\LOG32ORTEST1.DBF'
  ) SIZE 1M
```

```
DATAFILE
  'C:\ORACLE1\ORTEST1\DATA\SYSTEST.ORA',
  'C:\ORACLE1\ORTEST1\DATA\USR1ORTEST1.DBF',
  'C:\ORACLE1\ORTEST1\DATA\RBS1ORTEST1.DBF',
  'D:\ORACLE2\ORTEST1\DATA\SCPDAT1ORTEST1.DBF',
  'D:\ORACLE2\ORTEST1\DATA\SCPDAT2ORTEST1.DBF',
  'D:\ORACLE2\ORTEST1\DATA\SCPDAT3ORTEST1.DBF',
  'E:\ORACLE3\ORTEST1\DATA\SCPDAT4ORTEST1.DBF',
  'F:\ORACLE4\ORTEST1\DATA\SCPIDX1ORTEST1.DBF',
  'E:\ORACLE3\ORTEST1\DATA\SCPIDX2ORTEST1.DBF',
  'F:\ORACLE4\ORTEST1\DATA\TMP1ORTEST1.DBF',
  'E:\ORACLE3\ORTEST1\DATA\RAW01_TEST.DBF',
  'C:\ORACLE1\ORTEST1\DATA\RAW_INDEX.DBF'
;

# Recovery is required if any of the data files are restored backups,
# or if the last shutdown was not normal or immediate.
RECOVER DATABASE

# All logs need archiving and a log switch is needed.
ALTER SYSTEM ARCHIVE LOG ALL;

# Database can now be opened normally.
ALTER DATABASE OPEN;
```

17.7   ORACLE7 ENTERPRISE BACKUP UTILITY

I have mentioned the Oracle Backup Utility several times in the preceding chapters. Exactly what is the Oracle/Enterprise Backup Utility (EBU) and how can it be used? Let's take a quick look at the facility and what it does for you.

The EBU facility provides an interface between the Oracle database and your backup software. It is not an interface to VMS-Backup, UNIX tar, dump, cpio, or dump. The EBU facility automatically recognizes third-party tools it is compatible with and based on command line or script input commands processes Oracle backups against multiple databases. EBU can make both hot (on-line) and cold (off-line) backups.

The EBU facility includes the following background processes:

obackup—Monitors all other processes and communicates with databases, spawns instance manager if it isn't already operating.

brio—Coordinates between obackup and the brdk and brtp processes. For parallel operations, there is one brio per parallel IO stream.

brdk—Handles IO to disk files. There is one or more brdk processes per concurrent IO stream as controlled by the mux process.

brtp—Handles IO to tapes, only one brtp per tape parallel IO stream (i.e., multiple tape drives used concurrently for the same backup).

brd—(Instance Manager) This is a daemon process that monitors the backup catalog and obackup. This process also cleans up for any abnormally terminated backup operations.

The EBU facility uses a central backup repository to track backups against multiple databases. The EBU facility is invoked via the obackup command

```
obackup [[{-ch{ecksum] -t[est] }]|
-noa[utoregister] | -s[ilent] |
-ob[k_home]=path ] command_filename
```

Where

-ch	Cannot be used with test, invokes checksumming for all files.
-t	Test runs scripts without actually doing backup.
-s	Silent, runs without screen output (I guess without sound would be -b).
-noa	No autoconfiguration. Disables the autoconfiguration for a specific job.
-ob	Specifies the pathname of the $OBK_HOME directory.

Registering a DB in EBU. A database must be registered in the EBU catalog before it can be backed up using EBU; an example registration sequence would be

```
register
db_name = "TEST1"
oracle_home = "/bto/sys/oracle/product/7.2.3"
oracle_sid = "ORTEST1"
pfile = "/oracle0/ORTEST1/admin/pfile/initORTEST1.ora"
log = "/oracle0/ORTEST1/admin/log/obkTEST1.log"
```

Once a database is registered, it can be backed up using commands similar to the following.

For on-line:

```
backup online database
db_name = "TEST1"
oracle_sid = "ORTEST1"
parallel = 3
```

For off-line:

```
backup offline database
db_name = "TEST1"
oracle_sid = "ORTEST1"
parallel = 4
```

For tablespace backup:

```
backup online
db_name = "TEST1"
oracle_sid = "ORTEST1"
tablespace = "APPL_DATA","APPL_INDEX"
```

For control file backup:

```
backup online
db_name = "TEST1"
oracle_sid = "ORTEST1"
control_file
```

Control file and tablespace backups can be done together, as can database and control file.

An example shell script for UNIX backup is included with the EBU facility in the directory

```
$ORACLE_HOME/obackup/admin/lightsout.sh.
```

Restoration of Databases Using EBU. The EBU facility also allows for restoration of the database either to its original locations or to another host. A restore can consist of one or more of the following items:

- Data files
- Control file
- Parameter (initialization file)
- Archive redo log file

Restoration of entire database:

```
restore database consistent
db_name = "TEST1"
oracle_sid = "ORTEST1"
parallel = 4
log = "/oracle0/ORTEST1/admin/log/obkORTEST1.log"
```

Restore of tablespaces and control file:

```
restore
db_name = "TEST1"
oracle_sid = "ORTEST1"
control_file
tablespace = "APPL_DATA","APPL_INDEX"
```

Restore with datafile move:

```
restore
db_name = "TEST1"
```

```
oracle_sid = "ORTEST1"
dbfile = "/oracle1/ORTEST1/data/appl_data01.dbf"
remap = "/oracle1/ORTEST1/data/appl_data01.dbf" to
"/oracle5/ORTEST1/data/appl_data01.dbf"
```

You can also do a point-in-time restore:

```
restore database
db_name = "TEST1"
oracle_sid = "ORTEST1"
to = "01/07/1997 13:00"
```

The EBU facility also provides utilities for maintaining the catalog and generating reports on backups. I suggest a complete review of *Oracle7 Enterprise Backup Utility Administrator's Guide*, Release 2.0, March 1996, Part No. A42580-2 (Oracle Corporation), before attempting to use the EBU facility. It contains important information that space constraints prevented me from covering in this section.

17.8 ORACLE8 RECOVERY MANAGER FACILITY

Oracle8 introduces the recovery manager RMAN, which is the Enterprise Backup Utility on steroids. RMAN allows backup of database files at the block level and automatically performs datafile compression by only backing up blocks that have been used or altered. In incremental mode, the RMAN only backs up blocks that have been altered or added in the database, greatly reducing the size of required backups.

RMAN also allows the following:

- Scripting with RMAN script language, backup, and restore operations.
- Reports on backup status and backup file status.
- Use of a recovery catalog to facilitate backup and restore operations.
- Parallelization of backup and restore operations.
- Backup based on specified limits (i.e., amount of redo generated against a file).
- Backup of database, tablespace, or individual data files.
- Batch backup operations.

RMAN uses a recovery catalog; however, you can use RMAN without a catalog from just the data stored in the control files, but you are restricted to a subset of RMANs capabilities in this mode. The catalog contains information on the following:

- Data file and archive log backup sets and pieces
- Data file copies
- Archived redo logs and copies of them
- Tablespaces and data files at the target database
- Named, user-created sequences of commands called stored scripts

It is a good practice to maintain a small database strictly for the recovery catalog and perhaps the Enterprise Manager catalog files. The catalog should be resynchronized with all remote databases on a periodic basis. If you don't use a catalog you cannot do the following:

- Point-in-time recover
- Use stored scripts
- Recovery if a control file is not available.

RMAN creates backup sets that consist of backup pieces. Backup pieces are parts of the backup set at a size that is predetermined and usually based on backup media capacity of operating system file size limitations. Backup sets can be written to disk or secondary storage, can include a backup control file, and can span multiple OS files (pieces). Backup devices that are supported on your system are cataloged in the v$backup_device dynamic performance table.

RMAN backup sets that contain archive logs are called, appropriately enough, archivelog backup sets. With Oracle8 you cannot write archive logs directly to tape, but a job can be scheduled using RMAN to back archive log backup sets to tape or other storage.

RMAN produces either full or incremental backups. A full backup is a backup of one or more data files that contains all blocks of the data file(s) that have been modified or changed. Full backups can be created out of

- Data files
- Data file copies
- Tablespaces (all data files for a tablespace)
- Archive logs
- Control files (current or backups)
- Entire databases

An incremental backup is a backup of one or more files and contains only blocks that have been modified. However, only complete control files are backed up in either incremental or full backups. Incremental backups can be made of

- Data files
- Tablespaces
- Databases

The incremental backup allows leveling of backups. Each level is denoted by an integer value, with the level of backup meaning that any blocks changed since the last incremental backup at this level will be backed up the next time this level is specified. This allows levels to be set based on time frames; for example, 0 being a monthly full, 1 being a once-a-week incremental, and 2 being a daily incremental. Of course, this also leads to complicated rotation of tapes or backup media, taking us back to the good old towers-of-Hanoi backup scenario nightmares.

RMAN also allows for image copies of data files, archive logs, or control files. Image copies can only be made to disk and cannot contain multiple files.

RMAN allows report generation. Reports can be generated based on

- What files need backup.
- What files haven't been backed up recently.
- What backup files can be deleted.

Each backup set can be associated with a tag that can be used to identify it in subsequent operations. The tag doesn't have to be unique. RMAN selects the most recent backup set in the case of backup sets with duplicate tags.

RMAN works against running or shutdown databases whether they are in archive log mode or not. However, if the database is not in archive log mode the entire database can only be backed up if it was shut down cleanly. Tablespaces can only be backed up in NOARCHIVELOG mode if they are off-line normal. There are no restrictions of this type on databases in ARCHIVELOG mode.

RMAN automatically detects corruptions and logs these in v$backup_corruption and v$copy_corruption dynamic performance tables. Corrupt blocks are still backed up.

Installing the RMAN Catalog

The catalog should be owned by a user with the resource role grant. I suggest a user in a small database dedicated to system administration functions such as the RMAN catalog and Enterprise Manager catalog. Create a tablespace for use by the RMAN user and assign that as the user's default tablespace with unlimited quota. For example, if we wanted our user to be named rman_dba, the steps would be as follows:

```
sqlplus system/manager
SQL>CREATE TABLESPACE rman_data DATAFILE 'file_spec' DEFAULT STORAGE
(clause);
SQL>CREATE USER rman_dba IDENTIFIED BY rman_dba
 2: DEFAULT TABLESPACE rman_data
 3: TEMPORARY TABLESPACE  temp
 4: QUOTA UNLIMITED ON rman_data;
SQL>GRANT RESOURCE,CONNECT TO rman_dba;
SQL>CONNECT rman_dba/rman_dba
SQL> @$ORACLE_HOME/rdbms/admin/catrman.sql
```

Once the catalog is built, the recovery manager can be utilized. The command is either rman, rman80, or RMAN80 depending on your operating system. There are literally dozens of commands for use with the RMAN facility. I suggest reviewing the *Oracle8 Server Backup and Recovery Guide*, Release 8.0, Beta2 (or most current release) (Oracle Corporation, 1997) before using RMAN. The following are some example scenarios showing how the commands can be made into scripts.

Connection to rman in UNIX on early versions can be tricky. On some UNICES the double quote (") character has to be escaped, and you need to use the double quote to log in to rman (at least on early versions). Assuming the database to be backed up is ORTEST1 with a TNS alias of ORTEST1, the user is as specified earlier, and the catalog database is ORRMAN, the connection to RMAN for the user SYSTEM password MANAGER would look like this:

```
$ rman ORTEST1\"system/manager@ORTEST1\"\
rcvcat \"rman_dbo/rman_dbo@ORRMAN\"
```

Intuitive, isn't it? You will be glad to know that the double-quotes requirement goes away in Version 8.0.3.

Here is an example session: A sample session from Recovery Manager (RMAN) is shown next.

The target database service name in the "tnsnames.ora" file is "ORTEST1." The recovery catalog database service name in the "tnsnames.ora" file is "ORRMAN."

```
% cd $ORACLE_HOME/rdbms/admin
% sqlplus sys/change_on_install@ORRMAN
SQL> grant connect, resource to RMAN_DBA identified by RMAN_DBA;
Grant succeeded.

SQL> connect rman/rman@ORRMAN
Connected.
SQL> @catrman.sql
SQL> exit
%
% rman 'target sys/change_on_install@ORTEST1 rcvcat rman/rman@ORRMAN'

Recovery Manager: Release 8.0.2.0.0 - Beta

RMAN-06005: connected to target database: ORTEST1
RMAN-06008: connected to recovery catalog database
RMAN> register database;
RMAN-08006: database registered in recovery catalog
RMAN-08002: starting full resync of recovery catalog
RMAN-08004: full resync complete
RMAN> run
2> {
3> allocate channel c1 type disk;

4> backup full format '/oracle16/ORTEST1/amin/backup/backup%s%p'
(database);
5> }

RMAN-08030: allocated channel: c1

RMAN-08500: channel c1: sid=12 devtype=DISK

RMAN-08008: channel c1: started datafile backupset
```

```
RMAN-08502: set_count=9 set_stamp=280246639

RMAN-08011: channel c1: including current controlfile in backupset
RMAN-08010: channel c1: including datafile number 1 in backupset
RMAN-08010: channel c1: including datafile number 2 in backupset
   .
   .
   .
RMAN-08010: channel c1: including datafile number 11 in backupset
RMAN-08010: channel c1: including datafile number 12 in backupset

RMAN-08013: channel c1: piece 1 created

RMAN-08503: piece handle=/oracle16/ORTEST1/admin/backup/backup91
comment=NONE
RMAN-08003: starting partial resync of recovery catalog
RMAN-08005: partial resync complete
RMAN-10030: RPC call appears to have failed to start on channel default
RMAN-10036: RPC call ok on channel default
RMAN-08031: released channel: c1
RMAN> exit
```

Incomplete restore scenario. The following shows the scenario for an incomplete recovery. The following scenario assumes that

- You wish to do an incomplete recovery due to an application error that was made at a specific time.
- There are three tape drives.
- You are using a recovery catalog.

TIP   It is highly advisable to back up the database immediately after opening the database resetlogs.

The following script restores and recovers the database to the time immediately before the user error occurred. The script does the following:

- Starts the database mount and restricts connections to DBA-only users.
- Restores the database files (to the original locations).
- Recovers the data files by either using a combination of incremental backups and redo or just redo. Recovery Manager will complete the recovery when it reaches the transaction from the time specified.
- Opens the database resetlogs.

Oracle recommends that you backup your database after the resetlogs (this is not shown in the example).

Ensure that you set your NLS_LANG and NLS_DATE_FORMAT environment variables. You can set these to whatever you wish—the date format of the following example is the standard date format used for recovery, e.g., for UNIX (csh):

```
> setenv NLS_LANG AMERICAN
> setenv NLS_DATE_FORMAT 'YYYY-MM-DD:hh24:mi:ss'
```

Next, start up Server Manager:

```
SVRMGR> connect internal
Connected.
SVRMGR> startup mount restrict
SVRMGR>exit

#  rman target internal/knl@prod1 rcvcat rman/rman@rcat cmdfile case2.rcv
run {
#  The 'set until time' command is for all commands executed
#  between the { and } braces. Means both restore and recover
#  will both be relative to that point in time.
#  Note that Recovery Manager uses the Recovery Catalog to,
#  determine the structure of the database at that time, and
#  restore it.
#
    set until time '1997-06-23:15:45:00';
#
    allocate channel t1 type 'SBT_TAPE';
    allocate channel t2 type 'SBT_TAPE';
    allocate channel t3 type 'SBT_TAPE';
#
    restore
      (database);
#
#  There is no need to manually catalog logs before recovery,
#  as Recovery Manager does catalog resync from the current
#  control file.
#
    recover
      database;
#
    sql 'alter database open resetlogs';
```

The preceding scenarios are just examples of how to use the recovery manager. Please consult your manual before attempting to use the facility for production work. The RMAN readme file contains valuable insights into RMAN use and has several additional scenarios.

17.9   BD_VERIFY UTILITY

In the final section of this chapter I want to cover the DB_VERIFY utility. The DB_VERIFY utility is an external command line-based utility that is used to perform a physical structure integrity check on an off-line (shutdown) database. The utility can be used against backup files and on-line files or pieces of on-line files. The utility is used to be sure a backup database or data file is valid before recovery. The utility can also serve as a diagnostic aid when corruption is suspected. Since it runs against a shutdown database it can perform checks significantly faster than export or other utilities. The utility is named differently on different platforms; for example, it may be called dbv (on SUN/Sequent) or something else on your system. Verify its name with the system-specific documentation you should have received (if you didn't, call your Oracle rep and complain). The utility only verifies cache-managed blocks.

The DB_VERIFY utility has the following general syntax:

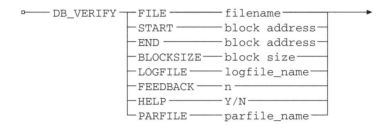

Where

FILE is the name of the database file to verify.

START is the starting block address to verify. These are Oracle block addresses.

If you get an ORA error giving a file number and block that is corrupted, you can use this to check that block.

END is the ending block to verify. This is an Oracle block number.

BLOCKSIZE is the Oracle block size if not 2k blocks.

LOGFILE specifies where logging data should be kept.

FEEDBACK - DB_VERIFY shows a dot for each n blocks verified.

HELP provides on-screen help.

PARFILE specifies the name of the file to read parameters from.

The following shows an example run of the DB_VERIFY against an Oracle 7.3 database file:

```
The following example shows how to get on-line help:

% dbv help=y

DBVERIFY: Release 7.3.1.0.0 - Wed Jul  2 10:17:10 1997

Copyright (c) Oracle Corporation 1979, 1994.  All rights reserved.

Keyword    Description      (Default)
----------------------------------------------
FILE       File to Verify   (NONE)
```

```
START      Start Block      (First Block of File)
END        End Block        (Last Block of File)
BLOCKSIZE  Logical Block Size (2048)
LOGFILE    Output Log       (NONE)
```

This is sample output of verification for the file, apl_data01.dbf. The feedback parameter has been given the value 100 to display one dot on screen for every 100 blocks processed:

```
% dbv file=apl_data01.dbf feedback=100

DBVERIFY: Release 7.3.1.0.0 - Wed Jul  2 10:17:10 1997

Copyright (c) Oracle Corporation 1979, 1994.  All rights reserved.

DBVERIFY - Verification starting : FILE = apl_data01.dbf

..........................................................

DBVERIFY - Verification complete

Total Pages Examined        : 7013
Total Pages Processed (Data) : 2174
Total Pages Failing   (Data) : 0
Total Pages Processed (Index): 523
Total Pages Failing   (Index): 0
Total Pages Empty           : 4586
Total Pages Marked Corrupt  : 0
Total Pages Influx          : 0
```

17.10 DBA SUGGESTED READING

The DBA is encouraged to obtain and review the following resources:

Oracle7 Enterprise Backup Utility Administrator's Guide, Release 2.0, Part No. A42580-2, Oracle Corporation.

Oracle8 Server Administrator's Guide, Release 8.0, Beta2, February 1997, Part No. A50648-1, Oracle Corporation, Chapter 23.

Oracle8 Server Backup and Recovery Guide, Release 8.0, Beta2, February 1997, Part No. A50610-1, Oracle Corporation.

Oracle8 Server Utilities Manual, Release 8.0, Beta2 (or most current), Oracle Corporation.

What's on the CD-ROM

The original manuscript contained Appendices A through G, and was over 1700 pages in length. Printing a book at this length would have required an increase in price from what the publisher had already announced, so we didn't include the appendices in the written portion of the book. Despair not! You'll find the appendices in their entirety and on the enclosed CD-ROM in Acrobat format. You can copy them onto your hard drive and reference them whenever you like, using Acrobat Reader, also included.

In addition to the appendices, a fully functional copy of the Visual Dictionary Light program from RevealNet, Inc. is included, and contained within are all the scripts shown in the book, plus a few bonus scripts. This set also provides a tool for viewing the scripts and copying them directly into NOTEPAD for transfer into a SQLPLUS session on your PC for easy execution. If you like the Visual Dictionay Lite product, you will love the full Oracle Administrator package, a demo of which (it can be booted 4 times and used during the full time of each boot session) is included. You'll also find a demo copy of the PL/SQL Developer product, from RevealNet and a final product, the Q diagnostic program, from Savant Corporation. I use the Q and Reveal-Net products on a daily basis, which is why I included them with the book; I am sure you will find them as useful as I do.

In the following sections the contents of each appendix are described so you can see what treasures each contains. The header information and a few pages of content from each are shown. Do not be confused! These are not the full appendices, just excerpts; the full appendices are on the enclosed CD-ROM.

APPENDIX A: EXAMPLE INTERVIEW QUESTIONS FOR ORACLE DBA, DEVELOPER CANDIDATES

You'll find sample questions on all of the following topics:

- DBA Sections: SQL/SQLPLUS, PL/SQL, Tuning, Configuration, Trouble shooting
- Developer Sections: SQL/SQLPLUS, PL/SQL, Data Modeling
- Data Modeler: Data Modeling
- All candidates for UNIX shop: UNIX

CD-ROM Excerpt: PL/SQL Questions

Score each question on a 1–5 or 1–10 scale.

1. Describe the difference between a procedure, function, and anonymous PL/SQL block.

   Level: Low

   Expected answer: Candidate should mention use of DECLARE statement, a function must return a value, while a procedure doesn't have to.

   Score: _____ Comment: _____

2. What is a mutating table error and how can you get around it?

   Level: Intermediate

   Expected answer: This happens with triggers. It occurs because the trigger is trying to update a row it is currently using. The usual fix involves either use of views or temporary tables so the database is selecting from one while updating the other.

   Score: _____ Comment: _____

3. Describe the use of %ROWTYPE and %TYPE in PL/SQL.

   Level: Low

   Expected answer: %ROWTYPE allows you to associate a variable with an entire table row. The %TYPE associates a variable with a single column type.

   Score: _____ Comment: _____

4. What packages (if any) has Oracle provided for use by developers?

   Level: Intermediate to high

   Expected answer: Oracle provides the DBMS_ series of packages. There are many that developers should be aware of, such as DBMS_SQL, DBMS_PIPE, DBMS_TRANSACTION, DBMS_LOCK, DBMS_ALERT, DBMS_OUTPUT, DBMS_JOB,

DBMS_UTILITY, DBMS_DDL, and UTL_FILE. If they can mention a few of these and describe how they used them, even better. If they include the SQL routines provided by Oracle, great, but not really what was asked.

Score: _____   Comment: _____

5. Describe the use of PL/SQL tables.

Level: Intermediate

Expected answer: PL/SQL tables are scalar arrays that can be referenced by a binary integer. They can be used to hold values for use in later queries or calculations. In Oracle8 they will be able to be of the %ROWTYPE designation, or RECORD.

Score: _____   Comment: _____

6. When is a declare statement needed?

Level: Low

The DECLARE statement is used in PL/SQL anonymous blocks, such as with stand alone, non-stored PL/SQL procedures. It must come first in a PL/SQL stand alone file if it is used.

Score: _____   Comment: _____

7. In what order should an open/fetch/loop set of commands in a PL/SQL block be implemented if you use the %NOTFOUND cursor variable in the exit when statement? Why?

Level: Intermediate

Expected answer: OPEN then LOOP then FETCH followed by the exit. Not specifying this order will result in the final return being done twice because of the way the %NOTFOUND is handled by PL/SQL.

Score: _____   Comment: _____

8. What are SQLCODE and SQLERRM and why are they important for PL/SQL developers?

Level: Intermediate

Expected answer: SQLCODE returns the value of the error number for the last error encountered. The SQLERRM returns the actual error message for the last error encountered. They can be used in exception handling to report or store in an error log table, the error that occurred in the code. These are especially useful for the WHEN OTHERS exception.

Score: _____   Comment: _____

9. How can you find within a PL/SQL block, if a cursor is open?

Level: Low

Expected answer: Use the %ISOPEN cursor status variable.

Score: _____   Comment: _____

(The full Appendix has over twenty pages of questions)

APPENDIX B: DBA SQL COMMANDS

This appendix lists all of the commands used in this book. Some general guidelines for the commands are:

- All commands that are standard SQL end with a semi-colon ";" in Oracle
- For all formatting commands from SQLPlus, such as SET, COLUMN, BREAK, etcetera, the semi-colon is optional.
- I have attempted to capitalize all commands, functions, etcetera, that are a part of standard Oracle SQL, SQLPLUS or PL/SQL in all scripts.
- I have tried to standardize the commands as wire diagrams because I find the new Oracle document standard of using brackets, curly brackets, parenthesis, and such abomidable except for short, generalized commands.
- The ultimate reference is, of course, the documentation. Where I know they goofed, I have tried to tell you; where I goofed, you will have to tell me.

CD-ROM Excerpt: DBA SQL Commands

Generalized CREATE COMMAND:

> CREATE object_type object_name
>
> create options,
>
> STORAGE (storage parameters).

STORAGE Clause for Tables, Clusters, Indexes and Default Storage for Tablespaces: the STORAGE clause specifies how an object uses the space that is allocated to it. Let's look at the format of the STORAGE clause.

```
>----STORAGE (-------------------------------------------------------------------------------)-----.,
                    |-- INITIAL integer ----------------------------------|
                    |                          |- K --|         |
                    |                          |- M -|           |
                    |-- NEXT integer ----------------------------------|
                    |                          |- K --|         |
                    |                          |- M -|            |
```

```
|-- MINEXTENTS integer -------------------------|
|-- MAXEXTENTS --------------------------------|
|                       |----integer-------|   |
|                       |-UNLIMITED-|
|-- PCTINCREASE integer (0-100) ------------|
|-- OPTIMAL integer --------------------------|
|                         |- K --|            |
|                         |- M -|             |
|-- FREELISTS integer ----------------------|
|-- FREELIST GROUPS integer ---------------|
```

Where:

INITIAL: This is the size in bytes of the initial extent of the object. The default is 10240 bytes. The minimum is 4096. The maximum is 4095 megabytes. All values are rounded to the nearest Oracle Block size.

NEXT: This is the size for the next extent after the INITIAL is used. The default is 10240 bytes, the minimum is 2048, the maximum is 4095 megabytes. This is the value that will be used for each new extent if PCTINCREASE is set to 0.

MINEXTENTS: This is the number of initial extents for the object. Generally, except for rollback segments, it is set to 1. If a large amount of space is required, and there are not enough contiguous space for the table, setting a smaller extent size and specifying several extents may solve the problem.

MAXEXTENTS: This is the largest number of extents allowed the object. This defaults to the max allowed for your blocksize for Oracle7 and Oracle8. In addition for Oracle8 if UNLIMITED is set, there is no upper limit.

PCTINCREASE: This parameter tells Oracle how much to grow each extent after the INITIAL and NEXT extents are used. A specification of 50 will grow each extent after NEXT by 50%, *for each subsequent extent*. This means that for a table created with one initial and a next extent, any further extents will increase in size by 50% over their predecessor. Under Oracle7 and Oracle8 this parameter is only applied against the size of the previous extent.

OPTIMAL: This is used only for rollback segments and specifies the value to which a rollback segment will shrink back to after extending.

FREELIST GROUPS: This parameters specifies the number of freelist groups to maintain for a table or index.

FREELISTS: For objects other than tablespaces, it specifies the number of freelists for each of the free list groups for the table, index or cluster. The minimum value is 1 and the maximum is block size dependent.

(The Appendix on the disk is over eighty pages of command formats and reference)

APPENDIX C: SQL AND PL/SQL SCRIPTS FROM BOOK

DBAs must know how to write and use SQL and PL/SQL scripts. The tools available to modern DBAs are all wonderful, including the Q product which is on the enclosed CD, however, there comes a time when the DBA needs a specific bit of information, a different cut at the same data, or, heaven forbid, a paper report they can show management or use in a report of their own. To accomplish this a DBA must know SQL and PL/SQL and the SQL*Plus formatting commands.

A general warning: each of these scripts has been test run, and they should execute properly, however, sometimes when switching from Notepad to Word to disk and back things like single quotes and other "minor" format items may get set for standard written text instead of what the computer expects to see. If you get the error saying the SQLPLUS, or other interface, doesn't understand or has a bad character, look to the single quotes first. If you have problems with some on UNIX due to Control-M characters (you shouldn't but it may happen) try reading the script from the CD into word and then save it as Text Only, this usually solves that problem. A final word, Oracle likes to add columns, remove columns, and change tables, views, and even statistics names, I have tried to ensure all of these are current, up to 8.0.2, but I can't say that in 8.0.3 or later things won't change.

The scripts in this book should provide a firm foundation from which the DBA can build an excellent toolbox of ready-made reports, scripot builders, and other items that all DBAs (at least with Oracle) should have. The key to scripts and their building and use are the SQL*Plus, SVRMGR, and OEM-SQL Worksheet interfaces. I prefer the SQL*Plus interface since every user can use it and it recognizes (naturally) all SQL*Plus formatting commands. This is followed by SVRMGR for the same reasons, bringing up the rear is the SQL Worksheet, simply because it hasn't been taught to recognize SQL*Plus formatting commands. Every platform has at least the first two tools, SQL*Plus and SVRMGR, usually both in GUI and command line form.

To Get into SQL*Plus:

SQLPLUS username/password@connect string @command file

Where:

username/password: This is the user's Oracle username and password, which is usually different from the Operating System username and password. If the user is assigned an autologin type of account, only the / is required.

@connect string: This is a connect string that connects the user to other databases than the default database. It can be used with SQL*NET or NET8 over networks to access other systems.

@command file: This allows the user to specify a SQL command file that is run automatically.

If the DBA account is what is known as an OPS$ account (not recommended), the format would be as follows.

SQLPLUS /

Since an OPS$ account allows the user to get into the Oracle system without specifying a password, if they are logging in from their normal account, the use of OPS$ accounts should be restricted to "captive" type users, that is, users who can only access the system via an appropriate secure menu system. Under Oracle7 and Oracle8 the OPS$ format is the default but the system manager can assign whatever prefix they desire by use of the OS_AUTHENT_PREFIX parameter in the INIT.ORA file.

Here are some tips on how to exit SQL*Plus. Use "exit" on most platforms. On my WINDOWS, WIN(95, and WINNT platforms I usually create multiple shortcuts, one for each database, from the SQLPLUS program icon. If you right mouse click on the shortcut you can get to the properties listing, from there on WINDOWS it is easy to edit the command line, from NT and WIN95 switch to the Shortcut tab and edit the target line to include a username and password as well as connect string. For example, on my NY platform one of my shortcuts has the target line:

D:\ORANT\RDBMS80\BIN\PLUS40W.EXE\ system/system_test@beq-test

This brings up the SQLPLUS program against the TEST (ORTEST1) instance. I also set the Start In: setting to the location of my SQL and PL/SQL scripts (usually C:\SQL_SCRIPTS). Off of the SQL_SCRIPTS directory I hang a "rep_out" directory with subdirectories for all instances. This is why you will see a majority of the scripts spooling out to "rep_out/&db/list_name" or "rep_out\&db\list_name," surprisingly it doesn't seem to make a difference which slash is used, the reports seem to get to the right place. It makes it easy to find reports, and I use the same format on all platforms.

To Get into SVRMGR:

$ svrgmr—or—svrmgrl (line mode)—or—svrmgr30 (NT, WIN95)—or—svrmgrm (motif mode)

You will get a normal prompt for svrmgr:

SVRMGR>

Just enter your connect command:

SVRMGR> connect internal/password

To exit SVRMGR just type "exit." The OEM SQL Worksheet has a self explanatory GUI interface.

Enough general verbage. Here are the scripts from the book; I hope you find them useful. They are also included in the Dictionary Lite product in a form I hope you find easy to use.

Script to build a database creation script:

```
REM FUNCTION: SCRIPT FOR CREATING DB
REM          This script must be run by a user with the DBA role.
REM          This script is intended to run with Oracle7 or 8.
REM          Running this script will in turn create a script to
REM          rebuild the database.  This created
REM          script, crt_db.sql,  is run by SQLDBA
REM          Only preliminary testing of this script was performed.
REM          Be sure to test it completely before relying on it.
REM M. Ault 3/29/96 TRECOM, REVELNET
REM
SET VERIFY OFF FEEDBACK OFF ECHO OFF PAGES 0
SET TERMOUT ON
PROMPT Creating db build script...
SET TERMOUT OFF;

CREATE TABLE db_temp
    (lineno NUMBER,   text VARCHAR2(255))
/
DECLARE
   CURSOR dbf_cursor IS
     SELECT
              file_name,bytes
     FROM
              dba_data_files
     WHERE
              tablespace_name='SYSTEM';
   CURSOR grp_cursor IS
     SELECT
              group#
     FROM
              v$log;
   CURSOR mem_cursor (grp_num number) IS
     SELECT
              a.member, b.bytes from v$logfile a, v$log b
     WHERE
              a.group#=grp_num
              AND a.group#=b.group#
     ORDER BY
              member;
   grp_member            v$logfile.member%TYPE;
   bytes                 v$log.bytes%TYPE;
   db_name               VARCHAR2(8);
   db_string           VARCHAR2(255);
   db_lineno             NUMBER := 0;
   thrd                  NUMBER;
   grp                   NUMBER;
   filename              dba_data_files.file_name%TYPE;
   sz                    NUMBER;
   begin_count           NUMBER;
   max_group         NUMBER;
   PROCEDURE write_out(p_line INTEGER,
```

```
                        p_string VARCHAR2) IS
      BEGIN
         INSERT INTO db_temp (lineno,text)
                   VALUES (db_lineno,db_string);
      END;
BEGIN
     SELECT MAX(group#) INTO max_group FROM v$log;
     db_lineno:=db_lineno+1;
   SELECT 'CREATE DATABASE '||name INTO db_string
     FROM v$database;
     write_out(db_lineno,db_string);
     db_lineno:=db_lineno+1;
   SELECT 'CONTROLFILE REUSE' INTO db_string
     FROM dual;
     write_out(db_lineno,db_string);
     db_lineno:=db_lineno+1;
   SELECT 'LOGFILE ' INTO db_string
     FROM dual;
     write_out(db_lineno,db_string);
COMMIT;
IF grp_cursor%ISOPEN
THEN
     CLOSE grp_cursor;
     OPEN grp_cursor;
ELSE
     OPEN grp_cursor;
END IF;
LOOP
     FETCH grp_cursor INTO grp;
     EXIT WHEN grp_cursor%NOTFOUND;
     db_lineno:=db_lineno+1;
     db_string:= ' GROUP '||grp||' (';
     write_out(db_lineno,db_string);
     IF mem_cursor%ISOPEN THEN
            CLOSE mem_cursor;
            OPEN mem_cursor(grp);
     ELSE
            OPEN mem_cursor(grp);
     END IF;
     db_lineno:=db_lineno+1;
     begin_count:=db_lineno;
     LOOP
            FETCH mem_cursor INTO grp_member, bytes;
            EXIT when mem_cursor%NOTFOUND;
            IF begin_count=db_lineno THEN
                    db_string:=chr(39)||grp_member||chr(39);
                    write_out(db_lineno,db_string);
                    db_lineno:=db_lineno+1;
            ELSE
                    db_string:=','||chr(39)||grp_member||chr(39);
                    write_out(db_lineno,db_string);
                    db_lineno:=db_lineno+1;
            END IF;
```

```
        END LOOP;
        db_lineno:=db_lineno+1;
        IF grp=max_group
        THEN
                db_string:=' ) SIZE '||bytes;
                write_out(db_lineno,db_string);
        ELSE
                db_string:=' ) SIZE '||bytes||',';
                write_out(db_lineno,db_string);
        END IF;
    END LOOP;
IF dbf_cursor%ISOPEN THEN
    CLOSE dbf_cursor;
    OPEN dbf_cursor;
ELSE
    OPEN dbf_cursor;
END IF;
begin_count:=db_lineno;
LOOP
    FETCH dbf_cursor INTO filename, sz;
    EXIT WHEN dbf_cursor%NOTFOUND;
    IF begin_count=db_lineno THEN
db_string:='DATAFILE '||chr(39)||filename||chr(39)||' SIZE '||sz||' REUSE';
    ELSE
        db_string:=','||chr(39)||filename||chr(39)||' SIZE '||sz||' REUSE';
    END IF;
    db_lineno:=db_lineno+1;
    write_out(db_lineno,db_string);
END LOOP;
COMMIT;
SELECT DECODE(value,'TRUE','ARCHIVELOG','FALSE','NOARCHIVELOG')
    INTO db_string FROM v$parameter WHERE name='log_archive_start';
    db_lineno:=db_lineno+1;
    write_out(db_lineno,db_string);
SELECT ';' INTO db_string from  dual;
    db_lineno:=db_lineno+1;
    write_out(db_lineno,db_string);
CLOSE dbf_cursor;
CLOSE mem_cursor;
CLOSE grp_cursor;
COMMIT;
END;
/
rem The next section could be converted to use
rem UTLFILE so the entire anonymous PL/SQL section
rem and this report section would become a stored
rem procedure, but to keep it generic I will leave as
rem is.
COLUMN dbname NEW_VALUE db NOPRINT
SELECT name dbname FROM v$database;
SET HEADING OFF PAGES 0 VERIFY OFF RECSEP OFF
SPOOL rep_out\&db\crt_db.sql
COLUMN text FORMAT a80 WORD_WRAP
```

```
SELECT text
FROM db_temp
ORDER BY lineno;
SPOOL OFF
SET FEEDBACK ON VERIFY ON TERMOUT ON
DROP TABLE db_temp;
PROMPT Press enter to continue
SET VERIFY ON FEEDBACK ON PAGES 22 TERMOUT ON
CLEAR COLUMNS
```

(The Appendix on the CD has this and several dozen other scripts, nearly 70 pages worth. These are also included in the Visual Dictionary Lite program from RevealNet, Incorporated.)

APPENDIX D: DCL AND SHELL SCRIPTS

In *Oracle7.0 Administration and Management* I provided numerous DCL and a few shell scripts to help in the management of Oracle databases. I provided more and better DCL scripts simply because I was spending a majority of my time supporting databases in the OpenVMS arena. Well, as they say, the worm has turned. Since that volume was published I have worked less with VMS and more with UNIX (of various denominations, Dynix, SCO, BSD, HPUX, Solaris). I'm afraid I don't have any new DCL scripts, but I will include the ones from the first book. However, I have written many useful UNIX shell scripts, so the number, and I hope, the quality of UNIX scripts has increased.

The first set of scripts we will show are Digital Command Language (DCL) scripts. It is logical to provide a central file to provide logical and symbol definitions. Therefore the first script will be a file that does just this. The file is called ORACLE_LOG.COM.

```
$! This command procedure DEFINES logicals used by the Oracle Management
$! menu.
$! MRA, REV 0, 10/23/92
$!
$! First, get logicals defined:
$!
$ DEFINE/NOLOG ORACLE$COM    M_ORA_DISK0:[m_oracle.dba_tools.dbstatus.COM]
$ DEFINE/NOLOG ORACLE$SQL    M_ORA_DISK0:[m_oracle.dba_tools.dbstatus.SQL]
$ DEFINE/NOLOG ORACLE$MENU   M_ORA_DISK0:[m_oracle.dba_tools.dbstatus.MENUS]
$ DEFINE/NOLOG ORACLE$DOC    DUA2:[NM91263.ORACLE6.DOC]
$ DEFINE/NOLOG ORACLE$ODDS   M_ORA_DISK0:[m_oracle.dba_tools.ddview.sql]
$ DEFINE/NOLOG oracle$log         DUA2:[nm91263.oracle6.log]
$ DEFINE/NOLOG ORACLE$EXP    m_ora_disk2:[m_ORACLE6.db_case.exportS]
$ DEFINE/NOLOG ORA$DBA_REP   M_ORA_DISK0:[m_oracle.dba_tools.dbstatus.reports]
$ DEFINE/NOLOG ORA$EXP_COM   DUA2:[NM91263.ORACLE6.COM.EXPORTS]
$ DEFINE/NOLOG ORA$ODDSFRM   M_ORA_DISK0:[m_oracle.dba_tools.ddview.sql]
$ define/nolog/TRANS=CONC         ORA$ARCHIVE M_ORA_DISK0:
$ DEFINE/NOLOG                    ORA_ANSI MH5102P
$ DEFINE/NOLOG                    ORA_LAND PRT_HBC5_R1_L
$ define/nolog ORA$IOUG
```

```
M_ORA_DISK0:[m_oracle.dba_tools.dbutil.sql]
$ define/nolog ora$com_rep
M_ORA_DISK0:[m_oracle.dba_tools.dbstatus.reports]
$ define/nolog ora_status_reports
M_ORA_DISK0:[m_oracle.dba_tools.dbstatus.reports]
$ define/nolog CASE_HP_CMD   "print /queue=plt_hbc5_draftpro"
$ define/nolog CASE_PS_CMD   "print /queue=prt_hbc5_r1_p"
$ define/nolog CASE_SDPRINT        "SYS$PRINT"
$ define/nolog  SDD$PRINT          "print /queue=prt_hbc5_r1_a"
$ define/nolog  SDD$WPRINT         "print /queue=prt_hbc5_r1_l"
$ define/nolog  SDD_QUEUE          "PRT_HBC5_r1_A"
$ define/nolog adhoccon            mmrd01"""sqlnet
sqlnet"""::"""task=ordnadhoc"""
$ define/nolog casecon                    mmrd01"""sqlnet
sqlnet"""::"""task=ordnkcgc"""
$ define/nolog DEVcon                     mmrd15"""sqlnet
sqlnet"""::"""task=ordnDEV"""
$ define/notran elcon                  "ELWOOD:oracle"
$ define tcpcase                "157.206.11.15:"""CASE""":4096,5,YES"
$!
$! Symbol definitions:
$!
$! Report related symbols:
$!
$ PREP            :== "@ORACLE$COM:PRINT_REPORTS.COM"
$ GREP            :== "@ORACLE$COM:GEN_REPORTS.COM"
$!
$! Menu related symbols:
$!
$ ddview          :== "''runmenu' ddview -m f"
$ dbstatus        :== "''runmenu' dbstatus -m f"
$ DBUTILS         :== "''RUNMENU' DBUTILS -M F"
$ DB_TOOLS        :== "''RUNMENU' DBTOOLS -M F"
$ DBTOOLS         :== "''RUNMENU' DBTOOLS -M F"
$ CASE_MENU  :== "''RUNMENU' CASE_MENU -M F"
$!
$! Specific Instance Startup and Shutdown symbols:
$! The instance specific ORAUSER must be run for symbol to work.
$!
$ start_kcgc             :== "@ORA_INSTANCE:startup_EXCLUSIVE_CASE.com"
$ stop_kcgc         :== "@ORA_INSTANCE:shutdown_CASE.com"
$ start_APPL             :== "@ORA_INSTANCE:startup_EXCLUSIVE_PROD.com"
$ stop_APPL         :== "@ORA_INSTANCE:shutdown_PROD.com"
$ start_ADHOC       :== "@ORA_INSTANCE:startup_EXCLUSIVE_ADHOC.com"
$ stop_ADDHOC       :== "@ORA_INSTANCE:shutdown_ADHOC.com"
$ START_RECDEV      :== "@ORA_INSTANCE:STARTUP_EXCLUSIVE_RECDEV.COM"
$ STOP_RECDEV       :== "@ORA_INSTANCE:SHUTDOWN_RECDEV"
$ START_RECRUN      :== "@ORA_INSTANCE:STARTUP_EXCLUSIVE_RECRUN.COM"
$ STOP_RECRUN       :== "@ORA_INSTANCE:SHUTDOWN_RECRUN"
$!
$! Management Menu related symbols:
$!
$ MAN            :=="@ORACLE$COM:MANAGE_ORACLE.COM"
```

```
$ DEV_DIR              :=="ORACLE.DEV"
$ LIMS_DIR             :=="ORACLE.LIMS"
$ KCGC_DIR             :=="M_ORACLE6.DB_CASE"
$ APPL_DIR             :=="M_ORACLE6.DB_APPL"
$ ADHOC_DIR            :=="M_ORACLE6.DB_PROD"
$ GORECDEV             := -
"@M_ORA_DISK0:[M_ORACLE.ORACLE6.DB_RECDEV]ORAUSER_RECDEV.COM
$ GORECRUN             := -
 "@M_ORA_DISK0:[M_ORACLE.ORACLE6.DB_RECRUN]ORAUSER_RECRUN.COM
$!
$EXIT
```

(The above is an example DCL (VAX/VMS) script; what follows is one of the Shell scripts provided. There are many more in the Appendix on disk.)

One of the first assignments I had after leaving the safe haven of being a house DBA and moving into consulting was the video on demand project that TeleTV, out of Virginia, put together. The pilot was in Rome, Italy on Sequent systems using N-Cubes as the video servers (I know, it was a tough job, but somebody had to do it). Anyway, while the systems had good system management tools and good backup tools, they had no DBA support tools to speak of. Pulling on my vast UNIX knowledge (right) I put together a menu system to allow the execution, printing, and viewing of DBA reports. Here it is; I hope you find it useful. At the end of the appendix I have also included a few shell scripts that do such things as kill Oracle operating side processes (other than core processes), list running instances and so forth.

```
#!/bin/sh
# dba_menu
# Oracle Database DBA Menu. Allows simple generation, viewing
# and printing of Oracle Database Reports and DBA activities
# Rev 0. 30/9/95 MRA - RevealNet
#
# first full path the report files
#
REP=/home/oracle/sql_scripts
#
# now set report output full path
#
REP_OUT=/home/oracle/sql_scripts/rep_out
SH_FILES=/home/oracle/sh_files
x="0"
while [ $x != "99" ]
do
#
tput clear
echo ""
echo ""
echo "                        Oracle Database DBA Menu"
echo "                        ----------------------------"
echo ""
```

```
echo "                        1. Generate a report, execute script"
echo "                        2. View a report"
echo "                        3. Print a report"
echo "                        4. See a reports function statement"
echo "                        5. grep Against the sessions report"
echo "                        6. Enter SQLPLUS"
echo "                        7. Enter SVRMGR (Must be from Oracle user)"
echo "                        8. tail the Alert log"
echo "                        9. Check SQLNet V1 TCPIP status"
echo "                       10. tail SQLNet V1 TCPIP log"
echo "                       11. Check SQLNet V2 TCPIP status"
echo "                       12. tail SQLNET V2 TCPIP log"
echo "                       13. Start/Stop SQLNET"
echo ""
echo "                       99. Exit menu"
echo ""
echo "          ------------------------------"
echo ""
echo "                            Enter Choice: \c"
read x1
if [ -n "$x1" ]
      then
              x=$x1
fi
case $x in

1)
cd $REP
tput clear
rep_name="none.sql"
echo ""
echo ""
echo "Please enter the name of the report to run from the following list:"
echo ""
echo "*********************************************************************** "
ls -C *.sql
echo "*********************************************************************** "
echo ""
echo "\n                        Enter choice: \c"
read rep_name2
        echo ""
        if [ -s "$rep_name2" ]
        then
                rep_name="$rep_name2"
        fi
echo "\n Enter Oracle user name to run report under : \c"
read orauser
stty -echo
echo "\n                        Enter Oracle password: \c"
read pw
stty echo
#
```

```
# get into SQLPLUS and run report, normally report will terminate
# automatically with output directed to REP_OUT
#
tput clear
sqlplus -s $orauser/$pw @$rep_name
#
;;

2)
cd $REP_OUT
tput clear
rep_name="none.lis"
echo ""
echo ""
echo "Please enter the name of the report to view from the following list:"
echo ""
echo "********************************************************************"
ls -C
echo "********************************************************************"
echo ""
echo "\n                    Enter choice: \c"
read rep_name2
            echo ""
     if [ -s "$rep_name2" ]
     then
             rep_name="$rep_name2"
     fi
      pg $rep_name
#
;;

3)
cd $REP_OUT
tput clear
rep_name="none.lis"
echo ""
echo ""
echo "Please enter the name of the report to print from the following list:"
echo ""
echo "********************************************************************"
ls -C
echo "********************************************************************"
echo ""
echo "\n                    Enter choice: \c"
read rep_name2
              echo ""
       if [ -s "$rep_name2" ]
       then
               rep_name="$rep_name2"
            lp $rep_name
     else
     pg $rep_name
        fi
```

```
echo ""
;;

4)
cd $REP
tput clear
rep_name="none.sql"
echo ""
echo ""
echo "Enter the name of the report to see the function for from following
list:"
echo ""
echo "**********************************************************************"
ls -C *.sql
echo "**********************************************************************"
echo ""
echo "\n Enter choice: \c"
read rep_name2
        if [ -s "$rep_name2" ]
        then
                rep_name="$rep_name2"
        fi
echo ""
grep -i FUNCTION $rep_name
echo "                        Press enter to continue"
read nada
;;

5)
$SH_FILES/grep_sessions
;;

99)
tput clear
exit
;;

6)
tput clear
echo "Enter Oracle User name for SQLPLUS session: \c"
read un
stty -echo
echo ""
echo "Enter Oracle Password: \c"
stty echo
read pw
sqlplus $un/$pw
;;

7)
svrmgrl
;;
```

```
8)
tput clear
$SH_FILES/ck_alrt
;;

9)
tput clear
tcpctl status>status.lis
pg status.lis
rm status.lis
;;

10)
tput clear
echo "Enter number of lines to display: \c"
read lines
tail -$lines /home/oracle/product/7.1.4.1.0/tcp/log/orasrv.log>tail.lis
pg tail.lis
rm tail.lis
;;

11)
tput clear
lsnrctl status>status.lis
pg status.lis
rm status.lis
;;

12)
tput clear
echo "Enter number of lines to display: \c"
read lines
tail -$lines /home/oracle/product/7.1.4.1.0/network/log/listener.log>tail.lis
pg tail.lis
rm tail.lis
;;

13)
tput clear
echo " S - Start SQLNET V1 and V2, X - Stop SQLNET V1 and V2: \c"
read strt_stp
if [ $strt_stp = "s|S" ]
then
      tput clear
      echo " Has the re-start of the SQLNET protocols been authorized by
STREAM? (Y or N):\c"
      read yn
      if [ $yn = "y|Y" ]
      then
            /home/oracle/start_tcpctl
      fi
fi
if [ $strt_stp = "x|X" ]
```

```
then
      echo " Has the stop of SQLNET protocols been authorized by STREAM? (Y or
N): \c"
      read yn
      if [ $yn = "y|Y" ]
      then
              /home/oracle/stop_tcpctl
      fi
fi
;;
*)
tput clear
echo ""
echo "                              Invalid Selection try again"
echo "                              Press enter to continue"
read nada
pw="0"
;;
esac
pw="0"
done
```

APPENDIX E: THE XX$ TABLES

The actual heart of Oracle is the K and X$ table structs at the heart of its code. The V$ dynamic tables are all based on these K and X$ structs. Normally you cannot see these structures, they cannot be directly selected from except from the SYS or INTERNAL user and cannot be described using the DESCRIBE command. The best possible look a user can get at these structures, without being a part of Oracle Corporation and seeing internal documentation, is to look at the definitions of the V$ tables as shown in the view V$FIXED_VIEW_DEFINITION by use of a code snippit such as this one:

```
column view_name format a25
column view_definition format a50 word_wrapped
set lines 80 pages 0
start title80 "V$ View Definitions"
spool rep_out\&db\v$view
select * from v$fixed_view_definition;
/
spool off
```

This code snippit produces output (for Oracle7) similar to:

```
V$ROWCACHE                     select
                               kqrstcid,decode(kqrsttyp,1,'PARENT','SUBORDINATE')
                               ,
                               decode(kqrsttyp,2,kqrstsno,null),kqrsttxt,kqrstcsz
                               ,kqrstusg,kqrstfcs,
                               kqrstgrq,kqrstgmi,kqrstsrq,kqrstsmi,kqrstsco,kqrst
                               mrq,kqrstmfl, kqrstilr,kqrstifr,kqrstisr from
                               x$kqrst
```

As you can see, the columns in the K and X$ tables are very descriptive, and their meanings are intuitive to the most casual observer (wink). One of the experts in the field of Oracle Internals is coming out with a book on then, perhaps he will cover these elusive structures so that us poor DBAs can understand them! In Oracle8, instead of the V$ tables being the lowest on the "V" view hierarchy, the GV$ tables take this distinction. The GV$ views (the G stands for Global) have a column added that corresponds to the instant numbers. This change to the V$ views was made to allow monitoring of a shared instance environment from a single instance. If you aren't using a shared instance environment this new feature isn't of any importance.

Anyway, the data dictionary tables you should be concerned with are actually derived from the K and X$ tables as well as from user and program input. These are collectively known as the XX$ tables (at least by me). I call them the XX$ tables because generally, not always, but most times, they end in "$." For example, COL$, TAB$, FET$ are all XX$ tables and are the base data dictionary tables that you as a DBA should be concerned with. The tables themselves are built when the database is created by the sql.bsq script that is located in the $ORACLE_HOME/rdbms/admin or $ORACLE_HOME/dbs directories or their equivilent on your platform. Essentially, any table owned by SYS is an XX$ table. The sql.bsq script has a comment line for virtually every column in every XX$ table. I suggest it is as another must read for the DBA. Luckily for you the sql.bsq script is only about seventy pages long.

If you are an experienced DBA and have monitored Oracle databases for tables with multiple extents you no doubt noted with dispair the data dictionary tables were your biggest culprit, especially in environments with numerous tables and other database objects. When you asked anyone with Oracle support about fixing this "feature," their answer was generally "That is an Oracle internal set of definitions, and if you change them we will no longer support you." Not anymore. Oracle will now support editing of the sql.bsq script to "improve" the storage values of the base Oracle data dictionary tables. However, **DO NOT** alter any of the table, cluster, or column names or any of the datatypes, or specifications. This eidt of sql.bsq for sizing must be done before you issue the CREATE DATABASE command. The following objects should probably have their storage initial extent values increased if you have a large environment (my current environment has around 1000 base tables, with supporting indexes, triggers, views, and packages):

Table	Initial Extent
ACCESS$	180K
ARGUMENT$	300K
COM$	100K
CON$	100K
DEPENDENCY$	180K
IDL_CHAR$	450K
IDL_SB4$	700K
IDL_UB1$	2M (yes, 2 megabytes)
IDL_UB2$	3M (yes, 3 megabytes)

OBJ$	450K
OBJAUTH$	180K
PROCEDURE$	32K
SEQ$	32K
SOURCE$	5M (yes, 5 megabytes)
TRIGGER$	300K
TRIGGERCOL$	60K
VIEW$	300K

The following Clusters should be adjusted:

Cluster	Initial Extent
C_COBJ#	350K
C_FILE#_BLOCK#	500K
C_OBJ$	1700K
C_TS$	180K

The following Indexes should be adjusted

Index	Initial Extent
I_ACCESS1	180K
I_ARGUMENT1	300K
I_CCOL1	57K
I_CDEF1	57K
I_CDEF2	98K
I_COBJ#	57K
I_COL1	475K
I_COL2	300K
I_COM1	57k
I_CON1	180K
I_CON2	100K
I_DEPENDENCY1	300K
I_DEPENDENCY2	180K
I_FILE#_BLOCK#	100K
I_ICOL1	57K
I_IDL_CHAR1	57K
I_IDL_SB41	180K
I_IDL_UB11	100K
I_IDL_UB21	100K
I_IND1	57K
I_OBJ#	100K
I_OBJ1	180K
I_OBJ2	300K
I_OBJAUTH1	180K

I_OBJAUTH2	180K
I_SOURCE1	1500K
I_SYN1	57K
I_TRIGGERCOL	100K
I_VIEW1	32K

Of course, if you really want to make your data dictionary efficient, you can also move the create index statements into a second script, drop the indexes from the SYSTEM tablespace, and recreate them in their own tablespace (I suggest SYSTEM_INDEX) on a separate disk platter or disk array. The sizes stated above are only suggestions. If you have an existing database that is similar to the one you wish to create (i.e., approximately the same number and type of objects) then run the extents report included on the companion disk and adjust your sizes according to its output.

(The actual appendix will also list the XX$ tables and their descriptions.)

APPENDIX F: THE V$ DYNAMIC PERFORMANCE TABLES

Under Oracle8 the V$ tables are actually views against the GV$ tables. The only difference being that the GV (Global View) tables have the instance value for systems using the parallel server option. Since a majority of sites don't use the parallel server option, I will cover just the V$ views and leave the discovery of the additional INST_ID column to you. The companion disk program "Visual Dictionary Lite" shows the actual view creation scripts for the GV$ views; these are direct selects from the GV$ definitions only without the INST_ID column. The definitions for the GV$ DPTs can be found by querying the GV$FIXED_VIEW_DEFINITION DPT (V$FIXED_VIEW_DEFINITION) using a query similar to:

```
COLUMN view_name FORMAT A30 HEADING 'View Name'
COLUMN view_definition FORMAT A40 WORD_WRAPPED HEADING 'View Definition'
SET LONG 1300 PAGES 0
SPOOL rep_out\gv$view
SELECT view_name,view_definition
FROM sys.v_$fixed_view_definition
WHERE VIEW_NAME LIKE 'GV%';
SPOOL OFF
```

The output from the query should resemble:

```
View Name                         View Definition
------------------------------    ------------------------------------------
GV$ACCESS                         select distinct
                                  s.inst_id,s.ksusenum,o.kglnaown,o.kglnao
                                  bj, decode(o.kglobtyp,      0, 'CURSOR',
                                  1, 'INDEX',    2, 'TABLE',      3,
                                  'CLUSTER',    4, 'VIEW',     5,
                                  'SYNONYM',    6, 'SEQUENCE',     7,
                                  'PROCEDURE',    8, 'FUNCTION',     9,
```

```
'PACKAGE',      10,'NON-EXISTENT',
11,'PACKAGE BODY',      12,'TRIGGER',
13,'CLASS',      14,'SET',      15,'OBJECT',
16,'USER',      17,'DBLINK',      'INVALID
TYPE') from x$ksuse s,x$kglob o,x$kgldp
d,x$kgllk l where l.kgllkuse=s.addr and
l.kgllkhdl=d.kglhdadr and
l.kglnahsh=d.kglnahsh and
o.kglnahsh=d.kglrfhsh and
o.kglhdadr=d.kglrfhdl
```

The Oracle documentation states that you can grant access to the V$ DPTs by running the utlmontr.sql script. Afraid the documentalists at Oracle need to get out more. The utlmontr.sql script has not been available since release 7.2. If you need to grant general access to these DPTs to your users then you must use dynamic SQL like the following:

```
SET HEADING OFF VERIFY OFF FEEDBACK OFF PAGES 0
DEFINE cr=CHR(10)
SPOOL v$grant.sql
SELECT 'GRANT SELECT ON '||view_name||' TO PUBLIC;'||&&cr||
FROM dba_views WHERE view_name LIKE 'V_$%' ;
SPOOL OFF
```

The script will produce a set of public grants to the underlying views to the V$ DPTs. You cannot grant directly against the V$ or GV$ DPTs since they are fixed tables, you must grant against their support views. We don't need to create public synonyms, this is already done for us. The script v$grant.sql only needs to be run once.

V$ACCESS

The V$ACCESS dynamic performace table (DPT) show objects in the database that are currently locked and the user processes that have the locks.

Contents of the DPT V$ACCESS

Name	Null?	Type
SID		NUMBER
OWNER		VARCHAR2(64)
OBJECT		VARCHAR2(1000)
TYPE		VARCHAR2(12)

V$ACTIVE_INSTANCES

The DPT V$ACTIVE_INSTANCES shows the actual instance names that map to the instance numbers for all of the GV$ views (if parallel server option is installed and the instances are parallel). This DPT was introduced in 7.3.

Contents of the DPT V$ACTIVE_INSTANCES

Name	Null?	Type
INST_NUMBER		NUMBER
INST_NAME		VARCHAR2(60)

(The actual appendix goes on for many more pages with detailed descriptions of the V$ tables.)

APPENDIX G: THE DBA_ VIEWS

Oracle has provided many windows into the data dictionary that are central to the Oracle database. These windows are the DBA_ series of views. A *view* is a look at a table or tables that may be displayed and may be updated. However, since the DBA_ views are looks into the data dictionary, they are not updatable. The following is a list of the DBA_ views, their descriptions, and their function. There are also USER_ and ALL_ views which for the most part are based on the DBA_ views but subset the data into that owned by the user in the case of USER_ and that which the user can access in the ALL_ views. Sometimes more information than is available in the DBA_ views is shown in the ALL_ or USER_ views, but not very often.

Normally, users will not have synonyms that point directly to the DBA_ views, but will instead have the USER_ and ALL_ views. However, most of the DBA_ views have public grants, so they can be accessed by placing "SYS." (SYS.DBA_TABLES) as a prefix. Before using the DBA_ views in functions or procedures the users must be granted a direct grant, not a grant through a role.

These views may change release-to-release of Oracle. Generally, the changes will involve addition of columns, consolidation of columns from multiple views into a single view, or addition of views. Please confirm the view structures before attempting to select against them based on this section alone. These view descriptions are from the Oracle8.0.2 beta 2 release. If the view is not identified as Oracle8 only it should be backwards compatible to at least 7.2.3.

DBA_ROLES VIEW

The DBA_ROLES view contains an entry for each defined role in the database and indicates whether or not the role is passworded. A related view is DBA_ROLE_PRIVS.

Contents of the DBA_ROLES view

Name	Null?	Type
ROLE	NOT NULL	VARCHAR2(30)
PASSWORD_REQUIRED		VARCHAR2(8)

DBA_PROFILES

The DBA_PROFILES view contains the complete definitions of all profiles in the database. This definition contains the profile name, resources and limits assigned to the profile.

Contents of the DBA_PROFILES view

```
Name                            Null?      Type
------------------------------  --------   -------------
PROFILE                         NOT NULL   VARCHAR2(30)
RESOURCE_NAME                   NOT NULL   VARCHAR2(32)
RESOURCE_TYPE                              VARCHAR2(8)
LIMIT                                      VARCHAR2(40)
```

Index

823

Q Diagnostic Center™
for Oracle® and Client

Call Savant to activate the copy of Q provided on your CD.

Savant is extending a special 10% discount for the readers of this book. Call for details.

Customer Support   800.956.9541
301.581.0511
qsupport@savant-corp.com

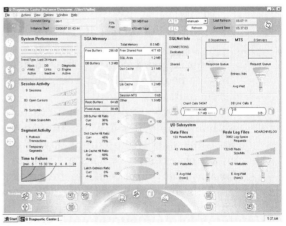

The Q™ Instance Overview Screen

S A V A N T

Included on the enclosed CD-ROM is the full suite of RevealNet demo products of interest to the DBA: Oracle Administrator, PL/SQL Developer, and Instant Messages. Each of these full-featured demos will allow at least four uses (a use is defined as a startup/shutdown of the PC upon which they are installed) before it deactivates. Note that the product does not erase itself or harm your hard drive in any way in this deactivation.

Included with the RevealNet demo products is the full-functioning Visual Dictionary Lite product, which is a fully executable product that is a companion to this book. No activation key is required for Visual Dictionary Lite; it is a self-contained program and never expires. The newer versions of the RevealNet products (released each quarter) are available at www.revealnet.com and can be downloaded from there. The Web site also contains the DBAPipeline, which is a great place to post questions and converse with other DBAs and developers.

The software product Q from Savant Corporation is also included in demo form on the CD-ROM. You need to call Savant to activate the copy of Q provided on the CD-ROM (and, as a reader, you can save 10 percent—see the ad at the back of the book for details). Q Diagnostic Center is an excellent diagnostic tool for Oracle 7.3 and lower database systems. The release of Q for Oracle8 is promised as of first or second quarter of 1998 and a new demo set can be downloaded from www.savant-corp.com at that time.

See the "What's on the CD-ROM" section for more details about Appendixes also found on the CD-ROM.

CUSTOMER NOTE: IF THIS BOOK IS ACCOMPANIED BY SOFTWARE, PLEASE READ THE FOLLOWING BEFORE OPENING THE PACKAGE.

This software contains files to help you utilize the models described in the accompanying book. By opening the package, you are agreeing to be bound by the following agreement:

This software product is protected by copyright and all rights are reserved by the author, John Wiley & Sons, Inc., or their licensors. You are licensed to use this software on a single computer. Copying the software to another medium or format for use on a single computer does not violate the U.S. Copyright Law. Copying the software for any other purpose is a violation of the U.S. Copyright Law.

This software product is sold as is without warranty of any kind, either express or implied, including but not limited to the implied warranty of merchantability and fitness for a particular purpose. Neither Wiley nor its dealers or distributors assumes any liability for any alleged or actual damages arising from the use of or the inability to use this software. (Some states do not allow the exclusion of implied warranties, so the exclusion may not apply to you.)